Psychology and Sex Roles

An Androgynous Perspective

Psychology and Sex Roles

An Androgynous Perspective

Alexandra G. Kaplan
UNIVERSITY OF MASSACHUSETTS

Mary Anne Sedney
PROVIDENCE COLLEGE

Little, Brown and Company
BOSTON · TORONTO

To my son, Jeremy Joshua Kaplan
AGK

To my parents, Mary McGettigan Sedney and Edmund J. Sedney
MAS

Library of Congress Catalog Card No. 79-90431

FIRST PRINTING

Published simultaneously in Canada
by Little, Brown & Company (Canada) Limited

Printed in the United States of America

Preface

When psychologists began to study sex roles, they focused on global sex differences, seeking to document the ways females and males differ psychologically. Underlying this approach was the assumption that these differences were a natural outgrowth of biological sex differences. Later, as researchers became slightly more sophisticated, they tried to understand the essence of female and male behavior: psychological "femininity" and "masculinity." Questions grew to encompass both biological and environmental sources of sex differences; but these questions were framed to suggest that masculinity was the desirable state for males, femininity for females. During the 1970s a major shift occurred. Masculinity and femininity were recognized as socially constructed stereotypes rather than biologically or environmentally determined components inevitably linked with males and females. People could be masculine, feminine, or both masculine and feminine, and psychological masculinity and femininity were to some extent independent of biological sex. Thus, the concept of androgyny was introduced to the psychological literature. Rather than focusing primarily on sex differences, recent researchers have increasingly been exploring the coexistence of femininity and masculinity in one person and the factors that differentiate masculine, feminine, or androgynous people of both sexes.

Psychology and Sex Roles: An Androgynous Perspective is part of this new direction. Building on the notion of androgyny as an *individual* characteristic, we develop androgyny as a *general model* around which issues in the psychology of sex roles can be organized. This androgynous perspective has several key elements. First, in contrast to the masculine bias in much existing research on sex roles, an androgynous perspective stresses the importance of examining both feminine and masculine dimensions. Second, as a holistic concept, it highlights the usefulness of including biological, intrapsychic, and environmental factors in understanding behavior. Third, the consideration of situational appropriateness at the base of androgyny leads to an emphasis on the study of factors that permit flexibility across situations and meaningful choices throughout life. Finally, this perspective acknowledges the relationship between society's values and the research carried out within that society. None of these elements is unique to androgyny, but all serve as cornerstones of this book.

By using androgyny as an integrating framework, we are expanding its use beyond the definition used by most psychologists. With this framework we hope to avoid the fragmentation that occurs when discrete issues of psychology and sex roles are considered outside a conceptual framework. For the sake of comprehensive coverage, we have included some topics not directly related to androgyny. Further, we have not included *all* possible topics on which androgyny has some bearing. Also, by focusing on androgyny and sex-related issues, we have limited our coverage of other major social considerations such as race and social class. We tried to produce a book that was sufficiently comprehensive yet selective enough that the material could be integrated around the concept of androgyny.

Our choice of androgyny as a central theme does not mean that we whole-heartedly endorse androgyny as the model of the future or the ideal psychological state. To argue that all people should be androgynous is no better than to argue that all women should be feminine or all men masculine. Instead, we use androgyny for the framework it offers, while examining its benefits and limitations within a particular culture.

Psychology and Sex Roles: An Androgynous Perspective was written as an undergraduate textbook and is designed to facilitate classroom teaching and learning. Thematic questions at the beginning of each chapter alert the reader to its major issues; summaries review this material from our perspective. The book requires an elementary knowledge of psychology; a more sophisticated background may enrich one's reading but is not essential. The chapters roughly follow the sequence we have used in teaching courses on the psychology of women and the psychology of sex roles over the past five years. In addition, the four parts of this book parallel the four main sections in Alexandra G. Kaplan and Joan P. Bean's *Beyond Sex Role Stereotypes: Readings Toward a Psychology of Androgyny;* thus the text and the reader can be used in tandem.

Although *Psychology and Sex Roles: An Androgynous Perspective* is primarily intended as a textbook, the nature of the material and the thinking that underlies it extend its usefulness beyond the classroom. The emphasis on the relationship between theory and research and the use of a consistent perspective provide a basis for generating topics that merit further study.

The book is divided into four sections, each with three chapters. The first introduces our perspective. We examine the concept of androgyny as it has been used by psychologists and discuss the ways psychological research—particularly on personal topics such as the behavior of women and men—is affected by the social context in which it occurs. Psychologists were not the first to use androgyny; we also explore its use in other disciplines, specifically religion and literature.

The second section focuses on three components of sex roles in which biology plays a prominent role: the sex hormones, reproduction, and sexuality. We emphasize the interrelationship of biology, psyche, and society as we stress the ways that the meanings and expressions of biological sex differences have been shaped by societal values and expectations. Throughout this section we are alert to the implications that biological sex differences have for an individual's potential for androgyny.

In the third section, we focus on the role of social influences—both within and outside the family—in the development of females' and males' behavior. We consider not only the ways stereotypic behaviors develop, but also potential paths toward the development of androgyny. The combined effects of biological and social influences are again considered when we examine some specific psychological sex differences and similarities in the cognitive, personality, and interpersonal domains.

Adulthood is the topic of the fourth section. We explore both interpersonal and occupational roles of women and men and the ways that current forces may limit these roles. In the final chapter we consider the factors that influence psychological adjustment for women and men and the role that therapy and self-help groups can play in expanding options.

A word about terminology: there is currently some discussion about the terms *sex* and *gender;* some authors designate the first as the biological term and the second the social term. We use the word *sex* to refer to the biological, psychological, and social aspects of femaleness and maleness, to emphasis their interrelatedness. When we wish to refer to a specific component of sex, we do so with the addition of descriptive words (i.e., biological sex, psychological sex, sexual intercourse, sex role, etc.). We limit the use of the word *gender* to discussions of gender identity, defined as comfort with and acceptance of one's physical body as male or female.

Many people have helped us over the past few years, and we are indebted to them. Joan P. Bean deserves thanks for her role in the early development of this project. Two students, Karen Burgess and Sandra Mandel, have been invaluable for their enthusiastic assistance with detailed bibliographic work and the numerous tasks of translating rough drafts into comprehensible print. Kenneth Bangs, Donna Benoit, Marie Scully, and Gale Storum have also helped with the often unexciting but necessary services in the library and at the typewriter.

Our colleagues and friends have been indispensible, lending us a hand, an ear, or a shoulder. These especially include Barbara Brooks, John Clayton, Edward Kaplan, Charlotte O'Kelly, David Kraft, Stephanie Kraft, Michael Spiegler, Barbara Tinker, and Robert Tinker. We thank Marian Ferguson, our editor at Little, Brown, for both her firm deadlines and her emotional support.

Reviewers' comments have also helped us in the development of our manuscript. In particular we would like to thank Barbara Brackney, Eastern Michigan University; Theodora F. Capaldo, Human Resources Institute; James K. Cole, University of Nebraska; Joan DiGiovanni, Western New England College; Margaret Jean Intons-Peterson, Indiana University; Roberta Klatzky, University of California at Santa Barbara; Kathryn Quina-Holland, University of Rhode Island; Juanita H. Williams, University of South Florida.

To one another we would like to say this: Co-authoring the book has not been an unmitigated blessing. There were times when criticism met with resistance and when support was overridden by self-interest. Yet somehow our friendship survived and was enriched by this collaboration. Perhaps the androgyny about which we were writing gave us a model for integrating affect and intellect, support and challenge.

Contents

ix

Chapter 8
Sex-Role Socialization Outside the Family 210

Chapter 9
Psychological Comparisons of Females and Males 235

PART IV
ADULT SEX ROLES

INTRODUCTION TO ANDROGYNY AND PSYCHOLOGICAL RESEARCH

PART

I

The Nature of Androgyny

1

Before you begin reading this book, take one minute and write down all the traits you can think of that describe the typical American female. Now, take one more minute and write down all the traits you can think of that describe the typical American male. We would guess that, even in this short time, you were able to come up with fairly long lists. If your lists agree with those which appear in the psychological literature (e.g., see Table 1.1) you might have described the typical female as emotional, intuitive, nurturant, sensitive, or dependent. Your description of the typical male might have contained such traits as assertive, independent, rational, competitive, or unemotional. If you compared your lists with those of your classmates, you would probably find that they are fairly similar. You might also notice that none of the traits on your "typical female" list appear on your "typical male" list.

Why can people generate lists of personality traits so easily when they know only the sex of the person? Because we asked you to describe a *typical* man and woman, you had to think in very general terms about traits that are commonly associated with each sex. By doing so, you were drawing on cultural stereotypes of males and females. A stereotype, according to the Random House Dictionary of the English Language, is a "simplified and standardized conception or image invested with special meaning and held in common by members of a group" (p. 1394).

Such "standardized and simplified" conceptions of women and men have regularly been found to exist in contemporary society (Komarovsky, 1950; Lunneborg, 1970; McKee & Sherriffs, 1957; Rosenkrantz, Vogel, Bee, Broverman, & Broverman, 1968). They stem from at least two sources. First is the belief that there is a direct link between personality attributes and sex. By knowing nothing more than someone's sex, it is considered possible to describe a number of characteristics that that person might reasonably be expected to have. Second, men and women are seen as having distinctly different personalities. If, for example, a person is described as being low in feminine-typed traits (e.g., unemotional, not particularly kind or gentle, not warm in relations with others), it is assumed that such a person would be high in masculine-typed traits (e.g., active, independent, making decisions easily; Fouchee, Helmreich, and Spence, 1979). When an adolescent male is exhorted to "be a man," the message is clear: Don't act like a woman.

Return now to your list of traits. Although you were able to make that list, doing so probably left you feeling a bit uneasy, perhaps a bit skeptical. For every "typical"

TABLE 1.1 Stereotypic Sex-Role Items (Responses from 74 College Men and 80 College Women)

Competency Cluster: Masculine pole is more desirable

Feminine	Masculine
Not at all aggressive	Very aggressive
Not at all independent	Very independent
Very emotional	Not at all emotional
Does not hide emotions at all	Almost always hides emotions
Very subjective	Very objective
Very easily influenced	Not at all easily influenced
Very submissive	Very dominant
Dislikes math and science very much	Likes math and science very much
Very excitable in a minor crisis	Not at all excitable in a minor crisis
Very passive	Very active
Not at all competitive	Very competitive
Very illogical	Very logical
Very home oriented	Very worldly
Not at all skilled in business	Very skilled in business
Very sneaky	Very direct
Does not know the way of the world	Knows the way of the world
Feelings easily hurt	Feelings not easily hurt
Not at all adventurous	Very adventurous
Has difficulty making decisions	Can make decisions easily
Cries very easily	Never cries
Almost never acts as a leader	Almost always acts as a leader
Not at all self-confident	Very self-confident
Very uncomfortable about being aggressive	Not at all uncomfortable about being aggressive
Not at all ambitious	Very ambitious
Unable to separate feelings from ideas	Easily able to separate feelings from ideas
Very dependent	Not at all dependent
Very conceited about appearance	Never conceited about appearance
Thinks women are always superior to men	Thinks men are always superior to women
Does not talk freely about sex with men	Talks freely about sex with men

Warmth-Expressiveness Cluster: Feminine pole is more desirable

Feminine	Masculine
Doesn't use harsh language at all	Uses very harsh language
Very talkative	Not at all talkative
Very tactful	Very blunt
Very gentle	Very rough
Very aware of feelings of others	Not at all aware of feelings of others
Very religious	Not at all religious
Very interested in own appearance	Not at all interested in own appearance
Very neat in habits	Very sloppy in habits
Very quiet	Very loud
Very strong need for security	Very little need for security
Enjoys art and literature	Does not enjoy art and literature at all
Easily expresses tender feelings	Does not express tender feelings at all easily

Source: From Inge K. Broverman et al., "Sex Role Stereotypes: A Current Appraisal," *Journal of Social Issues*, Vol. 28, No. 2 (1972), Table 1, p. 63. Reprinted by permission of the Society for the Study of Social Issues.

trait that you listed, you undoubtedly realized that you knew many men or women to whom that trait did not apply. Furthermore, your complete list of "typical" male or female traits does not accurately describe a single individual you know. Assumptions about stereotypical male and female characteristics, then, begin to break down when applied to actual people.

If you agree that your lists do not seem to fit with your knowledge of real people, then you are beginning to think along the lines suggested by the concept of androgyny. Sandra Bem (1972) raised a related point when she introduced the concept of androgyny to psychology. She entitled her paper, "Psychology looks at sex roles: Where have all the androgynous people gone?" Where, in other words, is the psychological study of all the people who have both feminine and masculine traits? Many people seem androgynous, many even think of themselves as androgynous. Yet these people have routinely been left out of the psychological thinking about females and males, as they are left out of the stereotypes. It has been Bem's intent, and that of psychologists who have followed her, to bring these androgynous people into the psychological fold. By doing so, these writers are challenging the two sources of sex-role stereotyping. They are claiming that there need not be a direct link between sex and personality, and therefore that personality differences between the sexes may not be nearly as distinct as is commonly believed. Rather than existing separately, masculinity and femininity may be able to coexist within individual persons.

What, exactly, is androgyny? How can androgynous people be identified? What are the differences between androgynous and nonandrogynous persons? What personality traits might androgynous people exhibit, and how might these people be expected to behave in the real world? These are the questions that we will address in this chapter. First, we will introduce *theoretical constructs* of androgyny, various writers' models, showing what they think androgyny entails. Next, we will discuss the *measurement* of androgyny, the ways that have been proposed for distinguishing between androgynous and nonandrogynous persons. Finally, we will address the *effect* that being androgynous has on behavior.

A central concern is how we can expect androgynous people to fare in contemporary society. Therefore, we will look closely at two key questions as we review available information on androgyny. First, are androgynous people being identified as accurately as is possible with the current procedures? Second, how do societal values and institutional structures influence the way in which we respond to an androgynous person? This chapter will move, then, from androgyny as a theory to androgyny as a set of measurable characteristics, and then to androgyny as it is expressed within the current cultural climate.

THE THEORETICAL CONSTRUCT OF ANDROGYNY

In its broadest sense, androgyny is a *holistic* concept, a way of thinking about the totality of a person's life experiences. Thus, a full exploration of androgyny includes a look at three levels of being: personality, behavior, and life style. This does not mean, however, that we can define *the* androgynous personality, way of behaving, or life style. The purpose of a theoretical discussion of androgyny is to provide a framework for thinking about the implications of this perspective, not to develop a blueprint for androgyny. In such a discussion we can begin to identify what is and is not consistent with the model of androgyny, while recognizing that "consistent" can contain great room for diversity.

The study of androgyny was stimulated by an awareness of the debilitating effects associated with rigid conformity to sex-stereotypic behaviors (Bem, 1972; 1975). It has therefore been suggested that an androgynous person would be healthier, more adaptable, or better adjusted, than the person whose behavior is firmly rooted in sex-role stereotypes. Androgyny, in other words, is often proposed as one model of well-being.

Components of an Androgynous Personality

In this book, androgyny will be considered to mean the combined presence of socially valued, stereotypic, feminine and masculine characteristics. To understand the implications of this seemingly simple definition, however, we will need some elaboration.

Consider the parts of this definition, one at a time. The word "androgyny" itself suggests a combination of femininity and masculinity. It is derived from two Greek roots: *andro* for male and *gyn* for female. To preserve the essence of androgyny, it must always be spelled with a "gyn" ending. If androgyny is misspelled as androgeny (as sometimes happens), then the root word is androgen, a male sex hormone, the female half of the term is lost, and the meaning is changed.

But not all components of femininity and masculinity are included in this definition of androgyny. The two delimiting concepts are *stereotypic* and *socially valued.* The use of stereotypic traits ensures that the characteristics included are commonly acknowledged to represent masculinity and femininity. They provide an answer to the question, "What do people mean by the terms masculinity and femininity?" Notice that this question does not address what women and men *do,* but rather the abstract clusters of traits that have been labeled feminine and masculine. In common parlance, of course, "masculine" implies "acting like a man" and "feminine" implies "acting like a woman." This is *not* the use of these terms suggested by the above definition. We are asking you to put aside this more common usage and think of femininity and masculinity more abstractly, as labels that are used for people's *expectations* about the behaviors of women and men.

To identify the components of femininity and masculinity, the majority of researchers on androgyny (Bem, 1976; Berzins, Welling, & Wetter, 1978; Spence, Helmreich, & Stapp, 1975) have turned to two major conceptual approaches. The first is the model developed by David Bakan (1966). Bakan proposes that masculinity and femininity are consistent with two fundamental modes of human interaction: masculinity with *agency* and femininity with *communion.* Agency is manifested in qualities of individual preservation: self-protection, self-assertion, self-expansion, the formation of separations, and the urge to master. Communion is manifested in qualities of interrelatedness: contact, openness, union, the lack of separations, and noncontractual cooperation. In general, agency is related to the advancement of the individual, whereas communion is related to the interrelationship between the individual and the broader community.

The second model is that offered by Parsons and Bales (1955). These authors conceptualize masculinity and femininity in terms of *instrumental* and *expressive* behaviors respectively. Instrumental behaviors, according to them, are directed toward a goal and reflect a cognitive emphasis on purpose and accomplishment. Expressive behaviors include supportive and affective responses and reflect concern for the well-being of others and an emphasis on caretaking.

Neither theory provided the actual feminine and masculine items in scales used to measure androgyny. However, the researchers' feminine and masculine items are similar to the constructs provided by Bakan and by Parsons and Bales. As Spence, Helmreich, and Stapp state: "Although these two types of items [feminine and masculine] were derived empirically on the basis of ratings of the ideal male and female, the agency-communion (Bakan, 1966) dichotomy (or the parallel instrumental-expressive distinction of Parson and Bales, 1955) is clearly reflected in their content" (1975, p. 38).

The inclusion of only *socially valued* traits further delimits the construct of androgyny. Is the person who sometimes acts helplessly dependent (stereotypically feminine) and at other times dangerously aggressive (stereotypically masculine) to be considered androgynous? This question poses something of a problem for students of androgyny. If androgyny is to serve as a model of well-being, such dysfunctional traits clearly do not belong. But can they arbitrarily be ruled out? Can we reasonably assume that someone who has the capacity to be both feminine and masculine will express the adaptive but not the maladaptive aspects of these stereotypes? There is some logical justification for believing this, if we consider that an androgynous person would not be determined to "prove" his or her masculinity or femininity. An androgynous person would not strive to be even more masculine, or even more feminine, if this involved hostile or self-destructive acts. The androgynous person would not be like the male who is so compelled to prove his masculinity by climbing to the top of his profession that he abuses his wife and family and becomes dishonest and manipulative with his colleagues. He or she would avoid thinking like the woman whose attempts to be feminine lead her to become so helpless that she becomes virtually incapacitated. People have carried masculinity and femininity to socially devalued extremes, but such extremes would not be incorporated into the construct of androgyny.

There is another dilemma in ascribing only socially valued traits to androgyny. In contemporary Western society, greater value is placed on masculinity than on femininity (Broverman et al., 1972; Kelly & Worell, 1977). If a person expresses only socially valued traits, might these weigh more heavily on the masculine side than on the feminine? Can a person balance masculinity and femininity in a masculine-oriented culture? We will address this question in subsequent portions of this chapter.

The next aspect of the definition of androgyny is the *combination* of feminine and masculine attributes. There are two basic ways in which this could occur. The first, which can be called the *dualistic* model of androgyny, consists of the separate coexistence of feminine and masculine characteristics. A person who reflects this dualistic model would express both feminine and masculine traits, but at different times. She or he might disagree forcefully and assertively with a colleague on a major issue of program development, but act comfortingly and caringly toward that same person's distress over a personal problem. Bem describes the dualistic model of androgyny as the capacity "for an individual to be both assertive and compassionate, both instrumental and expressive, both masculine and feminine" (1977, p. 196).

The second way in which feminine and masculine traits could be combined constitutes the *hybrid* model of androgyny. In this model, rather than merely coexisting, masculinity and femininity become fully integrated, or blended. Thus, at any one time, a person could react in a way that is characteristically neither masculine or feminine, but that results from the combination of the two.

The traits that would be created from this process might best be understood by an agricultural analogy, the development of hybrid corn. Hybrid corn is created by cross-fertilizing two varieties of corn, such that the offspring inherit the most desirable qualities of each. The newly created hybrid strain resembles the stock of neither parent, but has combined aspects of both to create a new variety with its own, unique characteristics.

There are many examples of behavior consistent with the notion of hybrid traits. A person might be assertive and forceful in an argument with a close friend, yet at the same time voice sensitivity to and respect for the validity of the other person's position. Bem provides another example, citing the person who "might even blend these (masculine and feminine) complementary modalities in a single act, being able, for example, to fire an employee if the circumstances warrant it but with the sensitivity for the human emotion that such an act inevitably produces" (1977, p. 196).

You may notice a certain clumsiness in describing the individual whose behavior is consistent with the hybrid model of androgyny. At best, it takes a rather long sentence to convey what is meant. This is due, in part, to the lack of readily available terminology for identifying "competitiveness tempered by warmth," or "assertiveness tempered by support." The absence of such labels is not a minor issue, because societies develop words to identify objects or characteristics that are important to them. If we had labels for such hybrid qualities, our awareness of them could increase, and they would then probably occur more often.

We have suggested elsewhere (Kaplan, 1979) the use of hyphenated terms such as "assertive-dependency" or "supportive-confrontation" to identify these hybrid characteristics. For example, "assertive-dependency" could signify the ability to recognize and accept one's legitimate dependency needs, along with the capacity to seek assurance that these needs would be met by significant others. Assertive-dependent people would not need to associate dependency with helplessness or weakness, or to deny their dependency in order to appear strong. They would not need to wait passively, hoping that their dependency needs would be met. Nor would they have to exaggerate expressions of dependency in order to force others to respond. Assertive-dependent people would act directly to effect the fulfillment of their dependency needs.

The hybrid model of androgyny appears to be more advanced or sophisticated than the dualistic model. It is possible, although there are no data on this issue, that an androgynous personality might develop sequentially, from a dualistic to a hybrid mode. In general, there seem to be distinct differences between the dualistic and hybrid forms of androgyny, and these differences might influence studies of the androgynous person.

Premises Underlying the Theoretical Construct of Androgyny

The transition from androgyny as a combination of stereotypic, socially valued feminine and masculine traits to androgyny as a model of well-being contains several premises about the characteristics of an androgynous person. These premises include the presence of a *broad repertoire of responses, flexibility in response to situational demands,* and *effectiveness* in dealing with the environment. We will examine each of these premises.

Broad repertoire of responses. The person who has incorporated both masculine and feminine characteristics should have a wider range of possible reactions for any situation than will someone whose reactions are based on what is considered appropriate for her or his sex. Additionally, the person whose behavior is consistent with the hybrid model of androgyny should evidence traits that are possible only when the masculine and feminine have been integrated.

Flexibility in response to situational demands. Having a broader repertoire of response possibilities, the androgynous person should be able to react according to what she or he feels is most appropriate for the situation, rather than according to the way a man or a woman is "supposed" to react. Thus, if an androgynous man were talking to a friend who seemed upset, he might encourage him to talk about what was bothering him, to express the feelings he was struggling to hold back. A more stereotypic masculine reaction might be to avoid commenting on the fact that the friend seemed to be in pain and talk instead about the game their team just won. Similarly, an androgynous woman talking with a man who seemed uncertain about whether or not to complain to his boss might offer to help him with this decision and make suggestions, even though women are "supposed" to support men in feeling strong and competent ("I'm sure you'll do the right thing").

Flexibility in response to situational demands requires the capacity to assess a situation and to determine the most appropriate response. In our two examples, the androgynous man and woman would not *always* offer emotional support or advice whenever they sensed a need. Rather, they would consider whether doing so felt right for *them* at that time, and whether such a reaction would be acceptable to the other person. They would have the *capacity* to respond as described, but they would use this capacity judiciously.

Effectiveness. Androgynous people should have greater success in their encounters with the world than other people. Such effectiveness would occur if androgynous responses were warmly welcomed by others, if people were praised or rewarded for behaving in an androgynous fashion, *or* if people were able to achieve their own goals by behaving androgynously.

Effectiveness, like flexibility, is in part influenced by the reactions of others. If, for example, the woman in our example consistently found that she could not offer advice to male friends without seriously harming the relationship, then she could act on this androgynous component of her personality only with great risk. Effectiveness, in other words, can depend on other people's willingness to accept the androgynous individual, who may not respond as they expect based on that person's sex.

But effectiveness can be determined by an individual's own standards for success, or by the standards of others. It may be difficult, however, to act on the basis of one's own beliefs if these beliefs are not shared by those with whom one interacts. Androgynous people may have to decide: Should I do what is best for me or should I behave as others expect me to? These are not necessarily opposing positions, but they can be. Because androgyny runs counter to cultural expectations about women and men, there is an inherent tension between androgyny and prevailing norms. This tension need not inhibit the androgynous person, but its existence should be taken into account.

Acting in accordance with one's own values has certain implications. It would mean that the person would shape the basic patterns of her or his life. She or he would not just "happen" to go to college, or become a housewife, or work as a plumber. Rather, the person would choose a role through weighing the pros and cons of available options and determining which is the most desirable for him or her at that time.

Clearly, however, such decisions are not made in a vacuum. The key word here is *available.* There are powerful environmental and personal constraints that can limit the awareness of possibilities, or the ability to pursue a preferred life style. Social class, race, and sex are three of the most fundamental environmental constraints. People who cannot afford to attend college, or who must begin working full time in adolescence, are less able to base a career choice on what they would most like to do. Third-world people who opt for certain career goals may find that genuine support for and opportunities in their chosen field are not available. Additionally, a man who decides to stay home and raise his children or a woman who wishes to be a high-level bank executive may find major stumbling blocks erected by others along the way.

Personal factors may also inhibit one's ability to recognize and pursue a consciously chosen way of life. People raised to think only about a future as a parent or as a professional may not be aware that there are other reasonable and valid choices for them. Those who are married and responsible for the daily care and financial support of children may feel prevented from making decisions about their own lives that might be detrimental to those dependent upon them.

None of these factors is insurmountable in any absolute sense. There are certainly men and women who have created life styles far different from that which is "typically" expected for someone of their sex. Likewise, there are poor and third-world persons who have overcome the barriers confronting them and found a way to construct their lives as they wish. There are also people who have found ways to pursue individual goals while keeping their family intact and happy. The point is that the "freedom of choice" consistent with an androgynous personality is not equally available to all. People with very similar androgynous *personality* characteristics may face vastly different situations when attempting to act on the basis of these traits.

The Relationship Between Androgyny and Other Sex-based Concepts

Because androgyny presents one view of the relationship between sex and personality, it is important to understand its relationship to other sex-based categories. Three primary aspects of sex roles are regularly used by psychologists: *biological sex, gender identity* and sex role identity, or what we shall call *psychological sex.* Because these terms are defined differently by different people, our use of them will be explained in the following descriptions.

Biological sex is perhaps the easiest term to define. It refers simply to one's physical existence as male or female (or, in rare cases, as hermaphrodite), including sexual and reproductive features that differentiate one sex from the other.

Gender identity, as defined by Stoller (1977), is a basic comfort with and acceptance of one's biological sex. A woman with a positive gender identity would be comfortable with her capacity for pregnancy, childbirth, and lactation, whether or not she ever chose to use these capacities. Men with a positive gender identity would be comfortable with their role in human reproduction and at ease with their sexual bodies. Notice that gender identity, as used here, does not include any mention of personality or behavioral characteristics that would be associated with one sex or the other.

Psychological sex signifies the cluster of personality and behavioral traits that characterize an individual. Three categories of psychological sex are considered possible: feminine, masculine, or androgynous. Psychological sex should be clearly distinguished from gender identity, as well as from sexual preference as homosexual or heterosexual. A man could be comfortable and certain about his identity as a male, and yet behave in ways that are stereotypically labeled "feminine." Such behavioral characteristics, under this formulation, would in no way challenge his essential "manliness." Similarly, women who are secure in their gender identity as females could exhibit traits that are commonly assumed to be "masculine." The presence of these attributes, however, would not discount their primary identity as women. Additionally, both women and men could evidence characteristics that draw from both the feminine and the masculine stereotypes. These individuals, with an androgynous psychological sex, would remain clear about their gender identity as females or males.

Another Look

Androgynous people, as we have seen, contain both feminine and masculine socially valued, stereotypic traits. As such, they differ from their sex-typed peers, whose personalities would reflect either stereotypic feminine *or* masculine attributes, but not both. Because of this difference, it is predicated that androgynous people would reflect a broader repertoire of responses, which they would express in a flexible, situationally appropriate manner. Further, androgynous people would be more effective than their sex-typed peers in dealing with their world. These aspects of androgyny—flexibility, situational appropriateness, and effectiveness—have been offered so far only as premises. It remains for studies of androgynous and non-androgynous people to determine whether these premises hold up under empirical investigation.

MEASURING ANDROGYNY

To discover whether or not human behavior is consistent with a theoretical construct (here, the construct of androgyny), we often need to translate the theory into observable, measurable components. These translations constitute the operational concept of androgyny.

The measurement of androgyny, far more than the development of theory, has been the focus of psychological researchers. This is indicated by the recent development of at least four such scales: The Bem Sex Role Inventory (BSRI, 1974); Spence, Helmreich, and Stapp's Personality Attributes Questionnaire (PAQ, 1974); Berzins, Welling, and Wetter's PRF ANDRO Scale (1978); and Heilbrun's Androgyny measure from the Adjective Check List (1976).

The purpose of these tests is to differentiate between androgynous and sex-typed individuals. Each test contains a feminine and masculine scale, which consists of items that have been found to be desirable for or typical of women or men. The respondent is asked to indicate the extent to which each item is typical of her or himself. One of several scoring procedures is then used to determine whether the respondent is sex-typed or androgynous.

Sex-role Inventories

Many tests were developed to measure masculinity and femininity before androgyny was introduced to psychology. They include the Terman-Miles M-F Test (1936), the M-F Scale of the Strong Vocational Interest Blank (1943), the Mf Scale of the Minnesota Multiphasic Personality Inventory (MMPI; Hathaway and McKinley, 1943), and the Femininity Scale of Gough's California Psychological Inventory (CPI, 1964). Such tests are routinely used to assess the extent to which a person's personality characteristics are consistent with masculinity or femininity. Although the newer tests, which are designed to assess androgyny as well as masculinity and femininity, have some points in common with the older tests, they differ in two fundamental ways.

The first variation concerns the *relationship* between masculinity and femininity. The older tests used a *bipolar* concept: femininity and masculinity were thought to be opposite ends of a single continuum (Constantinople, 1973). If femininity and masculinity are considered opposites, the more feminine the individual, the less masculine she or he would be. The bipolar concept is thus like a seesaw: the more one side goes up, the more the other side must come down.

The bipolarity of the older tests is inherent in the test items. For example, a respondent might be given the following item:

Forceful ___ ___ ___ ___ ___ ___ ___ ___ ___ Gentle

The task would be to check the point on this scale that most closely represents one's relative degree of forcefulness or gentleness. On such an item a person cannot indicate that she or he can be both forceful *and* gentle. Although a check at the middle point might be interpreted to represent this position, in fact, such a score would indicate neither forcefulness nor gentleness. There is no way to indicate the combined presence of both.

Tests for measuring androgyny reject the concept of *bipolarity*. They are designed around the recognition that femininity and masculinity are *independent* (Bem, 1975; Constantinople, 1973; Spence, Helmreich and Stapp, 1975). That is, a person's score on a feminine trait is unrelated to her or his score on a masculine trait. A person would not be asked to choose between the presence of a feminine or a masculine attribute. In these newer tests, then, respondents might be given the following items:

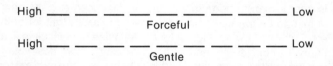

```
High ___  ___  ___  ___  ___  ___  ___  ___  ___ Low
                        Forceful

High ___  ___  ___  ___  ___  ___  ___  ___  ___ Low
                         Gentle
```

They could then indicate that they are high in both attributes, high in one but low in the other, or low in both.

The old and the new tests also use different criteria for determining the *selection of items* to be included in the feminine and masculine scales. The primary basis for selection in the older tests was differential responses by females and males. Thus, masculine items represented the typical male response, and feminine items represented the typical female response. In this approach, even a question such as, "Which do you prefer, baths or showers?" could be included in a MF Scale, if it could be demonstrated that males would typically respond one way and females another.

The old method of item selection violates one of the basic tenets of androgyny, that masculinity and femininity are abstract terms for clusters of traits, rather than terms that refer to the behaviors of men and women. Thus, it should be no surprise that the newer tests designed to measure androgyny reject this method. Instead, the basic criterion for item selection in most androgyny measures is sociocultural definitions of femininity and masculinity. Feminine items represent traits that are considered valuable or typical in women, and masculine items represent traits that are considered valuable or typical in men. The newer tests, then, reflect consensually validated stereotypes of masculinity and femininity, rather than the extent to which traits are endorsed by men or women.

The Bem Sex-Role Inventory (BSRI). The BSRI (Bem, 1974) was one of the first tests designed specifically to measure androgyny. It consists of sixty items, twenty masculine, twenty feminine, and twenty assessing social desirability. The Masculine scale contains such items as "analytical," "dominant," "self-reliant," and "willing to take risks." In the Feminine scale there are such items as "affectionate," "flatterable," "loyal," and "gullible." The Neutral scale, used to access social desirability, contains such items as "conventional," "jealous," "moody," and "tactful."

The respondent is asked to rate each item on a scale from 1 to 7 on the basis of how characteristic that item is for her or him. Originally, the BSRI was scored in terms of the difference between the means of the feminine and masculine scales. The closer this difference was to zero, the more androgynous the person was.

Bem's method of test construction directly reflects the definition of androgyny as being comprised of socially valued traits. Items were chosen for the Feminine and Masculine scales on the basis of their endorsement as socially desirable traits for women or men respectively. To determine social desirability, one hundred college students (50 women and 50 men) indicated on a seven-point scale the extent to which each of 400 personality characteristics were desirable for males or females (Bem, 1974). For example, they were asked, "In American society, how desirable is it for a man to be truthful?" or, "In American society, how desirable is it for a woman to be truthful?" No judge rated the same trait for both men and women. Personality traits were chosen for the feminine or masculine scales if both males and females considered them to be significantly more desirable for men or women. From among the items that met this criterion, twenty were selected for the Feminine scale and twenty for the Masculine scale.

Bem also included a third, Social Desirability scale. This scale was designed to determine whether individuals who took the BSRI were responding more on the basis of what they thought was a "good" response than on the basis of self-description. Items were selected for this scale if they were rated by males and females as no more socially desirable for females than for males, and if males and females did not differ significantly in their ratings of the social desirability of that item. Of the items that met these criteria, twenty were selected; ten represented positive personality traits, and ten represented negative personality traits.

The Personal Attributes Questionnaire (PAQ). The PAQ (Spence, Helmreich, and Stapp, 1974) was developed from an extended version of the Sex Role Stereotype Questionnaire (Rosenkrantz, et al., 1968). The PAQ (see Table 1.2) consists of three scales: Masculine (M), Feminine (F) and Masculine-Feminine (M-F). Items used on these three scales depended on judges' ratings of how *ideal* each was for members of both sexes and of how *typical* each was for one sex or the other. The Feminine items were those rated as ideal for both sexes, but more typical for women than men, whereas the Masculine items were those rated ideal for both sexes but more typical for men than women. The M-F items were those rated as both ideal and typical for one sex or the other, but not both. On the original version of the PAQ there were eighteen F items, twenty-three M items and thirteen MF items; the shortened and more widely used version has eight items on each scale. (See Table 1.2.)

The twenty-four items of the PAQ are rated by respondents on a five-point scale according to "what kind of a person you think you are." Although these items are constructed in a bipolar fashion, they are conceptually distinct from the bipolar

TABLE 1.2 Items on the PAQ

Scale

M–F	Not at all aggressive	A__ B__ C__ D__ E__	*Very aggressive*[a]
M	Not at all independent	A__ B__ C__ D__ E__	*Very independent*
F	Not at all emotional	A__ B__ C__ D__ E__	*Very emotional*
M–F	Very submissive	A__ B__ C__ D__ E__	*Very dominant*
M–F	*Not at all excitable in a major crisis*	A__ B__ C__ D__ E__	Very excitable in a *major* crisis
M	Very passive	A__ B__ C__ D__ E__	*Very active*
F	Not able to devote self completely to others	A__ B__ C__ D__ E__	Able to devote self completely to others
F	Very rough	A__ B__ C__ D__ E__	*Very gentle*
F	Not at all helpful to others	A__ B__ C__ D__ E__	*Very helpful to others*
M	Not at all competitive	A__ B__ C__ D__ E__	*Very competitive*
M–F	Very home oriented	A__ B__ C__ D__ E__	*Very worldly*
F	Not at all kind	A__ B__ C__ D__ E__	*Very kind*
M–F	*Indifferent to others approval*	A__ B__ C__ D__ E__	Highly needful of others approval
M–F	*Feelings not easily hurt*	A__ B__ C__ D__ E__	Feelings easily hurt
F	Not at all aware of feelings of others	A__ B__ C__ D__ E__	*Very aware of feelings of others*
M	*Can make decisions easily*	A__ B__ C__ D__ E__	Has difficulty making decisions
M	Gives up very easily	A__ B__ C__ D__ E__	*Never gives up easily*
M–F	*Never cries*	A__ B__ C__ D__ E__	Cries very easily
M	Not at all self-confident	A__ B__ C__ D__ E__	*Very self-confident*
M	Feels very inferior	A__ B__ C__ D__ E__	*Feels very superior*
F	Not at all understanding of others	A__ B__ C__ D__ E__	*Very understanding of others*
F	Very cold in relation to others	A__ B__ C__ D__ E__	*Very warm in relation with others*
M–F	*Very little need for security*	A__ B__ C__ D__ E__	Very strong need for security
M	Goes to pieces under pressure	A__ B__ C__ D__ E__	*Stands up well under pressure*

[a] Italics indicate the extreme masculine responses for the M and M–F scales, and the extreme feminine response for the F scale.

Source: From J. T. Spence and R. L. Helmreich, *Masculinity and Femininity, Their Psychological Dimensions, Correlates, and Antecedents*, Table II, pp. 231–233. Copyright © 1978 by Janet T. Spence and Robert L. Helmreich. Published by the University of Texas Press. Reprinted by permission.

items on the older tests that we criticized earlier. On the older tests, each bipolar item had femininity as one end of the pole and masculinity as the other end. This is *not* the case for the M and F scales of the PAQ, in which each item is scored as masculine or feminine, rather than as a choice between the two. For example, a person who rated him- or herself as "not at all independent" would receive a low masculinity score on that item, but this would have no bearing on her or his femininity score.

The PRF-ANDRO Scale. This measure of androgyny was not as much created by its authors (Berzins, Welling, & Wetter, 1978) as it was resurrected from an earlier personality measure, the Personality Research Form (PRF; Jackson, 1967). The original PRF consisted of twenty scales, each containing twenty items. From this pool of 400 items, Berzins, Welling, and Wetter selected those most consistent with the femininity and masculinity scales of the BSRI. Items consistent with the masculine definition were chosen if they seemed more desirable in men than in women, and the reverse for the feminine items. To determine the accuracy of the authors' choice, the selected items were presented to 177 student judges who were asked to indicate how desirable each item was for a man or for a woman. Highly significant differences were found between these two ratings, suggesting that the femininity and masculinity scales represented separate socially desirable traits. The final test consists of twenty-nine masculine items and twenty-seven feminine items. (See Table 1.3.) Respondents are asked to rate the extent to which each item is true for themselves.

The Masculinity-Femininity Scale of the Adjective Check List (ACL). The Adjective Check List was derived by Heilbrun (1976) from the earlier Gough and Heilbrun Adjective Check List (1965). The original ACL consisted of 300 adjectives from which the respondent was to select those which she or he considered typical of her or his behavior. The Masculinity-Femininity scale is comprised of twenty-eight masculine and twenty-six feminine items, selected from the original 300.

Heilbrun's method of item selection differs in important ways from that used in the other new measures of psychological sex. Essentially, Heilbrun followed the method used in the older tests, selecting items endorsed by men for the masculine scale and items endorsed by women for the feminine scale. He carried this procedure one step further, however, by including only those items selected by males who identified with masculine fathers and females who identified with feminine mothers. Thus, he is not only associating femininity and masculinity with the behaviors of women and men, respectively, but is limiting this association to supposedly truly "masculine" males and "feminine" females. Items endorsed by these individuals were selected for the scales *whether or not* they reflected socially desirable characteristics (Kelly & Worell, 1977). Thus, the M and F scales of the ACL differ in two ways from those of the other tests designed to measure androgyny; they define masculinity and femininity in terms of the responses of males and females, and they include both socially desirable and socially undesirable traits. Both of these variations violate aspects of the construct of androgyny.

Procedures for Scoring the New Sex-role Inventories

There are two procedures currently in use for scoring the newer sex-role inventories. We will discuss them in some detail, because there is a fair amount of controversy over which method is more appropriate.

The first method, which was originally used in scoring the BSRI, is based on the *difference* between an individual's scores on the feminine and masculine scales. This method reflects Bem's operational definition of androgyny as "the

TABLE 1.3 The PRF ANDRO Scale (A Measure of Psychological Androgyny Derived from the Personality Research Form)

Masculinity Scale items (MASCUL)
Items keyed true

When someone opposes me on an issue, I usually find myself taking an even stronger stand than I did at first.
I try to control others rather than permit them to control me.
I will keep working on a problem after others have given up.
I feel confident when directing the activities of others.
I don't mind being conspicuous.
I would never pass up something that sounded like fun just because it was a little bit hazardous.
I am quite good at keeping others in line.
My goal is to do at least a little bit more than anyone else has done before.
I seek out positions of authority.
I usually make decisions without consulting others.
If I have a problem, I like to work it out alone.
I will not go out of my way to behave in an approved way.
When I see a new invention, I attempt to find out how it works.
When I am with someone else, I do most of the decision-making.
I delight in feeling unattached.
I don't care if my clothes are unstylish, as long as I like them.
When two persons are arguing, I often settle the argument for them.
I prefer to face my problems by myself.
If I were in politics, I would probably be seen as one of the forceful leaders of my party.

Items keyed false

Adventures where I am on my own are a little frightening to me.
I would make a poor judge because I dislike telling others what to do.
I usually try to share my problems with someone who can help me.
I avoid some hobbies and sports because of their dangerous nature.
I am only very rarely in a position where I feel a need to actively argue for a point of view I hold.
I prefer a quiet, secure life to an adventurous one.
If I get tired while playing a game, I generally stop playing.
I feel incapable of handling many situations.
Surf-board riding would be too dangerous for me.
It is unrealistic for me to insist on becoming the best in my field of work all of the time.

Femininity Scale items (FEMIN)
Items keyed true

When I see someone who looks confused, I usually ask if I can be of any assistance.
I don't want to be away from my family too much.
The good opinion of one's friends is one of the chief rewards for living a good life.
People like to tell me their troubles because they know I will do everything I can to help them.
Once in a while I enjoy acting as if I were tipsy.
I make certain that I speak softly when I am in a public place.

Femininity Scale items (FEMIN) (continued)
Items keyed true (continued)

I believe in giving friends lots of help and advice.
I think it would be best to marry someone who is more mature and less dependent than I.
I am usually the first to offer a helping hand when it is needed.
To love and be loved is of great importance to me.
I would prefer to care for a sick child myself than hire a nurse.
One of the things which spurs me on to do my best is the realization that I will be praised
    for my work.
When I see a baby, I often ask to hold him.
Sometimes I get others to notice the way I dress.
I like to be with people who assume a protective attitude toward me.
Seeing an old or helpless person makes me feel that I would like to take care of him.

Items keyed false

I get a kick out of seeing someone I dislike appear foolish in front of others.
I dislike people who are always asking me for advice.
I would not like to be married to a protective person.
I get little satisfaction from serving others.
I prefer not being dependent on anyone for assistance.
I seldom go out of my way just to make others happy.
When I see someone I know from a distance, I don't go out of my way to say "hello."
People's tears tend to irritate me more than to arouse my sympathy.
I am quite independent of the people I know.
It doesn't affect me one way or another to see a child being spanked.

equal endorsement of both masculinity and femininity personality characteristics" (1976, pp. 51–52). Bem describes procedures for determining whether or not Feminine and Masculine scale scores are significantly different from one another. If the Feminine scale score is significantly higher than the Masculine, the person is feminine, whereas the person is masculine if the Masculine scale score is significantly higher. If there is no significant difference between the two scores, the person is androgynous.

This method, however, soon came under criticism from Spence, Helmreich, and Stapp (1975). These authors pointed out that when a difference score is used, no consideration is given to the magnitude of each scale score. That is, a person could be categorized androgynous if—to use two extreme examples—her or his average feminine and masculine scale scores were each 1 (i.e., the person responded 1—"never or almost never true" to each of the items), *or* if the two average scale scores were each 7 (i.e., the person responded 7—"always or almost always true" to each of the items). According to these researchers, only those who contain strong components of femininity and masculinity should be considered androgynous.

Instead of a difference measure, then, Spence, Helmreich, and Stapp proposed that tests be scored by means of a *median split* procedure. In this system, scores for all of the people who took the test together are listed by scale (i.e., feminine and masculine) from highest to lowest. A cutoff is made at the median, the point dividing the highest 50 percent of the scores from the lowest 50 percent. Those who score above the median on both the masculine and feminine scales are considered androgynous. Those who score above the median on the masculine but not on the feminine scale are categorized masculine, whereas those who score above the median on the feminine but not the masculine scale are categorized feminine. This procedure introduces a new category, "undifferentiated," to identify people who score below the median on both scales. (See Figure 1.1.)

Although the median split procedure remedies one of the difficulties inherent in the difference score, it in turn introduces other problems (Sedney, in press). First, classification is not based on significant differences between one's femininity and masculinity score. One could be above the median on one scale and below the median on the other scale with as little as a one-point difference between the scores. Second, one's classification using the median split procedure may vary, depending on the nature of the group from which the median cutoff points were derived. Although many researchers (e.g., Spence and Helmreich, in press) recommend that representative samples be used to determine the medians, medians based on small, nonrepresentative groups are frequently used. This, in turn, can affect the obtained results. A person who scores feminine when tested in a group of Army recruits could, with the same responses, score androgynous when tested with a group of college sophomores, assuming the groups' median cutoffs were different. For the individual taking the test, this means that she or he could consider her or himself androgynous, or sex-typed, relative only to those with whom she or he was tested. Such peer-group comparisons may have some importance, but they do not speak to the broader issue of identifying one's psychological sex. For psychological researchers, the change in cutoff from sample to sample means that it would be difficult to describe general characteristics that differentiate one category of psychological sex from another. In order to use the median split technique

FIGURE 1.1

Scheme for Classifying Individuals on Masculinity and Feminity Scores by a Median Split.

| | | Masculinity | |
		Above Median	Below Median
Femininity	Above Median	Androgynous	Feminine
	Below Median	Masculine	Undifferentiated

From J. T. Spence and R. L. Helmreich, *Masculinity and Femininity, Their Psychological Dimensions, Correlates, and Antecedents,* Table 3–1, p. 35. Copyright © 1978 by Janet T. Spence and Robert L. Helmreich. Published by the University of Texas Press. Reprinted by permission.

to derive scores that do not depend on the features of a specific population, it would be necessary to develop national norms, based on scores of a representative sample of the American population. At the time of this writing, however, such standardization procedures have not been published for all tests. Despite these weaknesses, Bem (1977) now concurs with Spence, Helmreich, and Stapp in advocating the use of the median split rather than a difference score.

We suggest, along with Downing (1979), that the most useful method of scoring consists of a combination of the difference score and the median split. The difference score could first be used to differentiate sex-typed from nonsex-typed persons. Then, for nonsex-typed persons, some cutoff (sample median, or an arbitrary one) could be applied to separate those who were high in both femininity and masculinity (i.e., androgynous) from those who were low in both (i.e., undifferentiated). This procedure resolves some of the difficulties we have discussed, but it does not address the lack of standardized norms.

Evaluating the Measures of Androgyny

Since there are at least four tests for determining psychological sex, and at least two methods for scoring these tests, how accurately can androgynous and sex-typed individuals be identified? That is, do categories differ depending on which scoring method is used or on which of the four tests a person has taken? There is also a more basic question to be asked regarding all four tests: How do the measures of androgyny relate to the assumptions underlying the construct of androgyny? That is, to what extent do scores from these tests indicate flexibility, situational appropriateness, a broad repertoire of responses, effectiveness, and the possible integration of femininity and masculinity?

Comparing scoring methods. Most of the research comparing the difference score and median split procedure focuses on whether these two methods categorize the same people as androgynous. In general, it has been found that from 25 to 50 percent of those categorized androgynous by one of the methods are categorized differently by the other. Bem (1977) tested a group of 375 men and 290 women on the BSRI, and then compared the results from the two methods of analysis. Of those who were categorized as androgynous by the median split, half of the men and a quarter of the women were categorized sex-typed, rather than androgynous, using a difference score. Similarly, Spence, Helmreich, and Stapp (1975), comparing scores from these two methods, found that more than half of those classified as androgynous with the median split did not score as androgynous using a difference score.

Such differences, although quite large, might not be a cause for concern if it could be demonstrated that one method is more valid than the other. That is, if we could determine that persons who score as androgynous using one procedure but not the other clearly evidenced androgynous traits, we would be able to choose between the methods. Both Bem (1977) and Spence, Helmreich, and Stapp (1975) have attempted to assess the relative merits of the two procedures, focusing largely on the relationship between scores using each procedure and self-esteem.

They both found that, using the median split, androgynous scorers were highest in self-esteem, followed, in order, by masculine, feminine, and undifferentiated. These findings played a major role in the decision to opt for median split rather than difference measures, because they confirmed the prediction that androgynous people would be highest in self-esteem.

However, using a difference score, Spence, Helmreich, and Stapp (1975) found that *masculine* scorers were highest in self-esteem, followed in turn by those who scored as androgynous and feminine. What do these competing findings suggest as to which is the more appropriate procedure? If we base our answer simply on our premises about an androgynous personality, then we would side with the median split. Androgynous people, considered to be more effective and adaptable in their daily lives, can reasonably be expected to be higher in self-esteem than their sex-typed peers. However, as several authors have pointed out (Antill & Cunningham, 1979; Bem, 1977; Kelly & Worell, 1977), the masculine component of androgyny may be more important than the combination of masculinity and femininity in leading to favorable outcomes including self-esteem. This is reasonable, because masculine behaviors tend to be regarded more highly than feminine behaviors in contemporary society. According to this line of reasoning, the *differences* measure would seem more appropriate than the median split.

Although the controversy between the two scoring methods seems to have been resolved in favor of the median split (Kelly and Worell, 1977), we believe that this decision is premature. Looking, for example, at the findings related to self-esteem, it seems that there is an intermediate but necessary question that has not yet been answered: Are androgynous or masculine people responded to in a way that would be expected to enhance their self-esteem? Additional studies examining the reactions of others to sex-typed and androgynous people could provide pertinent data on this point and thereby suggest which method most closely supports reasonable expectations on the relationship between such variables as self-esteem and psychological sex.

Comparing the four tests. Because there are four measures of androgyny, a question inevitably arises: Are people's scores affected by which test they take? That is, if someone scores as androgynous on the BSRI, will she or he also score as androgynous on the PAQ or the ACL or the PRF ANDRO? Two considerations bear on this question. First, do all four tests measure essentially similar dimensions? In other words, do the masculinity and femininity scales of each test cover basically the same range of attributes? Comparisons of the four tests suggest that the measures do in fact tap similar dimensions. High positive correlations have been found between the masculinity and femininity scales of the BSRI and the PAQ (Spence & Helmreich, 1978), between the M and F scales of the BSRI and the ACL (Wiggins & Holzmuller, 1978), and between the M and F scales of the PRF ANDRO and the BSRI (Berzins et al., 1978).

Second, will people be *categorized* similarly across the four tests when the scale scores are analyzed by means of a median split? Comparisons of categories show substantially less agreement among the tests than did the comparisons of the scale scores. Kelly, Furman, and Young (1978) found that only 30 percent of their subjects would be categorized similarly using the four different tests. And Gayton, Havu, Ozmon, and Tavormina (1977) found similar category scores for only 42 percent of their subjects.

The essential similarities between the scale scores, then, seem to become substantially reduced when the scores are reported in terms of categories. Kelly and Worell (1977) account for this by the fact that categories are only "broad typologies" and thus are not nearly as precise as the scale scores. It is this lack of precision that tends to exaggerate the differences between the tests. They suggest, along with others (Bem, 1977; Cronbach & Furby, 1970; Strahan, 1975) that for greatest accuracy, scale scores rather than categories be used in analyzing results from these tests. This suggestion is useful for researchers, but for the people taking the tests some information about psychological sex—whether they are androgynous, feminine, masculine, or undifferentiated—would still be desirable. Therefore, we can assume that some sort of classification will continue to be used. However, we need to keep the uncertain reliabilities of these classifications in mind.

Comparing the measurement and the construct. With the exception of the ACL, the tests designed to measure androgyny all conform to the *definition* of androgyny as presented earlier in this chapter. However, none of these tests is able to assess the *premises* associated with the construct of androgyny. Most of these premises deal with behavioral correlates of an androgynous personality: flexibility, situational appropriateness, effectiveness. Yet the measures of androgyny, like other personality inventories, do not assess what people do, but rather what they *think* they do. In general, there seems to be a low relationship between the ways people describe themselves and their actual behaviors (Mischel, 1975). Thus, it cannot be concluded with certainty that the person who describes him- or herself as both "active" and "nurturant" actually behaves in accordance with these attributes.

There is another difficulty with the tests that measure androgyny. Even if they accurately assess the presence or absence of certain traits, they do not measure the relationship between these traits, or the conditions under which they may or may not be expressed. Take, for example, the traits of "independence" and "compassion." Even if a person who scores high on both these attributes really does behave in both an independent and compassionate manner, he or she will not necessarily express these traits in flexible, situationally appropriate ways. Such a person might *always* be independent within intimate relationships (even when she or he would really like to be taken care of) or *always* compassionate with colleagues (even when he or she strongly disagrees with them). Such a person would not be using independence and compassion in conformity with the assumptions of androgyny.

Nor do the measures of androgyny assess a person's capacity for integrating masculine and feminine attributes. A person could have high scores on both dimensions, yet express them in distinct and separate ways. To continue with the above example, test scores would not indicate whether a person has the capacity to integrate independence and compassion, for example by maintaining an independent stance with a close friend while expressing sensitivity to and understanding of the other person's reaction. It could be said that at best these tests measure the dualistic model of androgyny, but not the hybrid model. The possibility that high levels of femininity and masculinity within a person could produce tension (cf. Vogel, 1979) rather than a potential for integration is not taken into account.

Further, these tests do not assess the context in which people live, which, as we saw earlier, might influence the effectiveness of an androgynous personality style and its utility as a model of well-being. Environmental factors could certainly influence whether an androgynous person will be able to behave in a manner consistent with her or his personality. For example, a person who behaves androgynously when employed in a supportive, nonauthoritarian work situation might act in a much more constricted fashion when placed in a competitive, demanding, achievement-oriented job. Or, a person who behaves androgynously in both settings could find great differences in her or his effectiveness and sense of competence. How other people's reactions affect the expression of androgyny is a critical consideration that is not assessed by these tests.

Also, none of the tests designed to measure androgyny check on the reasonableness of defining androgynous people as those who have incorporated socially *valued,* but not socially *devalued* characteristics. Is it possible, for example, that personalities containing the former will also regularly contain the latter? Kelly, Caudill, Hathorn, and O'Brian (1977) attempted to answer this question by asking respondents to rate themselves on valued as well as devalued characteristics. Devalued aspects from the masculine stereotype included cruel, rude, arrogant, impatient, dictatorial, and dogmatic; devalued aspects from the feminine stereotype included overly emotional, bitchy, frequently crying, indecisive, fickle, and vulnerable.

Their findings offered only partial support for the notion that androgynous individuals have incorporated socially valued, but not socially devalued, characteristics. The responses of the males were as would be predicted. Androgynous males rejected undesirable sex-typed characteristics more than did other respondents. Androgynous females, however, did not differ from other females in their rejection of devalued traits. This suggests that the distinction between people who do and do not express socially devalued traits may not be as easily made as the definition of androgyny implies. Androgynous females, in particular, who may not be rewarded as often as men for the sex-typed components of their personality, may find the distinction between valued and devalued traits especially difficult to make.

Finally, all of the tests designed to measure androgyny are inherently limited in that they are based on two currently existing constructs, masculinity and femininity. However, as Bem points out, this feature of androgyny

contains an inner contradiction and hence the seeds of its own destruction. . . . To the extent that the androgynous message is absorbed by the culture, the concepts of masculinity and femininity will cease to have distinct and substantive content, and the distinction to which they refer will blur into invisibility. Thus, when androgyny becomes a reality, the *concept* of androgyny will have been transcended. (1976, pp. 59–60)

What this transcendent version of androgyny will consist of, and how it might be measured, remain questions for the future.

Another Look

The two fundamental differences between older and newer measures of psychological sex reflect fundamental tenets associated with the construct of androgyny. We saw that recent tests are not based on the older notion that femininity and masculinity are poles of a single continuum. Instead they reflect the position that masculinity and femininity are independent and therefore should be assessed separately. In addition, item selection for the newer measures is based on the social desirability of the items for females or males, rather than on the older method of determining which items were responded to differently by men and women.

The newer sex-role inventories, however, are similar to their predecessors in that both are paper-and-pencil measures based on self-report. As such, they assess personality traits that may or may not correspond to people's behavior in real-life settings. Specifically, these measures do not take into account social influences on the expression of personality traits. Nor do they reflect ways in which feminine and masculine attributes may be integrated or whether these attributes will be expressed in a flexible, situationally appropriate manner. Thus, they may measure a person's potential for androgyny, but not whether the person is behaving androgynously.

At the time of this writing, there are at least four tests for identifying androgynous individuals, and at least two methods for scoring these tests. The questions of the relationships between these tests, and especially the differential results based on the two methods of scoring, have occupied a great deal of research time. This has understandably generated some confusion about how to determine "real" androgynous and sex-typed individuals. We feel that this confusion reflects the methods that have been chosen to study androgyny, rather than difficulties inherent in the construct of androgyny. We would suggest that, in addition to *measuring* androgyny, psychologists should emphasize in-depth descriptions of androgynous people, with special attention to the effect of social context. Such studies might provide useful guidelines that could diminish some of the existing confusion about the most appropriate ways to measure androgyny.

CHARACTERISTICS OF SEX-TYPED AND ANDROGYNOUS PEOPLE

Studies of the characteristics of androgynous and sex-typed people have two fundamental, and overlapping, purposes. The first is to check the validity of the instruments measuring psychological sex. Do people who score as androgynous on a sex-role inventory react as the model predicts they would? An answer of no could indicate either that the concept of androgyny needs further refinement, or that androgynous and sex-typed people are not being properly identified by that instrument. If the answer is yes, the findings support both the model and the measure.

The second fundamental purpose of such studies is to expand knowledge about the personality and behavioral traits that typify androgynous and sex-typed people. It is central to the construct of androgyny that androgynous people will behave in a healthier, more adaptive fashion than will their sex-typed peers. This is, of course, an extremely global statement, so researchers have attempted to determine whether or not, on a specific task or with a particular measure of emotional well-being, androgynous individuals outperform the others.

Androgyny and Flexibility of Behavioral Repertoires

The earliest studies of the personality characteristics of androgynous and sex-typed individuals sought to determine whether or not androgynous people exhibit situationally appropriate flexibility (Bem, 1975; Bem & Lenney, 1976; Bem, Martyna, & Watson, 1976; Bem, 1977). These studies, all carried out in laboratory settings, looked at flexibility and appropriateness in response to specific tasks.

In the first set of studies, Bem (1975) compared the behaviors of androgynous and sex-typed people on tasks that called either for the masculine trait of independence or the feminine trait of nurturance. The premises underlying the model of androgyny would lead us to predict that both androgynous and masculine people would perform well on the masculine task, and that androgynous and feminine people would perform well on the feminine task.

To measure independence, Bem assessed the ability of subjects to hold their own opinion in rating the funniness of a series of cartoons when placed with a group of confederates who rated funny cartoons as unfunny and unfunny cartoons as funny. Independence, then, was defined as the ability to resist peer pressure when it disconfirmed one's own perception. Findings from this study indicated, as the model would predict, that there were no significant differences between the responses of masculine and androgynous subjects, and that both agreed with the confederates on fewer trials than did the feminine subjects. These findings held for both male and female subjects.

To measure nurturance, Bem looked first at the responses of subjects who were placed alone in a room with a baby kitten. Nurturance was defined as the extent to which subjects interacted with the kitten when they had only the kitten to play with, or when they could choose to play with the kitten from among a number of other interesting objects in the room (magazines, puzzles, etc.). In this study, findings for the female and male subjects differed. Responses of the male subjects were consistent with the assumptions associated with the concept of androgyny. Both feminine and androgynous males evidenced greater involvement with the kitten than did the masculine males. For the female subjects, however, contrary to prediction, feminine and androgynous females were *not* more responsive to the kitten than were the masculine females; in fact, the feminine females were significantly *less* responsive than the androgynous females.

Two aspects of these findings cannot be explained using the concept of androgyny; the relatively high level of nurturance displayed by the masculine females, and the strikingly low level of nurturance displayed by the feminine females. To better understand these findings, Bem, Martyna, and Watson (1976) did two additional studies on nurturance. In the first study, subjects were left alone in a room with an infant; nurturance was defined as the extent to which the subject interacted with the infant. Findings from this study agreed with predictions based on the model of androgyny. Feminine and androgynous females and males did not differ significantly, and both were significantly more nurturant than the masculine subjects. Bem and her colleagues therefore concluded that findings from the kitten study applied only to interactions with an animal, rather than to those with another human being.

In the final study of nurturance, subjects were given the role of interviewer with a confederate who, the subjects were told, would simply talk about him or herself as a part of a study on interpersonal closeness. Subjects were instructed to respond to the confederate, but not to talk about themselves. The confederates described themselves as rather typical lonely transfer students who were having a hard time adjusting to their new college setting. Nurturance, in this case, was defined as the number of empathic responses the subject gave to the "lonely student." Again, the male subjects performed as predicted. Feminine and androgynous males did not differ, and both were significantly more responsive than the masculine males. However, feminine females were significantly more nurturant than the androgynous females, who in turn were more nurturant than the masculine females.

From this set of studies, it appears that androgynous males are capable of independence and nurturance, when these traits are called for. Androgynous females also demonstrated both independence and nurturance, although they were less nurturant than the feminine females when faced with a lonely student. Masculine and feminine males performed as predicted, but the feminine males were less nurturant with the kitten, and more nurturant with a lonely student than was predicted.

Other studies from Bem's laboratory (Bem & Lenney, 1976) took a somewhat different approach to the study of response flexibility. These studies sought to determine whether androgynous subjects would be more likely than sex-typed subjects to choose either masculine- or feminine-typed tasks when they were offered a choice between the two. Androgynous subjects, the authors speculated, could base their choice on which task offered the greater monetary reward (the measure of situational appropriateness), rather than on which task was considered more appropriate for someone of their sex. Thus, subjects were asked, for example, to choose between ironing a cloth napkin (feminine) or nailing two boards together (masculine). In every case, the task that was considered appropriate for that person's sex was given the lower monetary reward. Results indicated that, as predicted, feminine- and masculine-type subjects were significantly more stereotyped in their choices than were the androgynous subjects, even when such choices were financially less rewarding. When forced to choose, then, androgynous subjects revealed the flexibility and situational appropriateness associated with the construct of androgyny.

Evaluation of the flexibility studies. Bem's studies support the greater flexibility of androgynous as compared to sex-typed individuals, within a laboratory setting. The next question to be asked is, Can these findings be generalized to the real-life experiences of androgynous men and women? Certain features of Bem's methods make such generalizations difficult. First, different subjects were used for each of the studies. This means that there is no information on whether specific individuals would be able to evidence both masculine and feminine responses. Would the same androgynous woman who chose to nail a board rather than iron a cloth also be able to withstand peer pressure when asked to evaluate the funniness of cartoons? Others who scored like her on the BSRI were able to do so, but this does not provide information about flexibility across tasks for any given individual.

Second, the situations presented to the subjects are only minimally related to choices that one might have to make in the real world. How often, for example, might one have to decide between hammering a nail or ironing a cloth napkin? How often would one be alone in the room with a tiny infant, but with no predetermined responsibility for that infant? The more realistic question, it seems, is How often does one *choose* masculine- or feminine-typed behaviors over a period of time in real life? Also, in Bem's studies, subjects were presented with masculine or feminine-typed tasks, which could increase the likelihood of responding in masculine or feminine ways. We do not know from these studies, however, how often individuals would *seek out* situations that called for masculine or feminine responses. The androgynous person who is capable of nurturance but avoids situations in which nurturance is called for would not be behaving androgynously.

Third, in the forced-choice situations, it was always the non-sex-appropriate option that was given the high financial reward. However, in real life, it is unlikely that this would always be the case. Androgynous behavior does not necessarily meet with praise and encouragement. Thus, the androgynous person might choose a feminine or masculine response because it seems more appropriate, rather than because it offers the highest reward. Situational appropriateness, in other words, is often determined by one's own standards, as well as by societal rewards. The androgynous person would take both of these factors into account, an aspect not reflected in Bem's studies on response flexibility.

Androgyny and Emotional Adjustment

It is often suggested that androgynous people would evidence greater emotional adjustment than their sex-typed peers. Jones, Chernovetz, and Hansson (1978) investigated this idea, looking at the relative adjustment levels of 1404 individuals as a function of their psychological sex. The general category of adjustment was divided into four basic components. The first dealt with specific personality traits, including extroversion, a sense of being in control of one's own behavior, high self-esteem, and the absence of alcoholism. The second concerned intellectual competence and creativity, the third considered resistance to feelings of helplessness, and the fourth dealt with experience in heterosexual relationships.

In general, the data from this study only partially supported the prediction that androgynous persons would demonstrate the highest levels of adjustment. This prediction was particularly disconfirmed by the findings for the male subjects. On many of the measures, it was the masculine and not the androgynous males who showed the highest levels of adjustment. For example, the androgynous males felt less control over their behavior, had more drinking problems, and were somewhat more introverted than their masculine peers. They scored lower on political awareness and somewhat lower on creativity. On the other hand, there were no significant differences between the androgynous and masculine males in resistance to feelings of helplessness, in self-esteem, or in experience in heterosexual relationships.

For the females, the study more clearly supported the prediction that better adjustment was associated with androgyny. Androgynous females were less extroverted than their masculine counterparts, but they also had fewer drinking problems. They tended to be somewhat more creative. They reported more intimate relationships and fewer sexual inhibitions, but they did not show greater knowledge about sexuality. No significant differences for the females were reported for a number of variables, including sense of control, resistance to feelings of helplessness, neurotic tendencies, and self-esteem.

This study suggests that when differences are found, masculine males and androgynous females are likely to score higher in emotional adjustment than their same-sex counterparts. These findings can be evaluated in terms of the research methods used, and the effect of social context.

Many of the traits included in the study represented agentic qualities: perceived control over one's behavior, political awareness, and extroversion. In addition, sexual intimacy was measured by the number of sexual contacts one had, the age at which these contacts occurred, and the presence or absence of intercourse. By contrast, there is a striking absence of traits that would be consistent with a communal model: a capacity for working collaboratively, the expression of care and concern for others, the ability to consider the interests of others as well as of oneself. Similarly, the *quality* of intimate relationships—how satisfactory they were, how deep the emotional ties became, the extent to which feelings were expressed—was not included in the measure of sexual intimacy. These aspects of methodology might have contributed to the finding that masculine rather than androgynous males were better adjusted. If a more representative range of behaviors had been included, the potential strengths of the androgynous men might have been more apparent.

On the other hand, the approach taken by Jones, Chernovetz, and Hansson is representative of the values that exist in contemporary society. Political knowledge, the ability to be outgoing with others, a sense of mastery over one's behaviors, are generally valued more highly than a capacity to work in harmony with others or a sensitivity to others' needs. Thus, it may be valid to say their findings suggest that in a culture valuing agentic attributes over communal ones, masculine males will be better adjusted than androgynous males.

This interpretation is also consistent with the findings that androgynous females, although not androgynous males, showed higher levels of emotional adjustment than their peers. Androgynous females, as compared to their sex-typed counterparts, are capable of exhibiting the masculine traits valued by society. At the same time, having also incorporated feminine-typed behaviors, they do not regularly violate cultural expectations of how a woman should respond. Feminine females, by contrast, lack valued masculine attributes, and masculine females might be held in disfavor for being "too manly," or for lacking expected feminine attributes. For men, it is the masculine males who are both acting in accordance with expectations for their sex and reflecting the masculine attributes valued by society. Androgynous males, who have taken on some of the characteristics of the lesser-valued feminine stereotype, might not be responded to as favorably.

Another Look

We saw that in controlled laboratory settings, androgynous persons generally behave in a fashion consistent with the concept of androgyny. That is, they are capable of performing masculine- and feminine-typed tasks, and can express both masculine independence and feminine nurturance. By contrast, sex-typed people, either feminine or masculine, tend to respond in keeping with sex-role stereotypes.

The *effect* of being androgynous in contemporary society, however, seems related to whether one is male or female. In at least one study, emotional adjustment was associated with androgyny in females, but with masculinity in males. This is consistent with other findings (e.g., Kristal, Sanders, Spence, & Helmreich, 1975) that in order to fare well in society, one must evidence some aspects of behaviors expected for one's sex, as well as some behavioral traits reflecting the higher-valued masculine attributes. Because of the value base of contemporary society, androgyny may lead to well-being more often for females than for males.

This conclusion, however, can be tempered by two additional considerations. First, one can choose to be involved in settings where feminine as well as masculine attributes are valued—those which are not rigidly hierarchical, or those where interpersonal skills as well as achievement are rewarded. Under these conditions, we can expect androgyny to be more closely associated with emotional adjustment for both males and females, although studies to test this prediction are necessary. Second, one can look to personal fulfillment as well as to external rewards for satisfaction. The decision to behave in accordance with one's own values, rather than society's values, could result in favorable emotional adjustment for all. The relationship among cultural values, emotional adjustment, and psychological sex is one that has barely been explored, but that merits intensive investigation. Such studies would give us a comprehensive understanding of the effects of androgynous behaviors on well-being in various contexts.

TOWARD THE DEVELOPMENT OF AN ANDROGYNOUS PERSPECTIVE

In the following chapters, we will use the construct of androgyny to shape our discussion of the psychology of sex roles. Androgyny, in general, concerns the capacity to exhibit personality attributes and behavioral characteristics that are not delimited on the basis of one's sex. More specifically, from an androgynous perspective one would seek out evidence of behavior that combines feminine and masculine attributes so as to be flexible, situationally appropriate, and effective.

In thinking about the psychology of sex roles from an androgynous perspective, we should keep a number of questions in mind. The answers to these questions will help us understand the characteristics of an androgynous personality.

1. *How does behavior vary as a function of psychological sex?* The research on androgyny has indicated that traits commonly associated with males or females, such as independence or nurturance, may vary more as a function of psychological sex than of biological sex. Therefore, we will explore how studies comparing characteristics of males and females might have had different findings had psychological sex been taken into account. This may entail reinterpreting existing data, or suggesting new directions for research.
2. *What is the potential range of human responses?* The construct of androgyny contains the premise that androgynous individuals will have a broader repertoire of behaviors than will those who are sex-typed. To demonstrate this, we need some sense of the range of potential behaviors. Therefore, we will emphasize studies that examine the varieties of human responses, and people's behavioral potential rather than just their typical behaviors.
3. *How flexibly and appropriately can people act in a variety of situations?* The construct of androgyny further assumes that androgynous individuals will respond flexibly in a situationally appropriate manner. To explore this assumption we require information on the conditions under which flexible, appropriate responses will be manifested. We will seek out studies that demonstrate such flexibility and document the use of this flexibility in making choices about the pattern of one's life.
4. *What evidence is there for the integration of feminine and masculine attributes?* The potential for integrating sex-typed attributes is a central component of the construct of androgyny. Therefore, we will emphasize studies that examine the capacity for such integration or contrast the results of integrated behavior with those of sex-typed behavior. Because there has been little research on the integration of sex-typed attributes, we will also point to areas where such research might be pursued.
5. *How do cultural forces affect the expression of sex-typed and androgynous characteristics?* The possibility of effectively expressing androgynous characteristics is affected by culturally based expectations and values regarding appropriate behavior for members of each sex. These cultural components are reflected in prevailing myths about men and women, in the institutional structure of society, and in stereotypes about the behaviors of women and men. We will therefore pay attention to existing myths, to determine how these may constrict or enhance the development of an androgynous personality. We will also look at social institutions—educational establishments, the family, the structure of the work world—for the effect these have on the expression of androgynous characteristics.

In general, then, we will be examining the literature on the psychology of sex roles for information pertinent to the development and maintenance of an androgynous personality. In some areas relevant data will be available; in others we can only point to the weaknesses in existing data and suggest additional lines of research.

Because androgyny has only recently been a focus of psychological inquiry, we will rely more on recent than on older studies. For each study, however, our ultimate concern will be to relate existing findings to the construct of androgyny.

SELECTED READINGS

Bakan, D. *The duality of human existence.* Boston: Beacon Press, 1966.

Kaplan, A. G. (ed.). *Psychological androgyny: Further perspectives.* New York: Human Sciences Press, in press.

Kaplan, A. G., and Bean, J. P. (eds.). *Beyond sex role stereotypes: Readings toward a psychology of androgyny.* Boston: Little, Brown, 1976.

Kelly, J. A., and Worell, J. New formulations of sex roles and androgyny: A critical review. *Journal of Consulting and Clinical Psychology,* 1977, *45,* 1101–15.

Piercy, M. *Woman on the edge of time.* New York: Fawcett Crest, 1976.

Spence, J. T., and Helmreich, R. L. *Masculinity and femininity: Their psychological dimensions, correlates, and antecedents.* Austin: University of Texas Press, 1978.

Cultural Values and the Psychological Study of Sex Roles

Not too long ago, a clinical psychologist presented a paper to a group of colleagues on the applications of androgyny to psychotherapy. She first made the common observation that many clinicians consider it important to help clients get in touch with their feelings and express them in appropriate ways. However, she went on to say, these same clinicians are usually unaware that, by and large, they tend to encourage the expression of masculine feelings in males and feminine feelings in females. For example, she had observed a number of therapists who hesitated to help boys recognize that when they were sad, it could be all right to cry. With girls no such hesitation had been evident. She then pointed to the detrimental effect of this sort of sex-typing in psychotherapy. "It is as important," she concluded, "for boys to feel free to cry as it is for girls to feel free to cry."

Immediately a hand shot up in the audience. "That is unethical," announced one of her colleagues. "You would be imposing *your* values on that poor child, encouraging him to do what *you* think he should do. Your suggestion would make him the laughingstock of his friends. You are talking politics, not therapy, and politics should never be a part of clinical work."

This vignette raises a position frequently heard in discussions of androgyny: Constructs such as androgyny, which challenge long-standing beliefs, reflect the personal values of the professional and thus are not in keeping with the goals of objective science. Let us follow this reasoning a little more carefully as it applies to psychotherapy and to research: (1) The goal of science, including psychology, is an objective, impartial understanding of the world. (2) Scientific observers, be they researchers or therapists, should lay aside their own values or beliefs before beginning their work. (3) Psychological inquiry appears not to be based on personal values when the results confirm the findings of other studies or agree with common observations of human response patterns. (4) Findings or approaches that differ from those frequently reported or that disconfirm common observations should be examined for bias. (5) If atypical findings or positions are reported by someone who associates her or his work with a specific value base, such as a feminist perspective, bias is even more likely.

As Mednick (1979) has pointed out, the belief that certain positions are more biased than others is well illustrated in the preface to Lewis' book *Developing Women's Potential:*

I believe I have an advantage, as a man, in writing about women. Most books and articles about women have been written by women, and many have been justifiably criticized for being too emotional and biased. It is difficult, and perhaps impossible for a female writer to be objective in discussing women's roles. In many cases, their views and arguments are in support of their own role, and perhaps are an attempt to justify it. The result may be interesting but not objective. In any case . . . I wish to emphasize . . . that my being a man should be of secondary concern. I am writing as a psychologist and I hope my views will be judged on that basis. (1968, p. viii)

The accusation that bias may be unique to studies about and by women, or to approaches that challenge prevailing assumptions is of special concern to students of androgyny. Androgyny, as was shown in Chapter 1, challenges cultural stereotypes about "appropriate" behavior for women and men. It also counters a long-standing tradition in psychological research that links emotional well-being to the learning of "proper" psychological sex traits: masculinity for males and femininity for females. It suggests that topics such as the similarities between the sexes or behavior that transcends sex-role stereotypes are at least as important to study as the topic of "sex differences," which has long occupied many psychologists. Many of the people who study androgyny make explicit the feminist perspective that underlies their work. Thus, their work is vulnerable to accusations of being "biased," or "political," or value-based.

To put such accusations into perspective, we will attempt to demonstrate in this chapter that values can be associated with *all* approaches to psychological research, not just those which challenge commonly held positions. In particular, we will explore the effects cultural assumptions about women and men have had on the psychological study of sex roles. We will address several specific questions, such as: What is the prevailing view of women and men in contemporary society? How does this view influence the topics psychologists choose to investigate, the research methods they employ, and the interpretations they make from their findings? What changes in the psychological study of sex roles are suggested by an androgynous perspective?

To explore these questions, we will first look at the nature of psychological research—the basic procedures used by most psychological researchers. Second, we will see how cultural beliefs about women and men have shaped the positions of each sex in society and the psychological study of sex roles.

THE NATURE OF PSYCHOLOGICAL INQUIRY

Psychological research is essentially modeled after the experimental method of the natural sciences. Scientists strive for an objective, empirically grounded procedure that provides data any researcher can replicate. We will briefly outline the components of this procedure, and then look at the extent of its objectivity.

Researchers rarely begin a study with an open-ended question such as, "Are there any differences in the ways mothers and fathers treat their children?" Instead, they formulate an *hypothesis,* a stated expectation about the relationship between several aspects of experience, or about expected differences between two groups of people. Hypotheses can be derived from several sources. Frequently, they are based on a *theory* about human behavior, and are formulated to test one aspect of that theory. Or, they can be based on repeated observations of daily life. Thus, a researcher interested in studying sex differences in parenting behavior might begin with the theory that behavior (e.g., parenting styles) is biologically determined—influenced, for example, by hormones, innate instincts, or specific features of the nervous system. From this theory, the researcher might generate the hypothesis that specific parenting behaviors are directly related to the presence or absence of certain hormones in the body. Or, the researcher might theorize that women spend more time with infants because they are more responsive to infants' emotional states. This could lead to an hypothesis that there will be a significant relationship between time spent with infants and accurate identification of emotional states. In both cases, the function of the hypothesis is to translate the theory into a specific relationship that can then be tested.

Next, the researcher would *operationalize* the specific aspects of the hypothesis. In the study of the relationship between hormone levels and parenting behavior, the relevant hormones and parenting behaviors would be identified in a form that could be directly measured. Thus, parenting behaviors might be operationalized in terms of the amount of time between the infant's cry and the parent's response. In the study comparing female and male responsiveness to infants, the researcher might operationalize responsiveness by showing parents pictures of infants and asking them to identify the mood expressed in each picture.

Having operationalized the variables, the researcher would then carry out the study. The variables at issue—hormone levels, latency of parental response to the infant's cry, frequency of response, and accuracy in identifying infant's emotional states—would all be measured. In each study, direct comparisons would be made between the two relevant variables. That is, the researcher would compute the relationship between hormone levels and latency of parental response, or between sex of parent, accuracy of observations, and the amount of contact with infants. Then he or she would determine the relationship's statistical significance: Did it occur at a level significantly greater than chance? In the hormone study, there might be a significant finding that higher levels of a specific hormone are associated with more rapid parental response to the infant. In the study of sex differences in responsiveness, a significant finding might be that females were more accurate than males in identifying the emotional states of infants and had also spent more time caring for infants.

The researcher ends her or his study by offering interpretations of the findings, and relating them back to the theory or observation that initiated the study. In the hormone study, the researcher might suggest that her or his findings support a biological basis for parent-infant interaction. In the study of emotional sensitivity, the researcher might conclude that women's more accurate awareness of infants' emotional states gives them a greater sense of competence when dealing with infants, and therefore increases the likelihood that they will spend more time with infants than do men.

Finally, the study is written up and submitted for publication. In most psychological journals articles are evaluated by professionals who are experts in the topic covered. Criteria for publishing an article include the clarity of the theoretical framework, the logical derivation of hypotheses from the theory, the accuracy of the procedures, and the appropriateness of the interpretations.

The Value Base of Psychological Research

At every step of the research process—the formulation of theory, the selection of hypotheses, the operationalizing of variables, the testing of relationships, the interpretation of results, and the selection of articles for publication—values and assumptions can shape the course of events (cf. Wallston, 1979). Such values and assumptions come from many sources. Some relate to an individual's own belief system, such as a commitment to using psychological research as a force for social change. Some are based on prevailing cultural attitudes toward the topic under study: shared beliefs about the causes of poverty or the source of observed behavioral differences between members of different races or sexes. Others come from professional norms regarding topics appropriate for study and approved methods of research. These professional norms—what Kuhn (1970) calls "paradigms"—form the "conceptual boxes" within which research is carried out. Individual, societal, and professional belief systems, then, all create the context within which research occurs. Together, they suggest that "reality" is not a fixed state that can be observed and studied in the same manner by everyone. Instead, reality can be seen as socially constructed, determined by one's perspective (Berger & Luckman, 1966).

These individual, societal, and professional considerations may influence researchers' commitment to a particular *theoretical orientation.* For example, Pastore (1949) found researchers' theoretical orientations to be directly related to their political beliefs. He compared the political orientations of researchers who argued for environmental determinants of behavior ("nurture") with those who argued for biological determinants of behavior ("nature"). He found that, with very few exceptions, those who favored "nature" held politically conservative views, whereas those who favored "nurture" were politically liberal. These professional positions, then, rather than being impartially determined, appeared to be part of the researchers' broader belief system. In each case, their findings could support their more basic view of the world. For the conservatives, data indicating the biological bases of behavior could be offered as evidence that existing patterns of response were innately determined and therefore not open to change. For the liberals, data supporting the environmental effect on behavior could suggest that behavioral change could occur through alternating environmental conditions.

Ryan (1976) has also illustrated the ways in which belief systems can influence the selection of theory and the resulting research focus. Here, the belief was not related to whether behavior is fixed or changeable, but to where the source of the change should lie. Ryan identifies two contrasting theoretical positions, *universalism* and *exceptionalism.* The universalist sees problems as caused by the social arrangements of a community or society, not by the individual or group characteristics of the people who exhibit the problems. Universalistic researchers would therefore investigate institutional, legislative, or economic conditions that created the problems under study. Thus, if a researcher were interested in identifying the causes of poverty, she or he would attempt to document the aspects of a society that created a class of poor people.

The exceptionalist sees problems as relating to categories of people rather than to societal structure. Exceptionalistic researchers, thus, would attempt to understand poverty by investigating the characteristics of poor people; they would try to determine what features of these people result in their being poor.

It should be clear that universalism and exceptionalism would lead to very different kinds of studies, and very different findings regarding the causes of poverty. Universalistic researchers might investigate the relationship between income distribution and work patterns. They might hypothesize that fewer people would be unemployed if the welfare system provided financial incentives for working, or if a "negative income tax" based on family size were given to poor people. In other words, the relationship between poverty and specific structures of society would be at issue.

Exceptionalistic researchers would focus on specific characteristics of poor people, such as their motivational level, the stability of their families, or the amount of "cultural enrichment" within their homes. They might then hypothesize that poverty could be reduced if training programs were made available to poor people, or if children were provided with early "enrichment" programs.

In both of these examples—the nature-nurture controversy and the universalistic-exceptionalistic split—the relationship between theory and beliefs is seldom recognized or acknowledged by researchers. It would be most unlikely to find a study in which the investigator stated clearly that he or she does not believe in social change, and therefore has chosen to examine the innate determinants of behavior. Also, the researchers' theoretical positions are not always derived directly from a specific belief system. However, as these examples illustrate, theory *can* be influenced by researchers' values.

We need to keep three points in mind when trying to understand the relationship between theory and values. First, it is important to recognize whether or not there is an implicit value base underlying a theoretical orientation. If such a value base exists, the researcher should make it explicit, so that others can evaluate the research within its context. Second, studies in which a value base is articulated are not more "biased" or "political" than those in which the value base is unexpressed. On the contrary, the clear statement of a value orientation may make it less likely that the value base will distort the work in unrecognized ways. Third, the fact that values can influence theory does not always mean that the resulting research is "distorted" or meaningless. It does mean, however, that it represents only one way of looking at the topic at hand. Other theories stemming from a different value base would lead the researcher to a vastly different, but not necessarily better or worse, line of investigation.

Researchers' *expectations* can also influence their findings, even when utmost care is taken to assess objectively only what "really" exists. Facts, in other words, depend on what scientists bring to the laboratory (Kessler and McKenna, 1978).

Rosenthal and his colleagues have presented many studies in which expectancies influenced results (Rosenthal, 1966; Rosenthal and Jacobson, 1968; Rosenthal and Rosnow, 1969).

In one study, college students were told that the rats they were using in classroom experiments had been bred to be either "maze bright" or "maze dull." Even though there was in fact no difference between the two groups of rats, the "maze bright" rats performed significantly better in a learning experiment than the "maze dull" rats. In other studies, graduate students administered Rorschach ink blots to subjects, and were told in advance what sort of responses to expect. Indeed, their subjects then performed as expected. In yet another study, experimenters who were told to expect high levels of aggression in their subjects obtained higher levels than experimenters who were told to expect lower levels. Similarly, a group of experimenters were told that subjects who were asked to rate the degree of success or failure represented by pictures of people's faces would rate more success than failure. Subjects working with these experimenters rated the faces as successful more often than did subjects working with experimenters who were told to expect unsuccessful ratings. In all of these studies, experimenters' expectations are somehow transmitted to the subjects and influence their behavior.

Researchers' values can also influence their *interpretations* of findings. In 1855 Jarvis found that mental illness was most prevalent among the poor, and especially among the Irish. Such findings can be understood in several ways. A universalist might conclude that stresses associated with poverty have increased the rate of mental illness. An exceptionalist might reason that a specific group of people are emotionally unstable because of certain unique characteristics. Jarvis, while making some mention of the role of environmental stress, placed primary emphasis on the nature of the Irish:

> The Irish laborers have less sensibility and fewer wants to be gratified than the Americans, and yet they more commonly fail to supply them. They also have a greater irritability; they are more readily disturbed when they find themselves at variance with the circumstances about them, and less easily reconciled to difficulties they cannot overcome.
>
> Unquestionably, much of their insanity is due to the intemperence, to which the Irish seem to be peculiarly prone. (Dohrenwend and Dohrenwend, 1974, p. 444)

The value base behind this interpretation has been pointed out by Grob:

> Like others coming from the same background, Jarvis saw the genteel New England society that he loved and valued being eroded ... In a very real sense, therefore, some of the points that he attempted to make ... were a reflection of his own social ideology. What Jarvis did was to take a series of statistics and read them in the light of his own moral assumptions. (1971, p. 56)

Finally, reviewers' commitment to a specific theory can influence their *evaluation* of the scientific merit of a piece of research. This point is well illustrated in a study conducted by Mahoney (1976). Mahoney drew up a series of fabricated studies, all based on a widely held theoretical position. All studies followed exactly the same method, but some reported findings that directly confirmed the initial theory, whereas others reported findings that either partially or fully disconfirmed the initial theory. Mahoney found that when the results confirmed the theory, the study was much more likely to be accepted for publication than when the results did not. However, the rejections were justified on the basis of inadequate research design or poor choice of statistical procedures, not on the relationship of findings to theory. The same procedures, then, were deemed adequate when they produced expected results, but inadequate when they produced unexpected results.

Researchers, then, may choose theoretical orientations based on their own belief systems, may indirectly motivate their subjects to perform so as to confirm their previous expectations, and may interpret their findings in line with their own basic assumptions. DeBeauvoir offers a clear summary of this position:

> It is doubtless impossible to approach any human problem with a mind free from bias. The way in which questions are put, the points of view assumed, presuppose a relativity of interest; all characteristics imply values, and every objective description, so called, implies an ethical background. Rather than attempting to conceal principles more or less definitely implied, it is better to state them openly at the beginning. (1953, p. xxvii)

The solution, then, is not to abandon theory, or to research only those areas in which there is no basis for formulating expectations. Instead, as DeBeauvoir argues, the possible relationship between values and research needs to be more openly acknowledged. If this were done, it could provide a context for evaluating conflicting findings, and for developing alternative theories and methodologies based on alternative belief systems.

We will follow DeBeauvoir's advice, and make clear the value base that underlies the androgynous orientation of this book. The position we espouse is not unique to androgyny. Much of what we believe is similar to that which is associated with a feminist perspective. We are not attempting to differentiate androgynous and feminist points of view; rather, androgyny may be considered one orientation within the feminist framework. We use androgyny as a model for clarifying feminist principles, not as an alternative.

The Value Base of Research on Androgyny

Researchers whose interests center on androgyny share with all others an orientation to inquiry that reflects some belief system. The belief system associated with the construct of androgyny has several components. Perhaps the most basic is that the biological sex of a person need not determine the personality traits that are encouraged, or the role that she or he is prepared for in society. Because of this belief, such researchers value an understanding of the capabilities—the strengths as well as weaknesses—of both sexes.

Also central to the value base underlying the construct of androgyny is the belief that individual characteristics need to be understood within their social context. One theme that shall be repeated throughout this book is that cultural attitudes, values, and institutional structures profoundly affect not only individual development, but also the psychological study of sex roles. Some of the people who study androgyny carry this value base one step further to indicate that cultural factors have generally worked to the advantage of men and to the disadvantage of women. Such people emphasize research directions that have direct implications for social change, and that suggest ways in which the currently existing inequity between the sexes can be altered.

The belief system underlying androgyny research stands in contrast to the prevailing cultural beliefs about women and men. These more widely held beliefs warrant examination, because they bear directly on traditional studies of psychological sex.

PSYCHOLOGY'S CULTURAL HERITAGE

Cultures around the world do not share with us the belief that biological sex need not be associated with personality traits and social roles. On the contrary, biological sex is a primary factor in determining one's place in society. Firestone (1970) has argued that the earliest and most fundamental division within society was the division between the sexes. This division, as Rosaldo and others have pointed out, is universal: "Every known society recognizes and elaborates some differences between the sexes. . . . It is everywhere the case that there are characteristic tasks, manners and responsibilities primarily associated with women or with men" (1974, p. 18). Even more than race or social class, sex has a bearing on one's place in society; a person is seen first and foremost as a woman or a man. It is the person's sex that sets the stage for the unfolding of his or her life.

Cultures not only decree this fundamental distinction between the sexes. They also establish inequality. Men and male attributes are accorded greater value than are women and female attributes. (Chodorow, 1971; Mead, 1967; Mednick, Tangri, & Hoffman, 1975; Rosaldo, 1974). This asymmetry in cultural evaluations is also seen as a universal phenomenon: "The secondary status of women is one of the true universals, a pancultural fact" (Ortner, 1974, p. 67). These two features of society, the distinction between the sexes and the superiority of males, are closely intertwined (Firestone, 1970). It is in line with institutionalizing the superiority of males that the distinction between the sexes has been stressed. This feature of society—a distinction between the sexes in which males are dominant and females are subordinate—is called *patriarchy*. A patriarchal society is one in which values, institutions, roles, and responsibilities maintain the assumed superiority of men and the inferiority of women.

The Devaluation of Women

How can this universal devaluation of women be accounted for? Ortner (1974) offers one explanation by arguing that women are symbolic of a phenomenon that is universally devalued—nature. According to Ortner, women are to nature as men are to culture. Culture, it should be remembered, is a distinctly human experience; thus, it represents a more advanced level of development than nature. Women, thought to be more tied to nature than are men, represent a lower order of being.

Women's closer links to nature occur on three levels, according to Ortner. First, women are seen as more ruled by their bodies than are men. The effect on women of their monthly menstrual cycle, and of pregnancy, childbirth, and lactation, renders them more reactive to their bodies than men. Women create with their bodies (nature), whereas men create with their minds (culture). Second, women's social roles are closer to nature than are men's. Women, in almost every culture, have primary responsibility for domestic chores and raising children. Their functions lie within the private sphere of home and family, rather than within the public sphere. And it is within the public sphere that the institutions of a culture evolve—the politics, education, economic structure, religion, law and so on. Third, women's emotional life is seen as closer to nature than that of men. Women are viewed as experiencing things in subjective, concrete, immediate ways, whereas men's reactions are seen as more abstract, objective, and distant. Men, in other words, are considered better able to transcend their own experiences and deal with universals, better able to work with the world of ideas (culture) than the world of people (nature).

Central to this devaluation of women is the fact that humanity, the world of people, is viewed from a masculine, rather than a masculine *and* feminine perspective. DeBeauvoir makes this point explicit: "Humanity is male and man defines woman not in herself, but as relative to him" (1953, p. xvi). The real world, the world that counts, is the world of men. Women stand apart from this world; they are the "other" (DeBeauvoir, 1953), the "outsider" (Gornick, 1971). For Gornick, woman as outsider becomes a "human being who, for mysterious reasons and in mysterious ways, is outside the circle of ordinary human experience" (p. 126). As outsiders, women become seen not as who they are but in terms of what they symbolize. In this connection, Gornick, a known feminist, recalls a luncheon at the end of which a male friend leaned back and commented casually: "Of course, you realize that if Women's Liberation wins, civilization will simply be *wrecked.*" Her reaction was immediate:

> No. It cannot be. I am not real to him. I am not real to my civilization. I am not real to the culture that has spawned me and made use of me. I am only a collection of myths. I am an existential stand in. The *idea* of me is real— the temptress, the Goddess, the child, the mother—but *I* am not real. (p. 144).

Thus, in a very basic sense, women's experience in a patriarchal society is that of being somehow less than fully human, outside the realm of the "real world." She is different from and less valued than the insiders, the shapers of the dominant culture, the men. For the most part, this experience is in reaction to *cultural* standards, and to *cultural* beliefs that decree women's place in the social order. It is society—a collective—rather than individual people that conveys to women their status as other, as outsider.

Some people, however, clearly articulate, indeed exaggerate, this vision of woman as less than fully human. These are the people who practice *misogyny,* the belittling of and even hatred toward women. It is not difficult to find representations of a misogynous vision in literature and philosophy. These extreme statements carry the somewhat more subtle cultural perspective to an inflated and distorted end. Two examples, the first from philosophy and the second from literature, will suffice to suggest the degree to which the devaluation of women can extend.

Nietzsche, a nineteenth-century German philosopher and one of the leading thinkers of his time, exemplifies this misogynist attitude in the following passage from *Beyond Good and Evil*:

> Woman has much reason for shame; so much pedantry, superficiality, schoolmarmishness, petty presumption, petty licentiousness and immodesty lies concealed in woman—one only needs to study her behavior with children!—and so far all this was at bottom best repressed and kept under control by *fear* of man. Woe when the eternally boring in woman—she is rich in that!—is permitted to venture forth! When she begins to unlearn thoroughly and on principle her prudence and art—of grace, or play, of chasing away worries, of lightening burdens and taking things lightly—and her subtle aptitude for agreeable desires! (Roszak and Roszak, 1969, p. 4)

The playwright Strindberg, also a product of the nineteenth century, provides another example of misogyny in his memoirs, *A Madman's Defense*:

> Woman is not a slave by any stretch of the imagination, for she and her children are supported by her husband's work. She is not oppressed, for nature has ordained that she should live under the protection of her husband while she fulfills her mission in life as a mother. Woman is not man's equal in the realm of intellect, and man is not her equal when it comes to bearing children. She is not essential to the great work of civilization, since man understands its tasks and purposes better than she does. Evolution teaches us that the greater the difference between the sexes, the stronger and more fit will be the resulting offspring. Consequently "masculinism" in woman, the equality of the sexes, is a retrogression and an utter absurdity, the last dream of romantic and idealistic socialism. (Roszak and Roszak, 1969, pp. 13–14)

It is our guess that few readers of this book, male or female, would agree with the above quotations. They reflect neither the prevailing views of Western society, nor the beliefs of the majority of people. Yet within Western attitudes toward men and women, such extremes are *possible*. They do not stand in opposition to more commonly held positions, but rather represent an extreme version of a patriarchal view of women.

Devaluation of Women in Contemporary Society

The cultural devaluation of women has many manifestations in contemporary American society. A few of these should illustrate the point: People value masculinity more than femininity, accord greater worth to what men do than what women do, and, as parents, prefer to give birth to boys rather than to girls. Research on each of these topics reveals a consistent pattern: the assumption of male superiority.

Devaluation of femininity. As documented in Chapter 1, researchers find general consistency in the traits that people associate with masculinity and femininity. But these two clusters of traits are not accorded equal worth. In general, agentic qualities associated with masculinity are valued more highly than are communal qualities associated with femininity (Bem, 1975; Rosenkrantz, et al., 1968; Sheriffs & Jarrett, 1953; Sheriffs & McKee, 1957). Americans place a premium on individual achievement, on "success," and on advancement even at the expense of others. People who demonstrate drive and ambition are more likely to be promoted than those who evidence interpersonal sensitivity and a concern for the welfare of others. People who hold positions of power and influence have far more prestige than people who work for the betterment of others. Although some theorists argue strongly for recognizing the cultural importance of affiliative concerns (e.g., Miller, 1976), this plea is not yet reflected in the reward systems of society.

Devaluation of women's work. If women and men were seen as equally competent, then judgments about the worth of a product should not depend on whether that product was made by a man or a woman. However, studies suggest that this is generally not the case. As researchers have documented, works of literature and art are valued more highly if they are identified as being by a man than if they are identified as being by a woman (Deaux & Taynor, 1973; Goldberg, 1968; Morris, 1970). Only if women and men are identified as clearly outstanding—prize-winning artists or successful lawyers—will the women's work be seen to equal the men's (Abramson, Goldberg, Greenberg, & Abramson, 1977; Pheterson, Kiesler, & Goldberg, 1971). This finding cannot be accounted for by male devaluation of females, for members of both sexes gave less value to the women's work. Rather, it seems that both men and women have absorbed cultural attitudes regarding male superiority.

Male job applicants are also rated more highly than are female job applicants. Fidell (1970) found that hypothetical female candidates were recommended for positions of lower rank than were hypothetical male candidates, even though the resumes of both sexes were identical except for the name. Similarly, Deaux and Taynor (1973) found that male applicants were judged to be more qualified for a job than were equally competent female applicants. Apparently, people assume that males will do better than females, even when there is no objective supporting data.

Finally, jobs held by men are accorded greater prestige than are jobs held by women. Touhy (1974), for example, found that subjects asked to rank the prestige of various occupations gave lower rankings when given the prediction that the number of women in the field would increase. This evaluation is also reflected in governmental ratings of the skills required for a large number of jobs, as listed in the Dictionary of Occupational Titles (Mednick, 1979). The Dictionary is regularly used by employers to determine job requirements and salary levels. Three digits are assigned to each job; the first refers to information skills, the second to skills in working with people, and the third to skills in working with objects. The highest rating is 1; 8 is the lowest for columns 1 and 3, and 7 for column 2. Table 2.1

TABLE 2.1   Ratings of Selected Jobs in the Dictionary of Occupational Titles (1977)

Female job	Rating	Comparison job	Rating
Foster mother	878	Restroom attendant	878
Child care attendant	878	Parking lot attendant	878
Home health aid	878	Pet shop attendant	877
Nurse-maid	878	Newspaper attendant	868
Nursery school teacher	878	Offal man	887
Homemaker (maid: general)	878		
Kindergarten teacher	878		
Nurse - midwife	378	Hotel clerk	368
General duty nurse	378	Dog trainer	228
Private duty nurse	378	Undertaker	168
		Marine mammal handler	328

Note: Scale: 0–8 (8 is low).

First digit: dealing with data (information); second digit: dealing with people; third digit: dealing with things.

Source: Reprinted by permission from Martha T. Shuck Mednick, "The New Psychology of Women: A Feminist Analysis," in Jeanne E. Gullahorn, ed., *Psychology and Women: In Transition* (New York: John Wiley & Sons, 1979).

illustrates some comparable ratings for jobs frequently held by men and women. These ratings reflect, more than any argument we could make, cultural devaluation of women's work.

Devaluation of girl children.   If women and men were valued equally, one would expect couples to be equally eager to give birth to a boy or a girl. However, it seems that this is not the case. Hoffman (1977) studied the sex preferences of over 1500 married women and about 400 of their husbands. She found that almost twice as many women preferred boys as preferred girls, while between three and four times as many men preferred boys to girls. Dinitz, Dynes, and Clarke (1954) reported similar findings. Of young married adults interviewed who stated a preference for the sex of their firstborn, over 92 percent wanted a boy. If they expected to have only one child, 91 percent of the men and 62 percent of the women stated a preference for a boy. This preference was sufficiently strong that, according to Hoffman, couples are more likely to have more children than they originally planned if they have only girls.

Another Look

As we have seen, there is a universal tendency for cultures to draw clear distinctions between traits and roles associated with men and women, and to accord greater value to that which is male than to that which is female. That which is male comes to be equated with "humanity," whereas that which is female is relegated to the status of other, or outsider. In general this results in women being granted a secondary status in society; at worst, it appears in the hostile and blatantly derogatory misogynist portrayal of women. These universal cultural patterns are not absent in contemporary American society. As documented by researchers, masculinity is valued more than femininity, what men do is valued more than what women do, and boy children are desired more than girl children.

Neither men nor women are immune from absorbing this cultural assumption of male superiority. It therefore seems reasonable to speculate that professional disciplines, such as psychology, will similarly reflect a greater valuation of males and masculinity than females and femininity. These manifestations of cultural sex bias in psychological research merit careful attention, because they can directly limit knowledge relevant to the psychology of androgyny. An understanding of men's and women's potential to respond flexibly to situational demands, to integrate feminine and masculine traits, and to deal effectively with others would not be possible if the available information described only selected aspects of male and female behavior.

THE PSYCHOLOGICAL STUDY OF SEX ROLES

The psychological study of sex roles began in the late nineteenth century, and was essentially equated with the study of sex *differences*. In the nineteenth century, at the height of the Victorian Era, sharp distinctions were drawn between the expected behaviors of women and men, and the devaluation of women was pervasive. These societal beliefs, in turn, were reflected by psychological researchers. The prevailing approach to the study of sex differences was *functionalism*, the idea that social customs persist because they are useful to society and necessary to the survival of the social order. Under the influence of Darwin's recently published *Origin of the Species* (1856), functionalists sought to demonstrate that the social order as they observed it was necessary for species survival.

In order to justify the social order, the functionalists concentrated on demonstrating the inevitability of sex differences and the superiority of men (Shields, 1975). If "scientific" justification could be found for the existing secondary status of women, then efforts at social change would, in the functionalists' view, be fruitless. Thus, they turned their attention to biological or instinctual differences between the sexes that might be directly related to observed behavioral differences.

For example, researchers attempted to document that women's lesser intellectual accomplishments were a direct result of having an inferior brain. They tried several approaches, but none met with clear success. One line of inquiry sought evidence that women's brains were smaller than men's and therefore less capable. However, Ellis (1904) and others pointed to evidence suggesting that, relative to body weight, women's brains were in fact larger than men's. Faced with such findings, researchers could have wondered why women were not therefore outperforming men. Instead, they shifted attention to the study of sex differences in the size of specific parts of the brain. Originally, they thought that the frontal lobes were the seat of highest intellectual functioning, and they stressed findings that men's frontal lobes were more developed than women's and that women had more highly developed parietal lobes. However, the parietal lobes later came to be seen by some as the primary seat of intellectual functioning. Again, the researchers could have wondered why women were not fulfilling their biological potential. Instead they indulged in a bit of biological "revisionism": "The frontal region is not, as has been supposed, smaller in women, but rather larger, relatively. . . . But the parietal lobe is somewhat smaller" (Patrick, 1896, in Shields, 1975, p. 741).

Another common area of inquiry, according to Shields, focused on explaining women's role as mother in terms of a "maternal instinct." It was argued that women's nurturant behavior was an innate characteristic, directly related to pregnancy and lactation. There was general agreement that a maternal instinct existed, although the existence of other instincts was questioned. William James (1950) emphasized the strength with which the parental instinct was expressed in women. Halleck (1895), although discounting most instincts, held to the maternal, calling it, according to Shields, "as primitive and unrefined as that of infant's reflexive behavior" (p. 750). Shields (1975) points to McDougall as the strongest proponent of the maternal instinct, as illustrated in the following statement:

> And, when we notice how in so many ways the behavior of the human mother most closely resembles that of the animal-mother, can we doubt that . . . if the animal-mother is moved by the impulse of a maternal instinct, so also is the woman? To repudiate this view as baseless would seem to me the height of blindness and folly. (Shields, p. 750)

Although contemporary psychologists no longer account for behavioral sex differences in terms of brain weight or maternal instincts, the functionalist origins of the study of sex differences still have some effect. The study of sex differences has remained a major focus of psychological research (cf. Maccoby and Jacklin, 1974). Even though there are many more similarities than differences between the sexes, it is primarily the differences that tend to be reported (Unger & Denmark, 1975). The publication policies of journals are influential here, because findings that are not significant (e.g., findings in which the sexes do not differ) are rarely published. Thus, many more reports of differences than of similarities find their way into the journals.

This overemphasis on sex differences, in turn, creates the impression that biological sex carries with it certain fixed properties (Mednick, 1978), and that sex differences in behavior reveal innate differences between the sexes. Additionally, because personality characteristics are so often attributed to a person's biological sex, insufficient attention is given to social factors that may create observed behaviors. For example, Mednick (1979) and Miller (1976) have pointed to power differentials between men and women in this society. Observed differences, by implication, may be related to power, rather than to biological sex. However, by focusing on biological sex, researchers are likely to underestimate the influence of societal features such as power (Sherif, 1976; Unger, 1977). For this reason, findings on studies of sex differences in general continue to support the status quo rather than to provide evidence that could prompt social change and alleviate sexism (Vaughter, 1976).

Assumptions of Male Superiority

The study of women by psychologists and other social scientists often supports cultural assumptions of male superiority (Bernard, 1974; Carlson, 1972; Mednick, 1979; Millman & Kanter, 1975; Parlee, 1975; Weisstein, 1971). This point has been made clearly and unambivalently. Mednick, for example, says, "Women have always been studied as a reflection of man, from a masculine point of view and in the service of the study of man's world" (1978, p. 79). Bernard, speaking of women as they are studied in the research on sex differences, asserts that the purpose of such research has been "to rationalize and legitimize the status quo . . . especially the inferior position of women" (1974, p. 11).

This "androcentric bias" is reflected in the *content areas* in which women and men have been studied. Bernard asks,

> How does it happen that the net effect of the vast corpus of research leads to the conclusion that men are superior to women on all the variables that are valued highly in our society, namely: muscular or kinetic strength, vigor, competitiveness, power, need for achievement, autonomy? In brief, the components of the archetypical macho variable, offensive aggressiveness? (1974, p. 12)

She then answers her own question:

> These are the variables that interest men. These are the variables they judge one another by. These are the variables that are rewarded in our society. These are the variables we need to know about in order to operate in our society successfully. These are the prestige variables. (p. 12)

As Bernard so graphically puts it, the general pattern of psychological research is to emphasize masculine, or agentic, variables. These are the traits which psychologists consider most important to study. The large bodies of research on such variables as achievement motivation, cognitive dissonance, locus of control, and attribution theory document Bernard's position.

Others (e.g., Carlson, 1972; Wallston, 1979) have pointed to a masculine-oriented, or androcentric bias in the prevailing *methods* used by psychological researchers. Carlson points out that aspects of this methodology, including separating, ordering, quantifying, manipulating, and controlling reflect essentially agentic approaches. By contrast, according to Carlson, psychologists place less emphasis on more communal methods of inquiry including "naturalistic observations, sensitivity to intrinsic structure and qualitative patterning of phenomena studied, and greater personal participation of the investigator" (1972, p. 20).

Finally, within the atmosphere created by the assumption of male superiority, far more men than women have been studied by psychologists. As several researchers have documented (Carlson and Carlson, 1961; Dan & Beekman, 1972; McKenna & Kessler, 1974; Schwabacher, 1972) men, far more often than women, serve as subjects in psychological studies. Prescott (1978) investigated the reasons researchers gave for using only one sex in their studies. Most reasons fell into what she termed a "scientific" category. These included prior knowledge that sex differences existed in the category being studied, a desire to reduce the variation in the subjects' responses, and the fact that sex differences were not a consideration in the theory or hypothesis being studied. Slightly more than a quarter of the respondents cited practical considerations such as the unavailability of subjects of the other sex, or the inability to deal with an increased sample size. The remaining respondents reported a lack of interest in sex differences, or a fear that their data would become "muddied" if sex differences were explored. Because women, far more than men, are excluded on the basis of such reasons, psychology has learned far more about men than it has about women.

Yet, although women were often ignored when data were collected, they were *not* ignored when conclusions from studies were drawn. As Parlee points out, there is a pattern that "experimental results from males can be generalized to everyone . . . while those from females can be generalized only to women" (1975, p. 127). Consistent with the cultural assumption that humanity is male, men in psychological research are equated with "people," but women represent only women.

This evidence of assumed male superiority in the psychological study of women has created a trend that Parlee (1975) has called "psychology against women." Studies falling under this rubric convey unrealistic, damaging portrayals of women. There are three ways in which this can occur. First, studies may compare men and women, but on variables more consistent with the male than the female experience. This research may present a *distorted* picture of women. Second, if the topic of research is considered inappropriate for women, or if the inclusion of women is considered too problematic, women may be left out of studies. In this practice, women's responses are *denied.* Third, some studies look exclusively at women, but they typically explore, implicitly or explicitly, problematic aspects of women's behavior. This creates a situation in which women are *demeaned.* Although we are by no means attempting to argue that *all* psychological studies are designed to distort, deny, or demean women, we feel that these tendencies are prevalent enough to merit consideration.

Women as distorted. One common result when the responses of women and men are compared is that women are cast in a more negative light. This can be a function of research design or interpretation of findings. Consider, for example, the issue of sex differences in persuadability. Typically, studies investigate the extent to which subjects will change their opinion when presented with contrasting facts by an "expert." However, as Eagly (1978) has documented, the content areas of most of these studies are politics and economics—areas in which men tend to have greater knowledge than women. People are generally more vulnerable to influence on topics about which they have little knowledge. Yet, when findings are reported that women can be influenced more easily than men, the effect of the content areas is frequently not taken into account. Instead, a general conclusion is drawn about women's greater susceptibility to persuasion.

Studies on internal and external locus of control serve as another example. These studies use a scale developed by Rotter (1966) to determine whether a person perceives her or his behavior as motivated by environmental (external) or personal (internal) considerations. Internal locus of control, reflecting self-confidence and mastery over the environment, is generally considered the more desirable state. In most studies, more males than females have been found to have an internal locus of control. What these researchers do not consider, when presenting such findings, however, is that the scale may be measuring a realistic appraisal of one's ability to determine one's own success or failure, rather than the subtle and pervasive personality dimension that it purports to measure (Parlee, 1975). In other words, women may be reporting accurately the amount of control society has over them. However, the conclusions drawn by researchers imply that externality is a problem associated with the female sex, rather than with a powerless position in society.

Distortions can also occur in the operationalizing of behavioral characteristics. For example, in studying sex differences in dependency a researcher may operationalize dependency as seeking help and physical contact (the more feminine forms of dependency) but fail to include seeking attention (the more masculine expression of dependency; Whiting and Edwards, 1973). Findings might then demonstrate that women are more dependent than men, but the results might well have been different if dependency had been defined more broadly. In addition, distortions can result from operationalizing variables one way when studying women and another way when studying men. McKenna and Kessler (1977), for example, found that in 244 recent studies of aggression, there was no overlap in the most frequently used methods for operationalizing aggression in studies of only male or only female subjects.

Other distortions are created when men and women are compared on a scale that is more relevant to the former than the latter. Gilligan (1977) has raised this point regarding Kohlberg's (1970) developmental measure of levels of moral reasoning. She argues that the tests used by Kohlberg stress legalistic issues—topics more familiar to males than females—and thus do not accurately measure women's levels of moral reasoning. In fact, when she presented women with questions of moral judgment based on issues relevant to them, such as abortion, a developmental sequence of moral stages more pertinent to women emerged.

Distortions in the psychological descriptions of women also appear in the ways research findings are reported. Parlee (1975) provides a useful example in her discussion of Garai and Scheinfeld's (1968) frequently cited study of sex differences in mental and behavioral traits. She notes that when males performed better on a given measure the authors report that "males were superior" but when females performed better, they simply state that "females scored higher than males." According to Parlee, this leaves the reader with the erroneous impression that males in general surpassed females on the traits measured.

Finally, distortions can occur in textbook generalizations on the accumulated results of a large number of studies. Eagly (1978) documented that social psychological textbooks "typically express the view that women are more easily influenced than men," and that this influence is seen as "large, strong, clear, . . . well established . . . and both general and consistent" (1978, p. 86–87). However, her careful review of the studies on which this frequent conclusion is based revealed that, in fact, with the single exception of conformity studies involving group behavior, there is little if any empirical support for the claimed sex difference. Further, additional research (Eagly, Wood, & Fishbaugh, undated) has shown that sex differences in the group conformity studies appear because men conform less in public than in private, not because women conform more in public. Thus, psychologists seem either to have "forgotten" the actual data, or to have jumped too quickly to erroneous interpretations, in drawing their generalizations.

Woman as denied. The fact that women are studied far less than men can mean that, on issues of major interest to psychologists, women's reactions are simply not known. In some studies, women are excluded because the topic at issue is not seen as relevant to them. This is true of studies on creativity, for example. Helson (1976) has documented women's virtual invisibility in such studies, noting that when women do appear, it is usually in response to the question of why they are *not* creative. Perhaps the cultural expression of creativity is not at issue for women because women can perform the ultimate creative act—childbirth. Women were also excluded from Allport's (1958) discussion of victimization, and from much of the literature on aggression (McKenna & Kessler, 1974, 1977), apparently because these topics were not considered relevant for women.

Women may also be excluded from many studies because their responses are not consistent with theoretical predictions and cannot therefore be explained. Studies on achievement motivation are a classic example of this phenomenon. When McClelland and his colleagues began to study achievement motivation in the 1950s, they soon observed that women's responses were erratic and unpredictable within their theoretical framework. They therefore decided to exclude women as subjects for their studies rather than investigate *why* women did not behave as predicted. In their definitive book on achievement motivation, *Motives in Fantasy, Action and Society* (Atkinson, 1958), the discussion of women is relegated to a single footnote.

The failure to investigate the females' responses on major psychological dimensions is not unique to the study of humans. Doty (1974), in an article entitled "A cry for the liberation of the female rodent," argues that the female's role in initiating sexual relations has been regularly overlooked by researchers. The female's behaviors are generally not included in studies of rodents' initiation of sexual behavior, leading to the conclusion that males, more than females, play the dominant role in initiating sex. When female behaviors are considered, however, this conclusion is placed in doubt.

Women as demeaned. Finally, there are studies that look exclusively at women, but focus on areas that reveal problems, or conflicts, or weaknesses, while neglecting parallel potential problems in men. Several major trends in the psychological literature illustrate this point. Research on hormonal cyclicity is a prime example. Several studies (e.g., Dalton, 1964; Ivey and Bardwick, 1968; Moos, 1968) have documented emotional and behavioral instabilities associated with women's hormonal cycle. Because virtually no attention has been given to possible relationships between hormonal cyclicity and emotional responses in men, readers can only be left with the impression that women, but not men, are influenced by the state of their hormones.

Another major research area that seems to have been reserved primarily for women is the interaction of home and work roles. Role conflict, the difficulties that can arise from having both home and job responsibilities, is studied mainly in connection with women, not men. Similarly, the effect on children of whether or not the parent works is essentially reformulated as "the problem of the working mother" (cf. Hoffman, 1974). It is striking, given the large numbers of men who occupy work and family roles, that little research attention has been given to role conflict in men, or to the effect on children of different work patterns in men.

Women also receive an inordinate amount of attention in studies of the relationship between parental characteristics and children's emotional disorders. When fathers are studied in this regard, it is usually in terms of what they do not do— the effect of the "overly passive father." When women are studied, however, the consequences of what they do become the focus of inquiry. This imbalance leaves readers with the impression that mothers, more than fathers, cause emotional difficulties in children.

APPLYING AN ANDROGYNOUS PERSPECTIVE

Within a psychology of androgyny, it is desirable to have as much knowledge as possible about the full range of response potential for both men and women. Traditional patterns of research, which restrict the study of men and women, do not therefore provide sufficient information. In some areas of inquiry, such as creativity, achievement motivation, and aggression, far more is known about men than women. In other areas—role conflict, the effect of parenting behaviors on children, the relationship between hormonal cyclicity and emotional stability, to name a few—knowledge of women far exceeds knowledge of men. There has also been, on the whole, more research on masculine-valued, agentic variables than on feminine-valued, communal attributes, and more men than women have been used as subjects in psychological research.

A psychology of androgyny would suggest measures to redress these imbalances. From an androgynous perspective, we would not initially assume that any one personality characteristic—nurturance, creativity, emotional instability—is any more typical of one sex than the other. Therefore, we would need to design studies in which we could discover the expression of any one characteristic in both sexes. Because of the present imbalances, in the short run more studies would be done on women, on dimensions from which they have been left out. This presents something of a challenge to researchers, for it asks them to consider studying atypical response characteristics in each sex. In the long run, this would mean that, especially for those characteristics that are considered more typical of one sex than the other, care would be taken to include equal numbers of both sexes in all studies (McKenna & Kessler, 1977). Thus, if we use appropriate research design and interpretation, sex differences that do exist could be documented rather than implied by virtue of the questions chosen for study.

For a psychology of androgyny, masculine-agentic characteristics and feminine-communal characteristics would be equally worthy of study. An understanding of androgynous persons requires information on the expression of both masculine and feminine attributes. However, such understanding is hampered if psychologists know more about the former than the latter. Researchers would need to increase their studies of the quality of interpersonal relationships, of cooperative and collaborative endeavors, of emotionality. These communal traits, as defined by Bakan (see Chapter 1) all deal with the relationship between the individual and his or her world. It would be especially appropriate, therefore, to research these forms of expression as they occur in every-day life, so that the actual nature of these relationships can remain intact. (cf. Wallston, 1979)

Research consistent with an androgynous perspective would also look at the interaction between *psychological* and *biological* sex differences. As we have seen, the study of biological sex differences alone can easily be misused to support the assumption of male superiority. An additional focus on psychological sex differences, by contrast, would provide information on the relative effectiveness of masculinity, femininity, and androgyny—all of which can occur in both women and men. Because effectiveness is partially a function of environmental response (see Chapter 1), researchers would need to consider characteristics of the environment as well as characteristics of the individual. They would need to take into account society's different responses to male and female expression of the same behavior. They would also need to look at what effect being masculine, feminine, or androgynous has in our society.

Studies that followed these general guidelines would do more than redress existing imbalances in knowledge about women and men. They would, in their broadest sense, move from a documentation of the status quo to an exploration of the full range of human potential. By changing the assumptions brought to bear on the study of women and men, psychology could provide an incentive for people to think about their full range of capabilities rather than understanding only those forces which currently restrict their mode of expression or their behavioral possibilities. In addition, by looking more closely at environmental factors that encourage or impede individual expression, psychologists could provide information pertinent to societal change as well as to personal change.

Evaluating Research Studies

Existing studies vary widely in their compatibility with an androgynous perspective. This variation can appear in topic selection, methodology, and data interpretation. In each of these steps, there are questions you might pose to assess the fit between the study and an androgynous perspective. You might ask these questions about the selection of subject matter:

1. Does the question chosen for study focus on sex-stereotypic traits, or is there an attempt to explore unexpected traits in women and men?
2. Does the research question allow both individual and environmental factors to be taken into account, or is undue emphasis placed on one aspect at the expense of the other?

3. If the study is investigating negative consequences of behavior, is it designed to identify these consequences in the behavior of both men and women?
4. Is the study designed to provide information pertinent to social as well as individual change, or is only one of these factors taken into account?
5. Does the author make explicit the relationship between her or his study and cultural assumptions about the nature of women and men?
6. Is the author sensitive to the ways in which her or his own belief system might have influenced the question chosen for study?

Here are some questions you might ask about the methods employed:

1. If men and women are being compared on a given characteristic, is there evidence that the research contains conditions more favorable to one sex than the other?
2. Are both biological sex and psychological sex taken into account? If not, is undue weight given to biological sex when psychological sex may be equally at issue?
3. If traits such as aggression or dependency are being measured, are these terms defined to include the ways they are expressed by both women and men?
4. Are traits such as assertiveness or dependency operationalized in the same way for male and female subjects, or are different methods employed for each sex?

Questions may also be asked about the appropriateness of data interpretation:

1. In the discussion of research findings, does the study give disproportional weight to findings that favor one sex over findings that favor the other?
2. Do the authors make generalizations about men or women for which they have no empirical support, or are they aware of the extent to which the findings apply to one sex or the other?
3. If only one sex is studied, are the findings applied to that sex alone, or are assumptions about sex *differences* offered or implied?
4. In interpreting findings, are both individual and environmental factors taken into account, or is one dimension stressed at the expense of the other?

The answers to such questions should help you assess the usefulness of a given piece of research in building toward a psychology of androgyny. If studies seem inappropriate, in terms of either the questions posed for study, the method employed, or the interpretations offered, you could then begin to consider other approaches that would be more consistent with a psychology of androgyny. Moving beyond the analysis of single studies, you could also begin to identify broad areas of inquiry in which data pertinent to a psychology of androgyny are inadequate. This could stimulate thought about new directions for research. There is a tremendous amount of writing on sex roles and related characteristics which a psychology of androgyny can neither ignore nor wholly embrace. A critical examination of this literature, identifying distortions and areas in need of additional study, seems to be in order.

SUMMARY

Any approach to research may be influenced by the researcher's own values and assumptions about the topic under investigation. Her or his value base can affect the choice of theory, the design of the study, or the interpretation of results. If the researcher does not acknowledge underlying values—if the studies purport to represent the "truth" rather than one way of viewing the truth—then this value base can create unrecognized distortions. However, if the value base is made explicit, and if links between initial assumptions and subsequent findings are made clear, then we can evaluate studies within their own framework and compare results with those of studies from a different orientation.

Cultural assumptions about women and men can influence the value base that researchers bring to the psychological study of sex roles. Two assumptions have been found to exist across all cultures: (1) that which is male is clearly distinct from that which is female; and (2) things that are male are more valuable than things that are female. This androcentric bias is reflected in contemporary Western society in the valuing of masculinity over femininity, men's work over women's work, and boy babies over girl babies.

The assumption of male superiority has influenced the psychological study of sex roles in several ways. At its inception, the study of sex roles was embedded in the study of sex differences, with findings used to justify observable evidence of male superiority. Since that time, evidence has continued to be found of an assumption of male superiority and the parallel devaluation of women in the study of sex roles. Findings have indicated that men are studied more than women, that emphasis is placed on masculine more than feminine attributes, and that comparisons are made between women and men on dimensions in which men are likely to perform better than women.

An androgynous perspective suggests ways to correct reflections of assumed male superiority in the study of sex roles. These include studying as many women as men, and studying feminine as well as masculine attributes. In particular, existing gaps in knowledge can be remedied by studying each sex on dimensions from which they have been traditionally excluded. Rather than emphasizing biological sex, a psychology of androgyny would explore the interaction between biological and psychological sex. Finally, a psychology of androgyny would be sensitive to both individual and environmental influences on personality and behavior, and would include information pertinent to societal as well as individual change.

A psychology of androgyny provides guidelines for assessing the fit between existing studies on sex roles and an androgynous perspective. This critical evaluation can indicate areas of research in need of reevaluation or further investigation. It is this perspective that will guide our presentation of the psychology of sex roles in the rest of this book.

SELECTED READINGS

Berger, P. L., and Luckman, T. *The social construction of reality: A treatise in the sociology of knowledge.* Garden City, N. Y.: Anchor Books, 1967.

DeBeauvoir, S. *The second sex.* New York: Bantam Books, 1953.

Kuhn, T. S. *The structure of scientific revolutions.* Chicago: University of Chicago Press, 1970.

Mahoney, M. J. *Scientist as subject: The psychological imperative.* Cambridge, Mass.: Ballinger, 1976.

Pirsig, R. M. *Zen and the art of motorcycle maintenance.* New York: Bantam, 1976.

Watson, J. D. *The double helix.* New York: Atheneum, 1968.

Androgynous Themes in Religion and Literature

3

To read about psychologists' study of androgyny, one might think that adrogyny is a fairly new concept, an idea developed by twentieth-century, Western psychologists to describe the integration of stereotypic masculine and feminine characteristics. Such a belief, however, would be a serious error. The concept of androgyny, as a mythological or literary representation of the unity of masculinity and femininity, is one of the earliest appearing and most sustaining of human history. In fact, according to June Singer (1977), androgyny may be the oldest archetype known to humankind.

But the idea that androgyny is the brainchild of the mid-twentieth century is not entirely without foundation. Androgyny has never been as widely discussed within Western societies as it is today. This popular awareness of androgyny can largely be attributed to the rise of the feminist movement (Friedman, 1978). It is true that some feminists take issue with the term "androgyny," preferring that the female root come first, as in "gynandry." Some feminists also react against the notion of the integration of feminine and masculine traits, arguing instead that women should strive for the full development of what is within themselves. Yet, it is the feminist quest for the elimination of sex stereotypic personality traits and social roles that has been at the forefront of the growing interest in androgyny. Androgyny, although certainly not endorsed by a majority of the population, is a concept that impinges in one way or another on most people's thinking about sex roles. As such, according to Friedman, it has become a "living myth."

In this chapter, we will trace the representations of androgyny within Western and Eastern cultures as it is reflected in religious teachings and in literature. We will begin at the beginning, with images of androgyny as they appear in myths about the creation of the world. From there, we will turn to the role of androgyny as a religious symbol of fulfillment or enlightenment. Finally, we will turn to portrayals of androgyny in Western literature, from the classical Greek era to the twentieth-century novel.

The primary purpose of these explorations is to describe the historical roots out of which the present concept of psychological androgyny has developed. The study of androgyny in religious belief systems provides examples of how people, within a religious framework, have strived to integrate femininity and masculinity. Such knowledge can help one to see ways of growing toward an androgynous personality. By studying androgynous themes in literature, we will see how writers of fiction have portrayed aspects of an androgynous personality, and how these androgynous characters have been responded to by those around them. We can use this in examining the relationship between androgynous individuals and their society. Although representations of androgyny in religion and literature do not speak *directly* to the issue of androgyny within contemporary society, they do provide some background information and, more importantly, an historical context for viewing the present-day concept.

IMAGES OF ANDROGYNY IN EASTERN AND WESTERN RELIGIONS

Although androgynous images have existed for a long time, there is a wide variety in the roles that androgyny has played in shaping major belief systems. This diversity is well illustrated by comparing the prominence of androgyny in Eastern and Western religious teachings. In Eastern religions, including Buddhism, Taoism, and Hinduism, androgyny has figured prominently in myths about the creation of the world, and in teachings about the paths to enlightenment. It has been much less important in the Judeo-Christian heritage of the West. The primary Western religious belief systems emphasize not androgyny but patriarchy, symbolized for example by God the "Father" and the creation first of man and then of woman. Androgynous themes do exist, even in the Old and New Testaments, but these have been elaborated on primarily by those who have practiced esoteric, mystical, or heretical forms of worship. Thus, a search for androgyny in Western religions leads not to the major religious texts, but to the writings of peripheral groups such as the alchemists, the Gnostics, and the Jewish mystical writers of the Kabbalah.

What accounts for the fact that androgyny has been so much more important in Eastern religions? Although there may be many ways to answer this question, we believe that one major reason is the difference in the religious visions of life as centered on unities or dualities. Take away, for the moment, the content of androgyny, the idea that it represents the integration of stereotypic sex-role traits. What remains is a form of *holistic* thought, a representation of unity as opposed to duality. Holistic thought emphasizes integration, or "wholeness," whereas dualistic thought emphasizes separations or diversity. In general, it seems that androgyny thrives in religions oriented toward holism, and is minimized in those religions oriented toward dualism.

Holism Versus Dualism

All people, whether they live in the East or the West, must come to terms with the fact that the world they live in is essentially a world of dualities. In the words of Eliade, "In his immediate experience, man is made up of pairs of opposites" (1965, p. 95). There is, first of all, the basic biological duality of the sexes; male and female. Researchers have also recently become aware of another human biological duality; the two halves of the brain (Ornstein, 1973; Sperry, 1964). As studies are increasingly demonstrating, the two hemispheres of the cerebral cortex are responsible for different modes of functioning. The left hemisphere, which controls the right side of the body, deals primarily with analytical, logical thinking. It is the seat of verbal and mathematical reasoning, of logical thought based on sequence and order. The right side of the brain, which controls the left side of the body, deals primarily with integrative, holistic functions. It is the seat of visual-spatial awareness, of musical ability, of tactile sensations and bodily awareness (Ornstein, 1972).

The duality of functions of the two halves of the cortex indirectly corresponds, according to Ornstein, to the two modes of consciousness that coexist within all persons. Such dualistic consciousness is reflected in the opposites used in describing the world: right and left, good and bad, up and down, light and dark, cold and hot, figure and ground, right and wrong—to name only a few. Personality traits are also seen as being organized dualistically: here we have active and passive, rational and emotional, analytical and intuitive, dependent and independent, for example.

Cultural differences occur, however, in the *conclusions* that are drawn from one's experience within a dualistic world. Some people, according to Eliade, "come to believe that these opposites also hold for the absolute, that ultimate reality is the same as immediate reality" (1965, p. 95). This is the thinking that pervades the Judeo-Christian tradition of Western cultures. Eastern religions, however, have a vision of an absolute that transcends the dualities of everyday life. Their gods reflect both masculine and feminine principles. Their religious beliefs espouse methods of meditation or contemplation by which one can rise above the dualities of this world to reach, according to Eliade, a form of perfection that ultimately consists of unity, of totality.

Androgyny in Creation Myths

Myths of creation have existed wherever people have questioned their origins—that is to say, everywhere. These creation myths yield themes that repeat themselves endlessly throughout the world (Singer, 1977). June Singer, in her book entitled *Androgyny: Toward a New Theory of Sexuality,* has presented in detail the androgynous components of creation myths East and West. The following discussion is derived heavily from her work.

In speaking of androgynous themes in myths of creation, we will use the concept of androgyny more broadly than in other chapters of this book. Here, its use derives from Singer's formulation: it stands for conceptions of unity-totality in which the integration of sex-role components is prominent but not exclusive. The unity of the sexes is understood here more symbolically than literally; it serves as metaphor for broader notions of totality or wholeness. This usage is necessary in discussing myths of creation, because creation, by definition, predates the human form as male or female. Myths of creation, whatever their specifics, all hark back to existence before humanity. The broader concept of androgyny, then, connects the themes that evolve from the earliest stages of creation to the creation of humankind.

Singer argues that all myths of creation that hold androgyny as central describe four specific stages of creation. These stages form the framework within which the myths can be explored.

Stage I. The first stage, according to Singer, is an absolutely unknowable condition "before time was." This is the stage described in the Old Testament as "formless and void," or in Taoism as "Darker than any mystery/the Doorway whence issued all Secret Essences." It contains all the potentialities of later existence, although nothing is differentiated.

Stage II. In this stage, the undifferentiated, chaotic formlessness coalesces into a unified figure, which Singer calls the "All in All." Sometimes this is an abstract figure without human form or shape, such as the *t'ai chi* of Taoism. In other religions, for example in the Old Testament, it may be a God of creation. These unified figures symbolize the potentialities of all that is yet to be created; in some cases they are also the Being responsible for that creation.

Stage III. At this stage, the transition between the force of creation and that which is created, a form emerges that is, in principle, androgynous. This form exists in a proto-world, the world of precreation, which is the model for the world of creation yet to come. Stage III thus marks the transmutation of the spiritual into the material. This earliest being can be thought of as the Primal Androgyne, a prehuman form containing all the dimensions, including maleness and femaleness, that will become differentiated with the act of creation.

Stage IV. At this stage, the world as it is known is created. The Primal Androgyne of Stage III has fallen to earth, split in two as male and female, lost its immortality, and become human. Yet there is a lingering tension between the two halves of the original single being, a pull toward further development in which their reunification can become possible.

The most significant aspect of the flow from Stages I through IV is the notion that in the beginning was totality. Although this totality is destroyed with the actual creation of the world, there remains a pull toward a return to the original state of wholeness. The diversity of this world, the dualities we have described, emerge as characteristic of only a small moment in time. They are a feature of this world, but not of Absolute Reality. The more enduring theme is not that of a differentiation between the sexes, but rather that of the Primal Androgyne, an image of the potential wholeness toward which all beings strive.

Eastern religions. In the Hindu religion of India, Brahman is held to be the only reality in the universe. Brahman here symbolizes the chaotic mass of the first stage of creation; it is, according to Singer, an "unknowable eternal principle, beyond life and death, beyond beginning and ending" (1977, p. 166). Brahman is beyond all the differentiating characteristics of the world, yet contains the potentiality for all of them. It precedes all appearance of creation. As described in the books of the

Upanishads, Brahman is manifested by pure light—the light that is seen as shining within the interior of humans is in fact the same light that shines from Brahman, from beyond all things (Eliade, 1965). Thus, for humans who are able to contact their "inner light," there is a direct connection between them and the force that is Brahman. This connection, for humans, allows them to actualize the androgynous potential that is Brahman.

From Brahman, according to the Hindu tradition, develops Purusha, the Primal Being of Stage III from whom develops the people of earth. All of the later dualities are contained within this prototypical figure, which represents the inner self of all human beings. Purusha, as was Brahman before it, is neuter. There is no sense here of the Creator as male or female; rather, it is as an all-encompassing force from which all things will develop. Neither sex is closer to the source of creation than the other; and the creation of neither is subordinated.

Related to the Hindu tradition just described are the Tantric traditions in both Buddhism and Hinduism. These are secret, esoteric disciplines that according to Singer, have been concealed or deliberately obscured to protect the uninitiated from the dangers inherent in their power. Creation, in Hindu Tantra, begins with cosmic union represented by the supreme being called Ishvara. This is the unknowable, indescribable original force that "contains all the dualities and polarities gathered into a state of total unity" (Singer, 1977, p. 180). From this amorphous force the image of Primal Unity (Stage III) develops, and is split into opposites in the act of creation. These oppositions become incarnated in the forms of Siva (representing the masculine) and Sakti (the feminine). It is the goal of the followers of the Hindu Tantra to reunify Siva and Sakti within their own beings.

In Taoism, practiced primarily in China, the force equivalent to the Brahman of Hinduism is the "Tao which cannot be named." This Tao, according to Singer, represents the "awareness of the Ultimate Principle in which the uncreated coheres, until creation gives it form and shape and endows it with energy" (p. 188). From this Tao, which is the nameless, faceless, essentially unknowable force of Stage I, develops the T'ai chi, the circle out of which the principles of reality eventually develop. The T'ai chi consists of two poles, light or Yang, and darkness or Yin. It serves as the androgynous form of Stage II; in it all dichotomies coexist until torn asunder in the act of creation.

Although Yin and Yang begin as the principles of darkness and light, these concepts are expanded in Taoism to represent all polar opposites. Yang is symbolic of masculinity, the active, creative principle, and Yin is symbolic of femininity, the passive, receptive principle. According to Western values, Yang appears to be more desirable than Yin. However, Taoism emphasizes not the contrast between these two forces, but their complementary nature. Neither Yang nor Yin can be effective without the simultaneous presence of the other. The creative is powerless unless coupled with the receptive. The two are seen as being present in all situations. Only the particular distribution of Yang and Yin gives each situation its unique characteristics.

Thus, in Taoism, masculinity and femininity are seen as two aspects of the One. Human nature, in turn, corresponds to the T'ai chi of the heavens, so that each person, although created in a form corresponding to one pole of the masculinity-femininity dichotomy, seeks to express her or his androgynous potential as contained in the T'ai chi.

Western religion. In Western religions, it is necessary to look at not one, but two, myths of creation. But why? Certainly there is one myth that is known to all: God created man in his own image, and Eve was subsequently born from one of Adam's ribs, to be a helpmate to Adam. However, the actual rendering of the story of creation is somewhat more complex. The book of Genesis contains two versions of the story of creation, not just the one that is so widely recognized. In the less-known version, which appears in the first chapter of Genesis, there is a portrayal of creation far more in keeping with an androgynous vision:

> Then God said, "Let us make man in our image, after our likeness; and let them have dominion over the fish of the sea; . . . So God created man in his own image, in the image of God he created him; male and female he created them. And God blessed them and God said to them, "Be fruitful and multiply, and fill the earth and subdue it. . . ." (Genesis 1:26–28)

Singer emphasizes that in this portrayal of creation, God is plural, not singular: "Let *us* make man in *our* image, after *our* likeness." This use of plurals implies, according to Singer, that the God of creation being described was both masculine and feminine. Further, the original Hebrew word for God used here, *Elohim,* is a combination of the feminine singular *Eloh,* and the masculine plural, *im.* The use of the masculine singular "him" in the second sentence of the above quotation appears only in translation, and does not accurately represent the combination of masculine and feminine suggested by the original Hebrew word.

It is true that the account of creation in the second chapter, the "first Adam, then Eve" version, has figured most prominently from Biblical times to the present. Singer accounts for this emphasis in historical terms. Much of the Old Testament was codified during and immediately after the period of Jewish exile in Babylonia. The Babylonians practiced a religion much like the religions of the East, in which an androgynous vision of creation figured prominently. The Jews placed a high priority on differentiating themselves from the many other religious peoples who surrounded them and on establishing themselves as the Chosen People who believed only in one God. Thus, Judaic beliefs that suggested a more androgynous origin, a creation based on the union of male and female, had to be supressed. However, traces of this earlier belief lingered, as the version of creation in the first chapter of Genesis testifies.

To find sources that delve further into the implications of simultaneous creation of man and woman, one must go to the writings of the Jewish mystics, the Kabbalists. They explain creation in a fashion that closely parallels the Eastern tradition. In the beginning was a limitless, boundless, indescribable force, called by the rabbis *En Sof.* From this force evolved the precreation—the androgynous human prototype who was given the name of Adam Kadmon. This is the Primordial Being, the possessor of all the dualities, from whom the Adam and Eve of Eden were to evolve. Thus, although the Judeo-Christian tradition remains rooted in a single God and a patriarchal version of creation, there is an androgynous version, which remains as an "underground" aspect of the Western heritage.

A similar, androgynous version of creation can be found in the writings of the Christian Gnostics, a heretical sect that flourished in the first two centuries after Christ. The gnostics' beliefs directly challenged the primary doctrines of the newly founded Christian religion. The Gnostic version of creation contains the four stages described earlier. The first, which can be described only in metaphors, consisted of the formless "time beyond time," the "beginning of beginnings." From this amorphous force, a single prototypical being is created, referred to as the Son of Man. This Son of Man is the Androgyne, the being that contains all opposites. Human creation does not derive directly from this figure, however; a jealous God simultaneously creates a monster, and it is from this monster that the world is created. This "ghastly parable on the Genesis creation myth" (Singer, 1977, p. 123) is yet another version of creation as emanating from an androgynous union of all diversities.

Androgyny and the Attainment of Enlightenment

Most religions prescribe a path, a ritual, or a way of life that, if followed, will lead to attainment of a higher state of being, cosmic or transcendental enlightenment. As with the myths of creation, the paths to fulfillment in the Eastern religions contain explicit elements of an androgynous vision. In western religions, androgynous aspects are far more subtle, and are downplayed; yet they are present. The role of androgyny in the seeking of the highest good demonstrates once again the prominence held by androgyny in religious beliefs.

Eastern religions. One prominent theme in Eastern religions is the need for unifying the masculine and feminine principles in order to reach the highest states of enlightenment. Both masculine and feminine forces are seen as residing in dynamic opposition in each person. Intense, prolonged practice in self-control is necessary to bring these forces into harmony. The unification of the masculine and the feminine within the self is an intense experience, available only to the most devout. It brings the person into harmony with the Divine Being, in whom all dualities exist as one.

In the Hindu Tantric tradition, the path to unification is most clearly enunciated in the practice of Kundalini Yoga, as first developed by Gopi Krishna. In the Tantric tradition, there are two primary opposites; the *static principle,* which encompasses wisdom and cognition, and the *dynamic principle* which encompasses movement and energy. To the Hindu Tantrics, the static principle is masculine and the dynamic principle feminine. For the Buddhist Tantrics, however, the static is feminine and the dynamic masculine. What is significant, then, is not the determination of which qualities are masculine and which feminine, but rather the importance of unifying these two opposing forces.

Kundalini Yoga is an arduous, demanding path toward the ultimate unification of the masculine and the feminine. The practice of Hatha Yoga must first be perfected, training a person to gain full control over his or her breathing, thought processes, and sexual desires. Once this lengthy training has been achieved, the person is ready for the act of unification, which is achieved through sexual intercourse without passion, without desire, and most significantly, without orgasm. The two partners spend a period of months together in some secluded spot until all traces of desire are gone and a state of detachment is reached. When they finally join in sexual union, the couple, through the arrest of breathing and the stillness of thought, allows their sexual energies to circulate within themselves, permitting them to "transcend time as we know it and to emerge into a Cosmic Time. . . . Through the transcendence of opposites, the Divine Androgyne once again comes into being" (Singer, 1977, p. 183). The two become transformed into Gods, and unite as father-mother of the world.

A similar path to the attainment of enlightenment is described in Taoism. In the Tao tradition, the ultimate goal is the unification of the feminine Yin, or the receptive force, with the masculine Yang, the creative force. As with the Tantric Hindu tradition, the path to enlightenment for the followers of Taoism consists of a long and disciplined period of training through Yoga, for cultivating the art of stillness through control of breathing and thought processes. Those who succeed in achieving a state of deepened consciousness, finding the "inner mystery," are then ready for the experience of the Yoga of Dual Cultivation. The Yoga of Dual Cultivation consists of sexual intercourse devoid of any sensuality or sexual desire. The purpose of this practice was to "distill within the adept's body a golden liquid from which the elixir leading to longevity, immortality, and mystical union with the Tao could be formed" (Singer, 1977, p. 197). In order to distill this golden elixir, the yogi draws into his body the yin forces of his partner (or the yang forces if the yogi is a woman and the partner a man). Through the intermingling of the masculine and the feminine, the highest states of consciousness can be achieved.

Western religions. In the prevailing Western Judeo-Christian tradition, androgyny does not symbolize the path to ultimate fulfillment. Individual faith or good works instead lead to greater glory, or salvation. However, just as in the myths of creation, androgyny is prominent in mystical and heretical visions of enlightenment. These alternative approaches are represented by the alchemists, the Kabbalists, and the Gnostics.

For Christian Gnostics, Christ was an androgynous figure. In one gnostic document, Christ is even represented as producing a woman from his side. This woman was seen as representing the feminine aspect of Christ. By giving this aspect human form, both sides, the masculine and the feminine, could become conscious of one another and make more likely the possibility of reconciliation.

Christ is also portrayed by the Gnostics as holding forth androgyny as the path to the Kingdom of Heaven. In the *Gospel According to Thomas,* this is made explicit:

> Jesus saw children who were being suckled. He said to his disciples: These children who are being suckled are like those who enter the Kingdom.
> They said to him: Shall we then, being children, enter the Kingdom? Jesus said to them: When you make the two one, and when you make the inner

as the outer and above as the below, and when you make the male and the female into a single one, so that the male will not be male and the female [not] be female . . . then shall you enter the [Kingdom]. (Singer, 1977, p. 126)

The alchemists, who were in some ways heirs to the Gnostic tradition, also worked within a material and spiritual framework that was androgynous. Although they are best known for their attempts to turn base matter into gold, they were simultaneously, although secretly, working to free spirit from matter and achieve perfection of the spirit, or Philosopher's Gold. The work of the alchemists consisted of reducing all matter to its essential elements and then recombining these elements to form new substances—most prominently, gold. This combination of analytic and synthetic techniques held for the spirit within matter, as well as for matter itself.

The work of the alchemists was androgynous in two respects. First, the integration of essential elements consisted in large part of combining opposites, including sun-moon, fire-water, living-dead, and certainly masculine-feminine. According to Metzner, "The first fusion of male and female energies, known as the *conjunction,* is the central process of alchemy" (Singer, 1977, p. 135).

Second, alchemists always worked in pairs, consisting of a woman and a man. This pairing, known as the "alchymical welding" represented the unification of the masculine and the feminine principles. Additionally, when men and women worked together, each helped the other find both parts of her or his nature, the masculine and the feminine. Thus, the unification of opposites in general, and of the masculine and the feminine in particular, was central in the alchemical search for the formation of the ultimate substance.

In the Kabbalistic doctrines of the Jewish Gnostics, again androgyny is central. This is illustrated, for example, in their portrayals of the Tree of Life, a symbol of earthly existence. In one such portrayal, emphasis is placed on the unity of wisdom (the masculine principle) and understanding or intelligence (the feminine principle). These two are called, according to Singer, "two friends who never part." Singer continues, "Their union produces the life energy that sustains the universe" (1977, p. 158). The rapid, intuitive thought of wisdom is assimilated into the more receptive, meditative understanding in order that true knowledge can be brought forth. According to Singer, these "two friends that never part" represent the androgynous core of all human beings.

Another Look

We have seen that androgyny, as symbolic of the unity of opposites, is a recurring theme in Eastern and Western religious traditions. Whether it appears in the central myths of creation and enlightenment as in the Eastern traditions, or only in esoteric, heretical religious practices, as in Western traditions, depends on the religious orientation to holistic or dualistic thought. In the Eastern religions, the dualities of this world are only a temporary transgression from the totality of Absolute Reality. Enlightenment, or the search to regain the holistic state embodied in Absolute Reality, entails methods for resolving the dualities of this world within the self. Toward this end, the entwining, within the individual, of masculine and feminine forces becomes central. For the dominant forms of Western religions, God is a masculine rather than an androgynous image, so that the path to religious fulfillment does not encompass the pursuit of wholeness. However, in the mystical, heretical traditions of Gnosticism, alchemy, and Kabbalism, which retain the androgynous image of God, androgynous forms of seeking the "highest good" become central.

The images of androgyny as put forth by these religious traditions have only an indirect relationship to psychological androgyny as described in Chapter 1. In the religious concepts, androgyny is more a state of being than a mode of interacting with the real world. It is a central aspect in the path to personal fulfillment (ultimately, to being at one with the Creator), not to material or interpersonal success within this world. In religious representations of androgyny, "effectiveness" would have to do with transcendent goals, and not with worldly accomplishments. "Situational appropriateness" would be seen in terms of the pursuit of enlightenment, not in terms of response to environmental demands. Therefore, although the religious traditions speak clearly to the importance of androgyny as a mythic representation, they say little to the utility of behaving androgynously in this world. In literature we again have broad themes and symbolic representations of human questions and answers. However, there we come closer to daily life and the worldly practice of androgyny.

ANDROGYNY IN LITERATURE

Literary works portray the undercurrents in society, the tensions that are experienced but not made manifest in daily life. The best literature, that which survives through the generations, also portrays universal themes—such as the "human condition"—which transcend any one historical moment.

Androgyny, according to Carolyn Heilbrun, is one such universal theme. In her insightful book, *Toward a Recognition of Androgyny* (1973), Heilbrun seeks to document androgynous themes in literature that have long been overlooked by the majority of literary critics. She identifies four periods in which androgynous themes were salient: the classical Greek era; the medieval era; Elizabethan England, specifically the writings of Shakespeare; and the modern era, beginning with the development of the novel as a literary form. Drawing heavily on Heilbrun's analysis, we will trace this portrayal of androgyny in literature, to document, as before, its persistence as an historical tradition.

Androgynous people, as portrayed in literature, are often seen as being at odds with their society, as representing deviant or unacceptable modes of being. Androgynous ways of being "seek to liberate the individual from the confines of the appropriate" (Heilbrun, 1973, p. x). But in moving outside of the appropriate one can easily come into conflict with one's culture. In fact, according to Friedman, "literature has often expressed the longing for androgyny through its portrayal of heroes whose identities have been in conflict with the norms and institutions of decidedly non-androgynous worlds" (1978, p. 9). Thus, literary descriptions of the androgynous person in "decidedly non-androgynous worlds" may reveal something of the tensions that exist in the real world between an androgynous person's own goals and the options that are available.

The Classical Greek Era

The classical Greek era represents, as well as any period, the juxtaposition between androgynous themes in literature and a "decidedly non-androgynous world." During this time, when Athens was at its prime, women of the city were subjected to severe restraints, being scarcely able to appear alone on the streets (Lucas, in Heilbrun, 1973, p. 6). They had become, according to Heilbrun, "the submerged part of the human race" (1973, p. 6). And yet, the literature of this period reveals a remarkable number of strong, powerful, female heroes: Clytemnestra, Cassandra, Antigone, Phaedra, Medea. These women showed courage and fortitude. They acted forcefully on their world, not indirectly through "feminine wiles," but quite directly, often with the use of brute force. They did not hesitate to respond in the ways that they saw fit.

According to several writers, (e.g., Bachofen, 1861, Davis, 1971) the image of the powerful woman as represented in these plays hearkens back to an earlier Greek era in which women held major positions of power and influence. This was a time in which, according to these writers, Greece valued the feminine principal. Female gods were also much more prominent than during the classical era; even the creation of the world during that time was attributed to a goddess. After this period ended, with the invasion of the Dorians from the north, apparently the image of women as powerful lingered on. Although it did not affect the actual structure of society or the way women were treated, this image had a great influence on the portrayal of women in literature.

According to Heilbrun, androgynous themes are represented in classical Greek literature in two primary ways. First, there are the many women who play central, powerful roles. As pivotal figures in many of the dramas, they represent humankind, not *"women."* Through their roles, they portray the fundamental, profound conflicts of human emotion: the intermingling of love and revenge, loyalty and betrayal. As Heilbrun puts it, "[They] fulfill their destiny by being altogether human rather than merely ladylike" (1973, p. 10). This is a far cry from the use of women in current psychological studies. As we saw in Chapter 2, modern researchers make generalizations to "people" regularly from men but seldom from women.

Second, throughout classical Greek plays, there is what Heilbrun calls the "celebration of the 'feminine impulse' " within strong and powerful women. The female characters reflect sensitivity and affection at the same time that they display decisiveness and direct action. They demonstrate that power and strength need not be dissociated from compassion and caring. In this sense, the female characters of Greek drama symbolize one form of the integration of feminine and masculine characteristics.

Although the women of Greek drama represent some aspects of our model of androgyny, however, they also diverge from the model in significant ways. The primary distinction pertains to our view of androgyny as encompassing only socially desirable characteristics. This, it will be remembered, specifically excludes extremes of femininity and masculinity such as incapacitating helplessness or brute aggression.

The women of Greek literature whom Heilbrun considers androgynous frequently resorted to acts of extreme destructiveness of self or others, including murder and suicide. Take, for example, Antigone, who attempts to bury her dead brother although she knows that by doing so she will be condemned to death. She is caught and sentenced, but does not regret her action. Rather, she courageously defends what she has done, placing her commitment to the law of God above the law of the state, even at the expense of her own life. In response to King Creon, whose decree has determined her sentence, she states:

> Can anyone
> Living as I live with evil all around me
> Think death less than a friend? This death of mine
> Is of no importance; but if I had left my brother
> Lying in death unburied, I should have suffered
> Now, I do not. (Sophocles, in Fitts, 1947, p. 473)

For Antigone, the pursuit of that which she firmly believed in was more important than life itself.

Can this difference between Heilbrun's and our own use of androgyny be reconciled? One approach toward this end would be to focus on the *motivations* of these characters, and not on their ultimate behavior. We take this focus with some caution, realizing that in real life it would not suffice to look only at motivations in identifying androgynous beings. With literature, however, this liberty can perhaps be taken more easily, because the actions of characters are symbolic and not meant to correspond exactly to real life.

Looking, then, at the motivations that stimulated some of the destructive behavior, we can see that for these characters, death is the servant of a broader cause, a moral purpose that from their point of view could not be ignored. They are not portrayed simply as murderous beings, whose killing reflects wanton destructiveness or personal gain. Rather, using carefully reasoned moral principles, they act deliberately. They do what they feel they have to do and are prepared to bear the consequences, even death. If one considers such reactions "socially desirable," then these characters are indeed androgynous.

There are also two specific links that we *can* make between Heilbrun's and our model of androgyny. First, both emphasize the *integration* of feminine and masculine characteristics. Although the specific characteristics vary from one model to the other, both models suggest the possibility, for example, of assertiveness tempered by compassion, or anger tempered by affection. Second, both models point to the importance of consciously choosing among recognized options and of controlling one's own fate as central dimensions of the androgynous personality. The female characters of the Greek dramas are not willing to be relegated to second-class status. Nor do they consider that their possibilities for action lie only with those behaviors considered appropriate for a woman. The actual behaviors of these women fall beyond those which we consider androgynous. Yet their integration of strength and compassion and their ability to make conscious choices about their future are useful literary examples of androgyny.

Images of androgyny also appear in the philosophic writings of Plato, specifically in *The Symposium*. In this treatise, Plato portrays the creation of human beings in a way that reminds us of the androgynous myths in the first half of this chapter. Originally, according to Plato, there were not two sexes, but three; man, woman, and a figure representing a union of the other two. As described by Plato:

> First of all, there were three kinds of men, not two as now . . . but also a third containing both . . . /The androgenes/ were shaped like complete spheres. Their backs and sides made a circle. They had four hands, with the same number of legs and two faces—completely the same—on top of a circular neck. These two faces were set on opposite sides of one head, with four ears. And there were two sets of sexual parts, and whatever else goes along with these arrangements. (Plato, in Bretlinger, 1970, p. 61)

These figures were powerful—so powerful that they threatened the gods. In revenge, the gods cut them in half. From this point on, each half has continually sought the other, "longing to grow into one." According to Plato, this search for the other half of oneself explains the intense love, friendship, and intimacy that can exist within a couple, as each seeks to find the missing elements of him- or herself in another. Metaphorically, Plato is representing the incompleteness that results when qualities associated with each sex are separated. The greatest strength, the fullest capacities, exist only when masculine and feminine qualities can be reunited.

The Medieval Era

Androgyny as exemplified in the medieval romances represents what Heilbrun calls "the re-entry of the 'feminine principle' as a civilizing force" (1973, p. 21). In the medieval romances androgyny was not symbolized by a search for wholeness, leading to the joining of masculinity and femininity within a *single person*. Rather, it was reflected by the necessary coexistence of masculinity (typically embodied in men) and femininity (typically embodied in women). Thus, the persons portrayed in medieval literature were not themselves androgynous. However, the message conveyed in many of the writings was that both masculinity and femininity were necessary for a *civilization* to reach the state of wholeness, which it must in order to thrive.

The extent to which this message is androgynous, even if the individuals portrayed were not, can be best illustrated by contrasting the androgynous writings, the romances, with the nonandrogynous writings, the epic poems of the same era. In the epics, masculinity flourished. As described by Heilbrun:

> In the epics, . . . women do not figure at all. The whole world of the epic revolves around the nation, the hero, and occasionally his friends. These men exist for service and glory; women, the feminine principle, even the civilizing habit of self-abnegation, have no place in the epic. (1973, p. 21)

The epics, then, portrayed the significant things of this world as uniquely masculine. In the romances, however, women enter the picture, and with them come personal sensitivity, compassion, affection, and romantic love. From man and the state, the focus shifts to the integration of personal love and societal needs. Although this integration did not typically occur easily, and was in fact frequently marked by conflict, both sides of the human personality were acknowledged and validated.

The well-known tale of Tristan and Isolde contains, according to Heilbrun, a major example of this androgynous theme. For the two lovers, their need for one another was the paramount force that determined their future. What is stressed in this tale is that neither feels complete without the other. Having drunk a love potion, they are "joined together in a union necessary to their very survival; apart, neither can be released from a great sense of need" (Heilbrun, 1973, p. 24). Heilbrun sees their situation as a "metaphor for the androgynous condition, the need of a merging of the masculine and feminine with equal passion" (p. 25).

The validation of the feminine principle in medieval literature was paralleled by the rise in the importance of women as religious symbols, specifically the Virgin Mary. Although formal church doctrine discouraged, or even forbade the worship of Mary, to the people of this epoch Mary became a figure of highest significance. By worshipping her, the people also directly challenged the patriarchal nature of the Church hierarchy and of its doctrines. In their religion as well as in their literature then, although masculinity prevailed and dominated both church and state, the people of the medieval era showed some recognition of the importance of qualities associated with femininity.

The Writings of Shakespeare

Heilbrun argues that Shakespeare was "as devoted to the androgynous ideal as anyone who has ever written" (1973, p. 29). This commitment to androgyny comes through in many facets of Shakespeare's writings, including the ease with which male and female roles can be reversed and the dangers that can accrue to men if they ignore the feminine side of themselves and pursue what Bakan (1966) would call "unmitigated agency." To Shakespeare, true humanity can be attained only by the equal balance of the masculine and the feminine.

Shakespeare's portrayal of the fluidity between male and female roles is expressed most clearly when men or women successfully disguise themselves as members of the other sex. It is as though, according to Shakespeare, once one assumes the facade of the other sex, one can then fully and convincingly behave as though one were a member of that sex. What differentiates the sexes, then, is appearance rather than more fundamental and enduring personality characteristics.

Take, for example, Portia, in *The Merchant of Venice*. Disguised as a male lawyer, she is fully able to be authoritative and decisive, and ultimately to control the events that are to decide her fate. In helping the suitor whom she loves choose the casket that will win her hand, Portia behaves in a way that never suggests, even for a moment, that her feminine attributes will unwittingly give her away or spoil her effectiveness. She can not only be fully a man, but indeed can be more in control, more influential than any of the "real" men with whom she is dealing. Portia seems to exemplify, *par excellence,* the androgynous quality of situational appropriateness. When masculine attributes are called for, she can demonstrate them, fully and effectively. When more feminine characteristics are required, these too come into play. Her disguise as a man is primarily to make her masculine role convincing to others (and to hide her true identity). Shakespeare's underlying message is not that one must be a man to be masculine, but rather that one person, Portia, is fully capable of being masculine or feminine, as warranted by situational needs.

The ease with which men and women can exchange roles is perhaps most poignantly demonstrated in *Twelfth Night.* In this play, male and female twins are so alike that the female Viola, in disguise as her twin brother Cesario, is so indistinguishable from her brother that "An apple, cleft in two, is not more twin than these two creatures" (Shakespeare, in Harrison, 1948, p. 877). What is telling about the symbolism in this play is that, as a man, Viola/Cesario is not just masculine within a specific situation, as was Portia, but is so successfully and fully masculine that another woman, Olivia, has fallen in love with her. When the brother appears and Viola's true identity is revealed, Olivia is easily able to transfer her affection from the sister to the brother.

Shakespeare's suggestion that male and female twins are so much alike that they are interchangeable even by one who loves them seems to imply that each must be androgynous; the masculine and the feminine must have been truly integrated. If the man were overly masculine or the woman overly feminine, such interchange would not have been possible. That one can substitute so fully for the other suggests that both must have transcended the sterotypes of masculinity and femininity. Whereas Portia represents the flexibility between femininity and masculinity inherent in the first, or dualistic stage of androgyny, the twins of *Twelfth Night* seem to represent the second, or hybrid stage, in which the masculine and the feminine have been blended.

The androgynous component of Shakespeare's writings is also reflected in the role of women, or more specifically of what Heilbrun calls the "feminine impulse" in preventing disaster caused by uncontrolled aggression. Heilbrun points out several ways in which this theme is portrayed. There are, for example, men such as Julius Caesar who are plunged into disaster because they fail to listen to the advice of women, or to the parts of their nature which the women represent. There are also men, Hamlet primary among them, who must destroy a woman, the representation of their feminine self, before they can proceed with the murder of others. Murder and destruction, then, result from denial of the feminine impulse. By contrast, it is the women who, according to Heilbrun, "possess the redeeming powers. It is they who make possible the brave new world" (1973, p. 33). Shakespeare, then, is recognizing the necessity for the masculine and the feminine to be integrated in order to avoid the pitfalls of uncontrolled lust and aggression. This is as full a statement of not only the *possibility,* but also the *necessity* of androgyny, as any we can imagine.

Androgynous Themes in the Novel

The androgynous works of fiction of the nineteenth and early twentieth centuries portrayed people whose identities were in conflict with the nonandrogynous norms of their society. In the mid-nineteenth century, with the rise of industrialization, women's roles suffered a marked constriction. Before, women had played a prominent economic role through the production of goods at home. With industrialization, however, came the rise of factories, and the separation of production from the family and the home. The men went to the factories while the women stayed home; and women's role as wife, mother, and homemaker became idealized. More than ever before, women's fulfillment was equated with being a successful mother and a dutiful wife.

In contrast to this norm arose novels that spoke out against systems which required that women marry. Heilbrun stresses the large number of women in these novels who were androgynous—androgynous because they represented people who refused to yield aspects of themselves to fit into a role that society had prescribed for them. The novels stressed dedication to one's inner beliefs rather than conformity, especially conformity based on sex. Although life for these characters was certainly not portrayed as easy or without conflict, they were able to maintain their own integrity throughout.

Heilbrun points to Hawthorne's *Scarlet Letter* as the most androgynous work of American fiction. The central character of this book, Hester Prynne, chooses to act on her love of Mr. Dimmesdale rather than the sexual code of her Puritanical culture. Becoming pregnant out of wedlock, she is ostracized by her community and forced to wear a scarlet "A" around her neck. Hester, although she suffers because of her fate, does not take on the demeanor of a shamed and alienated woman. Rather, with a "strong, calm, steadfastly enduring spirit" (Hawthorne, 1971 edition, p. 232) she rebuilds a life for herself and her daughter in a cottage in the woods. In her later years, after voluntarily returning to her community, she even becomes a figure of some respect. The scarlet letter, which she continues to wear by choice, "ceased to be a stigma . . . and became something to be sorrowed over, and looked upon with awe, yet with reverence, too" (pp. 310–11). Women sought out her counsel, asking her why they were so wretched and what they could do about it.

Hester can be considered androgynous in terms of her dedication to her own convictions, convictions that enabled her to have great love for Dimmesdale and her daughter while maintaining strength and decisiveness. In this way, Hester represents a character who can hold fast to her personal integrity, and thus remain in control of her life. That she could do so even when it meant violating the strictest codes of her community highlights her androgynous character all the more.

Many more novels portraying androgynous characters were written in England than in America during the nineteenth century. It is probably no accident that most of them were written by women who in their own lives violated social expectations that any career strivings be subsumed by the roles of wife and mother. These women included Jane Austen, George Eliot, Emily Brontë, and to a lesser extent, Charlotte Brontë. Each of them, in her own way, portrayed the price paid by society for the polarizing of the sexes. And each created women who were able to transcend social stereotypes and seek both the masculine and the feminine within themselves. Similarly, the men to whom their characters were married became able to recognize their own wholeness, to acknowledge the feminine as well as the masculine within themselves.

One portrayal of this androgynous vision in fiction can be found in Emily Brontë's *Wuthering Heights*. As described by Heilbrun, the love between Catherine and Heathcliff is symbolic of an androgynous ideal; however this androgynous love is more potential than actual because at the end it is abandoned.

The love between Heathcliff and Catherine can be considered androgynous because for both of them it symbolizes wholeness. Rather than joining polarized and unequal beings, their relationship allows each to see a reflection of the self in the other. Each makes the other more complete, more fully human. Catherine puts it this way: "I love him . . . not because he's handsome, Nelly, but because he's more myself than I am. Whatever our souls are made of, his and mine are the same" (Heilbrun, 1973, p. 80). Heathcliff, speaking to the dying Catherine, reflects much the same sentiment: "How would *you* like to live with your soul in the grave?" (p. 81).

Although each sought wholeness or full humanity with the other, with Catherine dead that wholeness for Heathcliff became impossible. No longer able to keep in touch with the feminine side of himself, he becomes a caricature of the "macho" male; violent, brutal, and excessively seeking after money and power. He can only despise his son, who embodies feminine characteristics. Androgyny, for Brontë, as for some of the medieval writers we have discussed, lay more in relationships than within individual persons. But although two persons are needed for the androgynous image to be fulfilled, there is no question that each with his or her androgynous counterpart is superior to each alone and locked into stereotypic roles.

The twenty years on either side of the turn of the century marked, according to Heilbrun, a change in the characterization of women in fiction. First, the new women characters represent what she calls "Woman as Hero." Second, these heroic women all appear in fiction written by men.

The hallmark of the new women heroes is their hold on autonomy throughout life. They represent, in Heilbrun's words, "the need of every human being to be himself [or herself] freely and strongly" (1973, p. 92). Their lives are self-determined, rather than being shaped by the destinies of others, as is so often the lot for women. Heilbrun continues,

> Woman, serving as metaphor for modern man striving to express himself, to *be* himself within a mechanical society, discovers her greatest wish is to *live,* a wish for which she will turn aside anything and everything, even that which we have decided is innate in women; the love of children and the passionate desire for a man. (p. 94)

These women are heroic because, in acting to fulfill their destiny, they are inevitably thwarted by elements beyond their control. In pursuit of their own needs they suffer, and in suffering they embody the tragic element that characterizes the hero of fiction. What is so striking is that they are women, not men. The reason for using women as heroes was perhaps best identified by Ibsen, who sought to portray in his heroes the conflict between emotions and authority. Because men typically represent authority it was only in women that this conflict could be articulated. Thus, to portray a person in conflict with societal authority it was necessary that the person be a woman.

Ibsen's Nora in *The Doll's House* exemplifies the woman as hero as just described. At the beginning of the play, Nora presents herself to her husband as the dutiful wife; spending no more money than he will permit her, hiding the sweets he has forbidden her so that he will not see her eat them, buying gifts for the family but asking nothing for herself. Although she had borrowed money when he was ill, something he would have strictly forbidden, she keeps this an absolute secret from him and seems to behave in complete compliance with his wishes.

The dramatic turning point occurs, however, when Nora discovers that her husband would abandon his commitment to her the moment his own reputation was at stake. Suddenly she realizes that their love was a facade, and confronts her husband: "You have never loved me. You only thought it amusing to be in love with me. . . . I lived by performing tricks for you, Tovald. . . . I have been your doll-wife, just as at home I used to be Papa's doll-child" (Ibsen, 1931 edition, p. 35). Faced with this realization, she makes a clear decision: "I must try to educate myself. You are not the man to help me in that. I must set about it alone. And that is why I am leaving you. . . . I must stand quite alone if I am ever to know myself and my surroundings" (p. 36).

Again, it is Nora's *motivations,* rather than her solution, that can be explored for their representation of androgynous themes. Nora faces squarely the dichotomy between her personal needs and her family role, and chooses to act on the basis of her recognition. Action and feeling are intertwined; she neither immobilizes herself in self-pity (in an extreme version of the feminine stereotype), nor acts impulsively with disregard for her feelings (in an extreme version of the masculine stereotype). Thus she integrates the feminine and the masculine, and although her resulting decision to leave her husband and her children may be considered extreme, her sense of self and her control over her own fate remain consistent with our model of androgyny.

The Bloomsbury Group

The Bloomsbury group, which existed in England during the 1920s and 1930s, consisted of a number of extraordinarily talented and vigorous writers, both women and men. At the center of the group were two sisters, Virginia and Vanessa Stephan, later Virginia Woolf and Vanessa Bell. Around them gathered some of the leading literary figures of their day; including their husbands Leonard Woolf and Clive Bell, Lytton Strachey, Roger Fry, and E. M. Forster. This group was remarkable in two related ways, according to Heilbrun: "First, it produced more works of importance than did any similar group of friends, and second, it was androgynous" (1973, p. 118). The androgynous nature of their lives and their works will be the focus here.

The members of the Bloomsbury group explicitly rejected the prevailing sex-typed norms. Instead, their lives centered on the notion that reason and emotion should be equal and integrated. Brilliance, sexuality, and deeply felt emotions were welcomed and validated in all members of the group, male and female. Sexual passion, for example, was considered a joyful emotion to be experienced freely, tainted neither by jealousy of other relationships nor by the domination of one partner over the other. They engaged in both homosexual and heterosexual relationships, but the focus was not as much on the sex of the partner as it was on the freedom to be sexual in nonoppressive ways.

This choice of a life style that defied sex-role stereotypes was a conscious one. As Roger Fry put it, "We can by a deliberate effort change our character. We can fix our minds on those defects which from long-inherited custom have become not only traditional but instinctive, and by so fixing our minds may ultimately correct them altogether" (Heilbrun, p. 123). Thus, they refused to behave in certain ways just because one was "supposed" to do so, and determined for themselves what was valid and what was not. The guiding principles of this evaluation were a respect for both reason and passion, and an abhorrence of violence. In the terms of psychological androgyny, they embraced the valued aspects of the feminine and masculine stereotypes while rejecting their extreme, destructive, forms of expression.

The members of the Bloomsbury group were concerned with androgyny as a way of life and as a quality of mind. In fact the importance of an androgynous mind for the emergence of creativity figured prominently in their thinking. Virginia Woolf, for example, asked rhetorically whether "there are two sexes in the mind corresponding to the two sexes in the body, and whether they also require to be united in order to get complete happiness and satisfaction" (1929, p. 102). She recalled, in this connection, Coleridge's statement, "The great mind is androgynous," and inferred from the statement that "it is when this fusion takes place that the mind is fully fertilized and uses all its faculties. Perhaps a mind that is purely masculine cannot create any more than a mind that is purely feminine" (p. 102). She continued,

> It is fatal for anyone who writes to think of their sex. It is fatal to be a man or woman pure and simple; one must be woman-manly or man-womanly. . . . Some collaboration has to take place in the mind between the woman and the man before the act of creation can be accomplished. Some marriage of opposites has to be consummated. (p. 108)

This "marriage of opposites" is revealed in Virginia Woolf's novels. In *To The Lighthouse,* for example, which Heilbrun calls Woolf's best novel of androgyny, the damaging quality of rigid sex stereotyping within a marriage is consistently portrayed. The central character in the novel, Mrs. Ramsey, who is a beautiful mother-goddess with eight children, smothers her favorite children with her love. She lives through them and for them, and although she longs to be more than the source of support for others, does not find such avenues available. She embodies all the loving in the family; while she is alive there is no room for her husband to share in this expression. Nor is he able to work to his fullest capacity. However, with her death, Woolf uses Mr. Ramsey to portray an androgynous being; a person who can love and affirm his children without dominating them, who can relate compassionately with another woman without demanding that the woman sacrifice herself for him. In contrast to some of the other novels discussed earlier, in this novel the union between two people signifies not androgynous wholeness, but a forced and arbitrary dichotomy between the sexes. Androgyny rather, is experienced within the individual, once he feels free to be the bearer of both the strength and the compassion.

Woolf's novel *Orlando* also contains a portrait of androgyny, expressed as the ability of one person, Orlando, to appear as male or female, as s/he traverses space and time. In using one person to portray the male and female roles *Orlando* is reminiscent of Shakespeare's *Twelfth Night.* In fact, the link between Woolf and Shakespeare is not accidental. As Heilbrun points out, Woolf's Orlando has the same name as one of the leading characters in Shakespeare's *As You Like It,* and in fact seems to represent aspects of both Orlando, a man, and Rosalind, a woman, in that play. Woolf's Orlando is brave, noble, and self-confident, like Shakespeare's Orlando; s/he is also joyful and loving like Rosalind. Woolf wrote in *Orlando,* although she could have as easily been describing Shakespeare's *Twelfth Night,* "A vacillation from one sex to the other takes place, and often it is only the clothes that keep the male or female likeness" (Heilbrun, 1973, p. 165). For Woolf, as for the other members of the Bloomsbury group, it is only the clothes that "make the man." Personality, life style, the sex of one's lover all transcend one's sex. Personal integrity, the conscious choice of options, and a nourishing of the masculine and the feminine within the self constitute a full, successful, androgynous life.

Despite the richness of their lives, life was not always easy for the members of the Bloomsbury group, especially when they came into conflict with the broader society. Strachey, for example, with his abhorrence of violence, refused to join the army during World War I. For this he was tried in court, and rather brutally ridiculed. Virginia Woolf, responding to myriad internal and external pressures, ultimately committed suicide. Whether or not her suicide was a direct expression of the pain that can result from living in a fashion that is demeaned by one's society, her death can be seen, at least in part, as a painful reflection of the tension that can arise between androgyny and the norms of society.

Another Look

Androgyny is a theme that can be found in literature from the writings of the classic Greek era to the novels of the twentieth century. In this literature there seem to be two primary forms for the concept of androgyny. The first is the search for wholeness—the integration of the masculine and the feminine. Ultimately, this wholeness is sought within the self, although it is frequently represented as the search by one person for his or her other half through an intimate relationship with another. This theme is typified in Plato's *Symposium,* and is also represented in the medieval tale of Tristan and Isolde and in such nineteenth-century novels as *Wuthering Heights.* In all of these works, personal fulfillment is incompatible with a dichotomization between the sexes. The coexistence of the masculine and the feminine is seen as necessary, and the pursuit of this integration forms the main theme for many of these works.

The second form is the woman as tragic hero, who places personal integrity and individual choice above societal sex-role expectations. These women symbolize the struggle of humankind in general. Capable of profound feelings, they often respond to their emotions in extreme ways. They are androgynous in part because they encompass both feminine compassion and masculine decisiveness, in part because they insist on maintaining their personal integrity despite social pressures to do otherwise. Thus, they are in control of their lives, even if this control leads them to painful resolutions.

Throughout this brief survey, we have attempted to illustrate the ways in which literary figures fit our model of androgyny; flexibility, situational appropriateness, effectiveness, and the integration of masculine and feminine stereotypes. At times this "fit" works well, whereas at other times it is admittedly a bit strained. This is due in large part to the requirements of literature, which sometimes seeks extreme portrayals to evoke reader's compassion. Some of the literary characters, then, might not seem androgynous if they were flesh-and-blood people, because their resolutions go beyond the expression of socially desirable traits. However, their motivations and sense of self effectively reflect androgynous themes within literature.

CONCLUSION

This survey of androgynous themes in religion and in literature provides information pertinent to an understanding of androgyny's place in contemporary society.

It is clear that androgyny, representing the integration of feminine and masculine traits, is a recurrent theme in both literature and religion. Both enlightenment, in the religious traditions, and a sense of personal power and control over one's fate in the literary traditions, are associated with people who seek to transcend society's sex-role stereotypes.

Neither the religious nor the literary portrayals of androgyny, however, speak to the effective, socially adaptive use of androgynous characteristics within everyday life. In fact, within both of these disciplines, there seems to be a tension between *achieving* an androgynous state of being and *behaving* in an androgynous fashion. Within the religious teachings of the East, androgyny is achieved in isolation from society. Those seeking enlightenment through intermingling feminine and masculine impulses need to withdraw from society, to seclude themselves in order to seek personal fulfillment. In the West, those for whom androgyny played a central element in their beliefs were isolated from the practices of the prevailing Judeo-Christian tradition. In neither the East nor the West were the androgynous religious concepts translated into an androgynous way of life.

Within literature, the tension that frequently emerged was between androgynous *motivations* and *solutions* that were at times not androgynous. Androgynous characters held to their own internal convictions, and were capable of acting on the basis of these convictions. Yet the choices open to them often pointed to painful resolutions, including suicide, the abandonment of their families, or isolation from society. They could not both act in an androgynous manner and remain in harmony with their culture. Literary representations of androgyny portray in graphic form the conflicts with society that the androgynous person may face.

This survey of androgynous themes in religion and literature, then, seems to give a decidedly pessimistic cast to the prospects for effective use of androgynous characteristics in daily life. However, the extreme form in which the difficulties of the androgynous characters is portrayed must be seen as a function of their being fictional, and not real people. In a far more modified form, though, androgynous themes in religion and literature serve as a reminder of the tension between an androgynous state and the confines of a nonandrogynous world. They support the implications in Chapters 1 and 2 that the fully effective expression of androgyny requires societal as well as personal change.

SELECTED READINGS

Bachofen, J. J. *Myth, religion, and mother right.* (1861; R. Manhum, translator). Princeton: Princeton University Press, 1967.

Eliade, M. *Mephistophenes and the androgyne: Studies in religious myth and symbol.* New York: Sheed and Ward, 1965.

Heilbrun, C. G. *Toward a recognition of androgyny.* New York: Harper Colophon, 1973.

Ornstein, R. *The psychology of consciousness.* San Francisco: W. H. Freeman, 1962.

Singer, J. *Androgyny: Toward a new theory of sexuality.* Garden City, N.Y.: Anchor Books, 1977.

Woolf, V. *A room of one's own.* New York: Harcourt, Brace and World, 1957.

BIOLOGY AND SEXUALITY

PART

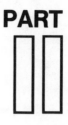

Biology and Behavior

The study of androgyny is the search for people's potential for integrating feminine and masculine characteristics to render them more flexible, more adaptable, and more effective in dealing with their world. Certainly, this potential is influenced by environmental conditions. As suggested in Chapter 2, societal beliefs about appropriate traits for women and men can influence development in a sex-typed or an androgynous direction. But the potential for androgyny may also be influenced by human biology. People are not just amorphous beings shaped by their environment. They also have bodies with distinct physical characteristics, a brain and nervous system, and hormones. These bodily features may affect a person's predisposition for certain general ways of reacting. For a psychology of androgyny, then, it is necessary to look at how response flexibility is conditioned by both environment and biology.

Some biological components are shared by all humans. Others vary as a function of a person's sex. In particular, the distribution of sex hormones, chemical substances manufactured by certain endocrine glands, differs for males and females. Sex hormones have been found to play a major role in the prenatal development of the physical characteristics that distinguish males from females. In recent years, a vast amount of attention has also been given to the potential role of the sex hormones in influencing psychological differences between the sexes (Kessler & McKenna, 1978). This question thus arises: Do the sex hormones make it more likely that men will be masculine and women feminine?

The possibility that biological features may bear on one's behavior might seem to threaten a psychology of androgyny. If biology can influence behavior, and if there are biological sex differences, might that not mean that the body places limits on one's capacity for androgyny? Does the existence of biological differences between the sexes suggest that men and women are constitutionally geared to respond in sex-linked ways? Indeed, if the answers to these questions were yes, people's potential for androgynous development might need to be reevaluated.

However, the fact that biology may influence behavior does not have to signal limitations on response potential. Biology can also be seen as only one of several conditions that influence behavior, with its final role determined by interaction with environment. One can ask, Can biological effects be minimized or even overcome by situational variables? Can life circumstances enable both men and women to develop in an androgynous direction despite any biological predispositions?

The possibility of biological, and specifically sex-hormonal influences on behavior, and the ultimate meaning of these influences when combined with environmental factors, will be the primary focus of this chapter. We will first look more closely at the implication of biological sex differences for a psychology of androgyny. How are biological differences between the sexes to be interpreted? What evidence is there that biological effect varies depending on the situation? What determines the relative effect of biology and environment in shaping sex-role related behavior?

Then, we will explore the prenatal process by which one becomes male or female. How absolute are the distinctions between males and females? What biological characteristics identify one as male or female? Next, we will turn to the relationship between biological sex and psychological sex to explore its extent. In particular, we will look at abnormalities in the development of biological sex. Finally, we will look at the biological bases of specific response patterns, including assertiveness and aggression, sexuality, and parenting behaviors. To what extent are existing sex differences in these responses influenced by biological factors? How much flexibility in these dimensions can be expected, in light of any biological influences? In all of these areas, our concern will be to identify possible links between biology and sex-role related behavior, and then to discuss the meaning of these links within an environmental context.

BIOLOGICAL RESEARCH FROM AN ANDROGYNOUS PERSPECTIVE

One primary reason that biological influences on behavior seem to threaten a psychology of androgyny is that biology is often seen as an immutable force. If biology can influence behavior, so popular thinking often goes, then this influence cannot be altered. Traits that are biologically based are seen as forever fixed within the individual. There is also a common assumption that if some biological attributes are associated with certain behaviors, then without those biological attributes, the behaviors will not occur. According to this line of thought, for example, if a link is found between male sex hormones and assertiveness, then women, without sufficient quantities of these sex hormones, are limited in their capacity for assertiveness.

It is therefore necessary to examine more specifically what it means to say that biology may influence behavior. There are many levels at which such an influence can occur. If, let us say, a person is hungry and therefore tries to find something to eat, we can conclude that the bodily state of hunger was responsible for the subsequent eating behavior. But we cannot conclude from this sequence that eating behavior is caused only by a bodily state of hunger or that hungry feelings will invariably be followed by eating. If there is no food available, then even under conditions of extreme hunger a person will not be able to eat. Also, people may eat because they are anxious, bored, or simply because it is dinnertime and they are expected to participate. Thus, although most people eat because they are hungry, eating is also affected by psychological states or social demands. Further, people may not eat at all even under conditions of extreme bodily need.

The same interplay of biological, psychological, and situational factors appears for biological influences on sex differences and behavior. Let us say for the moment (prior to fuller discussion of this topic later in the chapter), that men have higher levels of male sex hormones (androgens) than women, and that males, in general, are more assertive than women. Let us also say that, in experiments with animals, if extra androgens are given to either males or females, their assertive behaviors will increase. What are the implications of these findings? In general, all else being equal, it seems that the higher the levels of androgen, the more likely the expression of assertive behaviors—just as, in general, the hungrier a person is, the more likely it is that she or he will find something to eat. But this does not mean that androgens are the only cause of assertion. Under some conditions, such as extreme threat, the need for assertiveness may be strong enough to overcome any sex differences in biological predisposition. Under other conditions, such as an argument with a friend, psychological factors such as one's need to be right, one's level of self-esteem, or one's affection toward that friend, may interact with biological predispositions in determining the extent of assertiveness. Or, in receiving hostile remarks from a stranger, there may be clear sex differences in the levels of assertiveness in one's response. However, even in this case, it would be difficult to say that hormones alone were responsible for the difference. Physical strength or the belief that one is expected to fight back, both of which are generally higher in men than women, might also be responsible for sex difference. Androgen levels might have been one determining factor, but they do not work in isolation.

Thus, hormone levels may be one of several factors associated with sex differences in behavior. Possibly, a critical level must be reached before some behaviors occur; if this critical level is not present, the behavior will not be expressed. Or, hormonal level may predispose people to behave in a certain way, but whether or not that behavior is actually expressed will be determined by background, situational or psychological factors. Likewise, the same behavior may be stimulated by hormonal factors *or* by situational factors even in the absence of hormonal input. There are a number of ways, then, that biology, psychology and environment can interact in determining response patterns. To acknowledge that biology plays a role in shaping behavior is not to say that it plays the only role, or that its role might not be modified or even overcome altogether by other factors.

For a psychology of androgyny, the crucial issue is whether or not the influence of hormonal or other biological factors is strong enough to produce regular and consistent sex differences regardless of environmental or psychological conditions. If it is, then there would be reason to believe that present behavioral sex differences would be difficult to alter in an androgynous direction. If biological influence can be overcome or modified, however, then development in an androgynous direction becomes a real possibility.

In order to address the extent of biological influence on behavior, we must have information on the effects of complex levels of biological, psychological, and environmental interaction. However, only a few studies take this approach. As Rossi (1977) has observed, although studies of animal behavior routinely explore the interaction between biological and situational factors, studies of human behavior typically explore only one dimension or the other. As a result, there is often one body of research that documents biological influences on a specific behavior, and another that documents situational influences on that same behavior. Conflicting positions readily arise, and researchers argue as to which is the "real" determining factor. The more crucial question, concerning the relationship between these two dimensions, is seldom addressed.

The nature of most research on the relationship between biology and behavior also makes interpretation of the findings difficult. Many such studies are correlational; that is, they address this question: If levels of sex hormones rise, does the corresponding behavior increase? Researchers who find such a connection frequently suggest that the hormonal condition "caused" the behavioral manifestation. However, as any statistics textbook will tell you, correlations do not imply causality. Sometimes there is a third factor that causes both of the correlated conditions to change. At other times there is simply not enough evidence to determine which of the factors being correlated was responsible for the change in the other. In the studies on sex hormones and behavior, the possibility that behavioral changes could be responsible for hormonal fluctuations is frequently ignored (Kessler & McKenna, 1978).

In addition, in the majority of studies on sex hormones and behavior the subjects are either animals, or humans with biological abnormalities. It then becomes difficult to draw conclusions about normal humans. Also, many of the behaviors studied in animals, such as sexual responses, are instinctual, and thus bear little relationship to the corresponding human behaviors. Most scientists agree that human behavior is more varied and is influenced more by environment than is animal behavior. Yet they still try to understand biological/behavioral relationships in humans by studying animals (Kessler & McKenna, 1978).

Studies of humans with abnormal conditions present other difficulties. Persons who have abnormally formed genitals are aware of their condition, and this awareness can influence their subsequent behavior. Family members may treat these people differently than they would have under more normal circumstances. Their expectations about these people may influence how they interpret behaviors or which behaviors they encouraged or discouraged. Often, such people receive a tremendous amount of medical attention, which can further affect their subsequent behavior. Although most studies compare the behaviors of biologically abnormal individuals with control groups who are similar except for the abnormality, it is highly unlikely that it is only the biological condition, and not conditions of their upbringing, that differentiates the two groups.

Thus, studies of biological influences on behavior must be reviewed with care. To say that biology affects behavior is not to say that it is the only influence, or that other factors may not prevail over biological ones. In generalizing to normal humans from animal studies or from studies of abnormal humans one must respect the differences between these groups. With these cautions in mind, one can view studies of biological influences on behavior from a reasonable perspective.

BIOLOGY IN NORMAL DEVELOPMENT

There are two main factors that influence human development as male or female: genetic composition and the distribution of sex hormones. Before birth, these two factors determine the sexual differentiation of the fetus as female or male and set the stage for later sex-related biological events.

Genetic Sex Differences

Sexual differentiation begins with the genes, located on the chromosomes. At the time of conception, the fertilized egg will contain twenty-three pairs of chromosomes, half of each pair inherited from the mother and half from the father. Twenty-two of these pairs, called *autosomes,* contain genetic material that will determine a wide range of individual characteristics. The twenty-third chromosomal pair are the sex chromosomes, which determine genetic sex. For females, the genetic sex is designated XX, and for males it is designated XY.

The Y chromosome has only about one-fifth the volume of the X chromosome, and contains a minimal amount of genetic material. As a result, males are more susceptible than females to a number of genetically linked ailments.

Four genetically based abnormal conditions are directly carried on the Y chromosome, so they will only appear in sons who have inherited them from their fathers. These fairly rare conditions include barklike skin, dense, hairy growth on the ears, nonpainful lesions on the hands and feet, and webbing between the second and third toes. Because females do not have a Y chromosome, they cannot be similarly afflicted.

In addition to these conditions, there are over thirty diseases to which males are more susceptible than females, including hemophilia, color blindness, and cerebral sclerosis. These diseases are carried as recessive traits on the X chromosome. If a female inherits one afflicted X chromosome, she will be a carrier of the disease, and can pass it on to her offspring. However, unless the disease is present on both of her X chromosomes, she herself will not be afflicted, because the dominant, healthy gene will prevail. For males, if the disease is present on their one X chromosome, then they will be afflicted, because there is no dominant gene on their Y chromosome to counteract the effect.

From conception through the later decades of life, more males than females die. The mortality rate is higher for male than female fetuses; although between 125 and 150 male fetuses are conceived for every 100 female fetuses, for white Americans there are only 106 male births for every 100 female births. For those groups in which pregnant mothers have poor nutritional conditions, the proportion of male deaths to female deaths is even higher. Following birth, within every age range, proportionally more males than females die. Although this imbalance decreases with advancing age, it always remains in favor of the female (Montague, 1968).

Male and Female Sex Hormones

Hormones are chemical substances manufactured by the endocrine glands, including the gonads (ovaries in females and testes in males), the adrenal gland, the pituitary, the thyroid, and the pancreatic islets. These hormones travel through the blood stream and serve as messengers to organs throughout the body.

The sex hormones are primarily manufactured by the gonads. The primary sex hormones produced by the testes are the androgens, of which testosterone is the most potent. The ovaries primarily produce two sex hormones, progesterone and estrogen. Although the androgens are commonly referred to as the "male" sex hormones and estrogen and progesterone as the "female" sex hormones, these labels are in fact only relative. The ovaries produce small amounts of testosterone, and the testes produce small amounts of estrogen and progesterone. In addition, a substance similar to but weaker than gonadal androgen in produced by the cortex, or outer layer, of the adrenal glands in both males and females. The chemical structures of the male and female sex hormones are also not completely distinct. Through a process known as biosynthesis, both evolve from an initial chemical substance called pregaenolone. This substance undergoes a number of changes to become testosterone, estrogen, and progesterone. Thus, although there are differences in the distribution of the sex hormones in normal males and females, there are also hormonal similarities.

Fetal Development

In "the old days," it was assumed that fetal development as male or female was determined only by genetics; a genetic XX structure produced a female, whereas a genetic XY structure produced a male. But recent and complex procedures for understanding fetal development have demonstrated that in fact there is a series of stages through which differentiation as female or male occurs. These stages are influenced first by genetic composition, and then by the distribution of the sex hormones. The influence of the sex hormones during fetal development is guided by what John Money has called the "Adam Principle" (Money & Tucker, 1975). This principle states that in the absence of a sufficient complement of male hormones, development will proceed according to the female pattern. In other words, in the absence of male sex hormones, femaleness, and not neutrality, will prevail. Although male sex hormones are necessary to produce a male, female sex hormones are not necessary to produce a female.

The stages of prenatal sexual differentiation are as follows:

Stage 1: *Genetic differentiation.* As described earlier, Stage 1 is determined by the fetal genetic composition, the female pattern, designated XX, or the male pattern, designated by XY. The Y chromosome can be inherited only from the father, but the X chromosome can be inherited from the mother or the father. These chromosomal patterns, XX or XY, determine the sexual differentiation of the next developmental stage.

Stage 2: *Gonadal differentiation.* At the fetal age of six weeks for males and twelve weeks for females, the chromosomal patterns determine the development of male gonads (testes) or female gonads (ovaries). Both ovaries and testes develop from the same fetal tissue, the ovotestis. The ovotestis is bipotential, consisting of a core portion that can develop into testes, and an outer rim that can develop into ovaries. In the presence of a Y chromosome, the core develops into testes and the outer rim atrophies. This will occur even when there are genetic errors as in XXY (Klinefelter's syndrome) or XYY as long as a Y chromosome is present. With an XX chromosomal pattern, the outer rim develops into ovaries and the core section atrophies. In genetic abnormalities such as

XO (Turner's syndrome), the ovotestis develops into neither ovaries nor testes, but remains as gonadal streaks. There is also a rare genetic condition in which both testes and ovaries develop. It is this condition that Money and Ehrhardt (1972) identify as "true Hermaphroditism."

Stage 3: *Hormonal differentiation.* Once the gonads have developed sufficiently, they begin to produce sex hormones. It is the presence or absence of gonadal androgens which is responsible for the continued process of sexual differentiation. If the production and absorption of testicular androgen is normal, differentiation will proceed as male. If testicular androgen is absent, as in the genetic female, differentiation will proceed as female. Also, if the testes in a genetic male produce androgen but the tissues of the body are unable to absorb it, differentiation will proceed according to the female pattern.

Stage 4: *Differentiation of internal reproductive structures.* The fetus is equipped with the potential for developing male or female internal reproductive structures. The female structures, including the uterus, fallopian tubes, and upper vagina develop from the Mullerian duct. The male structures, including the vas deferens, the seminal vesicles, and the ejaculatory ducts, develop from the Wolffian duct. (See Figure 4.1.) In the absence of gonadal androgens the female structures develop from the Mullerian duct, and the Wolffian duct atrophies. For normal male development to occur, however, two hormonal components are necessary. Gonadal androgens stimulate the development of the Wolffian duct into the male internal reproductive structures. In addition, the presence of the Mullerian inhibiting substance is necessary for the Mullerian duct to atrophy. If it is not present, then both male and female internal reproductive structures will develop (Federman, 1967; Williams, 1968).

Stage 5: *External genitalia.* The development of the external genitals—the lower vagina, clitoris, and labia for women, and the penis, scrotum, and uretheral tube for men—is the final stage in prenatal sexual differentiation. (See Figure 4.2.) Again, development in the male or female pattern is based on hormonal input. In the absence of testicular androgens, the female external genitals will develop. If testicular androgens are present and absorbed, the masculine pattern will predominate (Jost, 1947, 1958). Unlike the internal reproductive structures which developed out of different fetal material (or different portions of the same basic substance) for male and female, male and female external genitals develop from the *same* fetal tissue. There is a genital

FIGURE 4.1

Sexual Differentiation in the Human Fetus.

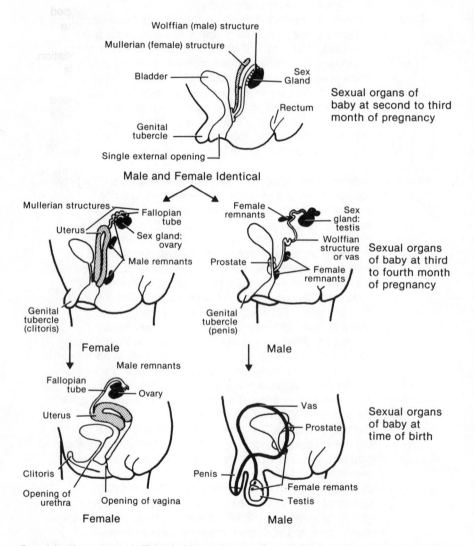

Wolffian (male) structure

Mullerian (female) structure

Bladder

Sex Gland

Rectum

Genital tubercle

Single external opening

Sexual organs of baby at second to third month of pregnancy

Male and Female Identical

Mullerian structures

Fallopian tube

Uterus

Sex gland: ovary

Male remnants

Genital tubercle (clitoris)

Female

Female remnants

Sex gland: testis

Wolffian structure or vas

Prostate

Female remnants

Genital tubercle (penis)

Male

Sexual organs of baby at third to fourth month of pregnancy

Male remnants

Fallopian tube

Ovary

Uterus

Clitoris

Opening of urethra

Opening of vagina

Female

Vas

Prostate

Penis

Female remants

Testis

Male

Sexual organs of baby at time of birth

From John Money and A. A. Ehrhardt, *Man and Woman, Boy and Girl,* Fig. 3.1. Copyright © 1972 The Johns Hopkins University Press. Reprinted by permission.

FIGURE 4.2

External Genital Differentiation in the Human Fetus.

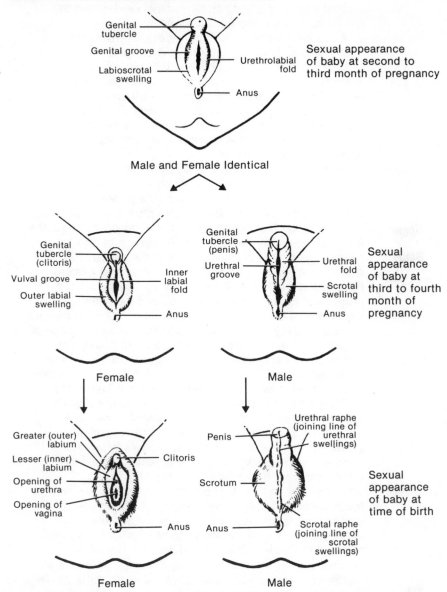

From John Money and A. A. Ehrhardt, *Man and Woman, Boy and Girl,* Fig. 3.2, Copyright © 1972 The Johns Hopkins University Press. Reprinted by permission.

tubercle that can become either a clitoris or a penis, a urethral fold that can become either the labia minor or the urethral tube, and a labioscrotal sac that can become the female labia major or the male scrotum.

Abnormal conditions, such as excess adrenal androgens, or synthetic androgens contained in drugs given to the pregnant mother, can influence the differentiation of the external genitals in the genetic female. Depending on the amount of excess androgens, partial to full masculinization can occur. Such persons can be born with a structure that can be called either an enlarged clitoris or a micropenis. Similarly, they could have a partially fused scrotal sac, or a partially fused urethral tube.

Stage 6:   *Brain differentiation.* When the vascular system is well enough developed to carry sex hormones throughout the fetal body, these hormones are absorbed by a portion of the brain called the hypothalamus. The hypothalamus is a small area at the base of the brain which, among other functions, regulates hormonal activity in the mature adult, through its effect on the pituitary gland. Hypothalamic control of the pituitary follows a different pattern in males and females. In normal females, the hypothalamus will have absorbed gonadal estrogens and progesterones prenatally. As a result, at puberty the hypothalamus will stimulate cyclical production by the pituitary of gonadal and pituitary hormones. When gonadal androgens are absorbed by the hypothalamus, however, this cyclical pattern will not appear at puberty. Prenatal hormones, then, "program" the hypothalamus for later differences in hormonal functioning in females and males (Money and Ehrhardt, 1972).

The process of sexual differentiation does not stop when fetal development is complete. The distinction between male and female is also influenced by what Kessler and McKenna (1978) call "gender attribution," the process by which it is decided whether someone is male or female. One additional stage bears on this process.

Stage 7:   *Sex of assignment.* Under normal circumstances, the birth of the infant immediately heralds the sex of assignment. It's a boy! or It's a girl! is usually the first proud statement on delivery. Bear in mind, however, that assignment is typically made on the basis of the external genitalia only. If the external genitals are unambiguously male or female, sex will usually be assigned without question. However, if the genitals have been partially masculinized, then a decision must be made as to whether the infant should be assigned as male or female. There are two ways of making this decision. One route is to determine the "real" sex of the child, by examining its internal reproductive structures and/or genetic sex. On this basis, for example, a child with very slight masculinization of the genitals could be labeled male if his genetic and internal patterns are male. The other route is to consider the feasibility of a child's healthy adjustment as female or male. For example, one could decide that corrective surgery of a genetically "male" child with minimal masculinization of the genitals could more easily replicate female than male genital structures. On this basis, one might decide to assign the child as female rather than male.

Parental attitudes following the assignment of sex are a major factor in influencing the healthy adjustment of the child to its assigned sex. Whether assignment is the natural result of the child's biological sex differentiation, or entails a decision, the parents must be clear and unambivalent in treating the child as female or male (Money & Ehrhardt, 1972). This parental consistency is necessary for the child's development of gender identity—a clear sense of self as male or female (see chapter 1). Parents who remain confused about the child's sex of assignment, or who give the child ambivalent messages about whether it is female or male, can disrupt the development of gender identity.

Another Look

Studies of fetal development illustrate that becoming a biological male or female is a gradual process, influenced by genetic composition and the distribution of sex hormones.

For each of the stages, there is a crucial period during which a specific aspect of differentiation as male or female will occur. After the stages that are influenced by genetic composition, differentiation will proceed as female unless androgens are present to structure development as male. Development may proceed in a unilateral direction, producing a person who, at every stage, has differentiated as a male or a female. Under abnormal conditions, however, persons may be born with both male and female biological components.

The biological distinction between male and female is not absolute. The fetus has the potential to develop as male or female, depending on genetic and hormonal conditions. In addition, although androgens predominate in males and estrogens and progesterones predominate in females, both sexes contain small amounts of the hormones of the other sex. There is also a range of individual differences within the basic hormonal distribution for each sex. Thus, although there are clear biological distinctions between females and males under normal conditions, these distinctions incorporate a number of biological similarities.

SEX HORMONES, GENDER IDENTITY, AND PSYCHOLOGICAL SEX

As we have seen, some people, biologically speaking, are not fully male or fully female. They provide an opportunity for exploring the interrelationship between biological sex, gender identity, and psychological sex. Gender identity, usually corresponds to one's biological sex. But if one's biological sex is not conclusively male or female, can one still establish a secure gender identity? Or can one similarly maintain a secure gender identity if born with an unambivalent biological sex, but assigned a different sex either in infancy or later in life?

The relationship between biological sex and psychological sex is much more controversial. To what extent is the personality of someone whose biological sex is unambivalent determined by biological or environmental factors? This is the issue at the heart of the nature-nurture debate. Are males more assertive than females because of their hormonal makeup or because of societal rewards for assertive behavior? Are females more nurturant because of their biological capacity for pregnancy and lactation, or because they are trained from an early age for a caretaking role? By studying persons with genetic or hormonal abnormalities we can examine the relative effect of biology and environment in shaping personality development. By and large, researchers have looked at the development of masculinity and femininity under several conditions of biological sex abnormalities. They have asked, can persons with an ambivalent biological sex develop feminine or masculine personality traits consistent with their sex of assignment? For our purposes, however, it would also be meaningful to look at the possible development of an androgynous personality in these people. Are there ways that the interaction of biology and environment produces conditions conducive to the development of androgyny?

Human Abnormalities in Biological Sex

Genetic abnormalities. Biological sex abnormalities can originate at Stage 1, the point of genetic differentiation. Rather than inheriting two sex chromosomes, persons with a condition called Turner's syndrome have an XO chromosomal pattern. Because one sex chromosome is missing, the gonads do not develop at Stage 2, but remain unformed. However, the remaining stages of fetal differentiation follow the female pattern, in accordance with the Adam principle defined earlier. At birth, they appear to be normal females and are so assigned. Lacking ovaries, these females are sterile, and require hormonal treatment to undergo the bodily changes that occur at puberty. They are typically short, and carry a risk of organ defects and retardation.

There have been no known cases of a YO chromosomal pattern, so it is assumed that this configuration is fatal. The Y chromosome, smaller than the X and containing little genetic material, apparently is not sufficient to sustain life. However, there are several other male genetic abnormalities, including XXY (Klinefelter's syndrome) and XYY. Because of the presence of the Y chromosome, and the subsequent production of gonadal androgens, the prenatal development of persons with these abnormalities follows the male pattern, and at birth they are assigned as males.

Those with an XYY pattern can be unusually tall and may be sterile. Those with Klinefelter's syndrome frequently have a small penis and are usually sterile. For the latter, androgen output is often low, so that hormones may have to be administered at puberty. They are at risk for psychopathology, and occasionally experience problems with gender identity (Money & Ehrhardt, 1972).

Sex hormone abnormalities. Sex hormone abnormalities can occur in genetic males or females from an overexposure to prenatal androgens or in genetic males from an inability to absorb prenatal androgens. The second condition is called either the androgen insensitivity syndrome or the testicular feminizing syndrome. Persons with this syndrome have adequately formed and functioning testes. However, because their bodies do not respond to the androgen that is produced, prenatal development after Stage 3 proceeds according to the female pattern. Thus, they are born with female internal reproductive systems and female external genitalia. Assignment of sex can sometimes be difficult with these individuals. In most cases, because their external genitals are unambiguously female, they are assigned as female. However, sometimes an astute physician may notice lumps in the labia that are caused by the presence of testes. The physician can then decide to assign the infants as male. This decision is usually unfortunate because the bodies of these males will never be able to respond to androgens, so hormonal treatment at puberty is not possible. According to Money, "they are obliged to negotiate life, looking unvirilized in physique and much younger than their chronological age" (1973, p. 260).

Hormonal abnormalities can also occur in persons exposed prenatally to excessive amounts of androgens. Two major sources of excess androgens have been reported. The first is overproduction of adrenal androgens, resulting in a condition known as the adrenogenital syndrome. This syndrome can affect both genetic males and genetic females, but it does not affect the internal reproductive structures and external genitals of genetic males. However, the excessive adrenal androgens in these males will lead to early pubertal development unless corrective treatment with cortisones is applied. Genetic females develop female internal reproductive structures, but their external genitals may be partially to fully masculinized, including a fully formed penis and empty but fully formed scrotal sacs. Assignment of sex is clearly difficult for genetic females with the adrenogenital syndrome. Some, on internal examination, are recognized and assigned as females. This would be followed by corrective surgery of the genitals and continual hormonal treatment to offset the effects of the adrenal androgens that would continue to be produced after birth. Others, with fully masculinized genitals, are assigned and reared as males.

The second source of excessive exposure to prenatal androgens, which affects only genetic females, was a drug given to mothers early in pregnancy to prevent miscarriage. The drug, which was given in the 1950s but discontinued after its effects became known, was an artificial progestin, containing a testosterone derivative that partially masculinized the external genitalia. The extent of such masculinization varied, but in almost every case was only partial. Therefore, these persons were usually assigned as females and given corrective surgery when necessary. No hormonal treatment after birth was necessary, because the effects of the drug ceased with birth.

This discussion demonstrates that sex of assignment is not always an obvious decision. In some cases assigned sex is distinct from genetic sex, and in some a decision is required as to what the sex of assignment should be. Table 4.1 lists

TABLE 4.1 Genetic sex, Hormonal distributions, clinical syndromes and sex of assignment

Genetic sex	XX	XY	XO
Excess androgens	Adrenogenital or progestin syndrome Assigned: male or female	Adrenogenital syndrome Assigned: male	
Insufficient sex-appropriate hormones		Androgen insensitivity syndrome Assigned: male or female	Turner's syndrome Assigned: female

the possibilities according to genetic sex, hormonal influence, and sex of assignment.

In turning next to the personality characteristics of people with genetic and sex-hormone abnormalities, we can explore the relative contributions of biological and environmental factors to gender identity and psychological sex. Do persons with identical biological abnormalities have similar personalities regardless of their sex of assignment? Do sex of assignment and biology interact in shaping personality characteristics? Does biological makeup seem to contribute anything to subsequent personality development?

Personality Characteristics and Abnormalities

There are two syndromes associated with the absence of a gonadal sex-hormone effect. They are Turner's syndrome, and androgen insensitivity syndrome, resulting from the body's inability to absorb gonadal androgen.

As we have said, those born with Turner's syndrome look externally like intact females, and are usually assigned as female. As documented by Money, their gender identity is invariably female (Money & Ehrhardt, 1972). In addition, studies suggest that they uniformly develop a feminine psychological sex. Money (1970) portrays these individuals as follows: "[These] girls not only conform to the style of femininity idealized in our cultural definitions of femininity, but they are also (long before they know the prognosis of their condition) maternal in their childhood play and adult aspirations" (p. 428). Elsewhere, Money and Ehrhardt report that:

Despite the handicap of their stature and infertility which all the older Turners girls know about, all but one explicitly hoped to get married one day. They all reported daydreams and fantasies of being pregnant and wanting to have a baby to care for one day. All but one had played with dolls exclusively, and the one preferred dolls even though she played with boy's toys occasionally. Twelve of them had a strong interest in taking care of babies, tending to their younger siblings, or babysitting for other parents; two had a moderate interest in such maternalistic activities; for the one remaining girl, information was missing. (1972, p. 107)

Additionally, Money points out that there was a "complete lack of tomboyish traits" and thereby concludes that these girls "develop a postnatal feminine gender identity with spontaneous ease" and "tend to be free of personality pathology" (1970, p. 428).

In comparison to normal matched controls, girls with Turner's syndrome ranging in age from twelve and a half to sixteen and a half differed on three counts. They had lesser athletic interest and skill, less display of childhood fighting, and a greater interest in personal adornment. On all the other attributes measured, girls with Turner's syndrome did not differ from the matched controls. They shared a limited manifestation of childhood sexuality, and had similar anticipations of romance, marriage, and motherhood (Ehrhardt, Greenberg, & Money, 1970).

The question arises as to whether girls with Turner's syndrome are invariably feminine in their psychological sex, or whether they could also develop an androgynous psychological sex. Money and his colleagues do not address this question, so tentative answers can only be inferred from their data. In general, these girls' strong commitment to a feminine identification, and their "complete lack of tomboyish traits" (Money, 1973), suggest that their capacity for androgyny may in fact be limited. If girls with Turner's syndrome had the potential to develop a masculine, androgynous, or feminine psychological sex, one would expect greater variability in their childhood play and anticipations of adult roles. The fact that, on both counts, the girls were consistently feminine suggests that there is some predisposition toward a feminine psychological sex.

The extent to which these girls' feminine development was influenced by environmental as well as biological factors is difficult to determine, since researchers have not documented characteristic features of their upbringing. It is possible that, if their parents were aware of their infertility, they might have gone out of their way to emphasize feminine traits in these girls in order to foster similarities in personality between them and other girls of their age. In this case, their feminine identity would be the result of a biological-environmental interaction. However, it is also possible that, knowing that these girls could never become natural mothers, the parents would have tried to develop more career-oriented aspirations in them. If this were the case, the feminine psychological sex of these girls would suggest a strong biological effect. Comparisons of girls with Turner's syndrome raised under different conditions of socialization would be necessary to sort out the relative effects of biology and environment.

Genetic males with androgen insensitivity who were assigned and reared as females seem, by Money's (1973) description, to be markedly similar in personality to females with Turner's syndrome. He describes the typical woman as one who "gives priority to marriage over a nondomestic career, who likes domestic activities . . . who anticipated the mother role in her childhood play and was definitely not a tomboy. . . . She is content in her role as a female and prefers and follows the feminine fashion in clothing styles and cosmetics" (p. 261). These persons have a clear gender identity as female and a feminine psychological sex, despite their XY genetic sex (Masica, Money, & Ehrhardt, 1971).

As with the girls with Turner's syndrome, there is not sufficient information for us to ferret out the relative contributions of biology and environment to the subsequent development of psychological sex. We also cannot make definitive statements about their potential for androgyny, although the limitations discussed under Turner's syndrome would seem to apply here as well. There may be some association between the absence of gonadal sex hormones and the predisposition for developing a feminine rather than a masculine or androgynous psychological sex for those raised as female.

Reports on the behavioral correlates of persons with androgen insensitivity reared as male are sparse, because the numbers are so small. Money states that "their masculine gender identity is characterized by a quality that has no name of its own and is the opposite of tomboyism, while not being sissyness" (1973, p. 261). The differences between these males and "sissyness" is not explained. In the same article, Money continues, "[These] men may be *adequately masculine* even to the point of overcompensation, to the extent that their physique permits, in the tradition of the most rugged masculine stereotype" (1973, p. 161, italics added). At the same time, they hesitate to take erotic initiative and are not noted for rivalrous aggression.

Conclusions about the gender identity and psychological sex of these persons must be drawn with caution, because of the limited amount of information available. Money implies that they do have a clear gender identity as males. There are not sufficient data, however, to infer their psychological sex with any reasonable clarity. In Money's terms, although they may be adequately masculine, there are "missing ingredients" in their masculine identity. His interest is in determining whether or not they are, in the final analysis, masculine rather than whether or not there may be evidence of androgynous response patterns. The intriguing possibility, that perhaps what Money sees as these "missing ingredients" are in fact not an absence but the presence of feminine characteristics that would render them androgynous must remain for further data to support or refute.

Let us now turn for comparison to genetic males and females with excessive androgens. One such grouping includes girls who were partially androgenized from prenatal exposure to artificial progestins. These girls have been studied in depth, from Ehrhardt and Money's (1967) first report to Ehrhardt and Baker's (1974) replication and expansion of earlier findings. The composite picture that emerges is of persons who consider themselves to be "tomboys" but are not dissatisfied to be girls. They are active and energetic, but no more aggressive or dominance-seeking than matched controls. They prefer utilitarian, simple clothing, but are not loath to dress up when necessary. They show no predisposition for primping, although they value cleanliness. Along with their distaste for female games, they show less interest, as youngsters, in doll play and other rehearsals of adult maternal roles. They anticipate marriage and a family, but balance this with planning for a career. They are further reported to reveal independence and self-reliance, to have minimal personality disturbances, to be good students, socially mature, easy to get along with, and flexible and reasonable in response to reasonable demands (Ehrhardt & Money, 1967).

Ehrhardt and Money (1967) state unequivocally that these girls are female in their gender identity; there is no evidence that any of them wish to be a boy. They further identify the psychological sex of these girls as "tomboyism," which they see as a variant of femininity (Ehrhardt, Epstein, & Money, 1968; Ehrhardt, 1969; Money, 1973). This tomboyism is specifically characterized by a vigorous energy expenditure in athletics and an indifference to the rehearsal of maternal roles in childhood doll play.

Rather than calling these girls tomboys, however, it seems far more appropriate to suggest that they be considered androgynous. Their absence of extreme sex-typed reactions, their high level of emotional adjustment, their ability to combine career and family in their future outlook, all speak to their *healthy* integration of masculine and feminine attributes. By calling them androgynous rather than tomboys, the emphasis shifts from demonstrating that they are still feminine even though they are tomboys (as do Money and Ehrhardt), to emphasizing that they represent a healthy combination of feminine and masculine characteristics.

Similar findings are reported for genetic females with adrenogenital syndrome (Ehrhardt & Baker, 1974). As described by their families, these girls, who ranged in age from 4.3 years to 19.9 years, show a similar elevation in activity level around athletic events, but no clear tendency to be disruptive or to fight with their peers. Like the girls discussed above, their childhood play reveals little rehearsal of adult maternal roles. They do not discount the possibility of becoming mothers, but are matter-of-fact about it, focusing instead on planning for future careers. They have a clear gender identity as female, and their personality, while not stereotypically feminine, is considered by their families to be within the range of what is appropriate for females. Thus, like the girls exposed to artificial progestins, they seem to evidence a behavioral repertoire consistent with the construct of androgyny.

Similar though less detailed descriptions can be found for genetic males with excess adrenal androgens (adrenogenital syndrome). Sex of assignment and gender identity are not at issue, for these persons are born with intact male internal reproductive structures and external genitals. In a group of ten males with adrenogenital syndrome studied by Ehrhardt and Baker (1974) ranging in age from 4.8 to 26.3 years, all evidenced a clear gender identity as male and a clear satisfaction with the male sex role. For the most part they did not differ from their male siblings, except for a more intense energy expenditure in outdoor play and sports activities. Money (1973) has also found that these boys are likely to be shy and rather hesitant in their relationships with females. Additionally they are "not prone to be fighters or otherwise aggressive. Rather, they tend to be gentle, as though protecting their smaller age mates against the power of their own precocious physique" (1973, p. 257).

From these brief descriptions it is difficult to determine whether the psychological sex of these boys is more consistent with masculinity or androgyny. However, Money's suggestion that they are fully masculine seems premature. Instead, their gentle, nonaggressive nature, combined with their excess energy expenditure in sports, suggests that they have at least the capacity for an androgynous identity.

They seem to evidence neither limitations in the development of their psychological sex, nor unhealthy extremes of masculine and feminine sex-role stereotypes.

Somewhat different behavioral characteristics seem to appear in males exposed prenatally to excessive amounts of estrogens. The effects of this unusual occurence were studied by Yalom, Green, and Fisk (1973) in the male children of diabetic mothers who were given dosages of estrogen to prevent miscarriage. Boys aged six and sixteen, who had been prenatally exposed to varying amounts of estrogen were compared to groups of matched controls to determine their relative degrees of masculinity and femininity on a number of traits. The findings in general indicated that the six-year-old boys differed from the controls only in being less assertive and less athletically able, whereas the sixteen-year-olds were significantly less masculine in terms of interest areas, assertion, visual-spatial ability, and personality characteristics. In contrast to the researchers' position that these boys were less masculine, might they be considered androgynous from our perspective? Although this question is not addressed in the study, the implication is that they evidence patterns of sex role extremes on several personality dimensions rather than androgyny. The researchers' conclusion is these boys were psychologically conflicted, caught between an aggressive, competitive orientation and an inability to express these strivings openly. The several case studies they offer seem to support this conclusion.

Sex Change and Psychological Sex

In all of the syndromes reviewed, the development of an unambiguous gender identity consistent with sex of assignment was possible, regardless of genetic or prenatal hormonal makeup. This identity was inhanced by surgical and postnatal hormonal treatment along with parental consistency about the "true" sex of the child. Persons with the same genetic and hormonal complements at birth, then, can be successfully raised as males *or* as females. From this evidence, Money proposes the concept of *bisexual potential* at birth, suggesting that environmental factors can predominate over biological predispositions in determining one's gender identity as female or male. As Kessler and McKenna have said, "What it means to be a male or a female is merely another way of asking how one *decides* whether another is male or female" (1978, p. 3). According to Kessler and McKenna, gender differentiation is not a biological fact but rather a social construction; the distinction between male and female is a "product of social interaction in everyday life" (1978, p. vii).

This position receives support from two cases of hormonally normal male infants whose assigned sex was changed to female (Money & Ehrhardt, 1972). One case, a male twin, underwent circumcision at seven months of age, and through medical error his penis was burnt off. The decision was made to reassign that twin as female, with appropriate surgical and hormonal corrections. Six years after this reassignment, Money and Ehrhardt (1972) found the female twin unambivalently female in gender identity and developing a feminine psychological sex. As described by the mother, the girl took pride in her feminine clothes and long hair, and valued neatness and cleanliness far more than did her identical twin brother. The son copied his father's behavior, but the daughter began to imitate the mother, helping her with household chores. Their preferences for toys differed; the boy asked for and received a garage with cars and gas pumps, whereas the girl asked for and received dolls, a doll house, and a doll carriage. Differences were also perceived in their play. Even though the female twin had been the dominant one prior to sex reassignment, by three years of age she acted like a "mother hen" with her brother, and the brother defended the sister if she was threatened. Consistent and conscious parental attention toward shaping the reassigned boy into a feminine female had apparently succeeded.

The other case involved an otherwise normal genetic male who was born with a microphallus the size of a slightly enlarged clitoris. Following many months of parental uncertainty, the decision was made to reassign the child as a girl. As early as two months after this decision, the parents noticed changes in the child toward more feminine behavior and definite differences in the ways they treated her and an older brother. Over the next few years the child, although described as a "tomboy," imitated her mother's household chores, showed a preference for and received girl's toys as presents, and did not wrestle with her father as did her brother. Although she continued to be high in physical energy and more assertive than her female peers, she seemed clearly to be developing preferences and behavioral traits consistent with a feminine sex-role orientation. Again, deliberate parental attempts to treat this child as a girl had their intended affect.

The situation confronting transsexuals also supports the independence of sex of assignment from biological sex. Transsexualism, according to Stoller, is the "conviction in a biologically normal person of being a member of the opposite sex" (1968, p. 89). Transsexuals, in other words, believe that they have been assigned the wrong sex. With available medical procedures, many of these persons are able to undergo surgical and endocrinological changes that will convert them to the other sex. This is especially true if the desired conversion is from male to female, which is by far the most frequently requested change (Bermant, 1972). Following a change in biological sex, these people seem easily to adapt a psychological sex consistent with their new biological sex (cf. Kessler & McKenna, 1978).

Another Look

In the syndromes with absent or unabsorbed sex hormones (Turner's syndrome and androgen insensitivity syndrome), we saw that those raised as female seem to have adopted a clearly feminine psychological sex, whereas those raised as male evidence some strikingly masculine traits, and possibly some feminine traits as well. Those with excess androgens (adrenogenital syndrome, and females exposed to prenatal androgens) and males exposed to prenatal estrogens through medication seem to behave in ways that are neither stereotypically masculine nor feminine. In particular, the girls exposed to artificial progestins seem to evidence characteristics consistent with an androgynous psychological sex. Insufficient data were available to determine whether the males who were exposed to androgens or estrogens evidenced androgynous characteristics or behaviors reflecting both feminine and masculine sex-typed extremes.

The most consistent theme across the studies of hormonal abnormalities and the two cases involving early changes in sex of assignment is that androgens seem to be associated with increased energy expenditure. This was true for both genetic males and females, and for those raised as male or female. In addition, the presence of excess androgens in genetic males or females, and the prenatal presence of androgens in the two persons subsequently raised as female seems to be associated with behavioral characteristics more consistent with androgynous than feminine or masculine psychological sex.

The connection between these cases and sex differences in the behavior of biologically normal persons must be considered, but with caution. In general, it suggests that sex differences in energy level are a function of the greater presence of prenatal androgens in males than females (cf. Ehrhardt & Baker, 1974). However, the relative effect of biological and environmental factors in shaping males' increased activity level complicates the determination of causality. In contemporary society, boys are encouraged and supported in energetic play more than girls. Thus, biological predispositions are reinforced by socialization. The possibility still exists, then, that if patterns of socialization ran counter to biological predispositions, boys could become equally or more docile than girls, and girls equally or more energetic than boys. To suggest that androgens create a predisposition for energetic play is not to say that they are necessary for such displays—that, under all environmental conditions, they will always lead to this form of activity. However, if society were oriented toward the development of androgyny, it might be profitable to increase opportunities for energetic activity in girls, thus compensating for a predisposition against such activity.

SEX HORMONES AND BEHAVIORAL TRAITS

The sex hormones have been studied not just in relation to gender identity and psychological sex, but also in relation to specific behavioral traits. At issue is the extent to which sex hormonal differences are responsible for observed sex differences in behavior. Are consistent behavioral patterns within each sex a function simply of hormonal makeup, or are they also shaped by environment? Does behavior vary more as a function of biological sex or of psychological sex?

The majority of studies on the relationship between sex hormone levels and behavior were done in the laboratory with nonhuman animals. This approach has certain advantages. It permits researchers to carefully control both hormonal levels and environmental factors. It also allows them a far wider range of hormonal levels and combinations than would be found naturally. However, there are disadvantages with this approach as well. The effect of a given hormone may vary depending on the species of animal used, the dosage administered, and the timing of administration, making general conclusions difficult to determine. Further, artificial hormones are not exact replicas of natural ones, but the effect of this difference on behavior is not fully known. Finally, although generalizations are regularly made from nonhuman to human populations (Harlow, Gluck, & Suomi, 1972), such generalizations can be made only with great caution. Humans depend less on sex hormones than do animals (Bleier, 1976), and are the only species conscious of its own behavior. Thus, findings of direct relationship between hormonal levels and behavior in nonhumans does not necessarily imply a similar relationship for humans. However, because humans are less tied to their biology than are animals, behavioral flexibility in animals not caused by hormonal levels would provide some evidence for a similar potential for flexibility in humans.

The behaviors we will discuss in this section are assertiveness and aggression, sexuality (including homosexuality and heterosexuality), and parenting. In all three areas, research with laboratory animals will be discussed, but for the first two there are also some data on humans.

It would be ideal to have a body of research on the hormonal underpinnings of assertive, sexual, and parenting behavior that gives equal attention to both sexes. Unfortunately, such information is not available. As might be expected from prevailing notions about the sexes, most assertiveness and aggression studies are of males or the impact of male hormones; almost all parenting studies look at females or the impact of female sex hormones. Sexual patterns are explored in both males and females, yet there is a general tendency to associate sexual drive ("libido") with male hormones (Money & Ehrhardt, 1972), and to ignore the active role played by females in sexual encounters (Doty, 1974).

There are also only a few studies that provide an examination of the interaction between biology and environment in affecting nonstereotypic behaviors. There is a growing awareness, however, that not only does the environment affect behavior in nonhumans (Larsson, 1973), but also that environmental stress can directly affect hormone levels in human and subhuman males (Rose, Gordon, & Bernstein, 1972; Ward, 1972). In addition, some scientists are realizing that sex-role expectations have prevented researchers from recognizing and studying unexpected or nonstereotypic patterns (Beach, 1947; Levine & Mullins, 1964; Sodersten, 1972). From these broadened approaches to research, data pertinent to the psychology of androgyny are beginning to emerge.

Assertiveness

Although scientists are usually aware of the importance of defining their terms, they are surprisingly unclear on the distinction between assertive and aggressive behaviors. Similar research designs have been used to explore behaviors ranging from rough and tumble play in the young to criminal behavior. There also tends to be no distinction made between traits that seem to be socially functional and those which seem to be socially debilitating. As a result, insufficient attention is paid to the stituational appropriateness of assertive or aggressive behaviors. Instead, there is a general, implicit assumption that assertiveness is better than nonassertiveness.

Two general statements can be made about the relationship between sex hormones and assertion. First, for most species, males tend to be more assertive than females. Second, across species and for both sexes, experimental or natural increases in androgen levels tend to increase measured evidence of assertive behaviors. These findings cannot be discounted as the biased conclusions of male researchers looking only to explain general patterns of male dominance. But neither should they be accepted as the total answer. An exploration of the behaviors studied under the label of assertiveness, and of the effect of environment on the basic relationship between androgens and assertive behavior can clarify these basic results.

One major line of research, which has been developed in the laboratory of William Young (e.g., Young, Goy, & Phoenix, 1964), has been to explore the effects of experimentally manipulated levels of androgens on the play behavior of infant monkeys. These researchers were interested in the effects of androgens on known sex differences in behavior. They used as their behavioral measures traits that Harlow (1962, 1965) had found to differentiate male and female monkeys. Specifically, Harlow had found that male monkeys were typified by threat behavior and rough-and-tumble play, whereas female monkeys were typified by passivity and rigidity. One study compared behaviors of infant monkeys under four hormonal conditions: (1) females androgenized in utero, (2) males castrated at birth, (3) intact males, and (4) intact females (Phoenix, Goy, & Resko, 1968). This study looked only at Harlow's two behavioral measures which typified males. It was found that intact and castrated males performed similarly to one another and to Harlow's male monkeys. The intact females evidence less masculine behavior than either the intact or castrated males, and the androgenized females were between the males and the females, but most similar to the former.

It is from studies of this sort that the basic relationship between androgens and assertion has been demonstrated. Male monkeys, whose nervous systems have been androgenized in utero, will demonstrate male behaviors even when castrated postnatally. In females, the prenatal addition of androgens results in more assertive behavior than that expressed by intact females.

It is necessary to look beneath the seeming simplicity of these results. Two major features were absent that would be of prime importance for the psychology of androgyny. The first has to do with basic research design: rather than measure those traits more closely associated with sex differences, the researchers might have examined the relationship between androgen levels and behaviors that are not so clearly sex-typed. For example, they might have asked these questions: Under what hormonal levels were animals of either sex playful and outgoing, but not rough and hostile with one another? Under what conditions were animals of either sex able to avoid playmates who looked threatening without otherwise inhibiting their contact with others? The second feature has to do with the observation and reporting of results. These researchers simply stated that the androgenized females were more similar to males than to intact females. But we know from Money's work, discussed earlier in this chapter, that human females slightly androgenized in utero behaved in ways that were neither typically female nor typically male, but seemed to demonstrate certain optimal combinations of both stereotypes. We wonder whether the androgenized female monkeys gave any indications of combined masculine and feminine characteristics, and if so, whether this was associated with greater flexibility and adaptiveness than evidenced by either the males or intact females.

Researchers are also beginning to explore environmental conditions under which testosterone levels and subsequent displays of assertiveness and dominance decrease. Much of the focus here has been on the role of stress. Robert

Rose and his colleagues have studied the effects of stress on male rhesus monkeys. In an ingenious study (Rose, Gordon, & Bernstein, 1972), they first placed male monkeys, individually, in all-female colonies where they became the high-status individual. Under this condition, androgen levels and assertiveness increased. These same male monkeys were then placed in all-male colonies with a preestablished hierarchy that relegated any newcomer to the bottommost position. Under these conditions, the males increased their submissive behaviors from 44 percent to 76 percent during the first hour. Although they were removed from the colony after two hours, two had received wounds serious enough to require suturing. Testosterone levels in the bloodstream, even during this brief exposure to defeat, dropped an average of 80 percent from baseline measures. For two of these males, these depressed testosterone levels were still in evidence nine weeks after this humiliating experience.

Rose and his colleagues have also begun to extend their work to the effects of stress on human males (Rose, Bourner, Poe, Mougey, Collins, & Mason, 1969), by comparing the testosterone levels of army men under high stress (awaiting imminent attack in Vietnam), moderate stress (rigorous basic training), and low stress (army volunteers doing routine jobs). As would be predicted from the studies with the rhesus monkeys, testosterone levels under high and moderate stress were strikingly lower than levels under low stress. No measures of the effect of these lower testosterone levels on the display of assertive behaviors were taken, but one would predict from the studies with monkeys that these would also decline.

These studies clarify some issues, but raise many others. They seem to demonstrate, fairly clearly, that not only do testosterone levels affect modes of interacting with the environment, but also that the environment can affect testosterone levels and perhaps subsequent behavior. The earlier statement on the relationship between testosterone and assertion can now be modified by noting (1) that testosterone levels vary as a function of environmental stress, (2) that these lowered testosterone levels are associated in monkeys with decreases in assertive behavior, and (3) at least for monkeys, these declines can remain in effect for more than two months. The questions to be raised from an androgynous perspective relate to the implications of these findings for human behavior. For monkeys, the nature of stressful situations is fairly clear, and for humans there are some conditions, such as preparation for combat duty, that can reasonably be assumed to produce stress. But what range of environmental conditions would produce effects on testosterone levels similar to those produced by stress? Does it include, for example, high-level decision making, the threat of physical danger, academic competition, or interpersonal conflicts? Cultural lore suggests that, with the possible exception of the last two, these situations would cause males, with their higher capacity for assertiveness, to function more effectively than females. But could it be that, at precisely these points, males lose their supposed advantage? There are not nearly enough data to provide answers to this question, because many issues remain to be explored. Are there individual differences in the effect of stress on testosterone levels and subsequent behavior? Under conditions of high stress, how do male and female reactions compare? Does stress effect female hormonal levels or behavior, and if so, how? This is the work of the future, but the findings, when they begin to accumulate, will go far in documenting the range of hormonal and situational factors associated with assertiveness in males and females.

In studies that seek to document the relationship between testosterone levels and clearly aggressive behaviors in the human male, findings tend to be equivocal. This is partly because of differences in the population studied, and partly because of variations in the way aggression is measured. When normal adult males are studied, findings sometimes point to a significant, positive relationship between hormonal levels and amount of aggression as measured by a battery of psychological tests (e.g., Persky, Smith, & Basu, 1971). However, in other studies this relationship is not found (e.g., Meyer-Bahlburg, Nat, Boone, Sharma, & Edwards, 1974). Similar conflicting findings can be found in studies using a prison population. In some, men who had committed the most violent crimes were found to have higher testosterone levels (measured some time after their criminal acts) than men who had committed less violent crimes (e.g., Rada, Laws, & Kellner, 1976). However, other studies reported only slight evidence for a relationship between expressed aggressiveness and testosterone levels in a population of male prisoners (e.g., Kreuz & Rose, 1972).

This ambiguity in research findings may be caused by the research methodologies that are used. Consider first the difficulties in determining testosterone levels. Because testosterone is known to undergo daily cycles, the researcher would need to take multiple measures to determine a person's average level. However, in many of these studies only one measure was taken, so we cannot know whether the level was a high, low, or average for that person. Testosterone levels may also vary as a result of situational factors. Thus, in studying the relationship between testosterone levels and criminal behavior, the preferred measure of testosterone would be taken at the time the crime was committed. For obvious reasons, this would be difficult to do. In addition, there are some problems associated with studying a prison population. For example, the stress inherent in a prison environment could cause all inmates to have depressed levels of testosterone, which would minimize individual differences. Thus, although there is some evidence for an association between increased testosterone levels and aggressive behavior, the strength of this association, and its situational variability remain unclear.

Sexual Behavior

There are many studies on the relationship between sex hormones and sexual response patterns in animals. In these studies (most often with the rat) researchers have documented a fairly distinct sex difference in sexual response. Female sexuality is characterized by a posture of *lordosis,* in which the animal is crouched with the rump up, whereas male sexuality is marked by a sequence of mounting, intromission, and ejaculation. In humans, for whom sexual response is more varied, research has tended to focus on the relationship between sex *drive* and levels of hormones. In reviewing this research, we will attend to evidence that suggests flexibility of sexual response independent of sex hormones, areas of overlap between male and female patterns of sexuality, and evidence of sexual behavior that transcends stereotypic expectations.

Researchers tend to agree that although the description in the last paragraph characterizes the typical sexual behavior of male and female animals, both sexes produce certain responses associated with the other sex (Bleier, 1976; Hutt, 1972; Money & Ehrhardt, 1971, 1972). Females in heat sometimes mount other females, and males, especially monkeys, may position themselves in ways suggesting lordosis.

Studies investigating the hormonal correlates of sexual behavior in animals typically expose the animal to some form of hormonal manipulation and then document the resulting sexual behavior. Drawing generalizations from all these studies is highly complicated, however, because of the many ways of manipulating hormonal levels (Money & Ehrhardt, 1971). Animals of either sex may be castrated prenatally or shortly after birth, or not at all. These animals may or may not simultaneously be treated with varying doses of sex-appropriate or sex-inappropriate hormones. At puberty or in later adulthood, these same animals may be castrated (if they had remained intact) with or without varying levels of sex-appropriate or sex-inappropriate injections. Thus, the relationship of sex hormones and behavior must be examined in terms of (1) the presence of castration, (2) the nature and amount of hormonal injections during the early critical period of sexual differentiation, and (3) the nature and amount of hormones injected at puberty.

The major conclusion drawn from reviews of this vast and rather varied group of studies (Gerall, 1973; Money & Ehrhardt, 1971) is that animal behavior is potentially bisexual. As stated by Money and Ehrhardt: "The evidence of animal sexology to date (Beach, 1947; Whalen, 1968) is that sexually dimorphic behavior is not uniquely male or female, respectively. Rather it is bisexual in potential, though predominantly male or predominantly female in manifestation" (1971, p. 243). The extent to which this bisexual potential is manifested depends on both environmental and hormonal factors. Past sexual experiences, the presence or absence of an attractive animal, social factors such as crowding or isolation all can influence the direct expression of sexuality. Additionally, animals' sexual expression will be influenced by early hormonal manipulation as well as their homonal status at puberty.

What evidence is there for the manifestation of bisexual response in animals? Even for intact animals, as we have said, sexual differentiation is not total. After hormonal manipulation by researchers, this bisexuality increases. Gerall (1973) summarizes the effects of androgens administered at puberty to female rats whose ovaries had been removed earlier, and who had been primed before birth with testosterone. These animals are born fully formed as males. If androgens are then given in sufficiently large doses in adulthood, they will display all the responses typically included in the male repertoire, including mounting, intromission, and ejaculation. Additionally, these animals give no evidence of female sexual behavior. Their sexual response, in other words, has been completely masculinized. Smaller doses of androgens have a lesser effect on behavior, depending on the amount administered and the age of the animal. Intromission and ejaculation may disappear, but these masculinized females continue to show mounting behaviors in excess of that demonstrated by their intact peers.

Similarly, a male rat castrated before the period of gonadal differentiation (which in rats occurs just after birth) and primed with estrogens and progesterones at puberty will demonstrate a fairly complete pattern of female sexual behavior (Money & Ehrhardt, 1971). Male rats injected with female hormones at puberty but not castrated earlier demonstrated a poor performance of male sexual behavior, but no female response. As described by Money and Ehrhardt (1971), their intromission and ejaculatory rates were lowered, and their mounting behavior was "bizarre"; they attempted to mount from the head or the side, rather than from the rear.

Male rats castrated neonatally and then injected with testosterone in adulthood will demonstrate frequent mounting behavior, but give little evidence of intromission or ejaculation (Goy, 1975). However, this behavioral effect might well result from the inadequate penile development caused by castration before the external genitals were fully developed (Beach, 1971; Whalen, 1968). In a variation of this procedure, Goldfoot et al castrated male rats at birth, and then injected them at puberty with androstenedione, a biosynthethic precursor of testosterone (Goy, 1975). Under the influence of this weaker male hormone, animals developed normal male genitalia and retained mounting, intromission, and ejaculatory behaviors, but they also evidenced the female lordotic response. These findings underline the trend that runs through much of this research; that masculine and feminine sexual responses are not mutually exclusive categories, even for animals, and that it is possible, albeit under unnatural hormonal conditions, to create a situation in which the two coexist.

Several cautions must be raised against concluding from this research that, although sexual behavior in animals does vary as a function of hormonal level, there is a clear and direct relationship between male and female hormones and masculine or feminine sexual responses. In neonatally androgenized females, subsequent doses of estrogen can lead to increased male mounting behaviors just as doses of testosterone do. Also, testosterone administered experimentally by researchers seems to have a greater effect on sexual behavior than does the normal testosterone of intact males. Laboratory studies, therefore, might not always provide an accurate base for generalizing to real-life situations. Money and Ehrhardt caution that "one must not equate masculine behavior with masculine hormone, nor feminine behavior with feminine hormone" (1971, p. 246).

The influence of androgens on male sexuality has been investigated in part by studies of the effects in men of inadequate androgen levels. Money and Ehrhardt (1972) cite the example of lowered sex drive in prepubertally castrated males, as well as in males afflicted with the androgen insensitivity syndrome. This lowered sex drive is a result not only of decreased hormonal levels, but also of inadequately developed male genitals. Postpubertally castrated men, whose genitals have fully matured, also evidence lowered sexual interest, which according to these authors, can be easily restored with testosterone replacement therapy. Findings such as these have led some to conclude that hormonal injections in physically intact males will ameliorate impotence or other sexual difficulties. Attempts to do this, however, have generally not been successful. Although hormone therapy may be able to ameliorate a clear hormonal deficiency, it apparently cannot counteract the broad range of causes, possibly including hormonal ones, that may be at the root of sexual dysfunction in human males with normal levels of testosterone.

Other support for the role of androgens in male sexuality has come from studies on the effects on sexuality of changes in the level of testosterone. Males' decreasing interest in sex with advancing age (Kinsey, Pomeroy, & Martin, 1948) has been associated with a gradual decline in testosterone. And yet, some men are able to remain sexually active throughout old age. These men, apparently, have found ways to overcome hormonally induced decreases in sexual drive.

Androgens have also been held to influence female patterns of sexual drive. Money and Ehrhardt, in fact, propose that "androgen is the libido hormone in both sexes" (1972, p. 222). Much of the evidence for this role of androgens again comes from studies of women in physically abnormal situations. Women who are given testosterone therapy tend to show an increase in sexual drive (Kane, Lipton, & Ewing, 1969). And, women who undergo adrenelectomies (which eliminate the androgens produced by the adrenal cortex) report a decrease in their sexual interest.

There is also some evidence for increased sexuality in women with the adrenogenital syndrome (Masica, Money, & Ehrhardt, 1971). As compared to genetic males with androgen insensitivity, the adrenogenital women had a much higher incidence of masturbation, and a greater number of erotic dreams, with both homosexual and heterosexual content. After cortisone therapy, the adrenogenital women did not report a higher sex drive than the androgen-insensitivity women, although the researchers conclude that "without such treatment there would undoubtedly have been a statistical difference between the two groups, since several adrenogenital women spontaneously remarked that, before cortisone therapy, their sexual drive had been stronger, and even too strong" (p. 137).

What of the role of estrogens and progesterones in women's sexuality? The evidence here is much less direct than was the case with testosterone. Unlike male castrates, women who undergo ovariectomies do not generally report loss of erotic sensitivity, although in some studies they do. Similarly, women treated therapeutically with estrogens do not seem to report an increase in their sexual interest. Thus, the female hormones lack the dramatic effect on sexuality associated with androgens.

The majority of studies on female sex hormones and eroticism examine fluctuations in sexual drive associated with the menstrual cycle. And most have found a cyclical pattern to women's sexuality (Sherman, 1971). However, the most common findings do not clarify the possible role of female sex hormones, because they report greatest sexual activity both at ovulation (when estrogen is at its peak) and premenstrually, when estrogen and progesterone undergo a rapid decline. Money and Ehrhardt account for this discrepancy by differentiating between the quality of sexual desires at these two times. They postulate that "at the ovulatory period, the feeling of sexual desire is likely to be a desire to surrender and to be occupied sexually. At the menstrual period, it is likely to be a desire to capture and envelop" (1972, p. 223). Thus, although the feelings associated with sexuality in women may vary as a function of hormonal levels, estrogen and progesterone do not seem to affect the level of women's sex drive.

Homosexuality

Some mention should be made about the possible influence of sex hormones on male and female homosexuality. As early as 1951, Ford and Beach stated,

> When the so-called male and female hormones were first discovered, some authorities concluded that homosexuality is caused by an abnormal amount of female hormone in males or of male hormones in females. There are a few clinicians who still hold this view, but the evidence against it is impressive. Attempts have been made to show that the urine of homosexual men contains an abnormal amount of estrogen. However, the differences between such men and "normal" men have been slight and unreliable, and in many cases no differences have been found (p. 236).

Yet the search for hormonal causes of homosexuality continues, producing as many conflicts in data and interpretation as any subject we have encountered. Some studies show normal or elevated testosterone levels in homosexual men as compared to heterosexual controls (e.g., Barlow, Abel, & Blanchard, et al., 1974; Birk, Williams, Chasen, et al., 1973; Brodie, Cartrell, & Doering, et al., 1974; Pillard, Rose, & Sherwood, 1974; Tourney & Hatfield, 1973). Others, however, have reported lower testosterone levels in homosexual males than in heterosexual controls (e.g., Kolody, Masters, Hendryx, & Tore, 1971; Loraine, Ismail, & Adamapoulos, 1970). Although some researchers have acknowledged these conflicting results (Doerr, Pirke, Kockott, & Dittman, 1975), others make statements to the effect that "recent findings in human plasma have indicated that in masculine homosexuals the testosterone levels are on the average lower than in normal males" (Straka, Sipova, & Hynie, 1975, p. 134). Behind this controversy lies the full force of societal attitudes toward homosexuality. Homosexuality is a political as well as a sexual issue, and whether researchers wish it or not, the direction of their work will influence the tenor of people's thinking. By looking at causes of homosexuality but not heterosexuality researchers are providing openings for the implication that homosexuality is pathological.

As with any other aspect of human sexuality, hormones may have some effect on sexual behavior, but are never the only determining factor. Unfortunately, for all the research into hormonal underpinnings of homosexuality, there has been virtually no attempt to explore the interaction of biological and environmental factors that might lead a person in a homosexual direction.

By contrast, research on homosexuality consistent with a model of androgyny might explore, for both heterosexuals and homosexuals, the interaction of cultural, familial, political, and hormonal forces that influence sexual object choice. By what routes does one become heterosexual or homosexual? How might individual differences in hormonal levels interact with changes in cultural attitudes, early experience, or legal dictates on sexual behavior? From this vantage point, both homosexuality and heterosexuality would be seen as influenced by a wide range of factors, including hormonal ones. Further, the onus of "pathology" would be lifted from homosexuality in androgynous research, because heterosexuals would serve not as "normal controls" but as subjects of inquiry in their own right.

Parenting

Our final topic regarding sex hormones is their relationship to parenting behaviors, more commonly called "maternal behavior." Parenting behavior, in most animal species and human cultures, is a female preoccupation (Oakley, 1972). This has stimulated an interest in documenting biological bases of maternal responsiveness in females. Around the turn of the century, speculation was rampant that women's maternal behaviors were caused by a "maternal instinct" (see Chapter 2). More recently, the focus has shifted to exploring the possible role of hormones in stimulating maternal responsiveness.

Examining the research on hormones and maternal responsiveness from an androgynous perspective, the central concern becomes whether or not there is a biological predisposition toward maternal behaviors in females, and if so, how this may be influenced by environment. Two specific questions bear directly on this issue: (1) What factors stimulate maternal behaviors in animals that have just given birth? (2) What evidence is there of a capacity for infant caretaking in females who have not given birth, and in males? Both of these questions have been studied extensively in small mammals, especially the rat. A summary of this research will suggest the relative effects of biology and environment on parenting behaviors. Although we cannot make direct comparisons from these studies to human responsiveness, we need to remember that humans are less, and never more, tied to their biology than are nonhuman species. Therefore, evidence in small mammals of flexibility in parenting responsibilities would suggest at least as much, if not more, flexibility for humans.

The acquisition of maternal responsiveness in female rats who have just given birth is influenced, in a developmental sequence, by both biological and environmental factors (Rosenblatt, 1969). During pregnancy, the large increases in circulating estrogens and progesterones seem to "prime" the female for later maternal behaviors. These behaviors, which in the rat include licking, retrieving, crouching in a nursing position, and nest building, are evidenced by pregnant females, but are not displayed as quickly as they are by mothers who have just given birth. After birth, however, stimulation from the newborn pups is necessary to sustain maternal behaviors even in their natural mothers. If the pups are born dead, for example, maternal reactions are greatly depressed. Similarly, it is the growing independence of the pups, rather than a decrease in hormonal levels, that seems responsible for the decline in maternal behaviors when these are no longer needed (Rosenblatt, 1969). Rosenblatt concludes that although both hormones and environment play a role in the onset of maternal behaviors for females who have just given birth, the mother's level of responsiveness is maintained and developed as a result of stimulation by the young. In his words, the new mother must be "motivated" by the young to respond to them.

If stimulation from newborn pups is necessary to produce maternal responsiveness in new mothers, is it also sufficient to stimulate parenting behaviors in virgin females and in males? From the many studies that have addressed this question, primarily with the rat, the general conclusion is a qualified yes (cf. Quadagno, Briscoe, & Quadagno, 1977). Although both virgin females and males require longer exposure to pups than do new mothers before showing maternal behaviors, with sufficient exposure, females (both mothers and nonmothers) and males both will display the full range of maternal responses. In addition, in a smaller enclosure (which increases the direct contact between adult and pups), the amount of exposure required to stimulate maternal behaviors in males is reduced (Quadagno, DeBold, Gorzalka, & Whalen, 1974). Quadagno, Briscoe, and Quadagno conclude from their review of this research that "in rodents both the male and the female will show all aspects of maternal behavior after prolonged exposure to pups" (1977, p. 76). Apparently, there is less differentiation by sex in maternal responsiveness than there is in mating behaviors (Quadagno et al., 1974).

This brief review suggests that it is exposure to the newborn that enhances caretaking behavior with newborn rodents. Hormonal factors increase the speed and ease with which these responses will appear, but are not a prerequisite.

These findings carry strong implications for sex differences in human parenting. They suggest that it is males' lack of exposure to infants, rather than just their low levels of female hormones, that is responsible for their low levels of participation in infant care. From animal studies we might reasonably expect that, given sufficient exposure, men could increase their facility in infant care. Nothing in the research on nonhuman males' parenting behavior suggests that men are biologically incapable of parenting.

Another Look

Studies on the relationship between the sex hormones and behavior show that there is a complex interaction between biology and environment in influencing response patterns. The evidence does suggest that the sex hormones predispose members of each sex to a readiness for certain kinds of behavior. In particular, the higher levels of androgens in males create a tendency for assertiveness, whereas estrogens and progesterones prime the female for caretaking behavior on the birth of her offspring. However, both of these predispositions can be partially or fully offset by environmental influences. Under some conditions of extreme stress, males' hormonal levels decrease and, in monkeys, there is a parallel decrease in their capacity for assertiveness. Studies with the rat have shown that in the absence of the increased sex hormones associated with pregnancy, both virgin females and males can develop the capacity for parenting behaviors if they have sufficient contact with newborns. Human sexuality has been shown to be shaped by both hormonal and environmental factors, although no studies have yet investigated how these two factors might interact.

In sum, there seems to be little evidence that biological conditions preclude the capacity for flexibility and situationally appropriate reactions that are consistent with the construct of androgyny. Rather, present findings indicate that both sexes are capable of assertive, or parental responses, but that compensatory training may be necessary to offset the effects of biological predispositions. However, as we will see in later chapters on sex-role socialization, members of each sex are still encouraged to reinforce rather than compensate for possible biologically based potentials. Thus, current social conditions are working against the development of one's androgynous potential.

Psychological research could also further the study of how environmental and biological interaction can increase the human potential for flexibility and non-stereotyped behaviors. Researchers would have to make a concerted attempt to study nonstereotypic response patterns in both men and women, and the forces that seem to have shaped those responses. Such documentation could go far in decreasing the still common assumption that biology is the primary determinant of current behavioral sex differences.

SUMMARY AND CONCLUSIONS

We began this chapter by raising questions about the relationships among biological sex, gender identity, and psychological sex. The essential question was, To what extent are gender identity and psychological sex fixed by one's biological sex? Or, put another way, How do environmental factors alter biological preconditions that may differ for females and males? This question was considered fundamental for a psychology of androgyny. If psychological sex is determined only by biology, then potential for androgynous development would be curtailed. However, if biological factors are variable, and if they interact with environmental considerations in shaping behavior, then androgynous development becomes possible.

As demonstrated in this chapter, the distinction between female and male is not absolute, even in terms of biology. The potential of the fetus to develop as male or female, and the presence of sex-hormonal similarities between the sexes create an overlap between what is male and what is female.

Most people have a clear gender identity as male or female. This clarity, however, is influenced not only by biological sex, but also by sex of assignment. In fact, some researchers argue that although one's gender identity is determined in part by biology, it is more strongly influenced by the sex that others consider one to be, or by the sex one considers oneself to be. Biologically normal persons can experience a change of assigned sex early in life and still develop a secure gender identity. Transsexuals, feeling a conflict between their gender identity and their assigned sex, find it emotionally easier to change the latter than the former.

Psychological sex is also influenced by both biology and environment. In terms of biology, most clearly documented is the relationship between male sex hormones and increased energy expenditure, especially in play activity. This relationship appears in humans with sex hormone abnormalities and in experimental laboratory studies with animals. There is also some evidence for an association between male sex hormones and sexual drive, and between female sex hormones and the rapid, easy acquisition of parenting behaviors. These relationships are clearest in animal studies; they do not appear in studies of humans with sex hormone abnormalities.

Very little research exists on how biological predispositions in normal humans can be influenced by environmental conditions. However, what research there is, combined with evidence from studies of animals and abnormal humans, suggests a strong possibility of environmental effect. We saw that testosterone levels, held to be responsible for males' greater assertiveness, will decrease in response to environmental stress. Also, male rats who are given sufficient exposure to newborn pups, will evidence all the caretaking behaviors exhibited by females who have just given birth. And, sex drive does not necessarily increase in the presence of increased androgen levels for those with sex hormone abnormalities or for normal humans.

We have identified no dimensions of femininity or masculinity that will invariably appear for all who are biologically female or male, respectively. And we have found no evidence of behaviors that cannot appear in normal members of either sex because of genetic or hormonal makeup. Between these two extremes are behaviors that may be more frequent in one sex than the other, but that will vary in expression depending on environmental circumstances. Unfortunately, little is known about the specific biological-environmental interactions that will make some responses more likely than others in males and females. Even less is known about the biological-environmental interrelationships that will be most conducive to androgynous, rather than to feminine or masculine, patterns of reaction. What can be said, however, is that psychological sex seems to vary in response to variations in biological sex and environment.

SELECTED READINGS

Bleier, R. H. Brain, body, and behavior. In J. H. Roberts (ed.), *Beyond intellectual sexism: A new woman, a new reality.* New York: Longman, 1976.

Caplan, A. L. *The sociobiology debate.* New York: Harper and Row, 1978.

Kessler, S. J., & McKenna, W. *Gender: An ethnomethodological approach.* New York: John Wiley, 1978.

Money, J. The differentiation of gender identity. Master lecture on physiological psychology: Manuscript No. 1330. Montreal, Canada: McGill-Queens University Press, 1977.

Ramey, E. Sex hormones and executive ability. *Annals of the New York Academy of Science,* 1973, *208*, 237–45.

Zubin, J., & Money, J. (ed.). *Contemporary sexual behavior: Critical issues in the 1970s.* Baltimore: Johns Hopkins University Press, 1973.

Reproduction Across the Life Span

Just before a small liberal arts college was to accept its first class of women, a high administrator was asked in an interview what the effect of adding women might be. The interview went something like this:

Q: How will the coming of the girls affect classroom procedure?

A: The male teachers' classroom methodology . . . will have to be retooled to conform to the demands of female psychology and biology. Take one fact: women menstruate. Girls taking exams just before their periods earn grades 15% lower than they usually do. Because women have one third fewer red blood cells than men, they ordinarily tire sooner and during menstruation may find it necessary to pause for rest more often. Women's brain is conditioned, as it were, by the womb, and the womb can be ignored only at the risk of treating women unfairly.

This interview did not take place in the nineteenth century, as one might have guessed, but in the early 1970s. Apparently, assumptions about the detrimental effect of women's menstrual cycle are alive and well, even today. We mention these assumptions at the beginning of this chapter because they illustrate general attitudes that directly link women's behavior to their reproductive biology.

The first of these assumptions is that women are controlled by their reproductive biology. Rather than being able to respond flexibly, as a situation requires, women must respond as determined by their biological state. An extreme reflection of this assumption was voiced by a nineteenth-century physician: "It is as if the Almighty, in creating the female sex, had taken the uterus and built up a woman around it" (Bart & Grossman, 1978, p. 337).

The second assumption is that this biological control hinders women's capabilities. At those times of the month, or during those stages of their lives when the influence of their reproductive biology is especially acute, women will be less competent, less appropriate, less effective than they otherwise are. Their reproductive biology, then, is seen as working directly against the development of their full potential.

The third assumption is that women therefore need to be protected from the harmful effect of their reproductive biology. Because women cannot respond in a situationally appropriate manner (for example, doing their best on an exam), the situation itself has to be altered or "retooled," to correspond to their lesser capabilities. Women, themselves, cannot be expected to rise to the occasion.

Finally, it is assumed that men are not similarly influenced by their reproductive biology. Before "girls" entered the institution described above, there had been no need to consider the relationship between biological events and academic performance. Women, but not men, are victims of their biology.

In this chapter, we will question the accuracy of these assumptions. We will examine three aspects of women's reproductive life; menstruation, pregnancy and menopause. For each of these events, we will ask, What is the relationship between biological events and women's behavioral and mood states? How is this relationship, in turn, affected by situational, attitudinal, and psychological factors?

To the extent that data are available, we will also discuss the relationship between reproductive biology and men's moods and behaviors in each of these three phases. Although men do not menstruate, at puberty they undergo hormonal changes that have some similarities to those responsible for the onset of menstruation in women. They may also experience hormonal fluctuations that could influence their psychological state. Men do not become pregnant, but they may be affected by the pregnancy of their wives. Men do not undergo the cessation of menstruation that occurs at menopause, but they do go through a gradual decline in hormonal levels in the middle years. Although possible links between reproductive biology and behavior in men have not been studied nearly as much as have similar links in women, the scarcity of data does not mean that such links do not exist. In examining the potential for androgyny in both sexes, one cannot assume that only women are at risk because of their reproductive biology.

THE MENSTRUAL CYCLE
Historical and Cross-cultural Attitudes to Menstruation

Women's menstrual cycle has been a source of curiosity from the earliest recorded time, across a wide variety of cultures. The most frequently described attitude to menstruation takes the form of a "menstrual taboo." A taboo, according to Ester Harding (1971), refers to something "unclean, holy, or set apart." This definition reveals the ambivalence with which menstruation has long been regarded. It is the subject of fear as well as awe; women who menstruate are to be isolated but also revered.

The element uniting fear and awe, isolation and reverence, is the *power* accorded to menstruation. Women's monthly flow of blood, appearing with mysterious regularity, suggested that women's bodies were controlled by powerful, unknown supernatural forces.

Primitive beliefs. The reactions of primitive and ancient cultures to menstruation reflect much more fear than awe. Examples abound of evils the power of menstrual blood was thought to wield. A first-century Roman, Pliny, describes potential harms that can accrue from menstrual blood:

> Contact with it turns new wine sour, crops touched by it become barren, grafts die, seed in gardens are dried up, the fruit of trees falls off, the edge of steel and the gleam of ivory are dulled, hives of bees die, even bronze

and iron are at once seized by rust, and a horrible smell fills the air; to taste it drives dogs mad and infects their bites with an incurable poison. . . . Even that very tiny creature the ant is said to be sensitive to it and throws away grains of corn that taste of it and does not touch them again (Delaney, Lupton, & Toth, 1976, p. 7).

Further evidence of the deadly impact of menstrual blood is given by Frazer in *The Golden Bough*

In Uganda, pots which a woman touches while the impurity of menstruation is upon her have to be destroyed. . . . Among the Bribri Indians of Costa Rica the only plates she may use for her food are banana leaves, which when she has done with them, she throws away in some sequestered spot; for were a cow to find them, and eat them, it would waste away. And she drinks out of a special cup for the same reason: if anyone drank out of the same cup after her, he would surely die (Weideger, 1975, p. 97).

The most common reaction of these peoples to the dangers of menstruation is to isolate the menstruating women until she is again safe. Frazier continues, "Among the Dogen of East Africa, . . . not only is a menstruating woman segregated in an isolated hut and provided with special eating utensils, but if she is seen passing through the village a general purification must take place" (Weideger, 1975, p. 97). At an extreme are the Carrier Indians of British Columbia who, according to Bettelheim, "at the onset of menstruation caused the girl to live for three or four years in complete seclusion in the wilderness, far from all beaten trails. She was considered a threat to anyone who so much as saw her; even her footsteps defiled a path or a river" (1962, p. 137). More moderate examples exist of cultures in which menstruating women were isolated in special huts, sent out to the wilderness, or forbidden from walking on paths used by men. Menstruating women have also commonly been prohibited from cooking or preparing food for men, from participating in religious activities, and from having intercourse.

But menstrual blood, as we have said, was revered as well as feared. Harding stresses the frequent connection made between women and the moon: "To primitive man, her monthly rhythm, corresponding as it does with the moon's cycle, must have seemed the obvious result of some mysterious bond between them" (1971, p. 66). This "mysterious bond" in turn became one source of the worship of women's fertility. Males, envious of women's menstruation, emulated their monthly bleeding through initiation rites of circumcision or subincision (Bettelheim, 1962). Menstrual blood was also thought to have curative powers; it has been considered able to cure, among other things, warts, goiter, hemorrhoids, epilepsy, leprosy, and headaches.

Several points, however, need to be stressed, to put the fear and awe accorded to menstruation in perspective. First, although the *image* or symbol of the menstruating woman and menstrual blood might have been worshipped, the flesh-and-bones menstruating woman never was. She was a pariah, isolated and restricted. Second, the impetus for this isolation of menstruating women was overwhelmingly the protection of men. Other women were permitted to have contact with a menstruating woman, but men were not. Men, in other words, seemed to fear women's potential power that derived from their menstrual cycles. The primary male reaction to these assumed powers was to try to control them.

Contemporary attitudes. Contemporary Western cultures do not continue the extreme reactions to menstruating women as we have seen in our examples from other cultures. Yet, more subtle forms of the same basic attitudes persist. Although menstrual blood is no longer feared, menstruation is still considered something shameful, something secretive—a "curse." Roughly half of all married couples refrain from intercourse during the woman's menstruation (Paige, 1973). Women tend to hide purchases of sanitary products in brown paper wrappers, and live with the monthly worry of being embarrassed by the stain or odors of menstrual blood. Even the common superstition of not walking under a ladder is said to derive from the fear of being stained from menstrual blood from above.

Women are also reminded of the debilitating effects that the menstrual cycle may have on their leadership capacities, or powers of decision making. Not long ago, a physician made headlines by calling attention to women's monthly "raging hormonal imbalances," which make women unfit for positions of top responsibility (Ramey, 1973). It is still assumed, then, that although cycling hormones may not make women dangerous, they do make them less than fully competent and capable.

On the other hand, women are constantly bombarded with reminders of the "normal" activities they are capable of performing during "that time." Many of these messages come through the media, sponsored by the manufacturers of sanitary products. They focus not on skills such as leadership or decision making, but rather on recreational activities that are considered to be within the woman's domain. The effect of this message is so strong that, according to one joke, a boy announced to his mother that all he wanted for Christmas was a box of Tampax. More than slightly surprised, the mother responded, "But why?" "Oh," the boy said excitedly, "then I can go swimming, and horseback riding, and hiking, and ride my bike, and play tennis as much as I want to!"

Menstruation, then, is seen as "perfectly normal" on the one hand, and a "curse" on the other hand. But neither extreme presents an accurate picture of most women's menstrual experience. Such distortions are rooted in ancient lore, and persist partly because of a conspiracy of silence among women themselves. This conspiracy of silence is illustrated by the ways preadolescent girls learn about menstruation. Materials, printed by the makers of sanitary products for girls just beginning to menstruate, minimize any physical discomfort or emotional changes associated with menstruation. Instead they emphasize thinking positive, acting normal, and above all keeping clean so that no one will "suspect" (Whisnant, Brett, & Zegans, 1975). Thus, if she has cramps, or feels a bit moody, the adolescent may begin to feel that she is somehow abnormal. This situation is compounded by the fact that many young adolescent girls look neither to their mothers nor to their friends for information, advice, or the simple sharing of feelings about menstruation (Whisnant & Zegans, 1975). Even in health classes menstruation is presented in technical terms which girls have difficulty relating to their own experiences.

If girls receive insufficient information about menstruation, boys are kept even more fully in the dark. They have little if any information at their disposal, virtually no one to discuss the events of menstruation with, and certainly no experience of their own against which to check what they hear. Thus, boys are fully vulnerable to absorbing the myths that are handed down to them. Opinions, such as the ones by the physician or the college administrator cited earlier, are the legacy of this lack of information. There is a pressing need, then, for both women and men to better understand the nature of the menstrual cycle and its effect on mood and behavior. Without such knowledge, men's and women's attitudes toward menstruation will continue to be shaped by prevailing myths and assumptions, rather than by reality.

Physiological Aspects of Puberty and Menstruation

Puberty. The onset of menstruation, menarche, is one of the major hallmarks of puberty for girls. It is typically preceded by other signs of physical maturation, including a growth spurt, the early development of breasts and female body contours, and the growth of axillary (underarm) and pubic hair. The age at which these developmental changes begin has decreased gradually in this country over the years, and now can be as early as nine years of age. Menstruation itself begins on the average at around age twelve and a half (Tanner, 1971).

The onset of puberty occurs about two years later in boys than in girls. It is characterized by a similar growth spurt, as well as a deepening of the voice and the growth of pubic, facial, and body hair. The testes and penis begin to develop to their mature size, and the production of sperm begins. Although there is no male equivalent to the onset of menstruation, it has been suggested that the onset of males' ability to ejaculate is the symbolic equivalent of menarche; both initiate the individual into adulthood (Matleson, 1975).

However, the beginning of ejaculatory capacity is not the "major hallmark" of puberty that menarche is for girls. There is little cultural lore or psychological research on the emotional and behavioral concomitants of boys' transition to adult sexual potential. Girls are acknowledged as having reached a "new state," whereas boys have no such culturally recognized demarcation. This situation may be one reason for the adolescent male initiation rites that imitate menstruation, as discussed earlier.

Yet there is reason to believe that boys' newly developed capacity for ejaculation, and their more frequent erections, may be the source of some emotional stress. Whereas girls can anticipate the timing of possible symptoms associated with the menstrual cycle, boys' erections occur irregularly and unpredictably. Thus, boys may suddenly feel out of control of their bodies, or vulnerable to having their emotions revealed in ways they had not anticipated. This, in turn, could lead to a certain amount of awkwardness, or social inhibition, especially when around female peers.

The possible association between pubertal developments and social difficulties for boys has received some confirmation in Jones and Bayley's (1950) study comparing the emotional characteristics of early- and late-maturing boys. Late-maturing boys were found to be more active, peppier, more talkative, more sociable, and more emotionally expressive than their early maturing peers. Although the authors call the behavior of the late maturing boys "childish" and "immature," it seems equally reasonable to consider that their more outgoing manner represented a social ease not shared by the early maturers. The onset of puberty, then, may be easier for boys if they are a bit older and psychologically more prepared to handle its interpersonal consequences.

For both sexes, the timing of puberty is regulated by the hypothalamus, which is a part of the brain stem. During prenatal development, as discussed in Chapter 4, prenatal hormones absorbed by the hypothalamus "program" it to increase hormonal production at puberty. This hormonal increase, in turn, signals the pituitary to initiate the bodily changes we have mentioned. Although there is some disagreement as to what causes the hypothalamus to stimulate the onset of puberty, the most widely accepted theory is that it is primarily a function of bodily weight (Frisch & Revelle, 1970).

Menstruation. The menstrual cycle, which some associate only with a monthly flow of blood, is actually a complex chain of events. Each month, the mature female's hypothalamus sets into motion a "negative feedback system," using hormones as messengers to regulate the ebb and flow of the process. Two of these hormones, estrogen and progesterone originate in the ovaries; the others come from the pituitary. There are three pituitary hormones involved in the menstrual cycle; follicle stimulating hormone (FSH), luteinizing hormone (LH), and luteotropic hormone (LTH). Their names derive from their functions. (See Figure 5.1.) These hormones communicate between the pituitary and the ovaries to alternately start and stop the biological events involved.

The menstrual cycle can be described as a twenty-eight-day cycle, starting on the first day of menstruation.[1] It is frequently divided into five stages based on changes that occur in the ovaries. (See Figure 5.2.) The first stage is the *follicular,* lasting roughly between Days 5 and 13. At this stage, FSH stimulates an ovarian follicle (a group of cells surrounding an egg) to bring that egg to maturity. As the egg ripens, the ovary begins to produce gradually increasing amounts of estrogen. When estrogen reaches a crucial level or peak, it signals the pituitary to cease producing FSH, and to begin producing LH. LH, in turn, stimulates the ovarian follicle to release its now ripened egg, which signals the second stage, *ovulation.* Although ovulation typically occurs at Day 14 in women with a regular, twenty-eight-day cycle, in women with irregular cycles it can occur at any day during the menstrual cycle (Ruble, Brooks, & Clarke, 1976). Once the egg is released, it remains viable for about forty-eight hours, during which time conception can occur. Sperm, however, can remain alive for up to four days, so that women's "unsafe period" (the time during which they can become pregnant) in fact extends from approximately four days before ovulation to two days after it.

Once the egg has been released from the ovary, the follicle collapses (much like a ruptured balloon) to form what is called the corpus luteum, or yellow body. This marks the onset of the third, or *luteal* stage, which lasts roughly from Days 15 to 25. Estrogen production, which had decreased slightly from its preovulatory

---

[1]Day 1 is usually considered the first day of menstruation, to aid women who are keeping track of their menstrual cycles. It is not, technically, the first day of the cycle.

FIGURE 5.1

The Hormone Feedback System during the Menstrual Cycle.

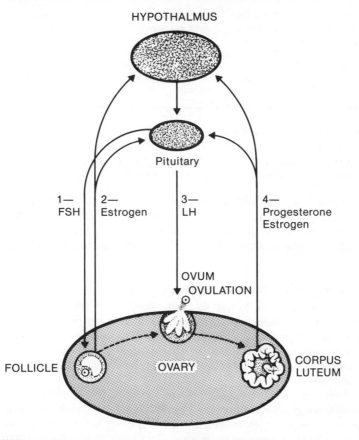

From Paula Weideger, *Menstruation and Menopause: The Physiology and Psychology, the Myth and the Reality*, p. 23 Copyright © 1975 by Paula Weideger. Reprinted by permission of Alfred A. Knopf, Inc.

peak, rises to a second peak during this phase. At the same time, the pituitary begins producing LTH, which signals the corpus luteum to begin the active production of progesterone. Progesterone also reaches its peak during the luteal stage. This high level of progesterone signals the pituitary to stop producing LTH and to begin producing FSH—starting the whole process once again.

During the luteal phase, the inner lining or endometrium of the uterus becomes endowed with an increased blood supply to nourish the fertilized egg that would become implanted in the uterus. This buildup continues only as long as progesterone, and secondarily, estrogen, are high. Once LTH ceases to be produced, however, levels of both estrogen and progesterone decline rapidly. This marks the fourth, or *premenstrual* phase of the cycle, lasting roughly from Days 25 to 28.

FIGURE 5.2

Changes in Hormone Levels over the Phases of the Menstrual Cycle.

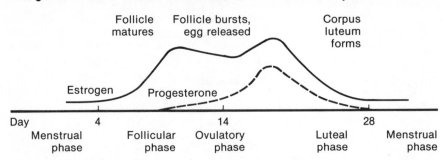

Reprinted by permission of the publisher from Janet Shibley Hyde and B. G. Rosenberg, *Half the Human Experience: The Psychology of Women* (Lexington, Mass.: D. C. Heath and Company, 1976).

Once these ovarian hormones have reached their lowest level, the buildup of the endometrium ceases, and the uterus sloughs off its increased blood supply. This marks the fifth, or *menstrual* phase (days 1–5). Although the average length of this cycle is twenty-eight days, it can be as short as twenty days, or as long as forty-five.

Psychological Correlates of the Menstrual Cycle

Many researchers have turned their attention to the relationship between hormonal cyclicity and women's psychological state. To explore this relationship from an androgynous perspective, our primary question would be, Is women's potential for incorporating masculine and feminine attributes and for behaving in flexible, situationally appropriate, effective manners, limited by their monthly hormonal fluctuations?

In order to answer this question, we need to ask, first, Is there a direct, predictable relationship between hormonal cyclicity and changes in women's mood? If there is, are the changes caused only by hormonal fluctuations, or are they also influenced by environmental conditions? For example, how do women's expectations of a relationship between mood states and stages of the menstrual cycle interact with hormonal changes in creating fluctuations in mood?

We also need to ask, If there are regular, predictable mood changes associated with menstrual cyclicity, how and to what extent do these affect women's actual functioning? Do changes in women's moods correspond to changes in their capacity for functioning appropriately and effectively? Do such changes always *decrease* functioning, or may they also enhance women's performance?

Mood and behavioral changes. A number of studies have found a direct relationship between hormonal and psychological fluctuations. Most studies report elation, activity, and increased sexual excitability at midcycle, and depression, irritability, and tension premenstrually (Coppen & Kessel, 1963; McCaulay & Ehrhardt, 1976; Sutherland & Stewart, 1965). Findings of premenstrual difficulties vary; from 15 to 95 percent of the women studied report having some premenstrual symptoms (Golub, 1976). In general, over 150 symptoms have been associated with premenstrual and menstrual distress (Sherman, 1971).

Three methods have been used to gather this data (Parlee, 1973). One approach is to look at women's memories of the behavioral and emotional symptoms they experienced at various phases of the cycle (e.g., Moos, 1968). Moos' questionnaire consists of forty-seven items, grouped into eight categories, each representing a possible menstrual-related symptom (see Table 5.1). Subjects are asked to rate on a six-point scale the extent to which they experience each of these symptoms during the menstrual, premenstrual, and intermenstrual (the remaining) phases. Using his Menstrual Distress Questionnaire (MDQ), Moos found that "approximately 30 to 50% of normal young married women are bothered to some extent by cyclical symptoms of cramps, backaches, irritability, mood swings, tension, and/or depression" (p. 863). A second approach is to examine in what phase of the cycle various problematic behaviors have occurred. Using this method, Dalton (1959, 1960, 1964) has found a greater-than-chance likelihood that women who suffer acute psychiatric illness, have accidents while flying airplanes, take their children unnecessarily to emergency rooms for treatment, or commit violent crimes are in the menstrual or premenstrual phase of their cycle.

A third approach consists of making thematic analyses of unstructured verbal material. Two studies that used this method are frequently cited. Ivey and Bardwick (1968) asked women to speak, for five minutes a day, about anything at all. They found frequent themes of anxiety, depression, hostility, and an inability to cope in stories told during the premenstrual but not the ovulatory phase of the cycle. Benedek and Rubenstein (1942) reported on the relationship between psychotherapy patients' dream material and phase of cycle. They were able to differentiate between ovulatory and premenstrual phases, using the themes of mutilation, death, anxiety, and depression that appeared in the patients' dreams only during the premenstrual phase.

TABLE 5.1 Background Data and Menstrual Cycle Variables on Total Sample (N = 839)

	Mean	S.D.
Background Data*		
Age	25.2	3.0
Education (yr.)	15.2	1.7
Length of marriage (yr.)	2.7	2.3
Menstrual Cycle Variables		
Length of cycle (days)	30.3	4.7
Length of menstrual flow (days)	5.5	2.0

Source: From R. H. Moos, "Menstrual Distress," *Psychosomatic Medicine*, Vol. XXX, No. 6 (1968), p. 857. Reprinted by permission of Elsevier North Holland, Inc.

*Of the total, 472 women have no children; 151, one child; 128, two children; 68, three children; and 30, more than three.

These studies report that hormonal cyclicity is directly related to mood fluctuations or the timing of specific problematic behaviors across the menstrual cycle. But researchers vary in the conclusions that they draw from such findings. Some feel that they suggest a causal relationship between hormonal and mood fluctuations (e.g., Bardwick, 1971). Bardwick argues, "Regular, predictable changes occur in the personality of the sexually mature woman, and these changes correlate with changes in the menstrual cycle. The personality changes occur in spite of individual personality and may even be extreme: *they are a consequence of endocrine and related physical changes*" (p. 26–27, italics added).

Other researchers are not so sure. Parlee points out that there is not yet sufficient evidence even to demonstrate a reliable relationship between hormonal and mood fluctuations:

> Psychological studies of the pre-menstrual syndrome have not as yet established the existence of a class of behaviors and moods, *researchable in more than one way,* which can be shown in a longitudinal study to fluctuate throughout the course of the menstrual cycle, or even a class of such behaviors which is regularly correlated with any particular phase of the cycle for groups of women (1973, p. 463).

The argument that Parlee and others make is based on criticisms of the studies we have looked at. They criticize the researchers' conclusions of a direct, causal relationship between hormonal and emotional cyclicity. They also point to the narrow focus of this research on the *problems* associated with menstrual cyclicity.

Consider, first, Moos' Menstrual Distress Questionnaire. As the title implies, Moos' intent was to document difficulties associated with menstrual cyclicity. Thus, he reported that 30 to 50 percent of his female subjects evidenced symptoms during the premenstrual phase, but he could as well have said that up to 70 percent of his subjects *did not* display menstrual-related distress. Moos also did not consider that his subjects' memories might have reflected their *expectations* of what they would experience during the various phases. However, when Parlee (1974) asked both male and female subjects to respond to the MDQ according to their expectations about women's menstrual-related symptoms, she found that these responses closely reflected the findings reported by Moos. Parlee concluded that the MDQ might primarily be measuring stereotypic beliefs about the psychological correlates of menstruation, rather than actual changes. Finally, Moos did not inquire about the possibility of positive mood states. The findings that women may feel pain, difficulties in concentration, and behavioral deficits during the premenstrual phase would take on different meaning if it were documented that, at the same time, they were also feeling affectionate toward others, self-confident, or successful.

Dalton's correlational studies also have methodological problems. For example, the behaviors she cited are not those which most women are likely to encounter in their lifetime. Her findings, then, pertain only to women who potentially could behave in these ways, not to the general population of women (Parlee, 1973). Also, because correlations do not imply causality, Dalton's findings do not "prove" that the women's hormonal phase caused their dysfunctional behavior. It is also possible, for example, that the stress of these events brought on an early menstrual period (Parlee, 1973; Ruble, Brooks, & Clarke, 1976).

Other weaknesses can be found in Ivey and Bardwick's study. Subjects were probably aware of the purpose of this study, since they filled out detailed questionnaires on their menstrual symptoms and recorded body temperatures to determine their time of ovulation. Therefore, it is very likely that, like the women in Moos' study, these women were influenced by what they expected their moods to be at various phases in their cycles.

Thus, although these studies reported evidence of negative mood states and problematic behaviors associated with the premenstrual or menstrual phases, weaknesses in method limit the usefulness of their findings. Specifically, there were no attempts to document the effect of women's expectations on their responses, or to measure any changes in daily behavior associated with mood fluctuations. Further, they said little about positive mood states that might have been associated with menstrual cyclicity. To examine these issues, we must look at additional research.

Situational and attitudinal influences. Studies examining the effect of hormonal fluctuations on a wide variety of behaviors suggest that women's actual daily behaviors are far less variable than their mood states. Sommer (1973) reviewed fifteen such studies, covering such aspects as production-line performance, athletic ability, activity level, reaction time, perceptual motor performance, and results of intelligence testing. She discovered few significant findings when performance levels at different phases of the menstrual cycle were compared. Sommer concluded, along with many of the researchers she cited, that "most objective performance measures failed to demonstrate a menstrual cycle related effect" (1973, p. 532). In a separate study, Sommer (1972) investigated the effects of menstrual cyclicity on women's intellectual performance. She found, in college-age subjects, no significant relationship between average test scores and stages of menstrual cyclicity.

Several studies are also beginning to document the effect of attitudes and expectations on menstrual-related symptoms. For example, Ruble (1976) arbitrarily told some women that, using sophisticated tests, she could tell that they were about to get their period; she told other women that they were between periods. She found that the women who thought they were premenstrual reported more symptoms than those who thought they were intermenstrual. In addition, it has been found that women who expect problems during the premenstrual phase are likely to have more of such problems (Paige, 1973), or to attribute problems during that time to phase of cycle rather than to other experiences in their lives (Koeske & Koeske, 1975). Attitudes toward menstruation itself can also affect premenstrual distress; women with less favorable attitudes tend to have more premenstrual complaints than those with more favorable attitudes (Levitt & Lubin, 1967).

Thus, both hormonal factors and expectations bear on the relationship between menstrual cyclicity and fluctuations in mood and behavior. Further, moods seem more readily affected than behavior. Despite periodic headaches, bouts of depression, or anxiety, women seem, in general, to be able to proceed with "business as usual." If this is true, then "raging hormones" may have little to do with determining women's destiny.

In addition, if women were not led to expect negative mood states during the premenstrual phase, they might pay less attention to these states. Mild anxiety or depression might be recognized, but accepted as a matter of course rather than as feelings that seriously impair aspects of one's life. Perhaps it is the "raging menstrual taboo," rather than hormones, which should be implicated in women's menstrual-related symptoms.

Increased knowledge about positive mood states associated with menstrual cyclicity could also help to put the negative mood states in perspective. Indications do exist that women's moods are elevated during the ovulatory phase (Bardwick, 1971; Benedek & Rubenstein, 1942; Coppen & Kessel, 1963; Ivey & Bardwick, 1968). Feelings of higher self-esteem, increased sexual desire, and elation are generally reported. However, these suggestive findings have not been pursued with nearly the vigor that findings on depressed mood have been. Certainly, there has been no attempt to label moods associated with the ovulatory phase as a "midcycle peak" to correspond with the label of a "premenstrual syndrome" (Parlee, 1973). For the study of androgyny, it is essential that the full range of women's mood and behavioral fluctuations be examined. This could provide knowledge about hormonal and attitudinal factors associated with competence, well-being, and strength in women, to balance those studies which focus on women's menstrual-related difficulties.

Studies of positive mood fluctuations during the menstrual cycle could focus specifically on the ovulatory phase, when these moods are reported to be at their peak. A number of pertinent questions could be explored. Do women who expect a midcycle emotional peak experience a higher mood elevation than those who do not hold such expectations? Are these emotional peaks associated with better performance or improved interpersonal relationships? Do women who are satisfied with their life circumstances report higher mood elevations than women who are dissatisfied? To the extent that hormonal and attitudinal factors influence women's premenstrual state, there seems reason to believe that these same factors would affect women's state at midcycle.

Studies could also explore the effect of positive mood fluctuations across the entire menstrual cycle. Because most studies focus only on negative mood, knowledge about how negative and positive feelings interact is scarce. It is not enough to know simply that negative or positive moods are low or high. At any given time, both mood states could be high or low, or one could be elevated while the other was depressed.

Initial evidence on the relation of both positive and negative mood states to menstrual cyclicity is provided by Rossi and Rossi (1977). As one aspect of their comprehensive study, Rossi and Rossi had sixty-seven female college or university students make daily ratings of positive and negative mood states over a forty-day span. Positive moods were included because "in the literature on menstrually linked moods, there is an implicit assumption with no empirical base to support it, that discomfort, pain, and depression associated with pre-menstrual and menstrual phases of many women necessarily means that women do not also feel happy and loving" (p. 282). Both positive and negative moods were subdivided into bodily-linked or psychological moods. Bodily-linked moods included feelings such as healthy (positive) or sick (negative); psychological moods included feelings like happy (positive) or depressed (negative).

In general, Rossi and Rossi found that changes in positive moods were not related to changes in negative moods. For example, although they found an increase in negative moods in the menstrual phase, there was not a corresponding decrease in positive moods at that time. Nor was the elevation of positive moods during the ovulatory phase accompanied by a decrease in negative moods. Thus, the effect of mood states at these times may be less than is suggested by researchers who have not explored the relationship between fluctuations in positive and negative moods.

Rossi and Rossi also compared patterns of mood fluctuations by the month (defined in terms of the biologically based menstrual cycle) and by the week (a social construction having no biological counterpart). They found that women's positive moods were influenced both by the menstrual month and the social week; they tended to peak on the weekend and reach their lowest point on Tuesdays. Negative moods varied more as a function of phase of menstrual cycle than day of the week. Thus, for their college-age sample, feelings of elation were influenced both by phase of menstrual cycle and by the increase in social activities that the weekend provided.

Mood and Hormonal Fluctuations in Men

In contrast to the large number of studies on the hormonal correlates of psychological fluctuations in women, there are few studies on hormonal or mood cyclicity in men. However, there is some evidence that male sex hormones undergo regular, cyclical patterns. The timing of these patterns varies from one study to another, but in general two distinct patterns have emerged: a three- to five-day cycle, and a twelve- to eighteen-day cycle (Harkness, 1974).

Even less evidence is available on the relationship between this cyclicity and males' psychological state. However, Ramey (1972) offers some informal evidence that males' moods also follow a regular, cyclical pattern. According to Ramey, low states for men are characterized by apathy, indifference, or a tendency to magnify minor problems. High periods are characterized by a feeling of well-being, a lower body weight, and a decreased need for sleep.

Not only may men's moods undergo regular fluctuations, but their feelings may be directly related to their bodily states. Rossi and Rossi (1977), who included fifteen university men in their study, found that the men felt achy, sick, and crampy as often as the women did, and that these states of physical discomfort were related *more* highly to negative psychological mood states in the men than in the women. The authors suggest that the women, who go through menstrual cycles every month, have learned to tolerate some physical discomfort without letting it affect their mood. Men, however, may have more of a psychological reaction, because their bodily changes are not predictable.

Several factors may account for the paucity of information on hormonal and psychological fluctuations in men. Although males' hormones may undergo regular cycles, there is no visible, monthly sign, equivalent to women's monthly menstrual flow. Thus, men themselves have no ready basis for expecting periodic changes in their mood and behavior. Cultural lore reinforces this individual experience. There are no myths or taboos regarding cyclicity in men; no prevailing expectations that men will regularly have some good days and some bad days, determined by their bodily states. The absence of information on cyclicity in men may also reflect the hesitation of male researchers to investigate this topic. Ramey (1972) suggests, along this line, that males hold to the myth of their own biological stability, and thus fail to seek evidence that might suggest that, like women, they are subject to periodic hormonal and psychological fluctuations.

Another Look

We have seen that both hormonal and environmental factors converge to create a cyclical pattern of women's emotional states. According to most studies, mood elevations occur at midcycle when estrogen levels are high, whereas moods depressions occur during the premenstrual and menstrual phases when both estrogen and progesterone are low. However, as we explained more fully in Chapter 4, this does not mean that all women will follow this mood cycle, or that hormones are the only factors to influence mood cyclicity. Strong societal expectations that women will become anxious or depressed premenstrually probably heighten their awareness of any changes in feeling at this time, and lead them to attribute such changes to phase of cycle rather than to other events in their lives.

There is much less evidence that these fluctuations in mood affect women's actual behavior. Although behavioral changes have been studied less than mood changes, most of the evidence suggests that women's performance levels are unrelated to their phase of cycle. There is reason to believe, then, that women's capacities for flexibility and effectiveness are not hampered in any measurable way by menstrual-related mood fluctuations. Conversely, there is little evidence to suggest that women are behaviorally constrained by their "raging hormones."

Much less is known about hormonal, mood, and behavioral cyclicity in men. There is some evidence that male hormones and moods undergo regular, cyclical patterns, but such evidence is still at a rudimentary stage. However, men's moods are affected by their bodily states more so than women's, because men have no basis for predicting bodily changes. Whereas women are trained to overreact to mood fluctuations that parallel bodily states, men are trained to underreact to them. For both sexes, a more realistic appraisal of the relationships among bodily state, mood, and behavior would promote more successful management of these changes.

PREGNANCY AND CHILDBIRTH

Pregnancy and childbirth represent major turning points in the lives of women. Biologically and psychologically, women undergo permanent changes. Virtually every system in the woman's body is affected by her pregnant state. The status of "mother," once attained, remains with women whether or not they are in close proximity to their children, and it can have a major effect on their self-image, producing an "altered state of consciousness" (Coleman & Coleman, 1971).

Unlike other biological turning points such as menarche and menopause, the changes of pregnancy are not a private experience. Pregnancy, far more than the other two stages, is an interpersonal event. Although women undergoing menarche and menopause are not readily identifiable by others, the pregnant woman, after the first few months, is obvious. Being pregnant, then, can affect virtually all of her personal interactions. Pregnancy, as compared to the other two stages, is also far more of a family experience. If the woman is married, her pregnancy will become a major aspect of her relationship with her husband. It will also have some effect on her relationship with members of her family of origin, particularly her mother. Finally, the pregnant woman has a new relationship—with the fetus growing inside of her—and fantasies about her relationship with her child once it is born.

The biological, psychological, and interpersonal events of pregnancy place major demands on women's capacities for communal and agentic responses. The future mother must deal directly with her abilities to nurture, her skills in and attitudes about the constant daily care of a helpless newborn. At the same time, she is faced with the task of maintaining some control over her own life apart from the demands of infant care, and the expectations of doctors, husband, and other family members. She must also try to maintain some control over the physical changes her body is going through, and the highly demanding, physical "work" of childbirth. Pregnancy and childbirth, then, are major challenges to a woman's capacity for androgyny.

In this section, we will explore cultural attitudes, biological changes, and psychological states that bear on women's experiences of pregnancy and childbirth. We will pay special attention to factors that affect a woman's capacity for both nurturance—caring for another—and independence—caring for herself. What circumstances seem to foster women's maximum growth in both of these directions? Do some factors of pregnancy and childbirth seem to mitigate development of the dual capabilities for nurturance and self-maintenance?

Contemporary Attitudes Toward Pregnancy

Contemporary American society gives a double message to the future mother. On the one hand, it describes pregnancy as a "state of bliss," a condition through which women can reach their ultimate fulfillment as women (Peck & Senderowitz, 1974). It sees pregnancy as a means through which women can confirm their status as adults in society, their independence from their families of origin, and their fertility. Pregnancy, then, is seen as confirmation of one's "womanhood."

On the other hand, pregnant women are frequently treated as needy, incapacitated, or even alien beings. Images abound of the pregnant woman craving for bizarre foods, being extremely moody and irrational, and being unable to perform her normal daily tasks. For many years, laws existed to "protect" pregnant women (or to protect others from exposure to pregnancy) by requiring that they leave their jobs as soon as they become visibly pregnant. Childbirth itself, usually occuring in the sterile confines of a hospital and without the presence of close family members, conveyed the image of the pregnant woman as ill, rather than as going through a normal, albeit difficult, process.

Pregnancy can also be responded to as a social stigma (Taylor & Langer, 1977). In studying responses to pregnant women, Taylor and Langer found that when strangers passed pregnant women on the street, they would stare and avoid contact with them. In an elevator, people were more likely to choose to stand near a nonpregnant than a pregnant woman. There is a subtle, daily reminder to pregnant women, then, that they are different, strange, or set apart.

Neither state of bliss nor time of illness and incapacitation describes the experience of pregnancy for most women. Thus, the exaggerated messages that women receive do little to help them cope realistically with their own feelings about their pregnancy. If women are concerned about respecting their own needs while caring for an infant, they may feel they are violating the image of "maternal bliss." If they feel more moody or more needy than usual, an overresponse to this by others can lead them to question their basic competence. Contemporary attitudes to pregnancy, then, do little to assist pregnant women in maintaining a realistic balance of their concerns about nurturance and independence.

Biological Aspects

Pregnancy. The biology of pregnancy begins with the ovulatory phase of the menstrual cycle. If the egg is fertilized by union with a sperm, it continues down the Fallopian tube, floats in the uterus for about nine days, and then becomes implanted in the lining of the uterus. The uterus, rather than sloughing its increased blood supply through menstruation, continues to be enriched by nutrients supplied by the mother's blood stream. Thus, the absence of a menstrual period is often the first visible sign that a woman may be pregnant, although some pregnant women continue to have short menstrual periods for one or two months.

In the early weeks of pregnancy, the placenta begins to develop. This is a large mass of tissue attached to the uterine wall and connected to the fetus by the umbilical cord. Through this cord, nutrients and oxygen that will sustain fetal development are passed from the mother to the infant, and waste materials are expelled. At the same time, the placenta serves as a barrier, protecting the fetus from certain harmful agents and organisms present in the mother, although some harmful agents, such as drugs, can be passed from mother to fetus. Maternal and fetal blood systems, however, remain completely separate (Friedman, 1978).

The placenta also functions as an endocrine gland, producing a variety of hormones during pregnancy, including vast amounts of estrogen and progesterone. Before the end of pregnancy, estrogen levels will be 1000 times as strong, and progesterone levels 100 times as strong as before pregnancy (Sherman, 1971). Under the influence of the placental hormones, the uterine muscle undergoes tremendous growth, necessary for the contractions that will occur at birth. These hormones also prepare the breasts for lactation after delivery, and are generally responsible for maintaining the state of pregnancy.

The nine months of pregnancy are typically described in trimesters. In the first trimester, the breasts begin to swell and the nipples become more sensitive. Other bodily changes might include a frequent need to urinate, increased fatigue, and a temporary diminuation in appetite. "Morning sickness" (nausea and vomiting) in early pregnancy may occur, but it is not nearly as frequent as it was thirty years ago (Guttmacher, 1973).

The fetus is at greatest risk during the first trimester, when it is undergoing rapid organ formation and maturation. Exposure to maternal illness, radiation, or certain drugs may harm it during this time. The first trimester is also the time when miscarriages, or spontaneous abortions, are most likely to occur. Spontaneous abortions occur quite frequently and may account for the termination of as many as one in five pregnancies (Friedman, 1978). A woman who has had one miscarriage is at no greater risk for subsequent miscarriages than is any other woman.

If a woman decides to abort her fetus, it is also far preferable that the abortion take place during the first trimester. Within the first twelve weeks, abortion can be performed by means of curettage (scraping of the uterine lining) or by use of a vacuum aspirator, which removes the fetal tissue through suction. After this time, a substance must be injected into the uterine cavity to induce labor. This process requires hospitalization and is a much more major undertaking.

During the second trimester, the pregnancy becomes visible. The abdomen swells, fetal movement can be felt, and the fetal heartbeat can be detected. The breasts become fully prepared for nursing during this time, and may emit a thin, yellow substance called colostrum. The physical symptoms experienced during the first trimester are usually gone, so for many women this is the most pleasant time of pregnancy. Sexual desire may also increase during this time, possibly as a result of increased vaginal lubrication.

During the last trimester, physical discomfort generally increases. Pregnant women are now carrying an extra twenty to thirty pounds, so their movements may become slow and encumbered. They may also experience some pain from the weight of the fetus bearing down on them. The fetus becomes quite active, which can interfere with the mother's sleep. And because of the woman's increased size, sexual intercourse may become awkward.

Childbirth. The average pregnancy lasts for 280 days, and most women give birth within ten days of this time. The onset of regular, frequent labor pains caused by uterine contractions marks the beginning of the process of childbirth. Labor pains have a characteristic all their own. They are marked by a gradual increase in strength, which remains at a peak briefly, and then decreases. The pregnant woman can feel the hardening and then softening of her abdomen as the pain rises and falls.

Labor is typically divided into three stages. During the first, which begins with the onset of labor pains, the cervix—a small opening at the end of the uterus through which the baby must exit—begins to dilate, or increase in size. This increase is caused by the uterine contractions, and takes place over approximately twelve hours for a woman who is having her first baby, usually less for a woman who has already given birth. The first stage of labor is considered over when the cervix has increased to a diameter of ten centimeters. Labor pains have been increasing in frequency and duration during this stage, reaching their peak of intensity as the cervix dilates the last two centimeters, a time often referred to as the "transitional phase."

During the second stage of labor, the baby exits from the uterus through the cervix, and moves down through the vagina. This process is also accomplished by means of uterine contractions, but the woman can play an active role here by pushing down with her abdominal muscles. The sensation accompanying this pushing is not nearly as painful as the first stage of labor, and is described by some women as pleasurable or even orgasmic (Ostrum, 1975). If the baby is in the typical head-first position, the pressure of the head on the vaginal opening causes it to stretch tremendously. Because there is a risk that the vaginal opening may tear as the baby is born, obstetricians in the United States frequently make a small cut, called an episiotomy, in the surrounding tissue to enlarge the opening. Gradually the top of the baby's head begins to appear as the vaginal opening stretches. The head and shoulders emerge first, after which the rest of the baby slides out easily and the baby is born.

The third stage of labor consists of the delivery of the placenta. This is accomplished with a few mild uterine contractions and usually takes only a few minutes. During this stage, there is a marked drop in estrogen levels. Progesterone levels are already low, having decreased during the second stage. If an episiotomy has been performed, it is closed with a few stitches, and delivery is completed.

Emotional Aspects of Pregnancy

The woman's reaction. The state of pregnancy has a profound effect on a woman's emotional life. It highlights a woman's awareness of her own body, and hence women often become greatly preoccupied with themselves during this time (Chertok, 1969; Nadelson, 1978). The feelings associated with this preoccupation contain aspects of both ecstacy and anxiety. Women may feel deep pride and joy regarding the future role of mother and the presence of a newborn infant. At the same time, they may worry about their capacity for motherhood or their physical and sexual attractiveness while pregnant. Ambivalence may arise over earlier decisions regarding a balance of home and career. Women who had decided to continue with their profession might regret the idea of time not spent with their newborn, whereas women who had opted to stay home might begin to fear the loss of their identity. In general, pregnancy is described as a time of emotional liability (Parks, 1951; Tobin, 1957), not so much as a sign of emotional distress, but rather as a natural reaction to the multitude of changes that are occuring.

The emotional reactions to pregnancy have been described as paralleling the biological states of pregnancy (Coleman & Coleman, 1971; Turner & Izzi, 1978). As a woman's body grows increasingly large, and as the time of birth grows nearer, women's feelings about themselves and others may change.

Initial feelings involve motivations to become pregnant. There are relative degrees to which pregnancy may actually be planned. Some women make a conscious choice to become pregnant. Others precipitate the event by failing to use birth control measures, although they had not made a real decision to become pregnant. These "semiplanned" pregnancies may occur when a woman is facing a transitional point in her life, such as a decision to return to school, or a change in profession, or a feeling that her marriage has reached a difficult stage (Shapiro, 1979). Unconscious factors may also affect motivations to become pregnant. These can include a woman's fantasy that a baby will guarantee someone to love her, a wish to experience the kind of mothering she never had by identifying with her infant, or a feeling that being pregnant will confirm her identity as a woman (Nadelson, 1978; Turner & Izzi, 1978).

During the first trimester of pregnancy, the woman deals with what it means to be pregnant and to be a future mother. According to Coleman and Coleman (1971), this stage involves the most self-reflection, and the most concern with formulating one's identity as a mother. Many women think about their own childhood, and how their style of mothering will compare with that of their own mothers. They may wish to be better mothers than their own mothers were, but may simultaneously experience guilt at the thought of succeeding where their own mothers failed. These thoughts exist even for women who have already had children, because there is the hope that one's ability to mother will improve with each successive child. During this stage, women may also begin the process that will continue throughout and after their pregnancy of working out a new relationship with their mothers (Shereshefsky, Plotsky, & Lockman, 1974).

In the second trimester of pregnancy, the focal point shifts to coming to terms with the reality of the baby inside one, made vivid by a new ability to feel the baby move. Concerns shift from one's identity as a mother to the integration of the baby into one's life. As a result, a married woman's attention centers now not on her mother, but rather on her husband. There is a strong wish for the husband to share in the experience of pregnancy, through feeling the fetal movements and watching the contours of his wife's body change. The pregnancy becomes much more of an interpersonal event than it was during the first trimester.

The second trimester is considered the most pleasant time of pregnancy. It is during this time that a woman is most likely to feel the "glow of pregnancy." The movement of the baby inside her, and the acknowledgement of others that she is pregnant can create eager anticipation of the baby that is to come.

At the same time, the woman becomes aware that her body is changing in ways that she cannot control. She also cannot monitor the progress of the growing fetus. Thus, she may feel some anxiety over the health of the fetus, and fear that her husband will no longer find her physically and sexually attractive. This fear is especially acute because of heightened sexual desires during this phase. Not knowing how bodily changes will affect her freedom of movement, a woman may also need reassurance that her husband will be able to care for her when necessary, and take over the chores that she is no longer able to perform.

During the third trimester, the woman begins to prepare herself and her home for the birth that is soon to occur. Although up to 50 percent of women in the first trimester indicate that they do not want their pregnancy, by the third trimester few women voice this sentiment (Coleman & Coleman, 1971). Much of their time is spent in active preparation for the baby, and in helping others in their family adjust to the imminent arrival.

During the third trimester, feelings related to motherhood and to self-control become pronounced. On the one hand, women may feel "an almost mystical identification with a primitive feminine principle within them, and a closeness with the reproductive, generative elements of the species and, indeed, of all living organisms" (Coleman & Coleman, 1971, p. 51). On the other hand, those who leave their jobs during this time may feel a direct threat to their self-esteem, fearing that they may never again regain their level of professional competence. The full meaning of both the expansive joys of motherhood and the possible restrictions that motherhood can entail become highlighted.

The man's reaction.   Many men feel an intense pride in learning of a pregnancy, seeing this as proof of their "manliness." This pride may be mixed with anxiety, however, if the man doesn't feel financially prepared to support a child, or if the couple is not married. Some women may also resent the pride that men express, if it implies that the woman has become the vehicle for the man's accomplishment.

During the first trimester, men begin to redefine their relationship to their wife. They become aware that they are no longer as central to their wife's feelings as they once had been. As their wives turn inward during this time, men may feel rejected and turn to friends for companionship. Men may be pleased by the demands their wives make of them, enjoying protecting them if they are feeling nauseous or excessively tired. However, if these demands become too frequent, men may become resentful.

The first trimester is also the time that men begin to consider their self-image as a father. For many, this image centers on their capacity as breadwinner. They may therefore reevaluate their job status, seek extra sources of income. These financial concerns often are not based on actual financial needs of the family; rather, they are stimulated by the man's growing concern about his own competence (Shapiro, 1979).

During the second trimester, men have the first opportunity directly to experience the growing fetus through feeling the fetal movements. This permits them a direct contact with the pregnancy that was not possible during the first trimester. Observable changes in their wife's body can also have a strong effect. Men may find themselves thinking back to their own childhood, or trying to imagine what it would be like to be pregnant. Men may feel an intense jealousy of the woman's capacity to be pregnant, or fearful of a woman whose body contains a living being within it. These more primitive feelings can be especially intense for men who are not sensitive to the feminine aspects of their own personality (Coleman & Coleman, 1971). However, if men are able to acknowledge the feminine longings that their wives' pregnancy evokes, this can be a time of personal growth and mutual support for the couple.

By the third trimester, most men have begun to resolve the conflicts around their own competence, competition with the newborn, and recognition of the feminine longings within their own personality. If these feelings are not adequately handled during the third trimester, men may find themselves becoming emotionally distant from their wives' pregnancy. But if these feelings are handled well, the couple may feel an intensity in their relationship that had not been present during the earlier stages of pregnancy.

Emotional and Situational Aspects of Childbirth

Childbirth is perhaps the most difficult and taxing work a woman will face during her adult life. Not only will she undergo many hours of discomfort and pain, but the bodily events of childbirth themselves are out of her control. Although a woman can have some effect on the physical conditions surrounding childbirth and on her attitude toward labor and delivery, she cannot change the course of her bodily processes once labor begins.

This loss of control seems to be the most important psychological dimension of the experience of labor and delivery (Coleman & Coleman, 1971). Many of a woman's emotional reactions to childbirth, then, center on the ways in which she, and other members of her family, attempt to shape and influence the processes of labor and delivery.

Some of the factors influencing the experience of childbirth are those over which a woman can have little say. For example, age and physical condition can have a determining influence. Young women (under the age of twenty) usually have shorter labors than older women (over the age of thirty), and first births are almost always longer than subsequent births. A woman who is in good physical health and who has had an adequate diet during pregnancy will probably have an easier labor than a woman who is not in as good physical condition.

But although labor may be shorter for women under twenty, there are some serious problems associated with the growing number of adolescents who are becoming mothers (Babikian & Goldman, 1971). Adolescent mothers are more likely than older women to have difficulties during labor and delivery, and to give birth to premature, low-weight infants. Infants born to adolescents are more likely to die than are infants born to older women; adolescent mothers themselves are more likely to die or to suffer illness or injury from complications of pregnancy (Alan Guttmacher Institute, 1976).

Cultural attitudes can also have an influence on a woman's experience of childbirth. Longer labors tend to occur in cultures in which pregnancy and childbirth are surrounded by fear and anxiety. Short, less difficult labors occur where there are more relaxed and casual attitudes toward childbirth (Mead & Newton, 1967). Childbirth has also been found to be shortened and less painful in cultures with a relaxed attitude toward sexuality (Rossi, 1977).

The two primary areas over which women can assert some influence are the physical surroundings of the birth and the management of pain. The vast majority of women choose to give birth in a hospital, under the care of a physician. Although their decision is usually motivated by the safety and medical attention a hospital can provide, there is some question about the value to health of a hospital delivery. Despite the sophisticated techniques of delivery practiced in the United States, fourteen industrial nations have lower rates of infant mortality (Seiden, 1978). Some women are also uncomfortable with the sterile, impersonal conditions surrounding hospital delivery. Because of these considerations, a few women are considering alternatives to traditional hospital deliveries. Some decide on a modified hospital delivery, in a "birthing room," in the presence of their husband as well as medical staff. Others, especially those who do not anticipate complicated deliveries, may give birth at home, with a doctor or midwife present, surrounded by family and friends.

A growing number of women are opting to gain mastery over the pain of childbirth by preparing for what is generally called "natural childbirth." Using either the "childbirth without fear" technique of Grantly Dick-Read (1953) or the method introduced by the French physician Lamaze (1958), these women learn to strengthen their bodies and control labor pains, permitting them to remain in control of the birth process and to refrain from using medication unless necessary. Husbands participate in the training along with their wives, and are encouraged to remain with their wives during labor and delivery. Under these conditions, childbirth becomes an experience for the couple, not just for the woman alone, and is treated more as a normal life event than as an illness.

A number of factors bear on a woman's choice of the physical conditions of labor and delivery. Women vary in their attitude toward and tolerance for pain. Those who place a premium on the avoidance of pain will probably decide to rely on local or general anesthetics to minimize physical discomfort. Also, some women want to play an active role in childbirth, whereas others are eager to place themselves in the hands of a competent physician.

Natural childbirth is not an option that is equally available to all women. Training classes, to some extent, tend to be oriented to middle- or upper-middle-class women (Ostrum, 1975). In addition, the focus on the active role of the husband might exclude young, unmarried mothers—women whose own sense of mastery over their pregnancy is likely to be lowest (Seiden, 1978). It is currently estimated that 10 percent of American women will become pregnant during the high school years, and most will keep their babies although not marry (Seiden, 1978). Therefore, although the use of natural childbirth has widened in recent years, it cannot yet be seen as a general, easily available method for all women to seek control over labor and delivery.

Decisions about the physical conditions of labor and delivery are best made on the basis of a woman's clear understanding of her own needs and wishes. There is no "best" way to undergo childbirth, no set of conditions that are optimal for everyone. There is some evidence that women who undergo and use training in natural childbirth will have a more personally satisfying experience of childbirth. On the basis of a comparative study of women who gave birth with and without training in natural childbirth, Chertok (1969) concluded that the women who actively and consciously participated in childbirth showed greater satisfaction with their experience and desire to have similar circumstances for any subsequent births. However, these results would probably not hold if women who did not wish to do so were coerced into natural childbirth.

Whatever steps women may have taken to control the circumstances surrounding their delivery, while in labor, they depend on the people around them (Coleman & Coleman, 1971). The attitudes of those others, including medical personnel and perhaps the husband, will greatly affect a woman's experience. Warm, caring, and frequent attention will go far in increasing a woman's feeling of pride, competence, and trust. Yet even with the best of care, labor can involve a certain amount of emotional stress. Because of the extent of their discomfort, some women may feel isolated, irrationally angry, or suspicious. Having to look mainly to others to provide comfort, women can come to feel that nothing anyone can do will be enough, and that nobody can understand what they are going through.

As labor moves toward transition and actual birth begins, many of these feelings dissipate. Once the baby begins to exit from the uterus the woman can take an active role in assisting the birth by bearing down with each contraction. The actual birth of the baby will produce a flood of emotions—relief, ecstacy, vitality. Despite the strains of the last many hours, women report feeling "transformed, renewed, and radiant" after delivery (Coleman and Coleman, 1971, p. 76). Whether or not they have given birth before, most women experience the moment of childbirth as an intense, exhilarating time.

Childbirth is also a powerful task; in Seiden's words, it is "an aggressive and libidinal task—tough and demanding" (1978, p. 91). To the extent that women are trained to be traditionally feminine, they are poorly prepared for the active work of childbirth. Newton (1974) has found that high femininity scores on traditional tests of masculinity-femininity have a low correlation with confident delivery, successful breastfeeding, and related attitudes and behaviors. Most women are taught to anticipate the "glow of pregnancy," but are given little training throughout life in mastery of pain and self-confidence; thus they may have difficulty bringing these qualities to the process of childbirth.

Similarly, especially if it is a first birth, the newly delivered mother has probably had little training in the daily care of the newborn. She may be assisted for a few days in the hospital, but after that most women are isolated in their homes with the demanding responsibilities of child care. Some researchers believe this is responsible for the feelings of irritability and unhappiness that are fairly common in the first few weeks after childbirth (Parlee, 1975; Rossi, 1968). Most women manage to cope; serious psychological depression seems to affect only about two women in every thousand (Brown & Shereshefsky, 1972). Yet the conditions of early infant care can place a great strain on women's feelings of mastery and self-confidence. Neither their education nor their immediate environment offers much assistance in easing women into motherhood.

The man's reaction. The fact that only women can bear children serves as a profound distinction between the sexes. There is some evidence that men may envy women's capacity for childbirth. In some cultures, for example, when their wives are in labor, husbands go through an imitation birth ritual known as *couvade.* They retire to their bed, act out the pain and struggles of labor, and finally go through the motions of giving birth. On occasion, they may remain in bed for days or even weeks, while being cared for by women in the community (Thurn, 1883). According to Bettleheim (1962), the practice of couvade serves men's need to fill the emotional vacuum created by their inability to bear children.

In contemporary Western society, there is no culturally determined role for the expectant father. In fact, in the majority of deliveries, the husband does not join his wife during either labor or delivery, but waits separately until the birth is announced. Some are excluded because of hospital regulations, while others may decline to participate, even if invited by the hospital staff to do so. Men may feel helpless and incompetent in the face of the ensuing events. Or, they may be disturbed by their wives' pain, or fear that they will feel ill if they witness the procedures involved. For the most part, training is needed to prepare a man to be a participant in childbirth.

For those men who do choose to join their wives, their role is at best a supportive one. There is no way that they can speed the process of birth, or share the pain of a contraction. For men accustomed to being "in charge," this may be a difficult situation. However, as the hours go on, they may find increasing pleasure in the real comfort they can provide their wives. If they have undertaken training in natural childbirth, they can help their wives pace their breathing and find a suitable bodily position. Even when they are not actively helping, they may be aware that simply by being there, they are giving support.

The actual delivery of the baby can be as much a peak emotional experience for the husband as it is for the wife. Without any assigned tasks during this time, he can be a total observer, and take in the full emotional effect of this event. It is also speculated that the husband's presence during labor and delivery will greatly increase the likelihood of his continued active involvement with the child after birth (Coleman & Coleman, 1971).

Another Look

Pregnancy and childbirth are times of major bodily and emotional changes for women. During pregnancy, a woman must adjust to the growing fetus inside of her, and the associated changes in hormonal levels and bodily contours. Emotionally, she is faced with forming a self-identity as a mother and anticipating the entry of the child into her current life. Issues of nurturance and independence prevail, as the woman deals with her caretaking abilities and her potential for maintaining an independent life apart from her child.

Men's reactions are based not on biological changes going on inside of them, but the changes they can observe in their wives. Pregnancy can stir up feelings of competition, of threats to their competence, of envy of the woman's capacity for childbirth. Men must also cope with their identity as fathers and the meaning the newborn will have for them.

Childbirth confronts both men and women with the need to cope with the bodily process of delivery over which neither has control. Women can attempt to structure the conditions of labor and delivery to best meet their needs, but men have no socially determined role in childbirth. They must therefore decide how active a position to take in assisting their wives. For both sexes, childbirth can be a time of stress, but also of great exhilaration.

Pregnancy and childbirth, then, are neither times of unmitigated bliss nor of helplessness and depression. For both sexes, they involve emotional changes and alterations in the life style, changes that are consistent with productive functioning and emotional growth. Acceptance of the emotional work of pregnancy and childbirth—the needs for dependency and mastery—can go far in making pregnancy and childbirth the rewarding experience that it can be.

MENOPAUSE

The final stage in the reproductive cycle for women is the menopause. This is a relatively short time, of one to two years, in which the ovaries cease producing eggs, ovarian hormones drop markedly, and menstruation ceases. Menopause, then, marks the end of women's reproductive capacity.

Menopause is a part of a broader process of physiological changes in later life known as the *climacteric*. The climacteric, which can last from fifteen to twenty years, is characterized by many changes in bodily systems and processes, and occurs in both men and women. During these years, men's levels of sex hormones gradually decrease, as does their potency and the production of sperm. However, men do not go through a rapid transitional period equivalent to the female menopause.

Because of the more dramatic nature of the menopause in women, their physical symptoms and emotional reactions during this time have received much more attention than parallel reactions in men. This greater attention is reflected in larger numbers of studies on the female menopause than on the male experience of the climacteric. It is also reflected in the greater prevalence of myths and assumptions regarding women's menopausal difficulties. This imbalance of knowledge creates a belief that women, far more than men, are hampered by the physiological changes of their later years.

This situation, for a psychology of androgyny, raises several questions parallel to those addressed in the discussion of the menstrual cycle. First, are women at greater disadvantage than men because of their physical and emotional symptoms associated with menopause? In other words, do the physiological changes associated with menopause serve as a barrier to women's androgynous development? Second, what are the relative effects of biological and societal factors in shaping women's experience of menopause? Are the difficulties associated with menopause inevitable, or do they also reflect culture-bound conditions related to women's role, and societal views about the older woman? In looking at the interaction between biological and environmental influences on menopause, our concern will be with those which affect women's potential for behaving flexibly and controlling their lives during the menopausal and postmenopausal years.

Hormonal Aspects

The onset of menopause usually occurs in women between the ages of forty-eight and fifty-two. There is a marked reduction in the levels of progesterone and estrogen produced by the ovaries, although the pituitary gland continues producing FSH and may even increase its production, since the ovarian hormones no longer trigger its cessation. The monthly release of a mature egg from an ovarian follicle becomes irregular and eventually ceases. Menstrual periods become lighter, shorter, and farther apart, and eventually cease. When a women has been without a menstrual period for twelve months, she is considered to have gone through menopause.

There are two common physical symptoms of menopause that are generally considered to be a direct result of hormonal changes: hot flashes and a reduction in vaginal lubrication. Hot flashes are caused by a rapid change in the diameter of blood vessels. They consist of a rapid sensation of warmth in the upper part of the body, and may be accompanied by patches of redness on the skin and sweating. They do not usually last long—from several seconds to a minute. There are several theories as to why hot flashes occur. One is that the large amounts of FSH circulating in the bloodstream cause a hormonal imbalance. Other theories associate hot flashes with insufficient amounts of estrogen or the rapid decline in hormone production. A final theory considers hot flashes a "withdrawal" symptom from the estrogen to which the body had become "addicted." (Weideger, 1975).

Emotional Aspects

Popular lore portrays the menopausal woman in mainly negative terms. She is thought to be anxious, irritable, depressed, disinterested in sex, irrational—in sum, impossible to live with. Perhaps each of these labels could be applied to some women undergoing the menopause. But it would be an error to assume that, taken together, they describe the typical experience.

Eighty to ninety percent of women have some symptoms during their menopausal years. However, this figure includes those women whose symptoms are primarily physiological; far fewer women also experience emotional difficulties. Of those who do, only 10 percent have symptoms that can be considered severe (Weideger, 1975). According to Neugarten and Kraines (1965) the most frequent symptoms mentioned specifically by menopausal women include headaches, irritability and nervousness, feeling blue, and feelings of suffocation (associated with hot flashes).

There is some evidence that women during the menopausal years undergo a certain amount of stress. When middle-aged women were compared to men and women at other ages who were also undergoing transitions (high school seniors and newlyweds), the middle-aged woman appeared the most distressed. They evidenced less satisfaction with their lives, had lower self-concepts, were more pessimistic, and had the most negative attitudes toward their spouses (Lowenthal, Thurnher, & Chiriboga, 1975).

But opinions vary as to whether middle-aged women's emotional problems are based in hormonal changes or in their life circumstances. Within the medical profession, there are many who view menopause as a "deficiency disease" resulting from low estrogen levels, and who therefore treat symptomatic women with estrogen replacement therapy (ERT), sometimes for the rest of their lives. Other physicians, while still linking menopausal difficulties with hormone levels, recognize the risks associated with ERT, including the higher likelihood of uterine cancer, and thus recommend ERT only for severe cases.

However, there is increasing evidence that emotional difficulties in middle-aged women are linked more to their social roles than to their hormone levels. Women themselves do not seem to associate their difficulties with menopause. In a study of 100 white women aged forty-three to fifty-three, only 4 percent indicated that menopause was a major concern (Neugarten, 1963). Losing their husband, getting older, fear of cancer, and children leaving home were cited far more frequently as sources of stress. In addition, the psychological state of these women did not vary depending on whether they were pre-menopausal, menopausal, or post-menopausal. Apparently the situations they faced in common had more to do with their emotional reactions than did their menstrual status. Yet these women were not immune to prevailing beliefs about menopausal difficulties. When asked how their reactions compared to those of menopausal women, virtually all saw their own situation as more favorable. They assumed that most menopausal women experience difficulties; they were the exception.

Other studies point to the importance of women's approach to mothering in influencing emotional difficulties in middle age. Bart (1971) studied the hospital records of 533 women aged forty to fifty-nine hospitalized for depression or schizophrenia, and also extensively interviewed twenty of the depressed women. She found that serious depression was directly linked to the experience of losing the maternal role. Further, the more central the role of mother was for these women, the more likely it became that they would be depressed. Women who were overprotective, or overinvolved with their children were more likely to be depressed than women who did were not.

Similarly, Levit (1963) looked at the emotional reactions of sixty-nine married women between forty-four and fifty-seven, half of whom were undergoing menopause and half of whom were postmenopausal. She found that very motherly women (as measured by projective tests) were more anxious during menopause than in the postmenopausal years, and concluded that the loss of childbearing capacity is more stressful for women who are highly invested in the mothering role than for women less invested in this role.

Depression in middle-aged women, then, is directly related to feelings of being useless, of having lost one's main purpose in life, and of having nothing to replace the role that has been outgrown. Women who have focused their adult years on childrearing seem to have lost their sense of self once the childrearing years are over. Social pressures on women to consider their primary fulfillment to come from their status as wife and mother play a large part in creating this situation. Further, these women are not helped by the fact that older women are not accorded respect or prestige in contemporary society (Bart & Grossman, 1978). Whereas men are generally permitted to age with grace, to be seen as wise and virile with advancing years, women become not wise but foolish, not attractive but sexually obsolete (Sontag, 1972). A woman's face may be her fortune, but only to the extent that it is youthful, wrinkle-free, and appealing to men. Older women cannot expect others to treat them in ways that will compensate for their own loss of self-esteem.

Psychological reactions to menopause are also directly linked to women's premenopausal personality (Bart & Grossman, 1978). In general, women who have been low in self-esteem and life satisfaction report more difficulties during menopause than do women who are higher on these dimensions. Difficulties during menopause are similarly linked to difficulties during other phases of the reproductive life cycle such as menstruation and pregnancy (Kraines, 1963). Thus, previous levels of adjustment play a major role in shaping women's emotional response to menopause. As Bart and Grossman put it, "The menopause itself does not turn a healthy, functioning woman into an involutional psychotic" (1978, p. 344).

Cross-cultural studies support this relationship between emotional reactions to menopause and women's status in society. Generally, in cultures in which women's status increases in middle age, women's sense of well-being also rises with advancing years. Increase in status is associated with strong ties to one's family or origin, an emphasis on the extended (rather than the nuclear) family, reciprocal mother-child relationships in later life, institutionalized roles for the grandmother and mother-in-law, and high values placed on age and on reproduction (Bart & Grossman, 1978). Having a formal and respected place as an older woman, then, makes a woman's adjustment to menopause easier.

However, even in contemporary Western society, it is not necessary for older women to become depressed. There is increasing evidence that, for women who are not fully enmeshed in the roles of wife and mother, the later years can be a time of growth, enrichment, and enhancement. For the majority of women, well-being is higher, and depression lower after the children have left home than when the children were young (Lowenthal, 1975; Radloff, 1975). Release from the responsibilities of child care can allow women to develop other parts of themselves, to seek out opportunities for which they previously had neither time nor energy. For women who have maintained a strong sense of self during the adult years, the middle years can be a time of expansion rather than constriction, permitting a fuller expression of an androgynous personality (Marecek, 1979).

Much less is known about the experiences of men during the climacteric. Men's reduced potency, however, can have a damaging effect on their sex life and on their sense of self in general. If a man's image is strongly connected to his sexual capabilities, he may come to feel inadequate in the later years. This feeling may be one reason some men turn from their wives to younger women to enhance their self-esteem. Men whose self-image has been closely linked to professional achievement may also become depressed if their advancements fall short of what they had wished and further opportunities for promotion seem limited. Like women, those men whose roles have been constricted during their adult years may find themselves distressed and dissatisfied once the opportunities in these roles become limited. However, the later years may also be a time of personal expansion.

CONCLUSION

The phases of the reproductive cycle—menstruation, pregnancy and the climacteric—all have biological bases, but occur within a social context. For a full understanding of a person's experience during any of these times, both factors need to be taken into account.

However, such a balanced perspective does not emerge from a review of the research reports. In discussing women, most researchers emphasize the biological determinants of their reactions. Thus, a composite picture emerges of women hampered and constrained by the physiological aspects of their reproductive cycle. In research on men, a pattern of denial emerges. There is far less of an attempt to identify males' emotional reactions during puberty or the climacteric, and even less of an attempt to associate these reactions with biological changes. For both sexes, cultural attitudes and expectations are seen as only secondary influences on experiences during these times.

As a result, both men and women are hampered in obtaining a genuine and complete understanding of their own reactions, including both capabilities and detriments, strengths and weaknesses. Women are described as being controlled by their bodies, men as free from the influence of bodily states. Women have learned to expect their moods to be regularly raised or lowered, and may learn to adapt to their emotional cyclicity, but they also are encouraged to place far greater weight on these mood swings than seems to be appropriate. Men have far less knowledge of predictable changes in mood, and thus are vulnerable to reacting in ways that are out of their control.

What emerges from our review is that at each stage of the reproductive cycle, both hormonal and environmental factors influence one's capacity for flexible, situationally appropriate, effective behavior. Each stage has some effect on women's moods (and perhaps men's too), based on the major bodily changes that are occurring. However, the extent of the effect, and the effects of mood on behavior largely depend on the cultural climate. There is no clear evidence that bodily related mood changes make women less competent. Rather, expectations about mood and related behavioral changes, women's status within society, and cultural lore regarding women and reproduction all have an influence on women's responses. The effect on women of bodily changes associated with their reproductive cycle is only one factor in determining their capacity for androgyny.

SELECTED READINGS

Bettelheim, B. *Symbolic wounds: Puberty rites and the envious male.* New York: Collier Books, 1962.

Denes, M. *In necessity and sorrow: Life or death in an abortion hospital.* New York: Basic Books, 1976.

Luker, K. *Taking chances: Abortion and the decision not to contracept.* Berkeley: University of California Press, 1978.

McFarlane, A. *The psychology of childbirth.* Cambridge: Harvard University Press, 1977.

Notman, M. T., & Nadelson, C. C. (eds.). *The woman patient: Medical and psychological interfaces.* New York: Plenum, 1978.

Weideger, P. *Menstruation and menopause: The physiology and psychology, the myth and the reality.* New York: Delta, 1977.

Sexuality

6

My lover's hold on me tightened; I felt my lover's lips fasten to mine like a vice. I felt passion rising in my lover like an evil flame, and then I was lifted into my lover's arms. "My dear," my lover said hoarsely, "why should we wait?" I was carried to a large sofa in the end of the room and as I struggled with every ounce of my strength, I knew that my resistance was merely exciting my lover.

My lover's lips were on my eyes, my ears, my throat. I felt my lover lay me down on the sofa, while I fought fruitlessly to regain my feet, knowing as I did that I was quite powerless. I heard my clothing begin to tear beneath my lover's hands.

Adapted from B. Cortland, *The Wings of Love,* in
Greer, 1970, pp. 185–86.

In the above vignette, the sex of the narrator has been carefully disguised. But is there any doubt that the narrator is a woman and "the lover" a man? We think not. In fact, we suspect that it would be difficult to read this passage without automatically thinking "he" every time "my lover" is mentioned.

The clarity with which male and female roles can be identified in this admittedly exaggerated vignette suggests the extent to which sexual behavior has become dichotomized on the basis of gender. In large measure, this dichotomization follows the patterns of traditional masculine and feminine sex-role stereotypes. It is the man who by and large takes the agentic role—the active pursuit of his interests. The woman's role is the communal one; attending to the emotional component of the relationship, responding to the man's needs in order to keep the relationship intact. It is the man who leads, the woman who follows.

How is this gender-based dichotomy manifested? What implications does it have for the integration of emotion and action, of agency and communion, in each participant in a sexual relationship? What effect does it have on men's and women's ability to control their sexual lives while respecting the wishes of their partner? How does it affect the capacity of men and women to respond sexually in a flexible, situationally appropriate manner?

These questions are all central to an androgynous perspective on sexuality. A person with this perspective would not assume patterns of sexual behavior to be dichotomized on the basis of gender. In an androgynous sexual relationship, there would not necessarily even be two distinct roles. Rather, personal needs and desires, combined with situational exigencies, would shape the pattern of sexual

140

responses. Each person would be able to feel a measure of control over her or his sexual behavior, while still respecting the wishes and needs of her or his partner. Sexual behavior would not necessarily be divorced from sexual feelings, and people would not feel a split between giving and receiving in sexual relationships. Personal satisfaction, combined with an appreciation of the partner's desires would be salient for both men and women.

In this chapter, we will examine the extent to which existing patterns of sexuality are consistent with this androgynous perspective. First, we will look at historical perspectives on female and male sexuality. Next, we will discuss the physiology of the human sexual response, with a concern for both similarities and differences in male and female patterns. Then, we will explore three forms of sexual expression for men and women; masturbation, heterosexuality, and homosexuality. Finally, we will look at two areas in which there is legal control over sexuality; prostitution and rape. For each topic we will examine prevailing notions about male and female sexuality, and discover how these notions affect the sexual behaviors of women and men.

CULTURAL AND HISTORICAL PERSPECTIVES

If one were to isolate the most prevalent theme about human sexuality across history, it would be that patterns of sexual expression are shaped around the needs and desires of men (Laws & Schwartz, 1977). This typically meant that men's sexuality was openly acknowledged and their need for sexual fulfillment recognized. Women were also seen as sexual, but their desires for sexual fulfillment were not necessarily validated. Throughout history, men have been permitted, at times required, to be sexual, but the permission accorded to women's sexual expression has varied, depending on the prevailing cultural ethos.

What can account for this widespread disparity in the permission accorded to male and female sexual expression? Scholars have looked to both cultural and intrapsychic forces for answers. Sherfey (1973) speculates that the suppression of women's free sexual expression was necessary for the transition from prehistoric to civilized societies. Basing her thoughts on Bachofen's *Myth, Religion, and Mother Right* (1861), she argues that before the development of stable, agricultural settlements, women were characterized by inordinate and uncontrolled sexual demands. "Not until these drives were gradually brought under control by rigidly enforced sexual codes," she states, "could family life become the stabilizing and creative crucible from which modern civilized man could emerge" (p. 139).

Dinnerstein looks not to historical patterns but rather to the structure of the nuclear family to explain her observation that "women are less free than men to seek 'selfish' sexual pleasure" (1976, p. 38). She believes that male and female sexual patterns were primarily determined by the different infantile experiences of males and females with their mothers. For both sexes, their first intense interpersonal relationship is with a woman, their mother. Both males and females, according to Dinnerstein, bring to their adult emotional relationships a pervading wish to reexperience this initial encounter. Men's quest to reenact this early relationship with other women provides the fuel for their intense heterosexual pursuits. But because women are of the same sex as their mother, they do not need to look exclusively to external sources to gratify this wish, because they "carry within [themselves] a source of the magical early parental richness" (p. 42). Thus, for Dinnerstein, males' greater sexual prowess is an innate part of life in a culture where women have exclusive responsibility for early childrearing.

Myths from antiquity and primitive cultures suggest that behind the tendency to control women's sexuality is a fear of the potential power of that sexuality. Images of women's capacity to destroy men's effectiveness through the use of their sexual prowess abound. One thinks of the biblical tale of Samson, who lost his strength when seduced by Delilah, or the Greek tale of Hercules, whose power was similarly destroyed by the intrigues of a woman. In the ancient Hindu and Chinese traditions, men were discouraged from sexual relationships with women when they needed to preserve their strength (Figes, 1970). Among the Arapesh of New Guinea, according to Margaret Mead (1967), men are told that they must "[resist] seduction by strong, positively sexed women. . . . 'You will sleep together, she will steal part of your body fluid, later she will give it to the sorcerer and you will die' " (p. 211). From these disparate traditions, a common theme emerges. Men are both sexual and powerful, but risk losing their strength if they yield to the sexual intrigues of a woman. For men to accept the image of woman as sexual is to place themselves in a position of great vulnerability.

Thus, the need to control women's sexuality derives from the subtle message that, if permitted free reign, it could endanger male power, and perhaps (according to Sherfey) even the structure of society. Denial and avoidance of women's sexuality seem to have emerged as the most successful ways to prevent this from happening.

Yet in thinking about women's sexuality, societies must somehow deal with these two images; women as nonsexual and women as highly sexualized. One way society has managed is to separate women into those who are sexual and those who are not. Thus, women have been dichotomized into the Virgin and the Whore (Laws & Schwartz, 1977). Consider the implications of this split: women are to be worshipped or to be used, to be idealized or to be vilified, to be protected or to be abused. There is a sense here that women's sexuality is not an integral part of their being, but rather exists only by virtue of their relationship to men. There is also a strong moral tone to this dichotomy; the Virgin is the "good" woman and the Whore is "bad."

Images of male sexuality have also been dichotomized, along the lines of sexual adequacy or sexual inadequacy (Fasteau, 1975). The sexually adequate man is one who is successful in attracting female partners and who can give pleasure to the woman with whom he is making love. The ability to "perform" sexually is frequently held forth as a major indicator of "manliness": the sexually active man is accorded respect and even envy by his peers.

The sexually inadequate man, by contrast, may find that his "masculinity" is being questioned. The inability to attract women, or problems with obtaining and maintaining an erection, can become a threat to a man's self-esteem, or can separate him from his more adequate peers. There is even some evidence that fears of sexual inadequacy are a primary source of suicide in adolescent males (Fasteau, 1975).

There are several major distinctions, however, between the sexual dichotomies of men and women. First, the value base is different. Men are respected for being sexual, women for being asexual. The "stud" does not have the negative connotation that the whore does. Second, male norms are responsible for the male sexual images, but females do not control the worth placed on their own patterns of sexual behavior. Rather, these values—in fact the very distinction between the Virgin and the Whore—are male creations. Thus, although members of both sexes are viewed in terms of their sexuality, men but not women control the images and values related to their own sexuality.

Historical Images of Male and Female Sexuality in Western Society

The theme that sexual norms are created to gratify the needs of men but not women recurs throughout Western history. This theme can take a variety of forms, as illustrated by two historical periods, the medieval era and the Victorian era.

The medieval era.   It is during the medieval era, which lasted roughly from the fifth to the fifteenth century, that one finds the birth of romantic love. Prior to that time, as we said in Chapter 3, the relationships of primary importance were those between men. Marriage was primarily an economic relationship, and little emotional feeling was expected to exist between women and men.

This pattern underwent vast changes beginning in the twelfth century, with the advent of chivalry, and the growing importance of Mary as a figure of worship. Love, as a spiritual and a worldly feeling, became highly valued. Knights fought not for the sake of fighting, as in earlier days, but in order to win their ladies' hearts. It was even believed during that time that "there could be no perfect knight who was not a perfect lover" (deRiencourt, 1974, p. 223).

Although romantic feelings still did not exist within marriages, both husbands and wives were expected to have lovers. These extramarital relationships were highly passionate. Although they frequently involved a sexual as well as a romantic connection, this was not always the case. Indeed, the most idealized form of love was that of unfulfilled desire; the perfect lover was one who was unattainable.

Because these nonmarital relationships were expected for both women and men, it might appear that their purpose was to gratify the needs of both sexes; however, this was not true. Lovers' relationships had both a worldly and a spiritual component, but the spiritual love, or love of God, was the ultimate goal. Worldly love, the love of women, was the main agent through which men could pursue the love of God and hence attain sprititual salvation (de Riencourt, 1974). Thus, women were the source of men's salvation; their romantic affairs were in the service of their lover's spiritual growth. The less these romantic liaisons were sexualized, the closer men could come to spiritual fulfillment—hence the idealization of distant and unattainable women.

Most women of this era welcomed and encouraged these relationships, despite the fact that they were serving men's needs. In part, their enthusiasm stemmed from the ways in which these relationships were carried out. Because it was recognized that the man's need for the woman was greater than the woman's need for the man, the sex roles became reversed. He was the humble wooer at the mercy of his beloved; she could take the initiative in accepting or rejecting him. She could place demands on him, while he would serve her humbly to win her favor (deRiencourt, 1964).

However, a few of the more literate women of the day protested against this abuse of female honor and the use of erotic love to satisfy men's needs. Jean Gerson, for example, a vociferous opponent of these liaisons, stated this position clearly: "All conventions of love are the works of men: even when it dons an idealistic guise, erotic culture is altogether saturated by male egoism. . . . Indeed medieval literature shows little true pity for women, little compassion for her weakness and the dangers and pains which love has in store for her" (in Huizinga, 1970, p. 128).

Thus, in one of the most romantic eras of Western history, and one of the periods in which women were granted greatest sexual freedom, erotic relationships were still shaped around the needs of men. Women's own sexual desires played a decidedly secondary role.

The Victorian era. The attitude toward sexuality in Victorian England stands in marked contrast to that of the Medieval era. During the Victorian period, sexual desires were held in strong disdain. This position was widely promoted by the writings of prominent physicians, most notably William Acton (Marcus, 1964). In his books, Acton expounded on the evils associated with sexuality and the dangers awaiting those whose sexuality was not properly contained.

Most of these warnings were directed at men, because their inherent sexual desires were far more widely acknowledged than were those of women. In writing about the male adolescent, for example, Acton warned,

> He does not know that to his immature frame, every sexual indulgence is unmitigated evil. He does not think that to his inexperienced mind and heart every illicit pleasure is a degradation, to be bitterly regretted hereafter—a link in a chain that does not need to be too strong to break (Marcus, 1964, p. 19).

For women, two distinct roles were proposed, in keeping with our earlier-made distinction between the Virgin and the Whore. Both roles were defined in relation to men's lustful desires. The first was that of wife and mother, and was discussed primarily as it applied to middle-class women. Victorian wives and mothers were thought to be free from sexual desires. Acton asserted, "The majority of women (happily for them) are not very much troubled by sexual feelings of any kind. What men are habitually, women are only exceptionally" (Marcus, 1964, p. 31). In case some married women did express sexual desires, however, Acton suggested to their husbands that these desires could easily be stifled by pregnancy and lactation. A pregnant woman, according to Acton, would experience no great sexual excitement.

Whatever the source of this view of married women's sexuality, its purpose was to protect their husbands from excessive enactment of their sexual needs. According to Marcus (1964) woman's task was to protect man from his sexuality. If women failed in this task, they would become the agent of their husbands' ruin. Popular notions of female sexuality, then, clearly served male needs, as defined by Victorian society.

The second role created for women was that of prostitute. In Victorian England, prostitution was a flourishing business. The vast majority of prostitutes were poor women, for whom prostitution offered social and economic advantages over the drudgery of the other work that was available to them. But there were also middle-class prostitutes, or courtesans, who were acknowledged as approrpiate mistresses for married or unmarried men. Prostitutes were seen as highly sexualized. However, it was assumed that they entered their chosen profession not to seek fulfillment of sexual needs, but rather for economic motivations. Their sexuality served as a useful outlet for men's gratification of their sexual desires. Taking a mistress was implicitly encouraged in Victorian society, in part to help men dispense with their sexual needs prior to marriage, in part to protect married women from their husbands' desires after marriage. The prostitute, then, although defined primarily in sexual terms, was not seen as deserving sexual gratification; her sexuality served only the interests of men.

Contemporary society. In contemporary society, sexual customs are not as fully oriented to meeting the needs of men as they were in the past (Laws & Schwartz, 1977). Instead both men and women are "objectified" by members of the other sex in terms of their sexual desirability. Women, as sex objects, are valued for their youth and their appearance. Men, as objects, are valued for their money or status in society, especially in the middle and upper-middle classes (Lipman-Blumen, 1976; Safilios-Rothschild, 1977).

As a result of this dual objectification, sex has become more a power game than a part of a mature, fulfilling relationship. Sexuality, for men, becomes an act of conquest (Fasteau, 1975). Finding and having a woman may become a more important goal than building a caring, loving relationship with that woman. Women, in turn, are encouraged to play "hard to get" so that men may feel that they have indeed conquered (Farrell, 1975). Once in a relationship, women may hesitate to show the extent of their affection, for fear of deflating men's competitive spirit (Safilios-Rothschild, 1977).

Both men and women are victimized by these current sexual arrangements. This victimization takes the form of denying to members of both sexes the opportunities to express both the agentic and communal aspects of their personality within an intimate relationship. The fusion of sexuality and intimacy—the acknowledgement of the emotional component of their sexual relationships—is difficult for men. Exposing their feelings can leave them feeling vulnerable and too dependent on their partner for emotional satisfaction. Men may even feel that the expression of love is incompatible with their "masculinity" (Balswick & Peek, 1971). For women, recognition of men's need to conquer engenders difficulties in maintaining an independent sense of self while in a relationship. They may feel a need to subordinate their own sexual desires to those of their lover—to engage in sexual relationships whether or not they wish to as "proof" of their affection. They may fear, or sense, that too great a demonstration of their competence will be threatening to their male partners. To the extent that women have conformed to men's objectification of them as sex objects, they will probably have neglected their own needs. Thus, contemporary patterns of sexuality make it difficult for men and women to accept both emotionality and an independent sense of self as legitimate aspects of an intimate, sexual relationship.

Another Look

Throughout history, women and men have been subjected to social norms about appropriate sexual behavior. For the most part, these norms clearly distinguish between expected sexual behavior in men and women, and tend to be shaped around the satisfaction of men's sexual needs. Men are encouraged to be sexual and are typically prized for their sexual exploits. Women, however, are considered "bad" if their sexual activity exceeds normal expectations. Thus, neither men nor women are free to define their own limits of sexual activity.

In the three historical periods we discussed, love and sexuality have been divorced from one another. In the medieval era the idealized form of love was asexual. In the Victorian era, sexuality as an emotional and pleasurable experience within marriage was strongly frowned upon, but sexual liaisons with prostitutes, free from emotional attachments, were readily available. In contemporary society, the objectification of men and women has served to structure sex as a game of power, which makes difficult concurrent expression of deep affectionate ties. For neither men nor women, then, is there encouragement for combined and sustained expression of emotional intimacy and sexuality within a relationship.

THE PHYSIOLOGY OF THE HUMAN SEXUAL RESPONSE

The scientific study of the physiology of the human sexual response is intrinsically linked to the pioneering research of Masters and Johnson (1966, 1970). Using systematic laboratory observations of sexual excitation in over 1000 subjects, Masters and Johnson have succeeded in documenting the specific bodily changes that occur in response to sexual stimulation.

The primary contribution of Masters and Johnson's work concerns their detailed accounting of the physiological features of orgasm. Their research speaks directly to several questions that are central to an androgynous perspective on sexuality: What are the similarities and differences in bodily responses to sexual stimulation in males and females? To what extent are commonly observed differences between male and female sexual behavior a result of physiological factors? What are the relative effects of bodily changes and social custom in shaping sexual response patterns of women and men?

Masters and Johnson's laboratory procedures for studying the human sexual response contained both strengths and weaknesses. Because all of their subjects were observed in the same setting and under identical conditions, individual variation based on mood or response to the immediate environment were minimized.

Although one might think that people would have difficulty engaging in sexual practices within a laboratory setting, apparently their subjects adapted with relative ease. Observations were made by means of precise measurements, instrument recordings, and photographic records whenever possible, so that the possibility of human error was greatly reduced.

The primary weakness of Masters and Johnson's research was in their selection of subjects. The researchers relied exclusively on volunteers, who tended to come from a white, academically oriented, upper-middle class community. There were virtually no subjects under the age of twenty-one, and only a few over sixty-five. Thus, aspects of sexual response that might vary as a function of age and social class did not appear in their data. In addition, the information they obtained pertains only to individuals who are orgasmic; subjects who could not reach orgasm through masturbation or intercourse were not included (1966, pp. 12, 32, 198). It is also possible that the nature of the laboratory setting affected subjects' sexual responses. Yet despite these limitations, their findings stand as a major breakthrough in the knowledge and understanding of the human sexual response.

Phases of the Sexual Response

Masters and Johnson were concerned with responses to sexuality affecting the entire body, not simply the genitalia. They documented a regular sequence of such bodily changes, which for simplicity is divided into four phases: (the following account is condensed and revised from Brecher and Brecher, 1966, and Masters and Johnson, 1966).

1. *Excitement.* For men, the first indication of sexual arousal is the erection of the penis, which can more than double its flaccid size. Masters and Johnson observe that this increase in size is proportionally less for large than small penises, a finding that Robinson (1976) terms "penile democracy." Erection is caused by the engorgement of blood vessels in the penis, a condition known as vasocongestion. Vasocongestion occurs in other male as well as female organs, and in considered "the primary reaction to sexual stimuli' (Brecher & Brecher, 1966). At the same time, the skin of the scrotum becomes thicker and tense, and the scrotal sac is raised and flattened toward the body. The testes, which are inside the scrotal sac, are pulled upward toward the body. (See Figure 6.1.)

   For women, sexual arousal is first indicated by the moistening of the vagina with a lubricating fluid, which can occur within ten to thirty seconds after the onset of sexual stimulation. This moisture comes from a kind of "sweating reaction" caused by the vasocongestion of the vaginal walls. The blood vessels emit a small amount of moisture that seeps through the semipermeable vaginal tissue.

   Changes also occur in the clitoris during this phase. The clitoris, located just in front of the entrance to the vagina (Figure 6.2), consists of a shaft with a bulb or "glans" at the tip that is highly endowed with sensitive nerve endings. The glans is covered with a hood or prepuce which in turn is attached to the inner lips (minor labia) of the vagina. During the excitement phase, the glans and

FIGURE 6.1

The Male Reproductive System.

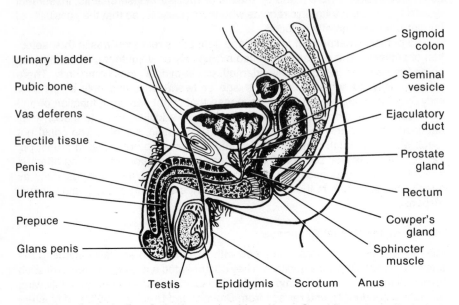

Urinary bladder

Pubic bone

Vas deferens

Erectile tissue

Penis

Urethra

Prepuce

Glans penis

Sigmoid colon

Seminal vesicle

Ejaculatory duct

Prostate gland

Rectum

Cowper's gland

Sphincter muscle

Testis   Epididymis   Scrotum   Anus

Adapted from drawing by Zena Bernstein reproduced from *Human Sexual Expression* by Benjamin A. Kogan, © 1973 by Harcourt Brace Jovanovich, Inc., by permission of the publisher.

shaft of the clitoris as well as the minor labia swell because of vasocongestion. At the same time, the cervix and uterus are pulled up and back, producing a "tenting" of the vaginal walls surrounding the cervix, and a "ballooning" of the inner two-thirds of the vagina. The vagina can increase in length by as much as one inch, and its walls become smoothed out and change in color from their normal purplish-red to a darker purple.

For women and some men, the excitement phase is marked by an erection of the nipples. For women, the breasts increase in size, and the areolas—the rings of darker skin around the nipples—become swollen and engorged. Additionally, for both sexes, the voluntary muscles tend to tense up, and the involuntary muscles may contract. The pulse rate speeds up, and there is a rise in blood pressure. For most women, and about one-third of the men, a "sex flush" appears at this time, beginning on the abdomen and spreading up over the breasts, often taking the form of a measle-like rash.

2. *Plateau.* Although set aside as a distinct phase, the plateau is basically characterized by a continuous increase in the processes begun in the earlier, excitement phase. The term "plateau," as Robinson (1976) points out, is also "singularly inappropriate" to describe this process of increasing responsiveness, unless, as he suggests, one thinks of an "inclined plateau."

The characteristics of this stage are related primarily to the continued engorgement of blood vessels and the increase in muscle tension.

FIGURE 6.2

The Female Reproductive System.

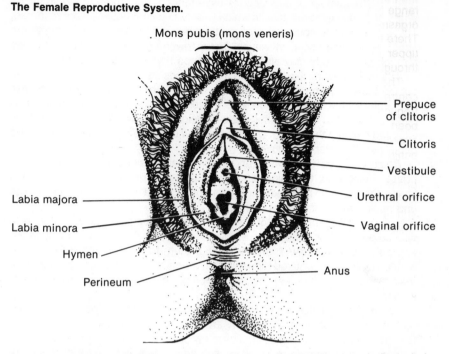

Adapted from drawing by Zena Bernstein reproduced from *Human Sexual Expression* by Benjamin A. Kogan, © 1973 by Harcourt Brace Jovanovich, Inc., by permission of the publisher.

For women, the changes are striking. Most significant is the development of what Masters and Johnson call the "orgasmic platform," or the swelling of the tissue surrounding the outer third of the vagina. This causes the diameter of the outer vagina to be reduced by as much as fifty percent, with the result that it becomes able to grip the penis. The uterus continues to increase in size, the clitoris becomes fully erect and retracts into the clitoral hood, and the outer lips of the vagina become engorged. The inner lips of the vagina change color; from bright red to deep wine for women who have had children, and from pink to bright red for women who have not. This color change is considered a definite sign that orgasm will occur within a matter of minutes if stimulation is continued. The only specific change for men is a slight increase in size at the base of the glans of the penis, and for some, a deepening of the reddish-purple color of the glans.

Bodily changes during this phase for both sexes include continued increases in the rate of breathing, blood pressure, and pulse rate. The sex flush becomes more pronounced, and there is a heightened tension of both the voluntary and involuntary muscles.

3. *Orgasm.* The orgasm, in women, is marked by rhythmic contractions of the orgasmic platform, occuring at first at intervals of four-fifths of a second and

then at longer intervals as the contractions become less intense. There is a range in the number of contractions experienced, from three to five in milder orgasms to one extreme case in which twenty-five contractions were recorded. There is a simultaneous series of contractions in the uterus, beginning at the upper end and moving in waves down toward the cervix. Other muscles throughout the body may also undergo these rhythmic contractions.

The male orgasm, like that of the female, consists of a sequence of rhythmic contractions occuring initially at intervals of four-fifths of a second and then less frequently as the intensity decreases. Fluid containing sperm cells, which had been collected in the seminal vesicles prior to orgasm (see Figure 6.1) is expelled first into the urethra with the first few contractions, and then out of the penis with the later contractions.

Bodily changes for both men and women reach their peak during the orgasm phase. Pulse rate, breathing, and blood pressure rise to their most intense levels, the sex flush becomes most pronounced, and muscles of the arms, legs and neck may contract in spasms.

4. *Resolution.* Within a matter of seconds, the body begins returning to its pre-stimulated state. Muscles relax, swelling decreases, the sex flush disappears, and pulse, blood pressure, and breathing return to normal. Somewhat longer periods of time are required for genitals in men and women to come down from their swollen state. If orgasm has not occurred, this process takes considerably longer.

The male resolution period is marked by a "refractory period" during which men are unable to become sexually aroused or have another erection. For a few men this period can be as brief as a few minutes but for most it is considerably longer, and it tends to increase with age. There is no parallel refractory period for women. Instead, women can be immediately stimulated to additional orgasms; Masters and Johnson found that six or even a dozen sequential orgasms were not unusual for some women. This demonstration of women's potential for multiple orgasms has become one of the most talked about results of their work.

Implications for Beliefs about Female and Male Sexuality

Masters and Johnson cannot be described as totally objective observers of the human sexual response. Rather, they present their findings in ways that seem clearly aimed at challenging prevailing assumptions about sexuality in women and men.

One of the clearest and most pervasive targets in their writings is the frequent assumption that men are more sexual than women. In Masters and Johnson's work, women, if anything, emerge as the more sexual beings (Robinson, 1976). Some of their emphasis on women's sexuality is implicit in the ways they present their findings. There is far more discussion of sexuality in women than in men, especially in *The Human Sexual Response* (1966). When they discuss sexual phases, they consider women's reactions first, and give a far less prominent role to men's reactions. Even women's sexual cycle was observed far more than men's. Although the number of male and female subjects was approximately the same, Masters and Johnson claim to have observed 7500 female sexual cycles but only 2500 male ones.

Masters and Johnson refer explicitly to ways in which women are more sexually responsive than men. For example, in tracing the progression of responses through the four stages, they report having found only one distinct pattern for men but three patterns for women. They claim that these three patterns are "only representative of the infinite variety in female sexual response" (1966, p. 4). Additionally, they look to the female capacity for multiple orgasms, as compared to the male refractory period between orgasms, as further evidence for their position. Finally, in their discussion of *Human Sexual Inadequacy* (1970), they give far more weight to problems in men than in women. Women emerge, rather, as the therapeutic agents for their male partners.

Masters and Johnson also attempt to challenge the assumption that women take longer to reach orgasm than men. They begin by stressing the essential similarity between the physiological responses of females and males during sexual stimulation. As was apparent in the discussion of the four phases, parallel responses between men and women in sequence of events, bodily parts affected, and causes of bodily changes are highlighted throughout. Masters and Johnson call clear attention to these similarities: "Parallels between the anatomical responses of the human male and female to effective stimulation have been established.... Aside from obvious anatomic variants, men and women are homogeneous in their physiologic responses to sexual stimuli" (1966, pp. 284–85).

Masters and Johnson are well aware that for most heterosexual couples engaged in intercourse, women take longer to reach orgasm than men. They account for the discrepancy between their findings and the experience of many people by stressing that intercourse does not provide maximum stimulation for women. Remember that the tip of the clitoris, containing a high concentration of nerve endings, is an extremely sensitive area. The walls of the vagina, by contrast, contain few nerve endings and are fairly insensitive to touch. Although direct stimulation of the clitoris is often too intense or even painful, indirect clitoral stimulation is a major factor in producing the female orgasm. The most immediate way for this to occur is masturbation, and Masters and Johnson are clear that masturbation is more effective than intercourse as a form of sexual release for women. The second most immediate route to female orgasm is through oral or digital manipulation of the female genitals by the partner. Using these methods, Masters and Johnson claim that there is no difference in latency to orgasm between men and women.

Masters and Johnson's statements on the importance of clitoral stimulation have been echoed by other writers discussing the nature of female sexuality (e.g., Laws & Schwartz, 1977; Rotkin, 1976). As these writers stress, clitoral stimulation and not intercourse is the "main sexual event" for women. This stands in marked contrast to most people's notions of sexuality; "having sex" is by and large equated with intercourse. Clitoral stimulation may be a part of foreplay, but unless a heterosexual couple has had intercourse, they have not "made love." What Masters and Johnson have implied, and later authors have made explicit, is that the primary sexual act is different for women and men. For men, intercourse is the most effective method for reaching orgasm, whereas for women it is the least effective. The fact that most people define "having sex" as having the man's preferred form of sex is perhaps the primary way that current sexual practices are still shaped around male needs.

Masters and Johnson's final challenge to prevailing assumptions about female sexuality deals with the myth of women's two orgasms, the vaginal and the clitoral. It was Freud (1925, 1931, 1933) who was primarily responsible for promoting the theory that women experienced two distinct kinds of orgasms, depending on whether the area stimulated was the vagina or the clitoris. According to Freud, vaginal orgasm was the only mature, adult sexual response. This position was embedded in Freud's theory of female psychosexual development. He maintained that during the Oedipal period, young girls practiced clitoral masturbation, which he identified as an "active" approach to sexuality. However, when they recognized that the clitoris is but a miniature and inadequate penis, the shame associated with this discovery led them to relinquish their clitoral masturbation and their active approach to sexuality. In puberty, when sexual interest was reawakened, girls maintained their avoidance of clitoral stimulation, and focused instead on vaginal stimulation and passive, or receptive, sexual aims. If this transition from clitoral to vaginal stimulation did not occur, then girls were considered sexually immature, lacking an appropriate feminine approach to sexuality.

Masters and Johnson use their findings on the four phases of sexual response to demonstrate that regardless of the source of stimulation, there is but one orgasmic response. Furthermore, the clitoris is primarily responsible for female orgasm, even during intercourse. The rhythmic thrusting of the penis inside the vagina produces friction on the inner lips, which in turn creates a rhythmic friction between the clitoral hood and the glans, stimulating the orgastic response. Thus, Masters and Johnson find no distinction in the bodily orgasmic response as a function of source of stimulation.

Although the physiology of orgasm does not depend on the source of stimulation, women may have different experiences of orgasm, depending on whether the primary area of stimulation was vaginal or clitoral. Seaman (1972), for example, found in her survey of 103 educated and sexually active women that several differentiated between their feelings of orgasm during intercourse and direct clitoral stimulation. For some, orgasm during intercourse produced a fuller, more complete feeling, whereas for others the clitorally based orgasm was preferable.

These differential experiences may reflect men's and women's reactions to vaginal and clitoral stimulation. For some women, the fact that their male partner is also being stimulated during intercourse may increase their pleasurable sensations. Others may resent that this sexual activity is geared primarily toward male pleasure, which would detract from their own enjoyment. Men may enjoy the stimulation of intercourse, but feel concerned if they cannot maintain their erection long enough for their female partner to reach orgasm. Further, not all men and women may be fully comfortable with clitoral stimulation to orgasm. They may feel that it is a substitute method, a sign that the woman is not capable of a "real" vaginal orgasm. On the other hand, some women may cherish the fact that this means of stimulation is just for them, and may therefore feel greater sexual excitement and orgasmic pleasure.

Another Look

Through detailed laboratory studies of the physiology of human sexuality, Masters and Johnson have documented that the bodily response to sexual excitation is essentially the same in women and men. Both the sequence of bodily changes and the timing of each of the four phases they identify are similar for members of both sexes. The primary exception to this similarity is that males experience a refractory period after orgasm which delays the recurrence of subsequent orgasms, while women have no such refractory period and thus are capable of multiple orgasms within a short time span.

Masters and Johnson present their findings in a way that challenges some of the prevailing assumptions about sex differences in the experience of sexuality. Specifically, they emphasize that women may be more, rather than less sexual than their male peers. In addition they stress that if women receive sufficient clitoral stimulation, there are no differences between men and women in the time necessary to reach orgasm. Finally, they document that, contrary to the Freudian position which has long influenced thinking about female sexuality, there is only one bodily response to orgasm, rather than a distinction between clitoral and vaginal orgasm.

Thus, studies of the physiology of the human sexual response suggest that members of both sexes respond similarly to sexual stimulation. Maximum sexual responsiveness is obtained by stimulation of the penis in men and the clitoris in women. If women do not receive sufficient clitoral stimulation, as frequently happens in intercourse, their likelihood of reaching orgasm will be curtailed, and they may consider themselves to be sexually unresponsive, or even "frigid." Cultural norms that equate intercourse with "making love" can diminish women's sexual pleasure.

CONTEMPORARY SEXUAL BEHAVIOR

There has been frequent talk in recent years of the existence of a "sexual revolution." This term implies that both men and women have become less constrained by social norms that had inhibited their sexual freedom. Those who celebrate the sexual revolution extoll their new-found permission to engage in sexual activity unhampered by previous limits.

However, the existence of a "sexual revolution" may not mean freedom from social expectation, but only a change in these expectations. Both men and women may now feel pressure to be sexually active, to engage in sexual relationships even if they do not feel inclined to do so. The "sexual revolution" may be as inconsistent with individual decisions about sexual behavior as earlier periods have been.

An exploration of changes in sexual practices is made possible by information provided by researchers who have attempted to document existing patterns of sexual behavior, beginning with the work of Havelock Ellis at the end of the nineteenth century. These studies provide data that are relevant to questions about sexual beahvior asked from an androgynous perspective: How much have sexual practices changed over the years? If such changes have occurred, have they equally affected men and women? Have changes permitted individual persons greater control over their own forms of sexual expression? Have they led to a greater integration of feeling and behavior? We will explore these questions as they pertain to three areas of sexual behavior: masturbation, heterosexuality, and homosexuality.

Masturbation

We have seen that during the Victorian era, frequent sexual expression of any sort was considered harmful. However, the most dangerous form of all sexual behavior was considered to be masturbation. Acton was unambivalent in his warnings about the evils associated with masturbation. These warnings were directed primarily against males, because female masturbation was thought to be infrequent:

> The frame [of a boy who habitually masturbates] is stunted and weak, the eye is sunken and heavy, the complexion is sallow, pasty, or covered with acne, the hands are damp and cold, and the skin moist. The boy shuns the society of others . . . [and] joins with repugnance in the amusements of his schoolfellows. . . . His intellect has become sluggish and enfeebled, and if his evil habits are persisted in, he may end in becoming a drivelling idiot. (Marcus, 1964, p. 19).

Because of the severity of probable outcomes, treatment was provided for the prevention and cure of masturbation. For males, a crude sort of chastity belt was designed, consisting of a padlocked metal cage surrounded by sharp spikes, which was fitted over the boy's gentials at night (Kogan, 1970). For females who were discovered to be masturbating, despite expectations to the contrary, treatment was more severe. Doctors would occasionally cauterize the clitoris with a hot iron or sew the vaginal lips together (Hastings, 1966).

Ellis' writings on autoerotism (1925) were one of the first attempts to challenge this view of masturbation. Ellis argued that there was no evidence to link masturbation with serious mental or physical problems. Further, he proposed that masturbation could even be a reasonable source of mental relaxation. He supported his position with evidence of masturbation among animals and among most known human civilizations. Finally, Ellis took exception to the Victorian belief that women lacked sexual feelings by suggesting that masturbation was equally or more prevalent in women that in men, supporting his contention with several examples of masturbation by women.

Ellis' position on masturbation received strong confirmation some forty years later in the research of Alfred Kinsey and his associates (Kinsey, Pomeroy, & Martin, 1948; Kinsey, Pomeroy, Martin & Gebhard, 1953). Kinsey and his associates conducted over 18,000 interviews in gathering their data. Although the subjects were not randomly selected, Kinsey attempted to derive a representative sample by getting subjects from organizations and insisting that all members participate in his study. Using these interviews, Kinsey found that masturbation had been practiced by virtually all of their male respondents (92 percent), and by more than a majority of the females (62 percent). Masturbatory activities, according to Kinsey's respondents, began early in childhood. Boys apparently began after observing others engaged in similar activities, whereas girls made the discovery of masturbation entirely on their own.

Somewhat different patterns in the progression of masturbatory activities were also observed between boys and girls. Girls who masturbated to orgasm outnumbered boys between the ages of five and ten. However, by age thirteen nearly 50 percent of the males but only 15 percent of the females had masturbated to orgasm. Furthermore, some women did not begin to masturbate until middle age, whereas 92 percent of the males had masturbated to orgasm by age twenty.

Kinsey also found a strong relationship between adolescent masturbation and the potential for orgasm during intercourse, especially for women. According to his data, one-third of all women who never masturbated to orgasm before marriage were unable to become orgasmic during their first five years of marriage. By contrast, only 13 percent of those who had premarital experience of masturbation to orgasm failed to be sexually responsive during these same early marital years.

These data do not demonstrate a *causal relationship* between adolescent masturbation and the capacity for orgasm during intercourse. They could be explained by positing that some women were sexually more responsive than others, expressed in adolescence by masturbation and in adulthood by orgasm during intercourse. However, in line with the general tendency to take a moral position in regard to his findings (Robinson, 1976), Kinsey argued that masturbation in fact helped women's sexual adjustment in adulthood. He suggested that girls who did not masturbate became accustomed to tensing their muscles and withdrawing from physical contact, habits that were difficult to unlearn after marriage (Kinsey et al., 1953). Thus, Kinsey's work brought the thinking on masturbation full circle, from a detrimental activity that should be avoided at all costs to a beneficial preparation for mature, adult sexuality.

There are no data on contemporary practices of masturbation or other forms of sexual activity comparable in scope to the findings of Kinsey and his associates. In fact, recent textbooks on sexuality (e.g., Katchadourian & Lunde, 1972) tend to rely primarily on Kinsey's findings in their discussions of human sexual behavior. However, a recent study by Hunt (1974), commissioned by the Playboy Foundation, offers some more current findings on masturbation, although from a smaller and more restricted sample. Hunt found a higher prevalence of masturbation in boys and girls at age thirteen: 60 percent for boys and 35 percent for girls. Proportionally, there was a greater increase in preadolescent masturbation for girls than boys as compared to Kinsey's data. However, Hunt's findings on the incidence of masturbation in adulthood are almost identical to those of Kinsey: 63 percent for women and 93 percent for men.

In general, there is only slight evidence that masturbatory practices have changed in the last thirty years. For adults, the incidence of masturbation seems to have remained essentially the same. For children, there are some reported increases. However, since the data on childhood consist of adults' retrospective accounts, differences between the findings of Kinsey and Hunt may simply reflect a greater willingness in Hunt's respondents to acknowledge earlier masturbatory activity (Hunt, 1974).

Further, in both samples and for almost every age range discussed, there is evidence of more masturbation by males than females. The finding that more than one-third of the female respondents in both studies did not masturbate is striking, since masturbation is the most effective way for women to reach orgasm (Masters & Johnson, 1966). Feminists writing on women's sexuality are looking to redress what they see as the feelings of guilt underlying this inhibition (e.g., Barbach, 1975; Boston Women's Health Book Collective, 1976; Dodson, 1974). These writers stress that masturbation is not only normal, it is a special way of enjoying oneself, of learning what is pleasurable and exciting. They counter the possibility of awkward feelings with suggestions on ways to explore one's body and experiment with different kinds of touching.

Men may also feel some guilt associated with masturbation, but their guilt is less likely to inhibit their masturbatory practice. Although less has been written directly to men about masturbation, they are also encouraged to accept it as normal and healthy (Kogan, 1970).

Heterosexuality

Research on heterosexuality is typically carried out within a framework in which marriage is the norm; studies are classified as representing premarital, marital, or extramarital sexuality. Within this perspective, findings in general focus on the relative amounts of sexual behavior displayed by women and men, and the varieties of sexual activities in which the couple engages. These data, then, tell more about what people do than what they feel. However, they are useful in documenting changes in heterosexual behavior, both for the couple as a unit and for the relative roles of women and men.

There is a gradual trend in this research toward increased recognition of women as sexual beings. Ellis (1925) was one of the first to challenge the Victorian assumption that sexuality was far more characteristic of men than women. He argued forcefully that women shared with men a capacity for intense sexual desire and enjoyment of sexual relations. However, some of Ellis' views on women's sexuality remained rooted in Victorian mores. He saw women's sexuality, for example, as elusive, veiled in mystery, while that of men was open and aggressive. To him, women's sexuality was essentially passive and receptive, whereas men's was active and instrumental. Finally, women's primary purpose in sexual relations was procreation, and Ellis remained firmly wedded to the centrality of motherhood in women's lives. Thus, it remained for later researchers to present a more balanced picture of the sexual needs of women and men.

Premarital sexuality. One of the most common derivatives of the assumption that males are more sexual than females is the "double standard" regarding premarital sexuality. Male sexual activity before marriage has seldom been frowned upon, but "good girls" have been expected to remain virgins. Remnants of this belief are reflected in Kinsey's data on the relative premarital sexual activity of males and females. In his sample, approximately one-third of the women had experienced sex before marriage, whereas 84 percent of the men had experienced it. Both the age and the social class of his respondents influenced the likelihood that they would have had premarital sex. For the women, nonvirginity at marriage was more than twice as frequent for those born after 1900 as it was for those born before 1900. Social class figured prominently in the data reported by the men. Ninety-eight percent of those with a grammar school education, 85 percent of those with a high school education, and 68 percent of those who had attended college reported having engaged in premarital sex.

More recent data suggest that the situation has changed more for women than for men. In Hunt's 1974 survey, 89 percent of the males reported premarital sexual experience (an increase of 5 percent from Kinsey's time) and 51 percent of the women reported premarital sex (an increase of 18 percent). Age, however, continued to influence the experience of the women. Of those who were between eighteen and twenty-four at the time of the study, 81 percent reported premarital sexual activity, while at the other end, of those who were fifty-five and over, 35 percent had had comparable experiences. Taken together, then, the data from Kinsey's and Hunt's studies reflect a consistent increase in the numbers of women who engage in sex before marriage.

Figures on the incidence of premarital sexuality must be read with some caution. For example almost half of the women in both Kinsey's and Hunt's samples had had premarital intercourse with only one man, the man whom they expected to marry. For many women, premarital sexuality is acceptable only if it occurs within a loving context (Kaats & Davis, 1970). Men tended to have more variety in premarital sexual partners; the average number of partners for men in both Kinsey's and Hunt's surveys was six. It therefore seems reasonable to assume that men place less emphasis on love as a precondition for premarital sexual relationships.

There is some evidence regarding factors that differentiate orgasmic from nonorgasmic women during premarital intercourse. Shope (1975), in a sample of unmarried college women, found that the orgasmic women were generally freer sexually; they had fewer inhibitions, became sexually aroused more quickly; and were generally more pleased with their sexual capacities. They tended to see themselves as equal in sexual interest to their male partners, utilized a variety of sexual positions, and prolonged sexual relations after their first orgasm. Their pleasure seemed to drive from the sexual experience itself. Nonorgasmic women were more likely to focus on the romantic and intimate aspects of their sexual experiences. The orgasmic women did not differ from the nonorgasmic women in terms of numbers of sexual encounters, numbers of partners, or the length of time in which they had engaged in premarital sex. Thus, they seemed to have a freer attitude toward sexuality, and a greater acceptance of their sexual selves, but less of a tendency to link sexuality with romantic feelings.

Marital sexuality. The study of sex within marriage did not play a prominent role in Kinsey's work. Heterosexual relationships in general were considered as one among six possible forms of sexual release, and marital sexuality was discussed in a single chapter toward the back of his volume on men. His investigations in this area focused on the frequency, length, and variety of sexual relations between married partners. Sexual intercourse between married couples was found to occur on the average of 1.5 times per week, with the age of the couples playing a major role in determining frequency. Couples between the ages of sixteen and twenty-five had sexual relations approximately 2.5 times a week; couples aged fifty-six to sixty had them 0.5 times.

Sex, in Kinsey's time, was also a relatively quick experience. Kinsey's data suggest that, on the average, about 75 percent of his male respondents reached orgasm within two minutes after intromission. Some variety in forms of sexual expression was reported. Oral sex, both fellatio and cunnilingus, was practiced by about 40 percent of the couples Kinsey surveyed. Kinsey did not report data on anal sex, stating that "anal activity in the heterosexual is not frequent enough to make it possible to determine the incidence of individuals who are specifically responsive to such stimulation" (1948, p. 579).

Hunt (1974) reported a marked increase in sexual freedom among married couples from Kinsey's time. In contrast to the two-minute "quickie" found in Kinsey's sample, sexual experiences in Hunt's study averaged about ten minutes, with the time increasing to about thirteen minutes for younger couples. More couples than in Kinsey's time also used a wider variety of sexual approaches. Between 58 and 63 percent of couples interviewed had practiced oral sex within the previous year. Fingering and kissing the anus had been practiced by a sizable minority of Hunt's couples, and about 25 percent of the couples under thirty-five had experimented with anal intercourse.

Whereas Kinsey did not emphasize attitudes toward sexuality, Hunt explored some of the factors related to sexual enjoyment in married couples. He found sexual satisfaction and marital success to be closely related, which he accounted for by better methods of birth control and greater acceptance, by women, of their sexuality. Acceptance of one's sexuality, and the corresponding freedom to engage in a variety of sexual practices, however, seem to vary as a function of social class (Rubin, 1976). Working-class women, according to Rubin, respond with some hesitation to their husband's requests to engage, for example, in oral sex. For these women, there is a lingering association between forms of heterosexuality other than intercourse and the label of "loose women." Middle-class women feel freer to expand their repertoire of sexual practices, but may feel guilty if they are unable to enjoy these less traditional forms of sexual experience.

Changes in patterns of behavior are only one measure of changes in the sexual climate for married couples. Although there is evidence of greater variety in their sexual practice, it is less clear whether or not satisfaction with sexuality in marriage has increased. On the one hand, the greater use of oral and manual stimulation, combined with the increased length of time during intercourse, should enhance women's potential for sexual enjoyment. On the other hand, pressure to engage in a variety of sexual practices could create difficulties. Some women are not comfortable with forms of sexuality other than intercourse. Others feel more obliged than before to have one, if not several, orgasms. Some men may feel inhibited if women take an active role in initiating sexual relations, and some may feel obliged to ensure that their female partner has at least one orgasm (Fasteau,

1975). There is a need for additional research into the feelings and attitudes accompanying the increased variety in sexual behavior. Are both members of a couple more aware of what forms of sexuality will increase their enjoyment? Can each pursue his or her own pleasure while still maintaining respect for the other's needs and desires? Do contemporary forms of marital sexuality increase the intimacy and affection within a couple? Studies addressing these questions would help us to see how increases in sexual behavior are associated with a more or less fulfilling sexual relationship.

Extramarital sexuality. Kinsey did not at first investigate extramarital sexuality, ostensibly because it did not at first occur to him that such practices existed (Robinson, 1976). However, once he turned his attention to this subject, it became evident that both men and women had had experience with extramarital intercourse. As in the other areas of sexual practice that Kinsey investigated, men were more active than women. Approximately half of the married men Kinsey interviewed reported having had extramarital intercourse; the same was true for only about one-quarter of the married women in his sample. Kinsey was not convinced that sex outside of marriage necessarily undermined the stability of the marital relationship. In fact, he implied that in certain circumstances, extramarital relationships could improve the sex life of a married couple. Women who had difficulty being sexually responsive with their husbands might be more readily stimulated under the novelty of an extramarital affair. This increased responsiveness could then enrich their sex life with their husbands. Men also might become better able to appreciate sexual relationships with their wives, after having had intercourse with other women.

The incidence of extramarital relationships does not seem to have changed dramatically between Kinsey's time and the present, with one exception. For both men and women under twenty-five, the percentage of those engaging in extramarital sex had increased—from 27 to 34 percent for men and from 8 to 24 percent for women (Hunt, 1974). As these figures also show, the change for women has been more marked than the change for men. Yet recent studies report that men are likely to have more extramarital partners than are women. Whether men simply have more opportunities to meet potential partners, or whether women require a closer emotional attachment before engaging in extramarital sex, some sex differences remain.

Birth control. The increased freedom for women to engage in heterosexual activity has been greatly enhanced by available methods of birth control. Fear of pregnancy is no longer a major part of women's heterosexual relationships. Because the risk of pregnancy falls only to women, most contraceptive devices are designed for them. Such devices increase women's control over the prevention of pregnancy, but also often expose them to health hazards. Although forms of male contraception other than the condom are possible, research that would lead to more varied contraceptive methods for men has lagged far behind research on contraception for women (Bremner & de Kretser, 1975).

Table 6.1 lists the available methods of birth control, their levels of effectiveness, and their advantages and disadvantages. It shows that no method is both

TABLE 6.1 Methods of Contraception

Method	What is it?	How does it work?	How is it used?
Diaphragm	• shallow rubber cup used with cream or jelly	• covers opening of cervix • holds spermicide close to cervix • prevents sperm from entering uterus	• diaphragm (with spermicide) placed in vagina
IUD	• small piece of plastic with nylon string attached • some contain copper wire or synthetic hormone, progesterone	• seems to interfere with implantation of fertilized egg	• IUD inserted into uterine cavity by medical practitioner • string checked periodically
Pill	• pills containing two synthetic hormones, estrogen and progesterone	• prevents ovulation • makes uterus and cervix less favorable to conception	• pill taken daily (some types require a week when no pills are taken)
Mini-pill	• pills containing one synthetic hormone, progesterone	• may prevent ovulation • makes uterus and cervix less favorable to conception	• pill taken daily
Sterilization	• surgical procedure • involves the cutting and sealing of tubes that carry the egg or sperm	• separates the tubes • prevents meeting of egg and sperm	• surgical procedure required (doctor's office or hospital)
Condom	• thin sheath of rubber or animal skin	• covers penis • prevents sperm from entering the vagina	• condom placed over erect penis
Vaginal spermicides	• cream, foam, jelly or suppository containing sperm-killing chemicals	Chemicals • kill sperm • prevent sperm from entering uterus	• spermicide inserted into vagina
Natural family planning	• means of planning or preventing a pregnancy by observing signs of ovulation, such as: - basal body temperature (BBT) - cervical mucus - changes in cervix	• identifies fertile and infertile periods	• signs charted daily • unprotected intercourse is avoided during fertile period or barrier method may be used

Douching

Washing out the vagina after intercourse is not an effective method of birth control, and may actually push the sperm into the uterus more quickly.

Remember:
1) Whenever possible, the selection of a birth control method should be discussed and decided upon jointly by the couple, with the needs of both being considered.
2) No method of contraception is 100% effective – the only way to be absolutely sure that pregnancy won't occur is not to engage in sexual intercourse. However, the birth control methods outlined in this pamphlet will greatly reduce the risk of pregnancy. If you believe you are pregnant, you should see a family planning clinic or a doctor as soon as possible for a pregnancy test and more information.

Method	How effective is it?[a]	What are the advantages	What are the disadvantages?
Diaphragm	17 out of 100 women will get pregnant	• can be used during menses to hold menstrual flow • use only when needed	• must be fitted by a medical practitioner • medical exam necessary • has to stay in the vagina for several hours • may be messy when used with cream or jelly
IUD	5 out of 100 women will get pregnant	• not connected with the act of intercourse • one-time procedure for plastic IUDs	• must be inserted by a medical practitioner • medical exam necessary • insertion may be painful or uncomfortable • may be expelled
Pill	4–10 out of 100 women will get pregnant	• not connected with the act of intercourse • may establish regular periods, may make periods shorter and lighter • may diminish cramps, acne and pre-menstrual tension • decreased incidence of functional ovarian cysts in some Pill-users	• must be prescribed by a medical practitioner • medical exam necessary
Mini-pill	5–10 out of 100 women will get pregnant	• not connected with the act of intercourse • may diminish painful periods • less serious side effects than the Pill	• must be prescribed by a medical practitioner • medical exam necessary
Sterilization	• when successful, the man or woman will be infertile • chances of failure are less than 2 out of 1000 men/women	• one-time procedure • no further need of devices or chemical preparations • removing fear of pregnancy may improve sexual relations	• requires surgery • non-reversible procedure
Condom	10 out of 100 women will get pregnant • used with foam, 5 out of 100 women will get pregnant	• no prescription needed • some protection against VD • may help to maintain erection • use only when needed	• interruption of foreplay • may slip, tear or spill • may decrease sensitivity • may be messy when used with foam
Vaginal spermicides	22 out of 100 women using foam will get pregnant (generally, foam seems best for spreading spermicide) • used with condom, 5 out of 100 women will get pregnant • figures for cream, jelly and suppository are not available	• no prescription needed • use only when needed	• interruption of foreplay • time limit on insertion • may be messy

[a] Rates are based on usage by 100 women for 1 year and take into account failure due to method and incorrect use of method.

TABLE 6.1 Methods of Contraception (continued)

Method	How effective is it?[a]	What are the advantages	What are the disadvantages?
Natural family planning	2–12 out of 100 women using Sympto-Thermal Method (combined BBT), 7–19 out of 100 women using BBT, and 10–25 women using Mucus Method will get pregnant	• totally reversible • no use of devices or chemicals • fosters awareness of woman's own menstrual cycles • approved by the Catholic Church	• requires high level of instruction and motivation • cannot determine safe period before ovulation occurs

Method	What are the side effects or complications?	What are the health factors or contraindications?	What are the long term effects on ability to have children?
Diaphragm	• possible allergy to rubber • spermicide may be irritating	Contraindications: • greatly relaxed vagina tipped uterus	• none
IUD	• may include cramps, painful periods, heavy flow and spotting • major complications include anemia, pregnancy outside the uterus (ectopic pregnancy), pelvic infection, uterine or cervical perforation, and septic abortion • ectopic pregnancy or severe pelvic infection could lead to infertility	Health Factors–inform medical practitioner of: • previous cancer or abnormalities of uterus or cervix • infection of uterus, cervix or pelvis • VD, severe menstrual cramps, unexplained genital bleeding, abnormal Pap smear, anemia, fainting, recent pregnancy or abortion Contraindications: • pregnancy • acute pelvic infection	• tubal blockage due to severe pelvic infection or ectopic pregnancy • may result in infertility
Pill	Side Effects may include: • nausea, headaches, tender breasts, missed periods, unexpected vaginal bleeding, darkened facial skin, weight change, change in sex drive and depression Complications-higher risks of developing: • blood clots in the legs, lungs, heart or brain • high blood pressure, gallbladder disease, noncancerous liver tumors	Health Factors: • smoking while on the Pill greatly increases risk of heart attack or stroke • migraines, depression, asthma, high blood pressure, heart or kidney disease, diabetes or epilepsy may become worse • adolescents should be menstruating regularly for 1 year before taking the Pill • Pill-associated risks increase with age, especially after mid-thirties Contraindications: • pregnancy • previous history of heart attack, stroke, angina pectoris, blood clots • cancer of the breast or uterus • liver disorders	• may be delay after stopping the Pill before ovulation returns • taking the Pill during pregnancy increases risk of fetal malformations • before getting pregnant, a woman should discontinue Pills and establish 1–3 regular cycles

Withdrawal

Withdrawing the penis from the vagina before ejaculation requires strict timing and self-control by the man. Since some sperm are released before ejaculation, pregnancy can still occur. This is not an effective birth control method.

[a] Rates are based on usage by 100 women for 1 year and take into account failure due to method and incorrect use of method.

Method	What are the side effects or complications?	What are the health factors or contraindications?	What are the long term effects on ability to have children?
Mini-pill	Side Effects may include: • irregular periods, missed periods, breakthrough bleeding, shorter and lighter periods Complications: • higher risk of ectopic pregnancy	Health Factors–may be more suitable for women: • over 35 who wish to use Pills • in their teens • with history of headaches, high blood pressure, bad varicose veins • who had experienced estrogen-related side effects of the Pill Contraindications: • undiagnosed genital bleeding • also those that apply to the Pill	• presently unknown • taking the Mini-Pill during pregnancy increases the risk of fetal malformations
Sterilization	Complications may include: *Female:* those of surgery such as bleeding, infection, or injury to other organs *Male:* infection, hematoma (trapped mass of clotted blood), granuloma (reaction to sperm antibodies), swelling and tenderness near testes	Health Factors: • client's general health Contraindications: • uncertainty about not wanting children in the future	• woman cannot become pregnant • man cannot father a child
Condom	• possible allergy to rubber	• none	• none
Vaginal spermicides	• spermicide may be irritating	• none	• none
Natural family planning	• none	Contraindications: • BBT: imprecise or absent thermal response to ovulation • Mucus: cervical conization	• none • possibility of fetal abnormalities due to fertilization with aged sperm or overripe egg

Breastfeeding

Ovulation does not usually occur in a nursing woman, but she could be fertile before she resumes menstruating, so this is not a reliable birth control method.

Source: "Guide to Birth Control" reprinted by permission of the Family Planning Council of Western Massachusetts, Inc. Additional copies of the Guide and other informed consent material are available through the Family Planning Council of Western Massachusetts, Inc., 16 Center Street, Northampton, MA 01060.

completely safe to the user and totally effective in preventing conception. Because of the risks involved, some women hesitate to use the more effective methods, such as the pill or IUD. Other women use birth control carefully but become pregnant nonetheless. Greater availability of contraceptive methods for men would permit couples to make a more reasoned choice about which one of them would use birth control, and with what method.

Homosexuality

Kinsey's findings on homosexuality, which held a prominent place in his writings, appeared at a time when most people believed that homosexuality between men was a rare and abnormal phenomenon, and between women virtually nonexistent. Well aware of these attitudes, Kinsey presented his data as a challenge to this perspective. The very fact that homosexuality was given as much or more coverage than marital sexuality raised it to the realm of the respectable. Additionally, Kinsey sought to indentify homosexual *acts* rather than homosexual *individuals,* to document that there was not a vast difference in the sexual practices of homosexuals and heterosexuals, and to dismiss as irrelevant any discussion about the causes of homosexuality. Homosexuality, then, was portrayed as but one of many varieties of normal sexual expression.

What captured the attention of most of his readers at the time was Kinsey's report on the prevalence of homosexual relationships between men. Accoring to his data, fully 37 percent of his male respondents had experienced at least one homosexual relationship leading to orgasm, although only 4 percent of these people identified themselves as exclusively homosexual. The data on women revealed a lesser incidence. Although 20 percent of his female respondents reported having had at least one homosexual experience, that experience led to orgasm for only 13 percent of these and only about 2 percent identified themselves as exclusively homosexual.

Although Kinsey's figures were widely criticized for overrepresenting homosexuals, their accuracy is suggested by the fact that more recent studies on the incidence of homosexuality, although from a sexually sophisticated population, report quite similar findings (Hunt, 1977). In the early 1970s, as in the early 1950s, more than one-third of the men and one-fifth of the women have been found to have engaged in at least one homosexual encounter.

Kinsey's approach to the study of homosexuality seems to have had less of an effect on further research in the field than he probably would have liked. To operationalize his emphasis on homosexual acts rather than homosexual individuals Kinsey devised a seven-point rating scale to measure frequency of homosexual encounters. The scale ranged from exclusively heterosexual to relative combinations of heterosexual and homosexual behavior.

However, there are several problems with his scale. The distinction, for example, between "incidental" and "more than incidental" homosexual or heterosexual practice presents a challenge to rigorous classifications, to say the least. In addition, Kinsey's scale, exclusively measuring sexual encounters, lacks two other fundamental components of homosexuality. For many, a homosexual orientation includes a general feeling of warmth, appreciation, and love toward members of the same sex, a feeling that can be called the *homoemotional* component of homosexuality. Also, for some people, a homosexual orientation can have a political dimension—the public acknowledgement of one's sexual preference and a life style in which one's identity as a homosexual plays a central role. This has been called the *homoidentified* component of homosexuality (Radicalesbians, 1976). Reducing homosexuality exclusively to sexual encounters prevents exploration of these broader aspects of the homosexual experience.

Kinsey's position that homosexuality is not a pathological form of sexual expression and that therefore the exploration of its causes is irrelevant has also been ignored by a number of researchers in the field. Instead, the emphasis on pathological components of homosexuality has led some writers to label many studies "homophobic"—having a basic derogatory attitude toward homosexuality (Basile, 1974; MacDonald et al., 1973; May, 1974; Morin & Garfinkle, 1978; Smith, 1971). Whether or not homophobia is widespread, studies on the causes and cure of homosexuality prevail in the literature. Studies on causality come from two differing theoretical positions. Those interested in the biochemical origins of behavior focus on the biological differences between homosexuals and heterosexuals (e.g., Evans, 1972; Heston & Shields, 1968; Margolese, 1970; Meyerson & Neustadt, 1942–43). The results from this accumulation of studies remain inconclusive (see Chapter 4). Those whose work is based on a psychoanalytic perspective focus on the psychodynamic and interpersonal underpinnings of a homosexual orientation (e.g., Berg, 1968; Bieber, et al., 1962; Kallman, 1951; Marmor, 1965; Wilbur, 1965).

Studies on the treatment or "cure" of homosexuality appear primarily in the research on behavior therapy, because behaviorists are more interested in changing behavior than in documenting its origins. The primary method of treatment involves some sort of systematic desensitization in which patients' mental images of homosexual stimulation are associated, by the therapist, with noxious mental imagery, such as nausea, vomit, or fecal matter (e.g., James 1964; Kolvin, 1967; Rutner, 1970).

An increasing number of researchers, however, are dissatisfied with this general approach to homosexuality. As Bell (1975) puts it: "If it were up to me, I would declare a moratorium on the usual conduct of research in homosexuality." (1974, p. 422). These researchers point to the need for a more broadly based exploration into the nature of the homosexual experience, with specific attention to those attitudes of researchers which might distort the nature of their research.

Other writers on homosexuality have directly challenged the "homosexuality as illness" model, stressing the value judgment implicit in a focus on psychopathology (Begelman, 1975). In line with this challenge, Davison (1976) and Russell and Winkler (1977) have suggested that psychotherapists should attempt to validate the healthy components of homosexuality by designing psychotherapeutic procedures aimed at facilitating, rather than eliminating, homosexual practices. Davison has gone as far as to argue that "we stop engaging in voluntary therapy programs aimed at altering the choice of adult partners to whom our clients are attracted" (1976, p. 160).

Documentation supporting the position that homosexuality is not a reflection of mental illness has come from several recent studies on the mental status of male and female homosexuals.[1] Saghir, Robins, Walbran and Gentry (1970), in a comparative study of eighty-nine homosexual men and thirty-five unmarried heterosexual men found no differences in the extent of psychopathology between these two groups. Similarly, a study of over 1500 homosexual males reported increased self-acceptance and feelings of adequacy as they grew older, a pattern not at all atypical of heterosexual men (Weinberg, 1969). Bell and Weinberg also found that, with the exception of a few specific subgroups within a sample of over 500 homosexual men, the homosexual men "tended to appear as well adjusted as the heterosexuals or, occasionally, even more so" (1978, p. 207).

Studies on the mental status of lesbians also suggest that in some ways these women appear to be as well or better adjusted than their heterosexual counterparts. Ohlson and Wilson (1974) compared sixty-four lesbian and sixty-four heterosexual women matched for age and educational status on responses to a standardized personality inventory (the MMPI). They found that "female homosexuals are more alert, responsible, less anxious, and more self-confident than female heterosexuals. At the same time, they are more cynical and tend to isolate themselves more often from the general society" (p. 311). Riess, Safer, and Yotive (1974) reviewed findings from projective and nonprojective tests on the mental status of lesbians. In general, the former produced more evidence of pathology than the latter, including signs of inhibited emotionality, disturbed maternal relations, and anxiety about the female role. The non-projective studies portrayed the lesbian woman as somewhat healthier than the heterosexual controls—better adjusted, more competent, more mature and independent, and higher in achievement strivings.

There remains a need for further research into the nature and diversity of the homosexual experience. Of major importance would be the ways in which homosexuals are affected by living in a culture that generally disdains their sexual orientation. This emphasis on the social context of the homosexual experience could lead to some specific research questions. Are there differences in interpersonal and vocational histories between homosexuals who have remained "closeted" and those who have "come out"? To what extent, and in what ways, is the life of a homosexual affected by the presence or absence of a strong peer group or subculture in which their sexual orientation is welcomed? What are some of the ways in which homosexuals directly experience critcism of their sexual orientation by heterosexuals, and how do these experiences affect their self-images and life styles? Moving from an exceptionalistic to a universalistic perspective, (see Chapter 2) would increase knowledge about the ways that homosexuals, as a group, are affected by the culture in which they live.

[1]In 1973 the American Psychiatric Association, by formal vote of its members, determined that homosexuality was not in and of itself a psychiatric disorder. In this decision they distinguished between two forms of homosexuality. Sexual orientation disturbance, which remains a psychiatric disorder, applies to "individuals whose sexual interests are directed primarily towards people of the same sex and who are either disturbed by, in conflict with, or wish to change their sexual orientation." This category is differentiated from homosexuality per se, which by itself does not constitute a psychiatric disorder (Riess, Safer and Yotive, 1974, p. 71).

Another Look

Victorian attitudes that acknowledged sexual desires in men but not in women have given way to a recognition of both men and women as sexual beings. Along with this shift in attitude has come an increase in women's expression of sexuality. In the 1970s, as compared to the 1940s, more women report masturbating to orgasm and engaging in premarital, extramarital, and homosexual activity. Thus, there seems to be a "leveling" of sexual behavior, with women moving toward although not equalling, male levels.

These changes do not necessarily mean, however, that people have greatly increased control over their forms of sexual expression. It is true that contemporary heterosexual practices seem to take women's needs into account more than in the past. This is evidenced by couples' taking longer while making love, and increasing the use of oral and manual stimulation, both of which increase the likelihood of women's sexual arousal. On the other hand, the prevailing permissive atmosphere may put more pressure on men and women to be sexually active and to be orgasmic than is comfortable for them. Feelings of guilt or inadequacy may arise if people feel that they are not meeting these newer standards.

In general, there is an abundance of research on sexual *behavior,* but much less on how people feel about their sexuality or interpret their sexual behavior in light of cultural norms. For a psychology of androgyny, studies dealing with the interrelationships between emotions and behavior, and between the individual and society, would be especially relevant, providing a context within which to interpret the findings of increases in sexual activity.

SEXUALITY AND THE LAW

Two forms of sexuality are regulated by the legal system; prostitution and rape.[2] Although both are "crimes," there are some major distinctions between the two. Only in rape are the rights of one person directly violated by the behavior of another, and only in rape is violence a frequent occurrence. What rape and prostitution have in common, however, is that both involve forms of sexual behavior. Thus, legal strictures against rape and prostitution reflect social control over violence and abuse, but also over sexual expression.

The experiences of prostitutes and rape victims, the motivations of rapists, and patterns of arrest for rape and prostitution, serve as concrete manifestations of the effect of societal beliefs on sexual behavior. What does the treatment of prostitutes and rape victims reveal about attitudes toward women's sexuality? How are men's roles in these two events influenced by prevailing assumptions about sexuality in men? What are the explicit and implicit goals in social regulation of prostitution and rape? We will address these questions in the following sections.

[2]There are also laws against homosexuality, but they are enforced only sporadically, so we will not consider them here.

Prostitution

Cultural attitudes. Prostitution has been called the "oldest profession," yet it has long held a paradoxical position in the many countries in which it has existed. On the one hand, prostitution is often deemed illegal, so that prostitutes can be submitted to periodic arrest and imprisonment. On the other hand, it seems to be not only tolerated but even encouraged. In order to understand this paradox, let us examine the prostitute's position in light of the assumptions about female sexuality that we have delineated in this chapter.

Prostitution, although a crime, is "victimless"—one person does not force her- or himself on the other without the other's consent. Abuse of another person's civil rights is therefore not the basis of considering prostitution criminal. Neither does the sexual *act* between prostitute and her male customer seem to be the locus of the criminal activity. When arrests for prostitution are made, it is most often the prostitute, but not her male customer, who is arrested.

Instead, the basis for deeming prostitution criminal seems to reside within the behavior of the prostitute herself. As we have pointed out throughout this chapter, women are seldom encouraged to be sexual. Yet prostitutes, by definition, are openly announcing and displaying their sexuality. According to Laws and Schwartz (1977), it is precisely because prostitutes openly display their sexuality that they are considered criminals.

The extent to which contemporary society emphasizes the "crime" of female sexuality is supported by data on the proportion of all women criminals who have been arrested for prostitution. In 1974, approximately 30 percent of all incarcerated females had been arrested for prostitution, and a full 70 percent of all women imprisoned at that time were first arrested for prostitution (FBI Uniform Crime Reports, 1974). The open acknowledgement of sexuality as evidenced by prostitution is the primary crime committed by women.

But prostitution is also permitted to flourish, and this, too must be accounted for. Such permission is consistent with the historically recurring portrayal of women as the Virgin or the Whore. These conceptually distinct images can in fact be seen as two sides of the same coin; one side the mirror image of the other (Janeway, 1971). Figes (1970) extends this logic to argue that by necessity these two images, the Virgin and the Whore, must coexist. The demonstration of the purity of the Good Woman (the Virgin) is not complete without the converse image of the Bad Woman (the Whore) with which to compare her. Evidence for this position can be found, for example, in the Victorian era, during which there simultaneously existed an emphasis on married women's asexuality, and a highly flourishing practice of prostitution.

Background of prostitutes. Which women tend to become prostitutes? Just as in earlier times women who fell at the Whore end of the Virgin-Whore dichotomy tended to be poor, so do most contemporary prostitutes. Typically coming from impoverished backgrounds, most prostitutes cite economic need as their primary motivation (Iga, 1968; Winnick and Kinsie, 1973). But poverty is not the only cause. Many prostitutes come from disorganized and rejecting households and as children experienced feelings of loneliness, alienation, and inadequacy. They frequently have led marginal lives and have been poorly integrated into socially acceptable groups (Clinard, 1958). In addition to the economic and emotional precipitants, many prostitutes come from homes in which a close female relative was herself a prostitute, or in which they were routinely exposed to the activities of prostitutes (James, 1971). Thus, environmental and intrapsychic forces combine to compel women toward prostitution.

James (1971), in a large-scale study of prostitution, pointed to the overrepresentation of black women among his subjects. Within his sample, 56 percent of the prostitutes were black, 36 percent were white, and 7 percent were from other racial or ethnic backgrounds. This high proportion of black women can be accounted for in part by their parallel overrepresentation among the poor, in part by the smaller number of job opportunities available to them. But it also is consistent with a cultural portrayal of blacks as more primitive, and hence innately more sexual (Grier & Cobbs, 1968). Black women, more than white women, correspond to cultural fantasies of the Whore, the woman who is nothing but her sexuality. Ultimately, it may be the black prostitute who permits the white woman to be cherished for her sexual purity.

Issues in the legalization of prostitution. The fate of prostitution has recently become a subject of some debate among writers concerned with the role of women in society. Those who see prostitution as one of women's legitimate choices for expressing her sexuality argue for the protection of prostitutes through the legalization of their profession. Others (e.g., Brownmiller, 1975) focus on prostitution as one form of the oppression of women and argue that it should be abolished.

There are some valid points on both sides of this debate. The latter position is derived from a political analysis of the role of prostitution within a patriarchal culture. From this perspective, prostitution is seen as existing solely to gratify the sexual needs of men. Prostitutes essentially perform a service for their male customers for which they receive an income but not protection under the law or fulfillment of their needs for intimacy and affection. Prostitution symbolizes in stark sexual terms, according to this perspective, males' domination of females. The position of the prostitute, then, becomes that of victim. From this viewpoint, the role of the prostitute would certainly be incompatible with androgyny.

Yet other evidence suggests that, within existing social structures, prostitution holds some rewards for the women involved and is therefore worthy of support. Because prostitutes are often the products of disorganized or rejecting families, the community of prostitutes can be a kind of substitute family, a shelter and security against a seemingly hostile world. These features emerge as salient in a study of prostitution in Lebanon, where prostitution is legal (Khalaf, 1968). Khalaf argues that although economic forces may have orginally driven the women he studied into prostitution, it is the security of their community that keeps them there. This notion of security is supported by his findings that, for the 130 women he studied, the average length of time in the profession was seventeen years, and 37 percent of his sample had been licensed prostitutes for twenty years or more.

From an androgynous perspective on prostitution one would seek information that is not yet available. One would ask, first, Can the "decision" to become a prostitute be considered to have been freely made within present social structures (cf. Libby & Whitehurst, 1977)? Any decision a woman makes about her social role is made within the context of cultural norms, and is further influenced by the restrictions placed on her by virtue of her class and racial background. The prevalence of poor and third-world women within the ranks of prostitutes suggests that they enter this career far more because of limited options than by deliberate choice.

Second, are there conditions under which prostitutes can fare as well or better than women who have opted for other roles in society? How do prostitutes compare, either with women from similar backgrounds, or with women at large, in terms of emotional well-being, economic security, self-image, or basic satisfaction with their life style? Winnick and Kinsie (1973) suggest, for example, that prostitutes see themselves as having a job just like any other people, and that in selling sexual favors they are honest while the rest of the world is corrupt. The prevalence and broader implications of such a position would be useful to explore.

The answers to these and similar questions would provide a basis for evaluation that is free from assumptions that prostitution is "bad" or "wrong" or "harmful" simply because these women are sexually exploited or because they are so clearly sexualized. The first step, then, in evolving an androgynous perspective on prostitution would be to greatly expand the study of prostitution to obtain more thorough documentation of the social position and personal attitudes associated with this way of life.

Rape

Cultural attitudes. Rape is not only illegal, but it is also a crime with a victim, in which one person, the rapist, forcibly and without consent imposes himself sexually on another. "Himself" is used deliberately here; in the overwhelming majority of rape cases, the assaulter is male and the victim female. Thus, the legal treatment of rape, and the reactions of rape victims reflect societal notions of male and female behavior, particularly sexual behavior.

As with prostitution, statistics on the incidence and prosecution of rape reveal a great deal about underlying societal attitudes. Rape, as measured by the frequency of reports to authorities, is a fast-growing crime (Burgess & Holstrom, 1974), perhaps the fastest-rising violent crime in the United States (McCombie, Bassouk, Savitz, & Pell, 1976). FBI statistics report a 68 percent increase in rape from 1968 to 1973, from 31,000 to 51,000 reported instances. The FBI further estimates that ten times that many rapes actually occurred. The APA Monitor (1978) estimated that only one out of every fifteen rapes is annually reported to the police. Once the rape is reported, according to this same source, only one in twenty rapists is arrested, one in thirty prosecuted, and one in sixty convicted.

One reason far more rapes occur than are prosecuted is women's hesitancy to report rape. Such a step can entail a great deal of personal stress. Memories of the rape experience remain vivid and painful in the retelling, police and court officials may be less than supportive in their inquiries, and the victim may fear further attacks after publicly acknowledging her experience. At a more fundamental level, many women may have unconsciously accepted the prevailing social message that if a woman has been raped, she must have wanted it. There is a theme throughout the reports on rape that women want to be raped, that they behave so as to invite rape, that they are perpetrators as well as victims of the crime (cf. Amir, 1971; Hilberman, 1976). This theme is rooted partly in psychoanalytic notions of women's sexuality, for example Helene Deutsch's emphasis on women's unconscious rape fantasies as evidenced in their dreams (1944). At present, it is played out in many court proceedings, in which evidence that a woman is sexually active, has dressed "seductively," or was alone in a dangerous place, could be used to support the innocence of the rapist (Amir, 1971; Brownmiller, 1975). If a woman is raped, then, she may be as guilty as a prostitute of violating the assumption that women are not sexual beings.

The legal treatment of the male rapist reflects, in a converse fashion, a basic attitude of permissiveness toward men's expression of their sexuality, even in this extreme form. This was most clearly articulated by a Wisconsin judge who in 1977 determined that an adolescent rapist was innocent because "rape was a normal reaction to the way the woman was dressed" (NOW Newsletter, 1978). (He was subsequently voted out of office, primarily because of this ruling.) Men are expected to be sexual, and even deviant expressions of their sexuality do not violate fundamental cultural mores.

In an attempt to free the treatment of rape from these prevailing notions about male and female sexuality, recent researchers have emphasized the concept of rape as an extremely stressful event brought about by violence to one's person, and only secondarily as an act of sexual abuse (McCombie et al., 1976; Notman & Nadelson, 1976). As Hilberman succinctly puts it, rape "is best understood in the context of a crime against the person and not against the hymen" (1976, p. 436). From this perspective, one would no more expect a woman to want to be raped than one would expect her to want to be robbed or murdered. Stress and violence, then, provide a basic context within which to examine the motives of the rapist and the reactions of the rape victim.

The rape offender. There is no one portrayal of the typical rapist, or scenario of the typical rape. The rapist may or may not have known his victim prior to the crime. In a study commissioned by the National Commission on the Causes of Violence, it was found that 10 percent of reported rapes occurred between members of extended families, 29 percent between acquaintances, and 53 percent between strangers. Rapes between family members or acquaintances are likely to occur within the home. Between strangers, rapes are equally likely to be initiated on the street, or in a setting that encourages acquaintances, such as a party or a bar (Amir, 1971). The rape may occur quickly and impulsively, or the rapist may entice the victim into a relationship more slowly, and then abuse her sexually. Amir identified four means used by rapists in approaching their victim; tempting them with money or a ride, coercing them with verbal threats, intimidating them through verbal or physical means, and intimidating them by means of a weapon or other object. These last two methods were used by two-thirds of the rapists Amir studied in a large-scale investigation of rape in Philadelphia.

Both aggressive and sexual motives seem to influence the rapist's behavior. Cohen (1971) identified four motivational factors associated with rape: (1) aggressiveness, in which the rape is an act of hostility against the victim; (2) sexuality, in which the rapist is compensating for feelings of sexual inadequacy; (3) sadism, in which the rapist expresses violence toward his partner in order to be aroused; and (4) impulsivity, in which rape is part of a pattern of acting out behaviors. Because of the role of aggression in motivating acts of rape, it is not surprising that Amir (1971) found that physical violence, including beating, choking, and gagging the victim was evident in all but 15 percent of the rapes he studied.

The backgrounds of convicted rapists are not dissimilar to the backgrounds of those convicted for other acts of violence. According to the FBI Uniform Crime Reports, 61 percent of the offenders are between the ages of sixteen and twenty-four; 47 percent are black and 51 percent white. The vast majority come from lower socioeconomic classes, and specifically from what Wolfgang (1967) has called a "subculture of violence." Members of this subculture—poor, marginal, unemployed, and disenfranchised—tend to hold values that run counter to those of the dominant society. For them, violence and physical aggression can become a way of life.

The rape victim. Although any woman is vulnerable to being raped, the majority of rape victims are of the same age, race, and socioeconomic status as the rapists. Those most likely to be raped are black, adolescent, urban, lower-class girls (Brownmiller, 1975). Recently, however, there has been a dramatic increase of rapes occurring on college campuses, primarily of women who had been hitchhiking. In recognition of this fact, the FBI now also lists the numbers of rapes committed at large universities.

Until recent years, most studies of rape victims focused on their individual psychodynamics (cf. Amir, 1971). However, with the newer recognition of rape as criminal assault, attention has turned to understanding the experiences and psychological consequences of rape for the victim (Burgess & Holstrom, 1974, 1976; Notman & Nadelson, 1976). Responses to rape, for these researchers, are understood in terms of an intense stress reaction in the face of a life-threatening experience.

Within this context, women go through a sequence of reactions. Just prior to the actual rape, some women are able to sense danger approaching, and they may attempt to verbally ward off the attack. Strategies include engaging the potential rapist in conversation, reasoning with him, stalling for time, and using flattery, bargaining, jokes, and in some cases, verbal threats (Burgess & Holstrom, 1976). In a study by Burgess and Holstrom of ninety-two women representing a variety of ages and social classes, only a very few of the women attempted to use physical force to prevent attack. One-third of the victims were unable to use any preventive strategy whatsoever. In some cases the victims were asleep or taken totally by surprise. In other cases, the women sensed danger but reacted with denial by becoming what the authors call "psychologically paralyzed."

During the rape itself, many victims used cognitive strategies to keep their mind off of what was happening. They talked to themselves, memorized details connected to the event, or recalled previous advice on how to handle such situations. They continued using verbal strategies to calm, reassure, or in some cases threaten the rapist. A few victims struggled or fought with their attacker, but they tended to cease resisting when they sensed that it was hopeless or that their struggle was actually exciting their attacker.

Reactions following the rape are powerful, painful, and varied. The immediate postrape reaction, called "disorganization" by Burgess and Holstrom (1974) includes a number of physical reactions such as soreness and bruising, general tension, sleep disturbance, stomach pains, and vaginal irritation. There is also a wide gamut of emotional reactions. Fear of violence and death are the most frequent emotional aftermaths, seconded by self-blame (Burgess and Holstrom, 1974). Notman and Nadelson (1976) point to guilt and shame as "virtually universal" postrape feelings. Both studies link this last reaction to societies' tendency to "blame the victim," which leaves her with the recurring sense that had she behaved differently, she could have prevented the rape. Neither study mentions the one reaction that one might most readily expect—anger. In fact, anger did not characterize the immediate postrape reactions of the victims studied. Notman and Nadelson (1976), taking a psychodynamic approach, speculate that cultural expectations of compliance and nonaggressiveness lead women to repress their anger, which is then turned into the more culturally validated feelings of guilt, shame, or self-blame.

The long-term aftermath of rape involves a period of "reorganization" (Burgess & Holstrom, 1974). Victims take steps to ease their emotional stress, including moving, changing their phone numbers, or going on vacation. Many of the women studied turned to family or close friends for emotional support. Yet the emotional upset generated by the rape experience continued. Twenty-nine of the ninety-two women studied by Burgess and Holstrom reported persistent, frightening nightmares. Other women developed phobias; fear of being indoors or outdoors (depending on where the rape took place), fear of crowds, or fear of people behind them. Two fears characterized almost all of the victims studied; fear of being alone and sexual fears. For women who were sexually active, fears associated with the rape increased when they resumed sexual relationships. Many women were unable to return to their normal pattern of sexual activity for some time. For women who had no prior sexual experience, the rape seriously inhibited their thoughts about future sexual activity.

Another look. Findings on the incidence of rape, leniency in dealing with rape offenders, and the emotional reactions of rape victims highlight the damaging effects of cultural assumptions about male and female sexuality. The male offender is denied external controls because of the widespread acceptance of males' sexuality. Female victims are doubly affected. Externally, they face a criminal justice system in which assumptions about their collusion in the act are evident, fueled by the notion that every woman desires to be raped. Internally, they have incorporated society's message that, in the words of one victim, "whatever a man did to a woman, she provoked it" (Burgess & Holstrom, 1974). Trained not to be aggressive, they hesitate to fight back, thus reinforcing their sense of their own complicity, and leaving them with feelings of guilt, shame, and self-blame, but not anger.

Thus, both the female victim and the male rapist are affected by cultural attitudes toward sexuality and aggression in women and men. Women would be far better able to protect themselves if they were encouraged to be aggressive when under attack, perhaps even receiving training in self-defense. They would perhaps also be seen by the legal system more as victims than as perpetrators if it were assumed that women could actively and consciously seek gratification of their sexual needs, eliminating the need for an unconscious wish for sexual gratification through rape. Men could more easily control their sexual and aggressive urges if abusive displays of these needs were clearly condemned by society and punished accordingly. The implicit acceptance of sexuality and aggression in men and not in women creates a scenario in which rape is becoming increasingly frequent.

SUMMARY

We began this chapter by raising questions about the implications of having different notions of sexuality for males and for females. We then looked at issues that affect the capacity of both sexes to develop both agentic and communal dimensions of their sexual lives and to maintain control over their sexual expression while respecting the need and wishes of their partner.

Historically, both elements of sexuality have been curtailed by cultural mores in which acceptable patterns of sexuality have been designed to meet male but not female needs. In the medieval era, the premium placed on romantic love as the route to salvation meant that ideal relationships were asexual. In the Victorian era, sex within marriage other than for purposes of procreation was discouraged. Women were assumed not to have sexual needs; men were warned against excessive sexual activity but supported in their use of prostitutes as sexual outlets. In contemporary society, both men and women are "objectified" in terms of their sexual appeal, so that sexual relationships become more a game of power than an opportunity for the integration of sexuality and affection.

Cultural acceptance of methods of sexuality further reflect the disparity with which male and female needs are recognized. Intercourse, which is generally equated with "making love," is more stimulating for men than women. Clitoral stimulation, which Masters and Johnson have found to be the most direct method for sexual excitement in women is typically considered as "foreplay" or "afterplay," but not as "having sex." This puts pressure on men to be able to sustain an erection in order to feel sexually adequate, and leaves women feeling sexually unresponsive if they do not have an orgasm during intercourse. Increases in the practices of sexual methods other than intercourse have to some extent lessened these problems for both sexes but have created additional difficulties. Men may feel obliged to ensure that their female lovers have at least one, if not several orgasms, and women may feel guilty about their inhibitions in regard to experimenting with a variety of sexual modes.

Patterns of sexual behavior also reveal that men feel freer than women to express their sexuality. Although women are more sexually active in the 1970s than they were in the 1940s, their frequency of engaging in such sexual practices as homosexuality, masturbation, and premarital and extramarital relationships remains below the level found for men. The freedom granted to male sexuality has also led to a greater incidence of rape and lenient treatment of rapists in the courts, as well as to greater penalties for female prostitutes than for their male customers.

Thus, it is difficult for individual persons to adopt more androgynous forms of sexuality within a culture that differentiates between the importance of sexual needs in women and in men. The freedom for each person to determine what is appropriate in terms of both his or her needs and the wishes of his or her partner awaits a situation in which society does not arbitrarily distinguish between appropriate forms of sexuality in women and men.

SELECTED READINGS

Bell, A. P., & Weinberg, M. S. *Homosexualities: A study of diversity among men and women.* New York: Simon and Schuster, 1978.

Bengis, I. *Combat in the erogeneous zone.* New York: Knopf, 1972.

Brownmiller, S. *Against our will: Men, women and rape.* New York: Simon and Schuster, 1975.

Bulloch, V., & Bulloch, B. *Sin, sickness and sanity: A history of sexual attitudes.* New York: New American Library, 1977.

Laws, J. L., & Schwartz, P. *Sexual scripts: The social construction of female sexuality.* Hinsdale, Ill.: Dryden, 1977.

Masters, W. H., & Johnson, V. E. *Human sexual response.* Boston: Little, Brown, 1966.

SEX-ROLE
SOCIALIZATION

PART

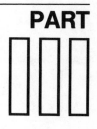

Family Influences on Sex-Role Development

One of the most common explanations among lay people for sex differences in behavior is that parents induce them. The pink or blue nursery that parents set up is seen as a symbol of ongoing efforts to socialize the little girl into femininity and the little boy into masculinity. Through example, subtle expectations, and direct training, parents are said to play a major role in the development of psychological sex. By implication, parents can lead their children toward androgyny, or toward sex typing, through their own actions.

Most psychologists seem to share this assumption of the importance of parents in sex-role development. The best evidence of this orientation is the large numbers of theories and research studies that focus on the relationship of parental sex-role characteristics or attitudes and similar characteristics in their offspring. In fact, much of the work in this area has traditionally focused on preschool children, suggesting that psychologists believe the foundation of sex-role development is laid in early childhood.

This chapter is divided into four major sections, presenting both the theories and research that represent psychological work on sex-role development in the family. The first part is a description and discussion of the major theories of sex-role development. Although some of the traditional theories have only limited applicability for explaining androgynous development, they will be examined thoroughly because of their major influence on work in this area. These theories, for all their limitations, provide the frameworks for establishing whatever knowledge is available about the development of psychological sex. Whenever possible, we will draw out the hidden implications these theories have for androgynous development.

In the second part of the chapter we will look at the empirical work on sex-role development in the family. Here the emphasis will be on the research evidence for parental influence on sex-role development. Do parents affect sex-role development? If so, how and when? Whenever possible, we will see how available data support—or don't support—the theories of sex-role development.

In two final sections we will integrate the theories and research as much as possible, and then discuss direct applications to childrearing practices.

Throughout the chapter the emphasis will be on factors that foster not only sex-typed but also androgynous development in the family. To what extent is learning "I am a girl" or "I am a boy" necessary for healthy psychological development? Is androgyny something that must be learned from androgynous parents or can one combine the feminine characteristics of one parent with the masculine characteristics of the other to form one's own unique, nonstereotyped sex role? Must one learn a stereotyped sex role before developing one's androgynous potential? How strong are parents' efforts to teach children stereotyped roles? Under what conditions can a person develop beyond a stereotyped home environment?

THEORIES OF SEX-ROLE DEVELOPMENT

There are three traditional theories of how sex roles develop within the family: psychoanalytic, social learning, and cognitive development theory. Although each theory has its problems, all three are important because they have virtually "cornered the market" of thinking in this area. Most writers and researchers on sex-role development have spent massive amounts of time trying to support or discredit these three major theories. Therefore, we must have some understanding of these three theories in order to begin understanding psychology's approach to sex-role development.

A central concept in the three traditional theories of sex-role development is *identification.* Although some authors prefer to use the term "imitation," most agree that the process is one by which a person takes on some of the characteristics of another and makes them a part of her or his own personality (Hall & Lindzey, 1978, p. 49). When talking about sex-role identification, psychologists are usually referring to the process by which a child comes to emulate certain behaviors of a parent, especially of the same-sex parent.

In discussing how sex-role identity develops, we must remember the distinctions among gender identity, sexual preference, and psychological sex described in Chapter 1. As we defined it there, sex-role identity is an alternative term for psychological sex. Thus, in the following sections, we will examine various explanations for the development of feminine and masculine personality characteristics and behavior.

Psychoanalytic Theory: Sigmund Freud

Sigmund Freud spent much of his life working with middle-class patients in Victorian Vienna. Within that cultural milieu, the roles and behavior of the sexes were quite distinct. Families were very patriarchal. Men were often strong and assertive, focusing much of their energy on work responsibilities in order to support their families. Women were often dependent and passive, centering their lives on home and family. These differences were considered right and natural.

Freud's task was to identify the causes of these observed psychological differences. In addition, he sought to explain how loving relationships for both sexes changed between infancy and adulthood. For female and male infants, the person who is most available as an object of identification, and the person who is their most important love object is a female, mother. In the preschool years, however, a shift occurs so that males feel similar to (identify with) males, while retaining females as their primary love objects. Although females retain that early sense of similarity to (identification with) other females, they must shift the main focus of their love from females to males. Within Freud's theory, "normal" development is defined as the development of femininity in women, masculinity in men, and heterosexuality in both sexes.

Freud used his larger theoretical framework as the basis for explaining both these shifts in relationships and the psychological differences he observed between the sexes. A fundamental aspect of his more general theory was that vast areas of the personality are within the "unconscious." Motivation is largely controlled by deep-seated, instinctual biological drives, particularly for sex and aggression. Personality develops, often outside a person's consciousness, in response to the interaction of those instinctual drives and cultural demands. Childhood is considered a particularly important time for development.

Freud's explanation for the psychological and interpersonal differences between the sexes was based on the anatomical differences between the sexes. Children's psychological reactions to the discovery of sexual pleasure associated with their genitals serve as the impetus for the development of sex-role identity.

In the first few years of life, according to Freud, girls and boys develop in similar ways, due to infantile sexuality and an inevitable strong attachment to mother, their original source of nurturance. Both sexes soon discover the pleasure they can derive from manipulating their genitals. Yet their development proceeds in different directions when they realize that the genitals of girls and boys are different. For the girl, the enjoyment of clitoral masturbation comes to an abrupt halt when she notices that boys have a larger, and thus supposedly superior, genital organ. Freud calls this

a momentous discovery which little girls are destined to make. They notice the penis of a brother or playmate, strikingly visible and of large proportions, at once recognize it as the superior counterpart of their own small and inconspicuous organ, and from that time forward fall a victim to envy for the penis. . . . She has seen it and knows that she is without it and wants to have it. (1925, p. 252)

The little girl sees her deprivation as somehow mother's responsibility. Until now, mother has been the person who met the girl's physical and emotional needs. This "perfect love" is marred, however, by the discovery that mother has failed the little girl in one important regard. The realization that mother, too, lacks a penis makes it even clearer to the girl that mother is responsible. The girls falls out of love with her mother and, in disappointment and anger, turns to father. Father does not share mother's failing, and the girl has the unconscious hope that he will provide the missing organ. The girl focuses her emerging sexual feelings onto father, hoping to share her love with him. The ultimate outcome of this love would be a new baby which, if it were male, would be a substitute for her missing penis. Even though the girl no longer focuses all her love on mother, she identifies with mother, in hopes of sharing some of mother's obvious success at winning father's favor.

Thus, by the age of six, the girl has gone from a close relationship with her mother to an identification with mother in order to gain father's love. Her love of the opposite-sexed parent, the Oedipus complex (named after the mythological Greek hero who killed his father and married his mother), is destined to fade with the passing years. Although the girl never totally relinquishes her attachment to her father, she eventually (after puberty) turns to other men. Through love relationships with men it becomes possible for her to remedy her deficit by producing a "complete" infant, a male child.

It is the girl's identification with mother, along with feelings growing out of penis envy, that accounts for her development of a feminine personality. A normal female, according to Freud, has inclinations toward jealously and feelings of inferiority as a result of her realization that she lacks a penis. Passivity is also a hallmark of the normal feminine personality as the girl accepts the passive sexual role she must play because she does not have the penis necessary to initiate active sexual relationships.

Even though boys possess the penis, they have their own tensions and conflicts in growing toward a masculine personality. Like the girl, the boy spends the first few years of life in a close relationship to his mother.[1] Initially one with her in the womb, he continues to experience her as the center of his existence and the source of satisfaction for his physical and emotional needs. For the male child who has not yet developed a sense of society's prohibitions, it is natural to focus his undeveloped sexual longings onto his mother. Once the boy discovers the pleasure available through manipulation of his penis, around age three, he begins to develop a sexual attraction toward his mother. Consequently, he enters into a rivalry with his father for mother's affection. This is the male version of the Oedipus complex. But the genital pleasure the boy is experiencing leads indirectly to new fears. Realizing that father already apparently has some attachment to mother and will not give her up easily, the boy develops castration anxiety. This is his fear that, in retaliation for his amorous strivings, father will remove the son's genitals and hence end his new-found pleasure. Noticing that girls are apparently already victims of castration makes the boy's fear seem more realistic. In order to reduce this growing anxiety, the boy unconsciously opts to abandon his Oedipal desires and identify with his father. By being masculine, like father, the boy can quell his fears as well as nurture his ability to one day procure a woman of his own.

Hence, it can be seen that Freud explains the development of femininity or masculinity as an indirect result of anatomy. Because the boy has a penis and the girl does not, they are destined to develop different types of relationships with each parent and, ultimately, to identify with the same-sex parent. If all proceeds normally

[1]Though Freud did not use the term "identification" in discussing this early mother-son closeness, other writers have. Stoller (1974), for example, points out that one of the most difficult tasks for male development is to separate one's identity from mother's femaleness. Men must struggle throughout life to combat their initial identity and assert their masculinity. This tension inherent in maleness may account for some men's apparent preoccupations with being extremely strong, independent, and (at times) hypermasculine. They fear that they will remerge into mother's femaleness. The female, on the other hand, has a more stable basis for her identity, since even her pre-Oedipal identification was with a female.

(in Freud's framework), this process of identification comes to fruition at puberty when the Oedipal feelings reemerge, but this time they are directed to opposite-sexed contemporaries.

Freud's theory has several strong points. He stressed both early family relationships and childhood reactions to anatomy in explaining the development of personality. He was one of the first to point out the intensity of early parent-child relationships. He also suggested that, just as sexual feelings are part of many adult intimate relationships, they also might be part of intimate relationships involving children. He must be credited with suggesting that, even if biology has few *direct* effects on personality (e.g., through the sex hormones), it can have *indirect* effects. These indirect effects can come about as children perceive their own bodies and compare them to the bodies of other children and adults. Few people would deny that a physically athletic, active, well-coordinated child reacts to him- or herself (and is reacted to) very differently than the child with an awkward, slow uncoordinated body. Similarly, psychological development probably does not proceed completely independent of other biological realities, including sexual anatomy. Children as well as adults quite likely assign some psychological significance to their physical bodies.

Despite these strong points, Freud's work has been challenged on both empirical and theoretical grounds. He has been criticized for basing his theories about child development on clinical work with neurotic adults. He rarely saw children or had the opportunity to test his ideas in the controlled, systematic manner demanded by psychologists. Also, some people who have subjected Freud's ideas to empirical analysis, have found evidence to contradict his conclusions.

It has been difficult to find evidence for the feelings of penis envy that are central to Freud's differential explanations for female and male development (Sherman, 1971). In a carefully controlled study of a representative group of many children (ages four and five) researchers saw no evidence of castration concern in either girls or boys (Kreitler & Kreitler, 1966). During interviews with mothers of children, Hattendorf (1932) found that, although the children asked many questions about sex, most of the questions concerned the origin of babies. Only three of the 865 questions by preschoolers suggested anxiety about the presence or absence of the penis—and all of these questions came from boys. Similar data were reported in other studies: castration anxiety is rare in normal children and the few cases in which it does occur tend to be boys (Friedman, 1952; Conn, 1940).

Another part of Freud's theory, that preschool girls prefer their fathers, has come under doubt. Sherman (1971) reviewed the evidence on this topic and found little support for the Freudian hypothesis. If a conclusion about children's parental preference can be made, it is that there is a slight tendency for both sexes to prefer the mother.

Freudian theory also suggests that appropriate resolution of the Oedipus complex through identification with a feminine-passive mother for girls and a masculine-dominant father for boys is necessary for psychological health. Williams (1973) offers evidence that this is not the case, at least for girls. In fact, high school girls who showed the best personal adjustment were more likely to perceive themselves as similar to a dominant father than were any other girls. Thus the evidence in these studies seems to contradict the Freudian explanation of sex-role development, particularly for females.

Some of Freud's followers disagree with him about sex-role development on theoretical rather than empirical grounds (cf. Blum, 1977). Alfred Adler (1927) and Clara Thompson (1942, 1943) thought that Freud was too literal in his discussion and did not give enough attention to the cultural context of development. According to these theorists, girls do not envy the penis itself but, rather, the male power that it symbolizes in Western society. The available data support such an interpretation, since many studies indicate that both females and males—adults as well as children—more often think it is preferable to be male than female.

Karen Horney (1967) suggested that Freud's own maleness limited his understanding of female development. She pointed out that his ideas of penis envy in girls closely parallel little boys' ideas about girls' anatomy, rather than the girls' ideas. Table 7.1 presents her analysis. According to Horney, Freud may have been revealing his unconscious "womb envy" by emphasizing what females do not have (penis) rather than what males do not have (womb).

In defense of Freud, he himself pointed out the tentative nature of his views and the lack of confirming data (1925). He felt compelled to present what he considered incomplete ideas about feminine development, because he feared that he would die before he could refine this aspect of his theory. Other people have also risen to his defense. In recent years, Juliet Mitchell (1974) has pointed out that Freud was simply analyzing a patriarchal society, not advocating it or claiming its inevitability.

TABLE 7.1   Horney's Comparison of Boys' Ideas and Freudian Ideas of Feminine Development

The boy's ideas	*Freudian ideas of feminine development*
Naive assumption that girls as well as boys possess a penis	For both sexes it is only the male genital which plays any part
Realization of the absence of the penis	Sad discovery of the absence of the penis
Idea that the girl is a castrated, mutilated boy	Belief of the girl that she once possessed a penis and lost it by castration
Belief that the girl has suffered punishment that also threatens him	Castration is conceived of as the infliction of punishment
The girl is regarded as inferior	The girl regards herself as inferior. Penis envy
The boy is unable to imagine how the girl can ever get over this loss or envy	The girl never gets over the sense of deficiency and inferiority and has constantly to master afresh her desire to be a man
The boy dreads her envy	The girl desires throughout life to avenge herself on the man for possessing something which she lacks

Source: From Karen Horney, *Feminine Psychology*, pp. 57–58 (New York: W. W. Norton & Company, Inc., 1967). Reprinted by permission.

Although Freud's theories of sex-role development have not withstood many empirical or theoretical analyses, his writings do contain some hints at an androgynous potential within people. Even while emphasizing the importance of biology in the development of sex differences, Freud wrote that everyone is born with a bisexual potential, a potential to develop in feminine and masculine psychological directions. He struggled with this notion throughout his career (1905, 1937), and his ultimate judgment was that he had failed to solve the enigma of similarities as well as differences existing between the sexes (1938). He felt that by explaining sex differences, he was making sex similarities unexplainable. Despite the fact that his observations presented problems for his theory, he could not help noting

In human beings pure masculinity or pure femininity is not to be found either in a psychological or a biological sense. Every individual on the contrary displays a mixture of the character-traits belonging to his own and to the opposite sex; and he shows a combination of activity and passivity whether or not these last character-traits tally with his biological ones. (1905, pp. 219–20)

Perhaps Freud found these observations problematic only because of the polarized assumptions he brought to his work. It seems that he conceptualized his task as explaining femininity in women and masculinity in men. Instances of androgyny thus became contradictions to his "knowledge" that women and men are different. If he had been trying to explain the existence of both feminine and masculine traits in either women or men, perhaps he would have developed the bisexual element of his theory more fully.

Social Learning Theory: Walter Mischel

Walter Mischel represents a group of psychologists, known as social learning theorists, which says that children learn many behaviors by imitating people around them. Hence, sex differences in behavior occur because children see females and males around them behaving in different ways and learn to behave as they do.

Mischel, a personality theorist and researcher at Stanford University, has spent much of his career trying to combat Freudian ideas that, in his opinion, pervade too much of psychology. Mischel does agree with Freud that sex-role behavior is acquired from other people, but he interprets this process somewhat differently.

According to Mischel (1966, 1970, 1976), there are two distinct aspects in the learning of any behavior, including sex-role behavior: acquisition and performance. *Acquisition,* the learning process, occurs primarily through observation of models —what a person sees others doing. The models can be real or symbolic (in stories, television, etc.). *Performance* of the observed behaviors occurs, however, only when one is motivated. In any situation, what one perceives as the possible consequences of an act determine one's motivation. Thus people rarely perform the whole range of behaviors they have acquired, because they anticipate aversive consequences for performing some of them. In fact, Mischel thinks that girls and boys acquire many similar behaviors but restrict their performance because of social constraints against behaviors that "belong to" the other sex.

Although Mischel thinks that children acquire sex-role behavior from a wide range of adult and peer models, he suggests that parents are particularly important models. Obviously they are the earliest, as well as the most powerful models in the child's life. But most children have both a female (mother) and male (father) model available. Why then do the sexes often develop in different directions? Why, for example, do a sister and brother who are exposed to the same parental models acquire and perform different behaviors?

Mischel explains the acquisition of sex-typed behavior in terms of the observer's (in this case, the child's) selection of a model (here, the parent) who is nurturant, powerful, and similar to her or him. Because both parents are likely to be powerful and nurturant in the eyes of the child, the child would probably acquire behavior of the same-sexed parent—the one whom the child is most likely to perceive as similar. To the extent that the same-sexed parent is sex-typed, the child will tend to develop sex-typed behaviors.

So far we have looked only at the child's acquisition of sex-typed behavior. Whether or not the child actually performs the behavior depends on her or his motivation. Mischel discusses motivation in terms of the consequences the child expects for performance. These consequences are called *reinforcement* and *punishment.* Reinforcement is anything, real or imagined, that increases the chances that a behavior will be performed. Some common reinforcements are praise, a feeling of competence, or social acceptance. Punishment, on the other hand, decreases the chances that a behavior will be performed. Possible punishments include physical harm, feeling foolish, and social rejection.

Children learn about these consequences for behavior both directly and indirectly. A direct punishment would be the spanking a girl receives for wandering too far from home. The result, the decreased chance that she will wander from home, can also occur when she sees another child being spanked for wandering, or when she is told that wandering will result in spanking.

Social learning is such a powerful force, according to Mischel, that it causes people to develop expectations about the consequences of behavior. These expectations, developed by observing the surrounding world, encourage or discourage people from performing the behavior they have acquired. The girl who hesitates to do her best in math class for fear of losing popularity, or the boy who pushes himself to be the toughest kid on the football team in order to meet parental expectations of a "real boy" show how anticipated consequences influence everyday performance.

The potential discrepancy between behaviors people acquire and those they perform was demonstrated in a set of laboratory experiments (Bandura, 1965). Preschool children watched a film in which an adult model exhibited unusual aggressive behavior toward a large, inflated plastic doll ("Bobo"). One group of children saw the model severely punished after this behavior, another group saw the model generously rewarded, and a third group observed no consequences. These groups differed widely in aggression when later given a Bobo doll to play with: children in the model-punishment group displayed fewer aggressive responses than the other children. In addition, boys showed more aggressive responses than girls, across all groups. These findings suggest that the groups and sexes differed in the aggressive behavior they acquired. However, when all the children were later offered an attractive reinforcement for aggressive behavior toward still another unfortunate Bobo doll, the group and sex differences decreased. Apparently, when all the children anticipated positive consequences (e.g., attractive reinforcement), they were motivated to perform the previously observed aggression. The earlier reluctance of boys in the model-punishment group and the average girl to perform aggression seemed to be contingent on the consequences they anticipated. The researcher postulated that even in the model-reward condition girls anticipated aversive consequences for aggression because of social learning previous to the experiment. When the anticipated consequences were made equivalent for all children, through promise of a reward, all displayed the behavior they had acquired. The researcher's conclusion was that children do not necessarily perform all behaviors they acquire.

By emphasizing the role of observation in learning, Mischel and other social learning theorists are acknowledging that learning sex roles is more complicated than simply receiving praise or punishment for "sex-appropriate" behavior. Watching others and hearing the "rules" for females and males are important for the child in developing a sense of what is appropriate for her or him.

Like Freud, social learning theorists paint a picture of development that emphasizes the ways stereotyped sex roles develop. Also like Freud, they posit that this process begins early in life, when parents are still the major influences on the child. Thus, Mischel does agree with Freud in suggesting that children are likely to develop sex-typed behaviors from their parents. However, Freud attributes such development to the child's internal motivation to identify with the same-sexed parent, which results from anatomy and family dynamics. Mischel's explanation focuses on more straightforward processes—perceiving similarity and anticipating consequences that are learned through direct teaching and observations. Learning sex-role behavior is, to Mischel, no different than learning other behavior. Hence, although parents are important sex-role models according to social learning theory, so too are siblings, peers, teachers, television characters, and, potentially, anyone else the child observes. As long as parents and models are sex-typed and as long as anticipated consequences depend on the child's sex, children will develop—acquire and perform—sex-typed behavior.

There is some empirical evidence to support social learning theory. In the laboratory, children tend to imitate the behavior of models, particularly those who are powerful, rewarded for their behavior, or similar to the child (Grusec & Mischel, 1966; Rosenkrans, 1967). Even more relevant for learning of sex-role behavior is the evidence that boys imitate adult male models more readily than adult female models, whereas girls have a similar (though less pronounced) tendency to imitate adult female models (Grusec & Brinker, 1972).

Yet this evidence for the social learning explanation of sex-role development has been questioned because it has often been gathered outside children's natural settings. Most of the studies on social learning involve interactions between children and nonparental models under controlled laboratory conditions. Maccoby and Jacklin (1974, pp. 296–97) list nineteen studies that they consider relevant to children's imitation of same-sex or cross-sex models; yet only three of these studies were done with parents and their own children. Even the studies that used parent-child pairs examined only behaviors that were not related to sex roles—such as children's willingness to imitate their parents' aesthetic preference (e.g., Hetherington, 1965). One cannot be sure whether the conclusions derived about nonsex-role behavior can be generalized to account for sex-role learning.

Even within the limited studies available (Maccoby & Jacklin, 1974), it is difficult to predict how the nurturance, power, and similarity of models will interact, as well as what other model characteristics are crucial. For example, one study found that children of both sexes imitated the dominant parent more than the passive parent, and girls imitated both parents more than boys did (Hetherington, 1965). Whom does the son of a dominant mother and nurturant father choose to imitate? Is dominance more important than the combination of nurturance and similarity?

An even more relevant question for the study of androgyny concerns nurturant parents who are sometimes dominant, sometimes egalitarian, and sometimes passive: Will the child choose one parent as a model or one type of behavior to imitate; or will the child imitate both parents or avoid the confusion by imitating a sibling? Do children learn differently at different ages? Are there individual differences in the extent to which children are influenced by models: Are sex-typed masculine children less likely to imitate any models than sex-typed feminine children? Many such questions remain, and although social learning theory addresses some of them it has by no means answered them all.

Social learning theory has implications for androgyny, although Mischel does not develop them explicitly. The idea within social learning theory that *both* parents serve as important models for the child suggests that both sexes can *acquire* feminine and masculine behaviors early in life. It is chiefly motivation that prevents people from *performing* the full range of behaviors that they know. It is as if most people have buried abilities that can be released when they modify the ways they think about the world. From this perspective, many people have acquired the skills necessary for androgyny but hesitate to perform them. If the sex-role rules of society were changed, both present and future generations might begin to expect different consequences for behavior that is now labeled as appropriate for only one sex. Under such conditions, both sexes might feel free to perform the wide range of behaviors they have acquired.

Cognitive Developmental Theory: Lawrence Kohlberg

Lawrence Kohlberg's cognitive developmental theory of sex-role development is both different from and similar to the theories of Freud and Mischel. The major thesis in Kohlberg's argument is unique: sex-role development is an outgrowth of cognitive development. Children think of themselves as a girl or boy, and then mold their behavior to maintain a stable sense of identity as a girl or boy. Identification with parents occurs as a result of these self-maintaining motives. Like Freud, Kohlberg sees sex-role development as the reflection of an internal developmental process. And, like Mischel, Kohlberg apparently believes that actual sex-role behavior is learned from environmental models.

Kohlberg is a psychologist at Harvard University whose central interest is the extension of Jean Piaget's ideas of cognitive development to explain a child's increasingly complex sense of morality. In one paper, however, Kohlberg (1966) extended the application of principles of cognitive development from moral reasoning to sex-role identity.

According to Piaget's general cognitive developmental theory, a child's cognitive organization of the physical and social world undergoes radical, but natural, transformations with age development (1952, 1954). For example, young children do not understand the principle Piaget calls "conservation"—that physical objects remain the same even when their appearance is different. Thus, before age six, children who observe water being poured from a four-inch to a six-inch wide container insist that there was "more" water in the first container because it looked deeper. Only after age seven do children develop the concept of conservation.

Kohlberg argues that, just as children's understanding of conservation changes as their thinking matures, so does their understanding of themselves and sex roles. A child's understanding of reality, including gender, is very different from an adult's more "logical" interpretation.

Within Kohlberg's theory, sex-role development begins at age two to three, when the child begins to label her- or himself as a girl or boy. The child at first does not apply the same categorization appropriately to others. So, although the majority of three-year-olds can label their own sex correctly, they have trouble labeling adults or dolls (Kohlberg, 1966). The child also does not conceive of sex as an unchanging characteristic until she or he is five or six. In one study (Kohlberg, 1966), children between four and eight were asked whether a pictured girl could be a boy if she wanted to, or if she wore boys' clothes. Most of the four-year-olds agreed that the switch was possible, but most of the seven-year-olds were sure that the girl could not be a boy even if she changed her appearance or behavior. Conceptions of sex roles develop as do other concepts, according to Kohlberg; four-year-olds also think that a pictured cat could be a dog if it wanted to, or if its whiskers were cut off, but seven-year-olds assert that the cat's identity is invariable. Other data supporting Kohlberg's contentions of age-related changes in sex-role concepts include young children's confusion about whether they will be a mommy or a daddy when they grow up. After all, in a child's view of the world, if age changes, maybe sex does, too.

So, whereas Freud saw preschoolers embroiled in Oedipal rivalry and Mischel sees them imitating sex-appropriate models, Kohlberg sees them more concerned with their own thoughts. The child spends the preschool years establishing a self-label as girl or boy, and coming to the realization that this aspect of her or himself is permanent. According to Kohlberg, the judgment, "I really am and always will be a girl," is the result of cognitive development quite independent of social sex-role training and parental identification.

Once the child has established this firm sex-role self-concept, she or he then uses it to develop sex-typed preferences and values—what is called sex-role identity. This later development is similar to that envisioned by Mischel, but the motivation is different. In social learning theory, children perform sex-role behaviors in order to get rewards, to fulfill society's expectations. In cognitive developmental theory, children are not seeking rewards but cognitive consistency. Mischel's little boy would theoretically say to himself, "I want rewards; I am rewarded for doing boy things; therefore I want to be a boy," and proceed with doing "boy things." Kohlberg's little boy would theoretically say, "I am a boy; therefore I want to do boy things; therefore doing boy things is rewarding," and proceed with doing "boy things" (Kohlberg, 1966). In other words, Kohlberg thinks that children learn sex-appropriate actions from other people, but that they perform them, not for rewards, but only to maintain their self-identity as girl or boy. The basic sex-role self-concept leads children to place different values on objects and activities: a girl comes to value girllike things and behavior because they help her maintain her self-image of girl, whereas a boy values boylike activities in order to maintain his self-image as a boy. This then leads to identification with the same-sexed parent simply because she or he shares that girllike or boylike quality.

Unfortunately, Kohlberg stops his analysis just as the child has developed stereotypic sex-role identification. Cognitive and moral development, however, continue into adolescence and perhaps later (Kohlberg, 1973). This presents intriguing implications for people interested in the development of androgyny. If it is true that people's thinking naturally becomes more complex and flexible as they get older, perhaps their thinking about sex roles also develops into more subtle, less stereotypic concepts. Kohlberg (1966), in fact, mentioned that young children are more stereotypic in their thinking than older children or adults. Perhaps people can grow beyond the global idea, "I am a girl and therefore find girl things rewarding," to "I am a woman, but I'm also a lawyer and thus find being assertive in the courtroom rewarding. In addition I am a friend and find being nurturant toward my friends rewarding." It may well be that in adulthood a person develops a more highly differentiated self-concept than "I am a girl or boy." If behavior does follow self-identity, as Kohlberg suggests, a nonstereotypic self-identity can lead to the development of less stereotypic and perhaps more androgynous behavior.

Kohlberg's theory is additionally provocative in terms of the link it suggests between one's certainty of being female or male and a stable identity in the general sense of "who I am." A fundamental component of "who I am" appears to be "I am female or male." Data described by John Money and his colleagues (Money & Ehrhardt; 1972; Money & Tucker, 1975) substantiate this aspect of the theory. Although gender can be reassigned (if medically indicated) without psychological harm up to the age of fifteen months, gender reassignment after the age of three of four is quite difficult. By that time, the child's self-categorization as female or male is so central to the sense of self that a shift cannot be effected without undermining the sense of self. Money concludes that it is very rare to find someone who has established a general sense of identity ("who I am") without labeling the self as female or male.

The suggestion that a sense of one's femaleness or maleness is fundamental to the development of a firm sense of self can be understood better if we recall the distinction between "gender identity" and "sex-role identity" (or psychological sex) explained in Chapter 1. Again, Kohlberg does not draw out the implications for androgyny, but they are present within his theory. The self-categorization as girl or boy may be the first step in establishing what is labeled "gender identity" (a recognition that one is female or male, and comfort with the accompanying physical body). Accordingly, such a self-categorization may be a necessary aspect

[handwritten margin note: gender identity vs. psychological sex]

of healthy development, although it need not interfere with later development of an androgynous psychological sex.

Kohlberg shares with the other sex-role development theorists a lack of clear, confirming data. A major review (Kurtines & Greif, 1974) has criticized Kohlberg's general cognitive model as somewhat difficult to specify and hence not open to thorough investigation by other researchers. These methodological criticisms could be applied to his work on sex-role development as well. Resolution of these difficulties would be especially useful, for one intriguing (yet unexplored) implication of his model is that a sex-role stereotypic stage is a natural by-product of cognitive development. We will return to this idea, after evaluating the three traditional models of sex-role development, when we discuss an alternative model.

Evaluation of Traditional Theories

Each of the major traditional models of sex-role development, in its own way, postulates that a great deal of sex-role behavior is learned within the family. According to Freud, children try to become like the same-sexed parent after going through a series of events that stem from a recognition of genital differences and accompanying family dynamics. To Mischel, children are more likely to acquire behavior from people whom they perceive as similar (e.g., the same-sexed parent), and to perform behaviors, such as "sex-appropriate" behaviors, that hold promise of reinforcement. To Kohlberg, children learn to behave in sex-typed ways in order to be consistent with their self-categorization as girl or boy.

These three theories, while offering an explanation for sex-role development, all share two major problems. First, none of the theorists provides confirming data based on good studies of naturally occurring parent-child interactions. Second, the traditional models all share a narrowness of vision.

Although we have pointed out the implications of each model for the development of androgynous behavior, the theorists themselves have limited their explanation to the development of sex-role stereotypic behavior. In concluding a review of the major theories of sex-role development, Mussen discussed the "major tasks" of the parents: to teach the child "appropriate sex typed responses" and to serve as a model of the "proper" attitudes and personality characteristics (1969, p. 728). He went on to describe these processes in detail, explaining how parents should reward sex-appropriate responses and punish opposite-sex responses. It is as if, once the child reaches school age and is acting appropriately as girl or boy, the traditional theorist breathes a sigh of relief that all is well, and promptly loses interest. Sex-role development has been defined as the development of "appropriate" sex roles and, hence, has not extended beyond early childhood. We will attempt to remedy this matter by discussing an alternative model of sex-role development.

Alternative Model: A Life Span View

One point neglected in the traditional models is the fact that people do not remain children. We know that most children can correctly label themselves as "girl" or "boy" by age three. By age four, most children can extend the gender labeling to others. Yet, the child does not perceive gender as a stable, unchanging aspect of identity until age five or six. What happens to sex roles after age six, when "proper" sex-role identification has been established?

The traditional models also do not tell us why children's ideas about sex-role behavior do not always match the behavior they observe in their parents. There is evidence that children of this age are disturbed by anything that conflicts with their somewhat rigid notions of sex roles, as when six-year-old Peter worried while his father held his mother's purse for a moment: "Why are you carrying the purse, Dad, are you a lady or something? You must be a lady, men don't carry purses" (Kohlberg, 1966, p. 116). Likewise, a five-year-old boy asked his father (a college professor who had not displayed any tendency at all toward sportsmen's heroics): "Oh, Daddy, how old will I be when I can go hunting with you? We'll go in the woods, you with your gun, me with my bow and arrow. Daddy, wouldn't it be neat if we could lasso a wild horse?" (Kohlberg, 1966, p. 136). In the face of such comments by children, one begins to wonder if children are going through some process of defining what constitutes manly and womanly behavior. Sometimes it seems that they build these categories in spite of what they see in their own families.

Although the traditional theories and research on sex-role development halt their investigations at this stage of youthful polarities, other theorists have taken a longer-range view. Jeanne Block (1973) has presented a model of sex-role development that is an extension of Jane Loevinger's (1966, Loevinger & Wessler, 1970) ideas of ego development. Loevinger conceptualizes personality development as an invariable sequence of stages, each more complex than the preceding stage, and all of them representing the person's attempts to cope with increasingly deeper problems (e.g., of self-ideal, morality, meaning, or existence). In a parallel fashion, Block conceptualizes sex-role development as the result of a person's efforts to attain an identity that permits her or him to deal with life's increasing complexity. Thus, the goal of sex-role development becomes a balance between agency and communion rather than the attainment of a rigid, sex-typed identity.

As Block explains it the person moves from the awareness that she or he is girl or boy to acquisition of a stereotyped sex role at the same time she or he is conforming to general society-defined roles (see Table 7.2). At this point, boys are encouraged to control their feelings, whereas girls are encouraged to control aggression. Later, the person becomes more introspective and develops her or his own values and ideas about the "kind of person I would like to be." At this time, rigid sex roles begin to be moderated, in order to fit one's individual values. This moderation leads one into the next stage, that of an awareness of potentially conflicting feminine and masculine elements within the self. At the highest level of sex-role development, the androgynous one, a person is able to integrate her or his feminine and masculine traits and values. Only when one learns to temper agency with communion, femininity with masculinity, can sex-role development be considered complete within Block's model.

In presenting their ideas on sex-role transcendence, Hefner, Rebecca, and Oleshansky (1975) have also taken a developmental approach (Table 7.2). According to them, a person originally has an *undifferentiated* conception of sex roles, during the stage characterized by global thinking: she or he is not aware of a female-male distinction, and experience is simply a mass of unorganized percep-

TABLE 7.2 Conceptions of Sex Roles Throughout the Life Span: Two Models

Block (1973)	Hefner, Rebecca, and Oleshansky (1975)
	Undifferentiated conception of sex roles
Development of gender identity	
Conformity to external role, development of sex-role stereotypes	Polarized notions of sex role
Examination of self as sex-role exemplar vis-a-vis internal values	
Differentiation of sex role, coping with conflicting masculine and feminine aspects of self	
Achievement of individually defined sex role, integration of both masculine and feminine aspects of self, androgynous sex-role definition	Sex-role transcendence

tions. With experience and the development of thinking, the child moves to *polarized* notions of sex roles. This shift includes an active acceptance of one's own sex-role, together with an active rejection of what is then conceptualized as the "opposite" sex. At this stage one is either female or male, and, hence, either feminine or masculine. Some people can make the transition, however, to a third stage of sex-role development, *sex-role transcendence.* This is a dynamic stage in which one can transcend the polarities in order to adopt more adaptive and personally relevant strategies.

In spite of the traditional emphasis on the development of polarized sex roles, a development beyond polarities can be found in other psychological theories. One of Freud's theoretical descendants, Carl Jung, noted that the middle years of life witness a return to the opposite-sexed traits that were rejected in childhood: women can reclaim their masculine selves, and men can reclaim their feminine sides. Jung does not see these changes as necessarily positive, he worries about what may happen in a marriage when the husband discovers his tender feelings and the wife her sharpness of mind. From an androgynous perspective, however, these changes need not signal a reversal of sex roles; they may reflect an extension of them. Perhaps decreased family responsibilities, an awareness of one's own mortality, increasing cognitive complexity, or simply continued contact with life requiring a variety of coping skills (cf., Sedney, 1977b), can impel one to develop additional behavioral skills and emotional styles. Perhaps Jung was the victim of his own polarities when he envisioned a reversal, men becoming feminine and women becoming masculine, in the second half of life. Women may, in fact, maintain the feminine characteristics that have dominated their lives, while broadening their self-definition and behavior to include some elements previously regarded as the sole property of men. Men may be doing the reverse. In other words, rather than simply maintaining a polarized view of one's sex role, or rather than changing to the other pole, perhaps adults in mid- to late life move closer to androgyny, toward a greater integration of so-called feminine and masculine aspects.

There are data to support these views. On the basis of projective data, Neugarten and Gutmann (1968) concluded that, with age, women become more tolerant of their aggressive egocentric impulses, and men become more accepting toward their nurturant and affiliative impulses. Lowenthal, Thurnher, and Chiriboga (1975) found that older women (close to retirement age) described themselves as more assertive than did younger women (high school seniors, newlyweds, and middle-aged women). Livson (1976) extended these results to include the question of psychological health. She found that the sexes were more similar in characteristics at ages forty and fifty than they had been in late adolescence. In addition, it was the healthy (according to psychological tests) women and men, rather than the unhealthy ones, who showed a dramatic rise in similarity by age fifty.

Pleck (1975) points out that decreases in sex-role rigidity as one progresses through life are understandable. A reliance on a rigid either/or concept of one's sex role may correspond to childlike stages of moral development in which one is limited to conventional role conformity. Only later does one progress to a more humanistic and principled morality (Kohlberg, 1973). To stop the analysis of sex-role development at the polarized stage is akin to endorsing this stage as the adult norm, which is not accurate. According to Pleck, sex-typed interests and traits reach their peak in adolescence. Adult life experiences can enlarge the concept of self beyond traditional sex-role labels.

Examination of the process by which sex roles develop in adulthood is only beginning, but it has exciting implications for those interested in the expression of androgyny. The questions have begun to be formulated. Psychologists are in general becoming aware that normal adulthood is a time of stress, change, instability, and development (Levinson, Darrow, Levinson, & McKee, 1978; Lowenthal, Thurnher, & Chiriboga, 1975; Sheehy, 1976). Perhaps some of this expanded thinking can be applied to the development of sex roles. For example, what effect do the normal milestones of adulthood, such as career advances, marriages, births, divorces, and deaths of family and friends, have on the development of sex roles in adulthood? How are the effects of some events (such as parenthood) different for women and men? What factors cause some people to increase their sex-role flexibility while others become more rigid and sex-typed? To what extent can one's emerging awareness of the complexities of self and reality overcome the effects of a strong sex-role socialization in childhood? Do all people, regardless of childhood experiences, have the potential to become more androgynous in adulthood? What factors seem to facilitate or impede such development? The questions are nearly endless, for perhaps the true potential in sex-role development has not yet been examined.

Another Look

We saw that the three traditional theories of sex-role development—Freud's, Mischel's, and Kohlberg's—differ in a fundamental way from the alternative model. Although the traditional theorists begin by asking "How does sex-typed behavior develop?" the alternative thinker asks, "How far can people go in sex-role development, and what factors facilitate full development?" These questions reveal differing assumptions. The traditional theorists assume that males and females should be psychologically different, and that stereotyped sex roles are "normal" and "good." The alternative model is based on the assumption that males and females can be psychologically similar, and that some people can move beyond the stereotypes of childhood.

The alternative model of sex-role development is more compatible than the traditional model with the androgynous perspective used throughout this book. It focuses the investigation of sex-role development on the ways children and adults can learn behavior that is flexible and situationally appropriate, and that represents an integration of femininity and masculinity. Nevertheless, questions about the development of sex-typed behaviors are relevant to an androgynous perspective. In order to expand individual persons' potential for androgyny we must understand how both stereotyped and androgynous sex roles develop.

The traditional and alternative models of sex-role development also differ in the predictions they make. For all their disagreements, the traditional theories all predict that girls will be similar to their mothers and boys to their fathers in sex-typing. A highly feminine mother would be expected to have a highly feminine daughter, whereas an androgynous father would be expected to have an androgynous son. Such an outcome would occur whether or not parents directly teach sex-role behavior.

The predictions derived from the alternative model would focus on adult rather than child behavior. One reason certain adults might be androgynous would be that their parents had given them a fundamental base for androgyny during childhood. Children, even with androgynous parents, may very well have stereotyped attitudes and behavior as they attempt to develop some notions of what constitutes maleness and femaleness. Within this model, a stage of sex-typing is not inconsistent with the eventual development of androgyny. Hence, it would be predicted that the children of androgynous parents, though sex-typed in childhood, are more likely than the offspring of sex-typed parents to be androgynous in adulthood.

To further examine the implications and strengths of the various models of sex-role development, we will discuss the available information on how parental behavior and attitudes relevant to sex roles influence the development of similar behavior and attitudes in their offspring.

PARENTAL INFLUENCES: THE EMPIRICAL VIEW

In order to get a picture of the effect parental characteristics can have throughout life, we will look first at the pressures toward androgyny, particularly the relationship of childhood socialization to adult sex roles. From there, we will look at some pressures toward sex typing from parents: parental expectations, task assignment, and parental behavior toward children. Finally, we will examine the child's side of the socialization equation as we look at children's resistance to nonstereotyped behaviors. Throughout this section, the emphasis will be on the empirical evidence that supports or discredits the theories we have described.

Pressures Toward Androgyny

A major study of sex-role development across the life span found that both parental sex typing and the quality of the parent-child relationship were implicated in sex-role development. In addition, there were discernible differences in the developmental processes at work in androgynous and sex-typed offspring. Block, von der Lippe, and Block (1973) compared information on a group of women and men in their thirties with data collected on the same people during childhood. The available information was quite extensive, including reports on family observations and intensive interviews at several time periods.

Children whose parents were psychologically healthy and available to them seemed to develop in adulthood toward a sex-role style consistent with their parents. When such families had a clear and conventional role division between parents, by adulthood the offspring became like the same-sexed parent. The families were harmonious and conventional. In healthy families with more complex, androgynous parental models, the offspring apparently took on characteristics of one or both parents and emerged as androgynous. In addition to the nurturance available in these families, there was an emphasis on the value of achievement. The parental relationship was characterized by shared responsibility in a somewhat unconventional way.

The offspring from both these groups seemed to fare rather well in adulthood, although the more highly feminine women were somewhat tense and lacking in spontaneity. As long as the family atmosphere was stable and loving, the offspring did not seem to run the risk of the extreme, socially undesirable aspects of either femininity or masculinity. In families marked by conflict and more difficult parent-child relationships, the adult offspring seemed to take on the extremes of sex-role behavior, often with detrimental results for their own psychological adjustment. When the same-sex parent was neurotic, rejected the child, and acted as a poor model, the child seemed to turn to the other-sex parent. If that parent behaved seductively, the child tended to develop the extreme of the "appropriate" sex-role identity as if in response to the parental seductiveness. The other-sex parent apparently molded the child's behavior to fit the traditional role. Males in this group, for example, were apt to be characterized by machismo, egotism, and undercontrol of impulses; females tended to be hedonistic, to reject conventional and achievement values, and to be narcissistic. If the same-sex parent was emotionally uninvolved and the other-sex parent had the negative aspects of their own sex-role (e.g., low confidence, depression, etc. in the mothers of sons; authoritarian stance, status and power-orientation, etc. in the fathers of daughters), the offspring tended to take on these characteristics exhibited by the other-sex parent. For example, males were submissive and very sensitive to criticism, and females in this group were critical, rebellious, and extremely insistent on autonomy and independence. In either case, whether the child accepted the negative extreme of the same-sex parent or of the other-sex parent, she or he experienced psychological difficulties.

Apparently, then, the primary factor in sex-role development is the quality of the parent-child relationship. Of secondary importance is the sex-typing of the parent. Unconventional sex-role behavior by the parents will foster androgynous development only when it occurs in the context of a stable and caring relationship. Perhaps the positive parent-child relationship provides the person moving toward androgyny with a firm foundation of self-confidence that enables her or him to comfortably adopt a somewhat unconventional sex-role style.

There is additional evidence that exposure to nontraditional parents or cross-sex typing during childhood is important for the development of androgyny in adulthood. These studies are not quite as good as the Block, von der Lippe, and Block study, since they involve adults' retrospective reports of childhood rather than actual childhood observations. Nevertheless, the retrospective reports corroborate the general findings of Block and his colleagues.

Liberal attitudes about sex roles among women seem to be related to observations of an egalitarian power relationship between the parents during childhood. Lipman-Blumen (1972) found that women with a contemporary sex-role ideology (assumed for our purposes to include a large percentage of androgynous women) tended to come from families in which most of the time neither parent was dominant or from families in which the mother was dominant. The traditional pattern of dominant father seemed to foster more traditional development in daughters. The contemporary/androgynous daughters may well have picked up their nontraditional attitudes from a nontraditional mother or from egalitarian parents. Vanfossen (1977) attributes similar findings among some college women to the fact that, as children in egalitarian families, they saw the importance of women in general and the degree of control over life events that women can expect and desire.

The addition by parents of "cross-sex" elements, such as independence and achievement in women, and warmth and nurturance in men, to socialization during childhood would enhance the development of androgyny. A moderate level of warmth is necessary for women, and cognitive support and encouragement of control is necessary for men. Alone, however, these elements readily result in the development of stereotypic behavior.

The evidence for these statements is found in the work of Kelly and Worell (1975), Woods (1975), and DeFronzo and Boudreau (1979). Kelly and Worell found that androgyny (as measured by the PRF ANDRO Scale; see Chapter 1 for a description) in college women was associated with recall of high maternal involvement and interest, low parental control, and parental emphasis on intellectual curiosity. For men, emphasis on control or cognitive stimulation was of little importance, but parental warmth and involvement were necessary for the development of androgyny. A similar pattern of results regarding androgyny was reported by Woods, who also used the PRF ANDRO Scale and retrospective reports of parental behavior among college students. Indirect support for these findings is offered by Stein and Bailey's (1973) conclusions about the development of achievement behavior in females (considered for the moment as a sign of androgyny). Stein and Bailey reviewed many studies and found that a female child is more likely to develop achievement behavior and independence when her parents are moderately warm and moderately to highly permissive, and when they reinforce and encourage achievement efforts.

In yet another report, college males' femininity scores (on the Bem Sex Role Inventory) were related to their recollections of their fathers' involvement with household tasks; females' masculinity scores were related to their mothers' participation in the paid labor force (DeFronzo & Boudreau, 1979). The nonstereotypic behavior of the same-sex parent seemed in this case to be particularly important for the development of nonstereotypic behavior in the offspring. Again, the development of androgyny would seem to be enhanced by the addition of "cross-sex" elements to socialization in the family.

The strength of the relationship between offspring's reports of parental characteristics and their own sex-role characteristics after childhood is apparent in work with large numbers of high school and college students (Spence & Helmreich, 1978). Androgynous students were quite likely to describe both their parents as androgynous. Even androgyny in only one parent was associated, though to a lesser degree, with androgyny in the offspring. For sons, there was a particularly strong association with the father's characteristics. For daughters, the influence of both parents appeared to be more nearly equal. Hence, the development of androgyny in a male is more likely to require an androgynous father. However, androgyny in either parent has an equal tendency to be associated with androgyny in a female. An additional finding in the Spence and Helmreich studies was the high likelihood of androgynous parents to be warm, democratic, and oriented toward family harmony.

All of these studies support the conclusions of the Block, von der Lippe, and Block study: androgyny in adulthood seems to be related to a solid personal foundation derived from a warm parent-child relationship, as well as exposure to nonsex-typed models. These models can be both parents involved in an egalitarian relationship, one or two androgynous parents, or, for girls, a mother who is a strong member of the marital pair.

The effect of parents' sex-typing on that of the offspring might not have been apparent if children rather than adults had been studied. Sherman (1971) reported that both girls and boys are often more like their mothers than their fathers. Mussen and Rutherford (1963) found no significant relationships between girls' femininity or boys' masculinity scores (as measured by the IT Scale) and their parents' sex-role scores on a personality test of masculinity-femininity. The IT Scale is a supposedly sexless paper doll on whom the child is expected to project her or his sex-role preference when asked to choose toys and games for "IT."

Such findings of more parent-offspring similarity in adulthood than in childhood suggest that the alternative model of sex-role development is a useful one. Whatever effects parents have on their children are sometimes not apparent until later in life.

Pressures Toward Sex Typing

The traditional and alternative models differ not only in the time in life during which they expect to see the results of sex-role development, but in their emphasis on sex-typed or androgynous development. What are the pressures from parents toward sex typing? How exactly do parents try to pass on their sex-role characteristics to their children? We will see that parents may convey the sex-role message through their expectations, the tasks they assign, and their direct behavior toward their children. After describing each of these processes, we will examine some of the ways children resist parental efforts that run counter to the stereotypes.

Parental expectations. "It's a girl!" or "It's a boy!" proclaim the proud parents through calls, cards, and cigars following the birth of a child. After determining that the child is healthy, the parent is most interested in an infant's sex. Parents greet the infant with already-formed ideas about how girls and boys usually behave. There is anecdotal data (Lewis, 1972b) that parents express their attitudes about sex differences even during pregnancy: if the fetus is active, kicking, and moving a great deal, the parents often interpret this as a sign that the child is male.

A team of psychologists (Rubin, Provenzano, & Luria, 1974) interviewed thirty sets of parents within twenty-four hours of the birth of their first child. Although hospital records showed that the daughters and sons did not differ in weight, length, or physiological condition, parents of daughters described their infant as significantly softer, finer featured, littler, and more inattentive than did parents of sons. Sons were described as firmer, more large-featured, bigger, and more alert than daughters. These characteristics mirror common sex-role stereotypes. Although fathers were more stereotyped in their ratings than mothers, the socialization process was apparent, in expectations of both parents, as soon as the child was born. Not surprisingly, parents continue to have different attitudes about daughters and sons as the child grows up.

Using written questionnaires, Lansky (1967) asked ninety-eight parents of kindergarten and preschool children about their attitudes toward children's choice of same-sex activities (e.g., girls playing with dolls; boys playing with guns) and cross-sex ones (e.g., girls playing with guns; boys playing with dolls). Both parents tended to express negative attitudes toward boys' cross-sex choices and neutral or positive attitudes toward girls' cross-sex choices. Again, the tendency to stereotype children was stronger for fathers than mothers. In a Canadian study using questionnaires, there were no differences between fathers and mothers. Both parents of six-year old boys expected greater sex differences in behavior than did both parents of similarly aged girls (Lambert, Yackley, & Hein, 1971).

These patterns of parental expectation have continued in recent years. Mothers of children between nine and eleven stereotyped many behaviors and temperamental characteristics in the expected direction (Tuddenham, Brooks, & Milkovich, 1974). Parents of preschoolers (ages three to five) expected their sons to play with masculine toys (judged so by college students) and daughters to play with feminine toys (Diepold, 1977).

It seems safe to say, then, that parents of young children, particularly fathers, do have firm ideas about behavior that is sex-role "appropriate." Although they have standards for girls' behavior, these seem to be more flexible than those for boys' behavior. One still wonders, though, whether parental attitudes bear any relationship to children's behavior.

For girls, at least, there seems to be a relationship between fathers' expectations and children's psychological sex, as measured by the IT scale. Parents were asked to indicate what kinds of activities they expected their children to engage in. For the first-graders studied, fathers of highly feminine girls were more likely to expect and encourage the girls to play sex-appropriate games than were fathers of less feminine girls. No relationship between mothers' expectations and girls' behavior, or either parent's expectations and boys' behavior was found in this study (Mussen & Rutherford, 1963). Of course, there is no way to tell whether the girls were highly feminine because their fathers expected them to play feminine games, or whether the fathers expected the girls to play feminine games because they were highly feminine.

Patricia Minuchin (1965) compared the behavior of nine-year-olds from "traditional" and "modern" families and found parental attitudes were related to sex-role behavior. One aspect of the classification of "traditional" families included mothers' belief in sex-appropriate roles (fathers were not involved in the study); part of the "modern" definition involved more open conceptions of sex roles in the mothers' statements. In traditional families, boys were more aggressive in their play than were girls, but no such sex differences were found in the modern families. On the measures of sex-typing, children with "modern" mothers were more flexible and less sex-typed than those with "traditional" mothers. Girls from "modern" families were the least sex-typed in their behavior.

It appears that not only do parents have firm ideas about how girls and boys ought to behave, but their attitudes tend to be related to the child's behavior. Although, in general, these sex-role demands appear to be *directed* more carefully to boys than girls, girls seem to be more *likely to respond* to the expectations, especially when they come from the father.

Trying to relate these findings to the theories of sex-role development is like trying to decide if a glass of water is "half-full" or "half-empty." Freud, Mischel, and Kohlberg would probably all be pleased to hear that mothers' "traditional" or "modern" attitudes about sex roles seemed to be reflected in some aspects of their children's behavior. In addition, Freud would be happy to know that fathers' sex-role attitudes have a special relationship to girls' femininity. Yet parental expectations about sex roles were not related to boys' behavior in the Mussen and Rutherford study. Also, except for Freudian theory, the traditional theorists would have predicted that the same-sex parent-child relationship would be the most important for reflecting similarity, and the findings are not consistent with such a prediction. We would have had an adequate test of our idea that sex-role development continues throughout life only if adults' sex-role behavior had been compared to the attitudes of their parents. That was not done. The life-span development perspective receives a small measure of support, however, from the apparent weakness of the relationship of parental attitudes and child behavior.

Task assignment. Parental expectations can affect children's sex-role development through the tasks assigned to girls and boys. Data in this area have been gathered from a variety of cultures.

Whiting and Edwards (1973) found that task assignment seemed to account for many of the sex differences they observed in children's behavior in different cultures. The central factor seemed to be the frequency of interaction with different categories of individuals (infants, peers, adults) that occurred in various tasks. Girls were more frequently assigned tasks that required them to interact with infants and adults, as well as tasks that involved the care of others (e.g., child care, helping with food preparation, etc.). Boys, on the other hand, were usually assigned chores away from the home (e.g., assistance with animals and crops) that increased their opportunities for interaction with same-sexed peers and decreased their chances for interaction with infants and adults. Hence, it is not surprising that girls were more frequently observed to be nurturant and compliant, behaviors encouraged in the home, and that boys exhibited a great deal of rough play, behavior encouraged in peer interaction.

Even more important from the androgynous perspective, however, was Whiting and Edwards' observation of the consequences of *different* task assignment for "feminine" and "masculine" behavior. In societies in which boys were assigned domestic chores and the care of infants, sex differences were reduced to the extent that boys scored high in offering help and support and low in responding to aggression. Although girls were not given "masculine" chores in any of the cultures surveyed, when they were not expected to be involved in infant care the magnitude of sex differences was reduced.

Carol Ember (1973) looked at differences within certain cultures (in Western Kenya) and found that boys who had to act as nurses and do domestic chores were more responsible, less aggressive, less dependent, and less dominant than boys who were not required to do such chores. Their scores on these measures, however, were not as extreme as girls'. Because these results were not apparent when Ember considered culturally defined feminine tasks *outside* the home (e.g., gathering firewood, picking vegetables, etc.), she concluded that it is the *kind* of task performed (those involving the care of others) rather than the cultural definition of that task (as feminine or masculine) that is crucial. Unfortunately, Ember did not look at girls who had been assigned "masculine" tasks, so we do not know whether such assignment would result in increased assertiveness or other "masculine" traits.

It looks as if the kinds of tasks children are assigned play a part in their sex-role development. To the extent that girls are assigned tasks requiring them to care for others and boys are assigned tasks during which they may readily interact with peers and wander from home, girls and boys will tend to develop different sex-role styles. One of the presses toward sex-typing within the family, thus, is the assignment of girls to caretaking tasks and boys to chores away from the home.

Parental behavior toward children. Do parents treat girls and boys differently? To most professional observers, the answer is a resounding yes! Nonprofessional observers, as well, frequently notice ways in which parents seem to treat girls and boys differently.

Adults can be influenced by the sex of children as young as infancy. Seavey, Katz, and Zalk (1975) observed adults' interactions with an infant about whose gender they were given varying information. When told the baby was a girl, women and men were more likely to offer it a doll than a football or a teething ring. When given no information about the baby's sex, men tended to take the safe route of offering it the neutral toy (teething ring) and handling it very little; women tended to offer it a sex-stereotyped toy (of either sex) and handle it quite a bit. Perhaps most notable of all was the fact that participants who were given no information about the infant's sex tried to find it out. This suggests that it is important for adults to know a baby's sex so that they will have clues about how to interact with it. The males' hesitancy to get involved with "Baby X" leads one to suspect that it is particularly important for them to know a child's sex. Fagot (1973) also found nonparental men more stereotyped in their ratings of two-year-olds. You may recall that in several of the studies we looked at, fathers tended to be more stereotyped in their reactions than mothers. Perhaps because they are not exposed to children as often as women, men are more responsive to concrete, simplistic labels of a child (e.g., sex) rather than the more subtle cues in the child's own behavior.

The remainder of this discussion will primarily concern parents' responses to their own children. There are numerous studies concerning parental behaviors related to sex-role training. We have tried to select those which focus on naturalistic parent-child interactions in the home. Whenever possible, we have used studies that included fathers as well as mothers, though fathers have been less often included in studies of infants.

One of the best-established behaviors on the part of parents is their active encouragement of sex-typed activities in their children (Maccoby & Jacklin, 1974). Boys are more likely than girls to receive negative pressures for cross-sex choices. Fagot (1977) systematically observed twenty-four sets of parents and toddlers (20 to 24 months) over five one-hour observation periods. Although parents did not differ overall in their responses to sons and daughters, they did differ in reactions to the behaviors they considered important for sex-role socialization. Parents responded positively when the child engaged in a behavior preferred for their own sex, such as block play or play with transportation toys for boys and doll play for girls. On the other hand, parents responded negatively when the child behaved in a way preferred for the other sex, such as doll play for boys or running, jumping and climbing for girls. However, boys were punished more for feminine behaviors than girls were for masculine behaviors, showing the greater pressure put on boys than girls in sex-role socialization.

Parents also show their encouragement of sex-typing in the toys and furnishings they select for their children. By simply recording the objects in children's rooms, Rheingold and Cook (1975) found striking differences in girls' and boys' rooms. Boys (aged one month to six years) had more vehicles, educational and art materials, sports equipment, toy animals, depots (garages, etc.), machines, live animals and associated paraphernalia, and military toys. Girls had a much narrower range of toys, and exceeded boys only in number of dolls, doll houses, and domestic toys. Boys' rooms were more likely to be decorated with an animal motif, whereas girls were likely to live with a floral motif and lace, fringe, and ruffles. The fact that these differences were found in homes of highly educated and well-to-do parents during the 1970s is even more striking, since this group (if any) would have been expected to be particularly aware of nonsexist childrearing practices.

Parents not only encourage or discourage specific sex-typed activities in their children, but they also seem to foster the more general personality characteristics differentially associated with females and males. For example, after the earliest months, boys seem to be permitted or encouraged to be more independent of their parents whereas girls are apparently kept closer through greater emotional warmth from the parents.

Initially girls are talked to and looked at more often, whereas boys are held and touched more frequently. In examining these factors, Lewis (1972a) made the distinction between *proximal* and *distal* stimulation of infants by mothers. Proximal stimulation involves more physical interaction, such as touching and holding; distal stimulation is a more distant type of interaction such as looking and talking. Although three-week-old girls and boys did not differ in their own behaviors, mothers tended to give infant boys more proximal stimulation and girls more distal stimulation. So, for example, if a baby girl vocalized the mother was likely to talk to her, whereas if a baby boy vocalized the mother was more likely to touch or hold him.

These patterns of maternal responses shift, however, so that by age one girls receive both more proximal and distal stimulation than boys. Lewis attributes the mothers' decreasing physical contact with sons as an indicator of their greater desire to instill autonomy in sons than in daughters. The "emotional weaning" occurs earlier for sons than daughters. Moss (1967), suggests another interpretation. Perhaps boys are held more initially because they cry more. Yet, he says, since boys don't quiet as easily as girls, mothers are not so frequently reinforced for holding their sons. Therefore, they soon begin to hold their sons less, whereas mothers of daughters are reinforced for close contact and begin to hold their children more.

These sex differences in early mother-infant interactions parallel findings about children's later autonomous behavior, as demonstrated by Goldberg and Lewis (1969). Children of both sexes who are nurtured a great deal early in life tend to seek continued closeness to the mother later on. In addition, girls who have received inadequate nurturing apparently try to remedy that deficit later by also seeking maternal contact. The study involved observations of mothers and their children at six and thirteen months of age. There were strong sex differences in the thirteen-month-old children's behavior toward their mother in a free-play situation. Girls were more dependent (returning to mother more often, maintaining more eye contact with mother, and generally staying close to mother), showed less exploratory behavior, and played more quietly than did boys. When the experimenter placed a barrier between mother and child, girls tended to cry and motion for help, whereas boys seemed to spend more time making active attempts to get around the barrier. Goldberg and Lewis examined their records of the interaction of the same mother-infant pairs at six months and found that the boys who were touched more at six months returned to their mothers more at thirteen months. Girls whose mothers touched them either very much or very little at six months were more likely to seek a great deal of physical contact with mother at thirteen months than girls who had had moderate physical contact.

Fagot (1974, 1977) found continued indicators of greater encouragement of autonomy in boys than girls for two separate groups of toddlers (roughly eighteen to twenty-four months old) and their parents. In the first study, the boys were significantly more likely to be left to play on their own than were girls. In the second study, where the emphasis was on parents' encouragement or discouragement of children's activities, parents were more likely to respond positively when girls asked for help, helped an adult with a task, or followed the parent around. The parents' responses were more likely to be negative when boys asked for help or helped an adult with a task. Toddler girls are apparently being encouraged to stay close to the parents, whereas boys are being discouraged for showing the same types of behaviors.

Other authors have chosen to look at later periods of childhood, continuing to find differences in the ways parents encourage closeness and autonomy in daughters and sons. Block (1973) asked parents of groups of children about their child-rearing practices. Parents of boys reported a greater emphasis on achievement and competition, control of feelings, and conformity to rules. Girls' parents, on the other hand, reported a greater emphasis on close interpersonal relationships, encouragement to talk about troubles, and more frequent physical affection, comfort, and reassurance. The issues stressed for boys seem to involve authority and control, whereas those for girls reflect relationships, protection, and support. Once again, fathers were found to be more extreme in their treatment of the sexes.

Additionally, young girls are treated as more fragile; parents more often engage in "rough and tumble play" with boys. There is a consistent trend for parents to elicit "gross motor behavior" more often from sons than daughters (Maccoby & Jacklin, 1974). Although the data are not complete (information on fathers' reactions is lacking), there is no consistent sex difference in parents' responses to children's aggression. Nevertheless, boys do receive more physical punishment than girls. Maccoby and Jacklin suggest that boys may need it more because of their higher activity levels and greater tendency toward aggression. There is also a tendency for parents to give boys more praise, reward, and positive feedback for their actions than girls (Maccoby & Jacklin, 1974).

In summary, than, adults are apparently aware of children's sex and sometimes respond differentially to girls and boys. Clearly many parents try to encourage "appropriate" sex-role development in their children. This encouragement, conscious or not, takes the form of encouragement of "sex-appropriate" and discouragement of "sex-inappropriate" activities. In more subtle ways they foster sex-role development by facilitating boys' autonomy via punishing too much closeness (after early infancy), rewarding boys' self-directed actions, and setting up more distance in the parent-child relationship. Although parents seem to feel comfortable about letting their sons alone, interactions with them around rough and tumble play serve to let the boy know he is a strong yet valuable person. With girls, parents seem to be more likely to encourage closeness even after infancy and discourage girls' efforts to move away. Parents' interactions with daughters seem more likely to give the girl the message that she is fragile and sensitive, such that there is frequent physical affection and talk about troubles.

Again, it has been seen that the presses toward "appropriate" sex role development are stronger for boys than girls, while fathers are more stereotyped in their reactions to children than mothers.

This evidence of direct parental involvement in children's sex-role training is consistent with the traditional theories to the extent that they see the parent-child relationship as a major vehicle for sex-role development. Yet the traditional theories do not deal with the possibility that parents make such direct efforts at fostering sex-role development as this evidence suggests. While they do not rule out the influence of such efforts, they are more likely to focus on the reasons behind the child's motivation for "picking up" the sex-role behavior of the parent her or himself.

Children's Resistance to Nonstereotyped Behavior

In the above section the emphasis was on the ways parents foster stereotyping in their children. Nevertheless, there is some evidence that children are partially responsible for their own socialization, as they sometimes indicate resistance to nonstereotyped behavior. The parent-child relationship is one of interaction, and children do sometimes shape the behavior of their parents (cf., Osofsky & O'Connell, 1972).

Boys seem particularly resistant to "sex-inappropriate" behavior when it is advocated or modeled. A highly-esteemed female teacher tried to talk four- and five-year-olds into giving up the sex-appropriate toy they had selected as a gift from the experimenter. Most boys and girls resisted the teacher's advice and retained their original selection. Boys resisted more strongly and revealed more anxiety (Ross & Ross, 1972). Some took the additional step of attempting to discredit the usually admired teacher ("Poor teacher, she must have a real bad throat," p. 345), or explain her advocacy away ("Teacher has too much to do today. You shouldn't ask her to do more things. Let's pretend we never asked her," p. 345). In another study (Wolf, 1975) six-year olds watched a videotape of a peer playing with a sex-inappropriate toy (doll for boys, fire engine for girls). Boys in particular were still inhibited in playing with the sex-inappropriate toy, in spite of the model's behavior. An adult was even less effective as a model, for children who saw an adult model play with sex-inappropriate toys were no more likely to play with such toys than were children who saw no model. Again, boys were particularly unlikely to play with the sex-inappropriate toys (Wolf, 1975).

Another indication of children's resistance to nonstereotyped examples is the lack of relationship that sometimes appears between parents' "liberal" sex-role behavior and that of their children. Sutton-Simon and Menig-Peterson (1977) observed children's (ages four and five) play behavior and toy and peer preferences, concluding that these are strongly sex-stereotypic and relatively unaffected by either parents' sex-role behavior or attitudes toward sex roles. Among a group of children between the ages of two and three years, the children's use of sex-role labels for self and others, as well as their preference for sex-role labels, showed no relationship to family demographic factors (social class, parents' work time outside the home, parental education) or to mother's scores on a measure of sex-role attitudes (Thompson, 1975).

We do not mean to say that children are totally immune to the effects of information that counters stereotyped sex roles. As noted in earlier sections, researchers sometimes do find a link between parental sex-role attitudes and behavior, and those of children. We wish to point out, however, that the relationship is neither as universal nor as unequivocal as psychoanalytic or social learning theories would predict.

An instance of children being affected at least to a degree by nonstereotyped models is found in a study by Flerx, Fidler, and Rogers (1976). After being exposed to nonsexist films and stories, children (ages three to five) became less stereo-typed in answering questions such as, "Who would like to set the table?" (boy, girl, or both); "Who can change a baby's diaper?" (man, woman, or both), than children exposed to sexist films and stories. On at least half the measures, however, children's measured attitudes did not change as a function of nonsexist materials. This study differs from the ones that found children more strongly resisting non-stereotypic messages in that it merely required children to answer questions about people in general. The studies described earlier were more personally relevant to the child. Perhaps it is easier for children (or adults) to change what they say about "how the world should be" than it is for them to change their own behavior.

These suggestions that children sometimes resist efforts to move them beyond stereotyped sex roles are consistent with the cognitive developmental and life-span development models. Perhaps some children feel more comfortable in the security of stereotyped sex roles for a time. Perhaps they need to stay with the stereotypes while they attempt to make sense out of the world and themselves. Whatever the reason, such childhood resistance need not preclude an eventual movement beyond stereotypes toward androgyny.

GROWING TOWARD ANDROGYNY

In light of the evidence presented here on the development of sex roles in the family, we have several suggestions for parents who might wish to foster the development of androgyny in their children. Some of these refer to the ways parents can influence their child's sex-role behavior.

Parents first need to become aware of their own sex-typed attitudes. Even "liberal" parents, as products of this culture, bring stereotyped notions to their perceptions of their children. Although there seems to be an increasing willingness to accept a wide range of behaviors and traits in girls, boys still seem to suffer from stricter parental notions of what is "appropriate" for males. Girls are presented with trucks and guns much more readily than boys are presented with dolls and tea sets. Weitz (1977) suggests that this may be due to parental fears of anything suggestive of homosexuality in their sons. The fact that similar worries about cross-sex behavior in girls are not apparent suggests that an alternative explanation is in order. Perhaps parental hesitation to encourage tenderness and nurturance in sons is a sign of the continuing negative value this society places on most feminine things. Awareness of such sex-role filters is a first step in granting daughters and sons equal treatment.

Although one's sex-role *attitudes* are surely difficult to change, actual sex-role *behavior* may be even more difficult to modify. Yet, it seems that the more parents themselves behave in androgynous styles, in the context of a warm relationship, the more likely it is that their children will develop in androgynous directions. The child needs not only to hear that girls and boys have equal potential but also to see firsthand that both mothers and fathers can cry, cuddle, and be competent.

An additional suggestion involves the possible necessity for differential treatment of girls and boys, in order to compensate for any sex-linked deficits. In light of males' possible biological predisposition for aggression (see Chapter 4), parents might do well to pay particular attention to encouragement of sons' interpersonal relationships. One way to do this may be to increase the boys' tasks in the areas of responsibilities for others and interactions with adults. There is a hint that boys need special help in learning to care for others.

But parents cannot take full responsibility for the child's sex-role development. Just as parents cannot teach a one-year old child the full adult forms of language, they may not be able to teach a young child to display the full range of sex-role behaviors. Just as parents can expose the child to good language that the child will later manifest, they can expose the child to sex-role behaviors that may only later be manifested. For some children, stereotyped sex roles may be merely a developmental phenomenon. There is a hint in the studies that have been done that a true integration of feminine and masculine qualities can happen most easily after childhood, although the groundwork can be laid in childhood.

SUMMARY AND CONCLUSIONS

The evidence for the various theories of sex-role development is not yet strong enough for any one theory to emerge as the "right" one. Children *are* affected by the kind of relationship they have with their parents, so that a close and caring relationship with a sex-typed, same-sex parent facilitates sex-typed development. Alone, this finding supports the Freudian view. Yet if the relationship with the other-sex parent is also warm and the parents behave in nontraditional ways, the child has a good chance of eventually developing in an androgynous direction. Freudian theory does not account for such a finding.

Although it is true, as Mischel would predict, that children sometimes imitate the behavior of models, they also sometimes do not. The child's resistance to a model is particularly likely to occur if the model is behaving in a "sex-inappropriate" manner for the child. So, although Mischel tends to talk about how a model's nurturance, power, and similarity affect the child's response, he might do well to add consideration of the sex-appropriateness of the behavior for the child.

Both Freud's and Mischel's theories lose support from findings that sometimes show little correspondence between parents' degree of sex-typing and that of their children even within normal families. They predict a high degree of relationship between parent and child in psychological sex.

Kohlberg's theory and the life-span perspective on sex-role development receive support from the fact that, despite parental efforts, children sometimes seem to be in a stereotypic stage of development. Perhaps stereotyping in children is only a reflection of cognitive simplicity. Androgyny may develop with cognitive complexity later in life. Kohlberg, however, does not really consider the implications of his model for development beyond the stereotypes. In actuality, the life-span perspective is not so much a different view as an extension of Kohlberg's model beyond childhood.

The life-span model of sex-role development is supported by findings of a link between parental behavior during childhood and adult sex role styles, even though such links are not always apparent during childhood. Yet, despite what this model might suggest, not *all* children are equally stereotyped. In fact, some studies (e.g.,

Minuchin) suggest a link between aspects of parental sex roles and attitudes even during childhood. Some children do seem to be more androgynous than others, even during their supposedly simple cognitive years.

Although none of the theories has enough strong support to emerge as "the winner," we must take into account the questions they ask. From an androgynous perspective, the life-span development model is most useful. It asks the questions that go beyond development of stereotyped sex roles. It includes the possibility that sex-role development is linked to other aspects of development so that as the person and the tasks she or he faces become more complex, so do conceptions of sex roles. Perhaps a new model will emerge that explains this process more completely but, in the meantime, the life-span development model encourages thinking and research on the androgynous potential.

Throughout this chapter several themes have emerged concerning sex-role development in the family. First of all, despite psychologists' apparent difficulty in explaining the process by which sex roles develop, it is clear that parents do try to influence that process. Although parents may not always succeed in directly and completely influencing sex-role development, their efforts to foster stereotypes would seem to interfere with androgynous development.

One theme running through much of this chapter has been of the differential influences of mothers and fathers. Although mothers clearly play a role in sex-role socialization, as a group they seem to be more flexible and responsive to a child's individuality. Fathers, on the other hand, tend to pay more attention to a child's sex in determining their own reactions and in setting standards. Simply put, fathers are more extreme in their stereotypes.

A third theme is the stronger pressures put on boys than on girls to develop in stereotyped directions. During childhood, at least, girls are permitted greater flexibility in the sex-role realm. Boys get the message, apparently, as evidenced by their stronger resistance to nonstereotyped behaviors.

An often neglected theme in child development in general is the fact that the parent-child relationship is one of interaction. Many researchers apparently see the influences as uni-directional, as they examine the effects of the parent on the child. Although such effects do exist, children are active members of the relationship, perhaps influencing the parents' treatment of them.

One of the questions posed at the beginning of the chapter concerned the degree to which awareness of sex as a category is necessary for healthy development. Although all the answers are not in, a child's strong, stable sense of her or himself seems to include a recognition and acceptance of her or his own gender. In developing toward androgyny, children should not deny their gender or the existence of biological differences between the sexes.

The importance of this strong, stable sense of self to healthy development is additionally apparent in the findings regarding the quality of the parent-child relationship. Children exposed to nontraditional adult examples can only profit in an androgynous way if those adults are psychologically healthy and available to the child. Without such a positive relationship, the offspring seems to have difficulty in taking the adaptive parts of the femininity and masculinity she or he observes.

Only in the context of parental warmth can children benefit—in the short or long run—from any cross-sex typing that is offered.

We would speculate, then, that the first step in development toward androgyny is the development of a strong sense of self, including an awareness of one's gender: "I am————, a female," or "I am————, a male." This self comes to be experienced as worthwhile and good through a warm and loving parent-child relationship. This positive and strong sense of self, in turn, enables the individual to select models and behaviors that are flexible and represent an integration of femininity and masculinity. The early family relationships, we maintain, can "inoculate" a child so that she or he can resist persistent cultural efforts to limit her or his behaviors through sex-typing.

SELECTED READINGS

Chodorow, N. *The reproduction of mothering: Psychoanalysis and the sociology of gender.* Stanford, Calif.: Stanford University Press, 1978.

Dinnerstein, D. *The mermaid and the minotaur: Sexual arrangements and human malaise.* New York: Harper and Row, 1976.

Gould, L. X: A fabulous child's story. *Ms.,* December 1972. Reprinted in M. Tripp (ed.), *Women in the year 2000.* New York: Dell, 1974.

Lamb, M. E. *The role of the father in child development.* New York: Wiley, 1976.

Lynn, D. B. *The father: His role in child development.* Monterey, Calif.: Brooks/Cole, 1974.

Levinson, D. J., Darrow, C. N., Klein, E. B., Levinson, M. H., & McKee, B. *The seasons of a man's life.* New York: Knopf, 1978.

Sex-Role Socialization Outside the Family

8

Although families may provide the foundation for the development of sex-role related behavior, children fairly quickly turn toward the world outside the family, the broader culture. Once the child has developed the notion, "I am a girl" or "I am a boy", she or he is soon—and continues to be throughout life—confronted with an array of messages about what "girlness" or "boyness" is. The media, schools, language, and even friends portray sex-role concepts and exert their subtle pressures on the developing person.

Opportunities to develop an androgynous self-concept and behavior that is flexible, adaptive, and situationally appropriate, and an integration of femininity and masculinity can be provided—or inhibited—by these cultural forces. To the extent that these socializing agents press toward rigid stereotypes, the child's movement toward androgyny will be impeded. Likewise, these aspects of the cultural context can help a person move toward androgyny.

Any attempts to foster increases in androgyny and decreases in sex typing throughout the society require an awareness of the full range of influences on sex-role development. Thus, in this chapter we will attempt to document some of the ways the culture influences socialization of sex roles. The schools, media, language, and friends are some of the carriers of these messages and, in this chapter, we will focus on each in turn. For each of these potential influences we will ask these questions: What messages do they give about sex roles? How strongly do children internalize these images? What distinguishes children who do internalize the messages from those who do not? How could sex-typed messages within these cultural couriers be changed to stimulate children's androgynous potential?

Despite the conclusions in the last chapter about the potential for sex-role development across the life span, the emphasis in this chapter is on factors affecting children. Our assumption is that children are particularly vulnerable to cultural sex-role messages because of their need for structure. Children's readiness to learn about their environment makes them especially sensitive to its messages regarding social roles and expectations, including sex roles. The child is faced with the task of making sense of the world, deciphering whatever order is there, and uncovering the rules for behavior.

Perhaps the closest thing to the child's task that adults can experience is the first day in a totally new environment, such as college or a new job. Recollections of such days for many people include the impression of being bombarded with new stimuli and trying to organize it: Who is who? Who does what? Where do I go? What do I do? Whom can I even ask? In such situations, it is common to welcome any imposed structure, be it some concrete instructions, an organizational chart, or a schedule to follow. Once people feel more knowledgeable and secure about the environment, they can tolerate more ambiguity but, temporarily, they often seek order. So it is for many children. As their experience expands to encompass a world wider than the family, they are particularly needy of structure. Many aspects of the culture provide such structure through information about how to act and who to be.

MEDIA

One of the major nonfamilial sources of information about sex roles is the media: books, television, movies, magazines, musical lyrics, etc. In this section we will focus on the potential influence of television on sex-role socialization. This selection reflects our impression of the importance of television in the lives of children from very young ages. According to one survey (Liebert, Neale, & Davidson, 1973), nearly every family in the United States has a television set. In the average home, the set is on over six hours per day. By the age of sixteen, average children have spent 15,000 hours viewing television, more time than they have spent in the classroom. It is one socializing influence that extends to all races and social classes and, in fact, is watched more often by people who are black and poor (Liebert & Schwartzberg, 1977). Keep in mind that the findings regarding portrayals of sex roles on television are closely paralleled by findings for other media, including children's picture books (Weitzman, Eifler, Hokada, & Ross, 1972), literature (Martin, 1971; Snow, 1975), and popular songs (Reinartz, 1975).

There are differences in both the quantity and quality of portrayals of females and males on television, and these differences seem to reflect sex-role stereotypes. In a careful observational study of ten of the most popular children's television programs, Sternglanz and Serbin (1974) found sex differences in the visibility of characters' assigned roles and environmental consequences of behavior. Half of the most popular programs had to be excluded from this study, because they had only male characters. Even when the all-male programs were excluded from consideration, male characters outnumbered females two to one. Male characters were more likely than females to be shown as aggressive, constructive (e.g., building, planning), and seeking help. Female characters were likely to be shown as deferent, following others, and as being punished for being very active. One area in which females did excel was the use of magic. Sternglanz and Serbin suggested that girls are being taught that the one way they can be effective human beings is to use magic, to manipulate others without their awareness.

Overall, although males tended to be rewarded for their actions, females tended to receive neither reward nor punishment. Apparently the few female characters who made it onto the air were then ignored unless they were exceptionally active (in which case they were punished). The message seems to be: Damned if you do and ignored if you don't.

This study of children's television did not include programs on public television, such as *Sesame Street, Zoom,* and *The Electric Company.* Yet, at least at their inception, these programs were also criticized for their stereotyped portrayals of the sexes (Bergman, 1972).

The images are not any less sex-typed on prime-time television. A New Jersey-based group called Women on Words and Images (1975b) studied the top-rated shows (adventure shows and situation comedies) in the 1973–74 season. As with shows designed especially for children, prime-time TV had about two male characters for every female. The range of occupations for televised males was twice as great as that for females. Even these limited feminine occupations were generally left to single women, since the majority of married women and mothers on television did not support themselves financially. Women were shown as more frequently incompetent than men, and more likely to express anger indirectly. The message is: There are more men around, and they are dominant, authoritative, and competent.

Television commercials exaggerate the stereotyped message even more. In about 200 television commercials that were coded, male characters again outnumbered females (McArthur & Resko, 1975). Perhaps more importantly, their roles differed: the men were portrayed as authorities in the majority of cases whereas women most frequently appeared as product-users. A typical scene was a female marveling at the effectiveness of some product for cleaning her clothes, walls, floors, dishes, or skin while a male voice-over expounded authoritatively on the virtues of the product. The female central figures were more apt to be defined in terms of their relationship to others (e.g., as spouse, parent, etc.), whereas males were more likely to be defined independently of others (e.g., as worker, professional, celebrity, etc.). In addition, female product-users were more likely than males to be portrayed using home products. Women on Words and Images (1975b) had similar findings in their own analysis of commercials: women take care of the house, their families, their shopping, and their own appearance, while men work and play harder and provide the voice of authority for the purchasing decisions women make.

One might argue that these findings reflect the early 1970s, and that things have changed. Not entirely so, at least according to our own informal observations. For one thing, many of the old prime-time programs that were the focus of research in the past have now been simply shifted to daytime slots. Admittedly, women are playing a more prominent role in recent prime-time television than they did in the past; particularly noticeable are women serving as the main characters in some shows. Yet, women still do not serve as half the characters on television. Even as main characters, many of the women still work under the direction of men and are portrayed in sexual terms, while others emerge as somewhat less than intelligent. In all fairness, however, one must remember that few male TV characters could serve as models of desirable behavior either.

The Saturday morning TV line-up, designed especially for children, still seems to be selling as many sex-role stereotypes as breakfast cereals. Between 8 A.M. and 12:30 P.M. one recent Saturday morning we viewed an array of programs that included very few female characters. *Sesame Street* was one of the worst offenders: in one episode males (but not females) were shown as baseball players, sports announcer, referee, player, mechanic, bus driver, and even objects such as a tooth, milk, and a carrot. On this same episode some of the few roles designated for females (but not males) included a witch and a worm. On another program, two girls were shown as competent in finding clues, although it was their leader, a boy, who put together all the clues and solved the mystery. On a different program that showed more blacks than is common on television, very few females appeared. Another showed a contemporary woman as the strong yet sensitive central character, but continued television's tradition of explaining her strength as derived from magic. In short, there seems to be a great deal of consistency between past and present television portrayals of the sexes.

This documentation of stereotyped portrayals on television is especially important because it is known that children do attend to and imitate some of the behaviors of filmed models. Bandura's "Bobo Doll" studies in the early 1960s (reported in Chapter 7) were the first systematic attempts to demonstrate a relationship between what children see on the screen and what they later do. A review by Liebert and Schwartzberg (1977) of the research in this area concluded that children are, indeed, apt pupils to the TV teacher. Although most attention was initially focused on the effects of televised violence, more recent efforts have been made to delineate some of the prosocial potential of television: increases in cooperation, sharing, and helping after viewing these classes of behavior on film.

Although we know of no studies on the *direct* effects sex-typed television portrayals have on children's behaviors and aspirations, we suspect a strong link. The findings regarding both the potential negative and positive effects of television in other areas lead us to believe that children are learning about sex roles through the stereotyped presentation of the sexes in the media. Documentation in this area should proceed, particularly to uncover some of the mediating factors: Are all children affected to the same degree by televised stereotypes? Are these effects less for children who have been "inoculated" by a more androgynous upbringing in other areas of their lives? Particularly important are inquiries into the effects of portrayals of androgynous children and adults on television. Can such portrayals help counteract the stereotyped images that pervade other areas of a child's life? Or do the other images obscure the less sex-typed portrayals? Does it help if adults (or other children, for that matter) view programs with the child and point out the more desirable characteristics presented? In keeping with researchers' general recent interest in TV's prosocial potential, it would be useful to see more information about the ways TV can help sex-role development proceed beyond stereotypes to androgyny.

SCHOOLS

The major function of the educational system is to prepare young people for adult roles. Although the intended purpose concerns teaching of mental skills such as the traditional "three Rs" of reading, writing, and arithmetic, other, sometimes unintended, factors work to prepare the person for a "fourth R"—her or his social role. Two economists, Samuel Bowles and Herbert Gintis, recently documented how schools prepare children for their roles as workers within the socioeconomic system:

> [Schools] create and reinforce patterns of social class, racial and sexual identification among students which allow them to relate 'properly' to their eventual standing in the hierarchy of authority and status in the production process. Schools foster types of personal development compatible with the relationships of dominance and subordinancy in the economic sphere. (1976, p. 11)

Some educators agree, among them Betty Levy and Judith Stacey: "Schools . . . remain effective agents of social control, perpetuating the existing class, racial, and sexual divisions in our society" (1973, p. 105). In this section, we will look at the kinds of influences schools can have on sex roles as well as at schools' potential for fostering androgyny.

Considering the effects schools may have on children leads to a paradox: the average girl prospers in elementary school while her male counterpart is struggling, but the situation is reversed in secondary school and beyond. At the beginning, girls' physical, emotional, and cognitive development is ahead of boys'. Hence, when both enter school at age six, girls are equipped to handle schoolwork more competently and comfortably than boys are (Frazier & Sadker, 1973). During the elementary years, boys make poorer grades, are required to repeat a grade more frequently, are disciplined more often, and predominate in referrals to child guidance centers (Lee, 1973). Even boys who do as well as girls on achievement tests get lower grades in school (Frazier & Sadker, 1973). But as girls progress through the school system, they lose academic potential, self-esteem, and occupational potential. For example, although girls start off intellectually ahead of boys (in math as well as in reading), in high school, girls' scores on ability tests decline. Males' IQ scores increase significantly more from adolescence to adulthood than do females'. Of the brightest high school graduates who do not go to college, 75 to 90 percent are women. Although many males are underachievers in the early grades, girls often cut back on their aspirations and achievements by the fifth and sixth grades. In terms of changes in self-esteem over the school year, children's opinions of boys grow increasingly positive and their opinions of girls grow increasingly negative. Fewer high school women than men rated themselves above average on leadership, popularity, and intellectual as well as social self-confidence. Girls' commitment to a career declines during high school, and this decline is related to their feelings that male classmates disapprove of a woman's using her intelligence. This is only part of a list of educational side-effects compiled by Frazier and Sadker (1973).

What happens in the schools to put boys at an early disadvantage, and girls at a later disadvantage? How does the change occur? Girls enter school with an apparently greater chance for success, but leave the school system not having achieved it. What can be learned from the apparently long-term positive effects of school on boys that can be applied to girls? With these questions in mind, we will look at the educational system from three perspectives: structure of schools, teacher-student interaction, and curricular materials.

Structure of Schools

Elementary schools structure their staff and activities along sex-role lines (Saario, Jacklin, & Tittle, 1973). Many aspects of the day's activities and tasks are designated as female or male; both inside and outside the classroom, space is also labeled as female or male. Nearly everywhere the child looks, the school world is organized on the basis of sex-related labels. There are girls' jobs and boys' jobs; lines for girls and lines for boys; boys' areas of the playground that are separate from girls'; different tables for girls and boys in the cafeteria; and even "girls' subjects" (reading) and "boys' subjects" (math), in which each sex excels. In fact, these messages are learned so well after a few years that, according to a study by Kagan (1964), children in second and third grades were able to label objects in the classroom "feminine" (e.g., blackboard) or "masculine" (e.g., map, pencil).

Hence, one of the first messages the child learns in school is that sex—female or male—is a tremendously important aspect of the world. The school's insistence on segregation by sex can increase the child's perception of the sexes as "opposite."

Students are also exposed to subtle sex-role messages in the person of the teacher. The majority of elementary teachers are female: 85 percent in 1975 (Howe, 1977). The evidence suggests that this is not an improvement over the past, since women represented roughly the same proportion of public elementary teachers in 1959–60 and again in 1970–71 (Howe, 1977; Lee, 1973). But, although the elementary classrooms may be female, most of the principals and administrators are male.

Further, after elementary school, as the age of the student and complexity of the material increases, so does the prestige and salary of her or his teacher; female teachers are most prevalent in the early years when material is simple and prestige is low, whereas male teachers predominate in the later years when the content is more difficult and the prestige is higher. Half of high school teachers are male (Howe, 1977), and statistics on college teachers reveal fully 70 percent to 80 percent are male (Astin & Bayer, 1975; Bernay, 1978; Howe, 1977). A disproportionate number of the males teach in universities, while women are overrepresented in two-year colleges. Likewise, in one study (Astin & Bayer, 1975) a larger proportion of the men (25 percent) than the women (9 percent) were full professors, while a larger proportion of the women (35 percent) than the men (16 percent) were instructors, the lowest academic rank. Despite affirmative action policies, these differences among college teachers have not changed in recent years (Bernay, 1978). Hence, the average student is confronted every day, particularly after elementary school, with the vision of men as more competent than women.

Thus, it can be seen that schools structure both many of their activities and their personnel along sex-role lines. Throughout the academic experience, students are subtly taught that sex is an important determinant for behavior, and that males can do more. At the same time, most young boys spend the school day in a classroom controlled by a female, and college-age women are most likely to find their classrooms run by males.

Teacher-Student Interaction

One reason often given for boys' frequent difficulties in the grade-school years is that female teachers emphasize feminine behaviors and traits. For example, it is said (Lee, 1973) that elementary schools value politeness, neatness, and cleanliness—characteristics expected of girls. Schools emphasize language skills (in which the average girl excels) and deemphasize physical skills (in which boys are more likely to excel). Teachers who are trained in methods of passive rather than active learning encourage listening and discourage speaking, which fits with the submissive, passive, and dependent behavior trained in girls and conflicts with the independence and aggression displayed by boys. The teacher's attempts to be the dominant figure fit with girls' willingness to be submissive, but boys are more often accustomed to being the dominant one themselves.

These opinions are supported by evidence. Both classroom observers and the children themselves in one study noted that the (female) teachers expressed greater approval of girls and greater disapproval of boys (Meyer & Thompson, 1963). Boys received up to ten times as many prohibitory control messages ("That's enough talking, Bill." "Put that comic book away, Joe.") as girls (Jackson & Lahadierne, 1971). Also, when teachers criticized boys, they were more likely to use a harsh tone than when talking to girls about similar infractions. Apparently, boys in the early school years are disapproved of more often and more harshly than girls.

Yet such a conclusion does not reveal the full picture. A number of systematic observations have shown that boys receive more teacher attention in general. Fourth- and sixth-grade teachers (female and male) interacted more with boys than with girls in each of the following categories: approval, instruction, listening to child, disapproval (Spaulding, 1963). Likewise, boys got more positive as well as negative feedback from teachers, and initiated more contacts with teachers than girls (Brophy & Good, 1974). Even when girls did raise their hands in class, they were significantly less likely to be called on.

On the basis of this evidence we can revise our tentative conclusion: Although young boys bear the brunt of the teacher's disapproval, they seem to receive most of the teacher's positive, encouraging attention as well.

When young girls do get the teacher's attention, it is more often than not for behaving in a sex-typed feminine way. In observations of fifteen nursery schools, boys received more attention and instructions when they were involved in tasks or engaged in disruptive behavior. Teachers were more likely to react to girls when they were within arm's reach than when they were further away (Serbin & O'Leary, 1975). Even when a girl was disruptive, she was less likely to receive attention from the teacher. Thus, girls were inadvertently being reinforced for passive, dependent behavior, whereas boys were being reinforced for more active, inquisitive, task-related behavior.

Teachers' reinforcement of sex-typed behavior extends beyond the nursery school and into elementary school. The average teacher in one study (Sears & Feldman, 1966), liked both instrumental and expressive qualities in boys, but emphasized only expressive qualities in describing which girls they particularly liked. Although the teachers liked bright boys who were friendly and self-sufficient, the boys of average intelligence they liked were affiliative, dependent, confident, and had good work habits. Girls, on the other hand, were liked by the teacher when they were friendly and conforming, no matter what their ability. It seems that teachers like a degree of independence in boys, at least in bright boys, but that independence in girls is not as likely to merit the teacher's approval, no matter what the girl's intellectual ability.

If we look at the study from the perspective of androgyny, we can see some interesting possibilities. Apparently it would be fairly easy for teachers to tolerate androgyny in boys: boys receive approval for affiliation as well as independence, dependency as well as confidence. Yet teachers seem to demand a more restricted range of behaviors from girls, showing little apparent respect for any independence-striving or self-orientation. This suggests that it might be fairly simple for teachers to reinforce androgyny in boys, but difficult to learn to encourage the full range of androgynous behavior in girls.

The evidence reviewed so far concerning teacher-student interactions has been concerned with nursery and elementary schools. Girls seem to be rewarded for feminine behavior, but apparently at the expense of a creative, adventurous approach to learning. An examination of teacher-student interactions in the early years suggests that, although greater restraint is put on boys in elementary school, teachers do seem to offer more to boys. The fact that boys are attended to when they behave independently suggests that they are being encouraged to develop intellectual curiosity, to trust their hunches, and to explore their world. These are all traits that begin to pay off in later grades, when control is less important, and that continue to serve them well in adulthood. Teachers' interactions with girls, on the other hand, seem more likely to teach them conformity and provide suggestions about what they cannot do. Adoption of such attitudes can carry girls only so far, and can stunt them in major ways when education becomes more self-directed.

What happens in more advanced classrooms that can help explain females' declines in achievement and goal-setting? Many teachers, as a sample of the American middle class, reflect and accept many societal stereotypes. As the content of the classroom becomes less skill-oriented (e.g., reading, writing, etc.) there are greater opportunities for teachers' own opinions about the sexes to appear overtly.

Particularly in high school, additional lessons in sex-role behavior are frequently available in the guidance counselor's office. These years are a time of crucial decisions, including future careers, schooling, and life style. Guidance counselors sometimes construe certain professions as "appropriate" for women and others as "appropriate" for men. They therefore tend to respond more positively to female clients who hold traditional feminine career goals than to those who wish to make their way in a profession usually reserved for men (Thomas & Stewart, 1971).

The vocational tests that serve as the foundation for many guidance counselors' suggestions have been shown to be sex biased (Harmon, 1973). Despite recent attempts to reduce this bias, the tests still do little to encourage career development toward novel choices. Students' scores are derived by comparing their statements to ones made by persons of the same sex in various occupational categories. If a particular category does not currently include a sufficiently large number of females (or males), scores are simply not available for that sex in that occupation. It would take a particularly aware guidance counselor to suggest "architect" to a female or "art teacher" to a male, when no scores for her or him in that category are available from the formal test.

Much of the available career educational material is sexist. Women on Words and Images (1975c) surveyed eighty randomly selected grade school, high school, and postsecondary sets of materials for students. They found five occupations presented as male for every two occupations presented as female, at both the elementary and secondary levels. Over two-thirds of the illustrated figures were male. Further, when females were shown in occupations, they were frequently stereotypically feminine ones. There was an emphasis on grooming and demeanor for women, and a frequent assumption that marriage and motherhood constituted woman's primary career.

There is less systematic information about observations of teacher-student interactions in the college classroom. However, Harris (1974) collected some noteworthy quotes by college teachers to their students: "The girls at [X University] get good grades because they study hard, but they don't have any originality"; "Women are intrinsically inferior"; "Somehow I can never take women in this field seriously"; "A pretty girl like you will certainly get married, why don't you stop with an M.A.?"

Curriculum

In the early years, when the curriculum is focused on basic skills, textbooks provide additional information about the roles and relationships of the sexes. If children believed portrayals in textbooks, this is what they would learn:

About 70 to 80 percent of the people in the world—adults as well as children—are male, whereas 20 to 30 percent are female.

About 85 percent of the important people (those about whom biographies are written) are male.

Even in the animal kingdom, two-thirds of the creatures are male; that proportion increases to four-fifths when one considers the world of fantasy.

There are six times as many occupations for men as there are for women. The possible male occupations (147 in one study of children's readers) include exciting things like fireman, astronaut, doctor, policeman; females stick to quieter occupations (25 of them, in the same study) like teacher, nurse, telephone operator, secretary. Females do not work outside the home if they are mothers.

Females are usually smaller and younger than males.

Males are active, adventurous, clever, brave, skillful, resourceful, strong, heroic, creative, powerful, autonomous, and assertive, and they fight their emotions. Females are passive, incompetent, dependent, domestic, docile, victimized, humiliated by males, and apt to display extreme emotions, particularly fear.

As children, girls cook, make purchases, sew, jump rope, hold dolls and the hands of younger children, and are frequently bewildered. Boys do woodwork, sail, climb mountains, go to the moon, plant things, run, play ball, swim, and help girls clear up their bewilderment.

This list is only a sample of the results of several authors' content analyses of elementary textbooks, including readers (Saario, Jacklin, & Tittle, 1973; Women on Words and Images, 1975a), math books (Federbush, 1974), and science and social studies books (Levy & Stacey, 1973). Perhaps girls' negative views of themselves in the upper grades is assisted by their textbooks. Maybe boys' greater tendency to be overactive and even aggressive in the classroom is simply a reflection of stimulation by all the active, assertive, independent heroes in their textbooks.

These stereotyped portrayals in textbooks increase as the child progresses through the elementary grades and beyond. Saario, Jacklin, and Tittle found that the portrayal of female and male roles (child and adult) in children's readers became progressively more stereotyped in the years from kindergarten to third grade. Many upper-level texts speak of humanity as if it were composed of "men." History is devoted to the study of "our forefathers" and "the men who built our nation." Even if the phrase is changed to "the people who built our nation," it does not change the fact that the majority of the people discussed in the history texts *are* male. In math, the males who are used as examples still build, experiment, and achieve; the females continue the sewing and cooking they began in the elementary textbooks. The illustrations in some science books show mostly males using scientific equipment and solving problems. Most of the novels studied in English class feature male protagonists. Discrimination against women remains a neglected topic in most social science books (Trecker, 1973).

The male orientation in textbooks includes not only who is represented but the types of topics included. Once students begin to learn about things, rather than simply how to do things (i.e., to read, write, and compute), they are faced with the sex-biased content of most academic disciplines. History consists of the study of wars and power struggles, with little attention to the intellectual, cultural, and social areas of life; psychology devotes a lot of its attention to achievement, aggression, and competition, drawing conclusions about "people" when its data were derived from males (Holmes & Jorgensen, 1971); athletics is football, basketball, and ice hockey rather than the horseback riding and figure skating that might be more prominent in females' experience.

As students move up the academic ladder, they have an increasing number of choices. Yet this can create an illusion of freedom. Despite the proclaimed autonomy, students are subtly channeled into sex-typed curricula.

Sex discrimination in school curricula is now illegal but many school systems retain vestiges of the past. Girls were channeled into the liberal arts, teaching, or training for low-paying jobs such as homemaking and clerical work, while boys were channeled into the sciences, preprofessional programs, or training for highly-skilled and high-paying jobs such as mechanic, machinist, or carpenter. College admissions standards often continue to be lower for males: men are accepted more frequently than women with identical qualifications (Frazier & Sadker, 1973; Sexton, 1976). The message to students is clear: Females and males differ in abilities, and males (even those with lower grades and aptitude test scores) are better suited for skilled positions and higher education than females are.

There are also strong sex-role–related lessons to be found in the structure of extracurricular activities and athletics. In high school, and even more in college, students elected to leadership positions such as class or student body president tend to be male. The powerful positions that are held by women are more often appointive (i.e., editor of the yearbook) rather than elective (Sexton, 1976). It is widespread knowledge that school athletic departments devote less money, staff, and equipment to women and provide them with a narrower range of offerings. Even with the recent legal challenges to this state of affairs, it will probably take years to change budgets, attitudes, and expectations so that females have an equal opportunity to enjoy competitive as well as noncompetitive sports. In the meantime, students will continue to learn that males somehow deserve more of the school's resouces and leadership positions.

The curriculum is also notable for what it does *not* include: information about sex discrimination, the struggles of women to obtain the vote, consideration of women's role in history, literature, the sciences. Such lack of information about their own background may be one of the factors contributing to females' under-achievement after the early grades.

Thus, the curriculum joins with the structure of schools and teacher-student interactions to convey and support sex-typed attitudes and behaviors. Although some authors have complained that schools "feminize" boys (Sexton, 1965; Gold-man & May, 1970), it seems more accurate to say that schools help boys recoup any losses they suffered in the earliest years that emphasized control; girls, how-ever, accumulate losses throughout their academic careers that offset any initial gains they had made.

The orderliness and control required in school is stressful for some boys and can create problems. In particular, the boy who is not academically inclined is trapped in a cycle of punishment, resistance, and further punishment. Many au-thors have suggested that the best remedy would be to bring in more male elemen-tary teachers, and require less control from boys. An androgynous perspective leads to an additional possibility. Since orderliness and control *are* a part of civilized adult life, schools need not discontinue stressing a moderate amount of these qualities. Perhaps a moderate emphasis on feminine qualities (the so-called feminization of the classroom) could be an advantage for boys, as long as it does not interfere with an active approach to learning. It forces them to slow down, temper their aggression, and learn some additional social skills. School could be seen as a way to help boys remedy their sex-role–related problems with overac-tivity (Pleck, 1975). Admittedly this addition of demands for feminine qualities poses difficulties for some boys—apparently those who have been most "mascu-line" before school. Yet there are long-term benefits for males in learning to deal with other people in appropriate ways. Simply put, males cannot go through life with the attention-seeking and physically aggressive behavior not uncommonly found in boys. Success in later family and work roles requires some sensitivity to the reactions of others, as well as restraint and self-control. If the goal is to help boys develop a broad repertoire of social skills, school personnel would need to look toward ways to enhance an appropriate degree of self-control in those boys who seem to require it.

For girls, the picture is more discouraging. The schools' fostering of sex roles and emphasis on feminine qualities represents nothing new for the girl. It is merely a continuation of the lessons she receives from parents and the world around her. Girls are apparently seduced, through rewards, into increasing cooperation with the system: passivity and dependency add to the same qualities that were reinforced outside of school, too. Girls who try to get out of this sex-role cycle do so at the risk of losing any positive attention they might have had for stereotyped behavior. It could be different, however. A girl's already-acquired socialization to control and dependency, and her willingness to cooperate when she enters school need not be perceived as an advantage for a harried teacher. Rather, it could be conceived as the beginnings of a sex-role deficit as potentially dangerous to her as the boys' overactivity and relative lack of skills. Viewed from this perspective, teachers who see their jobs as nurturing both a willingness to respect the needs of others *and* an appropriate degree of independence and assertiveness would notice the need for the latter in many entering girls. This awareness could be followed by deliberate attempts to remedy the deficit.

Another Look

Although we have looked at findings concerning the relationship between sex roles and education, we have not yet commented directly on the *form* of the studies done, the types of questions asked, or the methods used. Issues in the approaches used will be examined, in order to highlight the ways that forms of research methods can determine outcomes.

First of all, much of the inquiry about the relationship between sex roles and education is focused on the elementary school when, at least by several indicators (grades, reprimands, referrals to child guidance centers), more boys than girls are obviously having a tough time. There has been less attention given to the later school years, when girls' declining scores and self-esteem suggest they are at a disadvantage (Frazier & Sadker, 1973). Instead of concentrating primarily on questions like: "Why can't Johnny read?", why haven't researchers asked, "Why doesn't Jane achieve?" A more useful research tactic might be to delineate both the costs and benefits different levels of the educational system have for the development of both girls and boys.

In reading discussions of the "feminization of the classroom," we are struck by most authors' ready assumption that this is a completely undesirable state of affairs, to be either disproved or eliminated. The teacher's feminizing influence is described as potentially making students passive, docile, and dependent—all negative aspects of the feminine stereotype. We wonder why there is no gratitude expressed to the female teachers for demonstrating warmth, cooperation, and compassion to students—for these, too, are "feminine" attributes. Researchers might do well to examine the ways that female teachers' interpersonal skills can foster similar skills in their students—female and male. This is an especially important area to document for, if changes in the sex-role aspects of schools are instituted, it will be necessary to know about the positive elements of female experience that stand to be eliminated. Social change artists must be aware of the desirable effects of female teachers so that they can work to retain them.

Part of the androgynous perspective is the assumption that there are positive aspects to both "feminine" and "masculine" traits. One who accepts this position may therefore wonder why researchers have not asked about the effect on girls of being cut off from male models. Just as little boys are deprived of male models when their fathers spend little time at home and their teachers are female, so are girls. Because of the current levels of sex stereotyping, it is also unfortunately true that children will probably observe independence, assertiveness, and ambition in adult males more than in females. Girls need to learn about these qualities at least as much as boys do. Therefore they need models who will express such qualities. Are girls more likely to exhibit these traits when they have had opportunities to interact with adult males? We know that boys, after all, besides being primarily socialized to masculinity, are often exposed to feminine influences. Girls, on the other hand, are confronted almost exclusively with feminine influences; they have fewer opportunities to observe and express "masculine" traits, and thus to develop this other aspect of themselves.

A second problem in much available research is that most of it has examined the circumstances under which stereotyped sex roles are developed and maintained. This procedure serves mainly to document the existence of sex-role pressures in the school. One cannot argue with the usefulness of knowing what problems exist before designing solutions. Yet, an awareness of sex stereotypes is necessary but not sufficient for a psychology of androgyny. It is time to move beyond description of an unfortunate state of affairs to possible remedies: What can people do through the educational system to undo sex stereotypes?

An exception to the dearth of studies on the effects of nonstereotypic classrooms is a study by Patricia Minuchin (1965). She examined the effects of "traditional" and "modern" schools on children's sex-role behavior. Traditional schools were those which stressed socialization toward the standards of society (including conceptions of sex-appropriate roles); modern schools stressed the individualized development of the child (including more open conceptions of sex roles). The study focused on about fifty fourth-graders in each type of school.

In general, Minuchin found more commitment to openness about roles and less sex-typing in both girls and boys from the modern than from the traditional schools. Children from the traditional schools were more likely to choose their own sex as having "the most fun and the best life" whereas children from modern schools were inclined to take a middle position—somewhere between "girls have the most fun" and "boys have the most fun." Yet they did not tend to state a preference for the opposite sex role. Unfortunately, for those interested in androgyny, the children were not given the option of responding that there were good things about being a girl as well as a boy.

Minuchin was also able to compare the influences of modern and traditional families in her study. The families seemed to have the greatest influence on the child's inner fantasy life, play, and personality organization, whereas the schools seemed to be more influential at the level of the child's attitudes toward sex roles.

Although our evidence comes from only one study, it suggests that there might be limitations in the effect of schools on sex roles. It seems that schools can expose the child to a variety of roles and activities, giving the child a less stereotyped view of the sexes in general. Yet these lessons in school are not easily applied to the child's sense of self. The difficulty could be caused by a variety of factors: perhaps the sex-role aspects of personality have already been formed before school; perhaps the existence of so many influences outside of school (peers, family, media, language, etc.) serve to erase the effects of even the most liberal school; perhaps the effects of the school are not felt immediately but will appear in several years, after the child has had a chance to consolidate the changes and integrate them into her or his decreasingly role-determined self-concept.

Changing stereotyped portrayals in the schools will not necessarily be welcomed by students. We are reminded of the studies, discussed in the last chapter, of children's resistance to nonstereotyped models. In addition, Jennings (1975) found that preschoolers preferred a story in which a character displayed sex-typed behavior (a girl who wanted to be a ballerina and a boy who wanted to be a mail carrier) to one in which the character displayed cross-sex behavior (a girl mail carrier and a boy ballerina). Nevertheless, children did recall the non-stereotyped story better. It seems that children do notice the sex roles portrayed in stories and, perhaps, remember the ones that run counter to expectations. The novelty effect might eventually diminish with time, so that children would be able to respond to stories irrespective of their sex-role portrayals. In the meantime, educators could develop methods to help children (at least initially) to enjoy less stereotyped textbook characters. Perhaps children who initially react with derision to a hero who cries could be more accepting if the story were accompanied by a sensitive discussion of the reality of sad feelings in adult males' (fathers, teachers, coaches, etc.) lives. A similar reality-based discussion of problems as well as possibilities could accompany a story about a girl who dreams of being a veterinarian, or one who stands up for her own rights.

To date, only limited solutions have been proposed for sex-role problems with the schools. The people who have suggested changes have usually been those who worry about the "feminization of the classroom." Their proposed solutions range from changing teachers' sex-linked expectations of children's behavior, to segregation of children by sex, to increasing the proportion of male teachers in the elementary grades (Lee, 1973), to masculinizing the schools (Sexton, 1969). A primary goal in such proposals seems to be to remove males from female influence. Such a solution seems rather drastic, particularly since much of the evidence suggests that the problem is an overabundance of sex-typing for both sexes in the schools and that, if anything, boys are already "overmasculinized" and girls "overfeminized."

However, to the extent that female teachers might experience difficulty handling the high energy level of some young boys, we would accept the viability of helping female teachers better understand the little boys' experience, particularly the pressure to be masculine. At the same time, teachers should be helped to understand the detrimental effects of pressures on little girls to be solely feminine. We would also suggest, at the higher levels of education where female teachers are rare, that teachers work harder to understand difficulties encountered by female students on their paths to autonomy and achievement.

Another possibility is that teachers be made aware of their own tendencies to react differently to female and male students. This awareness is a first step in teachers' striving to change their behavior. Perhaps they could attempt to be more responsive to girls, particularly when girls display independence. They might even wish to seek out any signs of assertiveness in girls. In addition, they could take care to pay less attention to aggression—particularly inappropriate levels—in boys.

In terms of curriculum, efforts should continue to open the full range of courses to all students, regardless of sex, and encourage children to take them. Yet more needs to be done than simply enrolling boys in cooking courses and girls in shop courses. We need to know how much curricular offerings reflect and encourage a full range of behaviors in all students: Would courses in women's studies help female students increase their knowledge about and pride in themselves? Are females as well as males represented in the content of the regular English, history, and social studies classes? Could students benefit from a course in self-defense? Are they receiving enough usable information about contraception? What about public speaking skills, particularly for female students who have been taught to fear self-presentation? Curricular revision should involve not only expanded opportunities for females to get their "male" needs met but also opportunities for all students to get their more person-oriented, "female" needs met.

COMMUNICATION

Even before making their first formal contacts with society through the classroom, children are exposed to other nonfamilial sources of subtle (and some not-so-subtle) messages about what it means to be female or male. One important bearer of these messages is language itself.

Language

Language is closely related to the world of polarized sex roles. Hence, it serves as an agent of sex-role socialization, as well as a potential agent for social change. In discussing these relationships between language and sex roles, we will first look at the properties of the English language itself, then at the different ways women and men use a given language. In order to complete the communication picture, we will also consider nonverbal aspects of communication. Finally, after examining what is known about language and sex roles we will raise issues about what we would like to know, from an androgynous perspective.

Properties of language. Words both structure and reveal thinking, as well as provide a means of communication with the next generation. The Eskimos' use of many different words for snow reflects and contributes to their awareness of subtle variations in winter climatic conditions. The English language, developed by people who lived in the temperate zones, has only one word for snow. The Aztecs, living in even warmer climates, had a single word to cover snow, ice, and cold (Miller & Swift, 1976). Accordingly, speakers of each of these languages would surely differ in their perceptions of winter weather.

Just as words for snow influence a people's perception of cold white stuff, so can the words used in discussing the sexes structure and limit thinking about the sexes. In fact, the English language is polarized in its consideration of the sexes. As Miller and Swift (1976) have pointed out, the meanings of the English words used to describe women and men reveal an emphasis on sex differences. For example, many people have used the words "feminine" and "masculine" as the personality equivalents of female and male without ever questioning this practice. In this way they communicate that qualities like toughness and timidity, gentleness and strength, intellectuality and emotionality are sex-related. The fact that the term "androgyny" is unfamiliar to most people suggests that, until recently, not many have even noticed the overlaps that occur in behaviors of women and men. Phrases such as "the opposite sex" are common, and can convey the message that the sexes are opposed, hostile, and in conflict, or at least strongly different from one another. At the same time, such a phrase denies the mutuality, equality, or human wholeness that potentially exists within the sexes. As another example, the existence and use of words like "sissy" and "tomboy" suggest that children's behavior should match a certain, different, standard for each sex.

In addition, as so often happens with polarities, only one pole emerges as positive. Here, not surprisingly in light of the greater power held by males in this culture, the connotations of qualities associated with males are more frequently desirable. In the foregoing examples, masculine, tough, strong, and intellectual males are more highly valued than timid, gentle, and emotional females. The fact that "sissy" has a more negative connotation than "tomboy" further suggests that feminine qualities (especially for males) are more distasteful and less tolerable than masculine qualities (even for females). Even words like "mistress" and "master" that originated as descriptive equivalents for the sexes have developed so that the connotation for the male form is more clearly positive than that for the female form. According to Miller and Swift, both words have their root in a word meaning "great" or "much." Although both do retain a sense of authority, in their most common uses "master" now denotes excellence in performance whereas "mistress" labels the "kept woman."

The generic use of the masculine form can contribute to the polarization of the sexes and the message that to be male is to be more important. According to those who compile dictionaries and rules of grammar, "man" means male but sometimes means all people, female and male; "he" and "him" refer to a male person but also refer to anyone whose sex is not specified. At best, the result of these double meanings is ambiguity. Do phrases like "the men who conquered the West," "early man," and "man and his environment" refer to male "men" or male and female "men"? One can never be sure. At times, the generic use of the masculine creates some bizarre sentences: "Since he is a mammal, man breastfeeds his young."

At worst, however, the generic use of the masculine constitutes a linguistic exclusion of women. Although the rule is that "man" can mean man and woman, the reality is that, for many people, it simply does not. To demonstrate this, two sociologists (Schneider & Hacker, 1972) asked several hundred college students to select pictures to illustrate an upcoming sociology textbook. Half the students were told to find pictures for chapters such as Social Man, Industrial Man, and Political Man. The other students were given corresponding titles such as Society, Industrial Life, and Political Behavior. Students in the first group selected significantly more pictures of males; those who received titles without "man" were more likely to choose pictures of both females and males. In a similar study, college students asked to write about a character referred to as "him" were less likely to use female story characters than students given instructions that included the words "their" or "his or her" (Moulton, Robinson, & Elias, 1978). These findings suggest that, even when "man" is used generically, the word is more likely to evoke images of males. Parallel results have been found in studies with children (Miller & Swift, 1976).

No one has yet examined the effect of the generic use of the masculine on factors such as students' self-image and aspirations. Try to remember (if you are female) your reactions as a girl when you first realized that you are "man" and that those many references to "him" in your textbooks silently include you. One can make a strong guess that, in the words of Miller and Swift: "Those who have grown up with a language that tells them they are at the same time men and not men are faced with ambivalence about their status as human beings" (1976, pp. 34–35). If you are male, remember or imagine your reactions to reading a passage that used the feminine form in a generic manner.

This convention reflects (and perhaps helps to maintain) a more general convention that most creatures are known to be male, that the male is the norm. Consider the little girl who hears talk of salesmen, chairmen, weathermen, workmen, postmen, and, yes, cleaning ladies. In her world, most doctors and lawyers are surely male, for there is mention of those occasional exceptions, the "lady doctor" and the "woman lawyer." What attitudes are formed, what conclusions drawn by the child who hears such language? The woman is the other, the special case, the exception who must be pointed out. If her presence is not noted she remains invisible. It is such aspects of language that may well contribute to a polarization of conceptions of, and hence of the relationships between, the sexes.

Use of language. Men and women often differ in some of the ways they actually use language. Despite myths to the contrary, many researchers have shown that men speak more often, speak at greater length, and interrupt more than women do. These differences are found in studies done with people alone, in single-sex and mixed-sex pairs, and in groups. They are found at all occupational levels, in real-life (e.g., wives and husbands) as well as experimentally created groups. In addition, after being interrupted, women are more likely to be silent than men are under similar circumstances (Deaux, 1976; Henley, 1977).

Robin Lakoff (1973) has suggested that the differences between female and male speech are so marked as to constitute separate women's and men's languages. Woman's language involves avoidance of strong expression of feelings, frequent expressions of uncertainty, and elaborate subject matter considered trivial to the "real" world. Despite the fact that women are stereotyped as the "emotional" sex, it is men who are accorded the privilege of using strong expletives. Lakoff noted women's tendency to use "tag questions" unnecessarily, to avoid commitment and express uncertainty. For example, sentences such as, "This course is interesting, isn't it?" and "That's a beautiful picture, isn't it?" leave room for the listener to disagree with the speaker. In fact, there is empirical support for the notion that females use more tag questions than males (McMillan, Clifton, McGrath, & Gale, 1977). Another way that "women's language" reveals uncertainty is through the use of rising intonation in some declarative sentences (Q: "When will dinner be ready?" A: "Around six o'clock?") and a greater tendency to phrase orders in terms of requests ("Won't you please close the door?" versus "Please close the door."). In woman's language it is also considered acceptable to employ words that make subtle distinctions about things that the "man's world" considers unimportant, such as color. Thus, although it is regarded as appropriate for a woman to discuss the relative merits of the "lavender" versus the "mauve" rug, eyebrows are raised at the man who uses such color words.

Repeated exposure to such differences in the verbal styles of women and men may well influence a child's view of relationships between the sexes, and eventually the child's own behavior. It would be useful to see this statement supported empirically. Perhaps children could be exposed to several sessions of various verbal styles by adults and then the children's feelings and attitudes toward these adults could be assessed.

Nonverbal Communication

Stereotyped sex roles are revealed, and perhaps perpetuated, in the nonverbal as well as the verbal aspects of communication. Touching, smiling, demeanor, and emotional displays all convey messages and relationships nonverbally.

From six months of age to adulthood, females are more likely to be touched by others than males are. Additionally, in adulthood, males initiate gestures of touch more often than women do (Deaux 1976; Henley, 1977). There are clear status connotations of these differentials. In the following pair, who is more likely to initiate touch and who is likely to receive the touch: master and servant? teacher and student? doctor and patient? It is difficult to imagine the servant, student, or patient putting an arm around the master, teacher, or doctor. Yet it is fairly easy to imagine the reverse. In addition, women respond more positively to being touched than not touched; for men, being touched does not seem to make a difference in their evaluation of the situation (Deaux, 1976). By itself, touching is not necessarily a gesture of dominance. In fact, among equals (e.g., among athletes) it connotes solidarity and is used reciprocally. Yet, when the touching remains one-sided with one member of a pair holding the permission to be the initiator, the message is that the toucher has some power over the touched. In one observational study, people of higher status (upper-class, male, older) touched those of lower status (lower-class, female, younger) significantly more often than the reverse (Henley, 1977).

Many of the sex differences in nonverbal communication can be interpreted as revealing the subordinate status of women and the dominant status of men.

Women display a full range of emotions and, in general, disclose information about themselves more readily than men do (Henley, 1977). Among nonfriends such revelations of emotional vulnerability frequently signal a lack of power. Women smile more often than men do—even when their message is not a positive one (Deaux, 1976; Henley, 1977). This suggests some parallels with the old image of the smiling, shuffling Uncle Tom. Subordinates smile to curry favor; dominants do not need to. Other differences in nonverbal styles of the sexes include males' staring and pointing, both dominance gestures, in contrast to the corresponding females' lowering or averting the eyes and stopping action or speech. Males more often take the powerful privilege of using a more informal demeanor, posture, and form of address with women, whereas women tend to be more formal in these aspects (Henley, 1977).

Such a power interpretation of sex differences in both verbal and nonverbal aspects of communication is relatively new. An alternative interpretation, and one emphasized until recently, is that women's use of tag questions, orders veiled as requests, greater tendency to listen, greater responsiveness to touch, willingness to self-disclose, and smiling demeanor all express their greater interpersonal sensitivity. The power interpretation need not preclude the interpersonal sensitivity interpretation. The two are linked, a reflection of one of the less desirable aspects of current society. In a situation of inequality, subordinates need to understand the dominants for their very survival. Hence, it has been suggested that, through practice, many women have developed their skills in reading small signals, both verval and nonverbal (Miller, 1976). The resulting interpersonal sensitivity may then be a side-effect of women's subordinate status in this society.

Another Look

Thus far, we have seen that there are messages about sex roles hidden within language, and differences in the ways women and men use communication. It seems reasonable to expect that children's conceptions of themselves and their sex are affected by what they hear and see in the communication of others, although few studies test the hypothesis directly. A fine-tuned analysis of the process by which these effects come about would provide a foundation for people who wish to introduce more androgynous language forms. A detailed documentation of the negative consequences of a sex-typed language might help convince more people of the importance of changing current sex-typed usages.

Information is lacking in other areas as well. There has been little examination of the effect generic masculine terms have on children. We need empirical information on the effect of this convention on socialization, self-image, school problems, and other areas of life.

An additional area for exploration is language as a function of status as well as sex. Are the sex differences in communication discussed above still present in dominant females and subordinate males? It would also be useful to examine the language of androgynous people. Is it typical of their sex or does it represent some integration of the usual female and male communication elements?

Another area of neglect has been women and language. Until recently, those studying language focused on its use by males. With the male thus defined as the norm, data on women were introduced as a "difference." To only discuss women when noting how they are different from men exacerbates a polarized view of the sexes, and constitutes an instance of the distortion of women discussed in Chapter 2. Studying language in both sexes equally could facilitate recognition of the many similarities between the sexes, thus keeping in perspective those differences that do exist.

Many writers seem to assume that men's language and usage are more effective than women's . It seems to us, however, that although the strength that seems to pervade men's style is useful, so is the sensitivity and "good listener" element of women's style. We wonder what combination of these styles is most effective in various situations, such as the classroom, intimate relationships, parent-child interactions, leadership roles, and helping roles. It would seem that, in most situations, an integration of the two styles would be more effective than either alone. In order to study this, it may first be necessary to point out the positive elements in women's language and the negative elements in men's language, aspects that are frequently overlooked. Along these lines, we would also ask whether the consequences of using these styles differ for women and men. Is men's language not readily acceptable when used by women, even in combination with women's language? Likewise, are the consequences for males using women's language different than those for females? If this is so, it would be necessary to increase the rewards for such combinations, so that speakers need not be limited by listeners' stereotyped expectations.

Regarding the relationship between language and social change, we wonder whether the use of more androgynous language styles would help to change current conceptions of power. Can communications that are both strong and personal help to create more egalitarian styles? Change at the individual level is interrelated with societal change, and both must change if either is to change. With current values, women's use of emotional expressiveness usually puts them in vulnerable positions and excludes them from powerful positions. Changes in values must accompany changes in language styles.

Efforts have been afoot for several years to change sexist aspects of verbal language. There is a movement in some quarters away from the generic use of masculine pronouns (e.g., s/he, her or him), as well as toward more sex-neutral titles (e.g., chairperson, police officer). Feminists have been largely responsible for these suggestions and they have received some support from professional organizations (e.g., APA) and some textbook publishers. More widespread uses of these changes—particularly among people in influential positions—is necessary, however, before they become part of the "mainstream language."

FRIENDS AS SOCIALIZING AGENTS

Friendship seems to be an almost forgotten topic in psychology. This is consistent with traditional psychology's tendency to focus on behaviors and characteristics valued by more men (e.g., achievement, aggression, power) and its corresponding lesser interest in areas where more women are skilled (e.g., intimacy).

Since families, schools, language, and the media have an influence on sex-role development, it is reasonable to think that friends do, too. Friendship can be defined as an intimate, caring, personal relationship, with or without overt sexual expression. A friend is more than a mere acquaintance, convenient companion, or familiar coworker. It is someone with whom one shares personal aspects of oneself, on a reciprocal basis. Friendship is a form of love. These definitions, as well as much of the work that follows, are based on the writings of Strommen (1977) on friendship.

Friendship patterns are influenced by developmental level. In early childhood, true friendship does not exist, partly because young children are incapable of taking on the perspective of another. In addition, the family, on whom the child is dependent, has the major effect on the child at this stage. During the school years, relationships are more personal as the child becomes capable of being more responsive to others. The reciprocal aspect of friendship becomes a possibility. At least in the past, friendships at this age were usually confined within the same sex.

As nonfamilial relationships become more important, there is pressure from peers to conform to sex-role standards (Hartup, 1970). Many schoolyards have been the scene of taunts such as, "He throws like a girl!" and social ostracism directed at the child who doesn't conform, including the boy who wants to jump rope and the girl who wants to play baseball. We know of no studies of whether such pressure persists in the current "enlightened" era, yet personal observation suggests that maximum sex-role flexibility is not yet the rule in children's groups. One boy recently expressed his opinion of females in words that were the ultimate put-down in his four-year-old view: "Girls wear diapers!" Six-year-old boys from a liberal academic community are sometimes heard to tease one another by saying, "You're just like a girl!"

One of the few personality theorists who discuss friendship, Harry Stack Sullivan (1953), has pointed out the importance of a "chum" in the preadolescent developmental stage (from as early as age eight and a half to puberty). A chum is a best friend of the same sex and, as friendship with this chum is the first truly equal relationship one experiences, it helps one develop a sensitivity to the needs of others. The intimacy with a chum thus provides the groundwork for later relationships. Sullivan seems to believe this initial, tentative exploration of another person can best be done with one who is similar in regard to sex.

Adolescence is the time when friends become truly important. One of the tasks of this stage is to break away from the family, and it is naturally difficult for a family to provide support for that. Conflict with family at that time is common. The adolescent increase in erotic feelings, hard for parents to deal with, is one more reason why the family cannot be the sole forum for development at adolescence. Friends provide understanding and assistance in the emotional and physical movement beyond family. In their willingness to criticize, friends help with "reality testing," checking out self-perceptions of limitations and strengths. They also can provide direct instruction in the intricacies of being an adult. This is particularly true regarding sex-related behavior, with the emphasis on increasing one's attractiveness to the other sex: how to dress, behave sexually, and, in general, learn the rules of social performance. At the same time, however, same-sex friendships may become ambivalent because of the simultaneous appearance of interest in the other sex.

Traditional psychological research has suggested strong sex differences in adolescent friendship patterns. It has been found that boys attracted friends because of their athletic or academic success, whereas girls were more often liked for their social achievements (Frazier & Sadker, 1973). Boys tended to experience their same-sex relationships with a "gang," a group that supported them in their struggles against authority. Girls tended to establish their relationships in twosomes and threesomes that were more intimate, and served as a source of emotional support in personal crisis. However, these are findings from researchers who studied adolescents in the 1950s and 1960s (Douvan & Adelson, 1966). High school students today are more mature in many ways, and may be experiencing the addition of more other-sex relationships as well. In fact, Komarovksy (1976) found that college males disclosed the most vulnerable aspects of their personalities to female friends (in nonsexual as well as sexual relationships), whereas in earlier studies college males shared more with male friends (Jourard & Lasakow, 1958). This cross-sex pattern of self-disclosure formerly was found chiefly among adults. Perhaps a similar broadening of relationships beyond sex-role limitations has occured among high school youth.

Even less is known about friendship in adulthood than in the other life stages. As we have said, with age there is an increased tendency to disclose the private aspects of oneself to someone of the other sex, and a corresponding decrease in the tendency to share oneself with same-sex friends. This probably reflects a cultural emphasis on adults as marital couples in most areas of their adult social life. Such all-encompassing binding of the pair tends to make relationships between the individual and others less likely. Many adults end up isolated within their families for all but the most mundane interactions. Nevertheless, in all stages of adulthood, women are more involved with friends than men are (Lowenthal et al., 1975). In that interview study, women (of various ages) showed greater involvement, indicated by the fact that they had more detailed conceptions than men of both real and ideal friendships. The women seemed to have thought more about their relationships and valued them more highly.

There is also a social-class difference in adult friendship patterns. Working-class women are more peer-oriented than couple-oriented, whereas middle-class women look to their husbands as the primary confidant (Komarovsky, 1967; Lopata, 1971, 1973). Within the working class, many women find their closest friends among their parents and siblings (Bott, 1971; Komarovsky, 1967; Lopata, 1973; Rainwater, Coleman, & Handel, 1959). As Rainwater, Coleman, and Handel put it: "Working class wives are family-type people and relatives are the people they like best" (1959, p.103). Yet this pattern has become less striking in recent years (Social Research, 1973). As the number of working-class women who work outside the home has increased, so have their social contacts outside the family. Whatever the source of her friendships, the working-class woman derives a great deal of support, satisfaction, and companionship from her friends. Komarovsky concluded that it was these confidantes that helped many of the blue-collar women she studied retain their emotional balance.

Unfortunately there is really very little information about the effects friends have on people's lives. For example: Can supportive friends facilitate individual development to more mature stages? Likewise, can friends serve as supporters of stagnation if they themselves do not welcome growth and change? How does the availability of same-sexed friends affect relationships with spouses? What benefits do accrue in the warmth and richness between intimate friends?

Some general theoretical writings can be used to develop speculations about some of the functions friendships serve across the life span. From an evolutionary perspective, Bowlby (1969) argues that attachments between humans exist as a function of the fact that their ancestors who survived were those who were willing to stay close to others and hence ward off predators. This is an interesting analysis and one suggesting that, by nature, humans probably strive for some relationships. Yet it is possible that modern relationships serve other functions as well. Some writers (e.g., Lowenthal, et al, 1975; Sullivan, 1953) think that friendship helps to establish the boundaries of one's identity, particularly for young people. People can find out who they are, in part, from the self-discoveries with which their friends help them. Jean Baker Miller (1976) sees friendship as serving a more general growth function. According to her observations, the individual develops only by means of affiliation. Relationships can give people strength.

If one thinks about the potential friends have for enhancing development, one begins to see intriguing possibilities. It is true that, for many people, young peers help lead them along the path of stereotyped sex roles, teaching them the rules for being female or male. Yet we wonder what effects an androgynous friend can have: Would he or she help guide the other through the complexities associated with flexibility rather than the rigid rules of sex-typing? Would she or he be able to offer support for a wide variety of adaptive behavior? One of the difficulties in moving toward androgyny is that occasionally one feels as if the rest of the world refuses to help. Especially at such times, a close relationship with someone who shares the androgynous perspective might be welcome. In fact, it is already known that similarity between individuals often serves as a kind of screening device: particularly among the young, people choose friends from among those similar to them. One group of researchers (Hill, Adelstein, & Carter) found that college student "best friend" pairs tended to have similar scores on the Bem Sex Role Inventory. It would be interesting to study people in the first stages of friendship and follow them as the friendship continues. This procedure would permit an investigation of how much sex-role similarity is present at the beginning and how much develops in the course of the friendship. It would provide information about the potential of friends to enhance each other's development toward androgyny.

SUMMARY AND CONCLUSIONS

We began the chapter by wondering what sex-role messages, if any, the child confronts outside the family. There is no doubt that children are innundated with information depicting and sometimes endorsing stereotypes. In the world of television, a stereotyped vision is presented to children: women are consistently underrepresented and portrayed negatively; androgynous characters are rare. The organization of schools, interactions with teachers and counselors, curricular materials, frequent female-male teacher status differentials, course content, and extracurricular activities all combine to explicitly and implicitly instruct students from grade school through college about appropriate behaviors for each sex. The very words and gestures that children observe and use to communicate subtly convey messages that the sexes are different and men are more important. Even friends, at least in the very early years, pressure each other to conform to sex-typed roles. Clearly, children grow up being exposed to a great deal of information and some pressure toward stereotyped sex roles.

Consistently, however, we have failed to find much evidence documenting a direct link between sex-typed media, schools, language and friendship, and children's actual adoption of sex-typed behavior. So, the second question posed at the beginning of the chapter (To what extent do children accept sex-typed cultural messages?) remains unresolved. The suspicion is strong that some influence is exerted, in the direction of increasing sex-role stereotypic attitudes and behavior. For example, we already know that children do imitate filmed models of aggression when the situation allows. Thus, the same effect may exist for filmed, and perhaps all visual and verbal models of sex-typed behavior. Nevertheless, more documentation is needed, particularly to delineate the parameters of the effects. Under what conditions do children respond to cultural sex-role instructions and under what conditions can they develop beyond the cultural messages available? Is it possible to "inoculate" children in the family against cultural pressures?

How does all this information fit in with the models of sex-role development presented in Chapter 7? In that chapter we presented the possibility that, rather than succumbing directly to others' pressure for sex-role socialization, children (and adults) form a concept of themselves as female or male (or potentially androgynous) and then develop behaviors to conform to that self-definition. If this is true, then perhaps the messages about sex roles conveyed through the culture operate by being available for people to incorporate them into their notions of sex roles. These cultural agents provide information to children regarding the *content* of a particular sex role. At the very least, they lead the child to some concept of what it means to be a "girl" or "boy." To the extent that children are trying to figure out what it means to be "girllike" or "boylike" they are particularly vulnerable to receiving such information.

From an optimistic perspective, perhaps if cultural messages provided children with more flexible examples of what it means to be girllike or boylike, children could more readily incorporate these more flexible concepts into their sex-role identities. Less stereotyped cultural messages can provide individuals with information about nonstereotypic options. In many places throughout this chapter we have discussed possibilities for providing children with less sex-typed, more androgynous information through media, schools, language, and peers.

In the following chapter we will examine some of the outcomes of biology and the differential socialization of girls and boys discussed in the past five chapters. There the emphasis will be on sex differences in cognitive, personality, and interpersonal realms.

SELECTED READINGS

Bowles, S., & Gintis, H. *Schooling in capitalist America.* New York: Basic Books, 1976.

Goffman, E. *Gender advertisements.* New York: Harper and Row, 1979.

Henley, N. M. *Body politics: Power, sex, and nonverbal communication.* Englewood Cliffs, N.J.: Prentice-Hall, 1977.

Miller, C., & Swift, K. *Words and women.* Garden City, New York: Anchor Press/Doubleday, 1976.

Women on Words and Images. *Dick and Jane as victims: Sex stereotyping in children's readers.* Princeton, N.J.: Women on Words and Images, 1975.

Women on Words and Images. *Channeling children: Sex stereotyping in prime-time TV.* Princeton, N.J.: Women on Words and Images, 1975.

Psychological Comparisons of Females and Males

Part of the impetus for interest in androgyny has been the existence of stereotyped beliefs about psychological differences between the sexes. The model of androgyny represents an attempt to open up the stereotyped expectations that restrict options for women and men. Yet development toward androgyny requires an accurate assessment of current validity of the stereotypes. It is necessary first to know to what extent the stereotypes are true—to what extent biology and culture combine to produce women and men who are "different"—before it is possible to help women and men develop similar skills and strengths.

A central question is, Are there elements of androgyny that will be particularly problematic for the average woman or man? If, for example, females are more likely to be emotional and males impassive, females passive and males aggressive, the average male may need extra work to develop the emotional aspect of his androgynous potential, and the average female might need help developing the ability to handle aggressive feelings. The road to androgyny is not the same for women and men in this culture, as long as psychological differences between the sexes persist.

In this chapter we will evaluate the validity of some prevailing myths and stereotypes regarding psychological differences between the sexes. Are there different areas of cognitive skills in females and males? Are men really more self-confident than women? Are men more comfortable than women about achievement? Are women more emotional than men? Do the sexes differ in their approaches to interpersonal relationships? Where there are differences, what is their origin?

PROBLEMS IN RESEARCH ON SEX DIFFERENCES

Sex difference research is one of the most problematic areas for psychologists interested in androgyny. On the one hand, it is important to find out whether sex differences are real and observable, or simply exist in some people's stereotyped conceptions of the sexes. Yet such information can easily be misused by people who view current sex differences as indicators of some natural, inevitable state of affairs. Findings of psychological differences between the sexes have limited value since they reveal only information about the average person today rather than the potential of those not limited by stereotypes. To address this problem, we will look carefully for studies comparing sex-typed and androgynous individuals, in addition to research comparing females and males. We will also be alert to findings of similarities between the sexes, and attend to cultural influences that may distort research findings.

The problems in sex difference research extend to methodology. As a first step in evaluating the evidence that will be discussed in this chapter, we will consider some of the difficulties facing studies in this area.

As in other areas of psychology, investigators of sex differences cannot help but be influenced by their stereotypes about the sexes when they design, implement, and interpret their research. The fact that they focus on psychological differences between the sexes at the expense of similarities reveals an assumption that the sexes are more different than similar.

Yet in almost all areas, differences *within* each sex are far greater than differences *between* the sexes. For example, an investigator reporting a finding that girls scored higher on a test of verbal skills than boys did can easily neglect the fact that many boys scored the same or higher than many girls. The most common statistical procedures rely on comparisons of the average person in one group with the average person in another group. This approach masks recognition of the range over which members of each group extend. Figure 9.1 illustrates the results of an imaginary survey of females' and males' grade-point averages (GPA) at a

FIGURE 9.1

Hypothetical Distribution of GPA for Females and Males in a Particular Sample.

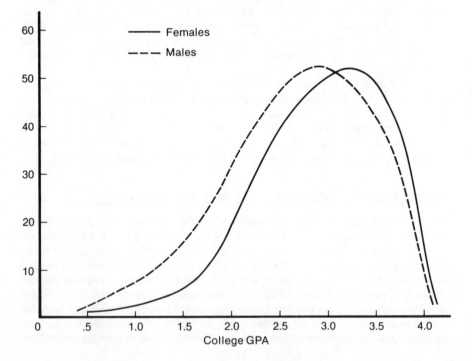

particular college. The average female apparently has a higher GPA than the average male. Yet the majority of GPAs, of both females and males, fall somewhere between 2.0 and 3.5, and many males do have higher GPAs than many females. Such overlap between groups is quite common, even when their average scores are significantly different. The finding of an average difference does not mean that each female's score is different from all the males' scores.

Researchers' assumptions about the existence of sex differences also influence their choice of terms. For example, researchers seem to be interested in "tomboyism" in girls, reflecting an implicit assumption that girls' and boys' behavior is different. Tomboyism is usually defined as girls acting "boylike": enjoying sports, climbing trees, preferring blue jeans to dresses, playing active outdoor games, etc. Yet half to three-quarters of young girls classify themselves as tomboys. If most girls are "tomboys" in childhood, why persist in studying them under this label (with its subtle implication of deviance)? As Hyde and Rosenberg (1976) point out, perhaps girls act primarily as children, just as boys do. Part of being a child—not only of being a boy—includes running, jumping, climbing, shouting, etc. Investigators of "tomboyism" apparently assume that these behaviors are usually expressed by boys and only rarely by girls. Hence, in reviewing research on sex differences, one should attend to stereotyped assumptions that are sometimes apparent in terminology.

An additional issue to confront in describing research on sex differences is that it has already been done on a very large scale. In a much cited, but sometimes criticized, review of this area, Eleanor Maccoby and Carol Jacklin (1974) summarized the results of approximately 1600 studies of sex differences done between 1966 and 1973.

Their conclusions were surprising: aside from sex differences in four areas (aggression, and verbal, visual-spatial and mathematical abilities) psychologists have not yet demonstrated the existence of consistent sex differences. In other words, the frequent assumptions about sex differences in sociability, suggestibility, self-esteem, analytic ability, motivation for achievement, timidity, anxiety, dominance, competitiveness, nurturance, and other qualities have not been supported by the data to date.

At first glance, the existence of such a summary should make the job of compiling information for this chapter easy: simply present Maccoby and Jacklin's work in summary form. However, despite the fact that their conclusions are widely cited, they are controversial. Therefore, we ought to look closely at their procedures before we accept their conclusions.

Jeanne Block (1976) has criticized their work on a number of grounds. Maccoby and Jacklin primarily referenced studies with children, although sex differences are generally more prevalent in adults. A greater attention to studies of adults may have resulted in evidence of more sex differences. In addition, Maccoby and Jacklin did not consider the quality of studies in their summaries, grouping together "good" and seriously flawed studies. Greater emphasis on the methodologically sound studies might have led to different conclusions. Maccoby and Jacklin also had problems with overly broad definitions of terms, according to Block. For example, are punishment and failure to grant a child freedom of movement (to friends' houses, etc.) both to be considered "restrictiveness"? To Maccoby, and Jacklin, they are, and girls are no more restricted than boys because sometimes boys are given more restriction and sometimes girls are. Yet an alternative set of definitions would have resulted in different conclusions: boys receive more punishment, whereas girls have more limitations placed on their independence. Finally, Maccoby and Jacklin's work contains many errors (studies misclassified, excluded, etc.) that, at times, make their conclusions questionable.

Thus, although Maccoby and Jacklin's work could serve as the "Bible" for a summary of sex difference research, conclusions in this chapter will at times differ from their often-quoted ones. We will use their results in any one area only after careful examination and in conjunction with other sources.

COGNITIVE ABILITIES

One possible explanation for the different types and levels of occupational achievement in women and men is that the sexes differ in their abilities. Perhaps there are more respected men than women writers, artists, accountants, engineers, and architects because of the average male's tendency to excel in verbal, mathematical, mechanical, and creative abilities. Likewise, perhaps many women choose the role of typist, keypunch operator, or clerical worker because the average woman is good at tasks requiring fine-motor and matching skills.

Females and males do not usually differ in tests of general cognitive ability that sample a balanced range of aptitudes. Yet "intelligence" is not a general, unitary trait but, rather, a set of separate abilities. It is when intelligence is broken down into these components that the sexes are sometimes found to differ.

Verbal Abilities

There is a small tendency for girls to excel in verbal abilities in the earliest years: girls have been found to say their first word sooner, articulate more clearly and at an earlier age, use longer sentences, and be more fluent (Maccoby, 1966). Recent studies report less clear-cut results but, whenever a sex difference in early verbal ability is found, it still favors girls (Maccoby & Jacklin, 1974).

During the early school years, there are not many sex differences in verbal ability. Girls do learn to read sooner, and they also do better on tests of grammar, spelling, and word fluency (Maccoby, 1966). From around age ten or eleven through adulthood, the differences are unmistakable and favor females in a wide variety of verbal skills: anagrams, reading comprehension, vocabulary, verbal creativity, understanding of complex logical relations expressed in verbal terms (Maccoby & Jacklin, 1974).

Quantitative Abilities

There are no consistent sex differences in quantitative abilities at the early ages, though boys move ahead in adolescence and afterward (Maccoby & Jacklin, 1974). Quantitative ability is measured through tests of counting (very early ages), arithmetic computation, arithmetic reasoning, and algebra. The sex differences in this area begin to appear between ages nine and thirteen, with a tendency for boys to do better; this difference becomes pronounced after age thirteen. These differences are apparent even when one compares high school senior girls and boys who have taken the same number of math courses. Thus they are not attributable only to experience in formal courses.

Visual-Spatial Abilities

A third cognitive area in which sex differences are consistently found is visual-spatial ability. This is the ability to correctly imagine three-dimensional objects when they are presented verbally or in only two dimensions. A person might be shown a drawing of a set of gears and then asked to determine the effects on the system of the movement of one gear. Another visual-spatial task might involve a drawing of a pile of blocks and instructions to ascertain how many surfaces would be visible if the pile were rotated 90 degrees. On such tasks, the sexes perform similarly until early adolescence, after which boys excel (Maccoby & Jacklin, 1974).

Analytic Abilities

A fourth type of ability is analytic—the ability to analyze a whole into its component parts, to separate a "figure," whether visual, spatial, or auditory, from its background. On measures such as the Embedded Figures Test (EFT) and the Rod-and-Frame Test (RFT) that have traditionally been regarded as tests of analytic ability, boys tend to do better than girls from eight years onward (Maccoby & Jacklin, 1974). The EFT requires subjects to find a simple geometric design hidden in a more complex design, whereas the RFT requires them to overcome the influence of the surrounding perceptual field in judging the position of their own bodies. Skill on both these tests was said by their creator to reflect a "field independent" cognitive style analogous to analytic ability (Witkin, Dyk, Faterson, Goodenough, & Karp, 1962). Witkin and his colleagues found evidence suggesting that females are field dependent (find it difficult to overcome the influence of the surrounding perceptual field, or to separate an item from its context), while males tend to be field independent (readily able to distinguish an item from its context). While it is true that when older children do exhibit a sex difference on the EFT and RFT, it is boys who are higher; some authors argue that this is merely a reflection of boys' greater visual-spatial abilities (Sherman, 1967). In fact, analytic ability (as measured by EFT) is highly related to and develops parallel to visual-spatial ability. In addition, when tactual and auditory versions of the EFT were developed (for use with blind people), and applied to adolescents, the usual sex differences favoring males did not appear. Thus, there seems to be some basis for concluding that girls' apparent difficulty with separating figure from ground on the EFT and RFT may occur because the tasks are visual-spatial (Sherman, 1967). The traditional tests of field dependence and independence seem to be measuring both visual-spatial and analytic abilities; the visual-spatial element seems responsible for apparent sex differences on such tasks.

On other types of tests designed to measure analytic ability, consistent sex differences do not appear (Maccoby & Jacklin, 1974). Here, analytic ability is defined broadly as an ability to "break set," or free oneself from an initial perception in order to discover new properties of a stimulus. For example, a subject might be given a set of color names, printed in the wrong color of ink, and be asked to report the color of ink for each word. This task requires her or him to suppress the usual response of reading the word itself. The ability to break set and analyze something in a new way is said to be an important component of problem-solving.

Areas of Similarity

Other areas of ability in which the sexes seem to be more similar than different include: concept mastery and reasoning, creativity, and moral judgment (Maccoby & Jacklin, 1974). Tests of concept mastery and reasoning usually involve assessing the degree to which people of various ages apply rules of logic when presented with a complex problem. On such measures, sex differences are not consistently found. When tests of creativity are primarily verbal (e.g., number of associations made to a particular word, number of uses a subject could think of for an object such as a cup), most studies show females doing better than males after the age of seven. But when the creative task is nonverbal (e.g., constructing original pictures, engaging in fantasy play) neither females nor males consistently do better. Hence, it seems that when creative abilities are studied separately from verbal abilities, sex differences are not found. The final item in the above list, moral reasoning, is included with intellectual abilities because, as commonly tested, it is regarded as an indicator of the development of complex forms of reasoning. Again, no consistent sex differences emerge.

Explanations for Differences in Cognitive Abilities

How does one explain the origin of the observed differences? Some authors have offered biological explanations, others environmental explanations, and still others a combination of the two.

One obvious biological explanation is a genetic one: females' genetic configuration is XX, males' is XY, as we saw in Chapter 4, and these differences result in physical development which results in behavioral differences. A major problem with this explanation is that, if it is accurate, one would expect the sexes' pattern of cognitive abilities to diverge from the first days of life, rather than only after middle childhood. Nevertheless, some authors have suggested that the visual-spatial ability in particular is genetically determined, by an X-linked recessive gene (Bock & Kolakowski, 1973; Stafford, 1961). Girls, with two X chromosomes, would not manifest strong visual-spatial ability unless they had inherited this recessive characteristic from *both* parents; otherwise, inheritance of the ability from one parent could by dominated by the lack of this genetic material from the other parent. Boys, with only one X chromosome (and a Y that has little genetic material), would manifest the ability whenever they received that gene, since there is no corresponding X to dominate it. The evidence does not yet provide a genetic explanation for females' greater verbal abilities (Maccoby & Jacklin, 1974). It is important to keep in mind that the relationships are not perfect. Boys are not born with a fully developed visual-spatial ability that exceeds that of most girls.

However, information from cross-cultural studies, particularly of visual-spatial ability, suggests that biological causes interact with environmental influences. Here, the evidence supports at least some experiential factors as precursors to that ability. If visual-spatial ability were totally determined by biology, one would expect males to be superior to females in all cultures. But this is not the case. In cultures that restrict children a great deal males do not exhibit their usual visual-spatial superiority, and when both girls and boys are given a great deal of freedom, the usual sex difference in this area decreases (Maccoby & Jacklin, 1974). These findings suggest that, at least in part, development of visual-spatial ability is related to the freedom to move around and explore one's environment. Girls as well as boys seem to benefit from such experience.

The idea that sex differences in visual-spatial ability may be as much a matter of sex roles as biological sex is further supported in a study by Nash (1975) of eleven- and fourteen-year-olds from middle-class urban public schools. The more masculine a child's actual-self or ideal-self rating, the higher her or his score was on the visual-spatial test. In addition, both girls and boys who said they would prefer to be boys scored higher in visual-spatial ability than the other children. It seems that children who saw themselves as having masculine characteristics and who valued masculine characteristics performed with the usual "male" skill on this task. It is impossible here to ascertain the direction of causality: perhaps children who preferred boys' toys and games (which generally provide more visual-spatial practice than girls' toys) developed special visual-spatial skills as a result of such experience; or perhaps children with a biological predisposition toward visual-spatial expertise enjoyed the masculine toys and games in which they excelled and hence developed a preference for things masculine and a view of self as masculine. Whatever the case, the implication is that some aspect of socialization to the male role, rather than simply biology, is related to visual-spatial ability.

Personality traits consistent with the concept of androgyny tend to be associated with optimum cognitive performance. Some writers have suggested that stereotyped sex roles inhibit intellectual development, and that persons who have moderate levels of both feminine and masculine characteristics perform better cognitively. In 1966, Eleanor Maccoby reviewed a number of studies and pointed out that people who excelled in analytic thinking, creativity, and general intelligence tended to display some of the interests and activities usually characteristic of the other sex. Because androgyny was not a familiar concept to psychologists in 1966, researchers did not examine the possibility that some children had both feminine and masculine interests. Yet, although the mere existence of cross-sex-typed interests is not equated with androgyny, to the extent that children with other-sex-typed activities also display elements of same-sex-typed behavior, this group includes androgynous children. To extend that line of reasoning, one might say that androgyny has a positive relationship with excellence in certain intellectual abilities, whereas extreme sex-typing relates negatively to such abilities. Children who fall at the extremes of femininity by being passive and inhibited are less likely to explore their environment and develop their own ways of thinking than other children. Children who fall at the extremes of masculinity by being very bold and impulsive would have a difficult time controlling their impulses sufficiently to take advantage of opportunities for education and training. Figure 9.2 displays these hypothesized relations. In either case, development of some intellectual skills could be impaired.

It looks as though moderate levels both of independence and of inhibition may be necessary for full development of one's intellectual abilities. For girls, this might mean being more assertive and independent than the feminine stereotype, whereas for boys it could mean tempering aggressiveness.

In her more recent writings Maccoby has not shown much enthusiasm for the validity of these hypotheses, partly because she does not see that sex differences in personality are as widespread as she once thought (Maccoby & Jacklin, 1974). Nevertheless, she points to new evidence continuing to suggest that more boldness and assertiveness seem to accompany greater intellectual abilities in girls. The area seems to merit further study by investigators using measures of androgyny.

Another Look

There are sex differences in verbal ability as well as in visual-spatial and quantitative ability that increase with age, from middle childhood or early adolescence onward. In the verbal realm, the average girl does better, whereas in the other two areas the average boy does better. Despite these differences, female and male abilities overlap a great deal. It is impossible to predict any one person's ability on the basis of her or his sex. There is no evidence of consistent sex differences in other aspects of cognitive abilities—analytic ability, concept mastery and reasoning, creativity, and moral reasoning.

FIGURE 9.2

Hypothesized Relationship of Inhibition-Impulsiveness and Intellectual Performance in Children.

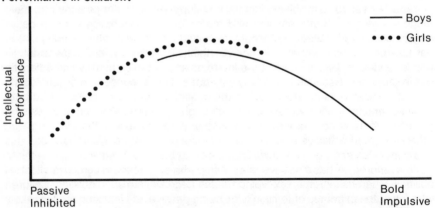

Regarding causality, there is some evidence of biological predisposition for visual-spatial ability, less for verbal ability. To the extent that visual-spatial ability is useful for quantitative performance, this biological predisposition may also affect quantitative ability.

Experience also plays a role in the development of cognitive abilities. In particular, current conceptions of sex roles seem to limit some children's development of certain abilities. As demonstrated in Chapters 7 and 8, families, schools, the media, language, and sometimes peers provide girls and boys with a steady stream of messages and pressures to adhere to their "appropriate" sex role. The best conclusion at this point seems to be that it is too soon to rule out either biological or experiential explanations for sex differences in cognitive abilities. Both must continue to be considered.

A person with an androgynous perspective on cognitive functioning should go beyond searching for documentation of sex differences and their causes. Once any biological explanations were verified, the search should be continued, to look for environmental ways to compensate for the differences in important areas. If the average female does approach quantitative tasks with a built-in handicap, what can be done to help her do well on such tasks? Likewise, what assistance can be offered to the average boy so that his verbal skills develop as fully as possible? Most people are not using their abilities to their fullest and hence have room to expand them. Such compensatory work should not be offered only according to gender, however. We should remember that the average pattern includes many girls with verbal deficits and boys with quantitative deficits.

More work should also be done on the cultural bases of intellectual functioning, particularly those related to sex roles. One might wish to examine the family and school backgrounds of children who excel in a wide range of intellectual skills. Do children with a modicum of both feminine and masculine characteristics find it easier than sex-typed children to enjoy the demands and benefits of school? What are some of the sources of these children's greater flexibility? Efforts must be made to specify how "sex roles" might affect intellectual performance. Perhaps it is through demands for female dependency, restrictions placed on girls' mobility, tolerance for boys' aggression, or communications that certain skills are "sex-appropriate."

Because most sex differences in cognitive abilities seem to increase with age, a researcher with an androgynous perspective would carefully examine children's cognitive environment from a developmental viewpoint. In order to help all individuals fulfill their potential, one would need to understand the experiential factors— such as sex-typed expectations—that inhibit or expand functioning in one sex or the other after a certain age.

In terms of developing the potential of both sexes, investigators could examine why, even in areas of average skills, many females achieve less than men in the long run. At the beginning of this section on cognitive abilities, we speculated that one reason for differential occupational achievements of women and men is their areas of particular abilities. If ability were the primary determinant of occupational achievement, one would expect that, because of their greater average verbal abilities, women would predominate in the top ranks of writers, reporters, editors, and college English professors. Likewise, men's greater mathematical abilities would suggest that they would be found in great proportions among cashiers and bank tellers. These examples make it clear that ability is only one part of the accomplishment equation. Personality and sociocultural factors are also important, as we will see in Chapter 11.

SELF-ESTEEM

A person's overall evaluation of her or his general worth is called self-esteem. Someone with authentically high self-esteem, a positive opinion of her- or himself would quite likely have an advantage over the person with low self-esteem. High self-esteem would seem to give one a better chance of feeling generally happy about the present and being more willing to try new things than low self-esteem.

Self-esteem Inventories

The most common method for assessing self-esteem is with paper-and-pencil tests. Subjects respond to a series of questions such as: On the whole I am satisfied with myself; I am able to do things as well as most people; I'm easy to like (Coopersmith, 1967; Wylie, 1979).

When self-ratings such as these are used, consistent sex differences in self-esteem are not found (Maccoby & Jacklin, 1974). Contrary to the continuing stereotype that males are more self-confident than females (Rosenkrantz et al., 1968; Broverman, et al. 1972), females seem to describe themselves no less positively than males do.

There is some suggestion, however, that the sexes differ in the *sources* for their positive feelings. When the global self-esteem measures are separated into questions concerning social abilities, athletic abilities, and academic abilities, sex differences sometimes emerge. At least throughout adolescence and college, females' self-esteem seems to be derived from positive interpersonal relationships to a greater degree than males' is. Young males' self-esteem seems to be tied more closely to physical activities and perhaps power over others (Berger, 1968; Rosenberg, 1965; Wiggins, 1973).

From an androgynous perspective, it would be useful to ascertain what patterns of sources of self-esteem exist at other stages of life among persons of varying psychological sex. For example, do successful career women still derive their self-esteem from interpersonal success or are they able to incorporate their professional triumphs into their self-concept as well? Does the addition of the parenting role cause men to value interpersonal skills more and hence base some of their self-evaluation on the success of relationships with their children?

Expectations

The results reported in the previous subsection are derived from people's responses to questionnaire items asking how they feel about themselves. Measures of expectations for performance can serve as more subtle indicators of self-esteem.

When people are asked to tell how they expect to perform in the future, or to evaluate and explain past performances, males reveal more apparently positive views of themselves than females do (Deaux, 1976; Frieze, 1975; Lenney, 1977; Maccoby & Jacklin, 1974). For example, when college students were asked to predict their grades for the next semester, males gave higher figures than females (Crandall, 1969). As it turned out, the men overestimated their performance and the women underestimated theirs. Females' self-confidence when predicting or evaluating their performance appears to depend more on certain situational factors than mens' (Lenney, 1977). In a comparison across a variety of tasks, college males' self-evaluations remained fairly stable and independent from changes in the social cues, whereas females' varied. Females' self-evaluations tended to be lower than males when they were given minimal or ambiguous feedback, or when their work was compared with others or evaluated by others. When feedback was clear or social comparison minimized, the sex differences in self-evaluation were minimized.

These patterns of female-male predictions also vary according to whether the task in question is "feminine" or "masculine." For example, girls expected to do better on tasks when they were told "girls generally do better." Yet, when the same tasks were labeled as "boys' " for other children, the boys predicted they would do better (Stein, Pohly, & Mueller, 1971). Also, female college students were less likely to underestimate their performance on female oriented verbal ability and interpersonal perceptiveness tasks than in other ability areas (Lenney, 1977). Such findings suggest that the general statement "males have higher expectancies for success than females" must be qualified by adding "on masculine tasks." Thus, although college males might expect higher grades than females, since in the past higher education (particularly its achievement and competitive aspects) has been considered a male purview, females might expect to be more successful at comforting a friend, since that is more readily defined as the female realm. This reinforces the finding noted earlier, that females tend to have higher self-esteem in areas specific to the feminine role, whereas males tend to have higher self-esteem in areas specific to the masculine role. If we can assume that many people pursue the tasks on which they expect to succeed rather than those which are riskier, we can expect sex-typed labels for tasks to limit some people's willingness to try them.

Attributions

Not only do the sexes differ in their expectations of success and failure; they also differ in their explanations for success and failure. Social psychologists suggest that people have four major types of explanations, or *attributions,* for performance: ability, effort, luck, or task difficulty. As shown in Table 9.1, these attributions vary along the dimensions of stability and source. Ability and effort are causes located *within* the person, whereas luck and task difficulty are causes *outside* the person. Likewise, whereas ability and task difficulty are relatively *stable* attributes, effort and luck are *unstable.* So, for example, a group of students might try to explain why they were accepted into law school. One using the ability attribution might say, "I'm bright and competent, particularly when it comes to analyzing things." The

TABLE 9.1 Possible Attributions for Performance

	Source of cause	
Variability of cause	*Internal*	*External*
Stable	Ability or lack of ability	Task ease or task difficulty
Unstable	Effort or lack of effort	Good luck or bad luck

Source: From I. H. Frieze, "Women's expectations for and causal attributions of success and failure" in M. T. S. Mednick, S. S. Tangri, and L. W. Hoffman, eds., *Women and Achievement: Social and Motivational Analyses* (Washington, D. C.: Hemisphere Publishing Corporation, 1975). Reprinted by permission.

student using task ease attribution could say, "Anyone can get into this school, it's not very selective at all." One who uses the effort attribution would remark, "I worked very hard all during college to get top grades and even spent two years intensively preparing for the Law Boards." Someone using the luck attribution might shake her or his head and say, "It's a mystery to me. Seems like I'm just lucky. Maybe it's because I happened to meet one of their faculty members on a plane trip and we just got to talking."

A number of studies suggest that males tend to invoke the "ability" attribution to explain their successes whereas females more often use the external attribution of task ease, or the unstable ones of effort or luck (Deaux, 1976; Frieze, 1975). Thus, in the preceding example of the law school applicants, a male would be more likely to use the "I'm competent" explanation for admission, whereas females would be more likely to say, "Anyone can get in"; "I worked hard"; or "I'm just lucky."

The findings regarding reactions to success are fairly clearcut; that is not the case for work on reactions to failure. For studies on attributions for failure, results are mixed. Thus, although the female's "A" would be attributed to luck, effort, or task ease, her explanations for a "D" are less predictable. There is some indication that, here, she would turn to an ability attribution, specifically, lack of ability (McMahan, 1971, 1972). Yet these results are not consistent. Other researchers have found that women attribute their failure, as their successes, to luck (Bar-Tel & Frieze, 1973; Feather, 1969). Perhaps one explanation for this discrepancy is that females vary in their hope for success: those who hope for success attribute failure to lack of ability, whereas those with no hope attribute either success or failure to luck (Frieze, 1975).

Women's lack of willingness to attribute success to their own abilities and men's corresponding unwillingness to attribute success to factors other than their abilities have interesting implications for self-esteem and strivings for the future. First of all, they suggest that males have greater self-confidence and readily take credit for their accomplishments, thus further enhancing self-confidence. Second, it seems that women would be less willing than men to confidently expose themselves to future chances for success. Those who attribute success to stable, internal factors maximize both their pride and security in their accomplishments. On the other hand, those who attribute success to unstable, external factors (luck) minimize both pride and security in achievement. Hence, people who ascribe past successes to stable, internal factors can face new situations secure in the knowledge that the ability that stood them so well in the past is still there. In contrast, people who view past success as due to unstable, external factors cannot have much confidence that those factors will help in the future. They might therefore become less willing to try out new challenges, despite past successes, and also deny themselves opportunities for the behavioral flexibility demanded for androgyny.

These findings regarding attributions must be read with caution, however, for they are usually based on traditionally masculine areas of success such as college achievement (Frieze, 1975). From an androgynous perspective, we would have to examine attributions for success in communal activities. Perhaps women would be more willing to take credit for their accomplishments in areas designated as feminine—expressive rather than instrumental ones. Women's differential attributions may not reflect personal feelings of inferiority, but rather, their evaluations of their performance on the masculine tasks that psychologists present. Perhaps women attribute interpersonal successes such as a satisfying and lasting friendship to their interpersonal abilities, rather than luck, task ease, or effort. Men, too, might reverse their attributions to external and unstable ones when the success is in the "feminine" area of close relationships. Once again, we are confronted with the narrowness of the existing research, which often seems to ignore those areas of human functioning in which the average female may feel more comfortable and competent.

Explanations for Differential Self-evaluations

The first explanation for differential self-evaluations in females and males is that other people evaluate females and males differently. In a classic study noted in Chapter 2, Goldberg (1968) presented college women with supposedly published journal articles, some with a female and some with a male author's name. The subjects rated the "male-authored" work higher than the same work when it was presented as "female-authored," even when the topics were in "feminine" fields. Men continue to rate men's achievements more highly, although the tendency for women to devalue women's work seems to have diminished in recent years. Females now sometimes rate women's competence more highly than men's (Deaux & Taynor, 1973; Morris, cited in Frieze, 1975).

The tendency to devalue women's work is decreased when their accomplishments are clear-cut, as noted in Chapter 2. For example, paintings signed by female artists were rated lower than the same paintings signed by male artists (Pheterson, Kiesler, & Goldberg, 1971). But when subjects were told that these were "prize-winning paintings," the women's paintings were not evaluated differently than the men's. Apparently a clear indicator of expertly judged success can help overcome the tendency to place a lower value on women's productions. By implication, books on the best-seller list by female and male authors would both be judged highly. However, it might be more difficult for the female-authored work to reach the best-seller list since, without that "stamp of approval," her work would be rated lower than a man's.

In terms of self-esteem these findings suggest that, until they are clearly successful, women's achievements are devalued by others, particularly men. To the extent that women receive and believe those evaluations, their self-evaluations would be expected to suffer.

Other people also seem to attribute females' and males' successes to the same factors that the women and men themselves do. Observers attributed good performance by a man to skill, but good performance by a woman to luck (Deaux & Emswiller, 1974). In a different study, students were asked to explain the causes for the success of either Dr. "Mark" or "Marcia" Greer (Feldman-Summers & Kiesler, 1974). In line with other research, Marcia's success was attributed to her hard work rather than her ability. Thus one explanation for the sexes' differential self-evaluations and attributions is that they reflect the judgments communicated by others.

A second contributing factor to females' and males' differential self-evaluations and attributions is the differing amounts of power they have over their own lives. Perhaps because of social pressures, external and unstable factors (luck, effort, and task ease) are needed for an able woman to be successful and recognized as such. Without these pressures, any male's ability is easily translated into overt success; luck, effort, or task ease do not have to enter into his personal equation for success, as his ability is frequently a sufficient factor. For females, ability may be necessary, but not sufficient, since so many factors (e.g., discrimination) control their lives to a greater extent than men's lives. In fact, college males tend to report feelings of more internal control over their lives than females do (Benton, Gelber, Kelley, & Liebling, 1969; Brannigan & Tolor, 1971; Feather, 1969).

A third factor that might contribute to females' lower self-evaluation involves internalization of sex-role standards. On the average, characteristics judged masculine are viewed as more socially desirable than those judged feminine (Rosenkrantz, et al., 1968). Women's tendency to devaluate their performance, relative to men, may reflect their internalization of lesser-valued feminine characteristics. If this is true, sex-typed feminine women would have lower self-evaluations than either masculine or androgynous women. Yet, there is a paradox here. Although the self-esteem of feminine women would suffer because they display characteristics that are not highly valued in this society, they would enjoy some benefits of accepting the feminine role that is expected of them. The self-esteem of women with masculine characteristics would benefit from the social value ascribed to these traits, yet their self-esteem would suffer because they are not totally accepting the feminine role that, devalued or not, is expected of them. Thus, one line of reasoning suggests that feminine women should have lower self-esteem than others because of their acceptance of these relatively devalued traits. Yet we could also argue that nonfeminine women should have lower self-esteem because of their rejection of the feminine role demanded of women by society.

For college students, there is an unmistakable relationship between self-esteem and androgyny (Bem, 1977; Hoffman & Fidell, 1977; Spence, Helmreich, & Stapp, 1975b; Wetter, 1975). This finding is particularly striking because the data were developed with a variety of general and social self-esteem measures, as well as all the major androgyny measures. Clearly, those people who report a combination of positively valued feminine and masculine characteristics also report feeling very good about themselves. Correspondingly, people at the other end of the scale, low in both femininity and masculinity (the "undifferentiated") usually report relatively low self-esteem.[1]

Yet there is a strong suggestion that the high self-esteem found in androgynous persons reflects their masculine characteristics to a greater degree than their feminine characteristics. Investigators have consistently found a strong relationship between self-esteem and masculinity—for both females and males (Bem, 1977; Hoffman & Fidell, 1977; Spence, Helmreich, & Stapp, 1975b; Wetter, 1975). The relationship between femininity and self-esteem is found less consistently, is generally lower, and usually is apparent for women but not men. Although Jones, Chernovetz, and Hansson (1978) did not find a relationship between self-esteem and psychological sex, their androgynous males did not fare as well as masculine males on some other indicators of internal stress. In addition, although androgynous subjects in many studies are high in self-esteem, they are no higher than sex-typed masculine subjects in some of these studies (Bem, 1977; Hoffman & Fidell, 1977). Further, average sex-typed feminine people never score as highly as the androgynous in self-esteem and sometimes even no higher than the undifferentiated (Bem, 1977; Wetter, 1975).

This pattern of findings suggests that acceptance of a high level of masculine characteristics is a necessary part of a positive self-evaluation for both women and men.

Yet, as pointed out in the paradox delineated for women ("Should I take on 'sex-appropriate' feminine characteristics or culturally-valued masculine characteristics?"), the cultural expectations of what is sex-appropriate must also be taken into account. Although college students tend to describe their "ideal" woman or man in less stereotyped terms than the "typical," males tend to idealize a stereotypically feminine woman. Whereas women's ideal woman was as masculine as their ideal man, men described their ideal woman as less masculine than their ideal man (Gilbert, Deutsch, & Strahan, 1978). Yet there is also some evidence that women who are competent and masculine in their interests are evaluated more highly by others than other women (Spence & Helmreich, 1972). College students were shown videotapes of a woman "job candidate" being interviewed and asked to rate her likability, adjustment, appearance, intelligence, etc. The depicted "candidates" varied in terms of their portrayed competence-incompetence (e.g., having an A versus a C average; being a leader versus a failure in campus activities) and femininity-masculinity of interests (e.g., fashion design versus physics as a major; gourmet cooking versus sports cars as a hobby).

---

[1]To say that "undifferentiated" individuals are relatively low in self-esteem is not the same as saying they are maladaptively low in any absolute sense. It could be argued that, among the normal college students studied, the range of self-esteem, including that for the "undifferentiated," is fairly narrow and chiefly reflects psychological health. It is not clear whether these undifferentiated "normal" college students have a greater likelihood than their compatriots of being in real psychological distress.

Both women and men rated the competent masculine "candidate" more highly and said they liked her more than the others.

These results conflict with the findings regarding ratings of the "ideal woman." They suggest that women who are competent and masculine in their interests are evaluated highest by others and thus stand a better chance of developing a very positive self-evaluation. Yet Spence and her colleagues were suspicious of these results. In terms of behavior outside the social psychology laboratory, would the successful woman physics major with her enthusiasm for sports cars be befriended unambivalently and more frequently than equally successful but more feminine women? Did subjects' questionnaire responses reveal their "real" feelings?

The investigators replicated the study (Spence, Helmreich, & Stapp, 1975a), but this time they asked some subjects to first describe the candidate and their reactions to her in their own words; only then did subjects complete the structured ratings. Under such conditions there was much less preference expressed for the masculine-competent woman. Instead, the feminine woman was rated more positively. The only group of subjects who did not give a lower rating to the masculine-competent candidate in the open-ended response consisted of women who had elsewhere revealed very liberal ideas about women's roles. Other investigators have also found evidence of penalties for sex-role reversals; this time for both sexes. For example, college students responded less positively, in a variety of situations, to passive men and dominant women than to dominant men and passive women (Costrich, Feinstein, Kidder, Marecek & Pascale, 1975).

One interpretation of these findings is that most college students today are sensitive enough to the demands of liberal thinkers that, superficially, they say they like women with masculine interests. Yet, when given a chance to think about the person they are rating, their deeper, more traditional values are revealed in a preference for more feminine women. We speculate that these apparently mixed feelings result in mixed messages to masculine competent women. People can easily say, "Sure, I like strong competent women—they're exciting and different," at the same time they select more traditional women as friends or dates. Peers may well give the masculine competent woman superficial support, a pat on the back perhaps, that fades when it is time for more far-reaching support, such as making the effort to establish a friendship or include her in social events.

As suggested in Chapter 1, such support for "sex-appropriate" behaviors may combine with the greater cultural valuation of many masculine characteristics. Together these factors may explain why both feminine and masculine characteristics seem to be related to self-esteem for women but only masculine traits are involved for men.

One sidelight of the Spence studies is their suggestion that peers' own attitudes affect their evaluations. Although in the deeper analysis, most college students preferred feminine women, profeminist women preferred masculine, competent women. Thus, one may enhance her chances for peer support by careful selection of a peer group. An adequate support system for nontraditional behaviors may be an important factor in helping one maintain positive self-feelings despite behavior contrary to old roles.

Another Look

On the surface, it seems that the sexes have few differences in their overall self-esteem ratings, although their positive feelings may have different, role-related sources. Yet more subtle indicators suggest that women have less confidence in themselves than men do, particularly on the masculine tasks psychologists usually study. Women tend to underestimate both their past and future performance, whereas men overestimate theirs. Men also seem to explain their successes in terms of the internal, stable factor of ability. Women, on the other hand, turn to external and unstable factors, such as luck, task ease, and hard work, which are not as reliable for help in the future.

These expectations and attributions about oneself are strikingly similar to others' evaluations. Further analysis suggests that women's different expectations and attributions may not only reflect others' evaluations but may also reflect reality: within this culture, women often have less control over what happens to them.

Current sex roles are related to self-esteem in other ways. People seem to use sex-role standards in evaluating both themselves and others, making masculinity a necessary, but not always sufficient condition for positive evaluations, particularly for women. Some recent studies suggest that what subjects tell psychologists on questionnaires is not always what they really feel. There seems to be a greater importance attached to femininity in women than subjects usually admit in superficial ratings.

ACHIEVEMENT MOTIVATION

Achievement is a problematic area for both women and men, albeit in different ways. For the average woman, there is evidence to suggest that she is not achieving to the fullest of her capabilities. For instance, Lewis Terman selected about 1500 California children in the 1920s because their IQ scores placed them in the top 1 percent (IQ = 135 or above) of the population. Following them throughout their lives, he found striking sex differences in the accomplishments of these exceptionally able people: by their mid-forties, seven women and seventy men had been listed in the prestigious *American Men of Science,* two women and ten men in the *Directory of American Scholars,* two women and thirty-one men in *Who's Who in America;* five patents had been taken out by the gifted women, 230 by the men; five novels had been written by women, thirty-three by the men; over 200 scientific papers were written by the women, 2000 by the men; thirty-two scholarly books by the women, sixty by the men (Terman & Oden, 1949). Earlier (when the subjects were about thirty), fully three-fourths of the women in an extremely select subsample of the larger group (IQ 170 or greater, representing .03 percent of the general population) worked as housewives or secretaries (Terman & Oden, 1947).

A major cause of women's underachievement lies in external barriers, such as discrimination, biases of others, and institutional limitations (O'Leary, 1974), as well as child-rearing responsibilities. Yet many women seem to internalize these barriers so that they contribute to their own weaknesses in this area.

Men, too, have problems with achievement in spite of (or perhaps because of) the fact that it has traditionally been a male domain. Because achievement is part of the male role by definition, men are faced with demands to be successful in the eyes of others. The stereotyped image of the hard-driving, pushing executive who loses warmth, leisure, and family to the demands of his job is reality for many men. Many working-class men, trapped in a system that requires higher education and a certain class standing, find it impossible to reach the standard of achievement promised by the American Dream. The result can be frustration, disappointment, alienation, and negative feelings about themselves (Rubin, 1976). Men sometimes find themselves being valued for their accomplishments rather than who they are. Just as women's options tend to be limited in terms of leading them away from achievement, men's options tend to be limited in that evaluation is often based on achievements, which may or may not be under their control.

Traditional Psychological Perspectives on Achievement

Psychologists have studied achievement under the label "achievement motivation" or "need for achievement," which was defined as a disposition to strive for success in any situation where standards of excellence apply (McClelland, Atkinson, Clark & Lowell, 1953). From this perspective, a person who worked hard to become a professor in a prestigious university, the top student in a class, or the best gymnast on the team would assumedly be motivated by a need for achievement. Theoretically at least, this striving for success would motivate a person in academics, athletics, friendship, career and all other spheres of activity. As long as some standard for success existed, a person high in need for achievement would strive to excel.

Psychologists have used projective tests to measure achievement motivation. In these, stories told in response to ambiguous pictures were scored for themes of achievement. For example, a person shown a picture of a child gazing at a violin might tell a story about the child's plans to become a famous concert violinist. Such a story would be scored as evidencing high need for achievement. Someone whose story depicted the child as disliking the violin practice demanded by parents would be scored as low in need for achievement.

Achievement motivation was a popular and apparently fruitful research area in the 1950s. Among white middle-class males, the projective measures of achievement motivation were reasonably well correlated with academic performance. When experimental conditions were designed to emphasize leadership and intellectual standards, males' scores in achievement motivation increased (Stein & Bailey, 1973). A general theory of achievement motivation postulating a positive relationship between actual achievement and strength of achievement motivation was constructed on the basis of such findings. Yet women did not behave as the theory would predict. Women scored higher than men in achievement motivation under neutral conditions, despite the fact that most women did not actually achieve more than men (McClelland et al., 1953). Females' need-for-achievement scores often did not correlate well with their actual achievement in academic settings either (Stein & Bailey). Also, unlike men, women did not respond to experimental conditions in which leadership and intelligence were stressed (Alper & Greenberger, 1967; French & Lesser, 1964).

Because women did not fit the theory, they were eliminated from much of the research, as mentioned in Chapter 2. Women were simply used as subjects less and less, because findings with them were so often "confusing." Males were the "norm" on which the theory was based; females were the "other," the exceptions who did not fit the theory.

A common explanation for eliminating women from the studies was that most women were simply not as motivated to achieve as men were. Such an explanation fit nicely with both women's anomalous behavior in the laboratories of achievement motivation theorists, and the fact that they do not achieve as often as men do in the real world. Using rather circuitous logic, social scientists could explain women's underrepresentation among professionals, geniuses, eminent scientists, politicians, writers, and corporate executives as a result of their low achievement motivation.

Changing Perspectives: Achievement in Specific Realms

More recently, some psychologists have suggested that some women *are* motivated to achieve, despite the fact that they don't fit the theory. For example, Stein and Bailey (1973) surveyed the earlier research and concluded that women are interested in excellence, but often in areas different from those for men. Pointing out that traditional research on achievement has focused on the leadership, college academics, and independence that this culture defines as the masculine domain, Stein and Bailey suggested that women's achievement motivation is frequently manifested in the interpersonal area that is defined as the feminine domain. In other words, some women may strive for marriage and popularity as a way to meet their need to achieve.

Achievement behavior may also be a function of one's attitudes and values, particularly regarding sex roles. Female high school students with traditional sex-role identities held lower educational aspirations than girls with less traditional identities (Doherty & Culver, 1976).

It seems then that some women are motivated to achieve, albeit at times in realms defined by the female role. Yet even among nontraditional women, who direct some of their achievement strivings to areas other than social skills, the average woman does not achieve as much as the average man. Actual achievement does not seem to be merely a combination of achievement motivation and values. Although there may be external barriers that should enter our equation, let us look at internal barriers. What internal factors cause women who are interested in achievement to so often achieve less than men?

Fear of Success

In the late 1960s, Matina Horner postulated that part of the explanation for women's underachievement lies not only in their striving for success but also in their "fear of success." Some people fear success because they expect negative consequences as a result of succeeding. For females, these consequences include social rejection or feelings of being unfeminine.

To demonstrate the presence of this motive, Horner (1972) gave college students a projective test. Female students were asked to make up a story in response to the sentence cue: "After first term finals, Anne finds herself at the top of her medical school class." For male subjects, the cue person was "John." The stories were scored for presence or absence of negative imagery related to the success.

Horner found that, in response to the successful male cue, more than 90 percent of the men showed positive feelings; they anticipated increased striving and a generally happy future for John. The majority of females (65 percent), however, depicted Anne's success in negative terms. Frequently Anne was faced with social rejection (loss of friends or dating possibilities), loss of femininity (fear of being a lesbian), or decrease in ambition (Anne drops out of medical school to marry a classmate, Carl, who does well with her help). Sometimes students went so far as to deny Anne's success (Anne is a code name for a nonexistent person created by a group of medical students who take turns taking exams for her) or simply present bizarre possibilities (Anne's classmates are so disgusted with her behavior that they beat her and maim her for life). On the basis of this evidence, Horner concluded that women more frequently experience a fear of success than men. Further, this fear can motivate one to avoid success in competitive situations, according to other studies done by Horner (1972).

Thus, Horner was suggesting that a woman with a high need for achievement may not actually achieve as much as a corresponding male, because she is more likely to be motivated by fear of success as well. As a woman, she expects negative consequences for the success she would like to seek. Men are not as likely to anticipate negative consequences for success, because achievement is an acceptable part of the male role. In fact, a nine-year follow-up of Horner's original subjects revealed that women who scored high in fear of success in college had married and had children sooner than the other women studied. Further, those women's pregnancies were more likely to occur when the women were faced with the prospect of success relative to their husbands (e.g., graduate school or a better job for the woman; career or academic setback for the man). Similar patterns of attempts at "marital balance" were not apparent for men (L. Hoffman, 1977a).

Although Horner's concept of fear of success became well known quickly, further research has suggested that it is not completely accurate. First of all, there has been some difficulty in replicating Horner's results with different groups of people. In particular, by 1970, about half the men in some samples were responding with fear-of-success imagery (Horner, 1972). At times, males have been shown to have more fear of success than females, even at the same university where Horner did her original research (Hoffman, 1974b). Overall, then, fear of success in women does not seem to be reliable enough across time and settings to explain women's consistent underachievement. Although evidence of fear of success has varied over the years and samples of subjects, the gap between actual female and male achievement has not.

A second problem with fear of success is its status as a deep-rooted personality trait. As originally conceptualized by Horner, this fear is a stable characteristic of the personality that is acquired early, at the same time sex-role standards begin to be formed. Horner assumed that the negative imagery in females' responses to the Anne cue is personalized; it reflects their fears about what would happen if they themselves were successful. Several people have disagreed with this perspective, pointing out that Horner's evidence concerns only females' responses to the Anne cue and males' responses to the John cue. Perhaps females' negative imagery did not really reflect a deep-rooted fear on their part, but merely their awareness that a successful female *does* sometimes experience difficulties in this culture. In fact, when females' and males' responses to both the Anne and the John cue were compared, both sexes gave more negative responses to the Anne cue (Monahan, Kuhn, & Shaver, 1974).

Several researchers (Condry & Dyer, 1976; Monahan, et al, 1974; Spence, 1974) have suggested that what originally looked like fear of success in Horner's female subjects may more appropriately be labeled realistic awareness of sex-role standards. Use of the word "fear" implies that the anticipated negative consequences are somewhat unreasonable. For example, a person who usually tries to avoid cats, and trembles and perspires when face to face with cats is said to have a fear of cats. Yet a person who avoids, and act anxious when confronted with a lion or tiger is usually viewed as having a realistic awareness of the power of these animals, rather than a fear. In the same vein, the label "fear of success" implies that women's expectations regarding the negative consequences of their success are unreasonable, or at least not experienced by other people (i.e., males). The awareness that these "fears" *do* have some basis in reality may be a first step in pointing to the necessity of making societal changes—beginning to cage some of the wild animals, as it were, that interfere with females' enjoyment of their success.

It seems then that Horner's work on fear of success has increased understanding of sex differences in achievement, although not exactly as originally outlined. Again, it appears that a woman's lower average level of achievement is not necessarily the result of a lack of motivation to or interest in success. Instead, sex-role standards, particularly the understanding that overt individual achievement is not an appropriate aspect of femininity, are implicated as the factors underlying females' frequent underachievement. Such an analysis suggests that males may also experience problems as a result of the male sex role. Part of that role includes expectations for high achievement. Either overachievement pressures or negative consequences for role deviation may affect men.

Socialization and Achievement

"Sex-role standards" is a general term and does not reveal the nature of the expectations and teachings involved. An examination of some of the childhood concomitants of later achievement reveals some of the ways these sex-role standards are translated in individual lives.

An orientation to achievement among females is clearly associated with certain childrearing practices that are antagonistic to the development of extreme femininity (Stein & Bailey, 1973). The development of achievement in females is related to a moderate degree of parental warmth or nurturance, permissiveness, some training for emotional independence, explicit parental encouragement of achievement efforts (e.g., positive reinforcement, pressure to accelerate, criticism for lack of effort), and the availability of female achievers as models. Many of these factors are opposite to the ones usually associated with training for the nonassertiveness, avoidance of competition, and dependency that are part of the feminine role.

The importance of a warm yet independent parent-daughter relationship for women's achievement is supported by a study of college women with a high career commitment (Tangri, 1972). Tangri found that women selecting occupations atypical for their sex seemed to have fairly warm relationships with their parents, but also had substantial areas of disagreement. This combination suggests that the women grew up in a caring family, but with enough independence to form their own opinions, make their own decisions, and develop their own life styles. So, while they were preparing to take up atypical and thus presumably difficult careers they could do so from a basis of emotional security. The delicate integration of parental distance and caring suggested in Stein and Bailey's review was apparently accomplished by the parents of Tangri's achieving women.

The distance between parent and child implied by these authors may have the added advantage of freeing the daughters from traditional sex-role expectations. Even if the parents themselves are traditional in their sex-role attitudes, daughters who grow up more independently have increased possibilities for formulating their own standards. In turn, girls who emerge with some freedom from stereotyped sex roles seem to have a better chance to achieve.

Another Look

Although the average woman and man achieve at different levels, this seems to be partially a result of sex-role standards rather than a lack of interest in achievement among women. Many women channel their achievement motivation into the affiliative realm acceptable for females in this society. In its emphasis on public achievement, psychology has tended to overlook the forms of achievement selected by many women. Because of this limited approach, it may also have ignored some males who "mask" their achievement in affiliation. Sex-role standards also become involved in the issue of achievement through socialization. Certain "feminine" characteristics, such as passivity and dependency, that are socialized in many females are antagonistic to the kinds of behaviors necessary for achievement.

A persistent theme in our discussion of achievement has been the demonstrated interplay between cultural standards (stereotypes) and research. The early researchers in achievement motivation were apparently so wedded to their own "masculine" definitions of "success" and "achievement" that they neglected other areas in which excellence can be achieved. Their ready acceptance of females' failure to exhibit behavior in keeping with their theory reveals their assumption that achievement is not really relevant to women. This omission of evidence concerning females resulted in a theory that was perhaps less valid or rich than it could have been. Consideration of the data for females would have complicated the theory, but rightly so; we are beginning to see that any worthwhile theory of motivation has to be complicated. It must include hesitations as well as hopes; expectancies as well as actualities; personal and societal standards; thoughts, feelings, and behaviors.

What implications does this information on achievement have for a psychology of androgyny? As society and psychology define achievement, it seems inconsistent with androgyny, since it is self-oriented. Achievement is also conceptualized as agentic, rather than communal. Psychologists' traditional assumption that achievement and affiliation are separate constructs reveals the belief that an integration of agentic and communal concerns would be difficult at best. From an androgynous perspective, we can say that this very integration is at the heart of the matter. In line with this perspective, research in the future could focus on possibilities for integrating achievement with affiliation, concern for self with concern for others. How can one incorporate the positive aspects of achievement, such as enhanced self-esteem and the improvement of the world through one's work, with a communal orientation? How can one achieve for oneself while continuing to respect others? Are there ways to prevent achievement from being one's major goal, or is self-enhancement so tempting that it overwhelms other goals?

To date, psychologists' definitions of achievement have been somewhat limited. Are there ways to achieve other than those now considered? As psychology has defined achievement, it often seems to contain competition as an integral part. Is this necessary? Can one be satisfied in achieving according to one's own standards or must achievement be measured "against" someone else's? Researchers might find it fruitful to examine the use of both self and other standards of comparison across the life span, as well as the costs and benefits of each in different spheres of life (e.g., athletics, career, recreation, social life).

EMOTIONALITY

The word emotion has its root in French and Latin terms meaning "to stir up" or "to disturb." To be emotional is to be "markedly aroused or agitated in feeling or sensibilities" (*Webster's*, 1971). Emotions are something to be wary of in our Western culture, which prizes rationality, for they make a person's behavior unstable and unpredictable by the usual rules of logic. Traditionally, emotionality has been stereotypically attributed to women. Reason and rationality, regarded as the opposites of emotion, have been attributed to men. Parsons and Bales' (1955) classic delineation of "expressive" and "instrumental" functions within the family maintains this distinction: the wife/mother performs the expressive tasks of making the home harmonious, while the husband/father takes care of the instrumental task of providing food, shelter, and clothing for the family. The distinction is sometimes taken even further when women have been deemed unsuitable for positions of power or responsibility because of the fear that their tendency toward emotional arousal would make them unable to act rationally.

Psychologists have also viewed emotionality in terms of disturbance by considering it as including anxiety and other signs of psychic discomfort. Sherman (1971) pointed out that this use of the term "emotion" excludes angry feelings as well as physical or verbal aggression. The negative label "emotional" thus remains a feminine stereotype separate from the "masculine" characteristic of aggression. Aggression is regarded as something people do rather than what they feel; men get something done (instrumental) whereas women feel (expressive).

There are three ways that psychologists measure people's emotions: direct behavioral observations, physiological recordings, and self-reports. Findings of sex differences vary with the measure used. There are no strong, consistent findings of sex differences in emotionality as measured by behavioral observations of children's activity level, frequency of crying, and reactions to feared stimuli (Maccoby & Jacklin, 1974). There is some suggestion of sex differences in measures of physiological arousal; for example, that women are more easily activated (cf., Duffy, 1962). Yet such findings are difficult to interpret because such physiological recordings are not systematically related to each other or to reported feelings. It is when emotionality is measured with self-report that females emerge as the more emotional sex. Fairly consistently, girls and women report more specific fears and general anxiety than do boys and men (Maccoby & Jacklin, 1974).

The meaning of these self-report results is unclear, particularly in light of the lack of evidence of consistent sex differences in the observational studies. From one perspective, these differences in self-reported fear and anxiety are not real, and merely reflect females' greater willingness to admit their fears. Other studies have suggested that boys are more defensive than girls, as they are less willing to admit to weaknesses (Maccoby & Jacklin, 1974). For example, boys are more likely to deny assumedly universal feelings such as hurt when rejected by friends. In general, males tend to be less self-disclosing than females in adulthood, too (Jourard, 1964).

A second perspective on the sex differences in self-reported emotionality is that, despite the possibility that the differences may merely reflect defensiveness, they do eventually affect behavior. A girl who grows up saying that she is afraid of snakes may be more likely to avoid camping and other outdoor activities because she truly believes she is afraid of snakes. Her brother, who might initially experience some of the same fear when confronted with a snake, may still spend a great deal of time in the woods, because he is less inclined to admit to "weakness." His experience then teaches him that snakes really are rare and usually avoidable. Viewed this way, females' greater willingness to admit to fear and anxiety can limit their behaviors and ultimately the situations to which they expose themselves.

A third perspective is provided by Jean Baker Miller (1976), who suggests that females' greater willingness to accept and acknowledge their emotions can be a positive force. Emotions, even negative ones, are an inevitable part of human experience and, in certain situations, acknowledgment of them can enhance growth. Sensitivity to one's emotional state can be informative for planning and reactivity. The discomfort that emotions signal can stimulate one to make changes in one's life and perhaps ultimately cope better. The awareness of anxiety and depression, for example, can motivate someone to get out of an unsatisfactory marriage or bad job, or work toward making the marriage or job more satisfactory. The process might be painful, but the result can be positive. People who are more distant from their emotions may be less willing to confront the vague dissatisfaction they sense, more likely to remain in a situation that could be improved, or more likely to leave precipitously without knowing why. In addition, the ability to admit and talk about one's emotions is an important aspect of intimate relations. To be close to someone and accrue the benefits of emotional sharing requires an ability to convey one's emotional state. Men, less schooled in their own emotions, may sometimes be handicapped in the interpersonal realm.

The study of emotionality from an androgynous perspective should receive a greater emphasis than it has in psychology thus far. First, the full range of emotions should be considered, positive as well as negative. Can men extend their apparent ease in expressing anger to other emotions? Likewise, can women extend their facility with most emotions to a greater comfort in handling angry feelings? Second, rather than accepting the cultural assumptions that emotions are maladaptive, researchers interested in androgyny should consider both the costs and benefits that accrue from a sensitivity to one's emotional state. Third, possibilities for integrating the valuable aspects of the emotional and rational principles should be examined. There is no inherent reason why reason must be divorced from feeling. We may find new and more adaptive styles of behavior when we have considered these possibilities.

INTERPERSONAL INTERACTIONS

The sex differences and similarities discussed so far have been those which function primarily on the individual level. Abilities, self-esteem, achievement motivation, and emotionality are seen by psychologists as traits existing within a person and remaining fairly stable from situation to situation. Yet a major portion of human experience occurs in interaction with other people. According to stereotypes at least, women and men function differently when relating to other people. To the extent that movies present an extreme version of a culture's values and attitudes, the John Wayne cowboy could be said to be the epitome of the masculine interpersonal style: tough, independent, and usually quick to "love 'em and leave 'em" when relationships get too close. Nicole in F. Scott Fitzgerald's novel *Tender Is the Night* represents extreme feminine interpersonal style: life lived wholly in terms of relationship, with independence expressed as moving from one relationship to another.

Psychologists have collected a tremendous array of data on interpersonal interactions. To facilitate a summary and interpretation of this wealth of research reports, we will use an organizing schema borrowed from Karen Horney (1937). Horney discussed what she called "interpersonal coping strategies," which represent solutions to the conflicts everyone experiences in trying to maintain a self and relate to others. Two of these are "moving toward people" and "moving against people." The word "moving" refers to an emotional as well as physical movement. Although our use of these terms will not coincide precisely with Horney's, we will use them as they are generally understood, and therefore our meaning should be clear.

Moving Toward People

Included in movement toward people are the behaviors psychologists have studied under labels such as dependency, altruism, nurturance, and compliance. Findings of sex differences in these studies depends to a large degree on the way the terms are defined. Dependency, for example, has been viewed as a passive tendency to remain close to others, an active seeking out of others, or a resistance to separation. It can be seen as negative, preventing one from engaging in more adaptive behaviors (e.g., staying close at the expense of trying new experiences), or as positive, enhancing coping (e.g., requesting help with a difficult task). Although all these activities are labeled dependency, they usually are not strongly related. Because these terms are so complex in their interpretations, our focus will be on some of the specific behaviors involved in moving toward people.

For infants and preschoolers, reports agree that there are few sex differences in movements toward people. Girls and boys are about equal in the degree to which they touch others, seek proximity to adults, and resist separations. Yet there does seem to be a qualitative difference in the children's reactions. Boys tend to be more active in their dependent behaviors; they are more likely to cry when a parent leaves the room and they make more trips to the mother when separated from her in experimental settings. Girls simply tend to remain nearer the parent (Maccoby & Jacklin, 1974).

Studies with older children reveal that, although both females and males display an interpersonal orientation, they do so differently. Girls are more likely to seek help and physical contact, whereas boys seem to seek attention, particularly negative attention (Edwards & Whiting, 1974). Maccoby (1966) concluded that girls showed more interest in social activities than boys did. In addition, girls' tastes in books and TV programs were oriented more toward the gentler aspects of interpersonal relations and less toward aggression and action than were boys'. Cross-culturally, boys are more often found playing at a greater distance from home than girls. Also, girls are more likely to comply with directives from adults (Hatfield, Ferguson, & Alpert, 1967; Minton, Kagan, & Levine, 1971; Stayton, Hogan, & Ainsworth, 1971).

Regarding peer relationships, Maccoby and Jacklin concluded that boys seem to engage in more friendly interactions than do girls. However, girls report more liking for the people with whom they interact than do boys. There is a tendency, during the school years, for girls to be involved in one or two intensive relations with best friends, and for boys to play in larger groups. Paradoxically, boys seem to be more susceptible to peer influence (Hollander & Marcia, 1970). The theme throughout these reports is that girls' relationships, although fewer, are more intimate. Boys' interactions are more likely to revolve around the game at hand, rather than the interpersonal relationship itself. Boys seem to depend on the peer group for values and interesting activities.

Regarding movements toward others in adulthood, there is not much data on dependency; most is on willingness to help others in distress and tendency to agree with others. Altruism, a willingness to help others, is greatly affected by characteristics of the situation studied (Deaux, 1976). It is exhibited more frequently by males when the helper is required to take the initiative in offering help. However results are mixed when the helper responds to a direct request, and seem to depend on whether the task is defined as feminine or masculine. Women are more likely to help if the request involves buying a "feminine" item in a store, and men if the item requested is "masculine." It appears that women and men offer help about equally, as long as they feel comfortable performing the task in question. Males' greater training to (and experience in) taking the initiative seems to enhance the likelihood that they will help strangers in public. However, most of these studies are done in public settings with strangers as the needy ones. If social psychologists were to study altruism in more intimate settings, such as within families, friendships, or even professional relationships, women's altruism might be more evident.

Another area of research among adults involves their responsiveness to social influence. Once again, the findings depend to a large extent on the situation studied. Females do not appear to be more easily influenced than males unless the situation involves group pressure (Eagly, 1978). When persuasive messages are presented in writing, or merely represent the opinion of someone who is not present, females appear to be no more susceptible than males to social influence. Yet, when studies are done in group settings and the source of the opinion is a group member or members, a substantial minority of studies find that females are more likely to conform than males.

Traditionally, social psychologists have attributed females' greater conformity to group pressure to the submissiveness of the female role. Eagly argues against such an explanation and instead suggests that the sex differences observed are due to females' greater interpersonal orientation. The submissiveness explanation views females' susceptibility to influence as a reflection of the passivity and dependency to which women are socialized. Yet Eagly points out that if females were so well trained to submit to influence they would conform even when the pressure occurred outside of a group. That is not the case. An explanation more consistent with the findings is that females are not necessarily more easily influenced, but that they are more concerned with the relational aspects of group situations than males are. There is a tendency among females, more than among males, to be concerned with maintaining social harmony and ensuring smooth interpersonal relations. Females' greater agreement in group settings may also reflect their low status in the group, due to cultural devaluation of their gender (Eagly, 1979).

An additional facet of women's stereotypically greater tendency to move toward others is sometimes said to be their empathy. When empathy is defined as recognition of feeling in another, consistent sex differences have not been established. Yet females do seem to be more likely than males to experience a vicarious emotional response to another person's feelings. Hence, although both sexes may be equally able to assess how another person feels, in females that assessment is more likely to be accompanied by similar emotional arousal. It has been suggested that the observed difference may be caused by females' greater tendency to imagine themselves in another's place, and males' inclination toward instrumental action—doing rather than feeling (M. Hoffman, 1977).

Moving Against People

Another interpersonal strategy considered by Horney is the tendency to move against people. This strategy usually includes an element of conflict and leads to the mastery of others. Psychologists have studied this strategy under labels such as aggression, dominance, and competition.

Aggression. Aggression is defined as the intent of one individual to hurt another. Conclusions in this area are limited by the fact that the majority of studies include only males (Deaux, 1976).

Males are more likely than females to describe aggressive behavior in dreams, to report aggressive intentions, and to report aggression in their customary behavior. Yet, when people are observed in the laboratory, sex differences are not so consistent, and they are apparently sensitive to situational factors (Frodi, Macaulay, & Thome, 1977). For example, when subjects are not first angered and are allowed to engage in direct, nonviolent physical aggression, average males are more aggressive than average females. However, when subjects are angered and then given opportunities for physical or verbal aggression, findings of greater male aggression are less consistent (Deaux, 1976; Frodi, et al.). Sex differences in aggression are also less likely to be apparent when the aggression is justified (i.e., "I'm going to shock this person in order to help out the experimenter who is doing the study.") or in a relatively anonymous situation (Frodi, et al).

The sex of the target person also plays a role in aggression. Usually, women are aggressed against less than men by both women and men in the laboratory (Frodi, et al.). Crime statistics, too, show that men are more likely than women to be the victims of murder, robbery, and assault (Stark & McEvoy, 1970). However, women's likelihood of being victims may be underestimated. Aggressive acts directed specifically against women, such as rape, incest, and wife abuse are neither always reported nor always included in lists of aggressive actions. In addition, phenomena such as discrimination against women could also be interpreted as a type of hostility. It has also been found that some of the protection from aggression afforded by being female is sacrificed when a woman deviates from the expected feminine role or is unattractive (Deaux, 1976). Thus, although the general conclusion is that males are more likely to be both the perpetrators and victims of aggression, females are capable of behaving aggressively and are certainly not immune from the aggression of others.

Dominance. Dominance is another form of movement against others. Although the purpose of dominance is not necessarily to hurt others, it is a form of mastery of others. Across the wide range of behaviors that might be labeled dominance, one finds that reports of sex differences seem to depend on the way dominance is defined and the age group under consideration. The weight of evidence suggests that when dominance depends on aggression or ascribed status, it is most often performed by males. When it does not, no sex difference is apparent.

For children, cross-cultural data suggests that boys are more likely to try to control others for their own ends, such as making another child run an errand for them. Girls are more likely to try to control another for some social good, such as warning another child to stay away from the fire (Whiting & Edwards, 1973). This is consistent with studies of American youngsters which suggest that boys are rated as "tougher" than girls as early as nursery school age, and that boys dominated girls in a coloring task (Omark & Edelman, 1973). More subtle forms of dominance among children include persuasion, manipulativeness, exploitation, and feigned submission, and there is no strong evidence of sex differences in the use of such strategies (Maccoby & Jacklin, 1974). Hence, when one considers the kinds of dominance that seem most closely linked to aggression, such as direct attempts to control another for one's own purpose, boys appear to be more dominant than girls. However, if the definition of dominance is extended to include a variety of efforts and of purposes, no such sex differences are apparent.

The "tough" dominance exhibited by more boys than girls is not necessarily an advantage after the childhood years when outright aggression is less socially acceptable. For example, among adolescents, leadership seems to be linked with attractiveness, popularity, athletic ability, and (for girls) stylishness (Marks, 1957). In adulthood, dominance is linked to status, and men are more likely to be high in status. Increased status can be a function of formal role (e.g., the president of the company would dominate the secretary), informal indicators (e.g., education, occupation, age, maleness), or expertise (Maccoby & Jacklin).

Men's dominance and status in the external world can affect dominance within the family, as was demonstrated in a study of newlyweds' reactions to conflict generated for the purposes of the study (Rausch, Barry, Hertel, & Swain, 1974). Although the sexes usually did not differ in their interactive style, the men were more likely to be independent and supportive in attempting to win their wives over, whereas the women were more likely to use coercion and to appeal to their husbands from a position of weakness. Raush et al. interpreted this difference in terms of a socially based power differential: the men could afford to be magnanimous, whereas the women were forced to resort to appeals.

The situational nature of the relationship between dominance and sex is revealed clearly in work by Kanter (1977) that will be discussed in depth in Chapter 11. Briefly, the conclusion there is that women holding real authority behave no differently than men with authority, and men without authority behave no differently than similar women.

Competition. Competition is the third form of movement against people. Unfortunately, psychologists' primary method for studying competition is rather narrow and its generalizability questionable. Most studies of competition rely on artificial games played in the laboratory by two players who basically have a choice of two strategies over the course of many trials of a game. Selection of the cooperative strategy usually means that a player minimizes her or his own winnings on one trial but increases the chances that both will be moderate winners in the long run. Selection of the competitive strategy maximizes one's own gains while minimizing the opponent's gains. The researchers assume that consistent use of the competitive strategy by one player will stimulate the other to adopt the same strategy; the result would be that both players lose in the long run. Cooperation is thus, by their definition, an adaptive strategy; competition a maladaptive one.

Results of such studies of competition do not clearly show one sex as more competitive, although Maccoby and Jacklin suggest there is a trend for males to be competitive more often. Such a normally minor trend becomes more significant when one realizes that this competitive tendency exists despite its long-term maladaptiveness.

Deaux suggests that the main difference between females and males in these games is their degree of interest. According to several studies, males appear to be more oriented toward the game itself and attempt to figure out strategies that will guarantee them the largest payoff. Females seem more concerned with the interpersonal setting than the game, as they are more likely to take advantage of opportunities for social conversation (not related to the game); they may also alter their strategy according to the partner's appearance. It is important to remember, however, that these sex differences may only be a function of the types of games used. The emphasis on mathematical odds may appeal more frequently to males who are more likely to exhibit mathematical interests. At the same time, females may more readily be bored by the repetitious nature of the games and turn to socializing as a welcome diversion. Hence, any apparently greater competition among males than females in these games may be artifactual rather than real. The mathematical and repetitious features inherent in these games are not always a part of real-world activities in which competition occurs.

Androgyny and Interpersonal Interactions

The preceeding discussion of sex differences in interpersonal behavior should not obscure the fact that there is great variability within each sex in these behaviors. One factor responsible for this variability may be psychological sex.

Bem's original series of studies of androgyny remains one of the few research efforts to examine actual interpersonal behavior of sex-typed and androgynous people (Bem, 1975; Bem, Martyna, & Watson, 1976). Subsequent research has been largely limited to subjects' reports of their behavior and dispositions on paper-and-pencil tests.

As explained in Chapter 1, Bem found that androgynous undergraduates are able to use both types of interpersonal strategies. They can comfortably move toward people when confronted with a lonely college student or an infant. Yet they can also move against others when their own opinions require it. With the exception of women in situations requiring initiative, sex-typed feminine persons do just as well when the situation calls for movements toward people, but perform less well when required to move against others by disagreeing with them. Sex-typed masculine persons display the opposite pattern: ease in moving against people but less willingness to move toward others.

Admittedly, these laboratory situations represent an oversimplification of the behaviors required in day-to-day interactions. The laboratory provides the safety of anonymity and thus movements against others may be easier. In the real world, however, one must often counter others in important interpersonal situations, where both parties know each other. Hence, attention to the feelings of the "other" is important, if relationships are to be maintained. Movements toward others are also artificial in the laboratory; they usually require more initiative in real life where the "others" are rarely actually presented to the subject. Also, sometimes movement toward one person requires movement against another, as when compliance with one group's standards involves noncompliance with another's.

Another Look

In drawing conclusions from the available information on tendencies to move toward people, it is important to note the large numbers of studies that find no sex differences in this area. Both females and males are clearly involved with others, although sometimes in different ways. Males are more likely than females to exhibit demandingness in relations in the early years, to engage in a large number of relationships in childhood, and to take the initiative in offering help, particularly when the task is consistent with socially defined masculine interests. Their apparent tendency to be more assertive in establishing and maintaining relationships indicates that they need and want interactions with other people. Females, once they have established a relationship, appear to be more interested than males in preserving its positive aspects. Females are also more likely to remain close in early childhood; to comply with adults' requests, and to form closer relationships, in childhood; and to respond to a request for help when it is consistent with feminine interests, to be empathic, to undertake more helping roles, and to facilitate group harmony by responding to group pressures.

Sex differences found in the movements against people favor males. Males are more likely to report aggression in a variety of situations. They also display more dominance behavior than females, particularly when the dominance has elements of aggression or relies on social status. Males are also more often competitive in laboratory games. Nevertheless, in certain situations, females are willing to meet aggression with aggression. They are also, as a group, willing to try to exert dominance when it can serve some social good.

A persistent theme in the research on interpersonal interaction is the importance of age and situation. Simple conclusions such as: "females are this way" or "males are that way" are rare. More frequent are statements such as: "At this age, under these conditions females (or males) tend to behave in a certain way."

There are two ways to interpret the situational effects. One is to conclude that there are few "real sex differences" in interpersonal styles. Differences attributable to characteristics of a situation are neither biologically based nor immutable. From this standpoint, for instance, to say that males are more likely than females to behave altruistically when initiative is required does not mean that males are inherently more altruistic. The explanation of these sex differences in situational rather than biological terms is actually accurate, and, as long as situations can be changed, so can these sex differences. Yet, such a perspective sometimes obscures the extent to which the sexes continue to be in different situations.

A second interpretation is that sex differences attributable to situational factors are important ones since, often, situations where women and men are found vary so markedly. To conclude, for example, that there is no "real" difference in the sexes' attempts to be dominant, because differences appear only when aggression or ascribed status is involved, is misleading. In reality, males are more often dominant than females, because aggression (or threat of it) and ascribed status (in which males are often higher) are frequently important factors. Likewise, although females may feel just as helpful as men toward strangers, initiative in giving unrequested help is often necessary and, hence, males end up helping strangers more often than women. Interpersonal interactions are often affected by factors such as power, roles, and initiative, and the sexes often differ along these lines. As a result, there are also frequent sex differences in interpersonal interactions. Social change, change in the situational aspects of women's and men's lives, is necessary to effect changes in these patterns of sex differences.

SUMMARY AND CONCLUSIONS

After examining the available information on sex differences in ability, self-esteem, achievement motivation, emotionality, and interpersonal interactions, one may conclude that, although psychological differences may not be as extensive as myth and stereotype suggest, some do exist. A brief summary follows.

1. There is a tendency for girls to have greater verbal abilities than boys in the early years. This tendency increases with age, and, by ten or eleven, girls have a clear edge in the verbal realm.
2. Although no sex differences are apparent in quantitative and visual-spatial tasks during childhood, boys do better than girls after early adolescence. When analytic ability is studied separately from visual-spatial ability, no consistent sex differences are apparent.
3. Sex differences are not consistently found in other areas of intellectual ability: concept mastery and reasoning, creativity when measured independently of verbal ability, and complex moral judgment.
4. Although there seem to be no sex differences in self-esteem when it is measured globally in paper-and-pencil inventories, the sexes seem to differ in the sources of their self-esteem: girls are more likely to derive self-esteem from interpersonal relationships and boys to derive theirs from physical activities and power over others. In addition, more subtle indicators suggest that men have greater self-confidence and more readily take credit for success on the masculine kinds of tasks studied. On the same tasks, women exhibit lower expectancies for success and more external and unstable attributions for success. Whether this lower female confidence can be extended to tasks in the neutral and feminine realms is an open question.
5. Both sexes appear to be motivated to achievement, although they often pursue achievement in different realms. Achievement motivation appears to be related to sex-role standards by way of the realm selected and expectations of consequences.
6. Women are more likely than men to report feelings of fear and anxiety, although there are usually no apparent sex differences in emotionality when actual behavior is studied.
7. Both sexes appear to be oriented toward other people, although sometimes they differ in the way they express it. In childhood, boys are more active than girls in seeking out and resisting separation from others. Yet the relationships in which girls are involved appear to be more intimate. In adulthood, males continue to benefit from their greater ease in taking the initiative by being more likely to offer help to a stranger in distress. Yet, when asked, females do respond. Women do seem to take greater responsibility for the social-emotional aspects of interactions, using their greater empathy and tendency to agree in order to facilitate group processes; and they take on roles requiring caring and giving more frequently.
8. Males are more frequently aggressive than females across the life span, although females are capable of behaving aggressively when provoked. Males

are also more likely to be dominant when dominance depends on aggression or status, or when it is for the purpose of controlling others. Females' dominance is more likely to be apparent when the goal will benefit someone else.

In presenting this information, we have seen several themes relevant to research on sex differences. First, we must say again that findings of differences between the sexes must be taken with the proverbial grain of salt. Any discussion of sex differences, including this one, tends to focus on differences and underemphasize the more common findings of sex similarities. We should not forget that females and males are more alike than they are different. Further, even findings of sex differences do not imply that every female is different from every male on that variable. Findings of sex differences reflect only average differences.

Second, any summary of sex differences is limited by the existing research. There is a consistent trend for this research to reflect a masculine bias. Thus, it has often concerned characteristics—achievement, aggression, self-confidence, dominance—in which men score higher. Further, the context frequently chosen for research—laboratory settings with strangers, tasks or achievement realms in which men often excel—seems to increase the probability that men will "do better" than women. Many areas have simply not been investigated, and some have not been investigated satisfactorily. This was apparent in the discussion of achievement where we pointed out that rarely has affiliation been studied as an expression of achievement. It was also apparent in the section on interpersonal interactions, where most of the interactions studied were with strangers rather than intimates.

A third theme in this chapter has been the importance of situation in affecting behavior. As we pointed out repeatedly, situational factors influence people's behavior so extensively that sex differences often vary according to the situation. It is therefore particularly important to remember that many of the results reported were compiled in a limited range of situations.

A fourth issue is that sex-difference research is subject to many problems of interpretation. As shown in Chapter 7, females and males differ not only in biological sex but also often in others' reactions to them, as well as the roles they play and experiences they have throughout life. Hence, many findings of sex difference may reflect the different experiences that females and males have had, as well as biological differences. Separation of causal factors is difficult. Rarely are a group of females and a group of males equivalent on all factors except sex. For example, females and males are socialized very differently in this culture. As another example, consider the college students who so often serve as the subjects in studies. Perhaps at a state university the females are from a higher social class than the males because families that pay for college are more likely to send sons to expensive private colleges. Also, many schools that accept higher proportions of males may have higher standards for females and hence the females at that institution would, on the average, be brighter. Because society is organized along sex lines, females and males in the same setting or situation may often represent different subgroups of the population at large. Hence, findings of differences between the sexes may reflect subgroup differences rather than general sex differences.

A fifth issue in sex difference research concerns the value-based interpretation of differences. It is important to avoid simplistic decisions about which sex has it "better" or "worse" on a particular dimension. A full understanding of sex differences requires consideration of the positive and negative aspects of a certain class of behaviors. For example, it would not be accurate to say males are handicapped by their greater tendency to aggression, for adaptation in certain situations requires a degree of aggression. Likewise, as pointed out earlier, females' greater sensitivity to their emotional states can be both helpful and a detriment. No behavior is clearly adaptive across all situations.

The questions at the beginning of this chapter concerned the relative strengths and weaknesses that females and males bring to the attempt to develop toward androgyny. Although average sex differences do exist in some areas, there is a great deal of overlap between the sexes. Nevertheless, attention to areas where sex differences have been established may be a first step for the person who hopes to be more androgynous, as well as for parents and teachers who hope to foster androgyny.

Once areas of average psychological sex differences are known, remedies can be attempted. For example, compensatory training could be made available in areas where the average female or male has less pronounced abilities. Further, efforts to change the situations that often limit the behavior of one sex or the other would be productive. Finally, attention could be paid to rewarding cross-sex-typed behavior, so that both females and males would receive social support for engaging in a wide variety of behavior.

SELECTED READINGS

Block, J. H. Issues, problems, and pitfalls in assessing sex differences: A critical review of "The Psychology of Sex Differences." *Merrill-Palmer Quarterly,* 1976, *22,* 283–308.

Hoyenga, K. B., & Hoyenga, K. T. *The question of sex differences.* Boston: Little, Brown, 1979.

Maccoby, E. E., & Jacklin, C. N. *The psychology of sex differences.* Stanford, Calif.: Stanford University Press, 1974.

Male Roles and the Male Experience. Special issue of *Journal of Social Issues,* 1978, *34* (1).

Psychological Bulletin often publishes reviews of sex difference research in particular areas; cf., Eagly, 1978 on conformity; Frodi, Macaulay, & Thome, 1977 on aggression; Haas, 1979 on language; Hall, 1978 on decoding non-verbal cues; Hoffman, 1977 on empathy; Lenney, 1977 on self-confidence in achievement settings.

Sherman, J. A. *Sex-related cognitive differences.* Springfield, Illinois: Charles C. Thomas, 1978.

ADULT
SEX ROLES

PART

Adult Roles in the Family

10

Part of this culture's social mythology is the association of certain roles and tasks with each sex. Woman: wife, mother, homemaker, nurturer. Man: husband, father, breadwinner, worker. Woman's roles are seen as the natural links to her "feminine" qualities of gentleness, nurturance, and compassion. "Masculine" traits such as competitiveness, assertiveness, and independence are often seen as requirements for adequate expression of man's husband and father roles.

At the foundation of such constructions of the sexes are the beliefs that "woman's place is in the home," and man's is, correspondingly, outside the home. Woman "tends the hearth," and man "brings home the bacon."

Although such simplistic prescriptions for adult roles are rarely invoked directly these days, they are still apparent in the doubts, difficulties, and barriers many people experience in building full adult lives. Attempts at personal change are not always as simple as they might be, because of institutions and laws that support outmoded designs for family life. Even when such external constraints are minimized, many people are still hesitant to violate the roles and rules associated with the constructions of the family that they have internalized. Can marriages be truly egalitarian? How can this be done, and at what cost to the comfort that accompanies continuation of familiar life styles? Is the struggle for change in the family necessary or worthwhile? How will children fare if they grow up in nonnuclear families or families in which both adults work outside the home? Can a woman who chooses to be a full-time mother build a meaningful life that preserves her self-respect as well as the respect of others? What are some of the consequences for adults who choose not to build their adult lives around marriage or childbearing? Is it possible to achieve true intimacy without the benefit of links to a nuclear family of one's own creation?

We do not promise to answer all these questions in this chapter, for there are no simple solutions. Instead, we will try to delineate some of the costs and benefits associated with variations of adult family roles.

In Chapter 1 we outlined the goals of androgynous development for the individual person: integration of femininity and masculinity, situational appropriateness of behavior, flexibility, and effectiveness of actions. In this chapter we will look for ways in which such goals can be met in the family. We will particularly look for ways in which personal options may be limited, and explore ways these limits can be decreased within the context of family roles.

In facing decisions about family life one is sometimes greeted with statements about natural constraints. Frequently one is told that current constructions of the family are "meant to be," "the best way," and "the way it has always been," because of the reproductive differences between the sexes. The argument is that, since women can bear and nurse children, they are meant to stay at home with the helpless child in order to foster its physical and emotional development. Biologically barred from such tasks and bonds, yet equipped with greater physical strength and aggressiveness, men are meant to protect the family and deal with the harsh world outside the family. Their role hence becomes worker and breadwinner.

So goes the myth. Yet reality has sometimes been surprisingly different, even in earlier times and less technological cultures. We will therefore explore some historical and crosscultural models of family life. Our purpose is twofold: we want to appreciate some of the options for family roles possible among humans, and also to understand some of the reasons for and consequences of present constructions of the family.

HISTORICAL AND CROSS-CULTURAL PERSPECTIVE

The loving nuclear family—father, mother, and children living in a single dwelling —is not universal either historically or across cultures. In contrast to today's sentimental view of the family, the idea of family during the Middle Ages, for example, was practical. Childhood was not construed as a separate developmental stage, and nurturance of children for long years was not deemed necessary. Across most classes, children were frequently apprenticed to someone outside the family by age seven. Most education was carried out in this way. Because the private and vocational were not considered separate entities, the apprenticeship taught the person both how to work and how to live with others (Aries, 1962).

The family was more clearly an economically productive unit than it is today. In the rural economy that characterized Western Europe and the United States before the Industrial Revolution, a household was the site of a broad array of functions and activities. Every home was part factory, producing food and cloth for both household and market (Janeway, 1971). Most work took place at home for women as well as men. Even among the gentry, women managed farms and workshops. Although specific tasks of family members might vary, all members generally took part in common economic activities. Men as well as women performed domestic tasks. Because children were part of the labor force from a very young age, they were regarded as an economic asset. Motherhood was valued for its clear economic contributions—the addition of new workers (Hareven, 1977). A similar pattern was found for a time in urban centers, too, as shops and factories of merchants and craftspeople were in the home.

Thus, for a large part of Western history, women did much more than tend to their families. This was partly due to the large number of other tasks they performed, and partly due to the view that childrearing was not a long-term job reserved only for women. Society, in the form of other households and masters, did much of the socialization of children.

This state of affairs changed, however, with the advent of industrialization. Once economically productive work began to take place outside the home, the public and domestic spheres became separate. The family functions became more specialized and focused on childbearing and childrearing. As explained by historians such as Tamara Hareven (1977) and Nancy Cott (1977), these changes affected sex roles, particularly in the emerging middle class.

First, home was transformed from a busy workplace and social center to a private family abode. Apprentices, business associates, and others involved with work were no longer part of daily household activities. Home became not a place where work occurred, but a refuge from the world of work.

A second result was the more rigorous differentiation in work responsibilities of family members. For the middle class who could afford it, home became the province of women and outside work the province of men. Housework became less valued because it was not paid for and did not produce visible goods for the marketplace.

Third, there was an increasing segregation of husbands from wives and fathers from children, since the father was away at work during the day. Mothers increasingly had sole responsibility for childrearing, for fathers were gone during the day. Also, industrialization brought many people to the city, frequently separating them from kin who had shared the tasks of childrearing.

Children at this time became less an economic asset and more an economic liability. Because they were not contributing to the family's productivity as much as they had in a rural economy, they were more clearly dependents. Gradually this concept expanded so that children were viewed as having special needs for nurturance and protection. Many poor children, forced to work in factories, did not share in these benefits. Yet the predominant cultural view and norm, even among the poor, was founded in the new middle-class belief in children's emotional neediness.

These changes also brought a greater amount of sentimentality to the family. Marriage and parenthood had made economic sense in the past: all members contributed to the family's productivity. The shift of economic responsibilities brought love and tender feelings to the fore as the justification for familial relationships.

Hareven (1977) points out, however, that the changes were not so dramatic at first for working-class families in which husbands, wives, and children were required to work outside the home. Simply put, wages were not sufficient to support many people on one salary. Although work conditions were deplorable, women and children remained economically viable members of the family. Children were an asset, because they contributed to the family's productivity. When women worked outside the home for long hours, their husbands shared household and childrearing tasks more (Hareven, 1977). Hence, at least initially, roles were less segregated than in the middle class. Yet, because the middle class frequently sets the values for a society, the middle-class pattern became the desired norm even for the working class.

There is an interplay between family, work, economics, and valuation of roles implied in this analysis. Women's and men's roles seem tied not only to their reproductive functions but also to social conditions. Women were not limited to the domestic sphere of wife and motherhood until economically viable work moved out of the home.

Analyses of other cultures suggest that as a society's economic basis shifts outside the home and men become less involved in domestic activities, women's social power declines. One anthropologist suggested that women's status is lowest in societies where there is a firm differentiation between domestic and public spheres (Rosaldo, 1974). The domestic domain includes activities performed within the localized family unit; the public domain includes political and economic activities that take place or have effect beyond the localized family unit, and that relate to control of persons or control of things (Sanday, 1974). Because of women's biological functions of bearing and nursing children, they are usually assigned domestic activities. When the domestic is separated from the public, the public activities along with the greater political and economic power involved are relegated to men. It is only when the domestic and public spheres are more integrated that men become more involved in domestic activities and women more involved in public activities. Under such conditions, adult roles are more likely to be egalitarian. Rosaldo suggests that when a man is involved in child care and cooking, in the domestic sphere, he cannot as easily establish an aura of authority and distance. At the same time, when public decisions are made in the household, women may have a legitimate public role. It seems that when the domestic and public are seen as separate activities assigned differentially to women and men, men more readily take on the authoritarian role.

The increased equality of the sexes associated with greater overlap of public and domestic activities may also be related to control of resources. According to an analysis of hunting and gathering societies, egalitarian relations were more likely to occur when women contributed to the needs of society and worked alongside men (Friedl, 1975). When hunting and gathering were communal activities so that both sexes had some control over how the resulting food resources were distributed, women's social status and power nearly matched men's. Women were most severely handicapped in societies where men provided almost all the food, and, hence, controlled its distribution. The resulting system of obligation, honor, and prestige served as a source of power over others not available to women.

In Western culture, we have seen that industrialization brought about a separation of private and public spheres. This, in turn, led to an increasing segregation of familial roles, a devaluation of the housework to which women were assigned, the conceptualization of children as dependent creatures, and the rise of sentimentality to justify the continuation of family relationships.

Another Look

A recurring theme throughout the cross-cultural studies is that women's role is less devalued when the roles of the sexes are not sharply differentiated. Both historically and cross-culturally, women's value declines as the domestic and public roles of women and men become separated. When women are cut off from playing a clear economic role in society, they have little chance to maintain power and respect in the larger society. Yet just involving women in the economically viable public sphere seems not to be enough. Women gain in power and prestige as men share in the tasks of the domestic realm.

The lessons from these cross-cultural and historical analyses are intriguing. Current constructions of the family, with a sharp distinction between the roles of the sexes and assignment of women but not men to most domestic tasks, are not inevitable. The current system seems to decrease the options open to women and men to the extent that it confuses current cultural practices with biological inevitability. It also seems to limit women's options especially, by assigning them a role that brings with it relatively little economic power. We will look again at these realities of power and economics, an inevitable part of family arrangements, when we discuss current varieties of family life.

PSYCHOLOGY'S PERSPECTIVE ON THE FAMILY

Before examining psychology's "knowledge" about the family, we must explore the ways that researchers have approached this topic. Since family life is a personally involving and emotionally charged issue for anyone, it should not be surprising that psychologists' approaches to this topic have been apparently influenced by their predispositions about "appropriate" family roles.

Psychologists have frequently confused the world as they see it with the world as it should be. For example, Freud developed his theory of personality while living in a patriarchal society. His view of personality development was based in the assumption that families consist of powerful fathers who work outside the home, nurturant mothers who perform domestic duties within the home, and children (Williams, 1977). The association of normality with development in such a nuclear family meant that the descriptive soon became prescriptive.

Maternal Responsibility

From these roots of Freudian theory and cultural milieu grew an acceptance of the idea that children need to have their mothers present during the formative years. Renee Spitz studied young children in institutions during the 1930s and concluded that

> Regularity in the emergence of emotional response and subsequently of developmental progress, both physical and mental, is predicated on adequate mother-child relations. Inappropriate mother-child relations (as in the foundling home) resulted regularly in the absence of developmental progress, emotional or otherwise, or in a paradoxical response (1949, p. 150).

Spitz neglected to consider the fact that not only were the children in the institutions deprived of their mothers, but they were also deprived of adequate stimulation and warmth from anyone. Although more recent interpretations of the Spitz studies acknowledge that the deleterious effects on the children were the result of institutionalization, sensory deprivation, and poor nutrition rather than maternal absence, the studies have been discussed under headings such as, "Later Consequents of Inadequate Mothering," in a 1960s edition of a popular child development textbook (Mussen, Conger, & Kagan, 1963, p. 168). Even after paying lip service to the notion that institutionalization rather than maternal absence is the problem, the authors concluded a review of studies of children in institutions with these words: "The weight of the evidence to date suggests that children raised by their mothers under normal family circumstances thrive better than children raised under relatively impersonal institutional conditions" (Mussen et al. 1963, p. 165). The most recent edition (1979) of that same textbook makes many efforts to be "nonsexist" in its interpretations. Yet, despite frequent use of the word "caretaker" in discussing adult-infant interactions, the authors often substitute "mother" (rather than "parent" or "father") for "caretaker," as in the following introductory passage:

> The infant becomes increasingly attached to the mother, and the mother to the child. Let us first examine the factors that foster the infant's attachment to its caretaker. In a later section, we will consider some factors that may facilitate—or hinder—the mother's attachment to the child (Mussen et al. 1979, pp. 156–57).

To those authors, apparently, "caretaker" is synonymous with "mother."

The message from psychologists to mothers is clear: It is your responsibility to raise the children and, if you leave them (perhaps even for eight-hour working days), do not expect them to thrive. This conclusion was reinforced by researchers who associated maternal employment with juvenile delinquency and dependency (discussed in Hoffman, 1963). The researchers failed to note, however, that the working mothers they studied were frequently poor, and their children's problems could as easily be ascribed to conditions associated with poverty—alienation, inadequate schooling, poor health—as to maternal employment.

The psychologist Harry Harlow continued this tradition of attempts to document the necessity of "mother love." In a series of studies, Harlow found that monkeys raised without mothers had impaired social development (less play, clinging to peers) compared to monkeys raised with their mothers. Interpretation of such studies as relevant to a necessity for "mothering" conveys the subtle message that human mothers hold primary responsibility for parenting. No efforts were made to study whether any adult monkey or set of adult monkeys could perform the same socialization functions. The researcher's bias is revealed in the following statement: "We are happy to state that we now believe that real mothering, monkey or human, is a very important social factor and that real mothering is here to stay!" (Harlow & Harlow, 1966, p. 271)

Such a conclusion is particularly ironic, in light of some of Harlow's findings that could lead to a very different conclusion. Some infant monkeys, deprived of other human contact, were offered terrycloth-covered or wire "surrogate mothers." Under conditions of stress, the monkeys preferred the softer terrycloth surrogate even if the wire surrogate had served as the feeding station. One interpretation, neglected by Harlow, could be that any soft, warm being—mother, father, or other —can provide the requisite comfort to infant monkeys. The use of the label "mothers" for the surrogates reveals his assumption that mothers are the ones who provide warmth and comfort.

We do not mean to imply that infants, human or monkey, should be allowed to fend for themselves. Rather, we wish to point out the ways in which researchers' own expectations about the appropriate constitution of families influence the questions they ask and interpretations they draw. The studies described by Spitz and Harlow do seem to suggest that a good, caring relationship with an adult is necessary for normal development.

However, interpreting such studies in terms of the necessity for constant maternal care of children has probably helped maintain current family patterns. These interpretations and others like them have been presented to the public through the media and to generations of college students through introductory and child psychology courses. It seems reasonable to expect that this research has helped to maintain an image of mother as primary childrearer, and to foster guilt in mothers who had to, or chose to, spend time away from their children.

Psychologists have also helped to preserve the assumption of maternal responsibility through some of their research on the causes of abnormal behavior. Until fairly recently, the focus has been on mothers more often than fathers in searching for precursors of abnormal behavior (Coleman, 1972). Paul Meehl (1962) pointed to "schizophrenogenic mothers" as one factor in the development of schizophrenia. He came to that conclusion after querying the mothers of schizophrenic and normal adults. His conclusions that mothers were responsible was inevitable, since his questions were not given to fathers. Again, mother emerges as the one responsible for childrearing, including its failures.

Distribution of Roles

Another way through which social scientists have helped to maintain traditional family roles is through their frequent assumption that women and men must play different roles in the family. Often these roles are portrayed as "complementary," but the emphasis is usually on the appropriateness of a husband's dominance. Parsons and Bales (1955) theorized that the husband's role is to be instrumental and the wife's, expressive. More recently, Vaillant (1977) wondered why the least well-adjusted men he studied had wives who were "devoted"; by implication, one should expect "devoted" wives to be associated with mental health in men. The primary situation in which fathers share the blame with mothers for their offspring's mental illness is that in which father is passive and mother dominant (Lidz, et al., 1957, 1958, 1963). Such an "inappropriate" distribution of roles is seen as pathological for the child. Current writings on family therapy (e.g., Minuchin, 1974) continue to present the normal family as one with strict divisions of roles—often made on the basis of sex.

Psychologists' acceptance of current family patterns as the best ones is further revealed in the questions they have *not* asked very often: What are the effects on a child of a father who is not involved in childrearing? What are the effects on mothers of their isolation within the home? How has the separation of work and home affected interpersonal relations, power within the home, and the development of children?

Another Look

It is clear that psychologists have both reflected and contributed to current images of the family. The questions asked, labels selected, interpretations presented, and questions ignored all reveal an overriding assumption that the family functions best when it exists as a haven from the outside world of work, when father takes responsibility for dealing with that outside world, when mother takes responsibility for the home and children, and when children serve as the focus of the home. Psychology's approach reveals an acceptance of two basic assumptions about the family: separation of work and family with differential assignment of the sexes to these realms; and separation of roles of women and men in marriage and parenthood.

In order to pursue the possibilities for androgynous family functioning, it is necessary to move beyond psychology's recent approach to the family. We will provide the groundwork for this by first examining the costs and benefits of current marital and parental roles. Later in the chapter we will discuss alternatives to these traditional roles.

MARITAL ROLES

Modern marriage is meant to serve as a reproductive unit that sustains and protects its members from the harshness of the outside world, while providing intimacy. Christopher Lasch has expressed this view of the ideal marriage and the family very well: "As business, politics, and diplomacy grow more savage and warlike, men seek a haven in private life, in personal relations, above all in the family—the last refuge of love and decency" (1977, p. xiii).

Intrinsic to many analyses of the ideal marriage is a complementarity of roles: two people can do better than one person, because the strengths and skills of one balance the deficits of the other, and vice versa. Parsons and Bales' (1955) description of the instrumental role of husbands and expressive role of wives fits such a pattern. Assumedly, such a pattern of roles within marriage is designed to benefit both partners.

Yet, elements of the popular culture protest such an assumption, suggesting instead that, in reality, marriage is more beneficial and desirable for wives than husbands. "Come and be my ball and chain," beckons Woody Guthrie in a song apparently to a prospective wife. Jokes abound about young women hot in pursuit of unwilling young men who prefer freedom to the trap of marriage. Many comic strips, such as "Blondie," are built around a bumbling fool of a husband who is repeatedly manipulated by his wife, and a wife who would gladly spend all his money on her frivolous desires.

However, recent work in the social sciences suggests that the opposite is true —marriage is more beneficial for husbands than wives. The difference in the apparent effects of marriage on women and men is so striking that Jessie Bernard (1972) has suggested that there are really two marriages: his and hers.

Marriage: His and Hers

Despite men's complaints against marriage, the average man seems to thrive in it. This is true according to a variety of demographic, psychological, and social indices Bernard examined. Although the physical health of married men is, on the whole, no better than that of never-married men, married men do have fewer serious symptoms of psychological distress and fewer mental health impairments. They are also less likely to be criminals, more likely to earn more money, and less likely to commit suicide. Further, once men have been married, they usually seek marriage again: at every age the marriage rate for both divorced and widowed men is higher than the rate for never-married men.

To determine whether marriage itself is responsible for these advantages, or whether healthy and successful men are simply more likely to marry, Bernard compared widowed to married men on some indicators. Deprived of marriage, widowers show greatly increased rates of mortality and psychological distress, when compared to still-married men. That this difference is not due only to the grief of bereavement is suggested by the fact that the increases are not as great among widowed women. Bernard concluded that, although selection is one factor in explaining the advantageous position of married men, the strongest factor is the beneficial effects that marriage has on men.

For women, marriage is not nearly so helpful. Despite the fact that a large proportion of women consider themselves and their marriages happy, the specifics of their marriages seem to bother many women. More wives than husbands report marital frustration and dissatisfaction; more report negative feelings; more have considered separation or divorce and have regretted their marriages; and fewer report positive companionship. Not surprisingly, in light of all this, more wives than husbands seek marriage counseling and initiate divorce proceedings.

Further, married women are more likely than married men to be in psychological distress. More married women than men show phobic reactions, depression, and passivity; more report anxiety and feelings of an impending nervous breakdown. These sex differences are not apparent when single women are compared to single men. In fact, Gove (1972) analyzed mental health statistics to show that women's greater frequency of mental health problems can be attributed to the rates for married women. If both married and single women were more likely than their male counterparts to report psychological distress, one could perhaps attribute the sex difference to the greater social acceptability of problems in women. Yet unmarried women do not report more problems and, actually, any sex differences in rates of mental illness in unmarried persons tend to show women as healthier (Gove, 1972).

Such findings are surprising, to put it mildly. They are in sharp contrast to both the general cultural image of the benefits of marriage to women and individual women's expectation of a blissful future when they marry. Various explanations have been offered for the apparently different effects of marriage on women and men.

Explanations for the Differential Effects of Marriage

Some writers suggest that marriage itself does not have differential effects on the sexes, but that different subgroups of women and men marry: the less healthy women and the more healthy men. Bernard described it as a "marriage gradient." (See Figure 10.1.) Although most spouses come from similar class and cultural backgrounds, men tend to marry women slightly below them in age, education, occupation, and other factors related to marital suitability. The result is that there is no one left for the men at the "bottom of the barrel" to marry, no one to look up to them. At the same time, the women at the top of the gradient, the "cream of the crop," are not so likely to marry, for there is no one for them to look up to. Hence, among the married, men are more likely than women to be healthy (to the extent that measurable factors such as higher education and occupation are related to mental and physical health), whereas among the never-married, women are more likely than men to be healthy.

This explanation could account for the finding that married men and single women are more likely to be free of psychological symptoms than their other-sexed counterparts (Gove, 1972). However, it does not fit with the finding that mental health statistics for the formerly married (divorced and widowed) are more similar to those for single than married people. According to the marriage gradient explanation, because divorced and widowed people had been part of the selection process, divorced and widowed men should be as healthy as the married men (since the "bottom of the barrel" males have been excluded) and the divorced and widowed women should be as unhealthy as the married women (since the "cream

FIGURE 10.1

The Marriage Gradient.

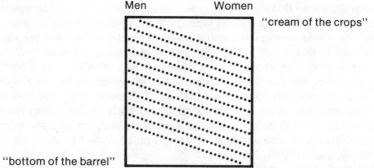

Figure 1, "The Marriage Gradient" (p. 33) from *The Future of Marriage* by Jessie Bernard (World Publishing Company). Copyright © 1972 by Jessie Bernard. Reprinted by permission of Harper & Row, Publishers, Inc. and Souvenir Press Ltd.

of the crop" females are not included). In fact, this is not the case. Thus, selection does not seem to account entirely for the different health statistics.

It seems then that there is something within marriage itself that has more beneficial effects on men than on women or, alternatively, more deleterious effects on women than on men. One of these factors within marriage may be power; specifically the power that is frequently associated with the role of husband. Women more frequently than men enter marriage expecting to redefine themselves and reshape their personalities to conform to the needs and demands of the spouse. And the wife more often moves to follow her husband's career than vice versa. Gradually, many wives give up aspects of their uniqueness to mold themselves to their husbands' wishes, in a process Bernard calls "dwindling." Research with couples reveals that more wives conform to husbands' expectations than the reverse (Bernard, 1972). Komarovsky (1973) studied senior men at an ivy league college and found that, although they gave lip service to a liberal view of woman's role in the family, they foresaw making few changes in their own lives to bring that to fruition. Specifically, only 7 percent were willing to modify their own roles significantly to facilitate their future wives' careers. Although many men agreed that a mother of a preschool child could appropriately take a full-time job, they added restrictions such as "provided, of course, that the home was run smoothly, the children did not suffer, and the wife's job did not interfere with her husband's career" (Komarovsky, 1973, p. 878). The assistance they were willing to give their wives extended from hiring a maid to adding "except . . ." (the laundry, diapers, or cleaning) to their statements of willingness. In other words, few changes would be forthcoming if the men had their way, even after children were born. For many couples, marriage involves many more changes for the wife than the husband.

Men who are highly oriented toward power as a general personality trait reveal that power in their marital relationships. Men who took a psychological test of the "need for power" as college freshmen in 1960 were queried again in 1974 when they were in their thirties. The men's college "power" scores were linked to their wives' career levels: wives of men high in the need for power tended not to have their own careers. In addition, the husband's conservative political views and position as a business executive were negatively linked to the wife's career level (Winter, Stewart, & McClelland, 1977). Apparently, men highly oriented toward power took a marital role in which their careers took precedence over their wives'.

Another factor that might contribute to the apparent difficulty that marriage entails for many wives is the conflict between ideals and reality. Bernard (1972) calls this idea the "shock theory of marriage." Girls often grow up with fantasies of a husband-to-be that few mortals could match. They entertain romantic notions with tales such as "Sleeping Beauty," and songs such as "Some Day My Prince Will Come" and "As Long As He Needs Me." But knights in shining armor are probably as difficult to live with as they are hard to find.

Many females are raised to be dependent on husbands who are pillars of strength. Quite a few, however, experience a period of shock when they realize that their husband is only human: he does not meet the implied husbandly guarantee of constant strength, knowledge, competence, and protection. This shock is greater because it occurs when the woman's role is changing; she is no longer the date who is catered to, but must become the wife who does the catering. She who grew up with the image of a superior spouse who would take care of her often finds herself taking care of someone who is unexpectedly needy. Because females are not always given the skills to be equal and strong partners, the reality of marriage may be surprisingly difficult for them.

Such cultural definitions of separate marital roles for husbands and wives have some advantages for the former. Daniel Levinson has studied forty men for several years and he writes about the roles some wives play, particularly during the twenties when a man is building his "Dream":

> The special woman helps him to shape and live out the Dream: she shares it, believes in him as its hero, gives it her blessing, joins him on the journey and creates a "boundary space" within which his aspirations can be imagined and his hopes nourished. (Levinson, Darrow, Klein, Levinson, & McKee, 1978, p. 109)

Such a relationship may be one reason so many married men thrive. Although Levinson did not study women, he admitted that in supporting the husband's dream the wife can lose her own and her development will suffer. Ideally, according to Levinson, both partners can have a dream at the same time they nourish the other's dream. Yet, in this less than ideal world, many women have put aside their own dreams in order to support their husbands'. Judging from the mental health statistics we cited, some seem to suffer later.

By far one of the most popular explanations proffered for the more negative effects of marriage on women than men is the differing job responsibilities they take on in marriage. When the domestic and work spheres were separated, women were assigned to the domestic domain. Until fairly recently, most women who married were expected to change their occupation to housewife. Bernard points out that this was akin to telling all men that, once married, they were to be janitors. Although many more wives are working outside the home now, the analogy has changed only slightly: it is as if someone were to tell men that with marriage, they were to *add* the job of janitor from 5 to 11 every evening, after their 9 to 5 job was finished. Recent evidence suggests that women who work outside the home continue to do most of the tasks of housewife: cleaning, cooking, laundry, child care (Pleck, in press; Stafford, Backman, & diBona, 1977). Public policy, such as that manifested in social security and federal income tax programs, encourages the continuation of woman's role in the house by according more favorable treatment to households with a single wage earner than to households in which both spouses have significant earnings histories (Flowers, 1977). In many circles, men are still seen as the basic breadwinners and women as the basic housekeepers.

There seems to be little doubt then that Bernard was correct when she suggested that the wife's marriage is clearly different from the husband's. Our discussion is not designed to deny that aspects of marriage are uncomfortable for men. For example, men are expected to shoulder the economic responsibility for the family. Yet the health statistics suggest that, however stressful the demands of marriage may feel to some husbands, the result is apparently not so harmful for them as for their wives.

One factor that may make marriage itself more difficult for both women and men is a rigid sex-role socialization that could well interfere with intimacy. In this culture, the sexes are raised to be different and are placed in a marital relationship that often enhances their differences, and then they are expected to be intimate. One spouse is placed in the home and the other in the world and they are told to grow closer to one another. Their activities and interests are led in differing directions, but they are expected to become better companions as the years go by. Within marriage also, one spouse is culturally assigned more power, although where there is unequal power and authority there is usually more distance than intimacy.

These paradoxical expectations for both distance and intimacy are particularly apparent in working-class marriages, which are sometimes characterized as "segregated" (Bott, 1971; Komarovsky, 1967; Rubin, 1976). As explained by Bott, couples in segregated marital relationships have quite distinct roles and carry out activities (tasks as well as leisure) separately, whereas couples involved in joint relationships carry out activities together and interchangeably.

The "ideal" marriage may be different in different classes. The middle-class ideal is to have friendships within marriage; a couple marries to share a life—and that often means sharing tasks, friends, leisure, etc. Even those aspects of each partners' work which are not shared (such as the husband's job) are shared verbally and peripherally, through socializing with his coworkers. This middle-class model, as Komarovsky (1967) presented it, assumes a certain equality and sharing of interests between the sexes. However, a substantial number of blue-collar couples with whom she spoke did not share this ideal. They emphasized what they saw as sex differences in personality that precluded such friendly, egalitarian relations between the sexes. These couples tended to think that friendship was more likely to exist between members of the same sex. In their minds, marriage offered the opportunity for sexual union, accomplishment of complementary tasks, and a mutual devotion, but the thought of marital "togetherness" during every leisure hour did not occur to them.

Komarovsky (1967) pointed out that marital differences between classes coincide with available information about sex-role socialization in those classes. When patterns of childrearing sharply distinguish between the sexes, there is a low probability of establishing marriages focused on friendship and interchangeability of female-male functions. If boys have been strongly encouraged to be "male" and have spent much of their time in a "male" subculture since early childhood, it is very unlikely that a wedding ceremony will bring their interpersonal styles, attitudes, and interests in line with those of a "female" subculture. Similarly, girls whose femininity has been strongly socialized might find it difficult to fit their interests with someone's from the male subculture.

There is a great deal of variability within the working class in both the ideals and reality of marriage. Both Seifer (1973) and a report by Social Research (1973) suggested recent shifts in these marriage patterns; marriage in the working class has taken on more of a middle-class tinge for couples in which the woman is becoming less housebound in her behavior. The increased feelings of independence and confidence that result from participation in the work force and in volunteer and community groups, lead to greater equality between partners and, eventually, to an increasingly friendship-based exchange.

Despite the difficulties for marital intimacy and communication that segregated roles can present, they may provide a model for enabling relationships outside the marriage. A striking finding in studies of segregated working-class marriages (Bott, 1971; Komarovsky, 1967; Rainwater, Coleman, & Handel, 1959) is the extent to which intimacy needs are fulfilled by friends and other family members. Often the social network—children, friends, and relatives—is more important to the lives of couples in a segregated than a joint relationship. Within more segregated relationships, a spouse is not expected to provide all the needed support, satisfaction, and companionship, and many people readily fill these needs through other sources. Such a pattern is particularly intriguing in light of the difficulties some couples experience in having the spouse meet all the intimacy needs sufficiently.

Another Look

We have seen that current constructions of marital roles seem to impose limitations on both sexes, though apparently more on women. The average wife's marriage appears to be less advantageous for her than the husband's is for him. A variety of factors seem to be responsible, including: the sexual politics that grants men greater power within marriage; wives' unreasonable expectations that husbands will protect them in all ways; and the role of housewife assigned to women.

Yet, despite these difficulties within marriages, couples continue to seek it. At the very least, marriage seems to provide a potential antidote for loneliness, a sense of continuity, and a possible means for personal development. Marital relationships can serve as training ground for other relationships, especially helping the members deal with the coexistence of conflicting feelings. Within marriage, one experiences the full range of feelings often found only separately in other relationships: anger and joy, love and hate, independence and dependence. The simple recognition of such "opposite" emotions can be instructive. Because of the continuity inherent in marital relationships, one is sometimes forced to go further and try to integrate these disparate feelings. Such demands are less frequently placed on a person outside the intense family arena. True, these mixed emotions can easily overwhelm one. Under such circumstances one may retreat from the marriage, regress to less intense involvement, or suffer unhappiness and maladjustment. Yet such conflict can also be a stimulus to grow psychologically richer and more emotionally complex.

The major problem, of course, is to translate the ideals into reality. In more pessimistic moments, many people wonder if it is possible—countless hours have been spent in discussions among friends of the problems and potentials of relationships between the sexes. Try to think of a couple in which both persons: (1) are happily married, (2) are doing what they want to do, and (3) possess a strong secure sense of self. The difficulty of finding people who meet these criteria leads some to suggest that marriage itself is at fault. Others suggest that the problem is the social context of marriage: a society that expects the sexes to be intimate while stressing their differences and putting more power in the hands of one sex than the other. These potentials and pitfalls of marriage remain relatively unexplored by researchers.

One of our goals in this book is to delineate the unanswered questions, the things that we need to know in order to pursue development toward androgyny. One primary set of questions focuses on marriage: How can people enjoy the benefits of marriage, the rich intimacy and growth, without losing themselves as individuals? One might begin by studying couples who have weathered marriage successfully. Another focus of inquiry is how women can cope successfully with the wife role, a role that society has sentimentalized yet devalued. How can marriage be less of a mental health hazard for women? Phyllis Chesler (1978) has suggested that only strong women can survive in marriage, for it takes strength to retain one's individuality while enjoying the benefits of that institution. In general, many of the most intriguing unanswered questions concern the ways couples have, or can, enjoy the positive aspects of marriage, without being overwhelmed by the negative.

PARENTAL ROLES

Parental roles seem to be particularly resistant to change in recent years. Immediately after marriage the majority of women continue to work outside the home today, and spouses tend to share household tasks, decision making, and a common experience (Rossi, 1968). However, the relationship often becomes more traditional with the addition of a child, as the wife stays home to care for it. Despite heralds of changing roles in the mass media, women still do most of the child care in two-parent families. Pleck (in press) reviewed the available research and concluded that there was no evidence of a recent significant change in the amount of child care and housework done by men. He also found no evidence that men with working wives did significantly more child care or housework than married men whose wives did not work outside the home. One is reminded of the study that found that a sample of middle-class fathers spent less than one minute per day in direct contact with their infants (Bronfenbenner, 1974).

One consequence of this disproportionate division of the parental roles would be that women get most of the joys and satisfactions of parenting. Rainwater et al. (1959) pointed out that, especially for women who lack opportunities for other satisfying work, the bearing and rearing of children can provide emotional rewards as well as a recognized social role. Yet women also bear an unequal share of any negative concomitants of childrearing.

Psychology has done its share in perpetuating the view that mothers are the chief parents. Until quite recently, fathers were rarely studied. Although there is now some evidence of the effects of fathers on children (cf., Lamb, 1976), we still know relatively little about men's experience of the father role and the effects of fatherhood on men. Thus, our conclusions about the male parental role will have to be more tentative than those about the female role.

Parenthood has a complex set of romantic and honorable connotations. Images of rosy-cheeked infants and young hands tucked trustingly into an adult's abound. Angela Barron McBride caricatured the positive aspects of her own ambivalent feelings about impending motherhood:

I began to think more and more about the warm, soft, tactile world of child-hood. Having a baby would be my chance for self-renewal. . . . I could feel those happy hormones tugging at my womb, confirming my lustiness, while I gave my husband a loving look, part earth mother, part Madonna. I would finally be a complete woman. My love affair with my child would be a pure, beautiful, holy relationship. Every day would brim over with bright colors and lullabies, cuddling and snuggling, balloons, and gurgling sounds. Oh, how we would sing and dance (1973, pp. 19–20).

Yet all is not supposed to be romantic, as revealed in Veevers' (1973) analysis of the more dutiful tinges to the social meaning of parenthood. Parenthood is sometimes conceptualized as a moral and religious obligation, as a civic responsibility to ensure the continuity of the species, and a response to natural instincts. It is also at times viewed as a sign of sex role acceptance: being a mother or father is proof of "femininity" or "masculinity" as well as of sexual competence. Parenthood is equated with normal adulthood and maturity, as suggested by these excerpts:

A woman who identifies with an unhappy mother might, in avoiding pregnancy, really be attempting to reject her femininity (Lantz & Snyder, 1969, p. 377).

Between the limits of childlessness and complete disregard for family size, every normal married couple will want to set its goal (Christensen, 1958, p. 475).

In a very real sense . . . the arrival of the first child symbolizes several things in our society; it makes the father a man and the mother a woman (LeMasters, 1957, p. 522).

For the developmental psychologist Erik Erikson, "generativity," defined as "concern in establishing and guiding the next generation" (1963, p. 267), is an important stage in normal adult development. Failure at this task will lead to "a pervading sense of stagnation and interpersonal impoverishment" (1963, p. 267).

Such images of parental roles combine to create a pressure toward parenthood and expectations that it will result in contentment at least. Contrast these images with the fact that infanticide was frequent and noticeable in Europe as late as the nineteenth century (Langer, 1972). Recent awareness of the prevalence of child abuse suggests that the parent-child relationship retains its potential for deep anger and hatred as well as love. Our own clinical work with fundamentally normal, healthy clients suggests that ambivalent feelings about the parental role are common. One young mother recently described the frustration and anger that coexist with the love she feels for her two preschoolers: "They're greedy monsters sometimes; so demanding! They act as if I exist solely for their benefit! I sometimes think they do things on purpose, to provoke me."

Part of the difficulty in recognizing such disenchantment with motherhood is the lack of preparation for any negative feelings about one's children. McBride concluded after watching other mothers and examining her own experience that,

"Jealousy, rage, envy, anger, depression, confusion, competition, guilt, sadism, and narcissism may not be as normal as apple pie, but they are normally present in all mothers" (1973, p. 49).

Individual tales of ambivalent feelings about parenthood may not be convincing to some people. After all, one might argue, it is not uncommon to find people who sound totally frustrated and disenchanted about their relationships with students, coworkers, friends, customers, etc. The phrase "greedy little monsters" could well characterize many people besides one's children at one time or another. Yet much of the available data suggest that negative feelings in the parent-child relationship can be particularly problematic.

Costs of Parenthood

Statistically, responsibility for young children in this society is associated with dissatisfaction, depression, and disturbance. Several recent studies of nonhospitalized populations have found that parents living with children experience high rates of depression and psychiatric disturbance. Low income, the presence of young children, and the presence of many children are factors that point to particularly high risk (Belle, 1979). There is a sharp difference between reported life satisfaction for young, married childless women (89 percent satisfied) and those with young children (65 percent satisfied). Indicators of psychological stress are greatest for both men and women during the early parental stage (Campbell, Converse, & Rodgers, 1976). For the average couple, marital satisfaction declines with the introduction of children, then rises during the postparental stage (Burr, 1970; Deutscher, 1959; Renne, 1970; Rollins & Feldman, 1970).

Despite talk of an "empty nest syndrome" among both psychologists and the public, any negative effects of a child's leaving home appear to be minimal and transitory (Harkins, 1978). Problems for the mothers' emotional well-being are more likely to arise if the offspring do *not* become independent when expected to do so. The "empty nest syndrome" appears to be primarily limited to women who had overprotective or overinvolved relationships with their children (Bart & Grossman, 1978).

Skolnick (1978) details the ways the addition of a child can disrupt a marriage: more frequent exhaustion, interruption of sexual relations, and increased competition of the child for the attention of the spouse. She cites one study reporting that following childbirth the amount of time the wife and husband converse with each other is cut in half. Nearly half of a group of professional and nonprofessional women listed restriction of freedom, opportunity, privacy, and mobility among the costs of parenthood (Beckman, 1978).

Motherhood

The costs of parenthood are often experienced more strongly by mothers, because mothers are usually more heavily involved in parenting. Despite talk in the media about increasing involvement of fathers, a group of middle-class parents described the majority of parental tasks as, ideally, the mother's primary responsibility (Kellerman & Katz, 1978). In these parents' views, basic physical caretaking and emotional support were to be carried out by mothers, education and guidance was to be a shared parental function, and fathers were to take responsibility for the more physically active, recreational spheres.

Bernard (1974a) suggests that anxiety, guilt, isolation, and stress are integral parts of motherhood as it is structured in this society. The anxiety results from the discontinuity between the demands of the maternal role and the socialization of females. The responsibilities of motherhood demand strength and power, but women are socialized into dependency. Rossi (1968) points out that although parenting requires "instrumental" skills, it is assigned to the woman, who is trained as a specialist in "expressiveness." Guilt is bred in mothers who are inevitably unable to meet the high expectations set for them. The mother is held accountable for many of her child's misdeeds: who has not glared at the mother whose child is screaming on a plane or in a store? The stress associated with motherhood is also comprehensible on purely physical grounds: children can be noisy and insistent, and care of them is often fatiguing. Isolation comes about as mothers are restricted to the home, with only young children for company. They often must confront the daily stress of parenthood without the companionship and support of other adults.

Not only parents but also children can be affected adversely by current constructions of parental roles. The lack of socially approved outlets for parental anger may be one reason children are sometimes beaten and battered physically and psychologically by their own parents. An additional by-product of the usual parent-child relationship is the increased likelihood of repeating current sex-role patterns in the next generation (see Chapter 7). In particular, the delegation of primary child care responsibilities to females creates an arrangement in which males must reject females and their own feminine aspects in order to ensure their male identification (Chodorow, 1978; Dinnerstein, 1976). According to this theory, women as mothers are first experienced by their infants as all-powerful beings. The infantile fear of this power and their dependency on the woman who wields it form the basis for males' later efforts to make themselves distinct from and to defensively denigrate women. Although female infants also experience the maternal power and their own dependency, they need not work so hard to assure themselves they are separate from the mother since they, too, are female. Hence, while men go on to seek closeness with women, they also often fear the dependency and femaleness that they associated with that closeness in infancy. Thus, the procedure of assigning child-rearing solely to women perpetuates the distance between the sexes.

The source of these negative effects is often seen as this culture's construction of parental roles, rather than parenthood itself. Bernard (1974a) distinguishes between the *reproductive* and *institutional* aspects of motherhood. The reproductive aspects—conception, gestation, birth, lactation—are constant across cultures and eras. The institutional aspects—such as responsibility for childrearing—are more variable. According to Bernard, the current institution of motherhood involves assigning sole responsibility for child care to the mother; requiring round-the-clock tender, loving care; and making such care her only activity.

Investigations of different ways of raising and caring for children suggest that these components of the institution of parenthood are among the worst possible.

Maternal warmth and emotional stability are lowest under conditions of maternal isolation and sole responsibility. A study of six different cultures revealed that in cultures where women were given the heaviest load of child care they were more changeable in expressing warmth than in other cultures and more likely to have hostilities not related to the behavior of the children (Minturn & Lambert, 1964). Mothers who spent a high proportion of their time caring for children were less stable in their emotional reactions to their children than those without such exclusive responsibility. The researchers speculated, "Mothers who are really isolated from their relatives and substitute caregivers may control expressiveness ... to avoid further wear and tear on their own frayed nerves and fights among siblings for their own praise and affection" (Minturn & Lambert, 1964, p. 283). Whiting (1961) reported that the attention and comforting a child receives is roughly proportionate to the number of adults in the household. Within this culture, well-run day care centers have found that about six hours of direct child care per day is an optimal maximum for the adult (Seiden, 1976). Full-time housewives surely exceed this.

The glorification of the mother role sometimes serves to mask some of the very real stress involved in the care of children. Young children are highly dependent on adults. They demand time, energy, and sacrifice, without guaranteeing support and satisfaction in return. Child care is hard work; it should not surprise us that it is associated with stress. By requiring mothers to spend long hours alone with their children without the support provided by other adults, this society seems to be incorporating some of the least useful arrangements—for both mother and child.

Fatherhood

Recent increased interest in the father role has resulted in clear documentation of the variations in paternal behavior that influence the child's sex-role adoption, moral development, academic achievement, adjustment, and interpersonal interactions (Biller, 1971; Lamb, 1976; Lynn, 1974).

Lynn (1974) documents the variety of practices—in some animals and across human cultures—of fathers' involvement with their offspring beyond procreation. Sometimes the father plays an important role. In several species of new-world monkeys, the father carries the infant almost all of the time. During certain seasons, mature males of one species of old-world monkeys hug the infant, groom it, play with it, hover about it, take it on their laps, and walk it. In the Israeli kibbutz, the father may become the child's favorite source of nurturance and affection. In communes in the United States in the early 1970s there was usually some man present who played the role of father to a child, even if it was not biologically his.

According to a study from the early 1950s (Tasch, 1952), most American fathers saw their role as anything but superfluous. Many of the fathers enjoyed spending time with their children, and regretted that their work limited that time. When companionship with the child was good, the father considered that relationship a major source of satisfaction in his life.

The father is clearly an important person in the life of even the infant and young child. There are surprisingly few differences in one- and two-year-olds' reactions to mothers and fathers in the psychological laboratory (Lewis & Weinraub, 1976).

Young children react more similarly to their fathers and mothers than to strangers (Kotelchuck, 1976). Although mothers sometimes report that their infants prefer them to fathers, direct observation reveals no consistent demonstrable difference in infants' protests over separation from mother or father (Lamb, 1976). Although infants do seem to prefer their mothers under stress, in most situations no consistent preferences are apparent (Lamb, 1976).

Nevertheless, there seem to be qualitative differences in the average mother-infant and father-infant relationships. At least in the early years, caretaking is the major way by which the mother interacts with the infant; the father's major mode for relating is through play (Lamb, 1976). For example, whereas mothers in a middle-class Boston sample were present with their children an average of nine hours per day, 75 percent of the fathers did not have any regular caretaking responsibilities. What is more, 43 percent of all the fathers in that sample reported they never changed diapers at all (Kotelchuck, 1976).

Yet fathers as a rule seem to be stricter and less comfortable with their children than mothers are. In one study, fathers gave reasons for their discipline less frequently than mothers did. Fathers were less likely to allow children to have their own way. They also seemed to lack the rapport that mothers displayed with their children, taking less time to answer questions and showing less affection. Perhaps not surprisingly, the children did not so often share confidences with fathers as mothers (Radke, 1946).

Men are often not confident about their abilities as fathers. When expectant fathers were interviewed, they were worried about whether they could handle the emotional and financial responsibilities of fatherhood (Liebenberg, 1967). Surprisingly, many of the men seemed to turn to their own parents more during the pregnancy. They wrote and telephoned their parents more than usual, and many wished to be at their parents' homes on Mothers Day. There was also evidence that some of the fathers envied their wives' pregnancies. Feelings of jealousy of the child were not uncommon after the birth.

There is also often a quantitative difference in the relationships fathers and mothers have with their children. The figures for fathers' interactions vary, but are usually strikingly low. For example, when microphones were attached to infants' shirts, it was found that fathers engaged in 2.7 vocal interactions with their babies per day (Rebelsky & Hanks, 1971). This constituted an average of 37.7 seconds per day. Even the *most* involved father averaged only 10.5 minutes of vocalization per day with his son. Fathers tended to decrease the time they spent vocalizing over the first three months, particularly with daughters.

Curiously, however, the quantity of time spent together is a poor predictor of the quality of the parent-infant relationship (Lamb, 1976). For example, as demonstrated above, fathers remain important figures to their young children, even when they spend very little time in interaction. In most families, there is clearly a special attachment between father and child. Kotelchuck (1976) found no relationship between the amount of most fathers' caretaking at home and father-child interaction in the laboratory. Except for the fathers who were extremely low in caretaking behavior, the children's reactions to the father in the laboratory (touching, proximity, etc.) did not vary as a function of the amount of time the father devoted to child care at home (Kotelchuck, 1976).

Hence, most fathers appear to be spending sufficient time interacting with their young children to ensure the establishment of a distinctive parent-child bond. It appears that only minimal interaction is necessary for the child to perceive the father as an important figure. Fathers are clearly capable of interacting with their young children but, as Lewis and Weinraub (1976) point out, do not often take advantage of that capability.

Such information about fatherhood is only a tantalizing beginning. There is much more to learn about fathers, particularly the effects parenthood can have on a man's development. The potential for expression of warmth and intimacy with children can perhaps help men develop their communal aspects that may have been masked by excessive agentic training.

Another Look

As we have seen, parenthood presents very different experiences for women and men. The average woman is heavily involved in the maternal role while she has children. Because there is psychological distress associated with responsibility for young children, she might be expected to suffer more than the average man who is less heavily involved in the parental role. Yet there is little available information on negative effects of fatherhood on men, or on the potential benefits they may be missing.

One way to catch a glimpse of what men may be missing in their frequent underinvolvement in parenthood is to look at some of the potential benefits of active relationships with children. McBride (1977) made the specific suggestion that aspects of family life, parenthood in particular, can foster the development of androgyny. According to her, the parent becomes more of a whole person as she or he regularly encourages the child's full human development. Repeated attempts to combine the authority and support necessary for child care can lead to the development of androgynous personality traits. She conceptualizes parenthood as a growth experience since parents are forced to reconcile their own seemingly disparate characteristics such as strength and tenderness, independence and sensitivity, courage and gentleness. Rossi (1968) touched on this theme, too, when she suggested the importance of recognizing and integrating the expressive and instrumental functions in each parental role: mother and father.

The family offers other potential benefits besides the enhancement of androgyny. Dinnerstein remarked on the sense of continuity family relationships can provide (Morgan, 1978). The intermingling of generations that parenthood provides can give one a sense of the reality of the life span and a greater appreciation of one's own potential for both change and consistency. Particularly since so many areas of life outside the family are age-graded, one can be helped to both live well and die well through the examples provided by family members.

Admittedly, to the extent that such potential benefits arise from close relationships, they can also be found outside the family. Yet families do provide a setting where emotional complexity, integration of personal characteristics, exposure to the human life span, and nurturance can readily occur. The questions for the future revolve around ways to construct family roles so that that potential can be realized more fully and by more people. There is variability across families and it would be instructive to carefully study a wide range of families: In what family arrangements do both children and parents seem to be developing most fully? Is it possible for fathers and mothers to be equally involved in childrearing? Do such arrangements decrease the stress of parenthood for mothers? It may also be instructive to look at the social supports available to families: To what extent does the availability of good day care (even if parents choose not to use it) increase parents' feelings of freedom? What community services make the jobs of parents easier? Do nonnuclear family arrangements (cooperative parenting, communal living) decrease the stresses associated with parenthood?

It is true that parenthood is currently experienced as very stressful by many adults. What remains to be seen is the extent to which one can enjoy parenthood, do it well, and avoid being overwhelmed by it.

PARTICIPATION IN BOTH FAMILY AND WORK

Despite the myth that home is women's sphere and work men's, it is not true for everyone. In fact, over half the mothers of school-age children now participate in the paid work force (Edwards, Reich, & Weisskopf, 1978). Also, some men are becoming more involved in family work. Even those young women who do not plan to depart from the housewife-mother role may find themselves adding paid responsibilities to their family ones at some point in the family life cycle, if only for economic reasons. In the same vein, men may find themselves with a greater-than-anticipated involvement in family responsibilities due to their wives' participation in the labor force.

In this section we will examine some of the consequences of loosening the sex-linked assignments of work and family roles. It is a particularly important area of inquiry for a psychology of androgyny, because less rigid psychological divisions between the sexes may coincide with less rigid divisions of labor. In fact, androgynous college women have been found to desire fewer children and to place more importance on competence at work than sex-typed women (Allgeier, 1975).

The view that husbands/fathers work outside the home while wives/mothers work inside the home has never been totally accurate for all segments of the population. The myth of the sex-typed family hid the fact that even in 1950, the heyday of the "feminine mystique" (Friedan, 1963), one-quarter of all married women who were living with their husbands were in the labor force. More than one-quarter of all women in intact marriages who had school-age children were employed. Further, 10 percent of married women with husband present and preschool children were in the labor force. The number of women who combine career and family roles has risen steadily since then (Van Dusen & Sheldon, 1976).

Despite the fact that working family women were not uncommon, some social scientists revealed a rather hostile attitude toward them in the questions they asked and conclusions they drew. Laws (1971) has pointed out, for example, this conclusion:

> As more and more enticements in the way of financial gain, excitement and independence from the husband are offered married women to lure them from their domestic duties, the *problem* is becoming more widespread and acute (Glueck & Glueck, 1957, italics added).

Another set of investigators studied a group of young women preparing for a profession (nursing) and characterized them with terms such as: hostile rejection of the homemaking role, excessive demand for striving, overpossessiveness, and hostile punitive control (Schaeffer & Bell, 1957). There is a history of a search for negative effects of women's employment on their children, marriages, and health that has only recently been questioned.

Consequences for Children

When parents work outside the home, preschool children must usually be placed in the care of others. And, because working parents cannot always be home when the children are dismissed from school, some arrangements also have to be made for young school-age children. Research in this area is generally presented under the heading of "working mothers." Yet it must be understood that this phenomenon would not cause concern for the children's welfare unless they had "working fathers" as well. We will first examine the information on working mothers, then attempt to piece together some idea of the consequences of paternal employment.

Maternal employment. Hoffman (1974a) summarized the effects of maternal employment on the child in six areas: modeling, emotional state of the mother, childrearing practices, supervision, maternal deprivation, and scholastic achievement. We already pointed out (Chapter 7) that working mothers serve as an important role model for children's, particularly daughters', concepts of the female role. Stein and Bailey (1973) found that achievement-oriented women were more likely than other women to have mothers who worked outside the home. Hoffman concluded that, for daughters, maternal employment is associated with less traditional sex-role concepts, more approval of maternal employment, and a higher evaluation of female competence. Effects on sons in this area are less clear-cut.

The working mother's emotional state depends to a large degree on her reasons for and satisfaction with her job. According to one study (Yarrow, Scott, DeLeeuw, & Hennig, 1962) mothers who chose not to work out of a sense of "duty" to their children had the lowest scores in "adequacy of mothering." Comparing professional women with housewives who had all graduated from college "with distinction," Birnbaum (1975) found that the nonworking mothers felt less competent in their child care skills than the working mothers. Hoffman (1974a) concluded that the working mother who obtains satisfaction from her work, has adequate arrangements for child and home care, and does not feel excessively guilty is likely to do quite well and sometimes better than the nonworking mother. If she feels very s10ilty about working, however, she may overcompensate and become overprotective. Levy (1966) pointed out, however, that one problem associated with full-time motherhood is "maternal overprotection"; maternal employment might generally help to avoid such a phenomenon if it can be accomplished with minimal guilt. Nye reported that employed mothers were more likely to enjoy activities and relationships with their children (1974a). He postulated that the change of scene offered by employment appears to allow for more enjoyment of time spent with the children. Skolnick (1978) pointed out another possible positive effect of maternal mood. She suggested that the intensity of full-time mother-child contact can be responsible for the expression of extreme feelings and anger in maternal child abuse. Perhaps the less intense interactions that might prevail if mother and child are separated for regular time periods can take the edge off such strong negative feelings.

Hoffman (1974a) has pointed out that few studies have examined working mothers' actual childrearing practices directly. It appears, though, that middle-class mothers tend to compensate for working with means such as reading with their children more than full-time mothers (Jones, Lundsteen, & Michael, 1967). With such exceptions, however, children of working mothers tend to receive more independence training and household responsibilities.

Consequences of maternal employment for supervision of children depend on social class. In the lower class, working mothers do provide less supervision, but their children seem, if anything, to be less likely to become delinquents. This may be because employment in the lower class is associated with stability and motivation to move into a higher social standing. In the middle-class, however, children of working mothers seem to have a higher rate of juvenile delinquency. It is not clear whether the cause is inadequate supervision or selection factors, such as those associated with the financial necessity for work (Hoffman, 1974a).

Psychologists who have noted the effect of parent-child attachment on later emotional and interpersonal development have been concerned about possible "maternal deprivation" associated with maternal employment. However, there is no evidence that school-age children perceive their mothers' working as rejection or that they are emotionally deprived (Hoffman, 1974a). One study compared children in day care from very young ages to children raised at home (Kagan, Kearsley, & Zelazo, 1978). The former group had been in day care eight hours a day, five days a week, from about three and a half months of age through twenty-nine months. These children were matched by age, ethnicity, social class, and sex with children reared at home. The day care was designed to be both nurturant and cognitively challenging. At twenty months, there were no important differences in the behavior of the two groups of children when placed in an unfamiliar situation with the mother, an unfamiliar woman, and the day-care teacher (for the day-care children) or a friend of the family (for the children raised at home). There was an overwhelming tendency for all the children to go to their mothers for comfort when tired, bored, or apprehensive because of the experimenter-induced provocation. Regular absence from the mother in day care, even throughout infancy, did not apparently interfere with establishment of a mother-child attachment. The two groups of children were remarkably similar in their cognitive, social, and affective development. Further, children in an Israeli kibbutz, who spent only a few hours each day with their parents, appeared more secure when left with their mother and a stranger than with their caretaker and a stranger (Fox, 1977). Mother-infant attachment seems to occur without a maximum of time together.

Overall, then, the consequences of maternal employment for the child seem to be positive. Children of working mothers can benefit from a positive female role model, a more contented mother, and a mother who fosters more independence. Supervision and attachment seem to be generally adequate. Problems seem more prevalent in the middle class, perhaps because mothers are less often able to justify their working by economic necessity. The ensuing guilt and conflict can present difficulties for mother-child interactions. However, most of the studies surveyed were done in the 1950s and 1960s, when maternal employment for noneconomic reasons was less readily acceptable. Changes in social acceptability of women working for their own reasons may have resulted in less maternal guilt and conflict among the middle class in recent years.

Paternal employment. Studies of the consequences of paternal employment for fathers' relationships with their children are less readily available. It is necessary to extrapolate from studies of full-time paternal absence and attachment. Conclusions drawn in this manner must be tentative.

As described in the section on fatherhood, a father-child attachment can survive even short periods of interaction. However, some minimal level of father-child interaction seems to be necessary for the bond to be built. For example, father and child had a difficult time forming a relationship if the father had been away from home and they were reunited after the child was a year old (Stolz, 1954).

The quality of time spent together seems to be important for the father-child relationship. Warm and accepting fathers tend to have children with high self-esteem, whereas rejecting and neglecting fathers seem to foster low self-esteem in their children (Lynn, 1974). Alienated adolescents view their parents as hostile and nonaccepting. Accepting fathers tend to have children who are accepted by their peers.

Although none of these studies examine consequences of fathers' normal unavailability to their children, they do imply that children benefit from more extensive and warmer relationships with their fathers. Since fathers' degree of absence does vary it would be helpful to assess the relationship between this factor and other aspects of the child's development. For example, degree of paternal absence at work could be related to factors such as the modeling, parental emotional state, childrearing practices, supervision, and parental deprivation studied for working mothers. Costs and benefits to children from paternal employment may be similar to those from maternal employment. The costs of paternal employment might be greater, however, because the average working father does not spend as much time interacting with his child as the average working mother (Edwards, Reich, & Weisskopf, 1978).

Consequences for Working Parents

Because sex-typed adult family roles are so deeply socialized, one would expect different effects on women and men of attempts to take part in both family and work roles. Frequently, the result is the addition of a role for a woman but not for a man. The woman generally takes on two full-time occupations, housework and worker, but the man's less extensive involvement in the home means his duties do not increase as much. Potentially then, current sex roles mean a greater possibility of conflict for women who attempt to combine work and home roles than for men who do so.

Many women are aware of this potential extra burden. One woman was overheard in a store discussing her reasons for not going out to work after the children entered school:

> It would mean getting up at 5:30. I'd have to fix their lunches, cook breakfast, get them dressed and off to school, get my husband going, make plans for dinner, and clean up the house. After work I'd have to cook dinner, clean up, and help the children with their homework. Then I'd do the laundry. Weekends would be spent doing errands and cleaning. I couldn't take it— never a free moment!

There is no doubt that, for this woman, eight to nine hours of work and commuting would have to be added to all her usual household duties. It is surprising, then, that so many women do decide to add outside work to their schedules.

Employed married women between the ages of twenty-eight and thirty-nine were able to describe both "costs" and "benefits" of their employment. Among the costs of work they listed were a lack of time, interference with needs of the children, and the routine of work (e.g., having to be there every day). The most salient benefits they saw were social interaction; achievement, challenge, and creativity; self-definition, esteem, or independence; economic rewards; mental stimulation; getting out of the house and into the world; and adding structure and pattern to life (Beckman, 1978).

Despite no consistent overall differences in reported happiness and life satisfaction (Wright, 1978), employed mothers generally seem to feel good physically and psychologically (Nye, 1974a). As a group, employed mothers report fewer physical symptoms than mothers who do not work, and they have a more positive image of themselves than do housewives (Feld, 1963). Among working-class women, those who work outside the home seem to have a greater sense of power over their lives (Seifer, 1973). When differences in mental health are found, they tend to show the employed woman as healthier (Nye, 1974a). Among highly talented college graduates fifteen to twenty-five years after graduation, the working mothers were higher in morale and self-esteem. The nonworking women had lower self-esteem and a lower sense of personal competence; they felt less attractive, expressed more concern over identity issues, and indicated greater loneliness (Birnbaum, 1975). Whereas the working women complained of a lack of *time* to do all the things they wanted, the homemakers complained of a lack of *challenge* and creative involvement in their lives.

These findings should not necessarily be interpreted as showing that outside work *causes* more positive feelings among well-educated women. It may be that the more confident women are the ones who choose to take jobs. To clarify the distinction between causes and consequences of work, it would be necessary to compare the health and happiness of family women before and after they took outside jobs.

Because men are expected to take on both family and work roles, there is little known about either the benefits or stresses of dual roles for men. The chief information in this area is indirect, but it suggests that responsibility for family and work roles is not particularly detrimental to men. As pointed out earlier, mental health statistics suggest that marriage (and thus probably family life) does men good: married men are less likely to experience mental illness than single, divorced, or widowed men (Gove, 1972). Of course, to understand this relationship more fully, it would be necessary to compare the psychological well-being of men with different degrees of actual family and work involvement. This may be increasingly possible as men display more variable commitments to family and work.

Interestingly, it sometimes turns out that men enjoy the changes in their roles that a wife's employment necessitates. Lein and her colleagues (1974) found that several of the husbands in the working couples they studied discovered that they enjoyed the extra time with their children and the sense of active participation in their development. Bernard (1974a) suggests that men whose wives contribute to family income have more options. They can support periods of unemployment or the risks involved in career changes.

Consequences for Marital Relationship

What effects do two major work commitments have on the structure of the marital roles? One of the major conclusions in this area is that there is a great distance between the egalitarian ideals couples voice and their actual practice (Rapoport & Rapoport, 1976). Epstein (1971) studied lawyer couples and found that although the wives had participated in family decisions more than traditional wives, their work within the law firm tended to be confined to the more routine, less prestigious tasks. Holmstrom (1972) studied twenty two-career couples. Although lip service was paid to equality between the sexes, actual decisions and arrangements were often based in the view that the man's career was more important. If ambition and plans were altered, it was the wife who typically made the bigger sacrifice.

Part of the problem cited by many men in transforming egalitarian ideals into reality is the constraints of current institutions. Men in Holmstrom's sample felt constrained in varying their own roles by the inflexibility of their work organizations. The inflexibility prevented them from accommodating to the requirements of a new organization of domestic work. Yet many women manage to work in the same organizations while juggling a full family commitment. Men seem to be not as practiced in the flexibility and sacrifices many working women display. Of course the stress on these women should not be minimized.

Related to the issue of egalitarian roles is the distribution of household responsibilities. Here findings are mixed. Rapoport and Rapoport (1976) found a great deal of variability in the dual-career families they studied during the 1960s. Frequently, however, the males did little beyond what males generally were doing to "help out" even in conventional families. Other studies they surveyed—including families in Scandinavian countries and Poland—had similar findings. Holmstrom (1972) found that wives in two-career families were not exclusively responsible for the performance of housekeeping or childrearing tasks. Frequently they had the assistance of hired help or their husbands. But no matter how much help the woman received, the domestic realm was defined ultimately as her responsibility. Pleck's (in press) review of the research led to a similar conclusion: there was no evidence that the average man with a working wife did significantly more child care or housework than the average married man whose wife did not work outside the home. Yet other authors disagree. Bahr (1974) concluded that, although employed wives tend to remain primarily responsible for household tasks, their husbands perform more of them than do husbands of nonemployed women, particularly if the wife is not highly committed to her work. These results need not be viewed as conflicting. Although men do share some of the household tasks when their wives work, in general they do not take on half the burden. More often than not, the wife does more work, as well as the very draining "work of worry" that signals true responsibility. Table 10.1 shows the minimal differences in the average daily time spent on household tasks by husbands and wives in families where the wife does or does not work outside the home.

Another stress faced by two-worker couples is simply work overload (Rapoport & Rapoport, 1976). There is often simply not enough time to fit in work, domestic tasks, entertainment, and leisure. One frequent complaint of two-worker couples is that they do not have enough time with their children (Gronseth, 1975; Rapoport & Rapoport, 1976). Frequently, entertainment and leisure must also be curtailed. This is unfortunate, since recreation can serve as a vehicle for dissipating the inevitable tensions that accumulate in close relationships. This might be one explanation for the greater conflict and lesser marital satisfaction in lower-class couples in which the wife is employed (Nye, 1974b). Bear in mind that this conflict is not necessarily a result of both spouses' working; it may reflect the lower level of financial resources that cause these lower-class wives to have to work.

TABLE 10.1 Average Daily Time Spent on Household Work

Number of children	Age of wife or youngest child	Nonemployed-wife families		Employed-wife families	
(1)	(2)	(3a)	(3b)	(4a)	(4b)
	Wife	*Wife*	*Husband*	*Wife*	*Husband*
	Under 25	5.1	0.9	3.5	1.4
None	25–39	5.9	1.2	3.6	1.4
	40–54	6.2	1.5	4.3	1.8
	55 and over	5.4	2.0	4.3	1.1
	Youngest child				
	12–17	7.1	1.7	4.8	1.7
Two	6–11	7.4	1.6	5.4	1.5
	2–5	8.2	1.6	6.2	1.7
	1	8.8	1.7	6.2	3.5
	Under 1	9.5	1.5	7.7	1.6

How to read this table:
Take, for example, a family with no children (col. 1) where the wife is between 25 and 39 years of age (col. 2 and row 2). If the wife is not employed (col. 3) she does an average of 5.9 hours per day (col. 3a) while her husband does an average of 1.2 hours per day (col. 3b). Even if the wife in this family works (col. 4) she still does 3.6 hours of housework (col. 4a) per day while her husband does an average of 1.4 hours per day (col. 4b).

Source: From Edwards, Reich, and Weisskopf, *The Capitalist System*, 2nd Ed., © 1978, p. 338. Reprinted by permission of Prentice-Hall, Inc., Englewood Cliffs, New Jersey.

In some couples, for both spouses to work may involve career sacrifice. Rapoport and Rapoport found that some couples accepted the idea of working less toward their own career goals, particularly after they reached a certain plateau. The one-career family might allow for greater career mobility, involvement, and higher eventual achievement for the working member. Whereas at one time, a career-oriented woman tried to decide whether she wanted a child badly enough to sacrifice some of her career, a man may find himself in a similar position today: is he willing to give up some of his career involvement so that he can enjoy his children and family life? The sixty- to eighty-hour work weeks that some professional and academic men are accustomed to are rarely possible when the men also share child care and domestic responsibilities, as well as leave time for involvement with their wives. If we add to this problem of hours the issues of potential competition and the necessity for joint decisions about careers, we can begin to appreciate some of the complexities that participants in dual-career couples face in their individual careers.

Another Look

Our study of working couples reveals how difficult true change is within the family. Children seem to survive nicely when both parents work outside the home, as do the individual spouses. Yet there are sacrifices, too—for example, in time spent in the individual careers and time spent together. Even in these couples who, on the surface, seem to be varying the traditional family roles, traditional roles remain substantially rooted. For the most part, the women still retain primary responsibility for the domestic, private sphere, even while they have added responsibilities in the public sphere. Women's movement out of the home does not seem to have significantly increased men's participation in the domestic realm. This may remind us of the historical and cross-cultural evidence we saw earlier concerning the importance of men's participation in the domestic sphere for equality between the sexes. From that perspective, it seems that, on the average, although families may be enjoying some benefits of women's increased public participation, they are not yet realizing the benefits of greater equality that might result from more fundamental changes in the work distributions of the sexes.

SINGLENESS

In the array of options that most people think of as the family, singleness is rarely considered. Yet one option exercised by an increased number of adults involves a search for protection and emotional sustenance outside the confines of marriage. Sometimes people deliberately eschew marriage, and sometimes singleness happens inadvertently, through death or divorce. Women, with their longer life spans and lower rates of remarriage, are particularly likely to be single at some point during adulthood. One author estimates that, at any one time, fully one-third of the adult women in the population are not married (Bequaert, 1976).

Despite their increasing numbers, single people remain a minority about whom society is ambivalent, at best. There has been a persistent belief among both social scientists and the public that people who do not marry do so because of some psychological deficit (Adams, 1976). Rather than a state freely chosen, singleness is often seen as an indicator of an "incapacity" for close relationships. "If you don't start being nicer to people, you'll end up a lonely old maid like your aunt," threatened the mother of an adolescent. Although strong elements of such images persist, they have been more recently mixed with scenes of "swinging singles." Attitudes toward singles run the gamut from envy and curiosity to pity.

On a broader scale, however, singles suffer from a lack of societal recognition. In a society that defines people as "————'s wife/husband" and "————'s mother/father," singles are an anomaly. To the extent that society is uncertain about the single's personal and social identity, she or he, too, might be expected to begin to feel like the "person who's not quite complete." This family-oriented culture sometimes seems to forget the existence of singles. The person-without-a-partner is often unwelcome at couple-oriented social events. The process can also be more subtle. For example, the head of an employee negotiating team stared blankly when a single woman pointed out that the new benefit package constituted a decrease in her pay, relative to her married colleagues. The employer would pay substantially more for the "family" than the "individual" health, dental, and legal insurance plans. More explicit efforts to pay salaries on the basis of need rather than experience and position would usually not be attempted.

Age, income, location, friendships, and degree of choice all influence the experience of singleness. Whatever their circumstances, most singles have to confront loneliness, a negative public image, and a lack of positive role models. Yet, someone who is struggling to make economic ends meet may despair of ever getting emotional ends to meet while single. A meaningless or exhausting job may leave a person with little of the extra energy needed to actively pursue close relationships that are not available at home. Isolation from other singles, old age, or a strong preference for marriage can all make the problems and anomie in singleness more difficult.

Perhaps the most consistent challenge facing singles is the dilemma of integration. All adults, in and outside families, must find ways to maintain a healthy degree of closeness with other people without compromising their own psychological identity. The dilemma has a different twist for singles, however; they tend to have an easier time than marrieds in holding onto their identities but a less clearly outlined solution to the interpersonal needs.

There is a strong suspicion in some circles that people who choose a single life style have a particularly strong interest in psychological autonomy (Adams, 1976). Many people choose singleness because they realize that a great deal of privacy and independence are essential to their well-being and happiness. Despite the norms in this culture favoring sociability, some people find that the joys of solitude outweigh the pains of occasional brushes with loneliness. In fact, women in one study reported that social isolation can be a teacher, a clarifier of goals and values (Bequaert, 1976). The person with an ever-present spouse or children may miss the opportunity to confront the noises of the self that readily fill silences. Much creative and intellectual work requires long periods of time alone, time that is not readily available to people immersed in families. Even doing nothing, all alone, can be a heady luxury for some people.

The striving for personal autonomy and identity is sometimes difficult for singles because their role is so ill-defined by society. Marriage and the new household that accompanies it unofficially indicate attainment of adulthood and separation from one's parents. Singles need some alternative processes to mark their adulthood and individuality. Interviews with singles suggest that housing can provide one such marker (Adams, 1976). For some singles, the establishment of their own clearly separate and independent homes also served as an explicit affirmation of their singleness. The message to the world was, "I am an adult who enjoys and deserves a comfortable homebase." These processes were apparent in both singles who lived alone and those in group living situations.

For most singles, the emphasis on psychological autonomy does not preclude close relationships with people. Married people have a built-in companion who is supposed to satisfy many of the intimacy needs. Singles' patterns of relationship have been found to be more fluid and flexible than the more exclusive, intensive attachments many married people have (Adams, 1976). Although relationships for many singles are qualitatively as rich as for marrieds, they differ in structure. Often this means, for singles, a greater variety in the sources of their relationships. They reach back further in time and across greater geographical distances, in a residual form of the extended family, as Adams' has said.

The number and range of these relationships serve an important role for singles. Such variety is necessary to increase the odds that companions will be available when needed. One potent side effect is a flexibility of possibilities. There are many degrees of intimacy and areas of special expertise. Without the false security of a spouse (and the implied guarantee of constant support and intimacy), singles often develop a wide range of relationships on which to draw.

Hence, there are both costs and benefits for people who elect a single life style. A strong sense of personal autonomy provides opportunity for development of an individual identity. Achieving intimacy becomes a challenge, but one that many single people manage with creativity and consistency.

SUMMARY AND CONCLUSIONS

Throughout this chapter we have seen that although adult family roles do have positive aspects, they also have a great many liabilities that seem to be associated with current constructions of the family. The difficulties built into today's marital, parental, and single roles are a handicap for persons who wish to aim for the integration, flexibility, situational appropriateness, and effectiveness that we see as associated with androgyny.

Women show the most obvious ill effects of these arrangements. Signs of psychological disturbance are statistically associated with the wife and mother roles, particularly when they are carried out as the primary ones and in isolation. Further, the extent of women's socialization to the wife and mother roles may be responsible for too much of an other-orientation and too little attention to self. Ironically, effective performance of women's family roles often requires agentic qualities such as stamina, responsibility, and independence in which women tend to be undertrained. Unfamiliarity with these qualities may also make the personal autonomy demanded in singlehood especially stressful for women.

Aspects of current family practices appear to be detrimental in some ways to men also, although this is less well documented. Men's generally lesser involvement in the family would seem to deprive them of full enjoyment of the pleasures and developmental demands of family life. The distance some men create between themselves and their families is perhaps partly a consequence of the socialization they receive. In the same way that many women might be poorly trained for the responsibilities of motherhood, many men might be inadequately trained for the intimacy of family relationships. Balswick and Peek (1971) suggest that many men are burdened by the inexpressiveness they have acquired. Men who are trained to deny and repress their emotions may often be found inadequate as husbands. They may also have greater difficulty in having their intimacy needs met outside marriage.

In thinking about these issues from a psychological and androgynous perspective, we focus on full development of options for each person. For a person to choose freely among life styles, she or he needs to feel competent in her or his capacities for both intimacy and independence. To the extent that socialization undertrains the sexes in either of these areas and directs them toward specific adult roles, free choice is not practiced and options are not real. Consistent planning for ways to meet these needs for separateness and togetherness seems to be necessary throughout the life span. Such awareness and planning is one way to increase the breadth of life-style options.

Attention must also be paid to the social context in which life planning and decisions are made. Laws, attitudes, expectations, and lack of cultural supports will likely remain as impediments to full exercise of options.

At the present time, the most visible change in family structures is women's increased movement out of the home and into the work world. As shown in the discussion of two-worker families, these changes are reflected primarily in the lives of women. The result is often additional burdens for the women. Although children do not seem to suffer and many women appear to fare better than when isolated in the home, there is still often a lack of equality in the work allocation within the marriages. A less obvious consequence of such one-directional change is further devaluation of communal, emotional, other-oriented qualities. It sometimes seems that in attempting to help women regain their agentic, self-oriented sides, social change artists lose sight of the valuable elements in women's traditional role in the family. For example, writers such as Van Dusen and Sheldon (1976) and Hoffman (1977) applaud the changing roles of women as the prescription for today's sex-role ills. They implicitly seem to accept the socially based value afforded independent achievement and self-oriented assertiveness. They imply that women will be better off when they leave their homes for the marketplace, this time as participants rather than consumers.

It seems then that women's moving into the labor force has not necessarily resulted in true change in family roles. For this to happen men must also become more heavily involved in the home sphere. The cross-cultural research discussed earlier in the chapter in fact suggests that relationships between the sexes are most egalitarian and divisions between the sexes are least pronounced in societies in which both men and women share extensively in childrearing and domestic tasks. Relationships are not egalitarian even when both sexes participate in the non-family production, if only women take on domestic responsibilities. One can speculate about the reasons for this pattern. It might be that frequent and regular interactions with family members help men develop their communal qualities and reduce divisions between the sexes. Without this involvement on the part of men, women's participation in childrearing sets them apart no matter what role they play in the paid labor force.

Changes in men's behavior are crucial to an adjustment of current home-work divisions, as suggested by research with dual-career families. Bernard (1974a) concluded that integrating a domestic and a worker role requires the cooperation of one's husband. One woman in Holmstrom's sample of dual-career couples went so far as to advise: "This really is the secret—to be careful who you marry" (1972, p. 137).

As changes in family roles come about, psychological research could contribute to their effectiveness by uncovering potential problems and solutions. For example, researchers could help establish the degree of adult-child interactions that maximize benefits while minimizing costs to both. There is a continued need for far-reaching examinations of the best child care arrangements. Are there certain children who thrive in a structured environment while others develop best in a more unstructured, family-type arrangement? Work might proceed in determining which children do best where. Perhaps one type of arrangement is best for infants, another for two-year-olds, and still another for the school-age child.

Other research could examine flexibility of adult family roles, including the cultural conditions that favor such flexibility. Efforts could be made to ascertain what institutional supports are necessary to assist such flexibility. Perhaps there are specific ways to help two-worker families, one-parent families, child-free couples, and single people select and enjoy their life-style options.

More systematic work also needs to be done in order to develop fuller appreciation of the benefits of family relationships. Many of the myths and images about the wonders of family life turn out to be untrue when reality is carefully examined. Yet, myths very often have a "kernel of truth." What is the truth in the myths about the family? Does parenthood promote the development of androgyny? If so, under what conditions? How? Can such conditions be created outside of parenthood? What is an optimal balance of dependence and independence in the family? What can family relationships teach people about the process of integrating contradictory feelings? Under what conditions do the inevitable conflicts of family life lead to growth and when do they contribute to a lack of movement or even disintegration?

One major question remains: How can we enable people to practice and enjoy family and work roles more fully if they so choose? An actual restructuring of society and its institutions seems necessary for current problems with marital and parental roles to be overcome. It is the differential assignment of the family and work spheres to the sexes that, in the final analysis, restricts personal options and is a major contributor to sex-role stereotypes and inequality of adult roles. Sigmund

Freud actually foresaw the issue when he remarked that the mark of the mentally healthy person is the ability both "to love and to work" (Erikson, 1963, p. 265). Figuring out ways to help all people—women and men—optimally perform both these tasks remains the major dilemma.

SELECTED READINGS

Adams, M. *Single blessedness*. New York: Basic Books, 1976.

Angelou, M. *I know why the caged bird sings*. New York: Random House, 1970.

Kagan, J., Kearsley, R. B., & Zelazo, P. R. *Infancy: Its place in human development*. Cambridge: Harvard University Press, 1978.

O'Kelly, C. G. *Women and men in society*. New York: Van Nostrand, 1980.

Rich, A. *Of woman born: Motherhood as experience and institution*. New York: Norton, 1976.

Rubin, L. B. *Worlds of pain: Life in the working class family*. New York: Basic Books, 1976.

Adult Roles at Work

Some type of paid work outside the home is a central part of adult life for most people. Work can bring order and meaning to life, as well as exaggerate the monotony and meaninglessness hidden in a technological society. It can provide opportunities to interact with others at the same time it isolates one from intimate relationships at home. For most people, work contributes to their sense of identity and their self-esteem—in both positive and negative ways.

In short, outside work is a mixed blessing long granted to men without question, and increasingly sought after by women. Ironically, although some women are looking from the confines of the home to the apparent opportunities for fulfillment in the workplace, some men and other women are longing for the flexibility of role and opportunity for personal growth that appear to be associated with freedom from paid work roles.

In this chapter we will examine these paradoxes associated with work. We will focus on the problems as well as the potential in paid work roles. An androgynous perspective requires exploration of the fullest range of options available to women and men so that they may both develop and use their potential, and enjoy work to the greatest possible extent. The concept of androgyny is built around the availability of choice—a wide range of skills and opportunities so that each person can freely make decisions. Any factors that interfere with the development and expression of these choices interfere with the expression of androgyny.

The emphasis in this chapter is on the ways current societal structures—particularly stereotyped sex roles—limit many people's full enjoyment of work and possibilities for change. What kind of paid work opportunities do women and men enjoy? How does the context of work affect one's enjoyment of it? Is it possible, or desirable, to integrate personal-familial roles with work-related roles? What kinds of relationships exist among stereotyped sex roles, economic conditions, and work? What sorts of changes in the workplace would facilitate more androgynous expressions of work roles?

VARIATIONS IN THE WORKPLACE

Imagine yourself a worker in an office filled with many desks that provide little privacy for the client interviews that are part of your job. Supervisors walking by can easily detect when you are making any forbidden "personal" phone calls. You were thirty-five minutes late for work this morning because there was a traffic accident along the way. Although you apologized to your supervisor, she or he told you to sit in the lounge for twenty-five minutes before starting to work, because work time can only be calculated in half-hour segments. Any nonwork-related conversations with your friend at the next desk are met by frowns from those around you. During break time and lunch time, the only periods when personal talk is permitted, the employees' lounge is filled with voices exchanging the details of home life and tales of clients encountered that day. Advancement happens on a fixed schedule and you know you have years before you are eligible for a supervisor's position yourself. At the end of the work day, your primary goal is to erase all thoughts of work from your mind, and direct your attention to your "real" concerns of family and friends.

Now imagine that you are a worker in a different office. This one has just as many desks, but they are enclosed with partitions for privacy. You were late for work that morning also. Your boss sympathized with the frustrations of sitting motionless in traffic. You are aware that you have a lot to get done today and might choose to skip your midmorning break or work a bit later to catch up. Without even thinking about it, you make a few phone calls to arrange for some repair work at your home and to check with the babysitter. Later in the morning you stop to talk with a friend at a nearby desk about plans for the weekend. The atmosphere in the office is pleasant and relaxed, and you hum to yourself as you sit down and become engrossed in your work. Your supervisor stops by to mention the good work you did in taking responsibility for a situation the day before. There are many opportunities for advancement with this company, and you look forward to new and challenging assignments in the months ahead. On the way home from work, you find yourself trying to puzzle through the details of a particularly knotty problem you have to confront the next day.

These examples are fairly accurate portrayals of two different jobs held by college graduates with similar degrees of training. These workers would be expected to have very different feelings about their jobs, and, perhaps, themselves. Quite possibly, their family lives would be very different also: the first worker might arrive home in a very different mood than the second. Personal and behavioral options are decidedly more restricted in the first job.

As most people experience it, work—and its accompanying satisfactions and dissatisfactions, joys and sorrows—is more than a job. The extent to which one looks forward to work, rather than dreading it, is related to factors such as pay, fringe benefits, social conditions, and health conditions. The sense that work is meaningful—and hence the worker is a valuable person—might hinge on the respect that others have for one's work, opportunities for advancement, the manner in which one is treated by supervisors, and one's autonomy on the job. Little things, like supportive coworkers and supervisors, opportunities to make personal phone calls, and even comfortable chairs, do a lot to convey a sense of respect for workers that enables them to feel and act as responsible adults.

Hence, discussions of work as one path for personal fulfillment must leave room for the fact that the experience of work varies greatly from job to job and setting to setting. Opportunities for personal flexibility are sometimes restricted by factors in the workplace.

Job Satisfaction

Amateur analyzers of occupational settings are sometimes tempted to dismiss variability in the quality of the workplace as a reflection of variability in the motivation in workers: "To many people, a job is just a minor part of themselves, something they do to earn a living. They aren't really emotionally involved in it. It's just something that they do."

Yet, for most people, this is not the case. After interviewing many people in a range of occupations and social classes concerning their feelings about their jobs, one journalist was struck with the importance to people of meaningful work (Terkel, 1974). As he put it, for many, work involves "a search for daily meaning as well as daily bread, for recognition as well as cash, for astonishment rather than torpor" (p. xi). Within this society, a job is a central feature of life for most people. It fixes one's place in economics, politics, and society, while influencing friendships, family relations, and even types of recreation (Kennedy, 1977).

Social scientists have come to similar conclusions in their investigations. A group of working-class men were found to change jobs frequently, in a search not only for higher pay, but also for work that could provide meaning, purpose, and dignity (Rubin, 1976). A sample of 1500 American workers revealed a desire for control over their lives and autonomy as well as feelings of personal meaningfulness in their work. They rated the following job factors, in order, as most important to them: (1) interesting work; (2) enough help and equipment to get the job done; (3) enough information to get the job done; (4) enough authority to get the job done; (5) good pay; (6) opportunity to develop special abilities; (7) job security; and (8) seeing the results of one's work (Special Task Force, 1978).

Factors such as these which are intrinsic to a job seem to be included in job satisfaction for women as well (Andrisani, 1978). Although black women studied were considerably less satisfied than white women, satisfactions with work stemmed from similar sources for both groups—something within the job itself or the interpersonal satisfactions it provided. Additional studies in this area show that workers with high job satisfaction tend to have jobs offering high pay, autonomy, prestige, opportunities for advancement, skill utilization, and skill development (Laws, 1976). People vary greatly in their likelihood of reaching similar levels of employment.

Occupational Segregation

In principle, there are no barriers in this "land of opportunity" to the types of jobs people of varying races, social classes, and sexes can hold. Yet, in reality, there are striking differences across race, class, and sex in wages paid and types of work done by the average person. Female workers tend to be concentrated in occupations that are predominantly female and lower paid; male workers are more evenly dispersed throughout the status and income hierarchy. This separate and unequal structure of the workplace has been called "occupational segregation."

Throughout this century, the proportion of women who work has steadily increased, so that by 1974, more than half of all women between eighteen and sixty-four years of age were in the labor force, as shown in Figure 11.1. Initially it was young single women who made up the majority of the female labor force. They were joined by older married women, then by mothers of school-age children, and, most recently, by still-increasing proportions of mothers of preschool children (Howe, 1977). Table 11.1 illustrates these changes.

These women are paid less, however, than men who work, despite similarities of education or work experience (O'Kelly, 1979). In 1965, women who worked full time earned 60 percent as much as did male full-time workers. By 1974, this proportion had not increased and in fact had dropped slightly, to 57 percent, in spite of passage of legislation designed to outlaw sex discrimination in wages. (See Table 11.2.) The female-male earnings gap remains even when women are compared to men with the same amount of work experience and education. In fact, in 1974 male high school dropouts earned 10 percent *more* than women with four or more years of college who were working full time. The women who benefit the

FIGURE 11.1

Women Workers in the Labor Force.

1890-1930: Persons 14 years and older in the total labor force.
1940-1974: Persons 16 years and older in the civilian labor force.

From Edwards, Reich, and Weisskopf, *The Capitalist System,* 2nd Ed., © 1978, pp. 336. Reprinted by permission of Prentice-Hall, Inc., Englewood Cliffs, New Jersey.

TABLE 11.1 Labor Force Participation Rates of Women by Marital and Child Status

| Year | Never married | Married, husband present | | | Widowed separated divorced |
		Total	With children 6–17 only	With children 0–6	
1890	36.9%	4.5%	—	—	28.6%
1940	48.1	14.7	—	—	36.2
1950	50.5	23.8	28.3	11.9	37.8
1960	44.1	30.5	39.0	18.6	40.0
1970	53.0	40.8	49.2	30.3	39.1
1974	57.2	43.0	51.2	34.4	40.9

Source: From Edwards, Reich, and Weisskopf, *The Capitalist System*, 2nd Ed., © 1978, p. 337. Reprinted by permission of Prentice-Hall, Inc., Englewood Cliffs, New Jersey.

least economically from their education, compared to equally educated men, are those who drop out of the labor force for extended time periods (to rear children, for example); these women are concentrated in much lower paying jobs than men at every educational level (O'Kelly, 1979)

The earnings gap is felt more strongly by black than white women. In terms of average income, white males earn more than black males, who earn more than white females, who earn more than black females. In order, median weekly earnings for these groups in 1977 were $259, $201, $157, and $147 (U.S. Bureau of the Census, 1977).

As race compounds sex differences in income, so does social class. For example, almost by definition higher social class is associated with higher income. Yet, although female-dominated fields such as teaching and nursing are rated as professions, their practitioners are frequently paid about the same as male laborers, a group substantially further down on the educational and social class scale (Safilios-Rothschild, 1976). Women laborers or women in unskilled jobs could be expected to earn substantially less than male laborers with similar social class ratings.

Some would argue that the earnings gap is justified because women do not have to support families as men do. Yet this is not true; the majority of women work because of economic need. Fully two-thirds of all women workers are single, divorced, widowed, or separated, or have husbands who earn less than $7000 per year. Half the women involved in divorce action do not receive alimony or child support; the median payment for the 50 percent who do is $1300 per year, hardly a livable income. Married women who work full time contribute on average 40 percent to family income (Griffiths, 1976).

There are also clear differences across sex, race, and class in type of work performed by the average person. As one goes down the occupational hierarchy, one is increasingly likely to find workers who are female and nonwhite. One

TABLE 11.2 Median Total Money Income of Males and Females[a]

Year	Full-time workers			Percent full-time[b]		All income recipients		
	Male	Female	F/M	Male	Female	Male	Female	F/M
1947	—	—	—	—	—	$2,230	$1,027	.46
1950	—	—	—	—	—	2,570	953	.37
1955	$ 4,246	$2,734	.64	63.1	31.1	3,358	1,120	.33
1960	5,435	3,296	.60	58.3	28.3	4,081	1,262	.31
1965	6,479	3,883	.60	59.8	29.3	4,824	1,564	.32
1970	9,184	5,440	.59	56.6	30.0	6,670	2,237	.34
1974	12,152	6,957	.57	55.9	30.4	8,379	3,079	.37

a Income in current prices of civilians 14 years or older.
b Year-round full-time workers—i.e., those working at least 35 hours per week and 50 weeks per year.

Source: From Edwards, Reich, and Weisskopf, *The Capitalist System*, 2nd Ed., © 1978, p. 340. Reprinted by permission of Prentice-Hall, Inc., Englewood Cliffs, New Jersey.

occupation—clerical work—accounts for over one-third of the entire female labor force (Howe). Women represent a majority in several occupations such as registered nurses (97 percent female in 1977), hairdressers (88 percent), preschool teachers (99 percent), sales clerks (70 percent), and secretaries (99 percent) (U.S. Bureau of the Census, 1977). At the same time, they are a minority in many other occupations: accountants (28 percent), physicians (11 percent), lawyers (10 percent), engineers (3 percent), carpenters (0.9 percent), electricians (0.2 percent), and plumbers (0.5 percent) (U.S. Bureau of the Census, 1977).

Sex differences are also frequently found in studies of actual behavior at work. Men are said to be more ambitious, more involved in their work, and more oriented toward the task at hand than women. Women are said to be less motivated and less committed to their work, and to be more concerned with relationships at work rather than with the task (Crowley, Levitan, & Quinn, 1973; Davis, 1967; Johnston, 1975). Findings such as these, and observations to support them, are sometimes used to explain why women are found so infrequently in high positions within organizations. Basically, women are said to be less interested in the actual work they do than men are.

This argument, which takes an exceptionalistic perspective (Chapter 2), is that women act less interested in their work because they are women. In the following pages we will examine some aspects of the work situation in itself that serve as alternative explanations.

Explanations for Variations in the Workplace

The existence of variations in the workplace is not a matter of debate to those who examine the figures or observe the world around them. The more important questions, however, concern the *why* of these inequalities. A variety of individual and cultural explanations have been proposed.

With their focus on the individual person, psychologists have tended to explain these variations in terms of differences in personality, motivation, or ability. For example, as demonstrated in Chapter 9, women's lower levels of achievement were explained as a sign of their low "needs for achievement." More recently, psychologists have tried to ascribe women's lower achievements to a "fear of success." Compared to the male professional ideal, most women and blue-collar workers are said to "lack career commitment." The cause is said to be something lacking in their personalities, rather than something lacking in their jobs or perhaps something more pressing and involving outside their jobs.

An additional psychological explanation for sex differences in work options is childhood socialization. Chapters 7 and 8 detailed a great many of the influences on children's development of sex-role related behaviors and attitudes, including parental child-rearing practices, schools, media, language, and peers. Basically, the average boy is more likely to be socialized to desire and actively pursue a career outside the family. As early as the second grade, children have been found to differ in their occupational choices (Siegel, 1973). Boys choose about twice the number of occupations that girls choose. Of twenty-nine girls, twenty selected either "teacher" or "nurse," but among thirty-two boys not more than three were in any single category, except for seven boys who chose "policeman." Although

young children appear to be quite stereotyped in their beliefs about sex appropriateness of occupations, people seem to become more liberal through college—
but then they become stereotyped again in adulthood (Gutek & Nieva, 1978).

Despite the intrinsic appeal of childhood socialization as an explanation for
occupational segregation, it does not tell the whole story, Even if one is blessed
with parents, teachers, and counselors who emphasize options and flexibility in
occupational choice, one must still confront—directly and indirectly, externally and
internally—societal and occupational structures that convey specific ideas about
the roles of women and men in the workplace.

The childhood socialization explanation for occupational development also
neglects the fact that change and development continue past childhood (Levinson
et al., 1978; Lowenthal, Thurnher, & Chiriboga, 1975; Vaillant, 1977). Many career
development theories such as those of Super and Holland seem to be based on
the assumption that, by their early twenties, people have carefully assessed their
skills, interests, and values, as well as the job market (Osipow, 1968). The result
is said to be a career choice that remains relatively stable, so that at fifty a person
will be doing the same kinds of things she or he was doing in her or his twenties.
Women's traditional roles as homemakers and childbearers clearly operate to
exclude them from adhering to such a "straight-and-narrow path." Yet it is becoming increasingly apparent that even most men do not follow such a path. Rather,
for both females and males, occupational development involves starts and stops,
changes and stability, reappraisal and growth, and sometimes regression and
stagnation. Occupational development involves more than a career choice. It also
involves coping (or not coping) with the joys, frustrations, barriers, disappoint-
ments, and accomplishments encountered.

Many psychologists' implicit attitude of acceptance toward differences in the
work experience for females and males has been revealed in their frequent failure
to examine these variations. Men have served as the standard for theories and
research about work. Despite the existence of groups of people who do not seem
to be developing their talents fully in the workplace, researchers in career development have traditionally focused on the group most likely to succeed in careers:
white, middle-class males (Laws, 1976). Male professionals tend to be used as the
standard for work motivation. They are found to work from an internalized devotion
to the task, independent of pay rates and a forty-hour work week. Work is often
presented as the central concern in their lives.

On the occasions when women have served as the focus for studies of career
development, the emphasis has been on middle-class women and the questions
have explored aspects of their pasts that caused them to "deviate" from the usual
feminine path. Frequently, questions were phrased and conclusions drawn in the
context of a "compensatory model" of career development in women (Almquist
& Angrist, 1970). The basis for this model is the assumption that women become
interested in achievement in order to compensate for their inadequacies in the
more "normal" (for women) affiliative realm. Lewis (1968) exemplified this view in
his description of girls planning a career as frustrated, dissatisfied, and less well-
adjusted than those content to become housewives. This was the view toward
career-oriented women emphasized in the 1950s and most of the 1960s (Helson,
1972).

As attitudes toward career-oriented women changed in the 1970s, so did the design and interpretation of psychological research. Recent studies portray achieving women in a much more positive light. Rather than trying to decide whether careers are good or bad for women, recent researchers have examined these women in more detail in order to capture the complexity of their motives and development, as well as social and institutional limitations to full development (Helson, 1972).

Another Look

We have seen that jobs vary tremendously in the financial and psychological rewards they offer. Factors within the job that are related to those rewards often vary with the sex, race, and social class of the worker. However, most psychologists' approach to development toward and success in the workplace has focused on the individual person. Success or failure has been attributed to elements of "personality," and to the effects of socialization on the child. The neglect of women workers, or treatment of them as "deviates" from a male norm of accomplishment has gone further to carry the subtle suggestion that each person is responsible for her or his position in the workplace.

Although each person is ultimately responsible, of course, for accepting or rejecting the challenges of the workplace, many external factors are exerting their influence almost continually. In the following sections we will discuss a number of these factors—elements of the organization, employees and supervisors, peers, and family—and how they influence development toward and behavior in the workplace.

Although these external factors will be discussed separately from the individual person, we do realize that the external and internal cannot really be separated. They overlap to form a self-perpetuating cycle. For example, sex discrimination could be considered an "external" factor that is "internalized" by an individual woman so that she reduces her aspirations at work. Her supervisors notice her low aspirations and use them as evidence to support continued sex discrimination. Investigations at the individual level of analysis would note only the low aspirations, whereas investigations at the external level might note the sex discrimination. Either explanation alone is incomplete, however, for the internalization does not occur without the external pressure, and the external pressures would be less effective if they were not internalized.

Thus, in looking at factors associated with the development of work attitudes and behavior we will focus on several levels of analysis. Findings to support one explanation need not preclude explanations at different levels.

ORGANIZATIONAL FACTORS IN THE WORKPLACE

Schools, government agencies, hospitals and corporations are all considered organizations. If one envisions an organizational power structure as a set of pyramids, one sees pyramids with both women and men at the base, increasing percentages of men as one moves up the pyramid structure, and finally almost all men at the top. In one recent survey of 163 American companies (reported in

Kanter, 1977), women held *none* of the management jobs in over three-fourths of those companies. For the banking industry, although the number of female and male bank tellers was nearly equal in 1969, over 80 percent of bank officers and financial managers were men (Kanter, 1977). As discussed in Chapter 8, schools are organized with female teachers predominating in the lower grades and males at the college level. Even in the lower grades, females are more likely than males to be found in the classroom than the principal's or superintendent's office.

At the Top: A Male World

In a book entitled *Men and Women of the Corporation* (1977), Rosabeth Moss Kanter analyzed the effect of organizational factors on the behavior of workers. These factors are useful in understanding sex differences in the workplace and, thus, Kanter's work will serve as our major source in this discussion.

Modern management theory stresses rationality and efficiency. Historically, institutions were designed to suppress irrationality, personality, and emotionality (Kanter, 1977). Emotion enters in only by way of the fact that worker's emotionality needs to be understood by management so that productivity can be enhanced.

In light of the overriding value on rationality and efficiency in organizations, there is little room for women who even hint of stereotyped femininity. The qualities valued by organizations tend to be those stereotypically associated with males. These qualities run directly counter to the stereotyped feminine concern with interpersonal intimacy and emotionality.

With this emphasis on rationality and efficiency, organizations would be expected to be highly structured. Yet there is a vagueness in organizational workings, particularly at the top. Jobs at the top are relatively unstructured, purposes have to be formulated, problems and procedures cannot always be foreseen. The criteria for "success" or "good" decisions are less certain at high management levels. In short, there is an aura of uncertainty at the top of organizations (Kanter, 1977).

In circumstances of uncertainty, people are forced to trust one another a great deal. Yet trust is difficult among strangers, or with people unlike oneself. For example, a student might more readily trust another student, particularly one of the same age, sex, race, and socioeconomic status, than a teacher or stranger from a different setting. The similar other is easier to trust because she or he is more predictable. It is for this reason, according to Kanter, that conformity and homogeneity are so highly valued in organizations. The three-piece-suited executives with identical shoes, attache cases, and haircuts may provide rich material for satire, yet their similarity serves a function. It increases their ease with and trust in each other. All else being equal, similar persons are better able to understand and count on one another.

Although such homogeneity makes sense from one organizational perspective, it presents problems for the entry of nonsimilar persons—women, minorities, and people from nonmiddle-class backgrounds. Even if an organization hires them, it is not likely to readily include them in the inner circles of decision making and power.

This male predominance both in numbers and values at the top of organizations is often reflected in actual policies. With few women in the board room to provide reality testing, myths about women's incompetence and lack of commitment can flourish. Such myths frequently serve as the foundation for organizational hesitancies to hire and promote women to top positions.

The emphasis on efficiency leaves little room for companies to provide "nonessential" services that cost money, such as on-site day care facilities. Yet such provisions for child care could well enhance parents' willingness to work, concentration at work (because they would be less likely to worry about their children), and enjoyment of work. Because women so often take the primary responsibility for child care, they would perhaps be most likely to benefit, and would perhaps then work more fully to their abilities.

The male orientation at the top of organizations may also be partly responsible for policies that have not permitted benefits for pregnancy leaves, maternity leaves, and paternity leaves. Often, women have been expected to mold their reproductive lives to the policies of the organization. Those who did not choose to do so dropped out of the work force, losing seniority rights and decreasing chances of promotions should they ever reenter the job market.

It seems that the male predominance at the top of organizations makes it more difficult for many women to be accepted and to function comfortably within organizations, particularly at top levels. At the same time, this predominance of males facilitates occupational enhancement of other males, particularly those who fit the masculine stereotype and reflect the "right" social class and ethnic background. This does not necessarily mean that women and other men would find it impossible to exist and thrive in organizations. It simply suggests that they would be working at a disadvantage.

Opportunity

Opportunity for advancement in a job is a self-fulfilling prophecy. The dog who is born of championship stock is, as a rule, fussed over, fed carefully, trained, and groomed in such a way that its chances of becoming a champion are greatly enhanced. In a similar way, those who expect and are expected to succeed generally receive and use a full range of opportunities for success.

The phenomenon can perhaps be more easily understood if we look at academic experience. Contrast the behavior of "A" high school students who know they can go on to college with that of "D" students for whom college is an impossibility. The "A" students are more likely to be given the better teachers, put in more interesting and stimulating classes, granted greater flexibility in scheduling, and respected by peers and teachers. Their behavior reflects these opportunities: they work hard, are interested in the material, learn a lot, maintain a good balance of socializing and studying, and readily move on to top colleges. At the same time, the "D" students are granted fewer opportunities: their classes are less interesting and teachers less committed, they are subjected to stricter enforcement of school rules, and they are looked down on by the achieving students. If they stay in school for long, they probably do so only because of the strong peer network they have established with others like themselves. School becomes a place where socializing takes precedence over academics. School officials say these students have a "bad attitude" and, in fact, they do. They do not end up with the grades, the recommendations, or the interest for going to college.

To what extent was the behavior of the low-achieving group a result of initial low talent or motivation, and to what extent was it a function of the opportunity structure that shut them out? This is the type of question posed by Kanter as she observed the range of work behavior in organizations.

Kanter's conclusion was that lack of opportunity in an organization plays a major role in the average differences found in the work behavior of women and men. In a long-term study of one organization, she compared the behavior of people at different ends of the opportunity scale. Those in jobs with good advancement prospects (e.g., from sales to management) tended to have high aspirations, a strong commitment, and a good sense of organizational responsibility. Those in dead-end jobs (e.g., clerical worker) had lower levels of aspirations, were concerned with security, engaged in low-risk activities, and took a greater interest in the social experiences work provided. People who were blocked from movement upward were more likely to seek satisfaction through connections with others. They talked more often and more openly about life outside, thought about leaving, and had a greater involvement in outside activities. Such differences remained even when factors such as job content, salary, or grade level of job were kept constant.

These phenomena are not confined to white-collar workers. A study of male workers in an automobile assembly plant found that they emphasized leisure and consumption of goods rather than their jobs (Chinoy, 1955).

Some people claim that the relationship between work behavior and opportunity is that the work behavior itself leads to the opportunities for advancement. To return to the example of the students, the "A" students were given the opportunity for college because they studied hard, were well behaved, and did well. Within organizations, this would mean that the young man in sales is promoted because he is such a go-getter, whereas the female file clerk is not promoted because she seems more interested in talking to her friends than in doing her work. However, more highly controlled studies, which can separate cause from effect, tend not to support this interpretation.

In the case of opportunity, it appears that opportunity can in fact be a cause of work behavior, rather than only vice versa. Opportunity for mobility did affect workers' behavior in one experimental study (Cohen, 1958). Men were put into groups and then their behavior related to some task was observed. In one type of group the men knew they were permitted to earn a place in a better group, whereas in the other type the men knew there was no chance for mobility. Keep in mind that the men were assigned to groups randomly, so that each group had a mix of personalities and abilities. Men who were in the mobile groups showed greater concern for the task, suppressed irrelevant communications, were less critical of higher groups, and were more oriented toward the higher groups than their peer group. The nonmobiles looked like the stereotype of the typical female worker: they centered their attention on the people in their group, neglected the higher groups, were openly critical of the upper groups, and were less involved in the task.

Findings such as these suggest that one's attitude and behavior at work can be a function of opportunities for advancement. Those with few opportunities to move up, a situation in many women's jobs, tend to lose interest in the task at hand. They tend to focus instead on the interpersonal aspects of the work situation and appear to be alienated from their jobs.

Power

Power is an important part of the working experience, both for those who have it and those who do not. As used here, power within organizations refers to autonomy and freedom of action, not necessarily domination of other people. The person with power in an organization is the one who can set her or his own schedule (within reason), make decisions about how to handle a job, set priorities for self and group, and engage the assistance of others. Prestige, the extras that make work easier and more enjoyable, and a sense of control often accompany powerful positions.

The manner in which the powerful exercise their power, in turn, directly affects those beneath them in the hierarchy. A harsh, demanding, arbitrary boss who offers little support, encouragement, or training can make work a miserable experience. At the same time, bosses can do much to make work both pleasurable and rewarding: they can treat one with respect, involve one in decision making, and help one develop further.

As discussed earlier, workers tend to prefer male to female leaders. Leaders of organizations also tend to worry about women's lack of potential for high-level positions. The word is that women don't make good bosses: they are overly concerned with details, too critical, too rigid, and controlling; they supervise too closely and take things too personally (Kanter, 1977; Laird & Laird, 1942). Workers at all levels of organization have differential views of female and male performance as bosses. In one case, subordinates, peers, and supervisors rated specific female and male managers along particular performance dimensions (Freston & Coleman, 1978). In some ways, the perceptions of male managers fit the male stereotype: males were seen as more task- than person-oriented, less actively seeking ideas of others, and more authoritarian. Yet they were also rated high on interpersonal skills such as trust and low on defensiveness. Many of the ratings of women managers also fit the female stereotype: nurturing, protective, cooperative, and collaborative. This stereotypic view was in conflict with the fact that the women were also seen as arbitrary and closed under stress.

The leadership styles of both women and men are seen to include interpersonal skills. Male leaders, however, are perceived as combining those skills with an instrumental ("get the job done") tactic, whereas women are said to combine it with rather rigid tactics.

Effective leadership has been found to be a function of both human relations skills and power within the system (Pelz, 1952). A boss who has warm relationships with workers can find no guarantee of high employee morale or productivity unless she or he can combine these assets with real influence upward in the hierarchy. Although working for a nice boss may be initially pleasant it can become discouraging if her or his low power results in organizational decisions adversely affecting the entire department, low opportunities for promotion of subordinates (since her or his recommendation carries little weight), and lower quality working conditions. Bosses with low power make unpopular and often ineffective leaders. As Kanter puts it, people prefer winners to losers, the bosses who can back up promises and threats as well as easily make changes in the situations of subordinates.

People's negative perceptions of female leaders may well reflect the low power women leaders often have within their organizations (Kanter, 1977). The management jobs women do hold frequently involve little real influence at the organizational level: supervising secretaries or clerical workers, staff jobs in personnel or public relations. Even at the management level, these positions are not where real decision making goes on.

Kanter details many of people's behavioral responses to powerlessness, and suggests that they are similar to the expected and sometimes actual behavior of women in responsible positions. Individual leaders who lack power upward in the organizational hierarchy turn to restrictive control over their subordinates. They become critical, bossy, and controlling, and they supervise subordinates more closely. Among male air force officers, those with low status and advancement potential tended to be more directive, rigid, and authoritarian (Hetzler, 1955).

People who lack real power also are more likely to turn to rules as a power tool. They are more cautious about making mistakes, and concentrate on getting everything right according to the rules. They are less flexible and demand conformity from those below them, out of a need to protect their own positions. For example, the teacher who is low on the college totem pole might become rigid about order, attendance, and assignments for students, as a response to her or his own vulnerability. The teacher who has strong alliances with the administration and some formal or informal influence on the running of the college can be more secure in her or his sense of power. This power is reflected in a more relaxed attitude to rules and regulations, so that she or he can be more responsive to the vagaries of student needs and situational shifts. The focus in the second teacher's class can more easily be placed on the task at hand: learning and development in students. A similar process exists in business organizations.

In short, simply being placed in a leadership position is no assurance that one will effectively lead. Respect, credibility, security, and opportunities for alliances are all part of effective leadership, and these require real power. The leader who has low power finds it harder to mobilize others and hence is cut off from further power. A downward spiral of decreasing power begins.

Women are not granted this necessary power as frequently and readily as men are. Power is acquired through a variety of sources—from mentors, high expectations of superiors, and reactions of subordinates, as well as one's own self-presentation and performance. Because of the differential expectations of the sexes inherent in sex-role stereotypes, women's options to effectively develop power in the workplace are more limited than men's.

Proportions

The experience of work is influenced not only by opportunities and power, but also by a person's status as a minority or majority member. Being a minority member limits a person's options in the workplace, both directly and indirectly.

Perhaps the easiest way to imagine the experience of minority status is to recall a situation in which you were the only woman or man or black or white in a social situation. Initially at least there is often a feeling of uneasiness or nervousness. As things loosen up you might be called on to speak for your group by giving the "woman's [man's, black's, white's] perspective" on some issue under discussion. As a minority you are at once more visible and less free to act (and be perceived) as an individual person. To extend the experience to the workplace, add the pressures of work itself, and multiply the result by eight hours a day, five days a week, fifty-two weeks a year. Work becomes an experience in which one is the outsider, the different, the exception, the "other." Such a context can easily affect both one's own behavior and the behaviors of the people with whom one works.

Because fewer women than men work, and because women's numbers are disproportionately low at the middle and upper levels of the status hierarchy, women are often a minority in the workplace. Such a situation is more likely to occur at the middle- and upper-status levels.

Minorities, by definition, are distinctive. They cannot help but stand out. Almost everyone will know the two plant supervisors who are female rather than the thirty who are male. Likewise, the twenty female professors at a college are more visible and more likely to be recognized than their 200 male colleagues. For example, a male teacher at College X was at a conference 1000 miles from the college. There he met a woman who said, "My friend ———— teaches at College X. Do you know her?" Immediately he replied, "Yes, she's the one who doesn't dress very well." Meanwhile the woman under discussion had no idea who her colleague at College X was from an intellectual or fashion perspective. The fact that she was one of very few female faculty members at College X increased her visibility. Likewise, the "lady doctor" and "woman lawyer" are quickly known throughout the small town when they set up practice. In each case, the females are "on display" nearly all the time, so that their work habits, social lives, and even style of dress are more noticeable than those of males.

Such exposure can have both advantages and disadvantages. If one is a candidate for political office, interested in attracting clients, or struggling to catch the notice of the person in charge of promotions, being a minority is a form of free advertising. Whenever being noticed is important, the token woman has one advantage. Yet the glow of the spotlight can become an uncomfortable glare when one makes a mistake that, for most people, would go unnoticed. Further, the very visibility that can be so advantageous in bringing the minority person to the attention of others serves also to decrease the probability that that person will be perceived as an individual. The token becomes the symbol for her entire group and her every act is taken as an indicator of how women perform (Kanter, 1977).

Minorities must contend not only with their high visibility, but also with the fact that their presence often produces a tightening of bonds in the majority group. The presence of one "different" person (the woman) makes all the "similar" people (the men) aware of what they have in common. Hence Kanter found that when male managers in one company had token women in their group, they were more likely to display elements of their "male culture": off-color jokes, sports stories, and tales of prowess. Yet, when the men were alone, these themes were less strong and were accompanied by company gossip and domestic talk. It is as if the presence of token females made the males more aware of, and more likely to show, the ways they differed from the tokens. Such exaggerated masculinity makes it difficult for the women to forget their outsider status.

A tendency seems to be to heighten the distinctions, to separate minorities from majorities. Yet Kanter found that sometimes the minority women were given an opportunity, through a "loyalty test," to join the majority. Basically such a test required the minority to choose sides: would she support "her" group or "their" group? Sometimes the test involved prejudicial remarks about other women in the presence of token women. Would the minority member stand up for her group, let the remark slide, or participate in the statements? Other test situations involved humor: would the token women allow themselves and their group to provide a source of humor for the group? On a broader scale, would the token women accept their situation as established by the majority or press for more advances?

Once minorities become visible and the majority group exaggerates its own distinctiveness, the way is paved for characterization of the minority members. The minority member is unusual, "strange," difficult for the majority members to predict and understand. In the context of such uncertainty, a frequent response is to revert to stereotypes. The majority looks on the minority in ways that are familiar and comfortable. The female manager is treated like a secretary, and expected to make coffee. The female professor is mistaken for a student and asked, in no uncertain terms, if the "professor has given his permission" for her to pick up the exams. The stereotyping extends beyond these sometimes (briefly) amusing cases of "mistaken identity." Men are accustomed to reacting to women in certain roles: wife, mother, daughter, sister. Not infrequently, they put the women with whom they work in similar categories, simply to structure the interaction along more predictable lines. Hence, token women sometimes find themselves in the role of mother, seductress, or pet (Kanter, 1977).

Since stereotypes can influence perceptions and such expectations can influence the actual behavior under observation, the majority members sometimes find their stereotypes being confirmed. If one expects women to be cute little pets who are giggly and frivolous, one will probably treat women in a light, joking, manner. It would not be surprising then if women react in similar ways, at least in this relationship. Hence, the stereotype is confirmed: women aren't serious enough for the "real" and important work of the company.

Confirming the stereotyped image of themselves is only one way a minority member may react to his or her minority status. Kanter has discerned several common responses in her studies of organizations.

One set of responses involves an acceptance of one's outsider status. Differences from the majority group are perceived and regarded as immutable. Relationships with colleagues are friendly but distant. The workplace is treated as a place where one can do the job, but where one doesn't really belong. The low priority given to personal relationships at work makes it harder for the worker to build the all-important alliances throughout the organization that can serve as a basis for power at work. Work becomes a somewhat lonely place where one remains an outsider without much support. No matter how competent or hard-working the person is, it is hard to imagine that superiors would single out that person for promotion.

For some minority members the context leads to conservative, low-risk behavior on the job. They hesitate to do anything to make themselves more visible than they already are. They almost seem to try to be invisible, to hide. They may hesitate to move out of their present work surroundings, because they wish to maintain their gains against stereotyped perceptions in their current setting.

Another response is to prove one's loyalty to the majority by becoming as much like them as possible. In this strategy one essentially denies one's minority status. One defines oneself as an "exception" and turns against one's own social category.

It is hard to escape the inner psychic costs of minority status in the workplace. The stress of being "not quite legitimate" may be subtle but is often present. At the very least, many women in token positions have to work twice as hard in order to overcome stereotypes and avoid mistakes in their highly visible positions. Self-distortion presents a nagging threat: "My boss told me I was seductive in dealing with clients. I *think* that simply reflects his expectations. He assumes a female will use her feminine wiles to make a sale, so that's what he sees. But maybe I *was* being seductive. . . ." The strength and uniformity of much of the majority group's perspective sows the seeds of self-doubt. It is difficult to attribute disturbing experiences and attitudes to your visibility, to majority group bonding, or to stereotyping when you are the only one who perceives it that way.

Although this list of responses is not exhaustive, it suggests that minority status can affect one's attitude toward and behavior on the job. These phenomena are not limited to token women in organizations. Male nurses, for example, have been found to be isolated from the other nurses and placed in stereotypical positions (jobs the women find distasteful or considered "men's work"), apparently as a function of their minority status (Segal, 1962).

Homemaking

Although the home is not usually considered an organization in the same sense as a school, hospital, or corporation is, work in the home is affected by status, autonomy, and structure, just as is work in more formal organizations. Whether they choose to combine it with outside work or not, most women are involved with homemaking. In recent years, women who choose to do homemaking full time have reported feeling "put down" by women moving to jobs outside the home. Feminists are blamed for devaluing the tasks that women perform in the home.

Yet the problems with homemaking seem to be broader than the feminists' devaluation. For example, homemakers appear to be in poorer mental and physical health than other women. Compared to women with jobs outside the home (most of whom are married and, hence, supposedly more likely to be at risk, according to Chapter 10), housewives are more likely to report having had a "nervous breakdown," to report nervousness, inertia, insomnia, trembling hands, nightmares, perspiring hands, fainting, headaches, dizziness, and heart palpitations (Bernard, 1972).

Part of the difficulties experienced by housewives may be related to the low status with which their work is regarded by society at large and by their own husbands. The role of housewife is not given high social rank in any of the common status ranking systems (Lopata, 1971). This is not surprising, for the role is unpaid and does not require extensive training as do the usual high-prestige occupations such as physician. At the individual level, Komarovsky (1973) found that depreciating remarks about housewifery were not uncommon, even among men with traditional views of women's roles. One conservative young man remarked, "A woman who works is more interesting than a housewife." Another said, "It must be boring sitting around the house doing the same thing day in, day out. I don't have much respect for the type of woman whom I see doing the detergent commercials on TV." (Komarovsky, 1973, p. 880). These comments become even more remarkable when one remembers that, at the same time, the young men expected their own wives to put home over career. Essentially the young men were saying: "Tasks in the home sphere are necessary and I expect my wife will love to do them, but they are also boring." The marital relationship in such cases can easily suffer as a man continues to be involved with a woman whose work neither he nor society respects.

Another difficulty that the housewife role presents is its isolation. The housewife's significant interactions are with her family who (after early childhood) expand their relationships beyond the family sphere.

Choice, too, may be a factor in a homemaker's satisfaction (or lack of it) with her role. Because of the limitations in the work world outside the home, some women may end up as homemakers against their real desires. These "under-duress" homemakers may be particularly at risk. Although the housewife relies on this role for her major gratification, her husband has two potential sources of gratification: home and work (Gove, 1972). If one is not satisfactory to him he can invest more energy in the other. Yet the housewife has no ready alternative source of gratification when things on the home front sour.

One of the most problematic aspects of housework seems to be its unstructured nature. In part, this is one of the benefits of the work, for Oakley (1974) found that housewives most valued the autonomy in their roles: "You can be your own boss"; "there's plenty of free time." However, as anyone who tries to work independently has found out, being one's own boss implies a necessity to supervise one's own work. There is also no boss to say, "You've done enough," or "Good job." Women thus often have to look to self-reward for this work, a requirement made difficult by the lack of any formal standards for housework.

The result of this fact can be seen in the tendency of the job of housework to enlarge, even with the addition of labor-saving devices and products. Formerly, women were content to present clean clothes to their families, but new products now make it possible, and hence necessary to many, for those clothes to also be soft and smell good. Likewise, the cooking tasks of housewives were at one time confined to substantial but simple meals. Increased varieties of prepared food and new appliances now lead to the expectation of more elaborate and international cuisine. As technology becomes available for housework, standards rise and routines become more elaborate. In part, this is a function of the unstructured nature of housework and the lack of uniform standards.

Another Look

In Kanter's analysis of structural factors affecting work in corporations, one confronts the strong effects of opportunity, power, and proportions. The context in which work takes place is a partial determinant of behavior in the workplace. Low opportunity is associated with limited aspirations, lower self-esteem, search for satisfaction outside of work, a great deal of complaining, discouraging peers from seeking advancement, a focus on extrinsic (rather than intrinsic) and social rewards of the job.

People placed in responsible positions but not granted much real power tend to behave in authoritarian ways, try to restrict subordinates' growth, evidence territoriality, and are less secure and more critical. Numerical minority status is associated with high visibility, exaggeration of differences with majority group, and tendencies to react to the minority group in stereotyped ways.

This analysis suggests that the work experience would be particularly difficult for people in low-opportunity, low-power, and token positions. Many jobs held by the lower and working classes as well as many blacks fit at least some of these descriptions. So do the jobs held by many women, across class levels and social lines. Hence, women are not the only ones to have their options for work satisfaction restricted by structural factors, but they are more likely to be affected this way.

Women's work options are not limited to formal organizations. Many women work in their own homes. Many aspects of the housewife role can serve as sources of difficulty for the woman. Isolation, and alienation from spouse, for example, can lead to depression. The lack of status in the role can result in low self-esteem, and the unstructured nature of the role can easily create anxiety.

It may be that some housewives find their work more satisfying and meaningful than the women in low-opportunity, low-power and low-proportion positions. Yet it seems that often neither the corporate nor the home setting provides a context for work that supports development of options, flexibility, choice, and opportunities to engage in work that is meaningful, satisfying and respected. Under such conditions, the goals of androgyny—flexibility, integration of masculinity and femininity, situational appropriateness, and broad repertoire—would be difficult to attain.

INTERPERSONAL FACTORS AND WORK
Employers and Supervisors: Their Effects in the Workplace

Workers' direct involvement with the organization is through the people who hire and supervise them. But the people in these positions of authority are not always as positive toward female employees as male (O'Leary, 1974). For example, many male executives are disinclined toward hiring women for management positions.

When asked, male executives rated their attitudes toward female executives in the mildly favorable to mildly unfavorable range (Bowman, Wortney, & Greyser, 1965). Many were worried that female managers would have a bad effect on employee morale. When asked their perceptions of women, a group of male managers said that women are less dependable because of biological and personal characteristics (Bass, Krusell, & Alexander, 1971). Criteria for evaluating job applicants also often differ according to the sex of the applicant. When evaluations of female and male applicants were compared, personality/appearance and skills/education were perceived as more important in evaluating the female, whereas motivation/ability and interpersonal relations were weighted more heavily in evaluating the male (Cecil, Paul, & Olins, 1973).

Expectations. Supervisors' expectations, in the form of sex-role stereotypes of female and male performance, would also be expected to affect their evaluation of actual performance. In the classroom, social psychologists have found that teachers' expectations about how smart children are can influence the children's grades and actual performance (Rosenthal, 1973). Teachers were told that some children (randomly chosen) were intellectual "bloomers" who could be expected to make great progress. In fact, at the end of the year these children received better academic grades than children not so labeled, and were more likely to have increased their scores on a general intelligence test (objectively scored) than children in a control group who were not so labeled.

It seems likely that employers' expectations about women and men can similarly affect their perceptions and the workers' performance. The supervisor who thinks of men as hard-working and serious about their jobs would probably be more likely to perceive a male in that light. The opinion that women are flighty and frivolous can readily result in perceptions of women in such a light. Given such perceptions and the self-fulfilling nature of the expectations, one can easily see who is more likely to get a promotion. Yet the supervisor responsible for evaluating the employees may not be aware of the subtle processes that underlie her or his decision. She or he probably truly believes that the male was a better candidate for promotion. The teachers in Rosenthal's study were not aware that their reactions to the children were affected by the artificially induced expectations.

Additional information about the effect of sex-related expectations on evaluation of performance was presented in Chapter 9. Particularly when accomplishments are not clearly defined, women's work tends to be evaluated lower than men's. We also saw that attributions for success vary according to sex: women's success tends to be attributed to luck, hard work, or task ease, and men's to skill (Deaux & Emswiller, 1974). It seems that women's accomplishments must be exceptional in order to be recognized.

Discrimination. Employers and supervisors can affect work options not only through their subtle expectations but also through outright sex discrimination. Discrimination refers to a tendency to treat certain people as a category rather than on the basis of individual merit. Women in some groups have become increasingly aware in recent years of the powerful effect sex discrimination has on their lives. In one sample of women on the faculty at a large Eastern university, 77 percent reported that they had been the victims of sex discrimination in careers (Young, MacKenzie, & Sherif, 1978). Reports of experiences of sex discrimination are less frequent in other groups, such as students at a large state university (Turner &Turner, 1975). Even among a large sample of adult workers, only 7.9 percent of the women felt they had experienced discrimination on the job. Although these women generally denied that discrimination had occurred, the investigators found that 95 percent of the women *were* discriminated against, both in income—losing an average of 71 percent of their salaries when compared with men of similar background and position—and quality of job (Levitin, Quinn, & Staines, 1971).

Effects of sex discrimination in the workplace can be both direct and indirect. Direct effects would include being blocked from a promotion, turned down for a job, or underpaid. Indirect effects involve one's self-concept, aspirations, and emotional state. The relationship between perceived discrimination and such reactions is rarely investigated. In one study college senior women who reported experiencing discrimination were more unhappy than women with low perception of discrimination (Turner & Turner, 1978). The high-discrimination perceivers were also more likely to report reacting with anger (rather than sadness) to tales of discrimination than low perceivers. Despite their unhappiness, the high-discrimination perceivers appeared to have a positive self-image: they were more likely to rate themselves as attractive, dominant, and helpful. Curiously, their perceptions of discrimination did not seem to result in lower aspirations. In fact their educational aspirations had increased over the four years of college, while the average level of educational expectation among low perceivers of discrimination remained the same. Thus it seems that, although perceived discrimination may make one unhappy and angry, such perceptions seem to enable one to continue to try. Whether or not it was wise for these women to keep trying in the face of discrimination, is a question that has to be answered in the long run and on an individual level.

Some authors have suggested that since sex discrimination does exist in this society women need to be aware of it (Turner & Turner, 1975). Such awareness of external barriers to achievement may enable women to confront the barriers more directly. Partial support for this idea was the finding that college freshwomen who were least sensitive to sex discrimination had high *educational aspirations* (compared to other women) but not necessarily high *educational expectations* or *occupational aspirations.* Perhaps their high educational goals were not being acted on, in part because of discrimination that they internalized. If they could have externalized the discrimination that did surround them, by labeling it as such, they might have found it more possible to act on their aspirations.

To the extent that awareness of discrimination has some positive consequences, white college women are at a disadvantage. Among a class of freshmen at a large Eastern university, white females were least likely to perceive occupational discrimination against women (Turner & Turner, 1975). Both black females and white males perceived significantly more occupational discrimination against women than did white females. The authors of that study suggest that, compared to black children, white female children are not socialized into the role of "a person who is discriminated against." As black children are growing up, they hear many explicit tales of race discrimination. White female children grow up hearing an ideology of equality between the sexes. Few girls' mothers explain any difficulties of their own to their daughters in terms of sex discrimination.

If this is the case, many females enter the work force unprepared for the sex discrimination that has been shown to exist among employers and supervisors. Recent superficial changes in sex-role ideology toward greater equality for women may, ironically, have a negative effect. Girls today may be growing up even less prepared to face discrimination than past generations were. In the past, sex discrimination may not have been mentioned at all, whereas today media coverage and public expectations suggest to the girl that, "thanks to Affirmative Action," women and men have equal opportunities. This insistence that sex discrimination is a thing of the past, not supported by data about continuing prestige and salary gaps, may cause females to believe that discrimination is a problem they will never face.

On the other hand, greater media attention over the past several years to the problems of sex discrimination may have served a "consciousness raising" function that has not been dissipated by talk of change in the opposite direction. In addition, the feminist movement's emphasis on increased assertiveness by women may have improved their abilities to actively respond to discrimination.

Peers: Their Effects on Work Behavior

One's friends and colleagues can both encourage and discourage exploration of occupational options. In many cases, it seems that peers serve to reinforce stereotypes. Among a group of midwestern adults, adults judged people who were in jobs that violated sex-role expectations (i.e., a woman in a "man's job," a man in a "woman's job") as having lower social standing than persons who followed sex-role expectations in terms of their jobs (Nilson, 1976). This suggests that the male telephone operator (a "woman's job") will have lower social standing than the male bricklayer (a "man's job"), while the female telephone operator will have higher social standing than the female bricklayer. In addition, however, a man in a female-typed occupation was penalized more for his role violation than a woman in a male-typed occupation.

Additional information suggests that more than negative sanctions for "rule-breakers" is involved. In one large company studied, female secretaries were somewhat hesitant to accept promotions into management ranks (Kanter, 1977) on the rare occasion when such an opportunity was presented. There was a great deal of camaraderie and solidarity within the secretarial group. To leave that group might bring forth charges of "disloyalty." What is more, once a woman moved up the hierarchy, she did not have a new female peer group to move into. Most of the women were concentrated in the secretarial ranks. Advancement for these women was a prospect marked by ambivalence, at best. They were faced with the choice of remaining in a relatively "dead-end" slot where the affiliative rewards were strong and guaranteed, or moving into a more prestigious position where the rewards were not guaranteed and one would quite likely be lonely. Whereas a man could find male peers at every level of the system, women found fewer and fewer female peers as they moved up the ranks.

Hence, for women, advancement often means loss of a supportive peer group, whereas for men it means only a change to a new peer group. As we saw earlier, the preference for similarity to self among executives makes it less likely that women will be readily accepted into the male groups. Kanter suggested that, if the sex ratios were reversed, men might be equally hesitant to accept promotions. At the present time, however, higher-level positions for women frequently are accompanied by a risk of the nonavailability of a supportive peer group.

This possibility receives further support from available information about successful women executives (Hennig & Jardim, 1976). These "pioneers," who were studied as they neared retirement, grew up in the 1920s. None married until at least their mid-thirties. Although they had had active social lives in college and the years immediately thereafter, their social life with peers was sharply reduced during their twenties. During this period they devoted a great deal of time to their work. At the same time, they developed a very close, mentor-type relationship with a boss. It seemed that this boss could provide the support and encouragement that their more traditionally minded peers were unable to do. Such intensive personal support was apparently an important factor in helping the women establish themselves in their careers. Yet, because most bosses are male, it is usually more difficult for women to enter into these mentor relationships.

Those "pioneers'" needs apparently could not easily be met by the usual people one thinks of as peers. Yet even among women who aspire to achieve today, peers seem to play a big role (Tangri, 1972). A group of college senior women, who planned to pursue innovative and prestigious careers, reported that their women friends had had a positive influence on their career choice. These women also reported frequent contact with people such as teaching assistants, who were usually male. Those men, generally a few years ahead on the career ladder, seemed to provide a measure of support and encouragement for the women's aspirations.

Family: Its Effects on Work Options

In the last chapter we examined marriages in which both spouses are employed outside the home. We found that this arrangement frequently meant a greater burden on women than men, even among some of the best-intentioned couples. The near-guarantee, then, that paid employment means two major roles, probably impedes many women from seeking the more prestigious jobs (which are usually more involving and demanding). In this way, women's family commitments frequently spell a diminishment of employment commitments. The fact that women bear the brunt of the family role means they are less likely to be able to take on a heavy burden in the work role. Men contribute to this state of affairs with their frequent unwillingness and inability to bear an equal share of the family tasks (Komarovsky, 1973).

Current stereotypes of the sexes and structures of family roles tend to foster husbands' occupational development and inhibit wives'. Studies of men's lives have pointed to the important role a wife plays in helping a man build his career (Levinson et al., 1978). The wife helps foster aspirations, provides psychological support, adds real physical assistance, at the same time she is taking major responsibility for cooking, child care, shopping, cleaning, and laundry. For example, if one is to believe book prefaces, many more women deserve authorship than are actually listed on book jackets. Authors' wives are frequently credited with inspiration, discussion, research, editorial work, organization, and typing.

There is an interesting contrast between the lives of the successful men who have served as the focus of recent studies of male development (Levinson, et al., 1978; Vaillant, 1977), and the successful women executives whose lives were carefully examined in another study (Hennig & Jardim, 1976). Although most of the successful men were married and apparently benefitting career-wise, none of the successful women studied married before their mid-thirties. Even then, half the group remained unmarried.

Many women may be strong enough to meet the challenge of two roles, even without the benefit of "wifely" support. Yet the stress is high and the pace hectic. Many women elect to decrease their career involvement, particularly at times when family responsibilities are at their highest. The cost of such a decision is frequently a loss of seniority, benefits, and less tangible rewards such as respect from employers. Such effects are not necessary, of course, and would probably be less likely if this culture valued human development and interpersonal relationships as highly as it values financial profit, productivity, and achievement. One expression of such a change in values would be more flexible work arrangements than the forty-hour week—for both women and men. If many people were allowed to increase or decrease work involvement at different points in the life cycle, any "time out" for family care might be less of a stigma and impediment to occupational development.

Another Look

Overall, interpersonal factors seem to be more likely to increase (or at least support) the development of occupational options for men, while frequently decreasing the likelihood of similar development in women. The available evidence suggests that many employers and supervisors react to women in the workplace with lower expectations, more negative attitudes toward women in high positions, and even outright discrimination. Although friends and the people with whom one works can serve as important supports at work, as women move up the occupational hierarchy they are less likely to find same-sexed peers than men are. In general, peers also often support adherence to stereotypic roles for both sexes, sometimes even providing negative sanctions for "rule-breakers." Current family structures may also help to inhibit women's work aspirations while supporting men's.

There is little direct information about the effects of these interpersonal factors on work behavior and occupational development. However, our analysis suggests that current occupational structure is self-perpetuating because people are discouraged from moving into fields dominated by the other sex. Because women are in fewer and lower-status occupations, they would seem to suffer more from these factors.

There is the additional suggestion that women may be aided in the long run through awareness of the effect of these interpersonal factors on their work. Men as a group have traditionally proceeded through personal occupational development with the help of employers, supervisors, peers, and family. Women as a group have not benefited from similar help to date. Such support is necessary, however, if their options in the workplace are to develop equally with men's.

INTERNALIZATION OF FACTORS IN THE WORKPLACE

Organizations, employers, supervisors, peers, and family members have now all been implicated in supporting women's occupational development less than men's. Yet these external agents would not be quite so effective if their messages weren't internalized by women.

In the words of one writer, it is difficult to tell which came first: someone saying, "You can't," and "You're not able to," or saying yourself, "I can't" and "I didn't want to anyway" (Kanter, 1977). If only to preserve a sense of personal integrity and control, people often respond to external barriers by changing their goal to one that is more attainable. The woman who finds she cannot have children might decide to adopt, and if that is not possible, decide to become more involved in her work. Likewise, a woman who starts out with the goal of being a supervisor might decide, after a few years of confronting discrimination and nonsupport, that she is content to stay in her present post or devote more energy to her family.

Decision processes are rarely so conscious or rational. One is not usually aware of the reasons she or he has decreased or changed aspirations. For this reason, it is difficult to observe the direct effects of external barriers. More often than not, one observes only the end-product. Hence, it has often looked as though women's lesser involvement in the workplace is a product of their own lack of motivation and skills or interests in other spheres.

Women are sensitive to pressures imposed by stereotyped views of femininity. They tend to choose occupations that conform to sex-role expectations, such as nurse, teacher, secretary (Gutek & Nieva, 1978). In making plans for the future, women are particularly vulnerable to what they think men want (Hawley, 1972). These perceptions reflect at least a degree of reality, for often feminine-typed jobs are easier for women to get into, and some men are threatened by female competence (Pleck, 1976).

The woman with a strong interest in a career is usually portrayed as one with a high need for achievement (Hoyt & Kennedy, 1958; Sedney & Turner, 1975; Tyler, 1964), success in past achievements (Astin, Suniewick, & Dweck, 1971), liberal sex-role attitudes (Lipman-Blumen, 1972; Turner, 1972), exposure to female role models who achieve (Almquist & Angrist, 1970; Baruch, 1972; Tangri, 1972), and encouragement from others (Cartwright, 1972). The general consensus is that jobs serve as outlets for expression of personality (Gutek & Nieva, 1978). By implication, women who opt for a low place or no place at all in the job hierarchy are simply expressing their personalities.

Personalities do not develop in isolation; frequently they develop out of conflict. Women's ambivalence about work and achievement can be seen as a product of conflicting expectations for them. Parents encourage their daughters' academic achievement but not their career planning (Standley & Soule, 1974). Girls grow up in a society that places highest value on external achievement, but are told that "something better" is reserved for them. Even when women are told that paid work is useful, the jobs they have frequently are dull, meaningless, and dead-ended.

Another externally originated factor that might be internalized and inhibit women's occupational development can be labeled "affirmative guilt." Affirmative Action policies were designed to ensure that women and minorities have the opportunity to apply for a full range of jobs. Ironically, although these procedures have not significantly increased income and the proportions of women in traditionally masculine jobs (O'Kelly, 1979), they seem to have added a new twist to an old conflict for women. The evidence at present is only anecdotal, but striking. Many women who get jobs or promotions in fields outside the traditional feminine ones tell themselves—or are told by others—that it was "only because of Affirmative Action." Two business majors, one female and one male, applied for the same job as they were graduating from the same college. The woman, with higher grades and a stronger record of extracurricular activities, got the job. Yet the male was comforted by faculty and friends who told him he was the victim of "reverse discrimination." Even after those students graduated, the "sad story" was recounted on campus and the myth lived on. Few remembered the woman's higher qualifications. One wonders how many other mistold tales served as the basis for women's statements such as: "I know I'll have an easier time getting a job than males will, and it's not fair"; "I feel terrible when I think of the men who will be passed over so that I get a job"; "It's easier for women to get into medical, law, or graduate school than men." Men, with their frequently expressed fears that they will lose jobs to women, help to reinforce such feelings.

Such statements do not reflect reality, yet they may well affect women's attributions for any success today. Within the Affirmative Action myth, it is nearly impossible for a woman to take full credit for her achievements. Even before Affirmative Action, when sex discrimination was more blatant, some women did manage successful careers. This fact sometimes seems to be forgotten in the frequent feelings of guilt and anger generated by the new guidelines.

One can only speculate about how such explanations may affect women's performance and future strivings. Attribution of success to external factors would seem to be risky. If it is only "luck" (i.e., Affirmative Action) that got her to be where she is now, a woman should perhaps be cautious in looking to the future. She can not count on such luck to continue. She feels like an outsider who does not deserve to be there. It is difficult to see how such thoughts and feelings could benefit women's occupational development.

WORK, SEX ROLES, AND ANDROGYNY

A recurring theme in this chapter has been the importance of job context in affecting both the development and expression of work behavior. In the past, psychology researchers looked to the person rather than the job to explain occupational segregation. Our analysis, however, suggests that workers' behavior cannot be understood without taking into account how the workers come to their present position and what the job is like.

Options are limited by internal and external barriers to occupational development: jobs that provide low power, opportunity, and proportions of one's own group; employees and supervisors with low expectations and discriminatory practices; and nonsupportive peers and family. Problems in the workplace—for both females and males—seem to be associated with limitations in these factors. Enjoyment of the full potential in work, likewise, would seem much more realistic if these conditions were combatted.

Although not all men work under optimum conditions, women are even less likely to find such conditions. The barriers to women's occupational development are higher and their jobs are less likely to provide the requisite opportunity, power, and numbers. Even housework, women's one delegated sphere, seems to suffer from low valuation, structure, and opportunity for change.

An androgynous perspective on work behavior suggests continued investigation of the interplay of the worker and her or his work context. More studies of whole organizations, such as the entire staff of a hospital from director to groundskeepers, would be helpful. The secretaries' "low achievement motivation" might be more easily understood if one found that there was nowhere for them to move within the hospital organization, for example. We also need to know more about the process by which external factors, such as organizational pressures, power structures, and peers become internalized. There are some people who have managed to resist the external pressures; how have they done it? Psychologists could also do more to study the intricacies of sex discrimination, both from the perspective of the perpetrator and the victim. Why are so few women aware of discrimination? Are they perhaps better off not being aware? How can awareness of sex discrimination be translated into effective action to combat it, rather than discouragement? What about the discriminator: how do well-meaning people practice discrimination subtly without being aware of it? What can be done to diminish discriminatory behavior on an individual level?

Ironically, the work experience is affected not only by current conditions of the sexes but by promises to affect conditions in the future. To the extent that the structure of the workplace affects people, it continues the process of sex-role socialization begun during childhood. Although parents are no longer telling the female she must be good, quiet, and interested in dolls, her boss is telling her to dress nicely, address him as Mr., and prepare the coffee. Day after day, work in a job that recreates the passivity, submissiveness, and dependency of the female role must exert a powerful and continuing force. Many of the jobs women hold act as "booster shots" for any childhood socialization that may be fading.

The very strength of the workplace in affecting people's behavior can be intimidating and discouraging to people who aim for change. Because work does affect people's behavior, solutions such as putting new people in the same old jobs are relatively useless. For example, if an androgynous woman were to become president of General Motors, there is no reason to expect that her behavior would be very different than a man's in a similar position.

The search for androgyny implies that integration of stereotypically masculine and feminine characteristics would be useful even in the workplace. Yet one wonders whether it is possible to add female-valued characteristics such as concern for others, warmth, and sensitivity to the male-valued characteristics such as dominance, independence, and ambition that seem to predominate in much of the workplace. The predominant values in many workplaces—efficiency, rationality, nonemotionality, and productivity—seem more in keeping with agentic than communal concerns.

In some circles it is said that the predominant values in the work world are oriented so strongly toward stereotypic masculine standards of aggression, profit, and competition that androgyny in the workplace is an impossibility. Admittedly, it is difficult to imagine the president of GM making decisions on the basis of the quality of employees' lives, relationships among employees, or the health of people who live around the company's plants. The tough question becomes whether or not it is possible to integrate agency and communion, instrumental and expressive concerns in the workplace, while remaining effective.

It seems that androgynous integration would be quite difficult without major changes in current organizational structures and values. Some of the areas where change is necessary are suggested by the analysis of current important factors in work behavior. Changes in these areas should increase the options available to women and men.

Some alternative organizational structures have been tried, with varying degrees of success. Nonhierarchical organizations represent an attempt to equalize the power within a group. Decisions are made as a group, and all share the responsibilities equally. Rotation of leadership roles, in which people take turns being "boss" serves both to equalize the opportunity structure and to guard against concentration of power in one person. Some organizations have tried to rearrange their priorities so that concern for others (e.g., a clean environment) is at least as important as profit.

Such changes are admittedly difficult, for they go against every traditional idea of organizations. Hence, attention to details, subtleties, and potential problems are necessary. For example, one publishing organization realized how power structures can be developed and maintained by having increasingly attractive offices as one moves up the hierarchy. As a reflection of their continuing efforts toward a nonhierarchical structure, they assigned offices by lot and planned to change frequently (*Mother Jones,* 1979).

A first step in changing the workplace—and a very difficult one—would be to decrease occupational segregation. Legal means are increasingly available to help people fight policies that restrict the types of jobs and amounts earned by both sexes. However, these methods are extremely slow, discrimination is difficult to obtain, and very few cases actually come to court.

The process of ending occupational segregation must be in effect not only in the courts and legislative bodies. It must be present at every step of the occupational development process, from childhood socialization, through policies of employers, to company policies that would be more responsive to women. Individual women must be made aware of the sex discrimination, in all its subtleties, as long as it continues to exist.

Options would be increased and work could well become more satisfying and meaningful if jobs were changed to give employees greater power and opportunity, and to employ more equitable numbers of females and minorities. Changes such as this would be massive, and would require real shifts in organizational decision making and promotion policies.

The major block to options for the average male concerns the decision of whether or not to work. Hence, his options would be enhanced if there were means available for men to be less involved in work. One solution would be to pay women fairly and advance them equitably, so that their incomes could support a husband and a family. Men should also be given more release time for family work, particularly at certain stages in the family life cycle. Such a procedure would help alleviate the burden of an either/or choice for men.

These major changes in the structures and procedures in organizations will probably be long in coming. Individual efforts at change will thus be limited. Perhaps the best hedge at the individual level against occupational limitations is life and career planning. The college sophomore who told her advisor that she didn't want to worry about what she'd be doing after graduation might have a very enjoyable college career, but a less enjoyable occupational career. For most college students today, work will be part of their futures. The meaningfulness and potential satisfaction of that work is very much affected by advance decisions and plans. Awareness of the variability within jobs should lead a person to be very cautious in selecting one.

SUMMARY AND CONCLUSIONS

Although work is a major part of the lives of both women and men, and although both sexes look to work for similar satisfactions, the sexes often differ in their experience of work. The types of jobs they hold, levels of achievements, salaries, and sometimes even approaches to their jobs frequently vary. The traditional psychological explanations for these variations have tended to emphasize internal factors such as personality, but external factors are also clearly implicated.

There is clearly a tangled web of barriers to a full range of options for women in the occupational sphere. We discussed the effects of organizational factors, employers and supervisors, peers, family, and the individual, and found all to be important. Yet we must remember that life is not lived or experienced in separate segments. These effects operate together and reinforce each other. Employers' attitudes are affected by employees' behavior, which is partly a function of family responsibilities. Those responsibilities are, in turn, increased by institutional pressures that divert husbands from their family work. This cycle sometimes seems to be discouragingly self-perpetuating. Yet some people have managed to break through it. One suggestion is that strong consistent pressure from any one segment can help break the rest of the cycle. Although there are no guaranteed ways to achieve long-term decreases in the barriers, the best bet would seem to be to press for change in as many segments of the cycle as possible. Full awareness of the extent of the barriers is perhaps the first step.

Pointing out that a few people have broken out of the cycle is somewhat risky. Some people might protest that the very existence of exceptional women proves that the barriers are not so high. We admit that many women do achieve and some lead full lives that integrate strong personal and work elements. Yet, as someone once remarked, the goal is not a society in which any *super* woman has just as much chance as a man of making it, but one in which any *ordinary* woman—of average ability and motivation for work—has as much chance as ordinary men have traditionally had.

SELECTED READINGS

Barnett, R. C., & Baruch, G. K. *The competent woman: Perspectives on development.* New York: Wiley, 1978.

Edwards, R. C., Reich, M., & Weisskopf, T. E. *The capitalist system,* 2nd ed. Englewood Cliffs, N. J.: Prentice Hall, 1978.

Howe, L. K. *Pink collar workers.* New York: Putnam, 1977.

Kanter, R. M. *Men and women of the corporation.* New York: Basic Books, 1977.

Olsen, T. *Silences.* New York: Delacorte Press, 1978.

Terkel, S. *Working: People talk about what they do all day and how they feel about what they do.* New York: Pantheon, 1974.

PSYCHOLOGICAL WELL-BEING AND CHANGE

12

Psychologists' values can easily come into play in the realm of clinical psychology. It is here that judgments about normality and abnormality are made and efforts at change are instituted. Is the housewife who feels depressed, lonely, and worthless suffering from the mental illness of "depression," or is she experiencing a normal reaction to her isolation and repetitious tasks? Should she receive individual psychotherapy that would help her adjust to her life by taking on volunteer work and some evening crafts courses? Should therapy focus on her relationship with her mother and how that affects her concept of the female role? Should the therapist perhaps work with the entire family, trying to shift their relationships so there will be more room for "Mom" to develop some autonomy?

What about the male college student who is suicidal because he feels that he is not really a male, but a female trapped in a male body? Is he an oddity who cannot conform to the male role? Or an especially sensitive man who cannot face the rigidities of stereotyped expectations? Should he be offered sex change surgery? Or should he be given opportunities to become more proficient at male behaviors so that he could be more comfortable with his maleness? Perhaps he could be helped by an exploration of his conception of the male role, with support from people who have more flexible ideas about what constitutes manliness.

There is an inherent tension in applying psychological principles through judgments about feelings of well-being and psychotherapy, because the practitioner is dealing with the interface between individual and society. Although mental health practitioners usually focus on the feelings and behaviors of the individual person, these are a product both of internal conflict and external pressures.

This interface of person and society is crucial for a psychology of androgyny, which focuses on behavior in its social context. A basic premise of the model of androgyny is that behavior that is flexible, situationally appropriate, and integrates femininity and masculinity will be effective and ultimately result in feelings of well-being. Extending this reasoning, one would predict that the sex-typed person would not be as likely to enjoy feelings of well-being, because her or his behavior would not be effective as frequently. But these arguments must also take into account the social context; feelings of well-being may be easier to achieve in a social environment that supports a full range of adaptive behaviors for either sex.

In this chapter, we will examine these considerations. We will look at the interface between the individual and societal sex-role standards as they affect personal feelings of well-being, professionals' standards of mental health, and possibilities for individual and societal change. Some of the questions we will explore are: Do androgynous people actually feel better and adjust more readily than sex-typed people? To what extent does one's sex typing affect judgments others make about one's mental health? How would mental health practitioners judge androgynous people who came to see them? How could sex-typed and androgynous people be helped in therapy? What changes in the social context would help remove barriers to individual options concerning sex roles?

A major focus of this chapter is change and its precursors. There are really two major types of triggers for change in a person and her or his life. First, there are personal feelings: "I am unhappy (or depressed, or anxious)." Second, there are others' judgments about one's feelings: "She (or he) seems to me to be unhappy (or depressed, or anxious)." Movements toward change are sometimes a result of decisions based on personal feelings, sometimes a result of decisions based on the judgments of others, and sometimes a combination of the two. In the following section we will consider personal judgments about well-being. Later, discussion will focus on some of the ways society has labeled and explained unusual behavior or dissatisfaction in the past and present. Then, we will consider some of the channels for change available through psychotherapy and social change.

SEX ROLES AND PERSONAL JUDGMENTS OF WELL-BEING

Self-reports of happiness, satisfaction, and low levels of symptoms (e.g., headaches, difficulties eating or sleeping, etc.) are all considered to indicate psychological well-being. The emphasis is on the person's own experience, rather than a mental health professional's "translation" of the self-reports.

Well-being in Various Populations

Who *does* feel good and who feels bad, in general? The best summary is that people who are under stress or low in power tend to feel worst. From other chapters, we know that people who are married tend to feel better psychologically than those who are single, although this advantage is not nearly as apparent for women as for men (Chapter 10). Among the married, men feel better than women. Further, responsibility for young children in this society is associated with dissatisfaction, depression, and disturbance (Chapter 10). People who are poor are less likely to feel good, for in a cross-sectional study in the Southeastern United States, the best predictor of a high level of psychosomatic symptoms was low socioeconomic status (Warheit, Holzer, Bell, & Arey, 1976). In another survey, although the average man's symptoms were much lower than the average woman's, men who were single or widowed, of low income, or black had symptom levels nearly as high as women's. Only among employed people with occupational status in the upper or upper middle class were women's symptoms as low as men's (Ilfield, 1977). For both sexes, psychiatric symptomatology was associated with social stress. One's educational level and attitude toward the stress are also implicated, for among a group of women undergoing marital breakup, higher education and a nontraditional attitude toward sex roles were related to a positive psychological outcome (Brown, Perry, & Harburg, 1977).

Overall, then, some of the stresses that can interfere with well-being include femaleness, singleness (especially for men), responsibility for children, low socio-economic status, minority status, and some aspects of marriage (for women). Power, in the form of high education and high socioeconomic status, as well as attitudes consistent with one's life style appear to help counteract the potential negative effects of life stress.

These two factors, life stress and low power, appear to be problematic for women more often than men. In a wide variety of studies, women tended to report more stressful life events, and these life stresses were associated with psychological symptoms. Further, psychological symptoms were most strongly associated with events the women could not control, whereas for men control was not so important (Dohrenwend, 1973). Johnson (1976) demonstrated that women's power is often more limited than men's, because women's relative lack of access to concrete resources often leaves them with only indirect, personal, and helpless modes of influence.

Women in general report more symptoms of psychological distress, even when their reports are not filtered through mental health practitioners (Gove & Tudor, 1973). The fact that men succeed in committing suicide more often than women might suggest a greater degree of disturbance among men, but women are more likely than men to attempt suicide, a clear sign of distress (Gove & Tudor, 1973).

To the extent that reliance on a feminine mode of response restricts one from engaging in instrumental actions, it would be predicted that feminine characteristics would limit one's power to deal with life stress. Further, the culture's lack of respect for the feminine, expressive mode often means that lower power would be ascribed to that mode. Hence, not only average females but also males who engage in a primarily feminine mode would be expected to cope poorly with stress and, ultimately, to show less psychological well-being. In addition, reliance on a primarily masculine response mode might interfere with the capacity to cope with life stress to the extent that expressive functions are useful for dealing with stress. As we discussed in Chapter 9, recognition of emotional states can serve as a cue for change and enhanced coping. Hence, the average masculine males and females who use a primarily masculine mode would also be predicted to have problems in coping and, ultimately, in psychological well-being.

Stereotyped Sex Roles and Well-being

In earlier chapters we reviewed some of the relationships between sex roles and psychological well-being. There is a general tendency for that which is masculine to be associated with well-being among college students in this culture. College men (a group whose average member is sex-typed masculine, according to Bem's 1974 studies of college students) seem to be more self-confident than women, in terms of expectations and attributions for success (Chapter 9). Acceptance of a relatively high level of masculine characteristics appears to be a necessary part of positive self-esteem for both sexes, although women seem also to need some positive feminine characteristics (Chapter 9). In more general terms, feminine characteristics, alone or in combination with masculine ones, seems to present some problems for college males' emotional adjustment (Chapter 1).

In the past, psychologists have found a relationship between high femininity and maladjustment in females. High femininity alone has been found to be associated with high anxiety and low social acceptance among female children and college students (Cosentino & Heilbrun, 1964; Gray, 1957; Webb, 1963). These studies were done in the preandrogyny days and, hence, did not consider separately those females high in femininity only and those high in both femininity and masculinity. Some evidence even suggests that high femininity in women is associated with poor performance of the traditional female tasks in marriage and motherhood (cf. Sherman, 1976).

For males, the picture from past research is more complicated and seems to change with age. Among a group of seventeen- and eighteen-year-old boys, high masculinity was associated with adjustment, high self-esteem, positive emotional state, and smooth social functioning (Mussen, 1961). Yet, when these same men were tested twenty years later, high masculinity was associated with lower levels of dominance, capacity for status, self-acceptance, introspectiveness, sociability, self-assurance, and perceived likelihood to be leaders (Mussen, 1962). Other studies of masculinity in postcollege adulthood have found masculinity in adult men to be associated with anxiety, guilt proneness, tough poise, neuroticism, and suspicion (e.g., Harford, Willis, & Deabler, 1967).

It appears that high masculinity, which is adaptive in the late adolescent male subculture, is not so adaptive in later adulthood, when demands and social relationships change. We will look at this point again in our discussion of androgyny and well-being. The more consistent link between high femininity and maladjustment in females may reflect the lack of cultural value for expressive qualities and the realistic necessity for instrumental skills.

Androgyny and Well-being

A fundamental premise in the model of androgyny is that androgyny is associated with well-being. In fact, androgyny does seem to be associated with behavioral flexibility. Bem's series of behavioral studies (Chapter 1) showed that androgynous people can both remain independent of group pressure and exhibit nurturance to others. To varying degrees, sex-typed persons had trouble in one realm or the other. Further, androgynous people could select the task that was most rewarding, whereas the sex-typed person was restricted in her or his choice by the sex-appropriateness of the task.

Yet, there remain contradictions between the premises of the model of androgyny and available information about androgyny and well-being. First, there is the male case. In terms of self-evaluation, men who incorporate feminine characteristics are more likely to feel some internal stress (Jones et al., 1978; Spence, Helmreich, & Stapp, 1975b). This may be a function of the social milieu of the late adolescent males who have been studied most frequently. Perhaps the hints in the androgyny research that androgynous and sex-typed feminine men seem susceptible to negative internal states reflects a phenomenon apparent in adolescence but not adulthood. Most of these studies are done with late adolescent college students, for whom an element of high masculinity is still a major aspect of social adjustment and positive self-esteem in men. Peers in this group are very likely not to look with favor on men who can cuddle kittens, bounce babies and comfort a lonely student as well as resist pressure to conform. As Costrich et al. (1975) pointed out, college-age students give negative evaluations to persons who do not conform to the stereotype.

A second set of contradictions between the ideals and reality of androgyny is found in clinical studies. Both Kaplan (1979) and Sedney (1977a) reported that in small samples of the (primarily female) psychotherapy clients they studied, the majority scored as androgynous on the BSRI. Sex-typed feminine females were less likely to be in therapy. The problems for the women who scored as androgynous seemed to center on a lack of situational appropriateness and failure to integrate their feminine and masculine tendencies.

The presence of both feminine and masculine characteristics in a person can lead to integration or conflict. The failure to use these characteristics in a situationally appropriate manner can be seen in cases reported by Kaplan (1979). "Molly," a woman in her fifties came to therapy because of depression about her husband's involvement with another woman. She was angry, but unable to channel it into an ultimatum or decision for action. She was warm and loving when her husband was rejecting, yet would "freeze up" when he reached out. She would make demands but fail to carry out the threatened consequences. Elements of masculinity and femininity were both present in her but they were not used appropriately.

"Susan," a college student, channeled her independence into a rebellious attitude toward school and a refusal to accept her own needs for nurturance. Yet in more intimate relationships her self-integrity seemed to disappear and no direct confrontation over differences was possible. Again, there was a failure to use the available feminine and masculine characteristics in a situationally appropriate manner.

In a study of middle-aged women's coping responses to stressful life events, Sedney (1977a) reported several instances of women who scored as androgynous but whose masculine and feminine response tendencies interfered with each other and generated conflict. For example, one woman decided to separate from her husband after learning of his extramarital affairs, yet agreed not to talk about the reasons for the separation, in order to spare him embarrassment. Thus she was forced to deal with the consequences of her assertiveness (being on her own) without any support from others, thanks to her continued concern for his well-being. The femininity interfered with the effectiveness of the masculine aspect of the response. Another instance of an apparent mismatch of masculinity and femininity concerned a woman who was informed by a government bureau that she owed them hundreds of dollars for overpayments sent her. She acted quite independently by selling her home and furniture, taking a new job out of state, etc. However, never did she challenge their opinion, defend herself, or consult a lawyer, though she felt she had received the payments in good faith. She was assertive and independent in some of her actions yet essentially passive in handling the *cause* of her difficulties. In another case, a woman was assertive enough to ask her father for an outline of financial arrangements for her future, yet was unable to deal with the rejection inherent in his reply. She became quite emotional, experienced a series of anxiety attacks, and was unable to bring the assertiveness to bear with him any further.

It seems that the mere presence of masculine and feminine qualities in a person does not automatically result in their appropriate use or integration. These contradictory elements can conflict and result in confusion and discomfort.

However, situational appropriateness and integration of femininity and masculinity are possible (Sedney, 1977a). For example, a woman whose neighbor was dying of cancer was able to use her assertiveness to express the emotions she felt in a very useful, adaptive way. She helped the family, dealt with doctors and talked about death with the patient. Yet, she was also able to maintain her own life, so that she was on vacation when the patient finally died in a hospital. She did what she could when she was needed, but did not become totally selfless and could pull back when her role was no longer needed. Another woman, who was unemployed, initially despaired and was prepared to sell her house, until she began to draw on her friends for advice and support. By being assertive enough to reach out for their help and reveal her dependency, she gained enough suggestions for temporary financial arrangements, new jobs, etc. that she was able to maintain her independence.

Another Look

Feelings of well-being seem to be associated with relative freedom from stress and perceptions of personal power. Women are less likely to experience either of these and, hence, are more vulnerable to psychological distress.

Components of psychological sex are apparently linked to feelings of self-esteem and well-being. For college students in this culture, self-descriptions in masculine terms herald greater adjustment for both sexes, although females seem also to benefit from some feminine elements. Alone, however, high femininity for females has been frequently linked with low adjustment. Questions about these relationships in adulthood, particularly in men, persist.

There are both gains and losses associated with the co-presence of femininity and masculinity. By incorporating both feminine and masculine characteristics into the self-description, people can broaden their behavioral repertoire, increase their flexibility, and expand their ability to deal with situations appropriately. Yet, even with these gains, behavioral effectiveness and psychological well-being do not necessarily follow.

The first potential negative aspect of having feminine and masculine characteristics is the increased possibility of conflict, both within the self and between self and society. Although conflict can stimulate growth, it can also result in discomfort, anxiety, and unhappiness. If one is unable to integrate masculinity and femininity, because of either a lack of skills or the belief that these tendencies are oppositional, one can experience increased conflict. The integration is particularly difficult because of a lack of examples and language to describe and reveal such possibilities. In addition, when someone displays tendencies usually associated with the other sex, a result can be conflict with society's standards, exhibited as a lack of social support. Few people are immune to such pressures.

A second possible problem with androgyny is increased ambiguity. For all their limitations, sex-role stereotypes do provide structure in life. The person who is stereotypically feminine knows how she is going to behave in many instances. She does not have to consider the vagaries of every situation she encounters, weighing the consequences of possible responses. The loss of such a rigid response style can be difficult for the person who has a low tolerance for ambiguity. For the androgynous person, a quick or easy response may not be possible. Greater complexity of perceptions and response style need not be adaptive in every situation, particularly when the response style goes against the cultural grain. Life is often more difficult when there are choices.

In light of these potential gains and losses it may be necessary to temper the model of androgyny with reality. Androgyny may well not be always adaptive in the current culture. Although the finer points of this remark may be open to question, it is necessary to recognize the potential for problems and to develop ways of dealing with them. We are not suggesting that people should not try to be androgynous. We are saying that although androgyny can relieve some problems associated with stereotyped sex roles it can also create new ones. This may be another way of saying that there are no magic solutions or simple paths to psychological well-being. Recognition of the complexity of meeting the demands of self, other, situation, and society may be a first step.

LABELING THE WELL-BEING OF OTHERS

Efforts at changing a person are not always brought about only by personal feelings of dissatisfaction. Sometimes, other people decide that the person needs to be changed. Psychological well-being cannot be discussed fully without considering who—aside from the person—decides who feels "bad" and what such decisions are based on.

Throughout history, various explanations have been proposed for behavior outside the norm of society. Judgments about normal and abnormal behavior, mental health and illness, reflect and support the cultural context in which they are made. These processes are sometimes easier to discern in retrospect. Hence, to illustrate some of the factors involved in labeling people as "not well" or "abnormal," we will look at two historical examples, witchcraft and hysteria. From these we will move to a discussion of current manifestations of these labeling processes in judgments about "mental illness."

Witchcraft: Power Through the Devil

During the late Middle Ages the Western world was in a period of instability: the feudal system was threatened by the discovery of gunpowder (which made the old feudal manors vulnerable); the plague was killing large numbers of people; the printing press, heralding massive changes in relationships between the elites and the masses, had been invented; and the Church was under attack for its abuses

(Zax & Cowen, 1976). During this time, the label of "witch" came into use. The threat of this label helped control people during a period of social instability. It also helped illustrate a norm by calling attention to how *not* to behave.

During the Middle Ages, witches were considered to have gained supernatural power through the Devil. Defined thus as heretics, they were subject to both ecclesiastical and secular discipline. To the people of that era, the mentally ill, witches, and heretics were synonymous (Veith, 1977).

The primary document explaining how to identify and punish witches was *Malleus Maleficarum* (The Hammer of Witchcraft), published about 1486 and written by two Dominican monks, Sprenger and Kraemer. Accusations based on this tome formed a major part of the Inquisition. Those who persecuted witches believed that witches were part of an organized sect bent on subverting the social order by using curses and their knowledge of herbs and poisons to kill rulers (Van Vuuren, 1973).

Sprenger and Kraemer held that women were especially susceptible to becoming witches because their sexual nature made them vulnerable to the advances of the Devil: "All witchcraft comes from carnal lust, which is in women insatiable. . . . And blessed be the Highest Who has so far preserved the male sex from so great a crime" (1948 edition, p. 47).

According to *Malleus Maleficarum,* women engaged in a wide variety of evils on orders of Satan. Themes included women's power and their sexuality. Women engaged in sex with the Devil (an act that cannot be seen by human eyes); taught young women how to bewitch their ex-lovers; caused sterility in animals and men; raised hailstorms, tempests, and lightning; foresaw the future; caused disease and famine; recognized the signs of death faster than a physician; and transported themselves through the air, sometimes on broomsticks (Van Vuuren, 1973).

In hindsight, it is difficult to ascertain what those accused of witchcraft actually *did* do to earn such accusations. It seems that there were several different groups of women who were particularly susceptible to being accused of witchcraft. Some writers have suggested that those labeled witches would be called mentally ill today. In fact, possession by the devil was said to result in wild behavior, unusual strength, making noises like an animal, and speaking strange languages (Rosen, 1968). People knowledgeable about herbs and poisons, as well as midwives, were also vulnerable to accusations of witchcraft. Old women and young, pretty women were other frequent victims (Van Vuuren, 1973).

Whatever reality was at the basis of witchcraft, the witch-hunts served to consolidate the power of the Pope. One result seemed to be to establish the superiority of God and the Church, within a context of fear and aversion of women. In a time of social upheaval, witch trials eradicated dissent, established conformity, and protected the established order (Rosen, 1968).

Thus, as the world was moving into the modern era, the label of witch was affixed to those who were outside, or who threatened the power and norm of society. What may seem to today's mind as preposterous and unfounded accusations were, at that time, vehicles that helped preserve the status quo. To the accusers, many of the accused, and observers, possession by the devil helped to make unusual and mysterious aspects of behavior comprehensible and controllable.

Hysteria: A Woman's Disease

Throughout recorded history, many of women's inexplicable physical, emotional, and behavioral conditions have been attributed to hysteria. Rooted in the Greek word "hystera" for the womb, hysteria was originally believed to be a result of a wandering uterus (Veith, 1977). Since then, the concept of hysteria has undergone many changes in its etiology and treatment. Yet, across time, it has continued to be applied more frequently to women, associated with their sexuality (in both causes and cures), and linked to instability.

Among the ancient Egyptians and Greeks, a broad array of physical and psychological symptoms were attributed to hysteria. Pains in the neck, head, and jaw, as well as general aches were some of the symptoms, as were convulsions, lethargy, drowsiness, loss of voice or vision, anxiety, palpitations, and excessive vomiting. Treatment usually focused on some method for attracting the wandering uterus back to its proper place, either through sexual intercourse or odorous preparations. The problem was seen as a physical one.

The uterine explanation for hysteria persisted through the seventeenth century. The signs continued to be physical afflictions, seizures, and sensory distortions, and treatment remained focused on returning the uterus to its proper position (Veith, 1977).

In the past several centuries, the emphasis has been more frequently on psychological causes, and hysteria has been labeled a "neurosis" (a major category of psychological disturbance less severe than psychosis). Around the time of the French Revolution, Pinel (1813) described states of restlessness, sadness, and loss of sleep and appetite, which he linked to excessive sexual behavior. In describing hysteria during the nineteenth century, Charcot (1877) emphasized sensory disturbances (including deafness and narrowness of vision), anaesthesia, and motor disturbances, and saw these symptoms in part as a reflection of the patient's suggestibility. Freud labeled many of his patients as hysterical, with symptoms such as headaches, fatigue, chronic depression, frigidity, paranoia, anaesthesia, and motor disturbances (Breuer & Freud 1895). He saw these symptoms as a result of patients' unconscious sexual conflicts.

There are several current uses of the term hysteria. In some circles, it is defined as a personality style that includes seductiveness, excitability, self-dramatization, immaturity, and dependency (American Psychiatric Association, 1968). Others focus on the hysteric's conversion of repressed psychological conflicts into physical symptoms, such as paralysis, involuntary movements, sensory disturbances, pains (Fenichel, 1945; Abse, 1974). Still another definition of one form of hysteria includes chronic medical problems and multiple somatic symptoms that are not medically explainable (Perley & Guze, 1962).

Our purpose has not been to ascertain whether or not a clinical entity of hysteria exists or is a useful distinction. Rather, we have attempted to demonstrate how variable and culture-bound the diagnostic/labeling process is. Most writers through the ages have been certain that they have identified the "real" disorder, whether it be somatic, psychological, or a combination of the two. And their contemporaries have agreed. Yet there is always a "new" view that appears at a later point in history and supplants the "old."

Hysterics are sometimes said to reflect an extension of the expected feminine role in a given era (Krohn, 1978; Lerner, 1974). For example, during the Victorian era, falling ill was one acceptable behavior—and, in fact, one of the few acceptable ways to channel conflict—for women, who were viewed as passive, naive, weak, and pure (Krohn, 1978). Today, diagnoses of hysteria are less likely to be based on physical symptoms, perhaps because it is less acceptable for females to fall ill. In middle-class urban settings, the diagnosis of hysteria is more likely to focus on personality traits that extend the feminine role: emotionality, seductiveness, and suggestibility.

By calling attention to persons who reflect the convention of society, the label of hysteric represents the values of society. The hysteric serves as an illustration of a norm, albeit in the extreme. "In living out the myths treasured by his reference group, the hysteric becomes a living advocate of the moral and stylistic positions of the culture" (Krohn, 1978, p. 208).

Modern Clinical Practice

What lessons can modern clinical practice take from the treatments of witches and hysterics of the past? First, this historical overview suggests that judgments about the normality and abnormality of behavior are changeable and fallible. Accordingly, contemporary clinicians need not lull themselves into security about their judgments with the belief that they have achieved "objectivity."

Second, clinical judgment is closely tied to culture. Reflections of cultural roles and values appear in the behavior that is labeled abnormal. A recurring theme in the history of abnormal behavior is aversion toward women and their sexuality, and it often occurred in cultures that devalue women. As the witch was the antithesis of the conforming passionless woman who was the norm in the Middle Ages, the hysteric has been the prototype of the feminine role in her own particular culture.

A third suggestion is that clinical judgment can serve purposes other than its apparent ones. It has a history of preserving the status quo. Hence, although clinicians may fully intend to help "depressed," "neurotic" and "schizophrenic" people by labeling them as such, they must remain aware that such labels may be performing social control functions as well. The very act of labeling someone's behavior as abnormal defines a power relationship: "I, the labeler, have the right and knowledge to judge you, the labeled."

Although the labels of witch and hysteric have been primarily applied to women, men have certainly not been exempt from labels of abnormality. At times, their criminal behavior has been judged the result of "insanity" and they have been incarcerated in mental hospitals for years longer than they would have been in jails (Ennis, 1972). Until quite recently, the mental health professions reinforced negative attitudes toward homosexuals by labeling their behavior a mental illness. On the international level, certain eras have seen men who wish to disagree with powerful political regimes labeled mentally ill.

The Politics of Clinical Judgment

Although many in the helping professions would prefer to think that psychological disorder represents "mental illness" that is analogous to "physical illness," the analogy has been shown to be unreasonable (Szasz, 1961). Histories of the field (e.g., Coleman, 1972) are sometimes presented in terms of the "Dark Ages" of "then," when cultures viewed disordered behavior as the work of gods, devils, wandering organs, deliberate intention, and other mysterious forces. "Then" is placed in contrast to "now," the enlightened era when the "truth" has been discovered: strange behaviors are really illnesses caused by psychological or physical forces that are potentially explainable.

The predominant psychological and psychiatric method for labeling abnormal behavior is according to a medical model. Abnormal behavior is viewed as a manifestation of a "mental illness" with a specific cause, set of symptoms, and appropriate treatment. Some of the major categories of nonbiologically caused disorders are: psychoses, neuroses, psychophysiological disorders, and personality disorders (American Psychiatric Association, 1968). Psychoses are said to be present when functioning is grossly impaired; they include schizophrenia and manic-depressive illness. Neuroses are characterized by anxiety without gross distortion of external reality or major personality disorganization. Among the neuroses are phobias (excessive fears), obsessions and compulsions (uncontrollable thoughts and rituals), hysteria, anxiety, and depression without impaired reasoning. Psychophysiological disorders are physical disorders of presumably psychogenic origin, and affect various physiological and organ systems (i.e., cardiovascular, gastrointestinal, etc.). Personality disorders are long-standing maladaptive behavior patterns without the specific symptoms, anxiety, or disability of the other disorders. Included here are passive-aggressive personality, antisocial personality, and explosive personality. Persons who come into conflict with society, such as criminals, alcoholics and drug abusers are often labeled as having personality disorders. On the surface, their behavior is bothersome to others but not to themselves.

Even within this medical model there seem to be "styles" of psychiatric diagnosis that are changeable and reflect prevailing theoretical orientations, available treatments, and other cultural factors (Blum, 1978). For example, British psychiatrists have tended to diagnose many more patients manic-depressive than the Americans, who have appeared to prefer the diagnosis of schizophrenia. Yet increases in the United States in diagnoses of manic-depressive disorders have followed the recent availability here of new medications for mania and depression.

Labeling abnormal behavior. Psychiatric diagnosis and its supporting services of psychotherapy and psychiatric medication can be regarded as political activities because of the role they play in exercising social control (Halleck, 1971). In general terms, clinicians direct their judgments of mental illness more frequently against the powerless: women and the poor. Poor people report more psychogenic symptoms, show more evidence of psychological disorder, and are overrepresented among mental hospital patients (Dohrenwend & Dohrenwend, 1969; Hollingshead & Redlich, 1958; Kleiner, Tuckman, & Lavell, 1960; Srole, Langer, Michael, Opler, & Rennie, 1963). In the years since World War II, women have predominated in first admissions to mental hospitals (public and private), psychiatric care in general hospitals, psychiatric treatment by general practitioners, and psychiatric outpatient care (public and private). Also, their physical symptoms are more often labeled psychophysiological than men's (Gove & Tudor, 1973). These sex differences in psychiatric symptomatology cannot be explained by a greater willingness among women to admit to socially undesirable characteristics. When sources of response bias are controlled, the sex differences in reports of symptoms increase rather than diminish (Clancy & Gove, 1975).

At first glance, such findings of differential rates of symptomatology suggest that women are more likely than men to have their behavior labeled and judged as "sick" or they are more frequently in distress, or both. Yet the picture is more complicated. Although women (since World War II) have had more psychoses, neuroses, and psychophysiological disorders, men predominate in personality disorders (Dohrenwend & Dohrenwend, 1974; King, 1978). When one also considers the much larger number of men than women labeled "criminals," it is clear that men are not immune to being labeled as deviant.

Nevertheless, there are differences in the implications of the labels given to women and men. The labels of psychoses, neuroses, and psychophysiological disorders that women receive are more likely both to be associated with personal distress and to be amenable to treatment. By definition, personality disorders are deeply ingrained. They are part of the character and hence are not particularly bothersome to the person him- or herself or amenable to change. The most common view of criminal behavior is similar. Despite superficial efforts to provide treatment for prison inmates, criminals are more frequently seen as "bad" people who need to be punished because their behavior is offensive to others. Another way of looking at the female-male differences in clinical judgments is to see them as saying "poor, sick girl" and "bad boy."

Both types of labels have costs and benefits. Although the "poor, sick girl" is to be pitied and understood, she is also subject to the social control that is sometimes a characteristic of psychiatric treatment. The social control efforts extended to the "bad boy" are more obvious and thus perhaps easier to resist, since one can potentially reject visible efforts at change more readily than subtle ones. Yet, he is often regarded as a "lost cause" from the beginning and is given little sympathy or opportunity for real change.

Sex roles and clinical judgments. Judgments by mental health professionals about what behavior is "normal" or "abnormal," "healthy" or "sick," are affected by sex-role stereotypes. There is a strong link between what people in general consider socially desirable behavior for the sexes, and judgments made by mental health professionals. In a study of clinical judgments, practicing clinicians with a wide range of experience rated a hypothetical healthy adult man, woman, or adult with sex unspecified on a set of bipolar descriptors (Broverman et al., 1970). Both female and male clinicians displayed a strong consensus about which behaviors and attitudes characterized a healthy male, a healthy female, and a healthy adult independent of sex, respectively. Also, their concepts of health for the sex-unspecified adult and for the man were not different. Their concepts of health for the woman, however, differed significantly from those of the adult. For example, clinicians suggested that healthy women differ from healthy men by being more submissive, less independent, less adventurous, more easily influenced, less aggressive, more excitable in minor crises, less objective, and more concerned about their appearance. Therapists seem to be no less free from stereotypes than the rest of the population, and perhaps they apply those stereotypes in their work.

The result of such ratings is said to be a "double standard" of mental health for the sexes (Broverman et al., 1970). A female has the choice of behaving as a "healthy woman" in which case her behavior is different from that of a "healthy adult," or of behaving as a "healthy adult" in which case her behavior is inconsistent with that of a "healthy woman." A man, on the other hand, is faced with no such choice, for by behaving as a "healthy man" he is also behaving as a "healthy adult."

More recent reports suggest decreasing consensus about standards of mental health for women, although male counselors continue to give stereotyped answers. In a replication of the Broverman study (with the improvement of giving counselors a wider range of choices than two for each item), female and male counselors in training continued to agree about the characteristics they expected for healthy adults and healthy men (Maslin & Davis, 1975). There was more variability, however, in their ratings of the adult woman. Male counselors held somewhat more stereotypic expectations for healthy females than for other persons. Female counselors held approximately the same expectations for all healthy persons, regardless of sex.

In light of the findings that clinical judgments are linked to expected behavior in a culture, one wonders how an androgynous person would be judged by a mental health practitioner. There are no studies to date of practitioners' reactions to androgynous clients, yet there is the risk that androgynous people would be seen by some clinicians as disturbed.

Because clinicians judging behavior seem to be influenced both by the behavior and by who performs it, there are contradictory predictions about their responses to androgynous clients. In describing the healthy adult, sex unspecified, they seem able to point out some qualities associated with effective action; thus, one would predict that they would respect the effectiveness of the androgynous person's behavior. Yet, even though some feminine behaviors are associated with effectiveness, clinicians would apparently not approve, for they seem reluctant to value feminine characteristics positively. Further, because clinicians do seem to have different standards for females and males, masculine behavior by a female might not be as readily approved as in a male, and feminine behavior by a male might also be sanctioned.

This discussion is speculative, of course, for there are no studies that test how these values affect therapists' actual practices. Our discussion of the politics of clinical judgment suggests, however, that clinicians would react not only to the client's behavior but to their own expectations for the sexes. Such reactions might take the form of selectively reinforcing sex-typed behavior in clients, or subtly encouraging clients toward sex-typed goals. Therapists' actual clinical practice will be taken up in the next section.

Another Look

Although labels for disordered behavior may change throughout history, their links with cultural values remain firm. Thus, today, females and males who report to the helping professions may be regarded differently. Therapists are not immune to the prevailing values of society, including sex-role stereotypes. Nevertheless, they may be becoming sensitive to the part these values play in their work. There is some suggestion of an increasing awareness among practitioners of at least what they "ought" to say.

Yet no remedy will do away with the politics of clinical judgment. The decision to label a person abnormal, which often involves a change in their status or deprivation of liberty, is not a psychiatric but a social judgment (Ennis & Litwack, 1974). There are no objective "experts" to make these decisions, for everyone is part of the cultural context.

INDIVIDUAL CHANGE THROUGH PSYCHOTHERAPY

So far in this chapter we have discussed both the political and personal sides of psychological well-being. We have looked at some of the effects of and criteria for labeling abnormal behavior, as well as some of the concomitants of personal reports of psychological well-being and distress. Although many people react to these labels and feelings by trying to effect change on their own in their lives, many others turn to psychotherapists for help in dealing with their problems.

Therapy is a process whereby one person (the client) experiencing emotional distress consults (voluntarily or involuntarily) a professional (the therapist) who is presumed to have the capability to help reduce that distress. The assumption is usually that the client has a problem in her or his approach to life, handling of relationships, or responses to stress. Once this problem is resolved, so the thinking goes, the client should be able to return to normal functioning and adjustment. Within such a framework, therapy usually focuses on finding ways to help the client adjust to the world as it is (to conform) rather than on changing the world itself.

The Perils of Therapy: Social Control

The therapeutic process is permeated with values (Beit-Hallahmi, 1974; Halleck, 1971; London, 1964). By offering counsel to a person, no matter how subtly or indirectly, the therapist cannot help conveying her or his own perspective on life. The conception of "the good life" is a very personal one, but one that is implicated in the ways therapists approach problems. We have already discussed therapists' biases in labeling problems. Now we will focus on how their values affect therapy itself.

It has been suggested that a client's beliefs and actions incline more and more toward the therapist's during the course of therapy (Pepinsky & Karst, 1964). In fact, clients judged most improved in therapy had modified their values regarding sex, aggression, and authority to more closely resemble those of their therapists. Unimproved clients tended to become less like their therapists in values (Rosenthal, 1955). The fact that the judgments of improvement were made by people other than the therapists suggests genuine exchange of personal standards of what is right and desirable took place from therapist to client.

Mental health professionals help define and carry out some of society's standards (Rawlings & Carter, 1977). Society has given them the power and prerogative to ultimately decide who is deviant, ill, needy, and entitled to their services. By accepting this mandate, therapists take on the role of judge about what kinds of behaviors need to be changed. They involve themselves further in making subtle distinctions between what behavior represents positive development, physical illness, madness, maladjustment, failure of will, wickedness, etc. They take on a form of the parental role in deciding who is good, who is bad, who should be rewarded, who should be punished, and who should be treated.

Since most psychologists and psychiatrists are white, middle class, and male (Chesler, 1972), the decisions they make tend to reflect white, middle-class, and male values. As products of a particular society, all therapists are likely to emphasize the prevailing values. Within such a context, any movements beyond the status quo—away from stereotyped sex roles—may be discouraged and perhaps perceived as pathological. Assertiveness in women may be perceived as "masculine striving," and expressions of dependency in men may be defined as "failure to accept the male role." A homemaker and mother's depression, and a man's alienation at work may be labeled as deviant, and attributed to the person's pathological inability to fit her or his role.

Despite these suggestions of stereotypes among practitioners in the mental health field, studies of their reactions to simulated case studies and therapeutic interactions find less evidence of evaluative prejudice against women (Abramovitz & Dokecki, 1977). One typical study involved the presentation of written case material to group therapists (Abramovitz, Roback, Schwartz, Yasuna, Abramovitz, & Gomes, 1976). The material described one client's (female or male) background and problems, then one group therapy incident in which the client was initially very quiet and then began to cry. Therapists were asked to describe what response they would make and what they thought of the client. The hypothetical client's sex did not seem to affect the majority of the ratings made by the therapists. The few differences involved reports of a better prognosis and more empathy for the female client, and a decision to throw the problem back to the whole group for the male client. Interpretation on the basis of these few findings is not justified, in face of the overwhelming number of "no differences" found in the study.

A major problem with such simulated studies, as even their authors point out, is in making generalizations. It is not clear whether there is any relationship between what therapists *say* they will do in a hypothetical case and what they actually do when confronted with the situation. The time for reflection and the knowledge that their therapeutic responses are being scrutinized in the simulated studies may permit therapists to give more "liberal," "nondiscriminatory" responses than they would make under pressure in a real situation.

In fact, more naturalistic studies do suggest that therapists' stereotypes often affect clinical practice. Relatively inexperienced and male therapists seem particularly vulnerable to these effects. Women were seen in therapy for more sessions than men when the young therapist was a male (Abramovitz, Abramovitz, Roback, Corney, & McKee, 1976). Men were more likely than women to be put in group therapy, preserving the women for the more intimate individual therapy (Brodey & Detre, 1972). Beginning male therapists were also more likely to give females than males diagnostic materials designed to elicit sexual-romantic themes (Masling & Harris, 1969).

Therapists thus do seem to be affected by clients' sex; they seem more willing to see the female in the "patient" role. Females are seen as better patients, according to two studies of residents of a small, short-term, inpatient psychiatric unit (Doherty & Liang 1976a, 1976b). Male patients were more likely to be rejected and rated as unimproved over the course of their stay by the staff. The women seemed to get more involved and adhered to the unit's norm of openness. Males who were disliked seemed to be those who violated the norms of the unit by being aloof and critical. Females who were disliked were those who apparently violated the norms for their sex by being nonaffectionate and outspoken. Most women, particularly the more feminine ones, seemed to be "ideal" patients.

At first glance these women seem to be at an advantage in treatment: liked by the staff and rated as improved, they seem to stand a good chance of benefiting from the hospitalization. Yet the positive ratings did not carry over into the staff's posthospital plans for women, although they did for men. Men recommended for further hospitalization were rated as more disturbed than other men or any women. Yet recommendations for women patients were unrelated to their impairment ratings. The decision to discharge women was related to their life circumstances; women who were discharged were more likely to be working, married, and older than those kept for further hospitalization. These variables were not related to plans for male patients.

It is difficult to decide whether female or male patients had a greater disadvantage in that hospital unit. Staff liked the women, saw them as improving—and then referred them to further hospitalization or discharge regardless of impairment. In fact, they were all less impaired than the men referred for further hospitalization. Staff did not like the men, saw little change in them and seemed to form opinions of them early on. Yet the men were sent out in a manner consistent with their impairment.

Therapists' conceptions of their clients' problems have implications for change. Caplan and Nelson (1973) identify two types of explanations of social problems —person-centered and situation-centered—that correspond to the exceptionalistic and individualistic distinction discussed in Chapter 2. A person-centered interpretation of marital problems would focus on the histories, dynamics, and emotions of the people involved. The person-centered observer would search for what it is about the two people that makes them unable to live happily together. A situation-centered observer facing the same problem might focus on the institution of marriage itself: what is it about the way this culture has institutionalized marriage that makes it so difficult for these two people to live happily together? The first approach would suggest work on internal factors; the second would lead to attempts to change social or external factors. Most psychologists have a tendency to use person-centered interpretations because it is the nature of their discipline to focus on understanding the individual rather than entire social systems.

Potential oppression in therapy through therapists' focus on individual culpability, their standards of right and wrong, and their own sociocultural narrowness of vision are illustrated throughout Phyllis Chesler's (1972) book, *Women and Madness.* Women, as more frequent users of therapy, as well as members of a society that tends to devalue them (cf., Deaux & Emswiller, 1974; Goldberg, 1968), are particularly vulnerable to the hazardous side of therapy. Chesler described several women's careers as clients, which included heavy doses of drugs, sexual involvement with therapists, and continued coercion to conformity. Although these negative side effects of psychotherapy do not occur in every case, they are not unheard of. The passivity and dependency to which many women are socialized make them relatively easy victims of a mental health system that frequently works as an instrument of ongoing socialization.

Therapy is not necessarily beneficial for men either. Because men rarely admit to emotional distress openly, their very presence in therapy marks them as abnormal and invites negative judgments from therapists. Further, because in this culture, the stereotypic view of men is that they are strong emotionally, it might be difficult for therapists to perceive men's pain. For many men, therapy can be a difficult experience because they are unaccustomed to asking for help and to being in a one-down power position.

The Potential of Therapy: Individual Change

Although therapy can serve as a social control mechanism that discards social misfits and subtly pressures the disenchanted back into their social role, it need not do so. Although there is a powerful conservative force built into most individual therapy approaches, positive change can be effected through individual therapy.

Kaplan (1976) has suggested that therapy can serve as a vehicle for resocialization in the direction of androgyny. Through some of the same processes that help induce social conformity in clients, therapists can also help clients move beyond conformity in an effective manner. This resocialization can take the form of recognizing feelings or reactions that have been either over- or underdeveloped as a result of sex-role socialization. The "missing parts" of one's repertoire can be added, as it were. Therapists can help those who have been trained to inhibit their anger to recognize it and use it constructively. For people who hold back expressions of dependency, therapy can provide a means for learning how to show neediness. The positive aspects of skills already present can be recognized and preserved. The possibilities are as endless as the deficits people bring to therapy.

For those who already have a broad repertoire of feminine and masculine characteristics, therapy can help them learn to read situational cues so that they can respond appropriately. Sometimes it is appropriate and effective to be aggressive; at other times, independence, nurturance, or sympathy would be a more useful reaction. One of the hallmarks of the androgynous person should be the ability to respond in any of a large variety of ways, using behavior that is reasonable for the circumstances. People may need help in learning how to identify appropriate types of behavior, as well as in feeling comfortable expressing new behaviors. With such training, they can begin to select and apply the appropriate response for each situation.

A sex-roles framework could be part of the process of assessing clients' problems. For example, a female client might be suffering from a psychophysiological disorder such as colitis. Close examination of the sex-role related aspects of her life might reveal stress associated with the conflict between her desires to be a warm, nurturant "good mother," and her desires for independent achievement in the paid labor force. By examining and learning to handle these conflicts she may well reduce her feelings of stress and, ultimately, her physical symptoms.

Therapy clients can also be helped to recognize some of the social sources of their problems. This can be a first step in dealing with the pains and pressures imposed by present cultural values. Victims of discrimination and misunderstandings perpetuated by stereotyped expectations can be helped to understand the social origins of their difficulties. Therapy can serve as a setting for talking about the experiences, sorting out feelings, understanding what happened, and figuring out what action to take.

Therapy can also serve the important function of supporting changes that do not conform to traditional stereotyped roles. Therapists' communications about feelings that are not socially sanctioned can provide a foundation for change: "You're not crazy to be depressed at home all day alone with an infant—however beautiful and lovable that infant is." "Your feelings of dissatisfaction about this prestigious job are not unusual and are sometimes helped by facing the issue of what you as an individual person want to do with your life." "Yes, being single is sometimes lonely, but you've often told me how lonely you feel in your marriage." These perspectives can give reassurance and support toward change.

Therapists can enhance the resocialization process by providing support for clients' attempts to recognize their full range of feelings and to arrive at new forms of behavior. Realizing that integration of feminine and masculine characteristics is often unfamiliar, difficult, and unheralded, therapists can assist the discovery process. At the same time, they can realize—and help the client realize—that androgyny may bring her or him into conflict with some of the sex-typed standards of society.

Viewing therapy in these ways makes some of its potential apparent. Therapy need not serve only to enhance conformity to old roles and values. It can help provide clients with the strength and skill to combat and continue to face a stereotyped society.

Feminist therapy represents the attempt by some therapists to overcome the potential negative aspects of psychotherapy. Within feminist therapy there is an emphasis on social rather than personal, external rather than internal, explanations for psychological distress and problems (Rawlings & Carter, 1977). Each person is encouraged to take responsibility for her or his life by recognizing the strength of social pressures. Therapists' values are made explicit. Whenever possible, the personal power between therapist and client approaches equality.

Issues in the Use of Therapy

Therapy is not so simple as our discussion of its potential would suggest. Above all else, it is a relationship, and relationships are notoriously complex. A full appreciation of the difficulties involved in helping people move toward androgyny through psychotherapy is not possible without considering some of the issues involved.

Who should do therapy? As we have seen, therapy seems to involve a convergence of clients' values toward those of the therapist. Some writers have suggested that, for reasons of both efficiency and ethics, clients and therapists should be prematched on values. This would diminish potential problems, like the assignment of the libertarian client to the ultraconservative therapist which would force the client to become more conservative or not benefit from therapy. Likewise, the vehemently antifeminist client would probably not do well with a feminist therapist. Nor would the feminist client achieve the full benefit of therapy with a therapist who holds traditional, sex-typed values.

However, the fact that most therapists are middle-class, white, and male, and thus probably represent a rather narrow range of values, would then limit the types of clients who could benefit from therapy. Although therapists might be educated to understand and appreciate diverse value systems, such efforts can be made unnecessary. If therapists represented a broader cross-section of society, a broad spectrum of clients could partake of therapy with greater ease and confidence. The possibility of having one's values superseded by those of an "alien" therapist would not be so great. Although some differences between therapist's and client's values may be helpful, large gaps could threaten the client's integrity.

In the meantime, until therapists who are representative of a full range of attitudes and values are available, therapists need to be particularly aware of the values they bring to therapy. It would help if they made their values clear to clients whenever possible and were ready to refer clients with strongly discrepant values elsewhere. Clients need to feel free to question therapists about their value orientations. Training programs for therapists could also help ameliorate value problems by providing opportunities for fuller understandings of the experiences and values of a wide range of potential clients. For example, male therapists in training could be exposed to information about female socialization and the effects on women of their subordinate status. Special efforts could also be made to help female therapists understand the negative elements of the male role, such as pressure to repress emotions and a lack of options for full family involvement.

Power, dependency, and anger. Therapy is, inevitably, a relationship with overtones of unequal power. By definition, the client is a person in some sort of distress who consults a therapist—"the expert." The client is asking the therapist for help and the therapist is trying to give it. Therapy is a model that assigns one person the role of authority and the other the role of needy person. This set of relationships has implications for power, dependency, and anger in clients of both sexes.

Therapy is a paradoxical relationship, similar to that between parent and child. It is constructed for the sole purpose of working toward its own demise. Ideally, therapist and client work together temporarily so that the client can exist without the therapist's help in the long run. The unequal power is supposed to decline as the client becomes more independent and self-sufficient. Yet there is an inherent contradiction as the client tries to move toward independence through dependence, toward more power through less power.

These conflicting tendencies at the core of therapy can present problems. Sometimes clients cannot tolerate the temporary dependence, and sometimes they are unwilling to take the leap toward separation when the time has come. Therapists themselves are certainly not infallible and, hence, sometimes do more to foster dependence than the independence that is the ostensible goal.

For many women clients, this relationship involving relatively low power and high dependency recreates many they have known. They stand in danger of falling into the old, familiar pattern of relying for the guidance, security, and evaluation on a powerful partner. Therapists need to be aware of this possibility. They need to be cautious, to increase women's chances of emerging from therapy changed in a positive way. It is all too simple for many women to follow the comfortable and familiar path, changing to fit the expectations of the latest partner, in this case the therapist. Care must be taken to preserve the woman client's autonomy and decision-making power. This could well involve a woman client's decision to remain more sex-typed than the therapist would prefer. To push a woman toward increased self-orientation is similar to saying, "I demand that you be independent!" An impossible request, for to carry it out is to defeat its purpose.

Within this relational context, women's anger in therapy takes on an added dimension. As in any intimate relationship, angry feelings are engendered in therapy. Therapists need to be cautious so that women's anger is expressed and recognized. An awareness of the relational and socialization factors that inhibit such expressions in women is necessary, but difficult to carry through to action. There are some fine lines of distinction to be learned before therapists and clients can confront, respect, and move beyond this anger.

For many men clients, the therapy relationship is an unfamiliar, and hence especially troublesome one. Their apparent reluctance to enter therapy may be partially due to an unease about admitting their vulnerability and to being in a dependent, low-power position. Although by avoiding therapy, men may avoid its potential hazards, they are denying themselves its potential benefits as well. If they choose to enter therapy, their lack of experience in being dependent in adulthood can lead to panic or the conviction that any hints of dependency signal a permanent return to childhood relationships. Therapists who recognize this potential dynamic may have a head start in helping the male who is overly trained in the masculine role to benefit from the therapeutic relationship. For men (and sex-typed masculine women), the very dependency inherent in therapy can be helpful if they learn that they can maintain their integrity while admitting their neediness.

It is all too easy for some men to play out their discomfort with the dependency and low power in therapy through angry confrontations. Men, especially those who are comfortable about expressing angry feelings, can use anger to try to regain independence and power. However, the blatant and nondiscriminatory use of anger is rarely likely to be therapeutic. If the expressions are severe enough, the result can be a premature termination of the therapeutic relationship.

Hence, although therapy can take people from where they are (psychologically speaking) toward their potential, therapy is frequently hindered by the very characteristics and patterns it seeks to change. Enhancing people's options for behavioral flexibility, situational appropriateness, and integration of feminine and masculine characteristics requires recognition of some of the predispositions and hesitations that the products of a sex-typed society bring to therapy. Without such awareness, the hazards of therapy become real possibilities.

Therapy and the sex-typed client. Therapists can use the concept of androgyny as an aid in diagnosis and assessment. A useful way to conceptualize problems is in terms of skills and deficits in the various aspects of instrumental and expressive, agentic and communal functions.

Sex-typed clients would be those who lack skills or motivation to behave in a nontraditional fashion. Although such clients might be suffering as a result of these deficits (i.e., the sex-typed feminine client who has lost any sense of her own desires; the sex-typed masculine client who has lost touch with real intimacy in his relationships), they may be enjoying a measure of support for their adherence to social expectations.

The direction for change might be apparent to the therapist in such a case, but she or he should proceed cautiously. Care must be taken to become aware of and respect both the clients' values and the reality of the social milieu. Perhaps the therapist could discuss these issues directly with the client, pointing out the possible consequences of change. The client might be giving up a "sex-role neurosis" only to confront some losses of social support. The problem is similar to the one in marital therapy, in which couples are sometimes warned in advance that talking about their problems directly can precipitate increased conflict.

Therapy and the androgynous client. If the client seems to be skilled and comfortable with both the feminine and masculine dimensions, yet is still experiencing difficulty, the therapist should look both to the individual and the social environment. The distress may stem from conflict between the client's own more stereotyped standards and the behavior patterns she or he has developed. Alternatively, the client might value both the feminine and masculine mode, but be having trouble integrating them or using them appropriately.

Another possibility is that the stress derives from conflict with a social environment that has more stereotyped expectations than the client can meet. Here, solutions may be possible, yet they are not as readily under the client's own control. She or he may be able to find other groups that are more supportive, though sometimes that is not possible. It is in the latter case that the client is facing the ultimate paradox of androgyny: the personally desirable expression that is not socially desirable. At this point both therapist and client are confronting the very real limitations of individual therapy. For all its potential as a resocialization tool, it cannot effect genuine social change at the cultural level.

Another Look

While psychotherapy can be beneficial to clients, it can also be harmful. Therapists can serve as agents of social control by encouraging adjustment to sex-typed norms. Therapists have been shown to react differently to female and male clients, and to hold stereotypic expectations for the sexes.

These results reflect the behavior of the average therapist. Yet, the therapist who works to remain sensitive to sex-role-related issues in therapy such as stereotyped expectations, power, dependency, and anger may help clients enjoy therapy's potential benefits. These benefits include support for countering a stereotypic culture, increased flexibility, development of new behaviors which had been "undertrained" in childhood, and greater awareness of sex-role pressures. In the long run, therapy clients may develop enough individual strengths that they may be better able to help effect change in the larger society.

CHANGE IN THE SOCIAL CONTEXT

We have pointed out that androgyny is not always associated with well-being because of problems with social pressures. Although psychotherapy, carefully carried out, can help clients learn to read situational cues and integrate their conflicting tendencies, broader change is needed to deal with the social context. Androgyny cannot really be effective in a society that devalues women and the feminine mode, that limits persons' options by treating them differentially according to sex, class, and race, and that grants greater power to one sex than the other.

The "social context" is experienced on at least two levels. There is a specific social network and the more nebulous larger society, with its values, demands, and limitations. One's social network includes all the people with whom one comes in contact: family, friends, coworkers, neighbors, bus drivers, clerks in stores, etc. (Speck & Attneave, 1973). Since, to a certain extent, one can choose at least some of the people with whom one comes in contact, this level is more readily controlled. Although it is not possible to create a life style in which one comes into contact only with similarly-minded people, a sort of supportive oasis can be created.

A supportive peer group can be particularly important for groundbreakers or others who are "outsiders" to the mainstream of society, such as persons striving toward androgyny. It can act as a cushion from the blows of the majority group and as an exchange for new ideas and skills.

The usefulness of such supportive groups can be seen readily in professional circles. A group of feminists who were learning to do therapy bonded together for many hours of discussion. Within that group they could at least deal openly with their difficulties in translating their feminist ideals into therapeutic reality. They could not have done this as easily with a more traditional group of peers, where fundamental value differences would have been the focus of struggles. Among the group who agreed on basic values and goals, it was possible to get on with work together. The group was not free of disagreement. Yet the differences were more likely to support and stimulate growth, since members shared some common values.

The benefits derived from selecting a group that can join in the struggle against the prevailing ideology are also seen in the phenomenon of "consciousness raising" (CR) or "support groups." More organized than the group of feminist therapists, CR groups were particularly prevalent during the earlier stages of the most recent wave of the feminist movement. In these groups, women discussed each other's personal experiences and problems in a usually supportive atmosphere. Members encouraged each other to view difficulties from a political and social rather than a personal perspective (Cherniss, 1972). Attributions were made to sexism and patriarchy, rather than to personal failings or psychological abnormalities. Women joined these leaderless self-help groups with the desire for societal transformation. Often significant changes in behavior resulted (Cherniss, 1972).

Similar groups for men disturbed by the problematic aspects of sexism for males were also developed. Although formal male or female CR groups are less apparent these days, they are credited with providing much of the impetus and many of the methods for combatting stereotyped sex roles at a personal level (Brodsky, 1973).

For the person who wants to become more androgynous and build a less stereotyped life style, a supportive peer group seems invaluable. Although some people may be strong enough to do it alone, for many, support is necessary. Family, friends, or coworkers who share androgynous goals and values can provide reassurance that "it's not crazy" to question stereotypes and that it is not easy. The support offered can be both emotional and specific. For example, it can help with problems such as these: How does one raise children who are androgynous when television, schools, and even one's own background seem to favor the stereotypes? Are there ways to balance or integrate work and intimacy? How does one maintain one's androgynous vision while immersed in the complexities of relationships? How can a self-orientation be integrated with an other-orientation? Are there new ways of handling work, anger, and dependency that are consistent with the goal of androgyny? Genuine peer support in struggling with these issues on a daily basis can sometimes be more effective than a therapist. It can also help protect one from the lack of support of a society that seems to hold different values.

Although one can select friends, a spouse, and even a work situation carefully so that one can find support for androgynous ideals, broader social change is less easy to achieve. Nevertheless, discussion of contextual barriers and supports to the development of androgyny must take into account the influence of prevailing cultural values.

The United States emerges as a culture with highly agentic, masculine values. College students in six countries (Norway, Sweden, Denmark, Finland, England, and the United States) were asked to describe their idealized self, the "kind of person I would most like to be." In the two countries that have a tradition of social welfare (Sweden and Denmark), there were fewer sex differences and less emphasis on agency than in the others. Further, men in the United States, the most capitalistic country of those studied, put greater emphasis than other men on agentic qualities like adventurousness, assertiveness, restlessness, ambition, self-centeredness, shrewdness, and self-confidence (Block, 1973).

The United States also emerged as more sex-typed than the others. College students' recollections of parental childrearing orientations revealed significantly greater emphasis on early and clear sex-typing in the United States. The agentic theme also continued to be apparent, in that American parents were perceived by their children as emphasizing competitive achievement, and attaching less importance to the control of aggression in sons (Block, 1973).

These findings do not necessarily mean that there are actual cultural differences in personality, as in "national character types." Yet they do reveal clear-cut differences in valued qualities. Further, these values held for the self by the average college student are consistent with the values reflected in a nation's social and economic systems. Capitalism in particular seems to parallel an agentic orientation.

The value attached to agentic or stereotypically masculine characteristics for both male and female students in the United States is particularly striking, as is the emphasis on sex typing. Although many of the qualities they idealized are certainly positive ones, one wonders what values are attached to communal or feminine characteristics. Broad social support for feminine characteristics or for deviation from the sex-typed norm seem hard to come by, particularly in this culture.

How can change in such deeply-rooted cultural values come about? Alice Rossi (1969) suggests at least two models: assimilation and hybrid. In the assimilation model, the present structure of society is considered stable and desirable. Minority groups are urged to accept the values and goals of the dominant group within that system as their own. The hybrid model, on the other hand, requires a restructuring of society, so that the lives of both the dominant and minority groups will be different. The world of jobs, laws, and politics would be changed as well as the lives of individual people.

As long as the dominant forces in this society emphasize agentic values and deemphasize communal values, change toward androgyny under the assimilation model seems frustrating at best and impossible at worst. Without change in the broader spheres of society, individual change is problematic. Only through a fundamental change in values, reflected in economic, legal, and social changes would the communal elements of existence be regarded highly enough so that individuals would be free to enjoy androgyny. Androgyny cannot really flourish unless communal values are given as much emphasis as agentic ones.

In order to comprehend the types of economic, legal, and social change required, it is helpful to imagine a society in which both agentic and communal values are prominent. First of all, basic physical needs of all people would be met, for when one is warm, well fed, and well clothed, emotional development is more readily achieved (cf., Maslow, 1970). Opportunities for jobs would not be limited by class, sex, or race but rather by skill and desire. Because the educational system would not channel people according to class, sex, or race, all would have the opportunity to develop individual skills. Flexibility in life planning would be possible because there would be no governmental interference with reproductive freedom and structures for intimate relationships. Widely available, high-quality day care, as well as institutional support for parenting leaves would permit parents flexibility to organize their family and work lives according to their desires. Close involvement with family and childrearing would be so highly valued that no penalties would be invoked for taking time for family responsibilities. A value on human life would be apparent when corporations accept lower productivity and profits as acceptable concomitants of business organized to enhance the lives of workers and consumers.

The fantasy could continue indefinitely, but the point by now should be clear: such a society is not around the corner. Although such dreaming sounds unrealistic even to our own ears, we have come to the conclusion that the full range of the potential benefits to be derived from androgyny are impossible without such fundamental social change.

CONCLUSIONS

We arrive at the end of this examination of androgyny and its implications for psychology feeling alternately invigorated and pessimistic. On the one hand, the concept still makes sense to us. It seems to have potential benefits for both sexes, to fit with some of the available data in psychology, to suggest enough hypotheses to last a researcher's lifetime, and to have positive practical implications for moving beyond sex-role stereotypes. Yet we are learning to temper that excitement with a growing awareness of the limits imposed by current social structures. Yes, it *would* be nice if people could be androgynous and live happily ever after. But this is not a fairy tale and these consequences cannot readily happen unless a massive reorganization of society removes the barriers.

In the meantime, the inherent tension between androgyny and current social structures needs to be recognized. Although there are potential advantages associated with androgyny, there are also disadvantages in the current climate. It may be useful to find alternative social structures within which to work. Those who elect to remain within traditional structures in the corporate, professional, and academic worlds, should be ready to face the continuing clash between androgyny and the prevailing social values.

SELECTED READINGS

Brodsky, A., & Hare-Mustin, R. (Eds.) *Women and psychotherapy.* New York: Guilford Press, in press.

Bruch, H. *The golden cage.* Cambridge: Harvard University Press, 1978.

Fasteau, M. F. *The male machine.* New York: McGraw-Hill, 1974.

Miller, J. B. *Toward a new psychology of women.* Boston: Beacon Press, 1976.

Rawlings, E. I., & Carter, D. K. *Psychotherapy for women: Treatment toward equality.* Springfield, Ill.: Charles C. Thomas, 1977.

Zeldow, P. B. Sex differences in psychiatric evaluation and treatment: An empirical review. *Archives of general psychiatry,* 1978, *35*, 89-93.

References

Abramowitz, C. V., & Dodecki, P. R. The politics of clinical judgment: Early empirical returns. *Psychological Bulletin,* 1977, *84,* 460–476. **349**

Abramowitz, S. I., Abramowitz, C. V., Roback, H. B., Corney, R., & McKee, E. Sex-role related countertransference in psychotherapy. *Archives of General Psychiatry,* 1976, *33,* 71–73. **349**

Abramowitz, S. I., Roback, H. B., Schwartz, J. M., Yasuna, A., Abramowitz, C. V., & Gomes, B. Sex bias in psychotherapy: A failure to confirm. *American Journal of Psychiatry,* 1976, *133,* 706–709. **349**

Abramson, P. R., Goldberg, P. A., Greenberg, P. H., & Abramson, R. H. The talking platypus phenomenon: Competency ratings as a function of sex and professional status. *Psychology of Women Quarterly,* 1977, *2,* 99–113. **42**

Abse, D. W. Hysterical conversion and dissociative syndromes and the hysterical character. In S. Arieti & E. B. Brody (Eds.), *American handbook of psychiatry* (Vol. 3). New York: Basic Books, 1974. **343**

Adams, M. *Single blessedness.* New York: Basic Books, 1976. **300, 301**

Adler, A. *Understanding human nature.* Garden City, N.Y.: Garden City, 1927. **184**

Alan Guttmacher Institute: *11 million teenagers: What can be done about the epidemic of adolescent pregnancies in the United States?* New York: Planned Parenthood Federation of America, 1976. **131**

Allgeier, E. R. Beyond sowing and growing: The relationship of sex typing to socialization, family plans, and future orientation. *Journal of Applied Social Psychology,* 1975, *5,* 217–226. **292**

Allport, G. *The nature of prejudice.* New York: Addison-Wesley, 1958. **49**

Almquist, E. M., & Angrist, S. S. Career salience and atypicality of occupational choice among college women. *Journal of Marriage and the Family,* 1970, *32,* 242–249. **312, 329**

Alper, T. G., & Greenberger, E. Relationship of picture structure to achievement motivation in college women. *Journal of Personality and Social Psychology,* 1967, *7,* 362–371. **252**

American Psychiatric Association. *Diagnostic and statistical manual of mental disorders (DSM II).* Washington, D.C.: American Psychiatric Association, 1968. **343, 345**

Amir, M. Forcible rape. *Sexual Behavior,* 1971, *1,* 25–36. **171–172**

Andrisani, P. J. Job satisfaction among working women. *Signs,* 1978, *3,* 588–607. **307**

Antill, J. K., & Cunningham, J. D. Self-esteem as a function of masculinity in both sexes. Unpublished paper, Macquarie Univ. Sydney, Australia. **21**

Aries, P. *Centuries of childhood: A social history of family life.* New York: Vintage Books, 1962. **272**

Astin, H. S., & Bayer, A. E. Sex discrimination in academe. In M. T. S. Mednick, S. S. Tangri, & L. W. Hoffman (Eds.), *Women and achievement: Social and motivational analyses.* Washington, D.C.: Hemisphere, 1975. **215**

Astin, H. S., Suniewick, N., & Dweck, N. *Women: A bibliography on their education and careers.* Washington, D.C.: Human Service Press, 1971. **329**

Atkinson, J. W., et al. *Motives in fantasy, action, and society.* New York: Van Nostrand, 1958. **49**

Babikian, H. M., & Goldman, A. A study in teen-age pregnancy. *American Journal of Psychiatry,* 1971, *128,* 111–116. **131**

Bachofen, J. J. *Myth, religion and mother right.* (R. Manhum, trans.). Princeton, N.J.: Princeton University Press, 1967. (Originally published, 1861.) **65, 141**

The page on which author and work are cited is shown in boldface.

Bahr, S. Effects on power and division of labor in the family. In L. W. Hoffman & F. I. Nye (Eds.), *Working mothers.* San Francisco: Jossey-Bass, 1974. **298**

Bakan, D. *The duality of human existence.* Chicago: Rand McNally, 1966. **6, 7, 51, 68**

Balswick, J. O., & Peek, C. W. The inexpressive male: A tragedy of American society. *Family Coordinator,* 1971, *20,* 363–368. **145, 302**

Bandura, A. Behavioral modifications through modeling procedures. In L. Krasner & L. P. Ullmann (Eds.), *Research in behavior modification.* New York: Holt, Rinehart & Winston, 1965. **186**

Barbach, L. G. *The fulfillment of female sexuality.* New York: Doubleday, 1975. **156**

Bardwick, J. *Psychology of women.* New York: Harper & Row, 1971. **119, 120, 121**

Barlow, D. H., Abel, G. G., Blanchard, E. B., et al. Plasma testosterone levels in male homosexuals: A failure to replicate. *Archives of Sexual Behavior,* 1974, *3,* 571; 575. **106**

Bart, P. Depression in middle-aged women. In V. Gornick & B. K. Moran (Eds.), *Woman in sexist society: Studies in power and powerlessness.* New York: Basic Books, 1971. **136**

Bart, P., & Grossman, M. Menopause. In M. T. Notman & C. N. Nadelson (Eds.), *The woman patient: Medical and psychological interfaces.* New York: Plenum, 1978. **111, 137, 287**

Bar-Tel, D., & Frieze, I. H. Achievement motivation for males and females as a determinant of attributions for success and failure. *Sex Roles,* 1977, *3,* 301–313. **246**

Baruch, G. K. Maternal influences upon college women's attitudes toward women and work. *Developmental Psychology,* 1972, *6,* 32–37. **329**

Basile, R. I. Lesbian mothers. *Women's Rights Law Reporter,* 1974, *2,* 3–25. **165**

Bass, B. M., Krusell, J., & Alexander, R. H. Male managers' attitudes toward working women. *American Behavioral Scientist,* 1971, *15,* 221–236. **324**

Beach, F. A. A review of physiological and psychological studies of sexual behavior in mammals. *Physiological Review,* 1947, *24,* 240–307. **99, 103**

Beach, F. A. Hormonal factors controlling the differentiation, development and display of copulatory behavior in the ramatergig and other related species. In L. Aronson & E. Tobach (Eds.), *Biopsychology of development.* New York: Academic Press, 1971. **104**

Beckman, L. J. The relative rewards and costs of parenthood and employment for employed women. *Psychology of Women Quarterly,* 1978, *2,* 215–234. **287, 296**

Begelman, D. A. Ethical and legal issues of behavior modification. In M. Hersen, R. M. Eisler, & P. M. Miller (Eds.), *Progress in behavior modification* (Vol. 1). New York: Academic Press, 1975. **165**

Beit-Hallahmi, B. Salvation and its vicissitudes: Clinical psychology and political values. *American Psychologist,* 1974, *29,* 124–129. **348**

Bell, A. P. Research in homosexuality: Back to the drawing board. *Archives of Sexual Behavior,* 1975, *4,* 421–431. **165, 166**

Belle, D. Mothers and their children: A study of low income families. In C. L. Heckerman (Ed.), *The evolving female: Women in psychosocial context.* New York: Human Sciences Press, 1979. **287**

Bem, S. L. *Psychology looks at sex roles: Where have all the androgynous people gone?* Paper presented at the UCLA Symposium on Women, May 1972. **5, 6, 264**

Bem, S. L. The measurement of psychological androgyny. *Journal of Consulting and Clinical Psychology,* 1974, *42,* 155–162. **12, 13–14, 27, 337, 338**

Bem, S. L. Sex role adaptibility: One consequence of psychological androgyny. *Journal of Personality and Social Psychology*, 1975, *31*, 634–643. **6, 13, 25, 42**

Bem, S. L. Probing the promise of androgyny. In A. G. Kaplan & J. P. Bean (Eds.), *Beyond sex role stereotypes: Readings toward a psychology of androgyny*. Boston: Little, Brown, 1976. **6, 16–18, 23**

Bem, S. L. On the utility of alternative procedures for assessing psychological androgyny. *Journal of Consulting and Clinical Psychology*, 1977, *45*, 196–205. **8, 20, 21, 22, 25, 248, 249**

Bem, S. L., & Lenney, E. Sex typing and the avoidance of cross-sex behavior. *Journal of Personality and Social Psychology*, 1976, *33*, 48–54. **25, 26**

Bem, S. L., Martyna, W., & Watson, C. Sex typing and androgyny: Further explorations of the expressive domain. *Journal of Personality and Social Psychology*, 1976, *34*, 1016–1023. **25, 26, 264**

Benedek, T. F., & Rubenstein, B. *The sexual cycle in women: The relation between ovarian function and psychodynamic processes*. Washington, D.C.: National Research Council, 1942. **119, 122**

Benton, A. A., Gelber, E. R., Kelley, H. H., & Liebling, B. A. Reactions to various degrees of deceit in a mixed-motive relationship. *Journal of Personality and Social Psychology*, 1969, *12*, 170–180. **248**

Bequaert, L. H. *Single women: Alone and together*. Boston: Beacon Press, 1976. **299, 300**

Berg, C. (Ed.) *The problem of homosexuality*. New York: Citadel Press, 1968. **165**

Berger, C. R. Sex differences related to self-esteem factor structure. *Journal of Consulting and Clinical Psychology*, 1968, *32*, 442–446. **244**

Berger, P. L., & Luckman, T. *The social construction of reality*. New York: Anchor Books, 1966. **35**

Bergman, J. Are little girls being harmed by "Sesame Street"? *New York Times*, January 2, 1972, Section D, p. 13. **212**

Bermant, G. Behavior therapy approaches to modification of sexual preferences: Biological perspective and critique. In J. M. Bardwick (Ed.), *Readings on the psychology of women*. New York: Harper & Row, 1972. **97**

Bernard, J. *The future of marriage*. New York: World, 1972. **279, 280, 281, 282, 288**

Bernard, J. *The future of motherhood*. New York: Dial, 1974.(a) **297, 303, 322**

Bernard, J. *Sex differences: An overview*. New York: MSS Modular Publications, Module 26, 1974.(b) **46**

Bernay, E. Affirmative inaction and other facts, trends, tactics for academic life. *Ms.*, 1978, *7* (November), 87–90. **215**

Berzins, J. I., Welling, M. A., & Wetter, R. E. A new measure of psychological androgyny based on the Personality Research Form. *Journal of Consulting and Clinical Psychology*, 1978, *46*, 126–138. **6, 12, 15, 16, 21**

Bettelheim, B. *Symbolic wounds: Puberty rites and the envious male*. New York: Collier, 1962. **113, 133**

Bieber, I., et al. *Homosexuality, a psychoanalytic study of male homosexuals*. New York: Basic Books, 1962. **165**

Biller, H. B. *Father, child, and sex role*. Lexington, Mass.: D. C. Heath, 1971. **289**

Birk, L., Williams, G. H., Chasen, M., et al. Semen testosterone levels in homosexual men. *New England Journal of Medicine*, 1973, *289*, 1236–1238. **106**

Birnbaum, J. A. Life patterns and self-esteem in gifted family oriented and career oriented women. In M. T. S. Mednick, S. S. Tangri, & L. W. Hoffman (Eds.), *Women and achievement: Social and motivational analyses*. Washington, D.C.: Hemisphere, 1975. **293, 296**

Bleier, R. H. Brain, body and behavior. In J. H. Roberts (Ed.), *Beyond intellectual sexism: A new woman, a new reality.* New York: Longman, 1976. **98, 103**

Block, J. H. Conceptions of sex role: Some cross-cultural and longitudinal perspectives. *American Psychologist,* 1973, *28,* 512–526. **192, 193, 204, 357**

Block, J. H. Issues, problems, and pitfalls in assessing sex differences: A critical review of "The Psychology of Sex Differences". *Merrill-Palmer Quarterly,* 1976, *22,* 283–308. **237**

Block, J., von der Lippe, A., & Block, J. H. Sex-role and socialization patterns: Some personality concomitants and environmental antecedents. *Journal of Consulting and Clinical Psychology,* 1973, *41,* 321–341. **196, 197, 198**

Blum, H. P. *Female psychology: Contemporary psychoanalytic views.* New York: International Universities Press, 1977. **184**

Blum, J. D. On changes in psychiatric diagnosis over time. *American Psychologist,* 1978, *33,* 1017–1031. **345**

Block, D. R., & Kolakowski, D. Further evidence of sex-linked major-gene influence on human spatial visualizing ability. *American Journal of Human Genetics,* 1973, *25,* 1–14. **240**

Boston Women's Health Book Collective. *Our bodies, ourselves.* New York: Simon and Schuster, 1976. **156**

Bott, E. *Family and social networks* (2nd ed.). New York: Free Press, 1971. **231, 283, 284**

Bowlby, J. *Attachment, Volume I: Attachment and loss.* New York: Basic Books, 1969. **232**

Bowles, S., & Gintis, H. *Schooling in capitalist America.* New York: Basic Books, 1976. **213–214**

Bowman, G., Wortney, B. N., & Greyser, S. H. Are women executives people? *Harvard Business Review,* 1965, *43,* 14–28; 164–178. **324**

Brannigan, G. G., & Tolor, A. Sex differences in adaptive styles. *Journal of Genetic Psychology,* 1971, *119,* 143–149. **248**

Brecher, R., & Brecher, E. (Eds.). *An analysis of the human sexual response.* New York: Signet, 1966. **147**

Bremner, W. J., & de Kretser, D. M. Contraceptives for males. *Signs: Journal of Women in Culture and Society,* 1975, *1,* 387–396. **159**

Brentlinger, J. (Ed.). *The symposium of Plato.* Amherst Mass.: University of Massachusetts Press, 1970. **67**

Breuer, J., & Freud, S. *Studies on hysteria.* In J. Strachey (Ed. and Trans.), *Standard edition of the complete psychological works of Sigmund Freud* (Vol. 2). London: Hogarth Press, 1964. (Originally published, 1895) **343**

Brodey, J. F., & Detre, T. Criteria used by clinicians in referring patients to individual or group therapy. *American Journal of Psychotherapy,* 1972, *26,* 176–184. **349**

Brodie, H. K., Cartrell, N., Doering, C., et al. Plasma testosterone levels in heterosexual and homosexual men. *American Journal of Psychiatry,* 1974, *131,* 82–83. **106**

Brodsky, A. The consciousness-raising group as a model for therapy with women. *Psychotherapy: Theory, Research, and Practice,* 1973, *10,* 24–29. **357**

Bronfenbenner, U. *American families: Trends and pressures.* Washington, D.C.: U.S. Government Printing Office, 1974. **285**

Brophy, J. E., & Good, T. L. *Teacher-student relationships: Causes and consequences.* New York: Holt, Rinehart & Winston, 1974. **216**

Broverman, I. K., Broverman, D. M., Clarkson, F. E., Rosenkrantz, P. S., & Vogel, S. R. Sex role stereotypes and clinical judgments of mental health. *Journal of Consulting and Clinical Psychology,* 1970, *34,* 1–7. **346, 347**

Broverman, I. K., Vogel, S. R., Broverman, D. M., Clarkson, F. E., & Rosenkrantz, P. S. Sex role stereotypes: A current appraisal. *Journal of Social Issues*, 1972, *38*(2), 59–78. **4n, 7, 244**

Brown, P., Perry, L., & Harburg, E. Sex role attitudes and psychological outcomes for black and white women experiencing marital dissolution. *Journal of Marriage and the Family*, 1977, *39*, 549–561. **337**

Brown, W. A., & Shereshefsky, P. Seven women: A prospective study of postpartum psychiatric disorders. *Psychiatry*, 1972, *35*, 139–159. **133**

Brownmiller, S. *Against our will: Men, women and rape*. New York: Simon & Schuster, 1975. **169, 171, 172**

Burgess, A. W., & Holstrom, L. L., Rape trauma syndrome. *American Journal of Psychiatry*, 1974, *131*, 981–986. **172, 174**

Burgess, A. W., & Holstrom, L. L. Coping behavior of the rape victim. *American Journal of Psychiatry*, 1976, *133*, 413–417. **170**

Burr, W. R. Satisfaction of various aspects of marriage over the life cycle: A random middle class sample. *Journal of Marriage and the Family*, 1970, *32*, 29–37. **287**

Campbell, A., Converse, P. E., & Rodgers, W. L. *The quality of American life: Perceptions, evaluations, and satisfaction*. New York: Russell-Sage, 1976. **287**

Caplan, N., & Nelson, S. D. On being useful: The nature and consequences of psychological research on social problems. *American Psychologist*, 1973, *28*, 199–211. **350**

Carlson, E. R., & Carlson, R. Male and female subjects in psychology research. *Journal of Abnormal and Social Psychology*, 1961, *61*, 482–483. **46**

Carlson, R. Understanding women: Implications for personality theory and research. *Journal of Social Issues*, 1972, *28*, 201–215. **46**

Cartwright L. K. Conscious factors entering into decisions of women to study medicine. *Journal of Social Issues*. 1972, *28*, 201–215. **329**

Cecil, E. H., Paul, R. J., & Olins, R. A. Perceived importance of selected variables used to evaluate male and female job applicants. *Personnel Psychology*, 1973, *26*, 397–404. **324**

Charcot, J. M. *Lectures on the diseases of the nervous system*. (G. Sigerson, trans.). London: New Sydenham Society, 1877. **343**

Cherniss, C. Personality and ideology: A personological study of women's liberation. *Psychiatry*, 1972, *35*(2), 109–125. **356**

Chertok, L. *Motherhood and personality*. London: Tavistock, 1969. **128, 132**

Chesler, P. *Women and madness*. New York: Doubleday, 1972. **349, 350–351**

Chesler, P. *The significance of feminism for female and male psychology*. Talk presented at the University of Rhode Island Honors Colloquium, November 9, 1978. **285**

Chinoy, E. *Automobile workers and the American dream*. Garden City, N.Y.: Doubleday, 1955. **316**

Chodorow, N. Being and doing: A cross-cultural examination of the socialization of males and females. In V. Gornick & B. K. Moran (Eds.), *Women in sexist society: Studies in power and powerlessness*. New York: Basic Books, 1971. **39**

Chodorow, N. *The reproduction of mothering: Psychoanalysis and the sociology of gender*. Stanford, Calif.: Stanford University Press, 1978. **288**

Christensen, H. T. *Marriage analysis: Foundation for successful family life*. New York: Ronald Press, 1958. **286**

Clancy, K., & Gove, W. Sex differences in mental illness: An analysis of response bias in self-reports. *American Journal of Sociology*, 1975, *80*, 205–215, **346**

Clinard, M. B. *Sociology of deviant behavior*. New York: Rinehart, 1958. **169**

Cohen, A. R. Upward communication in experimentally created hierarchies. *Human Relations*, 1958, *11*, 41–53. **172, 316**

Cohen, M. L. The psychology of rapists.

Seminars in Psychiatry, 1971, *3*, 311. **172**

Coleman, A. D., & Coleman, L. L. *Pregnancy: The psychological experience.* New York: Herder and Herder, 1971. **125, 129, 130, 131, 132, 133**

Coleman, J. C. *Abnormal psychology and modern life* (4th ed.). Glenview, Ill.: Scott, Foresman, 1972. **277, 345**

Condry, J., & Dyer, S. Fear of success: Attribution of cause to the victim. *Journal of Social Issues,* 1976, *32,* 62–83. **155**

Conn, J. H. Children's reactions to the discovery of genital differences. *American Journal of Orthopsychiatry,* 1940, *10,* 747–754. **183**

Constantinople, A. Masculinity-femininity: An exception to a famous dictum? *Psychological Bulletin,* 1973, *80,* 389–407. **12, 13**

Coopersmith, S. *The antecedents of self-esteem.* San Francisco: W. H. Freeman, 1967. **244**

Coppen, A., & Kessel, N. Menstruation and personality. *British Journal of Psychiatry,* 1963, *109,* 711–721. **118, 122**

Cosentino, F., & Heilbrun, A. B. Anxiety correlates of sex-role identity in college students. *Psychological Reports,* 1964, *14,* 729–730. **337**

Costrich, N., Feinstein, J., Kidder, L., Marecek, J., & Pascale, L. When stereotypes hurt: Three studies of penalties for sex-role reversals. *Journal of Experimental Social Psychology,* 1975, *11,* 520–530. **248, 250, 339**

Cott, N. F. *The bonds of womanhood.* New Haven: Yale University Press, 1977. **273**

Crandall, V. C. Sex differences in expectancy of intellectual and academic reinforcement. In C. P. Smith (Ed.), *Achievement related motives in children.* New York: Russell-Sage, 1969. **245**

Cronbach, L. J., & Furby, L. How should we measure "change": Or should we? *Psychological Bulletin,* 1970, *74,* 68–80. **22**

Crowley, J. E., Levitan, T. E., & Quinn, R. P. Seven deadly half-truths about women. *Psychology Today,* 1973, *7,* 94–96. **311**

Dalton, K. Menstruation and acute psychiatric illness. *British Medical Journal,* 1959, *1,* 148–149. **119, 120**

Dalton, K. Effects of menstruation on school girls' weekly work. *British Medical Journal,* 1960, *1,* 326–328. **119**

Dalton, K. *The premenstrual syndrome.* Springfield, Ill.: Charles C. Thomas, 1964. **49, 119**

Dan, A. J., & Beekman, S. Male versus female representation in psychological research. *American Psychologist,* 1972, *27,* 1078. **46**

Darwin, C. *The origin of the species.* Chicago: Encyclopedia Britannica Press, 1955. (Originally published, 1856). **44**

Davis, E. G. *The first sex.* Baltimore: Penguin Books, 1971. **65**

Davis, K. *Human relations at work.* New York: McGraw-Hill, 1967. **311**

Davison, G. C. Homosexuality: The ethical challenge. *Journal of Consulting and Clinical Psychology,* 1976, *44,* 157–162. **165**

Deaux, K. *The behavior of women and men.* Monterey, Calif.: Brooks/Cole, 1976. **226, 227, 228, 244, 245, 260, 261, 263**

Deaux, K., & Emswiller, T. Explanations of successful performance on sex-linked tasks: What's skill for the male is luck for the female. *Journal of Personality and Social Psychology,* 1974, *29,* 80–85. **248, 324, 350**

Deaux, K., & Taynor, J. Evaluation of male and female ability: Bias works two ways. *Psychological Reports,* 1973, *32,* 261–262. **42, 247**

DeBeauvoir, S. *The second sex.* New York: Bantam Books, 1953. **38, 40**

DeFronzo, J., & Boudreau, F. Further research into antecedents and correlates of androgyny. *Psychological Reports,* 1979, *44,* 23–29. **197, 198**

Delaney, J., Lupton, M. J., & Toth, E. *The*

curse: A cultural history of menstruation. New York: Mentor, 1976. **113**

Deutsch, H. *The psychology of women.* New York: Grune and Stratton, 1944. **171**

Deutscher, I. Socialization for post parental life. In A. M. Rose (Ed.), *Human behavior and social process.* Boston: Houghton Mifflin, 1959. **287**

Dick-Read, G. *Childbirth without fear.* New York: Harper & Row, 1953. **132**

Diepold, J., Jr. *Parental expectations for children's sex-typed play behavior.* Paper presented at the meeting of the American Psychological Association, San Francisco, August 1977. **199**

Dinitz, S., Dynes, R. R., & Clarke, A. C. Preference for male or female children: Traditional or affectional? *Journal of Marriage and Family Living,* 1954, *16,* 128–130. **43**

Dinnerstein, D. *The mermaid and the minotaur: Sexual arrangements and human malaise.* New York: Harper & Row, 1976. **141–142, 288, 291**

Dodson, B. *Liberating masturbation: A meditation on self love.* New York: Bodipex Designs, 1974. **156**

Doerr, P., Pirke, K. M., Kockott, G., & Dittman, F. Further studies on sex hormones in male homosexuals. *Archives of General Psychiatry,* 1976, *33,* 611–614. **106**

Doherty, E. G., & Culver, C. Sex role identification, ability, and achievement among high school girls. *Sociology of Education,* 1976, *49,* 1–3. **253**

Doherty, E. G., & Liang, J. *Outcome of short-term mental hospitalization, psychopathology, and sex: A double standard?* Paper presented at the meeting of the Society for the Study of Social Problems, New York, August 1976.(a) **349**

Doherty, E. G., & Liang, J. *Sex of patient and rejection by psychiatric hospital staff.* Paper presented at the meeting of the American Psychological Association, Washington, D.C., September 1976.(b) **350**

Dohrenwend, B. P., & Dohrenwend, B. S. *Social stress and psychological disorder.* New York: John Wiley, 1969. **344, 345**

Dohrenwend, B. P., & Dohrenwend, B. S. Social and cultural influences on psychopathology. *Annual Review of Psychology,* 1974, *25,* 417–452. **37**

Dohrenwend, B. S. Social status and stressful life events. *Journal of Personality and Social Psychology,* 1973, *28,* 225–235. **337**

Doty, R. L. A cry for the liberation of the female rodent: Courtship and copulation in *rodentia. Psychological Bulletin,* 1974, *81,* 159–172. **49**

Douvan, E., & Adelson, J. *The adolescent experience.* New York: John Wiley, 1966. **231**

Downing, N. E. Theoretical and operational conceptualizations of psychological androgyny: Implications for measurement. *Psychology of Women Quarterly, 1979, 3,* 284–292. **20**

Duffy, E. *Activation and behavior.* New York: John Wiley, 1962. **258**

Eagly, A. H. Sex differences in influencability. *Psychological Bulletin,* 1978, *85,* 86–116. **47, 48, 261**

Eagly, A. H. *Analysis of sex differences in influenceability.* Paper presented at the meeting of the Association for Women in Psychology, Dallas, March 1979. **261**

Eagly, A. H., Wood, W., & Fishbaugh, L. *Sex differences in conformity: Surveillance by the group as a determinant of male nonconformity.* Unpublished manuscript, University of Massachusetts, Amherst, Mass. **49**

Edwards, C. P., & Whiting, B. Women and dependency, *Politics and Society,* 1974, *4,* 343–355. **260**

Edwards, R. C., Reich, M., & Weisskopf, T. E. *The capitalist system* (2nd ed.). Englewood Cliffs, N.J.: Prentice-Hall, 1978. **292, 295, 308**

Ehrhardt, A. A. Early androgen stimulation and aggressive behavior in male and female mice. *Physiology and Behavior,* 1969, *4,* 333–338. **95**

Ehrhardt, A. A., & Baker, S. W. Fetal androgens, human CNS differentiation, and behavioral sex differences. In R. C. Friedman, R. M. Richart, & R. L. Vande Wiele (Eds.), *Sex differences in behavior.* New York: John Wiley, 1974. **94, 95, 98**

Ehrhardt, A. A., Epstein, R., & Money, J. Fetal androgens and female gender identity in the early-treated adrenogenital syndrome. *Johns Hopkins Medical Journal,* 1968, *122,* 160–167. **95**

Ehrhardt, A. A., Greenberg, N., & Money, J. Female gender identity and absence of fetal hormones: Turner's syndrome. *Johns Hopkins Medical Journal,* 1970, *126,* 237–248. **93**

Ehrhardt, A. A., & Money, J. Progestin-induced hermaphroditism: IQ and psychosexual identity in a study of ten girls. *Journal of Sex Research,* 1967, *3,* 83–100. **94, 95**

Eliade, M. *Mephistopheles and the androgene: Studies in religious myth and symbol.* New York: Sheed and Ward, 1965. **56, 57, 59**

Ellis, H. *A study of British genius.* London: Hurst and Blackett, 1904. **44**

Ellis, H. *Studies in the psychology of sex.* Philadelphia: F. A. Davis, 1925. **154, 156**

Ember, C. R. Feminine task assignment and the social behavior of boys. *Ethos,* 1973, *1,* 424–439. **201**

Ennis, B. J. *Prisoners of psychiatry: Mental patients, psychiatrists, and the law.* New York: Avon, 1972. **344**

Ennis, B. J., & Litwack, T. R. Psychiatry and the presumption of expertise: Flipping coins in the courtroom. *California Law Review,* 1974, *62,* 693–752. **348**

Epstein, C. Law partners and marital partners: Strains and solutions in the dual-career family enterprise. *Human Relations,* 1971, *24,* 549–564. **297**

Erikson, E. H. *Childhood and society.* New York: Norton, 1963. **286, 304**

Evans, R. B. Physical and bio-chemical characteristics of homosexual men. *Journal of Consulting and Clinical Psychology,* 1972, *39,* 140–147. **165**

Fagot, B. I. Sex-related stereotyping of toddlers' behavior. *Developmental Psychology,* 1973, *9,* 429. **202**

Fagot, B. I. Sex differences in toddlers' behavior and parental reaction. *Developmental Psychology,* 1974, *10,* 554–558. **203**

Fagot, B. I. *How parents reinforce feminine role behaviors in toddler girls.* Presented at the meeting of the Association for Women in Psychology, St. Louis, February 1977. **202, 203**

Farrell, W. *The liberated man.* New York: Bantam, 1975. **145**

Fasteau, M. F. *The male machine.* New York: Delta, 1975. **142–143, 145, 158–159**

Feather, N. T. Attribution of responsibility and valence of success and failure in relation to initial confidence and perceived locus of control. *Journal of Personality and Social Psychology,* 1969, *13,* 129–144. **246, 248**

Federal Bureau of Investigation Uniform Crime Reports. *Crime in the United States.* Washington, D.C.: U.S. Government Printing Office, 1974. **168, 172**

Federbush, M. The sex problems of school math books. In J. Stacey, S. Bereaud, & J. Daniels (Eds.), *And Jill came tumbling after: Sexism in American education.* New York: Dell, 1974. **219**

Federman, D. D. *Abnormal sexual development.* Philadelphia: W. B. Saunders, 1967. **85**

Feld, S. Feelings of adjustment. In F. I. Nye & L. W. Hoffman (Eds.), *The employed mother in America.* Chicago: Rand McNally, 1963. **296**

Feldman-Summers, S., & Kiesler, S. B. Those who are number two try harder: The effects of sex on attributions of causality. *Journal of Personality and Social Psychology,* 1974, *30,* 846–855. **248**

Fenichel, O. *The psychoanalytic theory of neurosis.* New York: Norton, 1945. **343**

Fidell, L. S. Empirical verification of sex discrimination in hiring practices in psychology. *American Psychologist,* 1970, *25,* 1094–1098. **42**

Figes, E. *Patriarchal attitudes: The case for women in revolt.* Greenwich, Conn.: Fawcett, 1970. **142, 168**

Firestone, S. *The dialectic of sex.* New York: William Morrow, 1970. **39**

Flerx, V. C., Fidler, D. S., & Rogers, R. W. Sex role stereotypes: Developmental aspects and early intervention. *Child Development,* 1976, *47,* 998–1007. **205**

Flowers, M. R. *Women and social security: An institutional dilemma.* Washington, D.C.: American Enterprise In-stitute for Public Policy Research, 1977. **282**

Ford, C. S., & Beach, F. A. *Patterns of sexual behavior.* New York: Harper Colophon, 1951. **106**

Fouchee, H. C., Helmreich, R. L., & Spence, J. T., Implicit theories of masculinity and femininity: Dualistic or bipolar? *Psychology of Women Quarterly,* 1979, *3,* 259–269. **3**

Fox, N. Attachment of kibbutz infants to mother and metapelet. *Child Development,* 1977, *48,* 1228–1239. **294**

Frazier, N., & Sadker, M. *Sexism in school and society.* New York: Harper & Row, 1973. **214, 219, 221, 231**

French, E., & Lesser, G. S. Some characteristics of the achievement motive in women. *Journal of Abnormal and Social Psychology,* 1964, *68,* 119–128. **252**

Freston, P., & Coleman, K. *Managerial style in the marketplace.* Paper presented at the meeting of the Association for Women in Psychology, Pittsburgh, March 1978. **317**

Freud, S. Three essays on the theory of sexuality. In J. Strachey (Ed. and Trans.), *Standard edition of the complete psychological works of Sigmund Freud* (Vol. 7). London: Hogarth Press, 1964. (Originally published, 1905). **185**

Freud, S. Some psychological consequences of the anatomical distinction between the sexes. In J. Strachey (Ed. and Trans.), *Standard edition of the complete psychological works of Sigmund Freud* (Vol. 5). London: Hogarth Press, 1964. (Originally published, 1925). **152, 181**

Freud, S. Female sexuality. In J. Strachey (Ed. and Trans.), *Standard edition of the complete psychological works of Sigmund Freud.* (Vol. 21). London: Hogarth Press, 1964. (Originally published, 1931). **152**

Freud, S. Femininity. In J. Strachey (Ed. and Trans.), *Standard edition of the complete psychological works of Sigmund Freud.* London: Hogarth Press, 1964. (Originally published, 1933). **152**

Freud, S. Analysis terminable and interminable. In J. Strachey (Ed. and Trans.), *Standard edition of the complete psychological works of Sigmund Freud* (Vol. 23). London: Hogarth Press, 1964. (Originally published, 1937). **185**

Freud, S. An outline of psychoanalysis. In J. Strachey (Ed. and Trans.), *Standard edition of the complete psychological works of Sigmund Freud* (Vol. 23). London: Hogarth Press, 1964. (Originally published, 1938). **185**

Friedan, B. *The feminine mystique.* New York: Norton, 1963. **292**

Friedl, E. *Women and men: An anthropologist's view.* New York: Holt, Rinehart & Winston, 1975. **274**

Friedman, E. A. The physiological aspects of pregnancy. In M. T. Notman & C. C. Nadelson, (Eds.), *The woman patient: Medical and psychological interfaces.* New York: Plenum, 1978. **127**

Friedman, S. M. An empirical study of the castration and oedipus complexes. *Genetic Psychology Monographs,* 1952, *46*(pt. 1), 61–130. **183**

Friedman, S. S. *Feminist definitions and debate: An overview.* Paper presented at the conference on Androgyny and Sex Role Transcendence, Ann Arbor, Michigan, May 1978. **55, 125**

Frieze, I. H. Women's expectations for and causal attribution of success and failure. In M. T. S. Mednick, S. S. Tangri, & L. W. Hoffman (Eds.), *Women and achievement: Social and motivational analyses.* Washington, D.C.: Hemisphere, 1975. **245, 247**

Frisch, R. E., & Revelle, R. Height and weight at menarche and a hypothesis of critical body weights and adolescent events. *Science,* 1970, *169,* 397–399. **116**

Frodi, A., Macaulay, J., & Thome, P. R. Are women always less aggressive than men? A review of the experimental literature. *Psychological Bulletin,* 1977, *84,* 634–660. **262**

Garai, J. E., & Scheinfeld, A. Sex differences in mental and behavioral traits. *Genetic Psychology Monographs,* 1968, *77,* 169–299. **48**

Gayton, W. F., Havu, G. F., Ozmon, K. L., & Tavormina, J. A comparison of the Bem Sex Role Inventory and the PRF ANDRO Scale. *Journal of Personality Assessment,* 1977, *41,* 619–621. **22**

Gerall, A. A. Influence of perinatal androgen on reproductive capacity. In J. Zubin & J. Money (Eds.), *Contemporary sexual behavior: Critical issues in the 1970s.* Baltimore: Johns Hopkins University Press, 1973. **103**

Gilbert, L. A., Deutsch, C. J., & Strahan, R. F. Feminine and masculine dimensions of the typical, desirable, and ideal woman and man. *Sex Roles,* 1978, *4,* 767–778. **249**

Gilligan, C. In a different voice: Women's conceptions of the self and of morality. *Harvard Educational Review,* 1977, *47,* 481–517. **48**

Glueck, S., & Glueck, E. Working mothers and delinquency. *Mental Hygiene,* 1957, *41,* 327–352. **292**

Goldberg, P. Are women prejudiced against women? *Trans-action,* April 1968, 28–30. **42, 247, 350**

Goldberg, S., & Lewis, M. Play behavior in the year-old infant: Early sex differences. *Child Development,* 1969, *40,* 21–31. **203**

Goldman, W. J., & May, A. Males: A mi-

nority group in the classroom. *Journal of Learning Disabilities,* 1970, *3,* 276–278. **220**

Golub, S. The effect of premenstrual anxiety and depression on cognitive functioning. *Journal of Personality and Social Psychology,* 1976, *32,* 99–105. **119**

Gornick, V. Woman as outsider. In V. Gornick & B. K. Moran (Eds.), *Woman in sexist society.* New York: New American Library, 1971. **40**

Gough, H. G. *California Psychological Inventory: Manual.* Palo Alto, Calif.: Consulting Psychologists Press, 1964. **12**

Gough, H. G., & Heilbrun, A. B. *Manual for the Adjective Check List and the Need Scale for the ACL.* Palo Alto, Calif.: Consulting Psychologists Press, 16 1965. **16**

Gove, W. R. The relationship between sex roles, marital status, and mental illness. *Social Forces,* 1972, *51,* 34–44. **279, 280, 297, 322**

Gove, W. R., & Tudor, J. F. Adult sex roles and mental illness. *American Journal of Sociology,* 1973, *78,* 812–832. **337, 345**

Goy, R. W. Early hormonal influences on the development of sexual and sex-related behavior. In R. K. Unger & F. L. Denmark (Eds.), *Woman: Dependent or independent variable?* New York: Psychological Dimensions, 1975. **104**

Gray, S. W. Masculinity-femininity in relation to anxiety and social acceptance. *Child Development,* 1957, *28,* 203–214. **337**

Greer, G. *The female eunuch.* New York: Bantam, 1970. **140**

Grier, W. H., & Cobbs, P. M. *Black rage.* New York: Basic Books, 1968. **169**

Griffiths, M. W. Can we still afford occupational segregation? Some remarks. *Signs: Journal of Women in Culture and Society,* 1976, *1*(3), 7–14. **309**

Grob, G. N. Introduction. In E. Jarvis (Ed.), *Insanity and idiocy in Massachusetts: Report of the Commission on Lu-*

nacy, 1855. Cambridge: Harvard University Press, 1971. **37**

Gronseth, E. Work-sharing families' adaptations of pioneering families with husband and wife in part-time employment. *Acta Sociologica,* 1975, *18,* 202–221. **298**

Grusec, J. E., & Brinker, D. B. Reinforcement for imitation as a social learning determinant with implications for sex-role development. *Journal of Personality and Social Psychology,* 1972, *21,* 149–158. **187**

Grusec, J. E., & Mischel, W. Models' characteristics as determinants of social learning. *Journal of Personality and Social Psychology,* 1966, *4,* 211–215. **187**

Gutek, B. A., & Nieva, V. F. *Career choice processes in women.* Paper presented at the meeting of the American Psychological Association, Toronto, August 1978. **312, 329**

Guttmacher, A. F. *Pregnancy, birth and family planning.* New York: New American Library, 1973. **127**

Haas, A. Male and female spoken language differences: Stereotypes and evidence. *Psychological Bulletin,* 1979, *86,* 616–626. **268**

Hall, C. S., & Lindzey, G. *Theories of personality* (3rd ed.). New York: John Wiley, 1978. **180**

Hall, J. A. Gender effects in decoding nonverbal cues. *Psychological Bulletin,* 1978, *85,* 845–857. **268**

Halleck, R. *Psychology and psychic culture.* New York: American Books, 1895. **45**

Halleck, S. L. *The politics of therapy.* New York: Science House, 1971. **345, 348**

Harding, E. M. *Women's mysteries: Ancient and modern.* New York: Bantam, 1971. **112, 113**

Hareven, T. K. The family and gender roles in historical perspective. In L. A. Carter, A. F. Scott, & W. Martyna (Eds.), *Women and men: Changing roles, rela-*

tionships and perceptions. New York: Praeger, 1977. **272, 273**

Harford, T. C., Willis, C. H., & Deabler, H. L. Personality correlates of masculinity-femininity. *Psychological Reports,* 1967, *21,* 881–884. **337**

Harkins, E. B. Effects of empty nest transition on self-report of psychological and physical well-being. *Journal of Marriage and the Family,* 1978, *40,* 549–558. **287**

Harkness, R. A. Variations in testosterone secretion by men. In M. Ferin, F. Halberg, R. M. Richart, & R. L. Vande Wiele (Eds.), *Biorhythms and human reproduction.* New York: John Wiley, 1974, 469–478. **123**

Harlow, H. The heterosexual affectational system in monkeys. *American Psychologist,* 1962, *17,* 1–9. **100**

Harlow, H. Sexual behavior of the rhesus monkey. In F. A. Beach (Ed.), *Sex and behavior.* New York: Wiley, 1965. **100**

Harlow, H. F., Gluck, J. P., & Suomi, S. J. Generalizations of behavioral data between human and nonhuman animals. *American Psychologist,* 1972, *27,* 709–716. **98**

Harlow, H. F., & Harlow, M. Learning to love. *American Scientist,* 1966, *54,* 244–272. **276**

Harmon, L. W. Sexual bias in interest measurement. *Measurement and Evaluation in Guidance,* 1973, *5,* 496–501. **217**

Harris, A. S. The second sex in academe. In J. Stacey, S. Bereaud, & J. Daniels (Eds.), *And Jill came tumbling after: Sexism in American education.* New York: Dell, 1974. **218**

Harrison, G. B. (Ed.). *Shakespeare: The complete works.* New York: Harcourt Brace, 1948. **69**

Hartup, W. W. Peer interaction and social organization. In P. Mussen (Ed.), *Carmichael's manual of child psychology* (Vol. 2). New York: John Wiley, 1970. **230**

Hastings, D. W. Can specific training procedures overcome sexual inadequacy?

In M. Brecher, & E. M. Brecher, (Eds.), *An analysis of human sexual response.* New York: New American Library, 1966. **154**

Hatfield, J. S., Ferguson, L. R., & Alpert, R. Mother-child interaction and the socialization process. *Child Development,* 1967, *38,* 365–414. **260**

Hathaway, S. R., & McKinley, J. C. The *Minnesota Multiphasic Personality Inventory.* New York: Psychological Corporation, 1943. **12**

Hattendorf, K. W. A study of the questions of young children concerning sex: A phase of an experimental approach to parent education. *Journal of Social Psychology,* 1932, *3,* 37–65. **183**

Hawley, P. What women think men think. *Journal of Counseling Psychology,* 1972, *19,* 308–313. **329**

Hawthorne, N. *The scarlet letter.* Boston: Houghton Mifflin, 1971. **70**

Hefner, R., Rebecca, M., & Oleshansky, B. Development of sex-role transcendence. *Human Development,* 1975, *18,* 143–158. **192, 193**

Heilbrun, A. B. Measurement of masculine and feminine sex roles as independent dimensions. *Journal of Consulting and Clinical Psychology,* 1976, *44,* 183–190. **12, 16**

Heilbrun, C. G. *Toward a recognition of androgyny.* New York: Harper & Row, 1973. **64, 65, 66, 67, 68, 69, 70, 71, 72, 73, 74**

Helson, R. The changing image of the career woman. *Journal of Social Issues,* 1972, *28*(2), 33–46. **312–313**

Helson, R. Creativity in women. In J. A. Sherman & F. L. Denmark (Eds.), *Psychology of women: Future directions for research.* New York: Psychological Dimensions, 1976. **49**

Henley, N. M. *Body politics: Power, sex, and nonverbal communication.* Englewood Cliffs, N.J.: Prentice-Hall, 1977. **226, 227, 228**

Hennig, M., & Jardim, A. *The managerial woman.* New York: Doubleday, 1976. **327, 328**

Heston, L. L., & Shields, J. Homosexuality in twins: A family study and a registry study. *Archives of General Psychiatry,* 1968, *18,* 149–160. **165**

Hetherington, E. M. A developmental study of the effects of sex of the dominant parent on sex-role preference, identification, and imitation in children. *Journal of Personality and Social Psychology,* 1965, *2,* 188–194. **188**

Hetzler, S. A. Variations in role-playing patterns among different echelons of bureaucratic leaders. *American Sociological Review,* 1955, *20,* 700–706. **318**

Hilberman, E. Rape: The ultimate violation of the self. *American Journal of Psychiatry,* 1976, *133,* 436–437. **171**

Hill, C. E., Adelstein, D., & Carter, J. Similarity of friends on the androgyny scale. Unpublished paper, University of Maryland. **232**

Hoffman, D., & Fidell, L. *Characteristics of androgynous, undifferentiated, masculine, and feminine middle class women.* Paper presented at the meeting of the American Psychological Association, San Francisco, August 1977. **248, 249**

Hoffman, L. W. Mother's enjoyment of work and effects on the child. In F. I. Nye & L. W. Hoffman (Eds.), *The employed mother in America.* Chicago: Rand McNally, 1963. **276**

Hoffman, L. W. Effects of maternal employment on the child: A review of the research. *Developmental Psychology,* 1974, *10,* 204–228.(a) **50, 293, 294, 295**

Hoffman, L. W. Fear of success in males and females: 1965 and 1971. *Journal of Consulting and Clinical Psychology,* 1974, *42,* 353–358.(b) **254**

Hoffman, L. W. Fear of success in 1965 and 1974: A follow-up study. *Journal of Consulting and Clinical Psychology,* 1977, *45,* 310–321.(a) **254**

Hoffman, L. W. Changes in family roles, socialization, and sex differences.

American Psychologist, 1977, *32,* 644–657.(b) **43, 302**

Hoffman, M. L. Sex differences in empathy and related behavior. *Psychological Bulletin,* 1977, *84,* 712–722. **261**

Hollander, E. P., & Marcia, J. E. Paternal determinants of peer orientation and self-orientation among preadolescents. *Developmental Psychology,* 1970, *2,* 292–302. **260**

Hollingshead, A. B., & Redlich, F. C. *Social class and mental illness.* New York: John Wiley, 1958. **345**

Holmes, D. S., & Jorgensen, B. W. Do personality and social psychologists study men more than women? *Representative Research in Social Psychology,* 1971, *2,* 71–76. **219**

Holmstrom, L. L. *The two-career family.* Cambridge, Mass.: Schenkman, 1972. **297, 303**

Horner, M. S. Toward an understanding of achievement-related conflicts in women. *Journal of Social Issues,* 1972, *28*(2), 157–175. **253–255**

Horney, K. *The neruotic personality of our time.* New York: Norton, 1937. **259, 261**

Horney, K. *Feminine psychology.* New York: Norton, 1967. **184**

Howe, L. K. *Pink collar workers.* New York: Putnam, 1977. **215, 308, 311**

Hoyt, D. P., & Kennedy, C. E. Interest and personality correlates of career-motivated and homemaking-motivated college women. *Journal of Counseling Psychology,* 1958, *5,* 44–48. **329**

Huezinga, J. *The waning of the middle ages.* London: E. Arnold, 1970. **144**

Hunt, M. Sexual behavior in the 1970's. *Playboy,* 1974, *21*(1), 60–61 686–687; (2), 54–55, 176–177. **155, 156, 157, 158, 159, 164**

Hunt, M. Changes in sexual behavior in the past generation. In D. Byrne & L. Byrne (Eds.), *Exploring human sexuality.* New York: Thomas Y. Crowell, 1977. **164**

Hutt, C. *Males and females.* Baltimore: Penguin Books, 1972. **103**

Hyde, J. S., & Rosenberg, B. G. *Half the human experience: The psychology of women.* Lexington, Mass.: D. C. Heath, 1976. **118, 237**

Ibsen, H. A doll's house. In E. B. Watson & B. Pressey (Eds.), *Contemporary drama.* New York: Scribners Sons, 1931. **72**

Iga, M. Sociocultural factors in Japanese prostitution and the "prostitution prevention law." *Journal of Sex Research,* 1968, *4,* 127–146. **168**

Ilfield, F. W. *Sex differences in psychiatric symptomatology.* Paper presented at the meeting of the American Psychological Association, San Francisco, August 1977. **336**

Ivey, M., & Bardwick, J. Patterns of affective fluctuations in the menstrual cycle. *Psychosomatic Medicine,* 1968, *30,* 336–345. **49, 119, 122**

Jackson, D. N. *Personality Research Form Manual.* Goshen, N.Y.: Research Psychologists Press, 1967. **15, 18**

Jackson, P., & Lahaderne, H. Inequalities of teacher-pupil contacts. In M. Silverman (Ed.), *The experience of schooling.* New York: Holt, Rinehart & Winston, 1971. **216**

James, B. Case of homosexuality treated by aversive therapy. In H. J. Eyesenk (Ed.), *Experiments in behavior therapy.* London: Pergamon, 1964. **165**

James, J. *A formal analysis of prostitution.* Final report to the Division of Research. Part I: Basic statistical analysis; Part 2: Descriptive report; Part 3: Formal semantic analysis. Department of Social and Health Services, pp. 1–468, Olympia, Washington, 1971. **169**

James, W. *The principles of psychology.* New York: Dover Press, 1950. **45**

Janeway, E. *Man's world, woman's place.* New York: Morrow, 1971. **168, 242**

Jennings, S. A. Effects of sex typing in children's stories on preference and recall. *Child Development,* 1975, *46,* 220–223. **223**

Johnson, P. Women and power: Toward

a theory of effectiveness. *Journal of Social Issues*, 1976, *32*(3), 99–110. **337**

Johnston, R. Pay and job satisfaction: A survey of some research findings. *International Labour Review*, 1975, *3*, 441–449. **311**

Jones, J. B., Lundsteen, S. W., & Michael, W. B. The relationship of the professional employment status of mothers to reading achievement of sixth grade children. *California Journal of Educational Research*, 1967, *43*, 102–108. **294**

Jones, N. C., & Bayley, N. Physical maturing among boys as related to behavior. *Journal of Educational Psychology*, 1950, *41*, 129–148. **115**

Jones, W. H., Chernovetz, M. E. O'C., & Hansson, R. O. The enigma of androgyny: Differential implications for males and females? *Journal of Consulting and Clinical Psychology*, 1978, *46*, 298–313. **27, 28, 249, 337**

Jost, A. Recherche sur la differentiation sexuelle de l'embryon de lapin 1. Introduction. *Archives d'Anatomie Microscopique et de Morphologie Experimentale*, 1947, *36*, 151–200. **85**

Jost, A. Embryonic sexual differentiation. In H. W. Jones & W. W. Scott (Eds.), *Hermaphroditism, genetic abnormalities and related endocrine disorders*. Baltimore: Williams & Wilkins, 1958. **85**

Jourard, S. *The transparent self*. New York: Van Nostrand, 1964. **258**

Jourard, S. M., & Lasakow, P. Some factors in self-disclosure. *Journal of Abnormal and Social Psychology*, 1958, *56*, 91–98. **231**

Kaats, G. R., & Davis, K. E. The dynamics of sexual behavior of college students. *Journal of Marriage and the Family*, 1970, *32*, 390–399. **157**

Kagan, J. The child's sex role classification of school objects. *Child Development*, 1964, *35*, 1051–1056. **215**

Kagan, J., Kearsley, R. B., & Zelazo, P. R. *Infancy: Its place in human development*. Cambridge: Harvard University Press, 1978. **294**

Kallman, F. J. Twin studies in relation to adjustive problems in man. *New York Academy of Science*, 1951, *13*, 270–275. **165**

Kane, F. T., Lipton, M. A., & Ewing, J. A. Hormonal influences on female sexual response. *Archives of General Psychiatry*, 1969, *20*, 202–209. **105**

Kanter, R. M. *Men and women of the corporation*. New York: Basic Books, 1977. **263, 313–316, 317, 318, 319, 320–321, 325, 329**

Kaplan, A. G. Androgyny as a model of mental health for women: From theory to therapy. In A. G. Kaplan & J. P. Bean (Eds.), *Beyond sex-role stereotypes: Readings toward a psychology of androgyny*. Boston: Little, Brown, 1976. **339, 351**

Kaplan, A. G. Clarifying the concept of androgyny: Implications for therapy. *Psychology of Women Quarterly*, 1979, *3*, 223–230. **8**

Katchadourian, H., & Lunde, D. *Fundamentals of human sexuality*. New York: Holt, Rinehart & Winston, 1972. **155**

Kellerman, J., & Katz, E. R. Attitudes toward the division of childrearing responsibility. *Sex Roles*, 1978, *4*, 505–512. **287**

Kelly, J. A., Caudill, S., Hathorn, S., & O'Brien, C. G. Socially undesirable sex-correlated characteristics: Implications for androgyny and adjustment. *Journal of Consulting and Clinical Psychology*, 1977, *45*, 1186–1187. **23**

Kelly, J. A., Furman, W., & Young, V. Problems associated with the typological measurement of sex roles and androgyny. *Journal of Consulting and Clinical Psychology*, 1978, *46*, 1574–1576. **22**

Kelly, J. A., & Worell, J. New formulations of sex roles and androgyny: A critical review. *Journal of Consulting and Clinical Psychology*, 1977, *45*, 1101–1115. **7, 16, 21, 22**

Kelly, J. A., & Worell, L. Parent behaviors related to masculine, feminine, and androgynous sex role orientations. *Journal of Consulting and Clinical Psychology*, 1976, *44*, 843–851. **197**

Kennedy, W. Work and dissatisfaction: Is money enough? In L. Phillips & H. L. Votey, Jr. (Eds.), *Economic analysis of pressing social problems* (2nd ed.). Chicago: Rand McNally, 1977. **307**

Kessler, S. J., & McKenna, W. *Gender: An ethnomethodological approach.* New York: John Wiley, 1978. **36, 79, 82, 88, 96, 97**

Khalaf, S. Correlates of prostitution: Some popular errors and misconceptions. *Journal of Sex Research*, 1968, *4*, 147–162. **169–170**

King, L. M. Social and cultural influences on psychopathology. *Annual Review of Psychology*, 1978, *29*, 405–433. **346**

Kinsey, A. C., Pomeroy, W. B., & Martin, C. E. *Sexual behavior in the human male.* Philadelphia: W. B. Saunders, 1948. **105, 154–155, 156–157, 158, 159, 164, 165**

Kinsey, A. C., Pomeroy, W. B., Martin, C. E., & Gebhard, P. H. *Sexual behavior in the human female.* Philadelphia: W. B. Saunders, 1953. **154–159, 165**

Kleiner, R. J., Tuckman, J., & Lavell, M. Mental disorders and status based on role. *Psychiatry*, 1960, *23*, 271–274. **345**

Koeske, R. K., & Koeske, G. F. An attributional approach to moods and the menstrual cycle. *Journal of Personality and Social Psychology*, 1975, *31*, 474–478. **121**

Kogan, B. A. *Human sexual expression.* New York: Harcourt Brace Jovanovich, 1970. **148, 149, 154, 156**

Kohlberg, L. A cognitive-developmental analysis of children's sex-role concepts and attitudes. In E. E. Maccoby (Ed.), *The development of sex differences.* Stanford, Calif.: Stanford University Press, 1966. **189–191, 192**

Kohlberg, L. Continuities in childhood and adult moral development revisited. In P. B. Baltes & K. W. Schaie (Eds.), *Life-span developmental psychology: Personality and socialization.* New York: Academic Press, 1973. **48, 194**

Kolody, R. C., Masters, W. H., Hendryx, J., & Tore, G. Plasma testosterone and semen analysis in male homosexuals. *New England Journal of Medicine*, 1971, *285*, 1170–1174. **106**

Kolvin, I. Aversive imagery treatment in adolescence. *Behavior Research and Therapy*, 1967, *5*, 245–248. **165**

Komarovsky, M. Functional analysis of sex roles. *American Sociological Review*, 1950, *15*, 508–516. **3**

Komarovsky, M. *Blue-collar marriage.* New York: Vintage Books, 1967. **231, 283, 284**

Komarovsky, M. Cultural contradictions and sex roles: The masculine case. *American Journal of Sociology*, 1973, *78*, 873–884. **281, 322, 327**

Komarovsky, M. *Dilemmas of masculinity: A study of college youth.* New York: Norton, 1976. **231**

Kotelchuck, M. The infant's relationship to the father: Experimental evidence. In M. E. Lamb (Ed.), *The role of the father in child development.* New York: John Wiley, 1976. **290**

Kraines, R. J. *The menopause and evaluations of the self: A study of middle-aged women.* Unpublished doctoral dissertation, University of Chicago, 1963. **137**

Kreitler, H., & Kreitler, S. Children's concepts of sexuality and birth. *Child Development*, 1966, *37*, 363–378. **183**

Kreuz, L. E., & Rose, R. M. Assessment of aggressive behavior and plasma testosterone in a young criminal population. *Psychosomatic Medicine*, 1972, *34*, 321–332. **102**

Kristal, J., Sanders, D., Spence, J. T., & Helmreich, R. Inferences about the femininity of competent women and their implications for likeability. *Sex Roles*, 1975, *1*, 33–40. **29**

Krohn, A. *Hysteria: The elusive neurosis.*

New York: International Universities Press, 1978. **344**

Kuhn, T. *The structure of scientific revolutions.* Chicago: University of Chicago Press, 1970. **35**

Kurtines, W., & Greif, E. B. The development of moral thought: Review and evaluation of Kohlberg's approach. *Psychological Bulletin,* 1974, *81,* 453–470. **191**

Laird, D. A., & Laird, E. C. *The psychology of supervising the working woman.* New York: McGraw-Hill, 1942. **317**

Lakoff, R. Language and women's place. *Language in Society,* 1973, *2,* 45–80. **226**

Lamaze, F. *Painless childbirth: Psychoprophylactic method.* London: Burke, 1958. **132**

Lamb, M. E. The role of the father: An overview. In M. E. Lamb (Ed.), *The role of the father in child development.* New York: John Wiley, 1976. **285, 289, 290**

Lambert, W. E., Yackley, A., & Hein, R. N. Child training values of English Canadian and French Canadian parents. *Canadian Journal of Behavioral Science,* 1971, *3,* 217–236. **199**

Langer, W. L. Checks on population growth: 1750–1850. *Scientific American,* 1972, *226,* 93–100. **286**

Lansky, L. The family structure also affects the model: Sex-role attitudes in parents of preschool children. *Merrill-Palmer Quarterly,* 1967, *13,* 139–150. **199**

Lantz, H., & Snyder, E. *Marriage: An examination of the man-woman relationship.* New York: John Wiley, 1969. **286**

Larsson, K. Sexual behavior: The result of an interaction. In J. Zubin & J. Money (Eds.), *Contemporary sexual behavior: Critical issues in the 1970s.* Baltimore: Johns Hopkins University Press, 1973. **99**

Lasch, C. *Haven in a heartless world: The family besieged.* New York: Basic Books, 1977. **278**

Laws, J. L. A feminist review of marital adjustment literature: The rape of the Locke. *Journal of Marriage and the Family,* 1971, *33,* 483–516. **292, 311**

Laws, J. L. Work aspirations of women: False leads and new starts. *Signs: Journal of Women in Culture and Society,* 1976, *1*(3), 33–50. **307, 312**

Laws, J. L., & Schwartz, P. *Sexual scripts: The social construction of female sexuality.* Hinsdale, Ill.: Dryden, 1977. **141, 142, 145, 151, 168**

Lee, P. C. Male and female teachers in elementary schools: An ecological analysis. *Teachers of College Record,* 1973, *75,* 79–98. **214, 215, 216, 223**

Lein, L., et al. *Final Report: Work and family life.* (National Institute of Education Project No. 3-3094). Cambridge, Mass: Center for the Study of Public Policy, 1974. **297**

LeMasters, E. E. *Modern courtship and marriage.* New York: Macmillan, 1957. **286**

Lenney, E. Women's self-confidence in achievement settings. *Psychological Bulletin,* 1977, *84,* 1–13. **244, 245**

Lerner, H. E. The hysterical personality: A "woman's disease." *Comprehensive Psychiatry,* 1974, *15,* 157–164. **344**

Levine, S., & Mullins, R. Estrogen administered neonatally affects adult sexual behavior in male and female rats. *Science,* 1964, *144,* 185–187. **99**

Levinson, D. J., Darrow, C. N., Klein, E. B., Levinson, M. H., & McKee, B. *The seasons of a man's life.* New York: Knopf, 1978. **194, 282, 312, 327, 328**

Levit, L. *Anxiety and the menopause: A study of normal women.* Unpublished doctoral dissertation, University of Chicago, 1963. **137**

Levitin, T., Quinn, R. P., & Staines, G. L. Sex discrimination against the American working woman. *American Behavioral Scientist,* 1971, *15,* 237–254. **325**

Levitt, E. E., & Lubin, B. Some personality factors associated with menstrual complaints and menstrual attitude. *Journal of Psychosomatic Research,* 1967, *11,* 54–67. **121**

Levy, B., & Stacey, J. Sexism in the elementary school: A backward and forward look. *Phi Delta Kappan,* 1973, *55,* 105–109. **214, 219**

Levy, D. M. *Maternal overprotection.* New York: Norton, 1966. **293**

Lewis, E. C. *Developing women's potential.* Ames, Iowa: Iowa State University Press, 1968. **32–33, 312**

Lewis, M. State as an infant-environmental interaction: An analysis of mother-infant interaction as a function of sex. *Merrill-Palmer Quarterly,* 1972, *18,* 95–121.(a) **203**

Lewis, M. Parents and children: Sex-role development. *School Review,* 1972, *80,* 229–240.(b) **199**

Lewis, M., & Weinraub, M. The father's role in the child's social network. In M. E. Lamb (Ed.), *The role of the father in child development.* New York: John Wiley, 1976. **289, 291**

Libby, R., & Whitehurst, R. (Eds.). *Marriage and its alternatives: Exploring intimate relationships.* Glenview, Ill.: Scott, Foresman, 1977. **170**

Lidz, T., Cornelison, A. R., Fleck, S., & Terry, D. Intrafamilial environment of the schizophrenic patient. I. The father. *Psychiatry,* 1957, *20,* 329–342. **277**

Lidz, T. Cornelison, A. R., Terry, D., & Fleck, S. Irrationality as a family tradition. *Archives of Neurological Psychiatry,* 1958, *79,* 305–316. **277**

Lidz, T., Fleck, S., Alanen, Y. O., & Cornelison, A. R. Schizophrenic patients and their siblings. *Psychiatry,* 1963, *26,* 1–18. **277**

Liebenberg, B. Expectant fathers. *American Journal of Orthopsychiatry,* 1967, *37,* 358–359. **290**

Liebert, R. M., Neale, J. M., & Davidson, E. S. *The early window: Effects of television on children and youth.* Elmsford, N.Y.: Pergamon, 1973. **211**

Liebert, R. M., & Schwartzberg, N. S. Effects of mass media. *Annual Review of Psychology,* 1977, *28,* 141–173. **211, 213**

Lipman-Blumen, J. How ideology shapes women's lives. *Scientific American,* 1972, *226,* 34–42. **329**

Lipman-Blumen, J. Toward a homosocial theory of sex roles: An explanation of the social institutions of sex segregation. *Signs: Journal of Women in Culture and Society,* 1976, *1,* 15–31. **145, 197**

Livson, F. B. *Coming together in the middle years: A longitudinal study of sex role convergence.* Paper presented at the meeting of the Gerontological Society, New York, 1976. **194**

Loevinger, J. The meaning and measurement of ego development. *American Psychologist,* 1966, *21,* 195–206. **192**

Loevinger, J., & Wessler, R. *Measuring ego development* (Vol. 1). San Francisco: Jossey-Bass, 1970. **192**

London, P. *The modes and morals of psychotherapy.* New York: Holt, Rinehart & Winston, 1964. **348**

Lopata, H. Z. *Occupation: Housewife.* New York: Oxford University Press, 1971. **322**

Lopata, H. Z. *Widowhood in an American City.* Cambridge, Mass.: Schenkman, 1973. **231**

Loraine, J. A., Ismail, A. A., & Adamapoulos, D. A. Endocrine function in male and female homosexuals. *British Medical Journal,* 1970, *4,* 406–408. **106**

Lowenthal, M. F. Psychosocial variations across the adult life course: Frontiers for research and policy. *The Gerontologist,* 1975, *15,* 6–12. **138**

Lowenthal, M. F., Thurnher, M., & Chiriboga, D. *Four stages of life.* San Francisco: Jossey-Bass, 1975. **136, 194, 231, 232, 312**

Lunneborg, P. W. Stereotypic aspects in masculinity-femininity measurement. *Journal of Consulting and Clinical Psychology,* 1970, *34,* 113–118. **3**

Lynn, D. B. *The father: His role in child development.* Monterey, Calif.: Brooks/Cole, 1974. **289, 295**

Maccoby, E. E. Sex differences in intellectual functioning. In E. E. Maccoby (Ed.), *The development of sex differences*. Stanford, Calif.: Stanford University Press, 1966. **238, 241**

Maccoby, E. E., & Jacklin, C. N. *The psychology of sex differences*. Stanford, Calif.: Stanford University Press, 1974. **45, 187, 188, 202, 204, 237–238, 239, 240, 241, 242, 244, 245, 258, 260, 262, 263**

MacDonald, A. P., Huggins, J., Young, S., & Swanson, R. A. Attitudes toward homosexuality. *Journal of Consulting and Clinical Psychology*, 1973, *40*, 161. **165**

Mahoney, M. *Scientist as subject: The psychological imperative*. Cambridge, Mass.: Ballinger, 1976. **38**

Marcus, S. *The other Victorians*. New York: Bantam, 1964. **144–145, 154**

Marecek, J. Social change, positive mental health and psychological androgyny. *Psychology of Women Quarterly*, 1979, *3*, 241–247. **138**

Margolese, M. S. Homosexuality: A new endocrine correlate. *Hormones and Behavior*, 1970, *1*, 151–155. **165**

Marks, J. B. Interests and leadership among adolescents. *Journal of Genetic Psychology*, 1957, *91*, 163–172. **263**

Marmor, J. (Ed.). *Sexual inversion*. New York: Basic Books, 1965. **165**

Martin, W. Seduced and abandoned in the New World: The image of woman in American fiction. In V. Gornick & B. K. Moran (Eds.), *Woman in sexist society*. New York: Basic Books, 1971. **211**

Masica, D. N., Money, J., & Ehrhardt, A. A. Fetal feminization and female gender identity in the testicular feminizing syndrome of androgen insensitivity. *Archives of Sexual Behavior*, 1971, *1*, 131–142. **93, 105**

Maslin, A., & Davis, J. L. Sex-role stereotyping as a factor in mental health standards among counselors-in-training. *Journal of Counseling Psychology*, 1975, *22*, 87–91. **347**

Masling, J., & Harris, S. Sexual aspects of TAT administration. *Journal of Consulting and Clinical Psychology*, 1969, *33*, 166–169. **349**

Maslow, A. H. *Motivation and personality* (2nd ed.). New York: Harper & Row, 1970. **358**

Masters, W., & Johnson, V. *The human sexual response*. Boston: Little, Brown, 1966. **146–147, 149, 150–151, 152, 153, 156**

Masters, W., & Johnson, V. *Human sexual inadequacy*. Boston: Little, Brown, 1970. **146, 151**

Matleson, T. M. *Adolescence today: Sex roles and the search for identity*. New York: Dorsey Press, 1975. **115**

May, W. Counselors', psychologists', and homosexuals' philosophies of human nature and attitudes toward homosexual behavior. *Homosexual Counseling*, 1974, *3*, 21–27. **165**

McArthur, L. Z., & Resko, B. G. The portrayal of men and women in American television commercials. *Journal of Social Psychology*, 1975, *97*, 209–220. **212**

McBride, A. B. *The growth and development of mothers*. New York: Harper & Row, 1973. **285–286**

McBride, A. B. *Does parenthood promote androgyny?* Paper presented at the meeting of the Association for Women in Psychology, St. Louis, February 1977. **291**

McCaulay, E., & Ehrhardt, A. A. Female sexual response: Hormonal and behavioral interactions. *Primary Care*, 1976, *3*, 455–476. **118**

McClelland, D. C., Atkinson, J. R., Clark, R. A., & Lowell, E. L. *The achievement motive*. New York: Appleton-Century-Crofts, 1953. **49, 252**

McCombie, S. L., Bassuk, E., Savitz, R., & Pell, S. Development of a medical center rape crisis intervention program. *American Journal of Psychiatry*, 1976, *133*, 419–421. **170, 171**

McDougall, W. *Outline of psychology*. New York: Scribners Sons, 1923. **45**

McKee, J. P., & Sheriffs, A. C. The differential evaluation of males and females. *Journal of Personality,* 1957, *25,* 356–371. **3**

McKenna, W., & Kessler, S. J. *Differential treatment of males and females as a source of bias in social psychology.* Paper presented at the meeting of the American Psychological Association, New Orleans, September, 1974. **46**

McKenna, W., & Kessler, S. J. Experimental design as a source of sex bias in social psychology. *Sex Roles,* 1977, *3,* 117–128. **48, 49, 50**

McMahan, I. D. *Sex differences in causal attributions following success and failure.* Paper presented at the meeting of the Eastern Psychological Association, Boston, April 1971. **246**

McMahan, I. D. *Sex differences in expectancy of success as a function of task.* Paper presented at the meeting of the Eastern Psychological Association, Boston, April 1972. **246**

McMillan, J. R., Clifton, A. K., McGrath, D., & Gale, W. S. Women's language: Uncertainty or interpersonal sensitivity and emotionality? *Sex Roles,* 1977, *3,* 545–559. **227**

Mead, M. *Male and female.* New York: William Morrow, 1967. **39, 142**

Mead, M., & Newton, N. Cultural patterning of perinatal behavior. In S. A. Richardson & A. Guttmacher (Eds.), *Childbearing—the social and psychological aspects.* New York: Williams & Wilkens, 1967. **131**

Mednick, M. T. S. Psychology of women: Research issues and trends. *Annals of the New York Academy of Sciences,* 1978, *309,* 77–92. **45, 46**

Mednick, M. T. S. The new psychology of women: A feminist analysis. In G. E. Gullahorn (Ed.), *Psychology and women: In transition.* New York: John Wiley, 1979. **32–33, 43, 45, 46**

Mednick, M. T. S., Tangri, S. S., & Hoffman, L. W. *Women and achievement.* Washington, D.C.: Hemisphere, 1975. **39, 42**

Meehl, P. Schizotaxia, schizotypy, and schizophrenia. *American Psychologist,* 1962, *17,* 827–838. **277**

Meyer, W., & Thompson, G. Teacher interactions with boys, as contrasted with girls. In R. Kuhlens & G. Thompson (Eds.), *Psychological studies of human development.* New York: Appleton-Century-Crofts, 1963. **216**

Meyer-Bahlburg, H. F. L., Nat, R., Boon, D. A., Sharma, M., & Edwards, J. A. Aggressiveness and testosterone measures in man. *Psychosomatic Medicine,* 1974, *36,* 269–274. **102**

Meyerson, A., & Neustadt, R. Bisexuality and homosexuality, their biological and medical aspects. *Clinics,* 1942, *1,* 932–957. **165**

Miller, C., & Swift, K. *Words and women.* Garden City, N.Y.: Anchor/Doubleday, 1976. **225, 226, 228**

Miller, J. B. *Toward a new psychology of women.* Boston: Beacon Press, 1976. **42, 45, 232, 258**

Millman, M., & Kanter, R. M. (Eds.). *Another voice: Feminist perspectives on social life and social science.* Garden City, N.Y.: Anchor Books, 1975. **46**

Minton, C., Kagan, J., & Levine, J. A. Maternal control and obedience in the two-year-old. *Child Development,* 1971, *42,* 1873–1894. **260**

Minturn, L., & Lambert, W. L. *Mothers of six cultures: Antecedents of child rearing.* New York: John Wiley, 1964. **289**

Minuchin, P. Sex-role concepts and sex typing in childhood as a function of school and home environment. *Child Development,* 1965, *36,* 1033–1048. **200, 208, 222**

Minuchin, S. *Families and family therapy.* Cambridge, Mass.: Harvard University Press, 1974. **277**

Mischel, W. A social-learning view of sex differences in behavior. In E. E. Maccoby (Ed.), *The development of sex differences.* Stanford, Calif.: Stanford University Press, 1966. **185**

Mischel, W. Sex-typing and socialization. In P. H. Mussen (Ed.), *Carmichael's manual of child psychology* (Vol. 2). New York: John Wiley, 1970. **185**

Mischel, W. On the future of personality measurement. Paper presented at the symposium *The future of personality measurement,* American Psychological Association, Chicago, 1975. **22**

Mischel, W. *Introduction to personality* (2nd ed.). New York: Holt, Rinehart & Winston, 1976. **185**

Mitchell, J. *Psychoanalysis and feminism.* New York: Vintage, 1974. **184**

Monahan, L., Kuhn, D., & Shaver, P. Intrapsychic versus cultural explanations of the 'fear of success' motive. *Journal of Personality and Social Psychology,* 1974, *29,* 60–64. **255**

Money, J. Sexual dimorphism and homosexual gender identity. *Psychological Bulletin,* 1970, *74,* 425–440. **93**

Money, J. Effects of prenatal androgenization and deandrogenization on behavior in human beings. In W. G. Ganong & M. Luciano (Eds.), *Frontiers in neuroendocrinology.* New York: Oxford University Press, 1973. **91, 93, 94, 95, 96, 100**

Money, J., & Ehrhardt, A. A. Fetal hormones and the brain: Effects on sexual dimorphism of behavior—A review. *Archives of Sexual Behavior,* 1971, *1,* 241–262. **103, 104**

Money, J., & Ehrhardt, A. A. *Man and woman, boy and girl.* Baltimore: Johns Hopkins University Press, 1972. **85, 86, 87, 88, 89, 90, 92, 96, 99, 103, 104, 105, 190**

Money, J., & Tucker, P. *Sexual signatures: On being a man or a woman.* Boston: Little, Brown, 1975. **84, 190**

Montague, A. *The natural superiority of women.* New York: Colliers, 1968. **83**

Moos, R. H. The development of a menstrual distress questionnaire. *Psychosomatic Medicine,* 1968, *30,* 853–867. **49, 119, 120**

Morgan, R. The changeless need. *Ms.,* 1978, *8*(2), 44ff. **291**

Morin, S. F., & Garfinkle, E. M. Male homophobia. *Journal of Social Issues,* 1978, *34,* 29–47. **165**

Moss, H. A. Sex, age, and state as determinants of mother-infant interaction. *Merrill-Palmer Quarterly,* 1967, *13,* 19–36. **203**

Mother Jones, January 1979, *4*(1), 5. **332**

Moulton, J., Robinson, G. M., & Elias, C. Sex bias in language use: "Neutral" pronouns that aren't. *American Psychologist,* 1978, *33,* 1032–1036. **226**

Mussen, P. H. Some antecedents and consequents of masculine sex-typing in adolescent boys. *Psychological Monographs,* 1961, *75*(506). **337**

Mussen, P. H. Long-term consequences of masculinity of interests in adolescence. *Journal of Consulting Psychology,* 1962, *26,* 435–440. **337**

Mussen, P. H. Early sex-role development. In D. A. Goslin (Ed.), *Handbook of socialization theory and research.* Chicago: Rand McNally, 1969. **191**

Mussen, P. H., Conger, J. J., & Kagan, J. *Child development and personality* (2nd ed.). New York: Harper & Row, 1963. **276**

Mussen, P. H., Conger, J. J., & Kagan, J. *Child development and personality* (5th ed.). New York: Harper & Row, 1979. **276**

Mussen, P. H., & Rutherford, E. Parent-child relations and parental personality in relation to young children's sex-role preferences. *Child Development,* 1963, *34,* 589–607. **198, 200**

Nadelson, C. C. "Normal" and "special" aspects of pregnancy: A psychological approach. In M. T. Notman & C. C. Nadelson (Eds.), *The woman patient: Medical and psychological interfaces.* New York: Plenum, 1978. **129**

Nash, S. C. The relationship among sex-role stereotyping, sex-role preference, and the sex difference in spatial visualization. *Sex Roles,* 1975, *1,* 15–32. **241**

Neugarten, B. L. Women's attitudes toward the menopause. *Vita Humana,* 1963, *6,* 266–273. **136**

Neugarten, B. L., & Gutmann, D. L. Age-sex roles and personality in middle age:

A thematic apperception study. In B. L. Neugarten (Ed.), *Middle age and aging.* Chicago: University of Chicago Press, 1968. **194**

Neugarten, B. L., & Kraines, R. J. Menopausal symptoms in women of various ages. *Psychosomatic Medicine,* 1965, *27,* 266–273. **136**

Newton, N. Interrelationships between sexual responsiveness, birth, and breast-feeding. In J. Zubin & J. Money (Eds.), *Contemporary sexual behavior: Critical issues in the 1970's.* Baltimore: Johns Hopkins University Press, 1974. **133**

Nilson, L. B. The occupational and sex related components of social standing. *Sociology and Social Research,* 1976, *60,* 328–336. **326**

Notman, M. T., & Nadelson, C. C. The rape victim: Psychodynamic consi-derations. *American Journal of Psychiatry,* 1976, *133,* 408–412. **171, 172, 173**

Nye, F. I. Effects on mother. In L. W. Hoffman & F. I. Nye (Eds.), *Working mothers.* San Francisco: Jossey-Bass, 1974.(a) **293, 296**

Nye, F. I. Husband-wife relationship. In L. W. Hoffman & F. I. Nye (Eds.), *Working mothers.* San Francisco: Jossey-Bass, 1974.(b) **298**

Oakley, A. *Sex, gender and society.* New York: Harper Colophon, 1972. **107**

Oakley, A. *Woman's work: The housewife, past and present.* New York: Vintage Books, 1974. **322**

Ohlson, E. L., & Wilson, M. Differentiating female homosexuals from female heterosexuals by use of the MMPI. *Journal of Sex Research,* 1974, *10,* 308–315. **166**

O'Kelly, C. G. The "impact" of equal employment legislation on women's earning: Limitations of legislative solutions to discrimination in the economy. *American Journal of Economics and Sociology,* 1979, *38,* 419–430. **308, 309, 330**

O'Leary, V. E. Some attitudinal barriers to occupational aspirations in women. *Psychological Bulletin,* 1974, *81,* 809–826. **251, 323**

Omark, D. R., & Edelman, M. *Peer group social interactions from an evolutionary perspective.* Paper presented at the meeting of the Society for Research in Child Development, Philadelphia, 1973. **262**

Ornstein, R. *The psychology of consciousness.* San Francisco: W. H. Freeman, 1972. **57**

Ornstein, R. (Ed.). *The nature of human consciousness.* New York: Viking Press, 1973. **56, 57**

Ortner, S. B. Is female to male as nature is to culture? In M. Z. Rosaldo & L. Lamphere (Eds.), *Woman, culture and society.* Stanford, Calif.: Stanford University Press, 1974. **39, 40**

Osipow, S. H. *Theories of career development.* New York: Appleton-Century-Crofts, 1968. **312**

Osofsky, J. D., & O'Connell, S. Parent-child interaction: Daughters' effects upon mothers' and fathers' behaviors. *Developmental Psychology,* 1972, *7,* 157–168. **205**

Ostrum, A. Psychological theories of childbirth. In S. Hammer (Ed.), *Women: Body and culture.* New York: Harper & Row, 1975. **128, 132**

Paige, K. E. Women learn to sing the menstrual blues. *Psychology Today,* 1973, *17,* 41–46. **114, 121**

Parks, J. Emotional reactions to pregnancy. *American Journal of Obstetrics and Gynecology,* 1951, 62, 339–345. **128**

Parlee, M. B. The premenstrual syndrome. *Psychological Bulletin,* 1973, *80,* 454–465. **120–121, 122**

Parlee, M. B. Stereotypic beliefs about menstruation: A methodological note on the Moos Menstrual Distress Questionnaire and some new data. *Psychosomatic Medicine,* 1974, *36,* 229–241. **120**

Parlee, M. B. *Psychological aspects of menstruation, childbirth and menopause: An overview with suggestions* for further research. Presented at the Conference for New Directions for Research on Women, Madison, Wisconsin, June 1975.(a) **133**

Parlee, M. B. Psychology: A review. *Signs: Journal of Women in Culture and Society*, 1975, (b) *1*, 119–138. **46, 47, 48**

Parsons, T., & Bales, R. E. *Family socialization and interaction process.* Glencoe, Ill.: Free Press, 1955. **7, 257, 277, 278**

Pastore, N. *The nature-nurture controversy.* London: Kings Crown Press, 1949. **35**

Peck, E., & Senderowitz, J. *Pronatalism: The myth of mom and apple pie.* New York: Thomas Y. Crowell, 1974. **125**

Pelz, D. C. Influence: A key to effective leadership in the first-line supervision. *Personnel*, 1952, *29*, 3–11. **317**

Pepinsky, H. B., & Karst, T. O. Convergence: A phenomenon in counseling and psychotherapy. *American Psychologist*, 1964, *19*, 333–338. **348**

Perley, M. J., & Guze, S. B. Hysteria—The stability and usefulness of clinical criteria. *New England Journal of Medicine*, 1962, *266*, 421–426. **343**

Persky, H., Smith, K. D., & Basu, G. K. Relation of psychologic measures of aggression and hostility to testosterone production in men. *Psychosomatic Medicine*, 1971, *33*, 265–277. **102**

Pheterson, G. I., Keisler, S. B., & Goldberg, P. A. Evaluation of the performance of women as a function of their sex, achievement, and personal history. *Journal of Personality and Social Psychology*, 1971, *19*, 114–118. **42, 247**

Phoenix, C. H., Goy, R. L., & Resko, J. A. Psychosexual differentiation as a function of androgenic stimulation. In M. Diamond (Ed.), *Perspectives in reproduction and sexual behavior.* Bloomington: Indiana University Press, 1968. **100**

Piaget, J. *The origins of intelligence.* New York: International Universities Press, 1952. **188–189**

Piaget, J. *The construction of reality in the child.* New York: Basic Books, 1954. **188–189**

Pillard, R. C., Rose, R. M., & Sherwood, M. Plasma testosterone levels in homosexual men. *Archives of Sexual Behavior*, 1974, *3*, 453–458. **106**

Pinel, P. *Nosographic philosophique ou la méthode de l'analyse appliquée à la médicine* (5th ed.). Paris: Brosson, 1813. **343**

Pleck, J. H. Masculinity-femininity: current and alternate paradigms. *Sex Roles*, 1975, *1*, 161–178. **194, 220, 282, 295**

Pleck, J. H. Men's new roles in the family: housework and childcare. In C. Safilios-Rothschild (Ed.), *Family and sex roles*, In press. **297–298**

Pleck, J. H. Male threat from female competence. *Journal of Consulting and Clinical Psychology*, 1976, *44*, 608–613. **329**

Prescott, S. Why researchers don't study women: The responses of 62 researchers. *Sex Roles: A Journal of Research*, 1978, *4*, 899–906. **46**

Quadagno, D. M., Briscoe, R., & Quadagno, J. S. Effect of perinatal gonadal hormones on selected nonsexual behavior patterns: A critical assessment of the non-human and human literature. *Psychological Bulletin*, 1977, *84*, 62–80. **107, 108**

Quadagno, D. M., DeBold, J. F., Gorzalka, B. F., & Whalen, R. E. Maternal behavior in the rat: Aspects of concaveation and neonatal androgen treatment. *Physiology and Behavior*, 1974, *12*, 1031–1033. **108**

Rada, R. T., Laws, D. R., & Kellner, R. Plasma testosterone levels in the rapist. *Psychosomatic Medicine*, 1976, *38*, 257–269. **102**

Radicalesbians. The woman identified woman. In A. G. Kaplan & J. P. Bean (Eds.), *Beyond sex role stereotypes: Readings toward a psychology of androgyny.* Boston: Little, Brown, 1976. **165**

Radke, M. J. *The relation of parental authority to children's behavior and attitudes.* Minneapolis: University of Minnesota Press, 1946. **290**

Radloff, L. Sex differences in depression: The effects of occupational and marital status. *Sex Roles,* 1975, *1,* 249–265. **138**

Rainwater, L., Coleman, R. P., & Handel, G. *Workingman's wife: Her personality, world, and lifestyle.* New York: Oceana, 1959. **231, 284, 285**

Ramey, E. R. Men's cycles: They have them too, you know. *Ms.,* 1972, 8–14. **124**

Ramey, E. R. Sex hormones and executive ability. *Annals of the New York Academy of Sciences,* 1973, *208,* 237–245. **114**

Rapoport, R., & Rapoport, R. *Dual-career families re-examined: New integrations of work and family.* New York: Harper, 1976. **297, 298, 299**

Raush, H. L., Barry, W. A., Hertel, R. K., & Swain, M. A. *Communication, conflict, and marriage.* San Francisco: Jossey-Bass, 1974. **263**

Rawlings, E. I., & Carter, D. K. *Psychotherapy for women: Treatment toward equality.* Springfield, Ill.: Charles C. Thomas, 1977. **348, 352**

Rebelsky, F., & Hanks, C. Fathers' verbal interaction with infants in the first three months of life. *Child Development,* 1971, *42,* 63–68. **290**

Reinartz, K. F. The paper doll: Images of American woman in popular songs. In J. Freeman (Ed.), *Women: A feminist perspective.* Palo Alto, Calif.: Mayfield, 1975. **211**

Renne, K. S. Correlates of dissatisfaction in marriage. *Journal of Marriage and the Family,* 1970, *32,* 54–67. **287**

Rheingold, H. L., & Cook, K. V. The contents of boys' and girls' rooms as an index of parents' behavior. *Child Development,* 1975, *46,* 459–463. **202**

de Riencourt, A. *Sex and power in history.* New York: Delta, 1974. **143, 144**

Riess, B. F., Safer, M. A., & Yotive, W. Psychological test data on female homosexuality: A review of the literature. *Journal of Homosexuality,* 1974, *1,* 71–85. **166**

Robinson, P. *The modernization of sex.* New York: Harper Colophon, 1976. **147, 148, 150, 155, 159**

Rollins, B. C., & Feldman, H. Marital satisfaction over the family life cycle. *Journal of Marriage and the Family,* 1970, *32,* 20–28. **287**

Rosaldo, M. Z. Woman, culture, and society: A theoretical overview. In M. Z. Rosaldo & L. Lamphere (Eds.), *Woman, culture, and society.* Stanford, Calif.: Stanford University Press, 1974. **39, 274**

Rose, R. M., Bourne, P. G., Poe, R. O., Mougey, E. H., Collins, D. R., & Mason, J. W. Androgen responses to stress II. Excretion of testosterone, epitestosterone, androsterone, and etiocholanolone during basic combat training and under threat of attack. *Psychosomatic Medicine,* 1969, *31,* 418–436. **101**

Rose, R. M., Gordon, T. P., & Bernstein, I. S. Plasma testosterone levels in the male Rhesus: Influence of sexual and social stimuli. *Science,* 1972, *178,* 643–645. **99, 101**

Rosen, G. *Madness in society: Chapters in the historical sociology of mental illness.* New York: Harper & Row, 1968. **342**

Rosenberg, M. *Society and the adolescent self-image.* Princeton, N.J.: Princeton University Press, 1965. **244**

Rosenblatt, J. S. The development of maternal responsiveness in the rat. *American Journal of Orthopsychiatry,* 1969, *39,* 36–56. **107**

Rosenkrans, M. A. Imitation in children as a function of perceived similarity to a social model and vicarious reinforcement. *Journal of Personality and Social Psychology,* 1967, *7,* 307–315. **187**

Rosenkrantz, P., Vogel, S., Bee, H., Broverman, I., & Broverman, D. M. Sex role stereotypes and self-concepts in college students. *Journal of Consulting* and *Clinical Psychology,* 1968, *32,* 287–295. **3, 14, 42, 244, 248**

Rosenthal, D. Changes in some moral values following psychotherapy. *Journal of Consulting Psychology,* 1955, *19,* 431–436. **348**

Rosenthal, R. *Experimenter effects in behavioral research.* New York: Appleton-Century-Crofts, 1966. **37**

Rosenthal, R. *On the social psychology of the self-fulfilling prophecy: Further evidence for Pygmalion effects and their mediating mechanisms.* New York: MSS Modular Publications, 1973. **324**

Rosenthal, R., & Jacobson, L. *Pygmalion in the classroom: Teacher expectations and pupils' intellectual development.* New York: Holt, Rinehart & Winston, 1968. **37**

Rosenthal, R., & Rosnow, R. L. *Artifact in behavioral research.* New York: Academic Press, 1969. **37**

Ross, D. M., & Ross, S. A. Resistance by preschool boys to sex-inappropriate behavior. *Journal of Educational Psychology,* 1972, *63,* 342–346. **205**

Rossi, A. S. Transition to parenthood, *Journal of Marriage and the Family,* 1968, *30,* 26–39; 361–376. **133, 285, 288**

Rossi, A. S. Sex equality: The beginnings of ideology. *The Humanist,* 1969, *29,* 3–16. **358**

Rossi, A. S. A biosocial perspective on parenting. *Daedelus,* 1977, *106,* 1–31. **81, 131**

Rossi, A. S., & Rossi, P. E. Body time and social time: Mood patterns by menstrual cycle phase and day of week. *Social Science Research,* 1977, *6,* 273–308. **122–123**

Roszak, B., & Roszak, T. (Eds.). *Masculine/Feminine: Readings in the sexual mythology and the liberation of women.* New York: Harper Colophon, 1969. **41**

Rotkin, K. F. The phallacy of our sexual norm. In A. G. Kaplan & J. P. Bean (Eds.), *Beyond sex role stereotypes:* *Readings toward a psychology of androgyny.* Boston: Little, Brown, 1976. **151**

Rotter, J. Generalized expectancies for internal-external control of reinforcement. *Psychological Monographs,* 1966, *80,* 1–28. **47**

Rubin, J. Z., Provenzano, F. J., & Luria, Z. The eye of the beholder: Parents' views on sex of newborn. *American Journal of Orthopsychiatry,* 1974, *44,* 512–519. **199, 252, 283, 306**

Rubin, L. B. *Worlds of pain: Life in the working class family.* New York: Basic Books, 1976. **158, 307**

Ruble, D. N. Premenstrual symptoms: A reinterpretation. Unpublished manuscript, Princeton University, 1976. **121**

Ruble, D. N., Brooks, J., & Clarke, A. *Research on menstrual-related psychological changes: Alternative perspectives.* Presented at the Conference on Bio-Psychologic Factors Influencing Sex-Role Related Behaviors, Northampton, Mass., October 1976. **116, 121**

Russell, A., & Winkler, R. Evaluation of assertive training and homosexual guidance service groups designed to improve homosexual functioning. *Journal of Consulting and Clinical Psychology,* 1977, *45,* 1–13. **165**

Rutner, I. T. A double-barrel approach to modification of homosexual behavior. *Psychological Reports,* 1970, *26,* 355–358. **165**

Ryan, W. *Blaming the victim.* New York: Vintage Books, 1976. **35**

Saario, T. N., Jacklin, C. N., & Tittle, C. K. Sex role stereotyping in the public schools. *Harvard Educational Review,* 1973, *43,* 386–414. **215, 219**

Safer, J., & Riess, B. F. Two approaches to the study of female homosexuality: A critical and comparative review. *International Mental Health Research Newsletter,* 1975, 11–13. **165**

Safilios-Rothschild, C. Dual linkages between the occupational and family systems: A macrosociological analysis.

Signs: Journal of Women in Culture and Society, 1976, *1*, 51–60. **309**

Safilios-Rothschild, C. *Love, sex and sex roles.* Englewood Cliffs, N.J.: Prentice-Hall, 1977. **145**

Saghir, M. T., Robins, E., Walbran, B., & Gentry, K. A. Homosexuality IV. Psychiatric disorders and disability in the female homosexual. *American Journal of Psychiatry,* 1970, *147,* 153–154. **166**

Sanday, P. R. Female status in the public domain. In M. Z. Rosaldo & L. Lamphere (Eds.), *Woman, culture, and society.* Stanford, Calif.: Stanford University Press, 1974. **274**

Schaeffer, E. S., & Bell, R. Q. Patterns of attitudes towards child rearing and the family. *Journal of Abnormal Psychology,* 1957, *4,* 391–395. **293**

Schneider, J. W., & Hacker, S. L. *Sex role imagery and the use of the generic "Man" in introductory texts: A case in the sociology of sociology.* Paper presented at the meeting of the American Sociological Association, New Orleans, 1972. **225–226**

Schwabacher, S. Male vs. female representation in psychological research: An examination of the *Journal of Personality and Social Psychology,* 1970–1971. *Journal Supplement Abstract Service,* 1972, *2,* 20–21. **46**

Seaman, B. *Free and female.* Greenwich, Conn.: Fawcett, 1972. **152**

Sears, P., & Feldman, D. Teacher interactions with boys and girls. *National Elementary Principal,* 1966, *46*(2), 30–35. **216**

Seavey, C. A., Katz, P. A., & Zalk, S. R. Baby X: The effect of gender labels on adult responses to infants. *Sex Roles,* 1975, *1,* 103–110. **201**

Sedney, M. A. *Sex roles and coping: Comparison of feminine, masculine and androgynous women's responses to stressful life events.* Paper presented at the meeting of the Association for Women in Psychology, St. Louis, February 1977.(a) **339, 340**

Sedney, M. A. *Process of sex-role development during life crises of middle-aged women.* Paper presented at the meeting of the American Psychological Association, San Francisco, August 1977.(b) **193**

Sedney, M. A. Comments on median split procedures in scoring androgyny measures. *Sex Roles,* in press. **19**

Sedney, M. A., & Turner, B. F. A test of causal sequences in two models for development of career-orientation in women. *Journal of Vocational Behavior,* 1975, *6,* 281–291. **329**

Segal, B. E. Male nurses: A study in status contradiction and prestige loss. *Social Forces,* 1962, *41,* 31–38. **321**

Seiden, A. M. Overview: Research on the psychology of women: II. Women in families, work, and psychotherapy. *American Journal of Psychiatry,* 1976, *133,* 1111–1123. **289**

Seiden, A. M. The sense of mastery in the childbirth experience. In M. T. Notman & C. C. Nadelson (Eds.), *The woman patient: Medical and psychological interfaces.* New York: Plenum, 1978. **131, 133**

Seifer, N. *Absent from the majority: Working class women in America.* New York: National Project on Ethnic America, 1973. **283, 296**

Serbin, L. A., & O'Leary, K. D. How nursery schools teach girls to shut up. *Psychology Today,* 1975, *9* (December), 57–58; 102–103. **216**

Sexton, P. Are schools emasculating our boys? *Saturday Review,* 1965, *48,* 57. **220**

Sexton, P. *Women in education.* Bloomington, Ind.: Phi Delta Kappa, 1976. **219, 220**

Sexton, P. C. *The feminized male.* New York: Random House, 1969. **223**

Shapiro, E. R. *Transition to parenthood in adult and family development.* Doctoral dissertation, University of Massachusetts, Amherst, Mass., 1979. **129**

Sheehy, G. *Passages: Predictable crises*

of adult life. New York: Sutton, 1976. **194**

Shereshefsky, P. M., Plotsky, H., & Lockman, R. F. Pregnancy and adaptation. In P. M. Shereshefsky & L. J. Yarrow (Eds.), *Psychological aspects of a first pregnancy and early postnatal adaption.* New York: Raven Press, 1974. **129**

Sherfey, M. J. *The nature and evolution of female sexuality.* New York: Vintage, 1973. **141, 142**

Sherif, C. W. *A social-psychological perspective on the menstrual cycle.* Presented at the Conference on Bio-Psychological Factors Influencing Sex-Role Related Behaviors, Northampton, Mass., 1976. **45**

Sherman, J. A. Problem of sex differences in space perception and aspects of intellectual functioning. *Psychological Review,* 1967, *74,* 290–299. **239**

Sherman, J. A. *On the psychology of women: A survey of empirical studies.* Springfield, Ill.: Charles C. Thomas, 1971. **105, 125, 183, 198, 257**

Sherman, J. A. Social values, femininity, and the development of female competence. *Journal of Social Issues,* 1976, *32*(3), 181–195. **337**

Sherriffs, A. C., & Jarrett, R. F. Sex differences in attitudes about sex differences. *Journal of Psychology,* 1953, *35,* 161–168. **42**

Sherriffs, A. C., & McKee, J. P. Qualitative aspects of beliefs about men and women. *Journal of Personality,* 1957, *25,* 451–464. **42**

Shields, S. A. Functionalism, Darwinism, and the psychology of women: A study in social myth. *American Psychologist,* 1975, *30,* 739–753. **44, 45**

Shope, D. E. *Interpersonal sexuality.* Philadelphia: W. B. Saunders, 1975. **157**

Siegel, C. L. Sex differences in the occupational choice of second graders. *Journal of Vocational Behavior,* 1973, *3,* 15–19. **311**

Singer, J. *Androgyny: Toward a new theory of sexuality.* Garden City, N.Y.: Anchor Books, 1977. **55, 57, 58, 59, 60, 61, 62, 63**

Skolnick, A. *The intimate environment: Exploring marriage and the family* (2nd ed.). Boston: Little, Brown, 1978. **287, 293–294**

Smith, A. H. Homophobia: A tentative personality profile. *Psychological Reports,* 1971, *29,* 1091–1094. **165**

Snow, K. Women in the American novel. In J. Freeman (Ed.), *Women: A feminist perspective.* Palo Alto, Calif.: Mayfield, 1975. **211**

Social Research, Inc. *Working class women in a changing world.* Chicago: McFadden-Bartell, 1973. **231, 283**

Sodersten, P. Mounting behavior in the female rat during the estrous cycle after ovariectomy, and after estrogen or testosterone administration. *Hormones and Behavior,* 1972, *3,* 307–320. **99**

Sommer, B. *Perceptual motor performance, mood and the menstrual cycle.* Paper presented at the meeting of the Western Psychological Association, Portland, Oregon, April 1972. **121**

Sommer, B. The effect of menstruation on cognitive and perceptual-motor behavior: A review. *Psychosomatic Medicine,* 1973, *35,* 515–534. **121**

Sontag, S. The double standard of aging. *Saturday Review,* 1972, 29–38. **137**

Sophocles. Antigone. In D. Fitts (Ed.), *Greek plays in modern translation.* New York: Dial Press, 1947. **66**

Spaulding, R. *Achievement, creativity, and self-concept correlates of teacher-pupil transactions in elementary school.* (Cooperative Research Project, No. 1352) Washington, D.C.: U.S. Department of Health, Education and Welfare, Office of Education, 1963. **216**

Special Task Force to the Secretary of Health Education and Welfare. Work in America. In R. C. Edwards, M. Reich, & T. E. Weisskopf (Eds.), *The capitalist system* (2nd ed.). Englewood Cliffs, N.J.: Prentice-Hall, 1978. **307**

Speck, R. V., & Attneave, C. L. *Family networks.* New York: Pantheon Books, 1973. **356**

Spence, J. T. The thematic apperception test and attitudes toward achievement in women: A new look at the motive to avoid success and a method of measurement. *Journal of Consulting and Clinical Psychology,* 1974, *42,* 427–437. **255**

Spence, J. T., & Helmreich, R. L. Who likes competent women? Competence, sex-role congruence of interests, and subjects' attitude toward women as determinants of interpersonal attraction. *Journal of Applied Social Psychology,* 1972, *2,* 197–213. **249**

Spence, J. T., & Helmreich, R. L. *Masculinity and femininity: Their psychological dimensions, correlates and antecedents.* Austin: University of Texas Press, 1978. **15, 19*n*, 21, 198**

Spence, J. T., & Helmreich, R. L. On assessing androgyny. *Sex Roles,* in press. **19**

Spence, J. T., Helmreich, R. L., & Stapp, J. The Personal Attributes Questionnaire: A measure of sex role stereotypes and masculinity-femininity. *JSAS Catalogue of Selected Documents in Psychology,* 1975, *4,* 127. **12, 14–15, 19, 20, 21**

Spence, J. T., Helmreich, R., & Stapp, J. Likeability, sex-role congruence of interest, and competence: It all depends on how you ask. *Journal of Applied Social Psychology,* 1975, *5,* 93–109.(a) **250**

Spence, J. T., Helmreich, R., & Stapp, J. Ratings of self and peers on sex-role attributes and their relation to self-esteem and conceptions of masculinity and femininity. *Journal of Personality and Social Psychology,* 1975, *32,* 29–39.(b) **6, 7, 13, 18, 19, 20, 21, 248, 249, 250, 337**

Sperry, R. W. The great cerebral commissure. *Scientific American,* 1964, *174,* 42–52. **56**

Spitz, R. A. The role of ecological factors in emotional development in infancy. *Child Development,* 1949, *20,* 145–156. **275–276**

Sprenger, J., & Kraemer, H. *Malleus maleficarum. The hammer of witchcraft* (M. Summers, Trans.). London: Pushkin, 1948. **342**

Srole, L., Langer, T. S., Michael, S. T., Opler, M. K., & Rennie, T. A. C. *Mental health in the metropolis.* New York: McGraw-Hill, 1962. **345**

Stafford, R. E. Sex differences in spatial visualization as evidence of sex-linked inheritance. *Perceptual and Motor Skills,* 1961, *13,* 428. **240**

Stafford, R. E., Backman, E., & diBona, P. The division of labor among cohabitating and married couples. *Journal of Marriage and the Family,* 1977, *39,* 43–58. **282**

Standley, K., & Soule, B. Women in male-dominated professions: Contrasts in their personal and vocational histories. *Journal of Vocational Behavior,* 1974, *4,* 245–258. **329**

Stark, R., & McEvoy, J., III. Middle class violence. *Psychology Today,* November 1970, 52–54; 110–112. **262**

Stayton, D. J., Hogan, R., & Ainsworth, M. D. S. Infant obedience and maternal behavior: The origins of socialization reconsidered. *Child Development,* 1971, *42,* 1057–1069. **260**

Stein, A. H., & Bailey, M. M. The socialization of achievement orientation in females. *Psychological Bulletin,* 1973, *80,* 345–366. **197, 252, 253, 255, 256, 293**

Stein, A. H., Pohly, S. R., & Mueller, E. The influence of masculine, feminine, and neutral tasks on children's achievement behavior, expectancies of success and attainment values. *Child Development,* 1971, *42,* 195–207. **245**

Sternglanz, S. H., & Serbin, L. A. Sex role stereotyping in children's television programs. *Developmental Psychology,* 1974, *10,* 710–715. **211**

Stoller, R. J. *Sex and gender.* New York: Jason Aronson, 1968. **97**

Stoller, R. J. Facts and fancies: An examination of Freud's concept of bisexuality. In J. Strouse (Ed.), *Women and analysis.* New York: Viking, 1974. **182**

Stoller, R. J. Primary femininity. In H. P. Blum (Ed.), *Female psychology: Contemporary psychoanalytic views.* New York: International Universities Press, 1977. **11**

Stolz, L. M. *Father relations of war-born children.* Stanford, Calif.: Stanford University Press, 1954. **295**

Strahan, R. F. Remarks on Bem's measurement of psychological androgyny: Alternative methods and a supplementary analysis. *Journal of Consulting and Clinical Psychology,* 1975, *43,* 568–571. **22**

Straka, L., Sipova, K., & Hynie, J. Plasma testosterone in male transsexuals and homosexuals. *Journal of Sex Research,* 1975, *11,* 134–138. **106**

Strommen, E. A. Friendship. In E. Donelson & J. Gullahorn (Eds.), *Women: A psychological perspective.* New York: John Wiley, 1977. **230**

Strong, E. K. *Vocational interests of men and women.* Stanford, Calif.: Stanford University Press, 1943. **12**

Sullivan, H. S. *The interpersonal theory of psychiatry.* New York: Norton, 1953. **230, 232**

Sutherland, H., & Stewart, I. A critical analysis of the premenstrual syndrome. *Lancet,* 1965, *1,* 1180–1193. **118**

Sutton-Simon, K., & Menig-Peterson, C. *The effects of parents' sex-role behavior upon children's sex-typing.* Paper presented at the meeting of the Association for Women in Psychology, St. Louis, February 1977. **205**

Szasz, T. *The myth of mental illness.* New York: Hoeber-Harper, 1961. **345**

Tangri, S. S. Determinants of occupational role innovation among college women. *Journal of Social Issues,* 1972, *28*(2), 177–199. **256, 327, 329**

Tanner, J. M. Sequence, temper and individual variation in the growth and development of boys and girls aged 12 to 16. *Daedelus,* 1971, *100,* 907–930. **115**

Tasch, R. J. The role of the father in the family. *Journal of Experimental Education,* 1952, *20,* 319–361. **289**

Taylor, S. E., & Langer, E. J. Pregnancy: A social stigma. *Sex Roles,* 1977, *3,* 27–36. **126**

Terkel, S. *Working: People talk about what they do all day and how they feel about what they do.* New York: Pantheon, 1974. **307**

Terman, L., & Miles, C. C. *Sex and personality.* New York: McGraw-Hill, 1936. **12**

Terman, L. M., & Oden, M. H. *The gifted child grows up.* Stanford, Calif.: Stanford University Press, 1947. **251**

Terman, L. M., & Oden, M. H. *The gifted group at mid-life.* Stanford, Calif.: Stanford University Press, 1949. **251**

Thomas, A., & Stewart, N. Counselor's response to female clients with deviate and conforming career goals. *Journal of Counseling Psychology,* 1971, *18,* 352–357. **217**

Thompson, C. Cultural pressures in the psychology of women. *Psychiatry,* 1942, *5,* 331–339. **184**

Thompson, C. Penis envy in women. *Psychiatry,* 1943, *6,* 123–126. **184**

Thompson, S. K. Gender labels and early sex role development. *Child Development,* 1975, *46,* 339–347. **205**

Thurn, E. F. *Among the indians of Guiana.* London: George Allen and Unwin, 1883. **133**

Tobin, S. M. Emotional depression during pregnancy. *Obstetrics and Gynecology,* 1957, *10,* 677–686. **128**

Touhy, J. C. Effects of additional women professionals on ratings of occupational prestige and desirability. *Journal of Personality and Social Psychology,* 1974, *29,* 86–89. **42**

Tourney, G., & Hatfield, L. M. Androgen metabolism in schizophrenics, homosexuals, and normal controls. *Biological Psychiatry,* 1973, *6,* 23–36. **106**

Trecker, J. L. Sex stereotyping in the secondary school curriculum. *Phi Delta Kappan,* 1973, *55,* 110–112. **219**

Tuddenham, R. D., Brooks, J., & Milkovich, L. Mothers' reports of behavior of ten-year-olds: Relationships with sex, ethnicity, and mother's education. *Developmental Psychology,* 1974, *10,* 959–995. **199**

Turner, B. F. *Socialization and career orientation among black and white college women.* Paper presented at the meeting of the American Psychological Association, Hawaii, September 1972. **329**

Turner, B. F., & Turner, C. B. Race, sex, and perception of the occupational opportunity structure among college students. *Sociological Quarterly,* 1975, *16,* 345–360. **325–326**

Turner, B. F., & Turner, C. B. *Correlates and consequences of personally experienced sexual discrimination.* Paper presented at the meeting of the American Psychological Association, Toronto, August 1978. **325**

Turner, M. F., & Izzi, M. H. The COPE story: A service to pregnant and postpartum women. In M. T. Notman & C. C. Nadelson (Eds.), *The woman patient: Medical and psychological interfaces.* New York: Plenum, 1978. **129**

Tyler, L. E. Development of career interests in girls. *Genetic Psychology Monographs,* 1964, *70,* 203–212. **329**

Unger, R. K. Status, power and gender: An examination of parallelisms. In J. A. Sherman & F. L. Denmark (Eds.), *Psychology of Women: Future directions for research.* New York: Psychological Dimensions, 1977. **45**

Unger, R. K. & Denmark, F. L. Introduction. In R. K. Unger & F. L. Denmark (Eds.), *Woman, dependent or independent variable?* New York: Psychological Dimensions, 1975. **45**

United States Bureau of the Census, *Statistical Abstract of the United States: 1977* (98th ed.). Washington, D.C.: U.S. Government Printing Office, 1977. **309, 311**

Vaillant, G. E. *Adaptation to life.* Boston: Little, Brown, 1977. **277, 312, 328**

Van Dusen, R. A., & Sheldon, E. B. The changing status of American women: A life cycle perspective. *American Psychologist,* 1976, *31,* 106–116. **292, 302**

Vanfossen, B. E. Sexual stratification and sex-role socialization. *Journal of Marriage and the Family,* 1977, *39,* 563–574. **197**

Van Vuuren, N. *The subversion of women: As practiced by churches, witch-hunters, and other sexists.* Philadelphia: Westminster, 1973. **342**

Vaughter, R. M. Review essay: Psychology. *Signs,* 1976, *2,* 120–146. **45**

Veevers, J. E. The social meaning of parenthood. *Psychiatry,* 1973, *36,* 291–310. **286**

Veith, I. Four thousand years of hysteria. In M. J. Horowitz (Ed.), *Hysterical personality.* New York: Jacob Aronson, 1977. **342, 343**

Vogel, S. Discussant's comments symposium: Applications of androgyny to the theory and practice of psychotherapy. *Psychology of Women Quarterly,* 1979, *3,* 255–258. **23**

Wallston, B. S. What are the questions in psychology of women? A feminist approach *to* research. Presidential address (Division 35), American Psychological Association, New York. September 1979. **35, 46, 51**

Ward, I. L. Prenatal stress feminizes and demasculinizes the behavior of males. *Science,* 1972, *175,* 82–84. **99**

Warheit, G. J., Holzer, C. E., Bell, R. A., & Arey, S. A. Sex, marital status, and mental health: A reappraisal. *Social Forces,* 1976, *55,* 459–470. **336**

Webb, A. P. Sex-role preferences and adjustment in early adolescents. *Child Development,* 1963, *34,* 609–618. **337**

Webster's Seventh New Collegiate Dictionary, 1971. **257**

Weideger, P. *Menstruation and menopause.* New York: Delta, 1975. **113, 117, 136,**

Weinberg, M. S. The aging male homosexual. *Medical Aspects of Human Sexuality,* 1969, *3,* 66–72. **166**

Weisstein, N. Psychology constructs the female, or the fantasy life of the male psychologist. In M. E. Garskof (Ed.), *Roles women play: Readings toward women's liberation.* Belmont, Calif.: Brooks/Cole, 1971. **46**

Weitz, S. *Sex roles: Biological, psychological, and social foundations.* New York: Oxford University Press, 1977. **206**

Weitzman, L. J., Eifler, D., Hokada, E., & Ross, C. Sex-role socialization in picturebooks for preschool children. *American Journal of Sociology,* 1972, *77,* 1125–1150. **211**

Wetter, R. E. *Levels of self-esteem associated with four sex-role categories.* Paper presented at the meeting of the American Psychological Association, Chicago, August 1975. **248, 249**

Whalen, R. E. Differentiation of the neural mechanisms which control gonadotropic secretions and sexual behavior. In M. Diamond (Ed.), *Perspectives in reproduction and sexual behavior.* Bloomington: University of Indiana Press, 1968. **103, 104**

Whisnant, L., Brett, B., & Zegans, L. Implicit messages concerning menstruation in commercial educational materials prepared for young adolescent girls. *American Journal of Psychiatry,* 1975, *132,* 815–820. **114**

Whisnant, L., & Zegans, L. A study of attitudes toward menarche in white middle-class American adolescent girls. *American Journal of Psychiatry,* 1975, *132,* 809–814. **114**

Whiting, B., & Edwards, C. P. A cross-cultural analysis of sex differences in the behavior of children aged three through eleven. *Journal of Social Psychology,* 1973, *91,* 171–188. **48, 200**

Whiting, J. W. M. Socialization process and personality. In F. L. K. Hsu (Ed.), *Psychological anthropology.* Homewood, Ill.: Dorsey, 1961. **289**

Wiggins, J. S., & Holzmuller, A. Psychological androgyny and interpersonal behavior. *Journal of Consulting and Clinical Psychology,* 1978, *46,* 40–52. **21**

Wiggins, R. G. Differences in self-perception of ninth grade boys and girls. *Adolescence,* 1973, *8,* 491–496. **244**

Wilbur, C. B. Clinical aspects of female homosexuality. In J. Marmor (Ed.), *Sexual inversion.* New York: Basic Books, 1965. **165**

Williams, J. H. Sexual role identification and personality functioning in girls: A theory revisited. *Journal of Personality,* 1973, *41,* 1–8. **183**

Williams, J. H. *Psychology of women.* New York: Norton, 1977. **275**

Williams, R. H. (Ed.). *Textbook of neuroendocrinology* (4th ed.). Philadelphia: W. B. Saunders, 1968. **85**

Winnick, C., & Kinsie, P. M. Prostitution. *Sexual Behavior,* 1973, *3,* 33–42. **168, 170**

Winter, D. G., Stewart, A. J., & McClelland, D. C. Husband's motives and wife's career level. *Journal of Personality and Social Psychology,* 1977, *35,* 159–166. **281**

Witkin, H. A., Dyk, R. B., Faterson, H. F., Goodenough, D. R., & Karp, S. A. *Psychological differentiation.* New York: John Wiley, 1962. **239**

Wolf, T. M. Response consequences to televised modeled sex-inappropriate play behavior. *Journal of Genetic Psychology,* 1975, *127,* 35–44. **205**

Wolfgang, M. E. (Ed.), *Studies in homicide.* New York: Harper & Row, 1967. **172**

Women on Words and Images. *Dick and Jane as victims: Sex stereotyping in children's readers.* Princeton, N.J.: Women on Words and Images, 1975.(a) **219**

Women on Words and Images. *Channeling children: Sex stereotyping in prime-time TV.* Princeton, N.J.: Women on Words and Images, 1975.(b) **212**

Women on Words and Images. *Help*

wanted: Sexism in career education materials. Princeton, N.J.: Women on Words and Images, 1975.(c) **218**

Woods, M. M. *The relation of sex role categories to autobiographical factors.* Presented at the Convention of the American Psychological Association, Chicago, 1975. **197**

Woolf, V. *A room of one's own.* New York: Harcourt, Brace, and World, 1929. **73**

Women on Words and Images. *Help wanted: Sexism in career education materials.* Princeton, N.J.: Women on Words and Images, 1975.(c)

Wright, J. D. Are working women really more satisfied? Evidence from several national surveys. *Journal of Marriage and the Family,* 1978, *40,* 301–314. **296**

Wylie, R. C. *The self-concept* (rev. ed.). *Volume II: Theory and research on se-lected topics.* Lincoln: University of Nebraska Press, 1979. **244**

Yalom, I. D., Green, R., & Fisk, N. Prenatal exposure to female hormones. *Archives of General Psychiatry,* 1973, *28,* 554–561. **96**

Yarrow, M. R., Scott, P., DeLeeuw, L., & Hennig, C. Child-rearing in families of working and non-working mothers. *Sociometry,* 1962, *25,* 122–140. **293**

Young, C. J., MacKenzie, D. L., & Sherif, C. W. *In search of token women in academia.* Presented at the meeting of the Association for Women in Psychology, Pittsburgh, March 1978. **325**

Young, W. C., Goy, R. W., & Phoenix, C. H. Hormones and sexual behavior. *Science,* 1964, *143,* 212–218. **100**

Zax, M., & Cowen, E. L. *Abnormal psychology: Changing conceptions* (2nd ed.). New York: Holt, Rinehart & Winston, 1976. **342**

INDEX

ability attribution, 245, 246, 248
abnormal behavior
  clinical judgment on
    politics of, 344–346
    sex differences, 345–346
    sex roles, 346–347
    personality characteristics and, 92–96
abortions, 48, 126
  methods of, 126
achievement
  androgyny and, 257
  motivation, 329, 331
    sex differences and, 49, 251–257, 311
  psychological measurement of, 252–253
  sex differences and, 214, 253
  social valuation of, 42, 46
  socialization and, 197, 204, 255–256, 293
Adam Principle, 84, 90
Adjective Check List (ACL), 12, 16, 21, 22
adolescence, 115–116, 194, 214, 295, 338–339
  friendship and, 230–232
adrenal glands, 83
adrenogenital syndrome, 92, 97, 105
  causes of, 91
  psychological characteristics of, 95
adulthood, 214, 227, 260–261
  family roles in, 271–303
  friendships and, 231–232
  sex roles in, 191–194, 196–198, 207–208, 338
  work roles in, 305–334
affirmative action, 215, 326, 330
aggression, 7, 46, 48, 49, 99–102, 186–187, 192, 194, 204, 211, 216, 220, 242, 257
  defined, 262
  sex differences in, 186–187, 200, 206, 237, 262
alchemy, 56, 62, 63, 64
altruism, sex differences in, 260–261
American Men of Science, 251
American Psychiatric Association, 166*n*
anal intercourse, 158
analytic abilities, sex differences in, 239–240
androcentric bias, 46
androgen insensitivity syndrome, 91, 92, 93, 94, 97
androgenital syndrome, 95

androgens, 6 (*see also* hormones; sex hormones; testosterone)
  defined, 83
  female sexuality and, 105
  fetal development, and, 85, 88
  male sexuality and, 104–105
  prenatal abnormalities and, 91–92
androgyne, the, 61
androgyny, 3–31, 33, 79
  achievement and, 257
  attainment of enlightenment and, 61–63
  biology and, 11, 80–82, 95–96, 98, 110
  the Bloomsbury group and, 72–74
  change in the social context and, 356–359
  clinical judgments and, 347
  cognitive abilities and, 241–242
  cognitive development theory and, 190
  in creation myths, 57–61
  definition of, 6–8
  development of, 98, 192–195, 233, 291
  dualistic model of, 7–9, 23
  emotional adjustment and, 6, 9, 21, 28–29, 194
  family functioning and, 278
  friendships and, 232, 250
  growing toward, 206–207
  holism and, 5
  hybrid model of, 8–9, 23, 69
  interpersonal interactions and, 9, 25–29, 264
  language styles and, 229
  in literature, 64–74
  measuring, 12–24
  in the novel, 70–72
  parenthood and, 11, 291–292
  perspective of, 29–31, 50–52, 222, 243, 247, 257, 259, 331
  pregnancy and childbirth and, 11, 125–126
  premises of, 9–11
  pressures toward, in sex-role development, 196–198
  psychoanalytic theory and, 185
  psychotherapy and, 351, 355
  in religions, 56–64
  research on, 20–29, 38–39, 264, 292, 338–340
  self-esteem and, 21, 27–28, 244, 248

393